The Foreign Policies
of Arab States

SECOND EDITION, FULLY REVISED AND UPDATED

The Foreign Policies of Arab States

The Challenge of Change

Bahgat Korany and
Ali E. Hillal Dessouki

---

with contributions by
Ahmad Yousef Ahmad, Gehad Auda,
Raymond A. Hinnebusch,
A. G. Kluge, Paul C. Noble,
Mohamed E. Selim,
I. William Zartman, and
Karen Aboul Kheir

Westview Press
BOULDER • SAN FRANCISCO • OXFORD

Copyright © 1984, 1991 by Westview Press, Inc.

Published in 1991 in the United States of America by Westview Press, Inc., 5500 Central Avenue, Boulder, Colorado 80301, and in the United Kingdom by Westview Press, 36 Lonsdale Road, Summertown, Oxford OX2 7EW

Library of Congress Cataloging-in-Publication Data
Korany, Bahgat.
   The foreign policies of Arab states : the challenge of change /
Bahgat Korany and Ali E. Hillal Dessouki ; with contributions by
Ahmad Yousef Ahmad . . . [et al.]. — 2nd ed.
      p.   cm.
   Includes bibliographical references and index.
   ISBN 0-8133-0874-7.   ISBN 0-8133-0875-5 (pbk.).
   1. Arab countries—Foreign relations.   I. Dessouki, Ali E.
Hillal.   II. Ahmad, Ahmad Yūsuf.   III. Title.
DS63.1.K656   1991
327'.0917'4927—dc20   90-24301
                                                                      CIP

Printed and bound in the United States of America

   The paper used in this publication meets the requirements
 (∞) of the American National Standard for Permanence of Paper
   for Printed Library Materials Z39.48-1984.

10   9   8   7   6   5   4   3   2   1

Contents

v

Tables and Figures

Preface
and Acknowledgments

The preparation of this second edition has been almost as seismic as the Middle East itself with its 1990–1991 Gulf Crisis. After all chapters had been written and edited, the Arab world and the world at large were faced with Iraq's invasion of Kuwait in an attempt to "correct" colonial history of border-demarcation and "state-creation." Later, by the time galley proofs had been prepared, coalition forces waged war against Iraq. From political and analytical points of view, at both the regional and global levels the Gulf Crisis has been an event of exceptional magnitude. Some of its immediate aspects needed to be incorporated into the analysis, if only in the conclusions of the different chapters. Moreover, the problematique of political change and its effects on foreign policy had to be more emphasized in both the book's long introduction and the last comparative chapter. In order to conclude the analysis as speedily as possible, we were forced to omit consideration of some pertinent topics, among them the issue of the war's effect on such groups as the Kurdish minority in Iraq.

There was a potential danger to guard against. The Gulf Crisis became a world media event—addressing it in that fashion could have entrapped parts of the book into becoming "instantaneous history" instead of being an analytical enterprise. Close as we still are in time to the Gulf Crisis, we should avoid losing sight of the forest for the trees. Indeed, we had to remind ourselves that this book is not primarily about "current events" and is destined not to replace, for instance, *The New York Times* or *Le Monde* but rather to help us grasp and situate what these influential mass-media organs offer. Consequently, patterns of foreign policy evolution and continuity have to be pointed out so that the magnitude of foreign policy change and the difference between the accidental and the much more permanent may stand out more clearly. Precisely so, the last chapter comes back to these crucial analytical issues in the study of Arab and Third World foreign policies.

Otherwise, this second edition pursues the same objectives as the first:

1. Fill the still existing gap in the literature on patterns of Arab foreign policies.

2. Link the empirical presentation with existing conceptualization and theoretical frameworks in the field of foreign policy analysis. Our hope is that this may prove useful and relevant to the understanding of the foreign policies of other Third World countries.
3. Maintain the unity of the book around a relevant framework followed throughout the chapters. In this case, the reader is informed about the specificities of the foreign policies of Iraq or Libya, Syria or the Sudan. But at the same time she/he is reminded of the existence of a general pattern of *Arab* foreign policy. This is why foreign policy is conceptualized as a role on the international scene, embracing both the specific performance or behavior and the general role-conception or orientation.
4. Maintain our commitment to providing information and being concerned with conceptual issues without making the reader—student or otherwise—suffer from unwarranted jargon.

Even though this book concentrates on the "survey" aspect of Arab foreign policies in order to be useful as a text, we have organized it around a main argument. As enunciated in Chapter 2, this argument draws attention not to leaders' idiosyncracies but to the weight of systemic-global factors (both constraints and opportunities, but especially constraints) in shaping the foreign policies of even the relatively "strong" Arab countries (for example, Egypt and Saudi Arabia). The 1990–1991 Gulf Crisis, and especially its aftermath regarding the organization of postwar regional order, gives additional credit, we feel, to this relationship of hierarchy between the global system and the Arab world. Global constraints do not, of course, preclude the subordinate regional and state-society dynamics to which the rest of the book is devoted, much less substitute for them. The dialectics between the regional-actor dynamics (including the impact of the leader) and their global contextualities are picked up in the book's last chapter.

The book will, we hope, prove useful not only to those interested in knowing more about Arab and Middle Eastern international politics but also to those interested in generating hypotheses and accumulating knowledge for theory-building. We also hope that our quest for relevance will make the book useful to practitioners—to functionaries of foreign ministries, journalists, and international civil servants.

We collaborated closely in the writing of Chapters 1, 2, and 13, and the order of our names on each chapter indicates which one of us took actual responsibility for the final version.

The first edition of this book proved its utility, thanks to our fellow authors who applied the framework in their different areas of expertise and responded positively to our queries. That this second edition is published is a result also of the use of the book by our colleagues who, sometimes with their students, offered comments and suggestions, both written and oral. We are indeed grateful to those specialists who published reviews of the first edition and who, while being extremely encouraging, did not hesitate to raise crucial questions to advance the nascent analysis of Arab foreign policies. We also hope that they, other colleagues, and graduate students join this "transnational" research enterprise.

Ali Dessouki would specially like to thank Mouna Aboul Kheir; Bahgat Korany thanks Canada's Social Science Research Council for financial support and Christiane Aubin, the efficient secretary of the Arab studies program. As with the first edition, Christiane tried to keep track of the typing and of the organization of bits and pieces. The support of our respective wives—Eglal Dessouki and Margaret Korany—was crucial; the exigencies of the Gulf crisis and the constant demands of the mass media made us draw on this support even more than usual.

Last but not least, through our copy editor, Steve Haenel, and especially editors Barbara Ellington and Libby Barstow, Westview Press has been indeed an ideal collaborator and firm supporter. This "transnational" enterprise between authors in the Arab world and North America was complicated in itself but was made increasingly so with the turbulent situation in the region. Barbara and Libby, too, had to put up with "change": both in the galleys and in the deadline. We thank them heartily.

Bahgat Korany
Ali E. Hillal Dessouki

The Arab World

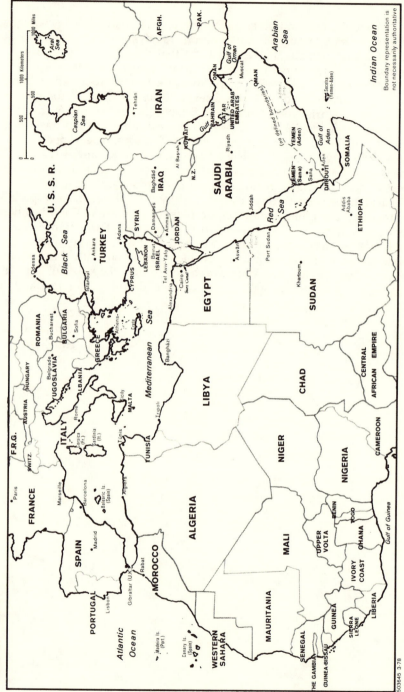

503845 3-78

Introduction

Arab states have been studied from many angles. We have books on Arab governments and politics, history and political evolution, ideologies and intellectual trends, inter-Arab relations and the great powers' policies in the region, but very little on Arab states' foreign policies or on how these countries view the world and their role in it.

This statement is confirmed by the results of our survey of the literature on Arab foreign policies, written in eight languages. The results, reported in Chapter 1, reveal for instance that in 1983, there was only one book in English dealing with Egyptian foreign policy, and it deals only with Egypt's Arab policy during the Nasser era (1952–1970). Similarly, no book exists on the Syrian foreign policy system with the exception of one on Syria's intervention in Lebanon.[1] We could not even find a systematic study of Lebanon's foreign policy. Books devoted to one Arab country usually have sections on external relations or foreign affairs, such as those by Majid Khadduri and by the Penroses on Iraq.[2] But this is not always the case; the two major books on Egypt published in the 1970s[3] have no such chapters. Finally, although scores of books on the domestic politics of Arab countries exist, there is but a single book on foreign policy–making in the Middle East, dealing with Israel and three Arab countries, and two other general international relations books.[4]

With a few exceptions, the existing literature suffers from a number of limitations. It is of a descriptive or prescriptive genre, rarely linked to recent conceptualization in foreign policy analysis. Most of it belongs to the tradition of diplomatic political history or commentary on current affairs.[5] Finally, other than statements about the role of leaders and personalities, there is almost no treatment in existing books of how foreign policy is actually made and implemented.

Four factors may account for this poverty in the literature. First is the underdeveloped state of the discipline of foreign policy analysis in Third World countries (which we examine more closely in Chapter 1). Between 1950 and 1965, Western scholars viewed these newly independent states as having no purposeful foreign policies of their own. Their external behavior was analyzed as a reaction to the great powers' policies toward them, and hence emphasis was placed on the international relations of the country rather than on its foreign policy proper. Moreover, theories of foreign policy analysis at that time dealt primarily with developed countries and were not applicable to developing ones. A second factor is the limited data available in a rapidly changing environment, in which foreign policy affairs are shrouded in secrecy and widely perceived as a matter of utmost national security. Third, students of Arab politics have focused more attention on regional dynamics than on single-actor behavior. There is no lack of analyses dealing, for instance, with inter-Arab relations or the Arab-Israeli conflict. The fourth factor concerns the present state of Arab (and Middle Eastern) scholarship in Europe and the United States.

An evaluation of this literature is not our objective here. We want only to emphasize the weakness in methodology and lack of analytical rigor; literature on the Arab countries has not as yet contributed to the body of social science as has, for instance, the literature on Latin America. Our field has been plagued by inadequate conceptualization, overemphasis on historicism and the uniqueness of the Islamic-Arab situation, and neglect of a truly comparative outlook.

Why should we study the foreign policies of Arab states? By Arab states, we mean those twenty-two states that belong to the League of Arab States, founded in 1945.[6] They are primarily distinguished by cultural-linguistic homogeneity. These countries occupy a strategic part of the world; their lands stretch from the Atlantic Ocean in the west to the Indian Ocean in the east, and from the Horn of Africa in the south to the "northern tier" in the north. They control a number of important waterways: the Suez Canal, Bab Al-Mandeb, the Gulf of Aqaba, the Gulf, and the Straits of Hormuz. They perform crucial roles in Islamic, African, and nonaligned councils. Finally, oil wealth has enabled some of them to accumulate enormous financial resources that may be placed at the service of their foreign policies.

We started our research with four main propositions on Arab foreign policies in mind:

1. Arab states share a number of norms and pan-Arab core concerns such as Arabism, the Palestine problem, and nonalignment. All Arab states—particularly those desiring to perform an influential regional role—address themselves to these core concerns. In addition to being part of the Arab collective political culture, these concerns have been used by Arab regimes as a legitimizing device and as a weapon to discredit opponents.
2. Arab foreign policies are primarily regional in orientation. This regional emphasis is the result of three factors. First, small or medium powers are usually regionally oriented. Second, the Arab-Israeli conflict is perceived as a common Arab problem. Third, the belief system of Islam or Arab nationalism encourages regional trans-state interactions.
3. There is an intimate relationship between domestic and external policies in most Arab countries. In Syria and Jordan, for instance,

the Palestine issue has direct implications for internal stability. For Saudi Arabia, the future of Jerusalem is a question intimately related to the regime's legitimacy. Among influential Arab states, Egypt provides an exceptional example of dissociation between domestic and regional foreign policies that allows the Egyptian leadership a noticeable degree of external maneuverability. The more a regime or leadership derives its legitimacy from a certain policy behavior, the less freedom of action it enjoys.

4. There is latent tension in the orientation of Arab foreign policies between the norm of pan-Arabism and the interests of each state, between role conception and role performance. There is growing discrepancy between the pan-Arab ideal and state behavior based on raison d'état. Thus one notices a difference between the sources of a particular policy, which are in many cases specific state interests, and the justification of that policy—usually articulated in pan-Arab rhetoric.

Beneath this rhetoric, what are the differences among the foreign policies of Arab states? Arab foreign policies can be classified according to a number of criteria. One is *orientation in the global system* (e.g., pro-U.S. or pro–Soviet Union). Although all Arab states are technically nonaligned, in most cases they tilt toward one or the other of the superpowers. A second criterion is *degree of involvement* in Arab politics (quietism versus activism). A closely related criterion is *distribution of resources and influence*, for in most cases activism is a function of a strong or rich country. A fourth criterion is *type of actor*. The Arab world has included a number of nonstate actors, such as the League of Arab States, the Provisional Government of the Republic of Algeria (GPRA), and the Palestine Liberation Organization (PLO). Another interesting example is Lebanon, a state that, for the last few years, not only has had no independent foreign policy, but whose territory has become an arena for the foreign policy of other regional actors.

On what grounds were certain countries chosen over others for this study? Our choice of nine actors (Algeria, Egypt, Iraq, Jordan, Libya, the PLO, Saudi Arabia, Sudan, and Syria) was influenced by four criteria: orientation, degree of involvement, distribution of resources and influence, and type of actor. The bias was toward "crucial" Arab actors whose foreign policies make a difference for the Arabs and the world. We made sure to represent countries from the Arab East (the Mashreq) and the Arab West (the Maghreb), rich and poor states, strong and weak, and a nonstate actor (the PLO).

The structure of the book reflects our concerns. The first chapter is conceptual and deals with three issues: various approaches to the study of the foreign policy of developing countries, a survey of the literature on Arab foreign policies, and the framework of analysis to be applied in the nine case studies. Thanks to the authors of the different chapters, the framework was followed closely. Depending on the availability of data or the importance of a particular variable to the analysis of an actor's foreign policy, the authors differed in their emphasis. Some put two variables together under one title. In certain cases, the impact of history was so important that the author felt obliged to discuss historical legacy. Notwithstanding these variations, all the case studies address the same major questions.

Chapter 2 analyzes the global system and Chapter 3 the regional system as they relate to Arab foreign policies. The objective of these two chapters is to outline how the external environment presents constraints or opportunities for different Arab actors. The nine case study chapters take up the nine Arab actors in alphabetical order. The last chapter deals briefly with some other Arab states, underlines patterns of Arab foreign policy for 1970–1980, and suggests some theoretical conclusions that may be of relevance to developing countries in general.

In the early hours of Thursday, August 2, 1990, Iraqi forces invaded Kuwait and eventually annexed it, and thus Kuwait became the nineteenth governorate of Iraq. Seven months later, on Thursday, February 28, 1991, President Bush declared that Kuwait was liberated and a cease-fire could be negotiated. The 209-day war created havoc in the Arab world and the Middle East at large. The events of this second Gulf war will affect the future of the region for a long time to come.

Militarily, a broad coalition, consisting of twenty-nine different states (including Arab, Muslim, African, Asian, European, North American, and South American) led by the United States, was established and maintained to force Iraq to leave Kuwait. More than half a million U.S. soldiers were sent to the battlefield. When war erupted, the coalition forces caused fundamental damage to Iraq's economic and military capabilities, sending it to the "pre-industrial age" according to a UN estimate.

Economically, the war was expensive and the United States requested economic help from Kuwait, Saudi Arabia, Germany, and Japan. Tourism in the region came to a halt. When roughly 2 million migrant workers were forced to return home, their countries lost these workers' financial remittances—money needed to offset the deficit in their countries' balance of payments. Additionally, in the last hours before withdrawal Iraqi forces set fire to Kuwaiti oil fields.

Politically, the crisis restructured existing alliances and groupings. For all practical purposes it destroyed the Arab Cooperation Council (including Iraq, Egypt, Jordan, and Yemen) and put immense strains on the Maghrebi Union (including Libya, Tunisia, Algeria, Morocco, and Mauritania). Even the Gulf Cooperation Council (GCC), which included Kuwait, Saudi Arabia, Qatar, Bahrain, the United Arab Emirates, and Oman, was affected; its leaders waited more than four months (from August 2 to December 22) to convene a summit meeting.

The second Gulf war represents a watershed in the development of the region. It demonstrated the fragility of Arab territorial integrity (raison d'état versus pan-Arabism or raison de la nation), heightened the conflict between pan-Arabist aspiration and individual states, and initiated a new round of the Arab cold war. It showed the divergent perceptions of national interest and national security maintained by different Arab governments. More specifically, the notion that one Arab country could constitute a threat to another Arab country became more pronounced, creating an atmosphere of mistrust. One particular feature of this crisis was the mobilization of the Arab masses. This war was not a conflict conducted by leaders and governments alone; rather, the influence of public opinion in countries such as Jordan and Algeria was crucial in foreign policy decision-making. Indeed, the attention the Iraqi media focused on issues such as Palestine, Israel, and Arab wealth proved effective. "Civil society" became increasingly salient even in some countries that were members of the coalition (for example, Egypt and especially Morocco).

In the postwar era, inter-Arab politics are likely to be restructured. In March 1991 a new grouping surfaced that included the GCC countries, Syria, and Egypt. Whether this grouping will prove transient or acquire elements of solidarity remains to be seen.

One prime victim of Arab fragmentation was the Arab League, which completed its move from Tunisia to its Cairo headquarters by the end of 1990 but lost its secretary general in the crisis. The neutrality and objectivity of Shazli al-Qulaibi (a Tunisian) in relation to the Iraq-Kuwait crisis was challenged, and this question led to his resignation. Until March 1991, pro-Iraqi states were following a policy of boycotting the meetings of the league, a situation that made the choice of a successor impossible, but with the end of the war the league members will certainly meet in the "new-old" headquarters in Cairo to prevent the crack from completely destroying their regional organization.

This Arab cold war will have its domestic repercussions. Arab governments may attempt to settle accounts with their adversaries. Economic and political destabilization policies are likely to be pursued against pro-Iraqi governments. However, the possibility of terrorist activities against the other camp remains. In all cases, Arab countries are likely to go through a period of turmoil and instability. It is still too early to predict the foreign policy consequences of this change in the regional landscape and in state-society relations and of the rising potential of domestic instability.

Another issue epitomized by the crisis is Gulf security. This issue finds its roots in the East of Suez policy adopted by the British in 1968. Since Britain's military withdrawal, the United States has followed a number of policies. For some time it considered the Iran of the shah as the guardian of the Gulf. Then the United States declared a policy of balance between Iran, Iraq, and Saudi Arabia. Presidents Carter and Reagan both issued major policy statements that considered the Gulf a vital U.S. interest. GCC members feel vulnerable in relation to either Iraq or Iran. Indeed, they could only establish the GCC after the two states went to war with each other.

Another issue on the agenda is the Palestine problem and the Arab-Israeli conflict. In 1990, Saddam Hussein made threats against Israel that made him a hero in Palestinian eyes. When the crisis erupted he emphasized the linkage between the Kuwaiti and Palestinian issues and followed this up by launching Iraqi Scud missiles against some Israeli cities. Such a linkage mobilized many Arabs in support of Iraq. Saudi Arabia and Egypt rejected the notion of procedural or simultaneous linkage. They rather referred to sequential linkage. In the postwar era, we can expect the Palestinian issue to receive more attention for at least two reasons. The first reason is moral; there is the need to be consistent. The liberation of Kuwait took place in the name of international legitimacy and Security Council resolutions. If international legitimacy is to be credible, it cannot be blatantly selective, and therefore those UN resolutions regarding the Arab-Israeli conflict need to be activated. The second reason relates to the stability of the region. There is the feeling that the Palestine issue is a time bomb, and its resolution is an essential ingredient of regional stability.

To sum up, although elements of continuity remain, the foreign policies of Arab states are presently facing major changes at the global, regional, and even state-society levels. We will pick up these concerns in the last chapter.

NOTES

1. Adeed I. Dawisha, *Syria and the Lebanese Crisis* (New York: St. Martin's Press, 1980).

2. Majid Khadduri, *Socialist Iraq* (Washington, D.C.: Middle East Institute, 1978); and Edith Penrose and E. F. Penrose, *Iraq: International Relations and National Development* (Boulder, Colo.: Westview Press, 1978).

3. Richard H. Dekmejian, *Egypt Under Nasser* (Albany: University of New York Press, 1971); Raymond W. Baker, *Egypt's Uncertain Revolution Under Nasser and Sadat* (Cambridge, Mass.: Harvard University Press, 1978). Recent books on Egypt's political economy establish more linkage with the country's international relations but still without analyzing its foreign policy. See Mark Cooper, *The Transformation of Egypt* (Baltimore: Johns Hopkins University Press, 1982); and John Waterbury, *The Egypt of Nasser and Sadat: The Political Economy of Two Regimes* (Princeton, N.J.: Princeton University Press, 1983).

4. R. D. McLaurin, Mohammed Mughisuddin, and Abraham Wagner, *Foreign Policy Making in the Middle East* (New York: Praeger Publishers, 1977). The more general and recent ones are L. Carl Brown, *International Policies and the Middle East: Old Rules, Dangerous Game* (Princeton, N.J.: Princeton University Press, 1984); and Tarek Ismael, *International Relations of the Middle East* (Syracuse: Syracuse University Press, 1986).

5. For instance, see the only book on Jordan, by Mohamed I. Faddah, *The Middle East in Transition: A Study of Jordan's Foreign Policy* (London: Asia Publishing House, 1974).

6. The twenty-two members are Algeria, Bahrain, Egypt, Iraq, Djibouti, Jordan, Kuwait, Lebanon, Libya, Mauritania, Morocco, North Yemen, Oman, Palestine, Qatar, Saudi Arabia, Somalia, South Yemen, Sudan, Syria, Tunisia, and the United Arab Emirates. Egypt's membership was suspended in 1979. *Arab Report*, published by the Arab League, 1984. (In 1989 the two Yemens merged into one country, but they are still in the process of consolidating this "unity.")

1

A Literature Survey and a Framework for Analysis

Ali E. Hillal Dessouki
Bahgat Korany

This book deals with the foreign policies of a number of developing or Third World actors. The study of developing countries' foreign policies has often been described as "underdeveloped" or "undeveloped." We have no intention of adding to the confusion of theories, models, and analytical frameworks already existing in the field. The objectives of this introductory chapter are rather: (1) to summarize the main trends and approaches in the study of developing countries' foreign policies, (2) to survey the literature on Arab foreign policies, and (3) to suggest a framework for analysis that takes into account the major conceptual contributions in foreign policy theory in the last two decades.

THE FOREIGN POLICY OF DEVELOPMENT:
APPROACHES TO THE STUDY OF
DEVELOPING COUNTRIES' FOREIGN POLICIES

For a long time the analysis of developing countries' foreign policies was dominated by three approaches:[1]

1. The psychologistic approach views foreign policy as a function of the impulses and idiosyncrasies of a single leader. According to this view, kings and presidents are the source of foreign policy; war and peace become a matter of personal taste and individual choice. Foreign policy is perceived not as an activity designed to achieve national or societal goals but, as E. Shills wrote in 1962, as "a policy of public relations"[2] whose objectives are to improve the image of the state, enhance the popularity of the leader, and divert attention from domestic troubles to illusory external victories.

There are at least three criticisms of this view. First, it makes foreign policy appear to be an erratic, irrational activity not subject to systematic analysis. Second, it ignores the context (domestic, regional, and global) within which foreign policy is formulated and implemented. There are certain systemic constraints that most leaders will not or cannot usually challenge. Third, it ignores the fact that because of their interest in political survival, most leaders downplay eccentricities that run counter to dominant attitudes, public mood, and political realities. For instance, in 1970–1973 President Anwar Al-Sadat of Egypt concealed his dislike of the Soviets in his public pronouncements. He even accused Egyptian critics of the Soviet Union of being traitors to the cause of the homeland. Under different circumstances (discussed in Chapter 5), Egyptian policies became increasingly influenced by Sadat's personal feelings. It has been argued that only those idiosyncrasies that neither challenge prevailing values nor threaten a regime's stability are likely to be expressed in foreign policy.

We cannot rule out idiosyncratic variables in many developing countries, but what is more important is to analyze how the context of policy-making encourages certain leadership types and not others; how it allows certain idiosyncrasies but not others; and how a leader's idiosyncrasies may alter the context, affecting the foreign policy orientation of other leaders.[3]

2. The great powers approach, dominant among traditionalists such as Hans Morgenthau,[4] views foreign policy as a function of East-West conflict. Briefly stated, the foreign policies of developing countries are seen as lacking autonomy; affected by external stimuli, they react to initiatives and situations created by external forces. The main weakness of this approach is its neglect of domestic sources of foreign policy. Moreover, it implies that developing countries lack purposeful foreign policies of their own.

3. The reductionist or model-builders approach[5] views the foreign policies of the developing countries as determined by the same processes and decisional calculi that shape the foreign policies of developed countries. The basic difference is quantitative; the former have fewer resources and capabilities and therefore conduct foreign policy on a smaller scale. This view is predicated on the assumption that the behavior of all states (big and small, rich and poor, developed and developing) follows a rational actor model of decision-making; that all states seek to enhance their power, and that all are motivated by security factors. The conclusion is that the foreign policies of developing countries are exactly like those of the developed ones, but at a lower level of material resources. This approach does not account for specific features of the developing countries such as modernization, the low level of political institutionalization at home, and dependency status in the global stratification system abroad.

Since the 1970s, students of Third World countries' foreign policies have looked beyond the idiosyncrasy variable to consider the structural factors of these societies. They have sought to identify the specific features of these societies that distinguish them from developed societies and to apply more rigorous analytical frameworks. These efforts have resulted in more interaction between students of comparative politics and foreign policy analysis—enriching both subdisciplines—and more interaction between theorists and those engaged in field research.[6] The net outcome has been the emergence of a new body of literature on what can be called "the foreign policy of development."

One common element of the new literature is the emphasis on domestic sources of foreign policy and on how the processes of modernization and social change affect the external behavior of developing countries. East and Hagen, for example, underline the resource factors, distinguishing between size factors (absolute amount of available resources) and modernization factors (the ability to mobilize, control, and use these resources). Modernization is perceived as the process by which states increase their capability to control and use their resources. The more modernized states thus have a greater capacity to act.[7] A second example is Weinstein's pioneering work on Indonesia, in which he defines three foreign policy objectives: defense of the nation's independence against perceived threats, mobilization of external resources for the country's development, and the achievement of objectives related to domestic politics (e.g., isolating one's political opponents from their foreign supporters, lending legitimacy to domestic political demands, and creating symbols of nationalism and national unity).[8]

An equally important element in the new literature is the emphasis on the political economy of an actor's position in the global stratification system. In this context, inequality becomes a core focus, for developing countries exist in a world social order characterized by inequality between states at the levels of socioeconomic development, military capability, political stability, and prestige. This results in the penetration of developing countries' decision-making processes from the outside, with external actors participating authoritatively in the allocation of resources and the determination of national goals.[9] Much has been written on the role of the International Monetary Fund (IMF), international private banks, multinational corporations, and the big powers' foreign aid in this regard.[10] The situation in most developing countries is characterized by domination and unequal exchange. It is a dependency situation involving highly asymmetrical patterns of transactions between states.

A proper analysis of the foreign policies of Third World countries should accept that foreign policy is part and parcel of the general situation of the Third World and reflects the evolution of this situation. In this sense, the foreign policy process cannot be separated from the domestic social structure or domestic political process. To understand a country's foreign policy, we have to open the "black box" of Third World society. The countries of the Third World are part and parcel of a world system; they are greatly affected by international stratification and inequality. Formal state sovereignty notwithstanding, a Third World society can be permeated, penetrated, and even dominated. It is thus important to see how external constraints and global structures (e.g., relations with big powers or multinational companies) affect its foreign policy-making process as well as its international behavior.

From reviewing the literature, it seems that developing countries are faced by three major issues in the conduct of their foreign policies. The first is *the aid/independence dilemma,* i.e., the trade-off between the need for foreign aid and the maintenance of national independence. Some leaders, such as Nasser, Nkrumah, and Sukarno, have been more concerned with independence; others, such as Sadat or Suharto, have attached more importance to foreign aid. The difference in emphasis cannot be understood only in terms of social background and political values; other structural factors, such as the characteristics of the global system, perceived security threats, and economic problems, are of equal importance.

The second issue is *the resources/objectives dilemma,* which is more pressing in developing than in developed countries. It refers to the ability of foreign policy–makers to pursue objectives within the realm of their country's capabilities. This seems a commonsense proposition; but examples abound of countries pursuing unfeasible objectives. In the 1940s, King Abdallah of tiny Transjordan followed an activist policy for unity with Syria; in the 1950s, Iraq, despite an obvious imbalance of resources, projected itself as an alternative to Egyptian regional leadership; and in the 1960s Egyptian resources were drained by the protracted war in Yemen against Saudi Arabia.

Third is *the security/development dilemma,* a modern version of the age-old guns-or-butter debate. Some scholars perceive foreign policy primarily as a process or an activity whose main objective is the mobilization of external resources for the sake of societal development. Students of Egypt's foreign policy, for instance, cannot escape this conclusion. Sadat's rapprochement with the United States and peace with Israel were motivated by economic troubles at home and the desire to attract foreign investment, as demonstrated in Chapter 5. For other states, such as Syria, threat perceptions and security considerations remain the paramount factors in their foreign policy, as shown in Chapter 12.

Although security threats of a military nature cannot be overlooked, particularly in regions—such as the Middle East and southern Africa—experiencing endemic long-standing conflicts, for most developing countries the real security threat is hunger and malnutrition. In its third annual report on world development in 1980, the World Bank stated that 78 million people are living in absolute poverty. The number likely increased in the 1980s because of the worsening economic outlook for developing nations and because of population growth. The earth's present population of 5 billion is expected to reach 6 billion by the end of the century. One of the most explosive forces in many developing countries is the frustrated desire of poor people to attain a decent standard of living. Poverty, population explosion, failure of developmental efforts, and food insecurity lie at the heart of the national security issue for these countries. Consequently, the concept of national security must be redefined and broadened to include nonmilitary as well as military threats.

THE STUDY OF ARAB FOREIGN POLICIES

1965–1981

The "underdeveloped study of underdeveloped countries" is nowhere more clearly demonstrated than in the analysis of Arab foreign policy, as conclusions reached in the late 1970s by nine specialists dealing with the Third World indicate.[11] As stated in 1977 by one of the present coauthors, "the systematic analysis of foreign policy in the Middle East is an underdeveloped area of study. Only in the last few years have academics undertaken foreign policy studies of Middle Eastern states."[12]

To go beyond general impressions and get a data-based view of the state of the art for foreign policy studies of the Arab countries, we conducted a survey of the literature for the seventeen-year period from 1965 to 1981. Books published on Arab foreign policies can be counted on one's fingers. Consequently, we inventoried articles from various periodicals as well as some unpublished Ph.D. dissertations.

Four initial criteria served as guidelines in selecting items for inclusion.

1. The item should go beyond pure information to shed light on the conceptual and empirical issues in the field of foreign policy analysis.
2. The item should be a scholarly work rather than one adopting a "propagandistic" or "current affairs" approach.
3. Consequently, the search for survey items should be restricted to the pages of well-established specialized journals.
4. Selection would be limited to those items published in English or French.

The strict application of these criteria—laudable as they were—resulted in a harvest of items too scanty to be informative or useful. Indeed, the scarcity of scholarly and systematic works on Arab foreign policy during a seventeen-year period is in itself a telling condemnation of the state of this subfield. We subsequently amended our criteria, making some realistic modifications. Rather than limiting ourselves to purely scholarly publications, we added periodicals dealing with current affairs but still possessing a recognized status among students of international relations. These additions range from *Foreign Policy* to *World Today*. We included articles in Arabic, German, Hebrew, Japanese, and Spanish. We also added some of the standard specialized magazines whose coverage

TABLE 1.1   Articles on Sixteen Arab Countries and Palestine, by Language of Publication, 1965–1981

Country	Arabic	English	French	Others[a]	Total
			Language of Publication		
Algeria	–	15	15	–	30
Egypt	2	40	8	2	52
Iraq	–	8	2	–	10
Jordan	–	1	–	–	1
Libya	–	14	7	–	21
Kuwait	–	2	–	–	2
Mauritania	–	–	1	–	1
Morocco	–	1	2	–	3
Oman	1	–	–	–	1
Palestine	–	2	–	–	2
Saudi Arabia	3	22	3	4	32
Sudan	–	5	1	–	6
Syria	–	3	–	–	3
Tunisia	–	2	3	–	5
United Arab Emirates	–	2	–	–	2
North Yemen	–	1	1	–	2
South Yemen	–	1	–	–	1
Total	6	119	43	6	174

[a]German, Hebrew, Japanese, and Spanish

of the area has been credible and of use to scholars in the field. (Examples are the bimonthly *Jeune Afrique*—Paris, the monthly *Middle East*—London, and the monthly *New Outlook*—Tel Aviv.)

The result was a total of 298 items. Because of our relaxed criteria, however, the articles did not fall into a neat classification between, for instance, internal, regional, and international politics on the one hand and foreign policy proper on the other. This again reflects the under-development of the foreign policy subfield. We distinguished instead between two categories of articles: those dealing *primarily with an Arab country's foreign policy,* and those dealing with what we dubbed *system dynamics,* i.e., inter-Arab politics, great power influences on one or two Arab states, or regional politics as such.

This categorization gave us 124 articles for system dynamics, leaving 174 articles that deal with the foreign policies of Arab countries (see Table 1.1). From the classification of articles in Table 1.1, several con-clusions are apparent: the dominant language for foreign policy studies is still English (articles in Arabic are much more numerous in the category of system dynamics); articles in French are concentrated—for obvious historical reasons—on the Maghreb, including Libya; and the distribution of the 174 articles among countries is very uneven. Egypt and, increasingly, Saudi Arabia are relatively overpublished. The six publications in lan-guages other than Arabic, English, and French focus on these two countries. Many other countries—even crucial ones such as Kuwait, Syria, or the Sudan, are underpublished. Particularly striking is the complete absence in our survey of any publications on Lebanon's foreign policy.

By the end of the decade 1965–1975, not a single book in Arabic, English, or French had been published on the foreign policy of Egypt—an overpublished country according to our inventory. The number of articles on Egypt for the same decade amounted to 23, totaling 369 pages—an average of about 37 pages a year.

From a *qualitative* point of view, the situation is even worse. Among the 23 authors of the articles on Egypt whose professional affiliations could be ascertained (12 in all), 10 had an academic background. The majority of articles were written under the pressure of events or for a specific occasion, without the benefit of in-depth research. As a result, these works neither reflect the recent advances in comparative foreign policy conceptualization nor attempt to link data and theory.

Our review of the literature published between 1965 and 1975 revealed three important theoretical problems. First, the works of this decade did not provide an operational definition of the "what" of foreign policy: the output itself. Authors tended to deal with goals, objectives, strategies, general declarations, and official statements, actions, and transactions—accepting all of these as foreign policy. No distinction was made between general orientation or world view and specific behavior or action. Second, with the exception of reporting gossip or practicing a modern version of the "great man" theory of history, the dynamics and intricacies of the foreign policy–making process were largely neglected. The "black box" remained closed. Third, although most authors attempted to intrepret and analyze the sources or determinants of foreign policy, their efforts suffered from conceptual fuzziness and a lack of explicitness.

The year 1975 was a watershed for the study of Arab foreign policy. The breakthrough came with a new generation of researchers who were graduate students at the time and who combined both the knowledge of the area specialist and the methodology of social science in their Ph.D. dissertations. Examples include Adeed Dawisha's Ph.D. dissertation at London University on Egypt; Nicole Grimaud's, Marlène Nasr's, and Ghassan Salama's dissertations at the University of Paris on Algeria, Egypt, and Saudi Arabia respectively; Mohamed Selim's work at Carleton University on Nasser's operational code; Walid Mubarak's study at Indiana University on Kuwait; and Ahmad Yousef's and Mustafa Elwi's dissertations at Cairo University on Egypt's foreign policy decisions in 1962 and 1967.[13]

Some of these dissertations were published, initiating a debate on the present state of theory in foreign policy analysis for developing countries and on the problems of relevant hypotheses and data collection in a context of agonizing social change and underdevelopment.

1982–1988

The survey of the literature for this more recent period did not result in any lessening of the original classification difficulties, which are in part due to the nature of the topic itself. In fact, many authors do not explicitly delimit the foreign policy output (that is, an actor's international orientation and/or behavior), and therefore many articles are of a general nature, combining foreign policy analysis with a discussion of other aspects of the Arab system. A large number of articles also deal with Islam and its transnational links. In short, an inflated number of articles may be found on a country without illuminating its foreign policy proper. The most notable case in this respect is that of Lebanon, given the vast number of articles on the civil war and its international ramifications (for example, Israel's 1982 invasion and the links between different groups and Syria, Iraq, or Iran). In a majority of these articles, Lebanon is discussed as a battlefield for various forces, whereas Lebanon itself as well as its foreign policy is not discussed. This is also true, although to a much lesser degree, in regard to Somalia and the Ogaden war, Morocco and the Western Sahara, Libya and the Chad war, the war in Southern Sudan, and the Iran-Iraq war.

There are also the articles written on a specific current or historical event. A large number of articles were written in 1982 and 1987 celebrating the twentieth and twenty-fifth anniversaries of Algerian independence. These are usually general and historical, dealing only in part with foreign policy. Other articles deal with change in the political regime of a given country, discussing the replacement of policy-makers and the change in the bases of legitimacy (including the use of international behavior in this respect). Examples of this type are the writings on Ben Ali's 1987 constitutional coup d'état in Tunisia.

Although the same criteria of inclusion/exclusion used for the period 1965–1981 were maintained for this period, a few exceptions were made. A number of articles not explicitly devoted to foreign policy were included because of their direct bearing on the subject: for example, change in policy-making groups and bases of legitimacy, the role of foreign capital and international debt problems.

In sum, the decision to include or exclude a specific work was made on the basis of three considerations; (1) the identity of the author and his/her known area of research; (2) the type of periodical the article was published in, so that an article published in *Foreign Policy* or *Foreign Affairs* would be included in most cases; and (3) the number of sources available on the country (one considered to be underresearched would be subject to more liberal inclusion criteria). The end result of the survey of 193 periodicals, therefore, was 216 articles, covering the period from 1982 to the summer of 1988. A breakdown of these articles is found in Table 1.2.

A comparison of Tables 1.2 and 1.1 reveals the following: (1) more countries have been covered, 22 as opposed to 17, (2) more periodicals

TABLE 1.2 Articles on Twenty-one Arab Countries and Palestine, by Language of Publication, 1982–1988

Country	Language of Publication				
	Arabic	English	French	Other	Total
Algeria	–	–	8	2	10
Bahrain	–	–	–	–	–
Djibouti	–	–	1	–	1
Egypt	5	26	16	7	54
Iraq	–	9	8	3	20
Jordan	1	1	–	–	2
Kuwait	1	5	1	2	9
Lebanon	–	6	4	1	11
Libya	3	13	17	2	35
Mauritania	–	–	–	–	–
Morocco	–	1	9	1	11
Oman	1	1	–	–	2
Palestine	1	2	3	1	7
Qatar	–	–	–	–	–
Saudi Arabia	2	10	4	3	19
Somalia	–	1	1	–	2
Sudan	–	2	1	–	3
Syria	2	7	8	2	19
Tunisia	–	1	5	–	6
United Arab Emirates	–	–	–	–	–
North Yemen	1	2	–	–	3
South Yemen	–	1	1	–	2
Total	17	88	87	24	216

have been used, 109 as opposed to 101, and therefore the number of sources used increased to 216 as opposed to 174 used for the previous period. In particular, we may note the increase of publications in languages other than English. Thus publications in Arabic increased from 6 to 17 and in French from 43 to 87. English is still the dominant language of study, although its relative dominance is receding as a result of the marked increase in studies in other languages. There is also a marked increase in the number of French publications, related to France's traditional geographical area of interest, the Maghreb, and to a number of current political problems, with which the articles deal as a question of *conjoncture.* Thus, there are a large number of studies on Syria, motivated by France's interest in the fate of Lebanon, and on Libya, due to its involvement in Chad, an excolony and a French-speaking country. Because this trend is so closely linked to contemporary events, there is no indication that it will continue in the future.

As for other languages, we can sum up the shift in the language of publications by noting that, in the period 1965–1981, there were three publications in English or French for every one publication in another language. For the period 1982–1988, the ratio became almost one publication in English or French to each publication in another language.

Although the quality of these publications is still modest, there is growing improvement and more use of foreign policy concepts in analysis.[14] An interesting addition to the literature on foreign policy has been the growing number of dissertations that focus on foreign policy problematique and are inspired by an analytical framework. Examples of these are dissertations by Mary-Jane Deeb,[15] M. El-Warfally,[16] N. Grimaud,[17] S. Mutawi,[18] Salwa Gomaa,[19] Said Ihrai,[20] and Gamal Zahran.[21] There are also a number of recent books concentrating primarily on foreign policy and decision-making, such as those by R. Khalidi,[22] B. Korany,[23] N. Safran,[24] M. Selim,[25] I. Saaddin,[26] and F. Halliday.[27] Another significant development has been the appearance of a number of Arabic publications that concentrate on foreign policy proper and use highly systematic data. These include the *Arab Strategic Yearbook* published by Al Ahram Centre for Political and Strategic Studies, the publications of the Cairo University Centre for Political Studies and Research, particularly its yearbook on Egyptian foreign policy, the publications of the *Arab Thought Forum* in Amman, and finally the *Arab Studies International Quarterly* in Washington, D.C. (1987–   ).

THE FRAMEWORK FOR ANALYSIS

To ensure coherence and continuity between the chapters of the book, the analysis of each actor's foreign policy has been based on the same fundamental concepts and categories. An important task is the precise description of foreign policy output. Does "foreign policy" mean general objectives, specific acts, critical choices and decisions, or all of these combined? In his oft-cited 1966 article, Rosenau deals extensively with foreign policy determinants (the independent variables) and their comparative influence, but neglects to define what he means by foreign policy as an output.[28] The 1968 article by the *International Encyclopedia of the Social Sciences* follows Rosenau's example and offers no definition. Even textbooks neglect this conceptual task.

Our solution is to conceptualize foreign policy output as a *role*. The role concept is very handy for our purposes, as it allows the disaggregation of foreign policy output into its relevant components: the actor's general objectives, orientation, or strategy (role conception) and the specific foreign policy behavior (role performance or role enactment). This breakdown of foreign policy output into general objectives and concrete behavior attracts attention to an important question in both foreign policy empirical analysis and theory building: How does the foreign policy role conception (general strategy and declaratory objectives) conform to or depart from the role performance (actual behavior)? What is the disparity ratio between "say" and "do," between conception and behavior? What determines the variations in disparity ratio between different regimes and countries? Is it a question of *intra-elite* conflict, with political elites agreeing on a consensual foreign policy orientation but disagreeing on the manner of implementation? Is it a question of *inter-role* conflict, with objectives and actions at the regional level conflicting with those at the global level? Or is it only a question of *role strain*, when the realization of foreign policy objectives is beyond the capabilities of the Third World actor or beyond the capabilities of a regime lacking the legitimacy to mobilize needed resources?

The introduction of role theory to foreign policy analysis inspires numerous theoretical leads that might help the field to sharpen and operationalize its conceptual distinctions, and thus proceed more quickly in overcoming its handicaps and limitations.

The contribution of role theory is not limited to its conceptual capital; it is also of empirical relevance. For instance, the election of former actor Ronald Reagan to the highest political office in the United States, and the crucial political roles played by Mao's wife, Jiang Qing, and Evita Peron, who both worked as actresses, establish a link between role theory and political analysis more direct than most leaders would like to consider. The empirical relevance of the role concept to foreign policy analysis can be quite explicit. Witness the assertion made by a prominent Third World leader—Gamal Abdal Nasser of Egypt—at the beginning of his career: "I always imagine that in this region there is a role wandering aimlessly about in search of a hero to play it. . . . It is we, and we alone in virtue of our position, who can play the part."[29] Nasser relates role to position or status. In retrospect, this quotation reminds us that if objectives are not tailored to capabilities, the result is foreign policy *crises or failures* (e.g., Egypt's 1967 war with Israel, initiated when the better part of the Egyptian army was in Yemen). Foreign policy crises can lead to foreign policy *change* (e.g., Sadat's replacing the USSR with the United States as Egypt's dominant role partner and his signing of a formal peace treaty with Israel with all its bilateral and regional repercussions). In other words—as Linton reminded us fifty years ago and as Nasser confirmed almost thirty-five years ago—opportunities and constraints, rights and duties, are inseparable properties of the actor's position and status.

The proposed framework of analysis consists of the following fourfold scheme: domestic environment, foreign policy orientation, decision-making process, and foreign policy behavior.

Domestic Environment

Each of the following factors is analyzed as either enhancing or constraining the foreign policy options of a country.

Geography. A state's geographic position has long been considered an important determinant of its foreign policy. The impact of geography, however, is not static. We know that states change their foreign policy and that the significance of geographic position varies over time. In the twentieth century, geographic considerations have been tempered by modern military weaponry and advanced communications technology.

This is not to suggest that geography has lost all significance. In many cases, certain national interests and objectives are obviously dictated by geographic considerations. The location of a country among its immediate neighbors contributes to the development of national identity. A state's potential development is also influenced by its geography: material endowments (size, topography, climate, and natural resources) play a vital role in determining whether a country will develop industry or agriculture or both; whether it can support a large population; and whether it has elements of power such as a strong economic base or easily defendable borders. A nation's access to natural resources within its boundaries affects its ability to enforce its own foreign policy demands and to resist pressures by other states. Finally, geographic factors influence the actions of a ruling elite. The significance of this influence depends upon the perception and interpretation of geographic factors by policy-makers.[30]

In the case of developing countries, two issues are of particular importance. The first is the issue of artificial boundaries: a number of African boundaries, for instance, were drawn along latitudes and longitudes in the colonial offices of London, Paris, and other European capitals. These political divisions ignore geographic, ethnic, and economic considerations. The second issue concerns the proliferation of ministates that lack the ingredients of independent existence. This situation results in continuous dependence on larger countries for economic aid, political support, and military assistance.

Population and Social Structure. The size, composition, and geographic distribution of a country's population are factors in the calculus of national power. Although a large population does not guarantee international influence, states with small populations are usually at a disadvantage. The size of population is not in itself a sufficient index of power. It is the composition of the population—its social cohesiveness, education, and distribution of skills—that really makes a difference. Like geographic factors, population is not a static element; it must be viewed in relation to the sociopolitical context. It may surprise many to know that in the wars of 1948, 1956, and 1967, little Israel mobilized combat forces that were larger in number than the combined forces of its Arab adversaries, whose total population was fifteen to twenty times greater than Israel's. The issue of social or national integration is particularly important in developing countries; most have ethnic, religious, and racial problems. The existance of minority groups in frontier areas further complicates matters for developing countries, especially when they seek help from a neighboring country.

Economic Capability. This factor refers to the natural resources of a country (availability) and to its ability to mobilize them at the service of its foreign policy (control). Economic capability affects both a state's objectives and its means of implementing them. Poor states, for instance, are likely to have a low level of diplomatic representation. In the case of developing countries, two questions are investigated: to what extent is the economic infrastructure (agriculture, industry, and services) capable of satisfying the economic needs of the population, thus reducing the need for foreign aid; and does economic development tend to enhance or decrease dependence on foreign sources?

Military Capability. This capability is both quantitative (number of troops and weapons) and qualitative (level of weapons systems and training, past experiences, and cohesiveness). Almost all developing countries depend for their armaments on a limited number of sources in the developed world. Arms sales have indeed been a major avenue for influence and penetration. Most developing countries, however, aspire to establish large, strong armies. The army is viewed as a symbol of national independence and as an embodiment of the nation's dignity. The literature underlines three areas where armaments and foreign policy interact: first, countries that follow activist or change-oriented foreign policies usually embark on a policy of arms acquisition; second, the existence of large armies may entice decision-makers to use the military instrument in their foreign policy; and third, the army acts as a constraint, influencing the choice between foreign policy options.

Political Structure. Here we discuss to what extent the political structure provides opportunities or imposes constraints on decision-makers. A political structure may constitute a resource, depending on its stability, legitimacy, degree of institutionalization, and level of public support. Conversely, political factionalization and domestic instability may constrain the conduct of a purposeful foreign policy.

The low level of political institutionalization and the high level of political instability in most developing countries have several results. One is the primacy of the executive, particularly in the development of a presidential center that dominates the policy-making process. The presidential center usually enjoys relative freedom of action due to the absence of a free press or a strong opposition. In these countries the link between domestic and foreign policy is more direct than in the developed countries: foreign policy is employed for the achievement of domestic objectives. This point will be further developed in our discussion of the decision-making process.

Foreign Policy Orientation

The concept of orientation refers to one component of foreign policy output; the other components are decisions and actions. Orientation is the way a state's foreign policy elite perceives the world and its country's role in it. Kal Holsti defines orientation as a state's "general attitudes and commitments toward the external environment, its fundamental strategy for accomplishing its domestic and external objectives and aspirations and for coping with persisting threats."[31] Taking the degree of involvement in international politics as a criterion, he identifies three basic types of global orientation: isolation, nonalignment, and coalition building or alliance construction. Orientations are necessarily stable, though by no means rigid or unchanging. They may change due to a radical alteration in the domestic political structure, the regional balance of power, or the global system.

The analysis of a country's orientation may address questions such as: What are the country's general objectives and strategy at the global and regional levels? How do we explain their adoption by the ruling elite? How do orientations change over time and what are the sources of change?

The Decision-Making Process

There has been an overemphasis in the literature on the personalized character of the decision-making process and on the lack of political institutionalization in developing countries. Although this emphasis is essentially valid, it gives a simplistic and reductionist image of the decision-making process. An individual leader may have the ultimate say in the choice between alternatives, but he or she must take into consideration a great number of variables and must weigh the responses of various influential domestic groups. Moreover, in many instances the primary unit of decision-making is not the president as an individual but the presidency as an institution. Individual politicians in developing countries are directly involved in foreign policy–making, but this process takes place in a specific social and institutional context. Even in the most authoritarian regimes, institutional arrangements constitute an intermediary variable between individual decision-makers and their environment.

In developing countries, the number and the relative influence of participants in the decision-making process vary according to type of political regime and issue area (for example, "high" versus "low" politics). These differences, however, do not affect the general decision-making pattern, which is dominated by the executive power around or through *el señor presidente* or *la monarchie présidentielle*. Robert L. Rothstein argues that the pattern of this political process is a function of two characteristics: conflict and poverty. Conflict is caused by the fractionalization of the polity into primordial or economic divisions that may be tribal, ethnic, religious, regional, or class-oriented. The frequency and the intensity of conflict are heightened by ever-increasing poverty caused by rising demands and insufficient resources. This situation leads to constant struggle between the various groups for control of the state.[32]

If foreign policy as an area of choice is a field of opportunities and constraints, the developing country enters this arena with the double burden of an "international system of increasing complexity" and a "domestic base that is less secure and less manageable."[33] The impact of underdevelopment on policy-making is heightened by the fact that "new and inexperienced elites [are] forced to decide critical strategic issues without much knowledge or expertise, without many useful precedents, and in the face of sharp economic cleavages and serious foreign pressures."[34]

The conceptualization of the decision-making process in developing countries as a "resource gap problem" involving group conflicts is a big step toward removing the blinders of psychological reductionism. It opens the door to further investigation of how and when an alliance between domestic and external groups can influience the resource gap and determine the decisions to be taken. It also explains the infiltration by outside groups into a developing country's decision-making process.

Foreign Policy Behavior

This includes the concrete actions, positions, and decisions that the state takes or adopts in the conduct of its foreign policy. Foreign policy behavior is the concrete expression of orientation in specific acts, and it is analyzed in this book in relation to the superpowers as well as to other regional actors.

The behavior of developing countries has been generally characterized by support for the United Nations and other international organizations, advocacy of change in the global system, promotion of the idea of a new international economic order (NIEO), and emphasis on regional issues.

In brief, we think that this framework for analysis has certain merits. It reflects conceptual advances in foreign policy analysis. It is interdisciplinary, relevant to the specific situation of developing countries, and applicable to the Arab countries with which this book is concerned.

NOTES

1. Bahgat Korany, "Foreign Policy Models and Their Empirical Relevance to Third World Actors: A Critique and an Alternative," *International Social Science Journal* 26 (1974), pp. 70–94.

2. Quoted in Franklin Weinstein, *Indonesian Foreign Policy and the Dilemma of Dependence* (Ithaca, N.Y.: Cornell University Press, 1976), p. 21.

3. *Ibid.*, p. 26.

4. See for instance his analysis of Afro-Asian neutralism. Hans Morgenthau, "Neutrality and Neutralism," *The Year Book of World Affairs* (London) 11 (1957), pp. 47–75.

5. James Rosenau, Michael Brecher, and Margaret Hermann all follow this approach.

6. For an overview of the field see Bahgat Korany, "The Takeoff of Third World Studies? The Case of Foreign Policy," *World Politics* 35, 3 (1983), pp. 465–487. See also John Stremlau (ed.), *The Foreign Policy Priorities of Third World States* (Boulder, Colo.: Westview Press, 1982).

7. Maurice A. East and Joe I. Hagen, "Approaches to Small States' Foreign Policy: An Analysis of the Literature and Some Empirical Observations," Paper

presented to the International Studies Association meeting, Toronto, Canada, February 25–29, 1976.

8. Franklin Weinstein, "The Use of Foreign Policy in Indonesia: An Approach to the Analysis of Foreign Policy in Less Developed Countries," *World Politics* 24 (1972), pp. 356–382. Other examples are Pat McGowan and Charles Kegley, Jr. (eds.), *Foreign Policy and the Modern World System* (Beverly Hills, Calif.: Sage, 1982) vol. 8 in Sage International Yearbook of Foreign Policy Studies; and Timothy Shaw, "Peripheral Social Formations in the New International Division of Labor," *Journal of Modern African Studies*, 2413 (Sept. 1986), pp. 489–508.

9. Bahgat Korany, *Social Change, Charisma and International Behavior* (Leiden, Netherlands: Sijthoff, 1976), pp. 140–159.

10. In general see Thomas Biersteker, *Distortion or Development? Contending Perspectives on the Multinational Corporation* (Cambridge, Mass.: MIT Press, 1978), pp. 1–26. For an analysis of Egypt's situation, see Ali E. Hillal Dessouki, "Policy-Making in Egypt: A Case Study of the Open Door Economic Policy," *Social Problems* 28, 4 (1981), pp. 410–416.

11. Korany, "The Take-off," pp. 465–466.

12. Adeed Dawisha, "The Middle East," in Christopher Clapham (ed.), *Foreign Policy-Making in Developing States: A Comparative Approach* (London: Saxon House, 1977), p. 70.

13. Adeed Dawisha, *Egypt in the Arab World: The Elements of Foreign Policy* (London: Macmillan, 1976); Nicole Grimaud, "La politique étrangère de l'Algérie," Ph.D. diss., University of Paris, 1982, forthcoming as a book in 1984; Marlène Nasr, "L'idéologie nationale arabe dans les discours de Gamal Abdel Nasser: 1952–1979," Ph.D. diss., University of Paris–Sorbonne IV, 1979 (Arabic edition published by the Center for Arab Unity Studies, Beirut, 1981); Ghassan Salama, "La politique étrangère de l'Arabie Saoudite," Ph.D. diss., University of Paris, 1979 (Arabic edition published by the Institute for Arab Development, Beirut, 1980); Mohamed Selim, "The Operational Code Belief System and Foreign Policy Decision-Making: The Case of Gamal Abdel-Nasser," Ph.D. diss., Carleton University, Ottawa, 1979 (Arabic edition published by the Center for Arab Unity Studies, Beirut, 1983); Walid Mubarak, "Kuwait's Quest for Security, 1961–1973," Ph.D. diss., Indiana University, 1979; Ahmad Yousef Ahmad, "Egypt's Role in Yemen 1962–1967," Ph.D. diss., Cairo University, 1978 (in Arabic); and Mustafa Elwi, "Egypt's International Behavior During the Crisis of May-June 1967," Ph.D. diss., Cairo University, 1981 (in Arabic).

14. Notable recent examples are L. Carl Brown, *International Politics and the Middle East* (Princeton, N.J.: Princeton University Press, 1984); Nassif Hitti, *The Foreign Policy of Lebanon* (Oxford: Centre for Lebanese Studies, Paper no. 9, 1988); and Tareq Ismael, *International Relations of the Middle East* (Syracuse, N.Y.: Syracuse University Press, 1987); Abdul-Rida Assiri, *Kuwait's Foreign Policy: City-State in World Politics* (Boulder, Colo.: Westview Press, 1990).

15. Mary-Jane Deeb, *Libya's Foreign Policy in North Africa* (Boulder, Colo.: Westview Press, 1991).

16. Mahmoud El-Warfally, *Imagery and Ideology in U.S. Policy Toward Libya, 1969–1982* (Pittsburgh: University of Pittsburgh Press, 1988).

17. Nicole Grimaud, *La politique extérieure de l'Algérie* (Paris: Karthala, 1984).

18. Sami Mutawi, *Jordan and the 1967 War* (Cambridge and New York: Cambridge University Press, 1987).

19. Salwa Gomaa, *Egyptian Diplomacy in the 1970s: A Study in a Leadership Issue* (Beirut: Center for Arab Unity Studies, 1988) (in Arabic).

20. Said Ihrai, *Pouvoir et influence: État, partis et politique étrangère au Maroc* (Rabat, Morocco: Edino, 1986).

21. Gamal Zahran, *Egypt's Foreign Policy 1970–1981* (Cairo: Madboli Bookshop, 1987) (in Arabic).

22. Rashid Khalidi, *Under Siege: PLO Decision-Making in the 1982 War* (New York: Columbia University Press, 1986).

23. Bahgat Korany, *How Foreign Policy Decisions Are Made in the Third World* (Boulder, Colo.: Westview Press, 1986).

24. Nadav Safran, *Saudi Arabia: The Ceaseless Quest for Security* (Cambridge, Mass.: The Belknap Press of Harvard University Press, 1985).

25. Mohamed Selim, *Nasser's Operational Code: A Study in Belief Systems and Foreign Policy* (Beirut: Center for Arab Unity Studies, 1983) (in Arabic).

26. Ibrahim Saaddin et al., *Decision-Making in the Arab Homeland* (Beirut: Center for Arab Unity Studies, 1985) (in Arabic).

27. Fred Halliday, *Revolution and Foreign Policy: The Case of South Yemen 1967–1987* (New York: Cambridge University Press, 1989).

28. James Rosenau, "Pre-theories and Theories of Foreign Policy," in Barry Farrell (ed.), *Approaches to Comparative and International Politics* (Evanston, Ill.: Northwestern University Press, 1966), pp. 27–93.

29. Quoted in Peter Willetts, *The Nonaligned Movement: The Origins of a Third World Alliance* (New York: Nichols Publishing Co., 1978), p. 9.

30. Norman Hill, *International Politics* (New York: Harper & Row, 1963), p. 226; and Harold Sprout and Margaret Sprout, *Foundations of International Politics* (New York: D. Van Nostrand Co., 1962), p. 288ff.

31. K. J. Holsti, *International Politics* (Englewood Cliffs, N.J.: Prentice-Hall, 1977), p. 109.

32. Robert L. Rothstein, *The Weak in the World of the Strong: The Developing Countries in the International System* (New York: Columbia University Press, 1977), pp. 181–182.

33. *Ibid.*, p. 62.

34. *Ibid.*, p. 90.

2

The Global System
and Arab Foreign Policies:
The Primacy of Constraints

Bahgat Korany
Ali E. Hillal Dessouki

In the early 1980s when the first edition of this chapter was written, the emphasis was on the dialectics between the global system on the one hand and the Arab regional system and its state components on the other. In general, the relationship between the dominant system and any of its regions (that is, its subsystems) is that of inclusion and subordination. But in the case of the Arab world at the close of the 1970s, with memories of the 1973 oil embargo still fresh and confirmed by the second oil shock following the Iranian revolution, an argument was implied in some writings of the period that the Arab subsystem could not be so subordinate. After all, oil prices had risen more than fifteen times in less than ten years, Gulf countries had accumulated international reserves and increased their investments in developed countries, and Saudi Arabia—for instance—was admitted to the exclusive club of the International Monetary Fund (IMF) board of directors. But our analysis indicated that in fact Arab subordination was still very much a reality, even if some specific aspects of passing context—what the French call *conjoncture* as distinct from structure—gave a different impression.

If anything, by the end of the 1980s this subordination had not only persisted but even increased. Oil prices continued their fall until they reached sometimes only 25% of what they were in 1980 ($10 compared to $40). Moreover, the Arab world had increased its subordination by being more fragmented and hence less effective at the international level. Despite the abundant cash of some of its countries, the Arab world is still very much a part of the Third World.

25

TABLE 2.1   Different Analytical Approaches to the Global System

	←————— The Ideological Debate —————→	
	Traditionalism	*Marxism-Leninism*
The historian's analysis of the nineteenth-century balance-of-power system; the works of Hans Morgenthau	The analysis of the European capitalist system; Marx and Engels
The Methodological Debate		
	Behavioralism	*Dependencia*
	Systems analysis inspired by social and natural sciences; the works of M. Kaplan and D. Easton	Adoption of a political economy approach that emphasizes the characteristics and role of the periphery; the contributions of S. Amin and F. Cordoso

This chapter starts by defining the global system and summarizing four approaches to its analysis (Table 2.1). Despite the vertiginous speed with which the Stalinist systems collapsed in Eastern Europe and a postbipolar international system rose, Marxist regimes and groups are still maintained in parts of the Third World and Marxism officially still shapes their perceptions of the global system. Moreover, many analysts in both North and South do apprehend national and international society in ways inspired by Marxism as both a "theory of history" and even a tenet of social practice. Though this intellectual influence is in the process of change, the four basic conceptual lenses of the 1980s are thus still lingering on. The "dependency perspective" is singled out as the most relevant in confronting the problematique that interests us here: international stratification and inequality and their effects on developing countries. However, this perspective is found wanting for two reasons: it addresses the linkage of global system and foreign policy in terms that are too general, and it lumps together the different parts of the Third World as if specific variations among different regions did not exist. After reviewing the literature on the global system/foreign policy linkage, the chapter concentrates on the specific features of the Arab world, demonstrating the primacy of constraints in the formation of foreign policy.

DEFINING THE GLOBAL SYSTEM

By global system we mean the pattern of interactions among international actors, which take place according to an identifiable set of rules. This simple definition contains three basic elements:

First, international actors include both states and nonstate actors: international organizations such as the Organization of Petroleum Exporting Countries (OPEC) and the Arab League, multinational companies (the Seven Sisters, Aramco), and national liberation movements (the PLO; Algeria's Provisional Government, 1958–1962). These actors differ in capabilities, characteristic structure, and objectives.

Second, relations among actors follow regular patterns of international conflict and cooperation. These patterns constitute a whole; the system is more than the mere sum of relations among its members. Moreover, relations embrace different issue areas: diplomatic, economic, cultural, and military.

Third, these relations are governed by a set of rules that are usually incorporated into international law, the deliberations of international organizations, and the practice of states. These rules can be well established, explicit, and written; or evolving, implicit, and more or less consensual. International law includes treaties as well as international practice and custom. Implicit rules should not be understood, however, as being less important, for they can be crucial in the functioning of the system, as is the case in the field of nuclear deterrence.

Although the literature basically agrees on the definition of the global system, no consensus exists on what is the best means of analyzing it. Approaches and schools of thought conflict on this issue.

APPROACHES TO THE ANALYSIS OF THE GLOBAL SYSTEM

Differences over how to study the global system are part of a larger debate in the sociology of international relations. Basically, the debate has turned on two major issues: the methodological-conceptual one (traditionalism versus behavioralism) and the ideological-substantive one (liberal versus Marxist, developed country versus dependency approaches).[1]

The Traditionalism-Versus-Behavioralism Debate

Students of political analysis believe that the study of the global system passed through a methodological-conceptual revolution in the 1950s under the impact of the behavioral movement in political science.[2] This behavioral movement was a reaction to *traditional approaches* to the study of politics, which were based on the following common assumptions:

- Both empirical (factual) and normative (value-judgment) questions are proper subjects of enquiry.
- Formal institutions, legal systems, and historical description of political events are the proper focus of research.
- Quantitative methods should be used sparingly, if at all.

- Conclusions are drawn on the basis of informed judgment and careful study or observation, not from statistical probabilities based on many observed cases.
- It is doubtful whether scientific methods, in any sense other than careful and systematic inquiry, can be successfully transferred to the study of human behavior.

The new *behavioralist* wave, on the contrary, focused on individuals and their behavior rather than on formal/legal structures. The behavioralists' greatest emphasis was on rigor and precision in research. Their objective was the elaboration of law-like generalizations, a theoretical base for the "science of politics."[3] To attain this objective, they followed four steps: (1) the formulation, at the outset of the research project, of explicit hypotheses defining the relationship between dependent and independent variables (the phenomenon to be explained and its possible determinants); (2) the development of quantitative indicators of variables to measure and test the relationship; (3) the use of mathematical-statistical techniques whenever possible to achieve maximum precision in testing the different hypotheses; and (4) the carrying out of necessary cross-national research and the collection of comparative data to make generalizations reliable.

Some welcome concerns of the behavioralists were the importance of rigor in social research, the relevance of concepts borrowed from other social sciences to promote interdisciplinary analysis, and the utility of discovering patterns of political behavior rather than being limited to individual cases. However, the behavioralists overdid their case to the extent that some founders of the movement (e.g., David Easton) became skeptical and raised the possibility of a "postbehavioral era." This self-scrutiny and skepticism were inspired by the excesses of the behavioralist school: a preoccupation with method to the exclusion of substantive issues, a focus on the most readily quantifiable hypotheses rather than on the relevant and meaningful ones, the promotion of expensive research tools such as computers and databanks and jargon incomprehensible to the policy-maker, and the relative neglect of some major ethical questions in a world of poverty, hunger, violence, and a nuclear balance of terror.[4]

Western Approaches, Marxism, and Dependencia

By the 1960s, a Third World perspective was coalescing around the dependency perspective to counterbalance established approaches. At first, this dependency perspective was associated with classical Marxism, and thus suffered from the poisoned atmosphere of the Cold War, but with the increasing excesses and failures of behavioralism in the late 1960s, young political scientists and politicians turned more and more toward the dependency perspective. By the early 1970s, the field of global system analysis included the schools listed in Table 2.1.

The traditional approach to the analysis of the global system concentrated only on inter-European politics, treating all events in the Third World purely as extensions of this major conflict. Indeed, traditionalists treated all international relations as inter-state phenomena, emphasizing the separation between domestic and external policies. They followed the so-called billiard-ball model of the state, which envisions borders as impenetrable barriers. Behavioralism attacked traditionalism for its methodological sloppiness and stressed the role of nonstate actors[5] as well as the linkage[6] between domestic and foreign policies. Methodological refinement notwithstanding, behavioralism was still as Eurocentric as traditionalism. Most importantly, however, behavioralists overemphasized academic neutrality, mistrusted "ideological issues," and hence made many of the substantive sociopolitical problems of the world taboo.

The drawbacks of behavioralism account for the general seductiveness of Marxism and the popularity of Lenin's theory of imperialism. Marxism focused on the impact of nonstate actors and linkages in an interdisciplinary way, emphasizing the "real life issues" of exploitation, inequality, and the hierarchy among major political actors. But even this approach was elaborated in terms of Europe, the system's center. Marxism also seemed to neglect the role of the superstructure in an age of populism and the interventionist corporatist state.[7] Marxism's frowning upon nationalism and its de-emphasis of the role of peasants (a massive proletariat is still absent in the predominantly agrarian Third World societies) were additional drawbacks.

Though sharing Marxism's emphasis on the importance of real-life issues and on the system's structural properties, dependencia tried to cope with deficiencies and anachronisms by bringing the "periphery" in. Building on previous advances in social analysis (e.g., rigor, interdisciplinarity, and the dialectical approach), the dependency perspective concentrates on the relationship between the global system and Third World societies, and hence comes nearest to our chosen problematique.

At this conceptual level, the late 1980s ushered in the third debate (after the first two of idealism/realism of the 1930s and 1940s, and traditionalism/behavioralism of the 1960s and 1970s). A major characteristic of this third debate is the increasing realization of the importance of an "ideological contamination" factor (that is, the absence of complete objectivity) in the choice of concepts and methods. Consequently, various interpretative lenses of looking at the world could be equally legitimate (the rise of a school of hermeneutics). There is thus a return to an emphasis on understanding and interpretation of social phenomena (more qualitative analysis) rather than an obsession with measurement and data tables (that is, numerology). In a nutshell, the big loser in this third debate is behavioralism with its empiricist approach and atomization of research. It is thus being replaced by an attempt to modernize traditionalism: neorealism. This latter approach incorporates some of the rigorous reasoning of the behavioralist era but signals a return to the use of history and grand theorizing about the global system.[8] Though some of its authors incorporate a certain brand of political economy,[9] it is centered on a big powers' approach to the international system.

However, neorealism's emphasis on interpretation and qualitative analysis, grand theorizing, discovery of historical patterns, mistrust of pure measurement and synchronic methods, consciousness of episte-mological-philosophical underpinnings of conceptualization, and redis-covery of the relevance of political economy could not but benefit the dependency approach and world system analysis à la Wallerstein.[10] Though some of this approach's details (for example, role of the state and patterns of state/society relations) have to be completed, its ma-crodimension and its emphasis on the subordinate place of the Third World in the hierarchical global system are vindicated.

As useful surveys of the perspective are now available,[11] we will limit ourselves to analyzing its basic propositions[12] (six in all) to see how they help in dealing with the global system and its influence on foreign policy–making.

THE MODIFIED DEPENDENCY PERSPECTIVE
EMPHASIZED HERE: ITS BASIC PROPOSITIONS

1. Present problems of Third World underdevelopment and devel-opment cannot be studied in isolation from their historical and global context. In a nutshell, Third World underdevelopment and development are part of a global dynamic: the process of change in the worldwide capitalist system.

2. Although internal structure and processes do play a role in Third World societies, most important changes in these societies are ultimately determined by external forces. This reveals the inability of Third World societies to exert much control over their own destinies, let alone over the larger world system. The use of the term "dependent" to describe this situation is amply justified both in practice and in theory.

3. Rather than being an isolated, mechanistic process, economic change is part of the general societal process and reflects the roles of different groups at the national and international levels. Two consequences follow: (1) the real object of our study is neither economics nor politics, but political economy, which is the interaction between the two; and (2) the state's sovereignty and frontiers are analytical concepts rather than barriers: in short, separation between the domestic and foreign policies of the penetrable Third World society is either a fiction or an aberration. Consequently, all social institutions—from the family and culture to religion and the media—are linked to the world political economy and the world domination patterns that underlie it.

4. The influence of the worldwide (capitalist) system is no longer exerted through an impersonal market, but through an important nonstate actor: the multinational company (MNC). Though the MNCs behave

with visible and deliberate purpose, they do not necessarily have the interests of the Third World at heart. For example, the industrialization that the MNCs sponsor is based on sophisticated technology (which has to be imported) and thus requires lots of foreign currency (which is scarce) but little local labor (which is plentiful).[13] The list of ensuing harmful effects can be extensive. Multinational companies drive out locally owned businesses; export scarce capital through profit remittances, transfer payments, and patent royalties; create unnecessary and alien consumption patterns; corrupt local politicians; and contaminate social values.

5. An examination of the pattern of international stratification—essential for an understanding of Third World foreign policies—shows that many local groups are consciously or unconsciously dependent on the existing system and hence unlikely to challenge it. These groups include landowners, the growing state bureaucracies, and the entrepreneurial bourgeoisie.

6. The road to change is therefore a difficult one. Some degree of dissociation of the dependent periphery from the system's core may be necessary as the only way to recreate another, more just structure.

The dependency perspective has three advantages as far as Third World foreign policy analysis is concerned. First, it emphasizes the role of structural factors that could account for foreign policy better than traditional approaches. For example, patterns of social organization and institutions could be emphasized instead of psychological or idiosyncratic factors. Second, it is a dynamic perspective that emphasizes both the role of social change in a global context and the linkage between the different levels of analysis—from the global to the subnational—through the hierarchical network of different social groups. The state is no longer seen as the compact and impermeable billiard ball traditionalists assumed it to be. And third, the advocates of dependency theory pushed aside rigid discipline boundaries to emphasize the close relationship between political, economic, historical, and sociological phenomena.

However, the perspective has two main drawbacks for an analysis of the linkage between the global system and foreign policy. For one, it is much more concerned with general patterns of national underdevelopment and development than with the systematic analysis of a dependent country's foreign policy. For instance, according to proposition 6 above, a country's policy-makers are advised to reverse dependency through dissociation from the system, but many questions remain unanswered. For instance, what form will the dissociation take? What groups can lead the effort? What specific policies should they adopt? This high level of generality is related to the second drawback: the perspective's homogenizing tendency to lump together all Third World societies. A common Third World position in the global system notwithstanding, there are variations among Third World regions. These variations[14] involve patterns of precolonial evolution and types of colonial relationship, social organization, and phases of development (e.g., Black Africa versus Latin America; India versus Honduras). In short, we need to sort out the common features of the Third World as a whole from the specific characteristics of its regions. Distinguishing general and specific traits will help make the analysis of the relationship between global system and foreign policy much more concrete. We shall deal with problems presented by each of these drawbacks in order to attune the dependency perspective to the analysis of Arab and Third World foreign policies.

What Elements Are Specific to the Arab World?

Despite common socioeconomic features and interests, the Third World is not a uniform group. Third World members vary in level of development (Brazil versus Upper Volta), GNP per capita (Argentina's $2,390 versus Bangladesh's $130), political orientation (Cuba versus Malawi), and historical experience (Senegal versus "noncolonized" Ethiopia). The Arab world, however, possesses several common elements that predominate over inter-Arab variations and make this group a distinct entity within the larger group of developing or dependent countries. These shared features include an Islamic component, cultural homogeneity, concentration of relevant resources, and the constant plague of a protracted social conflict (the Palestine-Zionist issue).

The Islamic Component. The coincidence between change in prevalent conceptualization (that is, rise of an interpretative-qualitative approach) and in global political reality (the decline in the East-West conflict) will increasingly single out the North-South dimension. As an offshoot, there could be more interest in the development of an "Islamic theory of international relations,"[15] that is, the development of "a set of abstract principles and values—a framework or set of guidelines."[16] What is interesting is that this Islamic conceptual lens could also be inspired by some tenets of the dependency perspective (as in the case of Iran or some radical Islamic groups). Moreover, some governments might be pushed by these groups to adopt an "Islamic foreign policy" to increase their legitimacy and mobilizational capacity. (Note the recent example of the secularist Saddam Hussein's emphasis on jihad against the coalition forces following the invasion of Kuwait.)

But even then, there could not be an identical foreign policy for the majority of Arab countries since other differentiating foreign policy determinants (geopolitical characteristics, level of economic resources, elite formation) will continue to have their impact in shaping individual countries' foreign policies.[17] Rather, it is the presence of Islam as a macrovariable, as a "conditioning situation" (to borrow the dependentistas' favorite term) that shapes the context within which foreign policy is debated and made. Its influence is greatest as a frame of reference within which specific foreign policy moves have to be decided. Other specificity aspects of the Arab world (cultural homogeneity, concentration of relevant resources, the Palestinian-Zionist protracted conflict) exist and tend to differentiate this region from the rest of the Third World.

Cultural Homogeneity. As a people, Arabs enjoy a high degree of linguistic and cultural homogeneity. Notwithstanding subnational variations due to the local history of each community, the greatest majority of the Arabs belong to the same religion, the same cultural tradition; they share a common history and converse in the same language. One of the dominant intellectual and political trends in the Arab world in the twentieth century has been Arab nationalism and the call for Arab unity. The pan-Arab trend was manifested in scores of cultural and literary clubs at the turn of the century, in political movements with branches in a number of Arab countries—the Ba'th party and the Arab nationalist movement are two, and in Egypt's policies of the 1950s and 1960s.

According to this pan-Arab ideology, the Arab world is one nation, and its division into separate states is an aberration resulting from "foreign designs." The daily circulation of Egyptian or Lebanese newspapers in different Arab countries, the use of common films and television programs, the presence of Arab students of all nationalities in the universities of Cairo, Baghdad, or Kuwait, and more recently the increasing labor migration: all indicate a level of exchange in the Arab world unparalleled in other Third World regions.

The high level of Arab interaction belies some established theories of the global system, e.g., Galtung's notion of a feudal pattern of international interactions.[18] According to this pattern, interaction is intense among top dogs (developed countries), quite high between developing and developed countries, and very limited among underdeveloped or dependent countries (the underdogs). Moreover, interaction among underdeveloped countries usually takes place through developed countries, according to Galtung.

Not only does Arab cultural homogeneity make Galtung's theory of the global system inapplicable to the Arab world, but it has also had political consequences at the regional Arab level. Arabs see themselves as having played a distinct and glorious part in the world civilization. They believe that they have a special role within Islam and the Moslem world. Islam was revealed to an Arab; its sacred shrines are in an Arab country; and its book, the Qur'an, can only be recited in Arabic. Because of their relatively early independence (mostly in the 1940s in the Arab East and the 1950s and 1960s in the Arab West), certain Arab countries (particularly Egypt) also played a significant role in the anticolonial movement in Africa and in the development of the nonaligned movement. In the 1970s, other Arab countries (Libya, Saudi Arabia, Algeria, and Morocco) played roles far beyond their immediate borders, as described in Chapters 4, 7, and 10.

A basic component of Arab political culture is the belief that Arab nationhood will be translated into Arab statehood, and that the present division of the Arab nation into several states is both artificial and temporary. This explains the enthusiasm with which the Arab masses accepted the union of Egypt and Syria as the United Arab Republic (1958–1961). This last case, in fact, confirms another important characteristic of Arab politics: intense involvement by the masses. It is almost as if inter-Arab relations are not really foreign relations but part of the politics of the extended family instead. Thus, Arab leaders tend to talk directly to the citizens of other Arab states. Moreover, pan-Arab issues (e.g., the Palestine problem) become a component of political legitimacy for many Arab regimes. The condemnation of Sadat's 1977 Jerusalem visit and the 1978 Camp David agreements was less an expression of opposition to peace with Israel than a protest against Sadat's go-it-alone diplomacy on a pan-Arab issue.

Arab cultural homogeneity has also led to occasional confrontation with the big powers. These powers are concerned over the potential emergence of a unified Arab state that could constitute an effective barrier to their influence in the region and their desire to control Arab resources. Both the West and the USSR clashed with Nasser on the occasion of the constitution of the United Arab Republic.[19]

The Protracted Palestinian-Israeli Conflict. All Arab countries—secular[20] and religious, radical and conservative—view the dispersion of the Palestinians as a blatant case of injustice against all Arabs. Already in 1960, the cofounder of the Ba'th Pan-Arab party and the former prime minister of Syria, Salah Eddin Al-Bitar, emphasized the "Western betrayal" and linked it to the foreign policy that the "Arab nation" should follow: "Western imperialism divided the Arab homeland, maintained it in a divided condition, took away Palestine, drove out its people, made it Jewish. . . . Thus the Arab position must reflect an attitude toward the West which is in harmony with the lack of Western justice."[21] The popularity among Arab public opinion of Saddam Hussein's attempt to link his evacuation of Kuwait with Israel's evacuation of occupied Arab territories was a reflection of this feeling of Western betrayal.

This perception of the Palestinian problem and of Western policy toward the Arabs is the major reason that Arab nationalists in the mid-1950s refused participation in Western alliances and adopted a policy of nonalignment.

Oil. If the popular image of the Arab as a bedouin has been replaced, it is by the image of the rich oil sheikh. The Algerians may be right when they say that oil is only another primary product, and hence that oil producers are like any other raw-material producers in the Third World. However, the realities of the 1970s indicated that oil has a very special impact on the global system. The shock of the 1973 oil embargo, associated in developed countries with long lines at petrol stations and talk of hard winters with minimum heating oil, showed that oil was special. (It is appropriate to note here that almost twenty years later, in addition to the upholding of international norms and principles, U.S.

TABLE 2.2   Arab Oil Power in 1971 and 1980

Country	1971		1980	
	Oil Production (bpd)ᵃ	Oil Revenue (millions U.S.$)	Oil Production (bpd)ᵃ	Oil Revenue (millions U.S.$)
Saudi Arabia	4.545	2,160	9.990	104,200
Kuwait	2.975	1,395	1.425	18,300
Iraq	1.700	840	2.645	26,500
United Arab Emirates	1.060	421	1.005	19,200
Qatar	0.430	198	0.470	5,200
Libya	2.765	1,766	1.790	23,200
Algeria	0.780	320	1.040	11,700
Total	14.255	7,100	18.365	208,300

ᵃBarrels per day

Source: Adapted from Michael Field, "Oil in the Middle East and North Africa," in *The Middle East and North Africa 1982–1983* (London: Europa Publications, 1982), pp. 98–134.

and Western speedy action against the invasion of Kuwait was motivated by that country's geopolitical position in the oil-rich Gulf region.)

The embargo by Arab oil producers could carry such clout for two reasons: they possessed a substantial percentage of world oil exports (see Table 2.2) and they acted in concert in the context of an energy-hungry world. The results of their action were a global systemic crisis and increased bargaining power for Arab oil producers. Saudi Arabia saw its international status change almost overnight from that of a purely Islamic leader to that of an oil power. The fact that Saudi Arabia was invited to sit on the IMF board of directors shows that Arab oil producers could, if they chose, influence many aspects of the global economy.

Oil wealth also gave impetus to the idea of a new grouping in the global system: the African-Arab-European dialogue. The rationale for this triangle of cooperation was to capitalize on the assets of the three groups: Africa with its enormous potential in agricultural and mineral sectors, but lack of technology, capital, and trained manpower; the Gulf Arabs with their oil and cash surplus; and the OECD (Organization for Economic Cooperation and Development) countries with their technology, skilled labor, and banking facilities for recycling petrofunds.

However, by the end of the 1980s these hopes did not materialize. The institutionalization of the Arab-African cooperation not only failed to pick up speed, but it even stopped altogether, and enthusiasm for the Euro-Arab dialogue was lost. This slowing of different facets of international cooperation around the Arab world coincided with the great decline in Arab countries' oil revenues (as Table 2.3 shows).

The table speaks for itself; many of these oil-producing countries have seen their revenues decline from the peak year (1980–1981) by more

TABLE 2.3 Government Oil Revenues of Arab OPEC Member Countries in the Middle East and North Africa (in million U.S. dollars)

	1977	1978	1979	1980	1981	1982	1983	1984	1985	1986	1987	1988
Saudi Arabia	38,000	36,700	59,200	104,200	113,300	76,000	46,000	43,700	28,000	20,000	23,000	21,000
Kuwait	8,500	9,500	16,300	18,300	14,800	10,000	85,900	10,800	9,000	6,000	7,000	7,000
Iraq	9,500	11,600	21,200	26,500	10,400	9,500	8,400	10,400	12,000	7,000	11,000	12,000
United Arab Emirates	8,000	8,700	13,000	19,200	18,700	16,000	12,800	13,000	12,000	7,000	9,000	8,000
Qatar	1,900	2,200	3,100	5,200	5,300	4,200	3,000	4,400	3,000	1,000	2,000	2,000
Libya	9,400	9,300	15,200	23,200	15,700	14,000	11,200	10,400	10,000	5,000	6,000	5,000
Algeria	5,000	5,400	7,500	11,700	10,800	8,500	9,700	9,700	8,000	4,000	5,000	5,000

Source: Peter Bild, "Oil in the Middle East and North Africa," in The Middle East and North Africa, 1990 (London: Europa Publications, 1990), pp. 134–173.

than half. Indeed, between 1981 and 1988 Saudi Arabia's revenue declined by more than 500%. In retrospect, then, the so-called petropower was a change of only short duration in the continuing history of international subordination (as we will see shortly concerning the limitation of resource power). These ups and downs (and more downs than ups in the 1980s) confirm the primacy of global constraints in the shaping of Arab foreign policies.

From 1956 to 1973, there have been eleven interventions by the big powers in the Arab East alone.[22] This high level of big-power attention may reflect several factors: the strategic position of the Arab world; Soviet interest in the warm waters of the Mediterranean; Western dependence on oil and fear of a Soviet threat; the influence of various transnational actors such as multinational oil companies and the Zionist movement; and the growing Arab market for arms and other goods. Whatever the reasons, the high level of big-power involvement in the region's affairs has blurred the distinction between purely regional and global issues. This brings us to the last point of this chapter: the impact of the global system on Arab foreign policies.

THE PRIMACY OF GLOBAL CONSTRAINTS

To the majority of international actors, the global system presents an arena of both constraints and opportunities. In the case of Arab countries— as with the rest of the developing or dependent countries—the constraints outnumber the opportunities. We will show the primacy of constraints in examining three main issues: the imposition of an arms control regime, the limits of oil as resource power, and Israel's extraterritoriality and Jewishness.

The Arms Control Regime

Arab-Israeli relations in the last thirty-five years have cost the Arab East six major wars, including the 1948 war at the creation of Israel, the 1982 Lebanese invasion, and the 1969–1970 War of Attrition between Egypt and Israel. With Iraq's invasion of Kuwait and its consequences for the Gulf countries, even Arab-Arab relations are becoming militarized. It is no wonder, then, that Israel and the countries of the Arab East have been the largest arms purchasers in the world during the 1970s and 1980s (Table 2.4). On both ethical and social grounds, any attempts are welcome that eliminate or at least limit wars that kill, maim, and waste needed development energies and funds.[23] But arms control regimes (a set of rules imposed by the great powers) have used the political context provided by the escalating Arab-Israeli conflict to buy influence and promote their own political objectives rather than to pursue political solutions.

A good example of the use of an arms supply and control regime as a means of domination over the recipients' policies is the May 1950

TABLE 2.4   Cumulative Value of Arms Transfers to Twenty Arab Countries, 1982–1986 (in million U.S. dollars)

Algeria	3,730
Bahrain	135
Egypt	7,640
Iraq	31,740
Israel	3,700
Jordan	3,355
Kuwait	1,120
Lebanon	585
Libya	10,160
Mauritania	40
Morocco	1,000
Oman	890
Qatar	830
Saudi Arabia	16,715
Sudan	470
Syria	10,830
Tunisia	580
United Arab Emirates	380
Yemen Arab Republic	1,485
Yemen, People's Dem. Republic	1,840
Total	97,225
%	100
Middle East and North Africa % of total arms exports	43.5
Middle East and North Africa % of total Third World arms exports	54.0

Source: Adapted from Hans Maull, "The Arms Trade with the Middle East," in *The Middle East and North Africa, 1990* (London: Europa Publications, 1990), pp. 126–133.

Tripartite Declaration on the Middle East by the three major Western powers of the period: the United States, Great Britain, and France. The statement recognized the need of the Arab states and Israel "to maintain a certain level of armed forces for . . . their internal security and legitimate self-defence to permit them to play their part in the defence of the area as a whole."[24] Thus arms were to be supplied according to the "good conduct" of each nation as judged by Washington, London, or Paris; no alternative arms supplier, of course, could ever be used. In this way, the declaration attained two objectives: it maintained a Western monopoly over the region, and it maintained the territorial status quo.

Israel welcomed the declaration. None of the Arab countries were consulted. In a joint statement, the Arabs reaffirmed their "pacific intentions," but stressed the "sovereign right of each State to evaluate its arms needs." However, when pan-Arabists like Nasser asserted this sovereign right (by negotiating the 1955 Soviet arms deal following the

West's refusal to supply such arms), immediate coercive measures were applied. These ranged from economic pressure and the withdrawal of aid to blatant military intervention (the 1956 Suez invasion). An immediate objective was to defeat this revolt against the system, or at least to impose a high price for disobedience and thus discourage its repetition elsewhere.[25]

The 1955 Soviet arms deal also demonstrates the opportunities that could be exploited by a dependent country; for Egypt's attempts to loosen the system's straitjacket control would not have been successful without an alternative power both available and ready to counterbalance the domination of the "capitalist core." In 1955, the Cold War context accelerated Soviet readiness to be involved, thereby helping Nasser to break free from the West.

This last point shows that a dependent or dominated state can still maneuver to maximize opportunities resulting from the system's structure and the global context; however, it is impossible to eliminate the constraints.[26] For example, by the early 1970s Egypt had changed its dominant international partner by establishing close military and economic cooperation with the Soviets. Yet Egypt was still very constrained in the type of weapons it could receive and by limits on their use. Thus in Sadat's mind the departure of Soviet experts in 1972 was a necessary prerequisite for launching the October War of 1973. Following the war, Sadat's Egypt changed dominant partners again and was reintegrated into the Western core, but constraints remained. We have only to think of Egypt's dependence on U.S. food shipments, the $1.3 billion in annual U.S. aid, and the borrowing facilities on the international market that Egypt would not have access to without the help of the United States.

To conclude, the present structure of the global system and the proliferation of "limited wars" have given the central powers huge leverage over their Third World subordinates. Though arms transfers and arms control measures have often been couched in moralistic and altruistic terms, historical evidence indicates that control of the arms traffic has been used as a privileged instrument of the central powers to exploit a favorable regional context. Their major aims were to promote their own political objectives and gain unilateral benefits against their global opponents—at the expense of local powers if necessary.

The Limitation of Resource Power

If any primary product could have an effect on the global system in the 1970s, it was certainly oil. In less than a decade, the price of a barrel of oil rose from $2 in 1972 to $42 at the end of 1981. From 1974 to 1976, OPEC countries increased their investments in U.S. commercial banks and in treasury and portfolio securities from $5.5 to $8.9 billion.[27] As a result, fragile and even vulnerable countries have come to occupy the center of world politics, as data on the increase of diplomatic representation and visits to Saudi Arabia as well as the hurry to send more than a half million U.S. military personnel to that country show. Stereotyped notions of "oil power" and "the Arabs are coming" aside, does the possession of oil by a few Arab countries open a range of opportunities for some developing states?

The 1973 oil embargo had a great impact because of its surprise effect; the oil-hungry system was quite unprepared for the sudden cutoff of supplies. But global demand can decline almost as quickly as it can rise, and this could shatter the oil-based economies of these countries. The impact of fluctuations shows how dependent the so-called oil powers are on the economies of the developed countries and on global economic policies as a whole.

For instance, between 1979 and 1982, oil demand in the noncommunist world dropped from 52.4 million barrels per day (bpd) to only 45.5 million.[28] Perhaps half of this decline was due to the worldwide recession— U.S. factories, for example, were operating at only 60% of capacity, but the developed countries' policy of conservation has turned out to be an even more important factor in the market place. Between 1973 and 1980, economic output in the major industrial countries increased by 19%, while total energy consumption grew by only 4%, and petroleum use actually declined. The problem for OAPEC (Organization of Arab Petroleum-Exporting Countries) is that the market loss due to conservation is irreversible. Even lower oil prices will not induce homeowners to rip the insulation out of their attics, or persuade automakers to build gas-guzzling cars.[29]

Developed countries have also demonstrated the fragility of oil power by entering the market as new producers with oil and gas fields of their own—in Alaska and the North Sea, for example. Because of this increased competition and sagging oil demand, OPEC's sales started to slide in 1982 for the first time in nearly two decades. By February 1983, OPEC's share of the noncommunist world's total oil supply stood at 46%, down from 68% in 1976.[30] Between 1979 and 1982, world demand dropped by 9.5 million bpd, and OPEC's production fell by more than 12 million bpd, to 17.75 million bpd. Yet according to one estimate, OPEC members need to produce about 21 million bpd to meet the needs of their own economies.[31] Even if the Arab oil producers are not yet in the same economic plight as Nigeria, which had to evict hundreds of thousands of foreign workers almost overnight, the writing is on the wall. Although they appear powerful, oil producers are in fact hostages to the global system and the short-term fluctuations of developed economies (as Table 2.3 showed).

Even before the 1982–1983 world oil glut, oil power could not guarantee the success of the 1975 Paris conference on North-South relations, nor achieve the global change insisted on by Algeria, nor establish the New International Economic Order (NIEO) that the Third World demanded. In this respect, Saudi minister of finance Abu Al-Khail's statement in 1975 is very relevant: "Saudi Arabia has surplus cash." But it is wealth rather than cash—as Adam Smith showed two centuries ago—that adds to a country's economic-military capabilities, and allows it to increase the ratio of global opportunities to global constraints. One may even argue that because of the present structure of the global system, even oil cash is recycled to Western countries, as data on Saudi arms purchases, imports, and Kuwaiti-Saudi financing of part of Operation Desert Shield show. In this sense, the system's core enjoys both the oil and its revenue.

The 1973 oil embargo also failed at the regional level to attain some of its most explicit objectives: the settlement of the Palestinian issue and the evacuation of Arab lands occupied by Israel in the 1967 war. It should be remembered that when OAPEC decided on the embargo, the resolution stated explicitly that this embargo and curb on production would not be lifted before Arab territories (Syria's Golan Heights, Egypt's Sinai, and Jordan's West Bank) were evacuated. A few months later, however, Secretary of State Kissinger managed to restore the status quo ante: normal oil flow without the return of Arab lands. This brings us to the Israeli issue as it relates to the primacy of global constraints.

Israel as an Extraterritorial Actor

It has been argued that the presence of Israel in the area encourages unity among Arab countries. This argument is predicated on the assumption that Arabs are united less by positive or constructive ideology than by their hostility toward Israel.

Leaving aside political rhetoric, this proposition can still be substantiated by the theory of conflict. According to this theory, when a group—a nation, a party, or a family—faces a serious external danger, it tends to downplay or forget internal conflicts in order to close ranks in the face of the outside threat. This model does indeed apply in both Arab and Israeli societies; the governments of both have occasionally used the conflict to cement national unity. Though important, this factor can be misleading if no account is taken of the other aspects of Arab-Israeli relations.[32] One such aspect is the specific character of Israel as an extraterritorial state.

Based on historical and sociological considerations, Israeli leaders insist on the conception of Israel as the embodiment of the Jewish dream of statehood. As a result a very complicated set of delicate and original problems, as Nahum Goldman, ex-head of the World Zionist Organization and World Jewish Congress, put it, faces Israel in its relations with the Diaspora.[33] In his three-volume classic on Israel's foreign policy, Michael Brecher dealt with this issue in relation to foreign policy analysis:

> The presence of externally based foreign policy interest groups is widespread in an age of "penetrated political systems": no state is totally immune from group pressures stemming from beyond its territorial boundaries. None is comparable to Israel in this respect, however. Israel is a self-conscious *Jewish* state; indeed that is its *raison d'être*; and Israel is the only Jewish state, indissolubly linked to world Jewry in the minds of her

leaders and of most Jews—and of most non-Jews in the Euro-American world as well.[34]

Among these Diaspora Jews, the over 6 million of North America stand out. Not only are they almost double the Jewish population of the state of Israel, but they have also provided Israel's basic means of political, financial, and economic support.[35] Without them,[36] Israel would not have achieved international recognition so quickly[37] and surmounted its political, economic, and military challenges so successfully.[38]

The result is that the influence of the central powers has been continuously felt in the daily evolution of the Arab system. From the very beginning, the creation of Israel and the subsequent conflict between Arabs and Israelis was determined by external events[39] such as the 1917 Balfour Declaration giving Britain's promise of a Jewish national home, the Hitler Holocaust and the subsequent Western desire to compensate the Jews by helping them to settle in Palestine, and then the decision to partition Palestine.

Even at the level of policy-making and implementation, European and American Jews participated directly in deciding the evolution of the Middle East. In the early years following the establishment of the state of Israel, the World Zionist Organization attempted to secure for its president, Nahum Goldman, an invitation to attend Israeli cabinet meetings. Israel's prime minister at the time, Ben Gurion, refused.[40] Goldman returned to this subject in his writings,[41] reviewing the proposals for a joint decision-making organ between Israel and the Jewish Diaspora (e.g., the establishment of a senate, in addition to the Israeli Parliament, where the elected representatives of the Diaspora would sit; the creation of a permanent assembly where equal numbers of Israelis and representatives of world Jewry would sit). In the absence of any common decision-making institution, Goldman found the existing practice unsatisfactory: periodic visits to Israel by leaders of Jewish organizations to discuss with the members of the Israeli government the current state of affairs. Israel's extraterritoriality has brought the global system even more concretely into the region's affairs. Possible lines of demarcation between regional interactions and global politics have become even more blurred.

The Debt Problem

It might seem contradictory to talk about a problem of debt when some of these countries (for example, the United Arab Emirates) in the early 1980s had the highest levels of per capita income. But with the continuing decline in oil prices and quantities sold, even some of these rich countries have started having balance of payments deficits and have had to borrow year after year on the international market to remedy these deficits. Even with their greatest trading partner, the European Economic Community, Gulf countries' non-oil exports are minimal and the Community enjoyed a $4.4 billion surplus at the end of the 1980s.[42] By the end of the 1980s, the United Arab Emirates itself had accumulated a debt of almost $9 billion and Saudi Arabia almost $17 billion. Indeed, by this time Gulf banks were angry that

> The Bank of International Settlements in Basle have [sic] classified their countries, with the exception of Saudi Arabia, in the high credit risk group. Kuwait, Bahrain, the U.A.E. are especially irked that they are being lumped together with other highly indebted Arab states in one Third World category.[43]

Then there is the case of Iraq which had to finance its increasingly costly war with Iran and whose debt by the end of the 1980s reached $60 billion. The 1990–1991 Gulf crisis worsens the situation terribly—not only that of Iraq but also of all other countries involved.

But the present situation of Iraq apart, Gulf countries could have a certain leverage in dealing with international creditors whether these are dominant countries or international financial institutions. But what solidifies the situation of international subordination is the case of what we might call chronic debtors—those countries that do not have enough resources to pay their accumulating debts and might continue to borrow to keep afloat. In these cases international constraints will continue to be primordial. Two cases stand out in this respect: Morocco (with a debt of about $21.6 billion) and Egypt (where the World Bank put its debt in 1988 at $40.262 billion and the former governor of the country's Central Bank put it above $50 billion). These two countries have even asked to be reclassified in order to join poorer countries in Africa and Latin America hard hit by debt so as to receive some acts of international clemency and payments facilities. Their demands have been refused. Consequently, their economic survival—as indeed that of Jordan or the Sudan—could depend on the level of resources provided internationally, and hence the primacy of their foreign policy remains internationally constrained.

CONCLUSION

At the beginning of the 1990s with the collapse of the Eastern bloc, the global system seems to be embarking on still another new phase: a postbipolar one. Whether this system will finally be unipolar (under the leadership of the United States) or multipolar (with the increasingly effective participation of Japan and a unified Europe), the fact of hegemony as a structural global characteristic of dependent countries does not itself radically change. The African proverb that insisted that when elephants fight, it is the grass that suffers may now have to be reworded to indicate that when elephants make love, the grass still suffers.

Indeed, the continuing integration of the erstwhile Soviet bloc into the global capitalist system might lessen the few opportunities that were open to dependent countries. Their diplomacy of weakness, which increased their maneuverability by balancing off the blocs against each other, is now even weaker. Moreover, not only do they lose the Eastern bloc as a source of aid and trade credits, but worse still, members of this vanishing bloc will actually be rivals in trying to get as much available global resources as possible. Consequently, the pie is both getting smaller and having to be distributed among a greater number of claimants. The ratio of global opportunities to constraints is, in fact, shrinking.

But this increasing primacy of constraints does not mean that dependent countries will be completely helpless in the face of systemic tyranny à la Kaplan or world hegemony à la dependencia. The adoption of such a deterministic view would imply that nothing other than the system counts in the making of a country's foreign policy. Global constraints notwithstanding, other factors continue to play an important part in the country's foreign policy orientation and behavior: national leadership patterns, economic and military capabilities, the size and composition of the population, the style of mobilizing and managing resources, and, of course, negotiating techniques in the global village. Even for a dependent country, the constraint/opportunity ratio could change as a result of the country's possession of the "right" resources and its leadership's will to use them. If maintained for some time, a foreign policy based on the use of these resources could eventually modify aspects of the systemic structure. It is thus the interaction between national capabilities and dispositions, on the one hand, and existing systemic structures, on the other, that determines a country's foreign policy and its degree of success.

NOTES

1. This debate, which has been raging for some time, has shaped the thought of professors, international civil servants, journalists, and students, affecting what and how many of us write.

2. The assumptions and propositions of the different approaches are scattered here and there in the basic books and articles of social science methodology and international relations theory. The best introduction to the international relations debate is still Klaus Knorr and James N. Rosenau (eds.), *Contending Approaches to International Politics* (Princeton, N.J.: Princeton University Press, 1969). Hans Morgenthau is most representative of the "traditional approach"; see his *Politics Among Nations*, 5th ed., rev. (New York: Alfred A. Knopf, 1978).

3. Good representatives of this school in international relations are Karl Deutsch, Bruce Russett, and J. David Singer. For a representative collection of papers, see J. David Singer (ed.), *Quantitative International Politics* (New York: Free Press, 1968); see also a collection of biographical and autobiographical studies of the main behavioralists, of their disciples, and of their main research projects in James N. Rosenau (ed.), *In Search of Global Patterns* (New York: Free Press, 1976).

4. Charles W. Kegley, Jr., and Eugene Wittskopf, *World Politics: Trend and Transformation* (New York: St. Martin's Press, 1981). Two points must, however, be emphasized here. First, the traditionalism/behavioralism dichotomy is not as neat or well-demarcated as our synopsis might suggest. Many social scientists cannot be classified as belonging to either school, having accepted some views of each. Second, the traditionalism/behavioralism debate has been concentrated in the West, especially in North America. Social scientists in the rest of the world have remained onlookers, uninformed or even unconcerned.

5. Robert O. Keohane and Joseph S. Nye, Jr. (eds.), *Transnational Relations and World Politics* (Cambridge, Mass.: Harvard University Press, 1972); Richard Mansbach et al., *The Web of World Politics: Non State Actors in the Global System* (Englewood Cliffs, N.J.: Prentice-Hall, 1976).

6. This concept has been popularized and systemized by J. Rosenau, *The Scientific Study of Foreign Policy* (New York: The Free Press, 1971).

7. Corporatism in its pure form entails the presence in society of various interest associations, yet these formal institutions are in fact controlled by the state or its representatives. Voluminous literature exists on the corporate form of state in the Third World. For a recent discussion of this issue in an Arab context, see John Waterbury, *The Egypt of Nasser and Sadat: The Political Economy of Two Regimes* (Princeton, N.J.: Princeton University Press, 1983), especially pp. 3–40, 307–388; a more general treatment in the context of developed (capitalist and socialist) countries as Gerhard Lembruch and Jack Hayward (eds.), *Interest Intermediation: Toward New Corporatism(s)*, a special issue of the *International Political Science Review*, vol. 4 (Beverly Hills, Calif.: Sage Publications, 1983).

8. Kenneth Waltz, *Theory of International Politics* (Reading, Mass.: Addison-Wesley, 1979).

9. Robert Gilpin, *The Political Economy of International Relations* (Princeton, N.J.: Princeton University Press, 1987); Robert Keohane, *After Hegemony: Cooperation and Discord in the World Political Economy* (Princeton, N.J.: Princeton University Press, 1984).

10. Immanuel Wallerstein, *The Modern World System I: Capitalist Agriculture and the Origins of the European World Economy in the Sixteenth Century;* and *The Modern World System II: Mercantilism and the Consolidation of the European World Economy 1600–1750* (New York: Academic Press, 1974 and 1980, respectively).

11. The most useful answers and evaluations are to be found in A. Foster-Carter, "From Rostow to Gunder Frank: Conflicting Paradigms in the Analysis of Underdevelopment," *World Development* 4 (1976), pp. 167–180; Richard Bath and Dilmus James, "Dependency Analysis of Latin America," *Latin American Research Review* 11 (1976), pp. 3–55; Antonio C. Peixoto, "La théorie de la dépendance: Un bilan critique," *Revue Française de Science Politique* 27 (1977), pp. 601–629; Gabriel Palma, "Dependency: A Formal Theory of Underdevelopment or a Methodology for the Analysis of Underdevelopment?" *World Development* 6 (1978), pp. 881–924; and J. Samuel Valenzuela and Arturo Valenzuela, "Modernization and Dependency: Alternative Perspectives in the Study of Latin American Underdevelopment," *Comparative Politics* 10 (1978), pp. 535–557.

12. John S. Gitlitz and Henry A. Landsberger, "The Inter-American Political Economy: How Dependable Is Dependency Theory?" in John D. Martz and Lars Schoultz (eds.), *Latin America, the United States and the Inter-American System* (Boulder, Colo.: Westview Press, 1980), pp. 45–70.

13. With the sudden influx of oil cash, this situation has been reversed in Saudi Arabia and other Gulf countries, which now import several million migrant

workers. Scarce foreign currency and abundant labor is still the norm in the Third World, however.

14. A good illustration of these variations is Edward Williams's "Comparative Political Development: Latin America and Afro-Asia," *Comparative Studies in Society and History* 11 (1969), pp. 342–354.

15. Abdul-Hamid Abu-Sulayman, *The Islamic Theory of International Relations* (Herndon, Va.: International Institute of Islamic Thought, 1987); Hafeez Maleek, "Islamic Theory of International Relations," *Journal of South Asian and Middle Eastern Studies*, 2 (1979), pp. 84–92; Ali Karaosmanoglu, "Islam and Its Implications for the International System," in Metin Heper and Raphael Israeli (eds.), *Islam and Politics in the Middle East* (London: Croom Helm, 1984), pp. 103–118.

16. Abu-Sulayman, *op. cit.*, p. 129.

17. For the different cases that substantiate this point, see the various chapters in Adeed Dawisha (ed.), *Islam in Foreign Policy* (Cambridge, London, and New York: Cambridge University Press, 1983). Especially to the point are the chapters by A. Dawisha on Iraq, A. Dessouki on Egypt, W. Zartman on Morocco, J. Piscatori on Saudi Arabia, S. Taher-Kheli on Pakistan, and R. Ramazani on Iran. On the role of Islam in this latter country after the 1979 revolution, see Mohammed Reza-Djalili, *Diplomatie islamique: Stratégie internationale du Khomeynisme* (Paris: Presses Universitaires de France, 1989).

18. Johan Galtung, "A Structural Theory of Imperialism," *Journal of Peace Research* 8 (1971), pp. 81–117.

19. For a solid and insightful tracing of how the different great powers of different historical periods have resisted moves toward Arab unity, see Galal Amin, *The Arab East and the West* (Beirut: Center for Arab Unity Studies, 1980) (in Arabic).

20. A protracted conflict involves economic, social, religious, political, and psychological dimensions at the level of the individual, the different social groups, the society itself, and even the global system. As Azar, Jureidini, and McLaurin have said, these conflicts are "hostile interactions which extend over long periods of time with sporadic outbreaks of open warfare fluctuating in frequency and intensity. These are conflict situations in which the stakes are very high—the conflicts involve whole societies and act as agents for defining the scope of national identity and social solidarity. While they may exhibit some breakpoints during which there is a cessation of overt violence, they linger on in time and have no distinguishable point of termination. It is only in the long run that they will 'end' by cooling off, transforming or withering away; one cannot expect these conflicts to be terminated by explicit decision. Protracted conflicts, that is to say, are not specific events or even clusters of events at a point in time; they are processes." Edward Azar, Paul Jureidini, and Ronald McLaurin, "Protracted Social Conflict: Theory and Practice in the Middle East," *Journal of Palestine Studies* (1978), pp. 41–61.

21. Salah Eddin Al-Bitar, *Arab Policy* (Beirut: 1960), pp. 23–27 (in Arabic).

22. Yair Evron, "Great Powers' Military Intervention in the Middle East," in Milton Leitenberg and Gabriel Steffer (eds.), *Great Power Intervention in the Middle East* (New York and Toronto: Pergamon Press, 1979), pp. 17–45.

23. Ali E. Hillal Dessouki, "The Effects of Arms Race and Defence Expenditures on Development: A Case Study of Egypt," Research paper, Cairo University, Cairo, 1980.

24. Paul Jabber, *Not by War Alone: Security and Arms Control in the Middle East* (Los Angeles and London: University of California Press, 1981), and "The

Tripartite Declaration," in Yaacov Shimoni et al. (eds.), *Political Dictionary of the Middle East in the 20th Century* (New York: Quadrangle, 1974), p. 388.

25. The 1957 Eisenhower Doctrine continued the same line of thinking. In 1967, "the renewal of U.S. interest in limiting the transfer of weaponry to the Middle East . . . came at a time when Israel had just achieved a position of clear regional military supremacy . . . [In] his address of June 19, 1967, President Johnson's call for limits on the 'wasteful and destructive arms race' was made while the Syrian, Egyptian, and Jordanian military machines lay practically in ruins," Jabber, *op. cit.*, pp. 181–182.

26. In the 1970s, arms purchases from the Soviet Union were not as taboo as they had been in the mid-1950s, but petrol sales were. Only the form of the constraint had changed.

27. Michael Field, "Oil in the Middle East and North Africa," in *The Middle East and North Africa 1982–1983* (London: Europa Publications, 1982, pp. 93–134.

28. *Time*, February 7, 1983, pp. 34–38.

29. *Newsweek*, February 7, 1983, pp. 50–54.

30. *Time*, February 7, 1983, pp. 34–38.

31. *Newsweek*, February 7, 1983, pp. 50–54.

32. For a further discussion of Israel's impact on the region, including Israeli influence upon Arab unity and disunity, see Bahgat Korany, "Structure et processus du système international arabe 1961–1983," in *Le Moyen-Orient: Enjeux et perspective* (Quebec: Presses de l'Université Laval, Collection Choix, 1983).

33. Nahum Goldman, *Où va Israël?* (Paris: Calmann Levy, 1975), p. 119.

34. Michael Brecher, *The Foreign Policy System of Israel* (London and New York: Oxford University Press, 1972), p. 137.

35. I. L. Kenen, *Israel's Defense Line: Her Friends and Foes in Washington* (Buffalo, N.Y.: Prometheus Books, 1981). Mr. Kenen has worked for U.S. support for Israel for more than forty years. At the time of publishing his book, he was honorary chairman of the American Israel Public Affairs Committee, which he helped establish in 1951, and editor emeritus of the *New East Report*, which he founded in 1957. His book has been described by Henry Kissinger as "fascinating and informative."

36. Nancy Jo Nelson, "The Zionist Organizational Structure," *Journal of Palestine Studies* 10 (1980), pp. 80–93; Walter Lehn, "The Jewish National Fund," *Journal of Palestine Studies* 4 (1974), pp. 73–96. See especially pp. 95–96 for the impressive data on the acquisition of territory in Palestine by the fund between 1905 and 1950.

37. Two notable analyses in this respect are Richard Stevens, *American Zionism and U.S. Foreign Policy 1942–1947* (New York: Pageant Press, 1962); and Evan Wilson, *Decision on Palestine: How the U.S. Came to Recognize Israel* (Stanford, Calif.: Hoover Institution Press, 1979). Wilson was a foreign service officer on the Palestine desk, watched U.S. policy in the making, and took part in its implementation. Drawing on heretofore unpublished documents, he describes how the White House, Congress, and the State Department were buried under an avalanche of paper from different Zionist groups engaged in a worldwide campaign of pressure politics. This pressure politics worked. In explaining his decision to recognize Israel, Truman said frankly to a group of State Department officials: "I am sorry, gentlemen, but I have to answer to hundreds of thousands who are anxious for the success of Zionism: I do not have hundreds of thousands of Arabs among my constituents." Wilson, *op. cit.*

38. Ghassan Bishara, "Israel's Power in the U.S. Senate," *Journal of Palestine Studies* 10 (1980), pp. 58–79. Mr. Bishara is the Washington correspondent of *Al-Fajr* (Jerusalem). See also Marvin Feuerwerger, *Congress and Israel: Foreign Aid Decision-Making in the House of Representatives* (London: Greenwood Press, 1979). Dr. Feuerwerger has several years' experience in Washington politics, having served as a legislative aide for the American Israel Public Affairs Committee, and as the principal deputy to President Carter's "advisor on Jewish Affairs." Feuerwerger demonstrates how Congress approves aid to Israel, often adding to administration requests. From 1970 to 1977, Congress increased economic aid to Israel by 30% over administration requests, at a time when Congress was cutting foreign and worldwide aid by almost 25%. Congress also eased Israel's burden by offering loans on easy terms and waiving repayment of major debts during this period. Congress earmarked foreign aid funds for Israel, a practice generally discouraged by the White House because it limits administration flexibility. See also the excellent review by John Richardson in *Journal of Palestine Studies* 10 (1980), pp. 80–85.

39. Historically, "Zionism was very much the child of the liberal and national movements of nineteenth-century Europe," Robert Freedman (ed.), *World Politics and the Arab-Israeli Conflict* (New York: Pergamon Press, 1979), p. 5.

40. Brecher, *op. cit.*, p. 143.

41. Goldman, *op. cit.*, pp. 136–139.

42. *The Middle East Magazine* (London), February 1990, p. 13.

43. *Ibid.*

3

The Arab System: Pressures, Constraints, and Opportunities

Paul C. Noble

The foreign policy of states is shaped by their national situations, by the values and perceptions of policy-makers, and by the global and regional environments in which they exist.[1] National and elite concerns influence what governments would *like* to do, but the environment shapes what they are *able* to do.[2] Systemic conditions shape state behavior in two ways. In the first place, they provide a set of opportunities or, more commonly, serve as a set of constraints, permitting states a certain range of possible action. Second, systemic conditions generate pressures that push or pull states in certain directions. Even if the system does not have a significant impact on the initial formulation of a state's policies, it has a decisive effect on whether those policies succeed or fail. These results are generally not lost on policy-makers and influence their subsequent behavior.

This chapter focuses on the Arab regional system, more particularly its core area, the eastern Arab world.[3] This area, more than any other, has been characterized by intense interaction as well as by extremely acute regional conflicts. The analysis is divided into two parts. The first part will examine the setting, namely the domestic and regional conditions that confront Arab states and underpin the regional system. The second part deals with the characteristics of the system proper, that is, its structural properties as well as the changing patterns of behavior and relationships among Arab states.

SETTING PROPERTIES

Two sets of conditions will be examined here: the domestic setting of Arab countries (unit properties) and the degree of homogeneity and interconnectedness between Arab societies (relational properties).

Unit Properties (the Domestic Setting)

A single state's internal conditions are not normally considered as a system property. However, when similar domestic conditions prevail among system members, and these conditions influence their international position and behavior, they require examination. One important characteristic of Arab countries has been their experience of extensive social change. For much of the population, substantial alterations in the conditions of life have occurred due to urbanization, increased access to education, exposure to mass media,[4] and the emergence of new social forces and sets of values.[5] As a result, Arab states have experienced a rapid increase in the number of people with some degree of political awareness as well as a substantial enlargement of the political arena.

These developments had two major consequences for domestic politics during the 1950s and 1960s. To begin with, they generated serious domestic political instability. Traditional regimes were overthrown in Egypt, Syria, and Iraq. The ruling elites of Jordan, Lebanon, Saudi Arabia, and Morocco felt insecure and suffered serious disturbances and/or periodic coup or assassination attempts.[6] New Arab regimes experienced difficulties in establishing their authority and legitimacy (Syria, Iraq).[7] The only exception to this widespread instability was Egypt, where President Gamal Abdal Nasser emerged as an unchallenged ruler enjoying extensive popular support.[8]

A second major consequence of the far-reaching social and political changes was the emergence of sharp ideological cleavages within Arab societies and an increasing focus on such issues.[9] The old social order, previously accepted as legitimate, was seriously questioned. The new regimes headed in radically new directions to justify their existence and generate popular support. The remaining traditional regimes felt increasingly threatened by the combined pressure of new social forces within their own countries and the challenge posed by the transformation of the political order in other Arab countries.

These domestic conditions altered the international position and behavior of members of the Arab system. Internal instability seriously weakened the *position* of key states, and the constant concern for political survival obliged Arab governments to devote much of their attention and energy to staying in power. This situation made it difficult to engage in any sustained activity in support of foreign policy goals. Furthermore, strong linkages between Arab societies exposed the unstable states to extensive intervention by other Arab governments. When conflicts occurred within the system, most Arab governments were exposed both to traditional forms of pressure and to externally generated subversive pressures as well. The simultaneous weakening of several states as a result of internal instability was an important factor contributing to the emergence, in the decade after 1955, of a highly unbalanced, virtually one-power system, dominated by Egypt.

Apart from shaping the pattern of power, the widespread internal instability also affected the *behavior* of system members. It contributed to rigidity in policy, as insecure governments were unwilling to deviate from established approaches, particularly with regard to long-standing opponents (e.g., Israel and the Western powers). Contrary to the widely held view that insecurity of tenure leads to external assertiveness, Arab states that were relatively weak or had conservative/moderate governments (e.g., Jordan, Lebanon, and Saudi Arabia) became introverted in the face of domestic instability.[10] By adopting this posture they sought to avoid antagonizing stronger Arab states and thus minimize outside pressure and intervention. Among unstable Arab states, only those that were relatively strong or led by reformist/radical governments (e.g., Syria and Iraq) tended to be assertive.[11] The most assertive of the Arab states during this period, however, was also the most stable: Egypt.

Finally, the transformation of the political and social order within Arab states added a whole new ideological dimension to Arab foreign policy and relationships.[12] Because most Arab governments were engaged in intense ideological conflict domestically, they became suspicious and intolerant of divergent regimes. They could not help but see these regimes and their own domestic opposition in the same light. These attitudes were intensified by the realization that regime stability and even survival were at stake. Some made an effort to reshape other societies in accordance with their own beliefs through a variety of propaganda and subversive activities. Naturally, this ideological revisionism increased the insecurity of most elites.

Because of the prominence of ideological issues, much of the conflict within the Arab system after 1955 centered on questions of legitimacy. This is not to say that the triumph of certain basic values was the sole or even the primary motivation of policy-makers. In fact, ideological issues were often used as instruments in a struggle for status and power. Whatever the motivations of policy-makers, however, legitimacy was a major stake in inter-Arab politics. Any regime that neglected this did so at its own peril. A further consequence of the focus on ideological issues was the emergence of sharp divisions between regimes espousing different value systems. This reduced the flexibility of the system and consequently the options of policy-makers.

During the 1970s, domestic instability declined. The most dramatic improvement occurred in the Fertile Crescent area, particularly in Syria. President Hafiz Al-Asad remained in power throughout the decade, far longer than any previous Syrian ruler.[13] A similar trend occurred in neighboring Iraq, where after a decade of instability following the overthrow of the monarchy in 1958, the Ba'thist government was able to maintain effective control throughout the 1970s.[14] The improvement in the domestic situation within Jordan was equally striking.[15] After nearly two decades of turbulence, culminating in a full-scale war with the Palestinian guerilla movements, King Hussein was able to reassert control over the country. The major exception to this trend was Lebanon, where the whole fabric of state and society broke down completely after 1975.[16] After the unsettled conditions of the 1960s, Saudi Arabia also enjoyed relative tranquility for much of the decade,[17] largely because of the tremendous influx of oil wealth. Under King Faisal the regime moved to provide both employment opportunities and some degree of responsibility to the burgeoning new middle class, thereby defusing a major source of potential opposition. Moreover, the position of the regime was enhanced by its activities in support of the Arab cause against Israel.

Improvement in the domestic political situations of key states had two main effects. First, it strengthened the position of these states in the regional arena. They became far less vulnerable to externally initiated propaganda and subversive pressures and consequently less on the defensive. Saudi Arabia, Syria, and Iraq, for example, were able to engage in more energetic and sustained foreign policy activity and to play more important roles in the system. Greater domestic stability also permitted these states greater flexibility in policy.[18]

Another change in the domestic setting was the declining importance of ideology to the leadership of several key states. This was evident in reformist and conservative states alike.[19] As a result of these developments, Arab foreign policies in the 1970s became more pragmatic, with tangible national interests prevailing over ideological considerations.[20] This pragmatic approach reduced the insecurity of regimes and opened a broader range of options for policy-makers. Greater flexibility led to the development of working relationships across previously rigid ideological divisions.

By the late 1970s, the Arab domestic setting appeared likely to undergo transformation once again. One aspect of this was the persistence of ideology as an issue in Arab societies even though its importance had declined at the leadership level. In effect, the Arab world was still in a period of transition. Although the old social and political order had been swept away or was being seriously questioned in most Arab countries, there was no consensus on what should replace it. Consequently, while the ideological debate died down for a period, it flared up again in a new form. The resurgence of Islamic fundamentalism refocused this debate within Arab societies,[21] and the Iranian revolution intensified it, particularly in the Gulf area. Arab governments were seriously concerned about these developments, and especially about the ideological cold war being conducted by Iran. Nevertheless, since fundamentalists failed to achieve a breakthrough in any Arab state, foreign policy remained pragmatic and ideological differences did not exacerbate inter-Arab relations.

The other main development during this period was the renewed manifestation of domestic instability.[22] This was noticeable in Syria, Iraq, Saudi Arabia, and some Gulf states, even Egypt. In Syria, economic difficulties, corruption, and intensified repressive activity fed the growth of popular disenchantment with the regime.[23] The majority Sunni community was increasingly dissatisfied with the dominant position enjoyed by members of the minority Alawi community. This dissatisfaction, combined with the secular orientation of the ruling Ba'thist movement, led to increasingly violent activity by Islamic fundamentalist groups, culminating in the Hama uprising (1982). The brutal crushing of this revolt dealt a severe blow to the opposition but the discontent remained.

In Iraq, the government of Saddam Hussein faced serious problems after the advent of Ayatollah Khomeini's Islamic fundamentalist regime in neighboring Iran.[24] The new Iranian authorities denounced Iraq's secular Ba'thist regime and exhorted religiously inclined elements to replace it with a regime based on Islamic precepts. While this appeal was directed in principle at all Iraqis, it constituted a scarcely veiled attempt to promote revolt among the underprivileged Shi'i majority. The danger of instability appeared to grow in the wake of Iranian military successes from 1982 on. Nevertheless, the regime's repressive capabilities and the sense of national identity proved stronger than religious or ethnic affiliation, at least in the case of the Shi'i community. Efficient internal security forces and the precariousness of the country's situation helped to avert other internal challenges for the duration of the war.

Other major Arab states also suffered in varying degrees from political instability during this period. After President Anwar Al-Sadat's assassination, his successor, Hosni Mubarak, sought to reduce existing grievances by pursuing more balanced foreign and domestic policies and by adopting a less imperial and confrontational style. Although taking a tough approach to extremist forces, he allowed greater freedom for moderate opposition forces, including religious elements. While opposition activity has been less intense as a consequence, Islamic elements have continued to make headway:[25] Many of the sources of discontent remain and could cause renewed instability.

In Saudi Arabia, accelerated modernization generated a backlash from conservative religious elements who felt that the Islamic character of the society was being seriously eroded.[26] This reaction was compounded by increased social inequality and corruption as well as by the growing Western influence that accompanied modernization. The problem was exacerbated by propaganda and subversive activities emanating from Iran. These pressures found expression in the uprising at Mecca and parallel Shi'i disturbances in 1979 and 1980; there were also periodic troubles surrounding the Hajj. After these initial difficulties, Saudi Arabia proved successful in containing both internal opposition and Iranian attempts at destabilization.

Despite renewed pressures, Arab states and regimes proved very resilient. None of the states, except Lebanon, fell prey to balkanization. Regimes were also able to overcome various challenges and maintain themselves in power throughout the 1980s. Their relative durability is attributable to several factors. At one level, vastly improved internal security and coercive capabilities were certainly an important element. Related factors include more sophisticated checks and balances among military forces combined with the difficulty of successfully coordinating a coup within a greatly enlarged officer corps. At another level, the oil boom strengthened the position of the state by furnishing regimes with vastly increased financial resources.[27] Even Arab have-not countries benefitted significantly in the form of substantial financial flows and worker remittances. Other contributing factors to the longevity of Arab regimes included inhibitions about challenging regimes in time of war or acute conflict (e.g., Iraq and to a lesser extent Syria) and the extremist character of the opposition forces in some cases.

In spite of the increased resilience of states and regimes, the potential for domestic conflict and instability remained substantial in the late 1980s. Although Islamic movements had not been successful in violent confrontations with state authorities, Islam continued to be a powerful force in these societies. While the impact of the Islamic regime in Iran was limited by its Iranian and Shi'i origins as well as by its increasing external and domestic difficulties, it could still generate significant difficulties wherever there was a substantial Shi'i presence (Lebanon, Bahrain, Kuwait, Iraq, Saudi Arabia).[28]

The danger of renewed instability has been heightened by economic developments in the latter half of the 1980s. During this period, softening world oil markets had harmful effects on the economies of virtually all Arab states. Oil-producing countries were the most directly affected as revenues plunged sharply.[29] While these states had several options available to cushion the effects on their economies, it was not long before domestic expenditures were cut as well, thereby slowing economic growth. In the short run these cuts have been bearable, but if continued over an extended period, they run the risk of alienating key support groups and impeding the regimes' ability to co-opt new social forces. The impact of the softer oil market on the have-not states has been even greater, especially since they had no means of cushioning its effects.[30] Some (e.g., Egypt and Syria) were affected directly, as their own limited oil revenues also fell. In addition, all have-not states suffered from substantial reductions in financial aid flows and worker remittances. Continued economic difficulties will undoubtedly increase social strains throughout the Arab world. This would create fertile ground for the mobilization of opposition to existing regimes. The situation would become very problematic if the issues of social reform and religious renewal came to be linked in the minds of the population of one or more countries. The combination of social unrest and religious revivalism would be an explosive mixture.

In any case, there will undoubtedly be some increase in instability in at least a portion of the eastern Arab world. Should this affect one or more leading actors, it would leave them in a weakened position vis-à-vis both regional challengers and other Arab states. It is unlikely that this would lead to assertiveness on their part, although others might be emboldened to take advantage of their weakness. Should the instability be restricted to periodic disturbances, its effects on the system would be limited. In fact, improved internal security and coercive capabilities, along with diminished transnationalism, will undoubtedly help govern-ments to contain instability and prevent regime change. Should such change occur, however, and should fundamentalist or other ideologically oriented forces achieve an influential position in a leading Arab state, the effects would be very disruptive.[31]

Relational Properties (the Arab Setting)

The domestic setting of the Arab system differs only *in degree* from that of other systems of developing states. However, relations between Arab societies differ *in kind* from those elsewhere. This has important implications for international politics and policy-making in the Arab world.

One special feature of the Arab setting is the degree of linguistic, cultural, and religious *homogeneity* among the peoples and elites of the area. This extensive homogeneity has generated a strong sense of kinship and even common identity. In fact, for a considerable period this sense of larger Arab identity rivalled individual national identities among important segments of the population of many Arab states. While the sense of Arab identity was strong throughout the 1950s and 1960s, it ebbed subsequently as specific national or even communal identities asserted themselves. Moreover, with the resurgence of commitment to Islam in many quarters, an increased sense of common Islamic identity emerged to rival Arab nationalism. Whatever the specific basis of iden-tification, however, the sense of kinship and larger common identity remained much stronger in the Arab system than elsewhere in the Third World. This has had a profound impact on the intensity of interaction within the system and gave rise to relations between Arab states which were qualitatively different from those in other regional systems.

The *intensity of the links* between system members is another distinctive feature of the Arab setting. Other Third World regions tend to be characterized by what Johan Galtung has termed a "feudal interaction pattern."[32] According to this model, developing societies of the periphery interact more intensely with developed societies of the center than they do with each other. Only limited links are supposed to exist among developing societies themselves. The Arab system, however, has been characterized by a high level of interconnectedness between its members at the societal as well as state level.

To begin with, *material links* are relatively strong. Physical or geo-graphic links are much tighter than in other Third World systems. The area involved is relatively small compared to other systems.[33] Trans-portation and communication links are much more developed than elsewhere, with extensive land, air, and radio connections.[34] During the 1950s and 1960s, economic links within the Arab system, although greater than in the rest of the Third World, were still modest.[35] At that time the eastern Arab world did not constitute much of an economic system.

Societal links constitute a more significant form of interconnectedness. These ties have taken several forms. One form has been an extensive movement of persons, including short-term visitors, students, and workers who take up residence in other Arab countries for varying periods. The most striking example is provided by the more than 2 million Palestinians who have migrated to various parts of the Arab world since the late 1940s.[36] After the oil boom of the 1970s, many more skilled and unskilled workers, clerical personnel, professionals, and teachers migrated to the more prosperous Arab countries.[37] This movement of workers declined significantly, however, with the recession in the oil industry in the mid-1980s.

Similarities in language and culture have contributed to the development of other types of societal links, including the growth of a variety of transnational associations. Above all, these similarities have made possible an extensive flow of information, ideas, and opinions among the people of the Arab world. The electronic media have been important instruments for the diffusion of news and ideas, particularly among attentive publics.[38] These have been supplemented by the flow of printed materials and by word of mouth. As a result, the eastern Arab world came to resemble a vast sound chamber in which currents of thought, as well as information, circulated widely and enjoyed considerable resonance across state frontiers. These transnational links have remained strong throughout the history of the Arab system and continue to characterize it today.

Linguistic and cultural homogeneity also contributed to the development of strong *political links* at both the state and societal level. As noted earlier, the population of the area developed a sense of kinship and larger Arab identity that transcended individual nationalities.[39] This was reinforced by the extensive flow of social communication and multiple channels of contact across state frontiers. Together these factors created an intense awareness of, and interest in, political developments throughout the system. Not only transplanted residents but also important segments of the indigenous population identified with leaders and political movements in other Arab states. The classic example of this phenomenon was Nasser's tremendous appeal throughout the Arab world.[40] The sense of belonging to a larger Arab community also reduced psychological inhibitions about transnational political ties. Throughout its history, the Arab system has been characterized by a variety of cross-frontier alliances between the government of one Arab state and individuals or groups in others. This form of political link has been utilized by all regimes. The prevailing climate also fostered the development of political and other movements with branches in several Arab states.[41]

Because of these links, the political systems of Arab states have been closely interconnected and permeable. Political developments in one segment of the system have set off reverberations in other segments, altering the local balance of forces and generating new assertiveness on the part of some of the contending elements.[42] These reverberations have frequently been accompanied by a substantial penetration of political systems, as leaders and groups in some states activated cross-frontier alliances to manipulate the internal politics of others. Thus, the Arab system of the 1950s and 1960s differed substantially from traditional state systems. In the traditional model, member states are assumed to resemble a set of billiard balls that come in contact only at their hard outer shell, with governments largely able to insulate their domestic systems from external influences.[43] Instead, the Arab system resembled a set of interconnected organisms separated only by porous membranes or, alternatively, a large-scale domestic system divided into compartments of varying degrees of permeability.[44] This gave rise to a transnational political process encompassing not only governments but also groups as well as individuals across the system.

These conditions had several important implications. The homogeneity and ensuing sense of kinship meant that the policies and behavior of member states were scrutinized more closely, and reacted to more sharply, than in other state systems. Differences over basic direction were treated not as a simple divergence in views but rather as behavior harmful to the interests of the community. The intensity of reaction tended to magnify the level of conflict. Furthermore, the sense of membership in a larger family led to pressures for solidarity when any segment of the community was in conflict with a non-Arab actor. Besides individual national issues, Arab governments therefore faced a number of Arab core issues.[45] During this period, the demands for conformity and commitment on these issues were extremely strong. A government's acceptability and status within the system depended on its response. Governments that aspired to play a prominent role in the system were obliged to take up general Arab causes to satisfy the larger Arab constituency.

Belief in a common Arab identity also gave rise to the view that political unity was a desirable objective. This in turn led to periodic pressures for mergers between various Arab states as a step toward overall unity. This climate of opinion constituted a permanent challenge to the legitimacy of existing states and the pressure to merge generated considerable insecurity.[46] Finally, linkages among Arab societies and political systems created a strong sense of vulnerability in most Arab policy-makers. Due to the larger sense of Arab identity and the identification of segments of their population with leaders or political movements in other Arab states, policy-makers felt that their political systems were exposed to external manipulation. Apart from the status or independence of states, the very existence of governments was at stake.

For some, these conditions provided an excellent opportunity to extend their influence but for most they constituted both a source of pressure and a major constraint on policy.

Many features of the setting persisted into the 1970s and 1980s, usually in much less intense form. Economic links were one exception. During the 1970s these increased considerably as a result of boom conditions in the petroleum industry. Large sums began to be transferred from wealthy oil-producing states to less well-off members of the system, particularly those on the front line with Israel. The Arab world became the only Third World system characterized by substantial intra-regional financial flows, which came to represent a very significant percentage of the total financial assistance received by system members.[47] Large numbers of workers also flocked from poorer Arab countries to the oil-producing states to fill positions generated by the oil boom. This in turn generated a substantial return flow of savings to their home countries. As a result, the Arab world came to constitute much more of an economic system. During the 1980s, however, the substantial decline in the demand for oil and the consequent slump in revenues brought a marked reduction in economic links within the eastern Arab world. Intra-regional financial flows dropped significantly as oil-producing states cut back on assistance programs. Large numbers of expatriate workers returned home as employment opportunities contracted sharply.[48] Naturally, this was accompanied by a major decline in the flow of remittances to their countries of origin. In spite of these developments, the eastern Arab world continued to constitute more of an economic system than any other Third World region.

Paradoxically, while economic links became more intense (at least until the mid-1980s), political links were weakening. One important contributing factor was the declining appeal of pan-Arabism.[49] This reflected not only the inevitable letdown after the exaggerated expectations raised by pan-Arab rhetoric but also disillusionment over the failures of policies pursued in its name. Another key factor has been the serious military-security, political, and/or economic difficulties confronting most system members during the 1970s and 1980s. As a result, elites and attentive publics became preoccupied with their own national problems and were less inclined to concern themselves with those of others.

These developments had a significant impact on relations between Arab states and societies. The most obvious manifestation was a sharp reduction in pressures for political union. As a result, the elites of many Arab countries felt less threatened and the state and territorial framework of the system acquired greater legitimacy. The decline in the intensity of identification with the larger Arab community also led to a reduction in commitment regarding Arab core issues. These issues no longer generated the same strong response across the Arab world. As the sense of Arab solidarity diminished, national and group interests were asserted to the detriment of community interests. The most striking example was

Egypt. During the 1970s, with the bulk of its energy and resources devoted to the conflict with Israel, Egypt ceased to be a driving force for solidarity in the system. By the late 1970s, due to the costs of the continuing confrontation, President Sadat decided to break ranks and come to terms with Israel. He did so with little regard for the interests of other front-line actors who were left in a more vulnerable position. Other manifestations of the same phenomenon were found in Lebanon and Syria. In Lebanon, much of the Christian community felt sufficiently threatened to develop open ties with Israel.[50] In Syria, hostility toward the Iraqi regime became so great that President Asad was prepared to align with an outside power, Iran, even though the latter posed a serious threat to several members of the Arab system.[51]

The weakened commitment to Arab core concerns was also evident in the behavior of Saudi Arabia and other conservative Gulf states from the late 1970s on. The rapidly developing economic and financial ties between these countries and the Western world created relationships of interdependence that they were loath to damage in support of Arab causes.[52] Furthermore, these governments were increasingly preoccupied with the threat posed by Islamic fundamentalism in Iran. Concerned about their vulnerability on the eastern front, they were less able to devote attention and resources to the problems of Arab states/actors on the western front and were unwilling to exert any serious pressure on the United States on their behalf. They did, however, provide considerable support to Iraq in its struggle with Iran.

Of equal if not greater significance was the decline in the permeability of Arab societies and political systems. This "hardening" of the Arab state was due in part to efforts by Arab regimes to better insulate their political systems from external influences.[53] This was carried out through tight control over the media, prevention of mass demonstrations, and increased internal security capabilities generally. Developments at the societal level, especially the weakening responsiveness to Arab core concerns, also contributed to this result. Attentive and mass publics alike now appeared preoccupied with the problems, both domestic and foreign, of their own societies, as well as with their own class or communal concerns. This change in political climate was reflected in the lack of any strong reaction within Arab countries to the Israeli invasion of Lebanon (1982), to the U.S. attack on Libya (1986), and to the ongoing Palestinian *intifada* (1987). While Arab regimes acted to limit local responses to these developments in order to restrict possible pressures for action, it is also clear that the intensity of popular concern for larger Arab causes had declined.

More specifically, the populations of the eastern Arab world appeared less disposed to identify with political leaders in other Arab states and much less likely to respond to cross-frontier appeals. Arab attentive and mass publics had become at least partially immunized to previous slogans and rallying cries due to the failure of the accompanying policies. Earlier transnational movements based on pan-Arab nationalism had either weakened, fragmented, or disappeared outright. In short, not only the automatic spillover effect of events but also the potential for cross-frontier mobilization had declined significantly. Arab regimes were now in a better position to insulate their political systems from regional pressures.

Despite these developments, Arab societies and political systems remain interconnected and even permeable to some degree. The policies and behavior of system members are still scrutinized closely by governments and attentive publics alike. Some segments of the population maintain a sense of attachment to the larger Arab community.[54] Pressures for solidarity in the face of external encroachments remain. Cross-frontier alliances, although not as widespread as before, are still utilized by governments. While the pan-Arab mystique has declined and transnational movements based on it have faded, there has been a clear increase in transnational responsiveness and cross-frontier ties based on Islam. Much of this centered on Shi'i movements or personalities who were responsive primarily to Iran. But at times it also extended to Sunni elements.

It would be premature, therefore, to predict an end to the permeability of Arab states. There remains a significant potential for transnational responsiveness that could be reactivated by new leaders who successfully articulate the ideals and aspirations of the Arab community. Alternatively, a new basis for transnational responsiveness might develop. The Islamic factor appears to have the greatest potential. If a movement with a pronounced Islamic character were to achieve a breakthrough in a key Arab state, this could have substantial repercussions for other Arab states. The problem of vulnerability to cross-frontier political pressures would return.

SYSTEM PROPERTIES

We turn now to the characteristics of the Arab international political system proper. The two principal sets of systemic properties examined are the basic structure or pattern of power (structural properties) and the patterns of behavior and relationships among Arab states (behavioral properties).

Structural Properties (Bases and Distribution of Power)

For much of the postwar period, the material capabilities of Arab states were quite modest. The *bases of power* were also very different from those usually found in state systems. In other systems, military and economic capabilities have been extremely important and have generally been employed coercively to achieve state objectives. In the Arab system, there were significant constraints on the use of these traditional instruments of statecraft. Arab states possessed modest military capabilities and had little or no ability to project military power beyond their borders. Even the strongest Arab military power, Egypt, had only a limited ability to employ force against other members of the system, principally because of the absence of land links between itself and the Arab states of southwest Asia. Among the important extrasystemic constraints, the most compelling was the likelihood of Israeli military action in the event of armed force being used against states in its immediate vicinity.[55] There was also a strong possibility of action by the Western powers in response to military pressure against any of their Arab allies.[56] For these reasons conventional military operations were unlikely except in peripheral areas such as North Africa (e.g., the Algerian-Moroccan War of 1963) and the rimlands of the Arabian Peninsula (e.g., the Yemen War of 1962–1967).

Nor were economic capabilities particularly significant during the 1950s and 1960s. The military and economic needs of Arab states were nowhere near as extensive as they later became. Hence, the financial resources of states were not as crucial to their international position. Furthermore, the low level of economic development limited economic interaction. There were few bilateral relationships of consequence: Opportunities to manipulate economic transactions coercively were limited therefore. Finally, none of the Arab states possessed sufficient financial resources to provide a level of aid or investment that would permit the development of influence relationships. In short, during this period the usefulness of military and economic capabilities as bases of power was clearly restricted. Arab states were definitely limited in terms of what they could do *to* one another or even *for* one another in material terms.

If the traditional instruments of statecraft were not widely used, the instruments of political warfare—propaganda, cross-frontier alliances, and subversion—were.[57] Conditions favoring the widespread use and effectiveness of such techniques prevailed within the Arab world. These included pronounced internal cleavages, political instability, and the extensive permeability of Arab societies. In these circumstances, the *political capabilities* of governments assumed great importance. There were two dimensions to this. One was the degree of domestic support that a government enjoyed. Any government in a weak position domestically would be extremely vulnerable to external propaganda and subversive pressures and unable to act in a vigorous and sustained manner in the regional arena. Second, the cross-frontier appeal of the leadership and policies of Arab governments was significant because of the uncertain stage through which Arab societies were passing. The people of the Arab world were searching for new directions, new models, new leadership. In this context, any leader or regime providing emotionally satisfying answers to the central issues confronting Arab societies could attract a following. Cross-frontier appeal could be translated into influence through propaganda and subversive activities designed to create internal pressures on governments to alter their policies or risk being overthrown.

TABLE 3.1   Demographic Capabilities, Eastern Arab World, Early 1960s[a]

Countries	Total Population (millions)	(%)	Literate Population (millions)	(%)	Secondary School Enrollment (thousands)	(%)	Overall (%)
Egypt	28.3	50.0	7.1	52.0	812.0	58.0	53.0
Iraq	7.7	13.5	1.8	13.0	220.0	16.0	14.0
Syria	5.1	9.0	1.9	14.0	161.0	11.5	11.5
Lebanon	2.3	4.0	1.6	11.5	72.0	5.0	7.0
Saudi Arabia	6.5	11.5	0.3	2.0	22.0	1.5	5.0
Jordan	1.9	3.0	0.6	4.5	89.0	6.0	4.5
Yemen	4.8	8.5	0.2	1.5	1.8	—	3.5
Kuwait	0.4	0.5	0.2	1.5	25.0	2.0	1.5
Total	57.0	100.0[b]	13.7	100.0[b]	1,402.8	100.0[b]	100.0[b]

[a]The figures represent an average of the relevant data for the years 1962 and 1965. The percentages indicate each country's proportion of the total for the eastern Arab World.
[b]Figures may not add up due to rounding.

Sources: UN Demographic Yearbook 1970 (New York: United Nations, 1971); *UNESCO Statistical Yearbook 1976* (Paris: UNESCO, 1977); and *UN Statistical Yearbook*, 1964, 1967, 1968 (New York: United Nations).

In short, political capabilities were probably the most important determinant of influence in the Arab system during the 1950s and 1960s.

During this period, the Arab system was also characterized by a distinctive *pattern of power*. Whereas in most Third World systems power and influence were relatively diffused, in the Arab system they were highly concentrated, giving rise to a virtual one-power situation. This concentration of power stemmed in part from Egypt's vast superiority in material capabilities. As can be seen from the accompanying tables, in all but one area Egypt accounted for half or more of the capabilities of the eastern Arab world. Egyptian superiority was most pronounced in the softer forms of material capabilities (see Tables 3.1 and 3.2).[58] The situation in regard to the traditional yardsticks of power was less clearcut, although the pattern of military capabilities closely followed the distribution of demographic and cultural/communications resources, as Table 3.3 makes clear. Egypt possessed almost half of the military capabilities of the whole eastern Arab world, with more than a 2:1 advantage over its closest competitor, Iraq. The pattern of economic capabilities was quite different (see Table 3.4). Economic power in the Arab East was more diffused than were other resources. Egypt's large population had the second lowest per capita income in the system and a lower level of foreign exchange reserves than Saudi Arabia, Iraq, and Lebanon. The inconsistencies in the rankings of the major Arab actors on different indicators reveal the unbalanced, and hence tenuous, economies in these states.

TABLE 3.2   Cultural and Communications Capabilities, Eastern Arab World, Early 1960s[a]

Countries	Higher Education Enrollment (thousands)	(%)	Book Production (units)	(%)	Radio Transmitter Facilities (kw)	(%)	Overall (%)
Egypt	160.0	69.5	3,325	68.0	3,770	53.5	63.5
Iraq	21.0	9.0	250	5.0	1,125	16.0	10.0
Syria	29.0	12.5	375	8.0	650	9.0	10.0
Lebanon	15.7	7.0	390	8.0	310	4.5	6.5
Saudi Arabia	1.9	1.0	300	6.0	415	6.0	4.5
Jordan	2.3	1.0	105	2.0	525	7.5	3.5
Kuwait	0.2	—	140	3.0	220	3.0	2.0
Yemen	—	—	—	—	40	0.5	—
Total	230.1	100.0[b]	4,885	100.0[b]	7,055	100.0[b]	100.0[b]

[a]The figures represent an average of the relevant data for the years 1962 and 1965.
[b]Figures may not add up due to rounding.

Sources: UN Statistical Yearbook, 1964, 1967, 1968 (New York: United Nations); *UNESCO Statistical Yearbook,* 1964, 1965, 1966, 1967 (Paris: UNESCO).

TABLE 3.3   Military Capabilities, Eastern Arab World, Mid-1960s[a]

Countries	Armed Forces (thousands)	(%)	Tanks (units)	(%)	Planes (units)	(%)	Overall (%)
Egypt	180	43.0	860	42.5	370	60.0	48.5
Iraq	82	19.5	535	26.5	80	13.0	19.5
Syria	60	14.5	350	17.5	94	15.5	15.5
Jordan	45	11.0	150	7.5	30	5.0	8.0
Saudi Arabia	20	5.0	30[b]	1.5	16	2.5	3.0
Lebanon	13	3.0	42	2.0	14	2.5	2.5
Yemen	10	2.5	30[b]	1.5	—	—	1.5
Kuwait	7	1.5	25	1.0	10	1.5	1.5
Total	417	100.0[c]	2,022	100.0[c]	614	100.0[c]	100.0[c]

[a]The figures represent an average of the relevant data for the years 1962 and 1965.
[b]Rough estimates.
[c]Figures may not add up due to rounding.

Sources: J. Hurewitz, *Middle East Politics: The Military Dimension* (New York: Praeger, 1969); N. Safran, *From War to War* (New York: Pegasus, 1969); and J. Sutton and G. Kemp, *Arms to Developing Countries 1945–1965* (London: International Institute for Strategic Studies, 1966).

With respect to hard material capabilities, the Arab system in the 1950s and 1960s stood between an unbalanced multipower system and a one-power system, although it more closely resembled the latter. Egypt's ability to use its hard material capabilities coercively was checked by physical and political constraints on the use of its military strength and by the absence of economic leverage.

TABLE 3.4 Economic Capabilities, Eastern Arab World, Early 1960s[a]

Countries	National Income (billions U.S.$)	(%)	Per Capita Income (U.S.$)	(%)	Electricity Production (millions kwh)	(%)	Financial Reserves (millions U.S.$)	(%)	Overall (%)
Egypt	3.90	38.0	140	3.0	4,790	60.5	205	14.5	29.0
Kuwait	1.30	13.0	3,439	72.0	610	7.5	110	8.0	25.0
Saudi Arabia	1.40	13.5	225	5.0	160	2.0	500	35.5	14.0
Iraq	1.40	13.5	192	4.0	1,000	13.0	210	15.0	11.5
Lebanon	0.86	8.5	378	8.0	660	8.5	230	16.5	10.5
Syria	0.81	8.0	164	3.0	560	7.0	45	3.0	5.0
Jordan	0.34	3.0	189	4.0	130	1.5	100	7.0	4.0
Yemen	0.26	2.5	55	1.0	2	—	5	0.5	1.0
Total	10.27	100.0[b]	4,782	100.0[b]	7,912	100.0[b]	1,405	100.0[b]	100.0[b]

[a]The figures for national income and per capita income are for 1963. The figures for electricity production and financial reserves represent an average of the relevant data for 1962 and 1965.
[b]Figures may not add up due to rounding.

Sources: UN Yearbook of National Accounts Statistics 1969, Vol. 2 (New York: United Nations, 1970); UN Statistical Yearbook, 1963, 1969, 1972 (New York: United Nations).

Although Egypt's military and economic capabilities provided only a limited basis of power, its political capabilities were enviable. They increased phenomenally during this period, becoming a highly effective instrument of influence. The Egyptian regime was extremely strong domestically, and Nasser's policies and accomplishments had tremendous appeal among the attentive and mass publics of most Arab states, enabling him to exert considerable pressure on other Arab governments. Its overwhelming political superiority allowed Egypt to achieve a position of commanding influence. This was not expanded to total dominance because Egypt had difficulty using its material resources to reinforce its political appeal. Nasser's hegemonic ambitions also antagonized those who might otherwise have been his allies.

During the 1970s and 1980s important changes took place in both the bases and distribution of power. With regard to the *bases of power*, there was a marked increase in the importance of material, particularly economic, capabilities. This can be traced to three factors, of which one was a dramatic growth in the economic needs of Arab states as a result of the intensified drive for modernization and rapid population growth. Second, the large pool of surplus capital in the region led poorer states to turn increasingly to the wealthy oil-producing states for assistance. The result was a substantial expansion of economic links and consequently a greater potential for financial strength as an instrument of influence.[59] Third, the importance of Arab oil, capital, and markets for the Western world gave the oil-producing countries more leverage within the international system. The newly developed capacity to exert pressure on the Western powers in support of Arab interests further strengthened the influence of these states.

By contrast, the change in the role of military capabilities was relatively limited. Admittedly, the growing seriousness of the military-security problems facing the Arab world enhanced the importance of military capabilities. The more serious military pressures became, the more vulnerable the states directly affected felt, thereby augmenting the leverage of those who could make a military contribution. However, no system member except Egypt or Iraq had sufficient military strength to contribute effectively to the security of others vis-à-vis Israel or Iran. Moreover, the possibilities for the coercive use of military power within the core area remained severely restricted.

While material capabilities were becoming more significant, political capabilities declined in importance. As the strength of identification with the larger Arab community declined and domestic political systems became less permeable, the potential for mobilizing support across state frontiers diminished. After Nasser's death, there was no leader who epitomized the ideals and aspirations of the Arab world and thus could effectively galvanize Arab opinion.[60] Nevertheless, despite the growing preoccupation of Arab elites and publics alike with tangible national concerns and the declining role of transnational political influence, it would be a mistake to underestimate the possibility of a resurgence. Arguments about legitimacy continue to be important in inter-Arab politics and Arab leaders disregard them at their peril. The potential for transnational responsiveness is substantial and new bases of appeal could emerge.

Along with this shift in the bases of power, a major change also occurred in the *pattern of power*. Previously, the concentration of capabilities and influence approached but never quite reached a one-power situation. Now, however, capabilities and influence were distributed more evenly, creating a more competitive multipower situation.[61] This diffusion of power was due in large measure to a decline in the material strength and political appeal of Egypt. This relative decline was most evident in the area of economic capabilities but later affected military capabilities as well. Of greater significance, however, was the dramatic reduction in Egypt's political capabilities as a result of the overwhelming defeat in 1967, the death of Nasser, and the major reorientation of Egypt's foreign and domestic policies under Sadat (particularly the adoption of an Egypt-first policy in regard to the Arab-Israeli conflict). All these developments lessened Egypt's prestige and seriously reduced its ability to shape opinion and mobilize support. Egypt's enforced isolation after the Egyptian-Israeli peace treaty was the culmination of this process.

While Egypt's capabilities were declining, those of other Arab states were on the rise. Spectacular changes occurred in the oil-producing states. Their financial resources and increased leverage with the Western powers generated important new instruments of influence. The greatest beneficiary of these developments was Saudi Arabia.[62] Because it had the highest production levels and largest reserves, its financial position was much stronger and its leverage over Western oil-consuming nations much greater. Iraq was another major beneficiary, although its oil revenues were lower than Saudi Arabia's and its internal needs much greater due to its significantly larger population. It achieved a substantial buildup of both financial and military capabilities by the late 1970s and seemed poised for a significant increase in status and influence.

Syria also experienced a significant increase in capabilities.[63] Although it lacked the economic resources of the oil-producing states, Syria occupied a key geopolitical position. It built up its armed forces until by the mid-1980s it had emerged as the largest Arab military power, with a small edge over Iraq. Furthermore, Asad established substantial political stability within Syria for much of the 1970s. Benefiting from this solid internal base, from the declining influence of Egypt, and from the continuing confrontation with Israel, the Syrian government was able to exercise unquestionable influence in the western Fertile Crescent.

This more competitive multipower pattern is reflected in Tables 3.5–3.8. With respect to the softer forms of material resources (Tables 3.5 and 3.6), the basic pattern remained unchanged. Egypt continued to enjoy a dominant but somewhat reduced position in terms of demographic

TABLE 3.5   Demographic Capabilities, Eastern Arab World, Mid-1980s[a]

Countries	Total Population (millions)	(%)	Literate Population[b] (millions)	(%)	Secondary School Enrollment (thousands)	(%)	Overall (%)
Egypt	49.5	45.5	18.8	39.5	3,201	45.5	43.5
Iraq	16.4	15.0	9.5	20.0	1,190	17.0	17.0
Saudi Arabia	12.0	11.0	6.1	13.0	604	8.5	11.0
Syria	10.6	9.5	4.2	9.0	875	12.5	10.5
Jordan	3.6	3.5	2.3	5.0	335	5.0	4.5
Lebanon	2.7	2.5	1.8	3.5	287	4.0	3.5
Yemen Arab Republic	7.0	6.5	1.5	3.0	84	1.0	3.5
Kuwait	1.8	1.5	1.2	2.5	239	3.5	2.5
People's Democratic Republic of Yemen	2.3	2.0	0.9	2.0	34	0.5	1.5
United Arab Emirates	1.4	1.0	0.7	1.5	62	1.0	1.0
Bahrain	0.4	0.5	0.3	0.5	38	0.5	0.5
Qatar	0.3	0.5	0.1	–	22	0.5	0.5
Oman	1.2	1.0	0.2	0.5	41	0.5	0.5
Total	109.3	100.0	47.6	100.0	7,019	100.0	100.0

[a]The data on total population and secondary school enrollment are for 1986 and 1985 respectively; the data on literacy are for various years (see below).

[b]Virtually all the data are taken from the *UNESCO Yearbook* except where the *World Tables* contained a more up to date figure. The data from the *UNESCO Yearbook* are for illiteracy; these were converted into literacy figures. The data are for the following years: Egypt (1976); Iraq (1972 and 1985); Syria (1970); Saudi Arabia (1982); Jordan (1979); Lebanon (1970); Yemen Arab Republic (1980); Kuwait (1980); United Arab Emirates (1975); People's Democratic Republic of Yemen (1980); Bahrain (1981); Qatar (1981); Oman (1970). Since Iraq data for 1985 were based on the 15-to-45 age group, the literacy rates for 1972 and 1985 were averaged.

Sources: U.N. Demographic Yearbook 1986 (New York: United Nations, 1988), Table 5, pp. 166–168 for total population; *UNESCO Statistical Yearbook 1987* (Paris: UNESCO, 1987), Table 13; and World Bank (IBRD) *World Tables* (3d ed.), vol. 2 (Social Data) (Baltimore and London: Johns Hopkins University Press, 1983) for literacy data; *UNESCO Statistical Yearbook 1987* (Paris: UNESCO, 1987), Table 3.7 for secondary school enrollment.

and cultural/communications resources. The situation was rather different in regard to the harder capabilities (Tables 3.7 and 3.8).[64] The economic indicators show an unbalanced multipower pattern, with Saudi Arabia accounting for a little over 25% of total capabilities and enjoying a clear lead over its nearest competitors. In the military sphere, there was also greater diffusion of power. Here too one finds a multipower pattern but a more balanced one, with Syria and Iraq virtually tied for the lead with around 25% of military capabilities and Egypt not far behind.

This new, more competitive, structure had certain distinguishing features. One was the lack of consistency in the capability profiles of the leading states. Those with the strongest military capabilities (e.g.,

TABLE 3.6   Cultural and Communications Capabilities, Eastern Arab World, Mid-1980s[a]

Countries	Higher Education Enrollment[b] (thousands)	(%)	Book Production[c] (units)	(%)	Radio Transmitter Facilities (KW)	(%)	Overall (%)
Egypt	739.0	57.0	1,895	56.0	9,353	19.0	44.0
Iraq	126.7	10.0	131	4.0	15,370	31.0	15.0
Syria	163.9	12.5	119	3.5	4,300	9.0	8.5
Kuwait	23.6	2.0	320	9.5	6,200	12.5	8.0
Jordan	53.8	4.0	392	11.5	2,432	5.0	7.0
Saudi Arabia	87.8	7.0	157	4.5	2,100	4.5	5.5
United Arab Emirates	7.6	0.5	64	2.0	5,270	10.5	4.5
Qatar	5.3	0.5	238	7.0	2,002	4.0	4.0
Lebanon	70.5	5.5	–	–	92	–	2.0
Bahrain	4.1	0.5	62	2.0	101	–	1.0
People's Democratic Republic of Yemen	3.6	–	–	–	851	2.0	0.5
Yemen Arab Republic	4.5	0.5	–	–	790	1.5	0.5
Oman	0.5	–	–	–	570	1.0	0.5
Total	1,290.9	100.0	3,378	100.0	49,431	100.0	100.0

[a]The data are generally for 1985 except where otherwise noted.
[b]The data are for 1985 except for the Yemen Arab Republic (1980); People's Democratic Republic of Yemen (1981); Saudi Arabia and Iraq (1983); Syria, Lebanon, and Jordan (1984).
[c]The data are for various years and have generally been averaged over two years: Egypt (1983, 1984), Iraq (1981, 1982), Syria (1983), Kuwait (1984, 1985), Jordan (1976), Saudi Arabia (1979, 1980), United Arab Emirates (1983, 1985), Qatar (1978, 1980), Bahrain (1982, 1983).

Sources: UNESCO Statistical Yearbook 1987 (Paris: UNESCO, 1987), Table 3.11 for higher education enrollment and Table 10.1 for radio transmitter facilities; UNESCO Statistical Yearbook, 1980, 1981, 1982, 1983–1984, 1987, 1988 (Paris: UNESCO) for book production.

Syria and Egypt) tended to be very weak economically. By the same token, those who ranked high on economic capabilities (e.g., Saudi Arabia, Kuwait, and the United Arab Emirates) possessed limited military capabilities. Moreover, several states suffered from internal difficulties that limited their political capabilities. In short, none of the leading actors had a strong, diversified power base that would maximize the effectiveness of their regional activities. Hence the new multipower structure represented more a *balance of weakness* than a balance of power, especially in the 1980s.

A second related feature was the partial regionalization of power. The absence of a dominant power provided opportunities for other major Arab states to develop their own local spheres of influence as well as to play a greater role in the affairs of the larger system. This was particularly true in the Arabian peninsula where, through financial

TABLE 3.7 Economic Capabilities, Eastern Arab World, Mid-1980s[a]

Countries	GDP[b] (billions U.S.$)	(%)	Per Capita GDP[b] (U.S.$)	(%)	Electricity Production (millions KWH)	(%)	Financial Reserves[c] (millions U.S.$)	(%)	Overall (%)
Saudi Arabia	92.6	34.5	8,022	9.5	31,150	28.0	17,010	48.0	30.0
Kuwait	21.3	8.0	13,019	15.0	14,196	12.5	5,398	15.5	13.0
United Arab Emirates	25.2	9.5	18,340	21.5	6,636	6.0	2,562	7.5	11.0
Egypt	36.9	13.5	760	1.0	22,870	20.5	1,702	5.0	10.0
Iraq	46.8	17.5	2,942	3.5	18,460	16.5	–	–	9.5
Qatar	6.5	2.5	20,737	24.0	3,425	3.0	753	2.0	8.0
Bahrain	5.1	2.0	10,091	12.0	2,056	2.0	1,454	4.0	5.0
Syria	16.0	6.0	1,523	2.0	6,757	6.0	311[d]	1.0	4.0
Oman	9.6	3.5	7,729	9.0	1,675	1.5	929	2.5	4.0
Lebanon	0.6	–	241	–	1,355	1.0	3,935	11.0	3.0
Jordan	3.8	1.5	1,084	1.5	2,304	2.0	716	2.0	1.5
Yemen Arab Republic	3.6	1.0	452	0.5	295	0.5	286	1.0	0.5
People's Democratic Republic of Yemen	1.1	0.5	532	0.5	280	0.5	233	0.5	0.5
Total	269.1	100.0	85,472	100.0	111,459	100.0	35,289	100.0	100.0

[a]The data are for 1985. Financial reserves figures are for the second quarter.

[b]GDP and per capita GDP data are derived from *World Tables* except for Iraq, Qatar, Lebanon, and the People's Democratic Republic of Yemen, which are derived from *National Accounts Statistics*. *National Accounts Statistics* contains some questionable figures, at least for Egypt. With the *World Tables*, GDP figures (current prices) in national currency were converted to U.S. dollars at the stipulated rate. This amount was then divided by the population figure for that year to obtain per capita GDP.

[c]Financial reserves include foreign exchange holdings and gold. Gold holdings were converted at $323 per ounce.

[d]The figure for Syrian reserves represents the last recorded amount (1983).

Sources: World Tables 1987 (4th ed.) (New York: World Bank, International Economics Department, 1987) and *National Accounts Statistics: Analysis of Main Aggregates, 1985* (New York: United Nations, 1988), Table 1 for GDP and per capita GDP; *Energy Statistics Yearbook 1985* (New York: United Nations, 1989), Table 34, pp. 384–407 for electricity production; *Monthly Bulletin of Statistics* (New York: United Nations, 1987), vol. 16, no. 4, 1987, Table 62, pp. 238–256 for financial reserves.

TABLE 3.8   Military Capabilities, Eastern Arab World, Mid-1980s[a]

Countries	Armed Forces (thousands)	(%)	Tanks (units)	(%)	Planes (units)	(%)	Overall (%)
Syria	402	24.0	4,200	34.5	500	23.5	27.5
Iraq	520	31.0	2,900	24.0	500	23.5	26.0
Egypt	445	27.0	2,159	18.0	427	20.0	21.5
Saudi Arabia	62	4.0	450	3.5	205	9.5	6.0
Jordan	70	4.0	795	6.5	121	5.5	5.5
Yemen Arab Republic	36	2.0	664	5.5	76	3.5	3.5
People's Democratic Republic of Yemen	27	1.5	450	3.5	103	5.0	3.5
Kuwait	12	1.0	240	2.0	76	3.5	2.0
United Arab Emirates	43	2.5	136	1.0	42	2.0	2.0
Oman	21	1.5	33	0.5	52	2.5	1.5
Lebanon	17	1.0	50	0.5	7	0.5	0.5
Qatar	16	0.5	24	0.5	17	1.0	0.5
Bahrain	3	–	–	–	–	–	–
Total	1,664	100.0	12,101	100.0	2,126	100.0	100.0

[a]The data here are for 1985.

Source: Based on data in International Institute of Strategic Studies, *The Military Balance 1985–86* (London: IISS, 1985).

assistance, cross-frontier alliances, and religious ties, Saudi Arabia surfaced as the predominant power.[65] Syria was successful for a time in establishing a limited sphere of influence in the western Fertile Crescent.[66] However, apart from the resistance of local states/actors, it also faced competition from Israel, Iraq, Saudi Arabia, and Iran. Iraq, too, attempted in the late 1970s to capitalize on its growing capabilities. It appeared inclined to compete for influence with Syria in the western Fertile Crescent and with Saudi Arabia among the Arab Gulf states.[67] The long and costly war with Iran severely limited its opportunities, however. Egypt, for its part, remained the principal force in the Nile Valley but faced increasing competition from Libya and Saudi Arabia with regard to the Sudan. In other words, while there were definite regionalizing tendencies in the pattern of influence, a significant element of cross-regional competition remained.

A third feature of the new structure was the absence of any effective leader or even a consistent hierarchy of powers. The status and influence of the leading actors fluctuated throughout the period with no one maintaining a consistently strong position. Thus, during the 1970s, Egyptian capabilities and influence declined, but Egypt remained arguably the principal actor in the emerging multipower system. However, its quasi-separate peace with Israel and subsequent enforced isolation effectively marginalized it for almost a decade. Egypt's increased activity in the Arab sphere in the latter half of the 1980s combined with its official reinstatement in the system (Casablanca Summit, May 1989) have undoubtedly provided it with new opportunities to exercise influence.

With its vast financial capabilities as well as economic leverage, Saudi Arabia emerged as a potential leader in the 1970s. However, it suffered from a number of limitations, including a narrow capability base and a strong sense of internal and external vulnerability.[68] Saudi Arabia's position became even more problematic in the 1980s due to a combination of softening world oil markets and threatening developments in the Gulf.[69] The former was responsible for a substantial decline in Saudi Arabian financial capabilities; the latter led to heightened feelings of insecurity and a concentration of energy and resources on the task of containing Iran's revolutionary Islamic regime. This preoccupation with the Iranian threat greatly restricted Saudi Arabia's ability to influence developments elsewhere in the system. It also led to increased dependence on the United States for support and protection. This sharply limited any leverage Saudi Arabia may have had vis-à-vis the Western powers, further reducing its influence in the Arab world. Given the divisions in the system and its own acute sense of vulnerability, Saudi Arabia was reluctant to provide leadership or exercise pressure on others for fear that they might respond with counterpressures of their own.

While Iraq's financial and military capabilities were growing during the 1970s, it was constrained by internal difficulties (e.g., the Kurdish problem), the conflict with Iran, and its relative isolation in the Arab world. An agreement with Iran in 1975 substantially reduced the first two constraints. Subsequent moves to moderate policy and improve relations with neighboring conservative regimes served to ease Iraq's isolation. With these obstacles removed, Saddam Hussein sought to capitalize on Iraq's growing capabilities as well as the partial vacuum created by Egypt's isolation. He attempted to assume the role of protector of Arab Gulf states in the face of increasing pressure from revolutionary Iran. However, after Iraq's military offensive was blunted and its forces driven back (1982), it found itself very much on the defensive. The long and costly war with Iran seriously weakened its position.[70] Preoccupied with avoiding defeat and ensuring regime survival, dependent on others for financial assistance, military equipment, and logistical support, Iraq was not in a position to exert much influence. After its semi-victory over Iran (1988) and the reduction of pressure on that front, Iraq began to be more active in the Arab system and sought to play a leading role once again.

A significant improvement in Syrian domestic political conditions along with an increase in military capabilities enabled it to assume a major role within the western Fertile Crescent during the 1970s. This in turn enhanced Syria's status and influence in the larger Arab system. However, from the late 1970s on, President Asad met with considerable local resistance (from Jordan, the PLO mainstream, and the Lebanese

Christian community) as well as competition from other regional actors in attempting to solidify Syria's position in the area. It also became relatively isolated in the Arab core system as a result of conflict with Iraq and Egypt and lukewarm relations with Saudi Arabia. Syrian support for Iran isolated it even further. At this stage, Syrian influence consisted essentially of a capacity to obstruct developments it opposed rather than to shape directions itself. By the late 1980s Syria's position had weakened further. Apart from continuing difficulties in establishing its predominance in the immediate subregion, it suffered from a deteriorating economic situation and diminished Soviet support.[71] Moreover, its archrival Iraq was in a much stronger position now that it had successfully concluded the war with Iran. This enabled it to put pressure on Syria even in its own sphere.

Overall, the inconsistent capabilities and fluctuating fortunes of the leading actors produced a leadership vacuum and an unstable hierarchy. This was true especially in the 1980s when these states not only suffered from certain persistent weaknesses but were also neutralized in varying degrees by serious regional challenges. In the late 1980s the position of some key states improved. If there is no resurgence of regional pressures and domestic economic and political conditions do not deteriorate, a more stable hierarchy will gradually emerge in the 1990s.

The emerging multipower structure of the 1970s and 1980s had several implications for the policies and relationships of system members. At one level, the diffusion of power, and particularly the balance of weakness that characterized much of the period, served to limit conflict. No single state had the capacity to engage in extensive revisionism or achieve a hegemonic position. Nevertheless, once extra-systemic pressures were reduced, the prevailing uncertainty about the power hierarchy could tempt one or more leading actors to assert themselves. At another level, the diffusion of power contributed to the increased fragmentation of the system. Prior to 1967, when Egypt enjoyed a position of commanding influence, Nasser was a focal point for cohesion although he also antagonized governments and created disruptions. His widespread appeal, and the respect or fear that it engendered, usually helped him to mobilize a number of Arab states in a common front against outsiders. Without this unifying pressure, there was a strong tendency in the 1970s and 1980s for system members to go their own way. The cohesion of the system suffered accordingly.

Behavioral Properties

Structural properties are basically pre-interactional in character and provide only a partial picture of an international system. Our ultimate concern is with the functioning of the system itself, that is to say the patterns of activities and relationships among participating states.

Level of Interaction. One distinctive feature of the Arab system has been the intensity of interaction among Arab governments. In fact, the

Arab world is arguably the only meaningful international political system among the various continental or macroregional groupings of states in the Third World. The latter are characterized by sporadic interaction and constitute geographic expressions more than genuine systems. In these areas, meaningful systems tend to be found only at the subcontinental level.

The Arab system, by contrast, has been characterized by considerable interaction throughout its history.[72] This stemmed in part from the extensive links within the system. Of particular importance was the interconnectedness and ensuing permeability of Arab political systems. These links led to a strong sense of involvement in Arab affairs as well as feelings of vulnerability on the part of most Arab governments. The extent of relations among Arab governments was reinforced by the sense of common Arab identity that generated strong interest in each other's affairs. As a result, the policies and behavior of Arab states were scrutinized closely, and reacted to forcefully, by Arab governments and publics alike. This process was intensified by the existence of pan-Arab core issues, which gave rise to strong pressures for solidarity among Arab governments. These conditions not only stimulated considerable interaction but also injected an intensity into inter-Arab relations that was not found elsewhere.

Sources and Level of Conflict: The Core System. A second key property of any state system is the level of conflict and consequently the degree of threat to which system members are exposed. During the 1950s and 1960s, the Arab world constituted a *revolutionary international system.* The policies of system members, especially the leading actor, Egypt, were extensively revisionist;[73] this posed a severe threat to a number of fundamental interests and values. Consequently, inter-Arab politics was characterized by a high level of conflict.

The system's revolutionary character was reflected in the *objectives* of member states. To begin with, there was extensive revisionism in regard to *distributional* issues (i.e., the allocation of tangible "values").[74] One subject of dispute was the *state and territorial framework.* As in most of the Third World, the shallow roots and questionable origins of many boundaries and state units, together with the existence of serious cleavages within societies, encouraged periodic challenges to the status quo. But the Arab world, unlike other regions, was also characterized by a widespread sense of common identity and an historical legacy of unity. This led to a belief that existing state units were artificial and should be merged into larger entities (e.g., pressures for various forms of union—Greater Syria, Fertile Crescent, Jordan-Palestine, Egypt-Syria, UAR-Iraq, Iraq-Kuwait).

Status and influence questions were even more acute and pervasive sources of conflict. Several features of the system stimulated revisionism by encouraging the belief that substantial modifications to the power structure could be achieved relatively quickly. The small number of actors meant that one or two alliances could significantly improve a state's power position. Widespread internal instability allowed governments to enhance their influence by helping friendly forces come to power in neighboring states. The concentration of capabilities encouraged Egyptian governments to believe not only that Egypt was entitled to a dominant position but also that this position was readily attainable. This perception led to a persistent Egyptian quest for power, which varied only in the degree of superiority sought and the nature of the methods used.

Egypt was by far the greatest source of disturbance in this sphere. From 1955 on, Nasser openly sought hegemony, in part to impose his views on directional issues and in part because he believed it was Egypt's due. Most Arab governments could accept Egypt's claim to leadership. However, they disagreed sharply on how much influence Egypt was to have and how it was to be exercised. This opposition would have been irrelevant if Egypt had been able to impose its will. However, the constraints on the use of its military strength combined with its economic weakness meant that Egypt could exert little in the way of material pressure to back up its considerable political capabilities. This, together with the resistance that its aspirations engendered, prevented it from achieving a clear hegemonic position. In any case, the situation encouraged persistent revisionism as Egypt strove for hegemony without ever fully being able to attain it.

Directional issues (i.e., questions of principle or basic orientation) were also a source of deep division and revisionism during this period. These directional issues included both the *ideological issue* of what constituted a legitimate domestic, political, economic, and social order and *foreign policy issues* concerning the proper stance toward outside powers.

Two main factors were responsible for the prominence of directional issues from the mid-1950s on. The first was the unsettled stage through which Arab societies were passing. There were sharp ideological cleavages both within and between Arab states about the direction their societies should take. The new regimes which came to power pursued radically new directions in both domestic and foreign policy. They not only called into question the basic values and policies of traditional regimes but also embarked on a campaign to force them to alter their course. Egypt in particular embarked on a sustained campaign to transform the political, economic, and social order throughout the Arab world.

The second factor accounting for conflict over directional issues was the extensive intrusion of outside actors. The bitter experience of colonial rule and the continuing pressures to which Arab states were subject made relations with the major powers emotionally charged from the outset. From the mid-1950s on, the differences between Arab states over these relations intensified as the Western powers sought to strengthen their presence in the face of growing Soviet involvement in the Middle East. Although policy toward Israel was also a sensitive issue, it was not as divisive. All members of the system, through conviction or fear of the political consequences, abided by the basic norm: no accommodation with or recognition of Israel. Difficulties did arise periodically over what further action, if any, to take and the inclination to engage in competitive posturing was strong. Second-ranking actors such as Syria and Iraq frequently challenged Egypt to adopt a tougher stand. The ensuing struggle generated considerable pressure on other Arab states to respond.

The revolutionary character of the system was reflected not only in the objectives of system members but also in their *techniques*.[75] Except among allies, little effort was made to shape the behavior of other governments through persuasion, diplomacy, or economic and other inducements. When differences arose, Arab governments relied primarily on unconventional coercive techniques. These included strong attacks on the leadership of other states, propaganda campaigns to mobilize opposition, and intense subversive pressures, including cross-frontier alliances with dissatisfied individuals and groups. The aim was to destabilize and ultimately overthrow opposing governments. Egypt, in particular, resorted extensively to such forceful techniques of political warfare. Many Arab regimes, therefore, faced a serious challenge not only to their basic direction and vital national interests but also to their very political survival.

In short, during the 1950s and 1960s the Arab system constituted a highly threatening environment. Revisionism was both extensive and far reaching in its scope as major challenges were posed to a wide range of fundamental interests and values. The fact that the leading Arab state was the principal revisionist force intensified the revolutionary character of the system. Not without reason Malcolm Kerr referred to this period as an era of acute cold war. The problem was compounded by the permeability of Arab societies and political systems. For a very few regimes this constituted an opportunity but for the vast majority it was an additional source of pressure and concern.

During the 1970s and 1980s, the level of conflict and revisionism within the Arab system declined significantly. Tensions over previously contentious *directional* issues eased, particularly in regard to *ideological* questions. Egypt and Syria were forced to reconsider their policies as a result of the dramatic changes in their national situation after the 1967 war. Both were faced with acute problems and were aware that the conservative regimes could be of considerable assistance in dealing with them. To obtain this support, they began to play down regime differences and halt political attacks.[76] In response to these signs of moderation, the leading conservative regime, Saudi Arabia, also became more flexible in its approach.[77] This trend was accentuated by domestic developments. In the two key "progressive" states, some disenchantment set in with the socialist economic experiment. This gave rise in the mid-1970s to measures of economic liberalization in Egypt and, to a lesser extent, Syria.[78] The conservative states for their part not only became more active in regard to social and welfare measures but also accepted a strong role for government in the direction of their national economies. This tendency toward convergence served to reduce further the salience of ideological differences in inter-Arab relations.

During the 1970s and 1980s, then, it was primarily lesser actors that were the sources of ideological criticism within the Arab system. As already noted, however, the ideological debate within Arab societies took a new twist as a result of the resurgence of Islamic fundamentalism. Attention then shifted from old controversies over socialism or other secular ideologies and increasingly began to focus on the role of Islam in state and society. This change has not yet engendered significant inter-state conflict in the Arab system. However, if Islamic fundamentalists were to rise to prominence in a key Arab state, this would undoubtedly lead to a new ideological cold war.

Conflict over *relations with the major powers* fluctuated during this period but on the whole was less severe than previously. In the early 1970s, due to the potential benefits, the two leading progressive regimes (Egypt and Syria) either abandoned or toned down their criticism of the conservative regimes over ties with the West.[79] This improved the climate of inter-Arab relations. After the 1973 war, this process was carried farther as the leading progressive regimes modified their policies. Egypt now sought eagerly to develop close relations with the United States, bringing its policy into line with the conservative states.[80] In the mid-1970s, the Syrian government, besides expanding economic links with the West, cautiously explored the possibilities for improved relations with the United States both in regard to the Lebanese problem and the Arab-Israeli conflict.[81] Iraq, for its part, maintained its strong opposition to the United States during much of this period. However, in the late 1970s, it too began to play down the issue in the interests of a rapprochement with the Gulf states. This was soon followed by cautious overtures to the United States in the wake of the Iranian revolution.[82]

From the late 1970s on, the situation deteriorated considerably as a result of two sets of developments. One was the deepening conflict between the superpowers both at the global and regional level. The other was the increased rigidity of superpower policies towards certain regional conflicts (e.g., the Arab-Israeli and Lebanese conflicts). As a result, the period was characterized by increased polarization not only among the superpowers but also between regional states and particular superpowers. Thus Syrian relations with the United States deteriorated sharply in the wake of the Camp David agreements, closer U.S.-Israeli ties, and U.S. policy in Lebanon.[83] Saudi Arabian fears of the Soviet Union intensified as a result of the invasion of Afghanistan and Soviet activities vis-à-vis Iran, South Yemen, Ethiopia, and Libya.[84] Egyptian opposition to the Soviet Union also increased for similar reasons. Intensified suspicions of the superpowers inevitably spilled over into inter-Arab relations.

By the late 1980s the situation had changed considerably. The emerging détente within the dominant system carried over to the regional level. The superpowers now displayed greater flexibility not only towards each other but also in relationships with regional states. This was most evident in the case of the Soviet Union,[85] which engaged in overtures to the moderate Gulf states and Israel as well as renewing relations with Egypt. This was matched by a constructive approach to regional conflicts. The United States also became a little more flexible in its approach to the Palestine Liberation Organization (PLO) and Syria.[86] Consequently, the issue of relations with the superpowers became less contentious, a trend that is likely to continue into the 1990s.

While these two sets of directional issues declined in importance, another—*policy toward Israel*—became the principal directional issue during this period.[87] Israel's sweeping victory in the 1967 war, its continuing occupation of parts of the territory of neighboring Arab states, and the emergence of a strong Palestinian national movement combined to place Israel at the top of the Arab foreign policy agenda. These events generated both a stronger sense of involvement in the conflict as well as a new mood of realism. The new mood crystallized gradually and guardedly in a willingness to reach an honorable settlement. As some governments departed from the previous rigid policy of no negotiations, no recognition, and no peace with Israel, the potential for conflict grew.

This situation was evident particularly after 1973. The shock of the war spurred the United States to press more actively for a resolution of the conflict[88] and induced Israel to display some flexibility, at least toward Egypt. Within the Arab world, the balance of forces began to shift in favor of a settlement, particularly among front-line actors. Syria now gave clearer indications that she was prepared to negotiate with Israel and conclude an agreement providing an honorable settlement could be obtained. Even the PLO leadership began to move hesitatingly and conditionally in the same direction. Still, serious divisions remained. Some actors (Iraq, Libya, the PDRY, Algeria, and the Rejectionist Front within the PLO) continued to oppose any settlement in principle and sharply attacked those who were willing to move in this direction. Even among those who leaned toward a settlement there were differences regarding both the terms of such a settlement and the process through which it would be arrived at. The divisions over these questions sprang largely from differences in national situations and were encouraged by variations in Israeli policy. Thus, President Sadat believed that Egypt stood a reasonable chance of achieving an honorable settlement on its own front and was ready to take initiatives and make concessions without receiving anything immediate in return.[89] Syria and the PLO were highly suspicious of Israeli aims and consequently were extremely cautious, even inflexible, in their bargaining positions, insisting on assurances that their basic national claims would be satisfied before they made any commitments or entered negotiations.[90]

These differences produced sharp conflict especially after President Sadat's unilateral initiative led to a virtual separate peace between Egypt and Israel. This treaty satisfied Egypt's purely national concerns but at the expense of Arab solidarity and the interests of other frontline actors. Not surprisingly, Egypt was subject to bitter attacks and forced into virtual isolation for much of the ensuing decade. Attempts to promote a settlement were effectively suspended over the next few years, thereby averting further conflict over this question. After the Israeli invasion of Lebanon, opportunities for movement developed once again, as the United States engaged in a new initiative (the Reagan Plan). Over the next three years, King Hussein and PLO Chairman Yasser Arafat made various attempts to explore these opportunities and initiate an opening to the United States but without success.[91] These efforts generated additional conflict as Syria vehemently opposed what it regarded as unilateral initiatives that would harm both Arab and Syrian interests. Subsequent Jordanian-Syrian coordination from late 1985 on left out the PLO, but the latter returned forcefully to the scene in 1988 after the extraordinary success of the *intifada*. The divergences in approach among front-line actors have now narrowed and the split with regard to Egypt has been healed. However, differences in policy and national ambitions remain and continue to cause strains in PLO-Syrian and, to a lesser extent, PLO-Jordanian relations. Hence, although conflict concerning directional issues declined overall, important differences remain.

There was also a reduction in conflict over *distributional* issues. *The state and territorial framework* was challenged much less than in the previous period.[92] The pressures that did occur were limited in scope.[93] The decline in serious challenges to the state and territorial framework was due in part to the stronger roots and increased acceptance these had developed over time. Stability owed more, however, to the decline of the pan-Arab mystique and the failure of earlier attempts at union, events that greatly reduced popular and elite enthusiasm for political union. States began to emphasize arrangements for functional cooperation (e.g., the Gulf Cooperation Council, the Arab Cooperation Council, and the proposed Maghreb cooperation arrangements)[94] rather than outright mergers. Even when agreements were portrayed as involving political unification, they never amounted to more than institutionalized cooperation or common fronts. Hence, fears of loss of autonomy or even absorption diminished substantially.

Status and influence considerations also generated less revisionism during this period. Egypt dropped its hegemonial aspirations and accepted a more modest definition of its status and influence. By the late 1970s the problem with Egypt was no longer its overbearing presence but rather its quasi-withdrawal from the system. The shift in Egyptian policy, together with the emergence of a more competitive multipower structure, reduced conflict significantly since there was no longer a dominant power exerting intense pressure throughout the system. Other key Arab states now felt less threatened. They were also able to acquire a larger say in the affairs of the system or even, as with Saudi Arabia and Syria, to establish local spheres of influence. This satisfied some of their aspirations for status and influence.

While this diffusion and partial regionalization of power eliminated one major source of conflict, it also created new ones. At one level the decline of the hegemonic power created uncertainty about the pecking order and led to a maneuvering for position among the rising powers. At another level, the attempts to establish subregional spheres of influence led to conflict between the principal local power and other states/actors in the area who were not prepared to accept its predominance. Thus, in attempting to dominate the western Fertile Crescent, Syria threatened other local actors. Its efforts throughout the period to control developments in Lebanon and to bring the Palestinian resistance movement under Syrian tutelage led to serious conflict with key Lebanese groups as well as with the leadership and mainstream of the PLO.[95] Saudi Arabia's greater assertiveness within the Arabian peninsula occasioned some conflict, particularly with the People's Democratic Republic of Yemen (PDRY),[96] but Saudi activities in the peninsula were less disruptive than Syria's actions to the north.

Certain Arab states whose opportunities for establishing a local sphere of influence were blocked by rivals constituted another source of conflict. During the 1970s, Iraq found itself blocked by Iran and Saudi Arabia in the Gulf area and by Syria in the western Fertile Crescent. Libya was hindered by Egypt in the Nile Valley and was unable to make any headway in North Africa. As a result, the Iraqi and Libyan governments tended to support disruptive activity within and outside their immediate regions, trying to secure a base for influence. While Libya remained a source of disturbance right through the 1980s, Iraq's policy fluctuated. In the late 1970s, a combination of substantially greater financial capabilities, a stronger domestic position, Egypt's isolation, and Iran's weakened condition created opportunities for Iraq to improve its position. President Saddam Hussein pursued these opportunities but in so doing adopted a conciliatory approach toward the Arab Gulf states.[97] Indeed he sought to enhance his country's influence in the area by portraying Iraq as a protector of Arab interests in the face of Iranian threats. During the remainder of the 1980s, Iraq's leadership ambitions were blunted as it found itself increasingly on the defensive in the war with Iran. This also led to a degree of financial and diplomatic dependence on the Arab Gulf states, especially Saudi Arabia.[98] After Iraq's semi-victory over Iran in 1988, the situation changed significantly. Iraq was now in a position to play a much larger role in the Arab system. This was manifested initially in a more confrontational stance toward Syria. Indeed, it already has been active in Syria's backyard, providing military assistance to Lebanese Christians in their efforts to pressure Syria to leave Lebanon.[99] Hence, although the challenge to the distribution of power was less serious during this period, revisionism persisted.

The greater moderation of the Arab system in the 1970s and 1980s was also reflected in the *methods* employed by system members. Less emphasis was placed on political warfare designed to destabilize or overthrow regimes. Instead, a greater effort was made to influence other governments directly through traditional techniques of statecraft, particularly diplomacy and economic rewards/pressures. This trend was evident mainly in the behavior of Egypt and Saudi Arabia. Under Sadat, the emphasis on "Egypt the revolution" gave way to that of "Egypt the state."[100] Sadat concentrated on improving relations with Arab governments to obtain maximum support. Saudi Arabia, while continuing to cultivate conservative and religiously oriented elements in other Arab societies, also sought to develop working relationships with certain of the progressive regimes.[101] In particular, it attempted, through financial inducement and the promise of diplomatic brokerage vis-à-vis the Western powers, to encourage further moderation among the progressive regimes.

Syrian behavior was mixed. During much of the 1970s it suspended political attacks and subversive pressures against the conservative regimes and Jordan. However, it engaged in intense political warfare with the rival Iraqi Ba'th regime and intervened heavily in Lebanese domestic politics.[102] During the 1980s, as it became more isolated Syria resorted to various measures of political intimidation or to the implied threat of such measures. These were employed not only in Lebanon but also against the PLO, Iraq, Jordan, and, in a more subtle way, against some of the Gulf states.[103] Iraq, for its part, engaged during the 1970s in subversive activities vis-à-vis Syria, the Gulf states, and the PLO. From the late 1970s on, it halted such pressures on the Gulf states and the PLO in order to improve relations with these actors at a time of deepening conflict with Iran and Syria.

During the 1970s and 1980s then, the Arab system was much less revolutionary than before. Egypt, formerly the principal source of disturbance, ceased by and large to engage in revisionist activity and reduced its involvement in the system. In the wake of this gradual Egyptian disengagement, other actors, notably Syria, Saudi Arabia, Iraq, and Libya, became more assertive. However, because of a more competitive multipower structure, none achieved a predominant position and thus none generated the amount of disturbance that Egypt had previously. In short, the Arab system became relatively moderate and policy-makers felt less threatened.

Sources and Level of Conflict: The Core-Periphery System. Paradoxically, at the very stage that conditions within the Arab system became less threatening, the larger regional environment was becoming more threatening. This environment was marked by two acute conflicts—the Arab-Israeli and Iran-Iraq conflicts. In terms of behavioral intensity, the Arab-Israeli conflict has been the most intense as well as most sustained conflict in any system of developing states. The 1967 war constituted a major watershed. At one level, Israel's sweeping victory left her in possession not merely of Palestinian lands but those of neighboring Arab states as well. This situation created more direct grounds for involvement of the front-line states in the struggle. At another level, the military-security problem became much more acute. Limited outbreaks of hostilities were now a frequent occurrence while the danger of full-scale hostilities remained ever present (1973, 1982). Throughout these clashes the Israeli military maintained a significant edge over Arab front-line forces.

The mid-1970s witnessed important steps toward conflict-resolution on one front—the Israeli-Egyptian. However, the combination of a new ultra-nationalist government in Israel (post 1977) and the quasi-separate Egyptian-Israeli peace settlement led to an intensification of Israeli pressures on the western flank of the core area. Egypt's defection from the Arab coalition created an even greater imbalance of power in Israel's favor. This had two important consequences. First, it allowed the Likud government to maintain, and toughen, its stand regarding the future of the remaining occupied territories. Indeed, in the years following the Egyptian-Israeli treaty, Israel seized the opportunity provided by the neutralization of Egypt to proceed with an expansionist policy in these territories (e.g., the formal annexation of Jerusalem in July 1980, the extension of Israeli law to the Golan Heights in December 1981, and the continuing extension of Israeli control of and settlements on the West Bank). Beyond this, the neutralization of Egypt enabled Israel not only to concentrate its forces on the other fronts but also to engage in more adventurous behavior in these areas (e.g., the intensification of military pressure on the PLO and Syria in Lebanon culminating in the invasion of 1982, the increased repression in the occupied territories, and the air attack on Iraq in June 1981). Israel at this time was supremely confident of its military superiority and was prepared to act accordingly. Thus, from the late 1970s on, the western front-line states faced an intensified threefold threat—a territorial threat, a military-security threat, and a power threat.

The impact of Iran on the Arab system was much less extensive, at least until the 1980s. During the 1970s, Iran began to adopt an increasingly assertive posture in the Gulf, coming into conflict primarily with Ba'thist Iraq. Tensions grew as a result of competing power aspirations in the wake of Britain's withdrawal (1971). This led not only to a war of words but also to the attempted destabilization of each other's regimes and eventually to border clashes. This pressure eased somewhat after the conclusion of an agreement in 1975 under which Iraq accepted a modification of the border in Iran's favor in the Shatt al Arab in return for a cessation of Iranian support for Iraq's Kurdish rebels.

Serious conflict broke out once again after the advent of a revolutionary Islamic regime in Iran (1979). The new regime soon engaged in sharp criticism and subversive pressures directed not only against Iraq but also the conservative monarchies for their alleged failure to govern according to proper Islamic principles. This was accompanied by efforts to incite rebellion among the Shi'i majorities of Iraq and Bahrain as well as the Shi'i minorities of Saudi Arabia and Kuwait. Iran now posed a substantial threat to all regimes in the area, not simply to Iraq.[104] This threat assumed even more serious proportions from 1982 on when Iran gained the upper hand in the Iran-Iraq war. Concern mounted about a possible Iranian victory and a collapse of the Iraqi regime, particularly after Iranian advances in 1986. At the same time, military incidents between Iran and various Gulf states stirred fears of wider military clashes.

By the early 1980s, therefore, the states of the eastern Arab world were involved in not one but two acute regional conflicts. They found themselves under mounting pressure not only on their western flank (Israel) but also on their eastern flank (Iran). Initially, the nature of the threats differed. While Israel posed a territorial and military-security threat, Iran constituted primarily an ideological and internal-security threat. By the mid-1980s, however, Iran too emerged as a military-security danger for an important segment of the eastern Arab world. Due to the immediacy and multidimensional character of the threat, the Iran-Iraq conflict at this point came to overshadow the Arab-Israeli conflict in the minds of many Arab decision-makers. This was reflected in the proceedings of the Arab summit held in Amman in November 1987.[105]

The simultaneous existence of two acute regional conflicts had a significant impact on Arab governments. For one thing, these conflicts created acute military-security problems for virtually all members of the system. The result was a militarization of foreign policy, including major arms buildups, and substantial strains on the economies of these countries.[106] Furthermore, the acuteness of these conflicts meant a much greater reliance on the major powers for military equipment, economic assistance, and diplomatic support. In most cases, this also led to the intensification of a special relationship with one or another superpower.

These core-periphery conflicts also contributed to further fragmentation and division within the Arab system itself. At the very least, the simultaneous existence of two acute conflicts created divided preoccupations as each set of states concentrated its attention and energies on the immediate problems on its own front. Beyond this, it served to intensify divisions within the system. As already noted, serious splits occurred among the states/actors of the western front regarding policy toward Israel. On the eastern front the situation was different. Here the conflict stemmed not from the front-line states themselves, which were very supportive of Iraq. Rather, the problem lay with Syria which chose to exacerbate its conflict with Iraq by aligning itself with Iran.

After almost a decade of strong external pressures on both fronts, conditions improved substantially in the late 1980s. This improvement was most noticeable on the eastern front where, after several years on the defensive, Iraq was able to drive back Iranian forces and bring the war to a successful close (1988). This qualified Iraqi victory, together with the internal difficulties and loss of momentum of Iran's Islamic revolution, eased the pressure considerably in this area. At the same time, it may lead Iraq to play a more active and assertive role in the system particularly vis-à-vis its archrival Syria. On the western front, the late 1980s witnessed a more limited improvement in the situation. While Israel maintained a decisive advantage in capabilities, the country's confidence in its ability to dominate its opponents and reshape its environment declined as a result of the bitter experience in Lebanon. The opening of a new front in the conflict in the form of a prolonged national uprising in the occupied Palestinian territories created additional difficulties. These developments placed Israel on the defensive and served to underline the instability of the situation. While pressures on the Arab front-line states remained, they were counterbalanced to some extent by emerging pressures on Israel.

These new conditions on the western front placed the Palestinian issue in the forefront and created opportunities for progress in the recognition of Palestinian national rights. By so doing, they may have altered the balance between front-line Arab actors in ways that could ease conflict between them over policy toward Israel. In particular, the weakening of Syria's position, due to factors previously mentioned, might reduce its obstructionism in this sphere. By the same token, the precariousness of Syria's situation will probably make it more adamant about preserving its presence and influence in Lebanon. Overall, then, the easing of pressures in the larger regional environment may, ironically, contribute to some renewed conflict in the core system.

Pattern of Conflict and Alignment

Another major development during the 1970s was a change in the pattern of conflict and alignment among Arab states and in the balance between the contending forces they represented.[107] For the decade prior to 1967, inter-Arab relations had been marked by acute conflicts between progressive regimes with a strong anti-Western bias and conservative regimes with close ties to the Western powers. This conflict created deep cleavages and rigidity, as there was little scope for developing relationships across directional lines.[108] Although the system was highly polarized in *directional* terms, it was by no means fully bipolar in *political-diplomatic* terms. The conservative regimes, apart from basic similarities in direction and policies, did not really form a cohesive bloc. Also, conflicts with Nasser ensured that there was always at least one major progressive regime that remained aloof from Egypt and conducted an independent policy.[109] In 1966 a common front developed among the progressive regimes, creating a political-diplomatic bipolarity that paralleled the divisions in the directional sphere.[110] Notwithstanding their differences, the progressive anti-Western regimes had the upper hand and kept the conservative pro-Western regimes on the defensive for most of the 1950s and 1960s.

By the early 1970s, changes were beginning to occur in this pattern of relationships. The two leading progressive states, Egypt and Syria, were faced with acute problems as a result of the 1967 war and were ready for détente. With the advent of détente, polarization along directional lines waned. This introduced more flexibility into the system and created more options for policy-makers. Saudi Arabia attempted to capitalize on the shift in direction within Egypt to develop ties with the new leadership.[111] Detente progressed to entente.

After the 1973 war, the evolution continued. Ideological issues ceased to be a force for polarization within the system. Instead, a more complicated triadic pattern of conservative (Saudi Arabia, the Gulf states, Jordan), moderate progressive (Egypt, to some extent Syria), and radical progressive (Iraq, Libya, the PDRY, Algeria) regimes emerged. Saudi Arabia tried to take advantage of developments in Egypt and Syria and use its increased financial capabilities and prestige to construct a broad-based coalition of conservative/moderate elements. By creating a favorable balance of forces, the Saudi regime hoped to make the area safe for conservatism.

The Saudis started with a substantial base of support among moderate regimes (e.g., the smaller Gulf states, Jordan, North Yemen, and the Sudan).[112] From this initial base, Saudi Arabia acted to create a broader coalition. The Saudi-Egyptian entente was strengthened considerably in 1973 when King Faisal employed the oil weapon to provide crucial support to Sadat in the confrontation with Israel. This close Egyptian-Saudi alliance constituted an important development in inter-Arab relations, as it linked the militarily strongest Arab state to the leading Arab financial power.[113] The axis was successful for a time in developing ties with the second Arab military power, Syria.[114] Initially, Syria was more closely associated with Egypt. However, after 1973 and particularly after the second Egyptian-Israeli disengagement agreement (1975), relations between Egypt and Syria deteriorated.[115] At the same time, Saudi-Syrian relations improved as modifications to Syrian policies produced considerable Saudi financial assistance. Syria remained associated with the Saudi-Egyptian axis for a time as a result of its links with Saudi Arabia.[116]

During the 1970s, then, a loose moderate coalition headed by Saudi Arabia and Egypt emerged as the leading force in the Arab system. It was opposed by several less influential actors, notably Iraq, Libya, Algeria, the PDRY, radical elements within the PLO, and leftist-nationalist forces in Lebanon.[117] Although these dissident actors were very clear about what they opposed, they were unable to act cohesively. Nevertheless, their combined opposition activities, even if not closely coordinated, were effective enough to hamper the initiatives of the influential moderate coalition.

The fortunes of this coalition largely depended on its capacity to influence the United States to bring about a comprehensive settlement of the Arab-Israeli conflict. Significant progress in this direction would have created incentives for Syria and the PLO to soften their opposition to the United States and draw closer to the Saudi-Egyptian axis. This would have strengthened the position of the pro-Western coalition and made it the dominant force in the system. However, the rigidity of Israeli policy and U.S. unwillingness to do much to change it proved a stumbling block. The inability of Saudi Arabia and Egypt to persuade the United States to pressure Israel into concluding an honorable settlement on all fronts seriously undermined their influence. Furthermore, the lack of progress toward a comprehensive settlement prompted Egypt to seek a quasi-separate peace with Israel. This split the coalition, as Saudi Arabia and many of the moderate governments were opposed to these moves. Failure to achieve a comprehensive peace placed the moderate pro-Western forces on the defensive.[118] The harder-line elements seized the initiative and called for action both against Egypt and its newfound ally, the United States. Under political pressure, Saudi Arabia and other moderate governments agreed to sanctions against Egypt but declined to take action against the United States. After 1978, Egypt became a virtual outcast and the other pro-Western governments remained largely on the defensive.

By the late 1970s, therefore, efforts to create a dominant coalition had failed and the Arab system became seriously fragmented. The overwhelming majority of system members were opposed to Egypt's unilateral actions but could agree on little else. The temporary convergence of views on this one issue masked important divisions that soon forcefully reasserted themselves. This was certainly true in regard to directional issues where the Arab world was split several ways over policy toward Israel.[119] Egypt had favored a settlement and was prepared to act on its own to procure peace. Jordan, Saudi Arabia, and the other moderate regimes clearly favored a settlement also and were prepared to make initial concessions but only in the context of a move toward comprehensive peace. Others—Syria and the mainstream of the PLO—appeared to be leaning toward a settlement providing it was comprehensive. They were unwilling, however, to make concessions or take any steps without assurances that a satisfactory settlement could be worked out. Still others—Iraq (at least initially), Libya, the PDRY, Algeria, and the Rejectionist Front within the PLO—rejected any settlement with Israel in principle.

While policies evolved somewhat in the course of the 1980s, disagreements over the proper approach to Israel continued to generate conflict. In addition, divergences over relations with the superpowers widened. As superpower conflict grew, polarization with regard to the Arab-Israeli conflict deepened and key Arab states reinforced ties with their respective superpower associates. These differences were reinforced by conflicts over status and influence as other leading states struggled for position in the wake of Egypt's disengagement. These divisions found expression in multiple conflicts rather than one dominant conflict. Furthermore, there was little, if any, solid alignment or cooperation in the system. The four leading states (Egypt, Syria, Iraq, and Saudi Arabia) were basically going their own way. Besides, none of these states, with the exception of Saudi Arabia, had enjoyed much success in attracting lesser power allies. In short, the Arab system was seriously fragmented at a time when it was facing its most serious regional challenges.

These centrifugal tendencies persisted throughout most of the 1980s. On the western flank, the front-line actors remained divided in their approach to the Arab-Israeli conflict.[120] Egypt remained an outcast for several years. The mainstream of the PLO strongly resisted Syrian attempts to establish its tutelage over the movement, generating bitter conflict especially after 1983. Jordan also distanced itself from Syria and sought to pursue its own path, at least until 1986. Syria responded by obstructing any initiatives on the part of Jordan or the PLO during most of the period. Jordan and the PLO cooperated for a while (1982–1985) in exploring possible openings to the United States. However, underlying suspicions and conflicting interests drove them apart. This split was reinforced by subsequent Jordanian attempts to marginalize the PLO and then, after the *intifada* began, to leave the PLO and Palestinian community on their own to face Israel. Renewed Egyptian efforts to organize a common front were hampered by the above-mentioned conflicting interests, by Syrian obstruction and, above all, by the rigidity of Israeli and U.S. policy.

On another front, the Syrian-Iraqi conflict intensified during the 1980s.[121] Concerned about Iraq's rising capabilities and ambitions as well as intra-Ba'thist feuds, President Asad developed ties with the new Iranian regime. These contacts were intended to keep Iraq off balance and prevent it from concentrating its attention on Syria. Syria went a step further in 1982, depriving Iraq of oil transit facilities, thereby increasing economic pressure at a time when Iraq was suffering military reverses. This exacerbated the conflict between the two regimes as well as increasing Syria's isolation in the system. The outbreak of the Iran-Iraq conflict also contributed to the fragmentation of the system, at least initially. As the situation worsened, the states of the eastern front devoted increasing energy and resources to the task of containing Iran. Preoccupation with the Gulf conflict led to a reduction in attention paid to the Arab-Israeli conflict as well as diminished support for the western front-line states. This intensified the centrifugal forces in the system.

Before long, however, the Gulf conflict proved to be the catalyst for new efforts at coalition building. At one level, Saudi Arabia and the smaller Gulf states had previously explored ideas for cooperation without any concrete results. Now the increasingly dangerous situation in the area provided the impetus for the creation of the Gulf Cooperation

Council (GCC) in 1981. This established an institutional framework for the Saudi-led coalition of Arabian peninsula states. At another level, as concern grew about Iran, several Arab states rallied to Iraq's side.[122] On the eastern front itself, Saudi Arabia, Kuwait, and other members of the GCC provided extensive financial assistance to support the Iraqi war effort. Jordan, which had initially turned to Iraq to counterbalance Syrian pressure, now aligned itself solidly with Iraq, furnishing transit facilities and logistical support. Egypt, moving to regain acceptance in the system, provided equipment, military advisors, and civilian manpower to free Iraqis for military service. There thus emerged a loose coalition encompassing three of the system's leading powers (Iraq, Saudi Arabia, and Egypt) together with several lesser states. Its aims were limited in character, namely to sustain Iraqi resistance, prevent its defeat or collapse, and ultimately contain Iran. Since the members of this grouping suffered from various weaknesses and were on the defensive vis-à-vis Iran, they were in no position at this point to provide leadership or attempt to shape outcomes on other issues. Nevertheless, it did establish a framework for further cooperation once the task at hand was achieved.

A smaller rival grouping also emerged beginning in the late 1970s. This was partly based in the eastern Arab world but extended beyond it. Syria was one of three main components of this grouping. Its position in the western Fertile Crescent enabled it to acquire a strong influence both in Lebanon and among certain Palestinian organizations. Its relative isolation in the core area, however, led it to seek allies elsewhere in the region. Libya and Iran became its principal associates since these two states also suffered from isolation and were both in conflict with opponents of Syria (Egypt and Iraq). Algeria and the PDRY became associated in varying degrees with this triad. This very loose grouping was thus drawn together by a combination of common interests and shared directional concerns (particularly opposition to the growth in Western influence in the region as well as to the perceived tendency to seek a settlement with Israel from a position of weakness). The two groupings were opposed on many issues but the polarization was far from complete. This was due both to the looseness of the groupings themselves and to the existence of crosscutting ties among states of differing tendencies. Thus Saudi Arabia maintained links with Syria throughout the period as did Jordan from the mid-1980s on. These ties were used to attempt to draw Syria away from Iran.

By the late 1980s, this grouping was fading as a force. Algeria slowly drifted away, adopting a different stance than Syria on the issue of the PLO, among other things. Libya, too, found itself in increasing difficulty both internally and externally. Facing strong pressure from the United States and suffering from continued isolation in the Arab world, it began to moderate its policies and attempt to improve relations with key Arab states. Conciliatory moves included a more evenhanded policy toward the Iraq-Iran conflict, an attempt to achieve detente with Egypt, and reduced support for extremist Palestinian groups. Iran, for its part, was weakened significantly by the unsuccessful war with Iraq. Its defeat and consequent loss of momentum greatly eased the pressure on Iraq and the eastern front-line states. Moreover, some differences developed with Syria over Lebanon. Hence, by the late 1980s, Syria could no longer count on effective support from its erstwhile regional allies, especially in confronting its principal opponents, Iraq and Egypt.[123] The setback to Iran also reduced Syrian leverage vis-à-vis Saudi Arabia and the other Gulf states since they no longer felt the same urgency about enticing Syria away from Iran.

The termination of the Iran-Iraq war thus marked another potential turning point in the pattern of Arab alignments. With the pressure on the eastern front eased considerably, the coalition supporting Iraq might conceivably dissolve, with Iraq, Saudi Arabia, and Egypt all going their own ways. Attempts have been made, however, to forge a more effective coalition that could provide leadership for the system on a broader range of issues. A partial institutional framework has been established through the creation of the Arab Cooperation Council (Egypt, Iraq, Jordan, Yemen Arab Republic)[124] to parallel the Saudi-led GCC. The new coalition has already been successful in restoring Egypt to full membership in the Arab League. It has also begun to turn its attention to other issues on the western front, notably the Arab-Israeli and Lebanese conflicts.[125] The main obstacle in this area would be Syria which, although in weakened condition, could probably block any arrangements it objected to, at least in Lebanon.

Even if this aspiring coalition does act in concert on certain issues, its cohesiveness will probably be undermined by national ambitions and the existence of subgroupings.[126] By the early 1990s, therefore, the eastern Arab world is more likely to be characterized by polycentrism than by unipolarity.

CONCLUSION

During the 1970s, a number of changes took place both in the Arab system and its setting. The previous concentration of power in one state gave way to a more competitive multipower pattern. The scope of revisionism declined as a more limited range of basic interests, policies, and values were challenged: This shift was accompanied by greater reliance on diplomacy and inducements rather than on political warfare or other coercive instruments of statecraft. This development was facilitated by a hardening of the Arab state and a consequent decline in cross-frontier alliances, external political mobilization, and the transnational political process generally. As the system became less revolutionary, the dominant conflict over directional issues and the role of Egypt gave way to separate conflicts of lower intensity. The reduced salience of directional issues and accompanying pragmatism softened the rigid lines of division in the system, creating more diplomatic options and alignment opportunities. All in all, the foreign policy environment of the core area became much less threatening for system members.

Circumstances changed for the worse from the late 1970s on. While intra-systemic pressures had lessened during the 1970s, pressures from the larger regional setting now intensified substantially. At the intrusive system level, as tensions between the superpowers deepened, their policies towards regional states and regional conflicts became more rigid. In the core-periphery system, the countries on the western flank of the core area were confronted with an overtly expansionist Israel that was becoming increasingly aggressive. Israeli policies and behavior not only endangered the security, territorial integrity, and even national integrity of these states but also threatened to reduce them to a subordinate and dependent position. The countries on the eastern flank were faced with different but equally serious pressures. The activities of the new Islamic revolutionary government in Iran threatened the regimes and social peace (i.e., intersectarian relations) of these states. The situation was exacerbated by a resurgence of Iranian military strength that endangered the security not only of Iraq but of the other Arab Gulf states as well. These increased pressures tended to accentuate the fragmentation of the system. Existing divisions (e.g., among the western front-line actors as well as between Syria and Iraq) persisted or became intensified. Moreover, with their attention and energies divided between two acute regional conflicts, the states of the eastern Arab world seemed unable to forge a common front to cope effectively with either. Problems were compounded by signs of domestic instability in several countries. These developments tended to produce a balance of weakness rather than a balance of power in inter-Arab relations. Thus during the 1980s the states of the core system were acutely aware of their vulnerability. Faced with threats from different quarters, governments remained divided in their preoccupations, indecisive in their behavior, and dependent on one or another superpower to cope with intensified regional pressures.

As the 1990s dawned, prospects for the Arab system appeared to improve in several areas. Progress was made both in easing intra-system conflicts and in overcoming the debilitating fragmentation of the 1980s. The situation on the eastern front was much less acute and threatening as a result of Iraq's victory over Iran. The emerging détente in the global system had carried over to the regional level. This reduced superpower polarization over regional conflicts, facilitated greater diversification in relations between Arab states and the major powers, and limited intra-system conflict over this directional issue. With the important exception of the situation on the western front, the overall regional environment was decidedly less threatening.

By mid-1990 the situation had deteriorated sharply. In the larger regional system, hopes for easing the conflict on the Arab-Israeli front were dashed as the Israeli government blocked the initiation of direct talks with Palestinian representatives. Worse still, the resumption of power in Israel by an ultranationalist government, the substantial strengthening of Israel's demographic capacity through Soviet-Jewish emigration, the decline of Soviet support for Arab front-line actors, and Israel's nuclear monopoly combined with its desire to prevent the growth of Arab nonconventional weapons capabilities all intensified Arab frustrations and security concerns. These were reinforced by apparent U.S. indifference to, or acquiescence in, some of these developments.

The core system itself experienced even more severe shocks as a result of the Iraqi invasion of Kuwait. The move dramatically altered the climate of inter-Arab relations. To begin with, the invasion underlined the pronounced imbalance of power that had developed in the Gulf region due to the rapid buildup of Iraqi military capabilities and a substantial weakening of Iran, the traditional counterweight. This imbalance posed a significant threat to Arab states in the immediate vicinity. Furthermore, Iraqi moves threatened to transform the Arab system into a revolutionary system once again. The invasion raised fears that Iraq had become highly revisionist because its objectives appeared to include not only alterations in the state and territorial framework and the elimination of opposing regimes but also substantial changes in the pattern of power within the system. Saddam Hussein was perceived to be positioning Iraq to intimidate and control Saudi Arabia and other Gulf states with a view ultimately to achieve a hegemonic position in the eastern Arab world. Equally worrisome were the techniques employed by Iraq. One concern was the use of massive military force to settle disputes and the accompanying prospect of the militarization of inter-Arab politics. The other was the initiation of a campaign of political warfare involving attempts at transnational political mobilization and the restoration of the permeability of Arab political systems. This campaign, invoking themes of Arab nationalism, Islamic identity, and social inequalities, attempted to delegitimize and destabilize opposing regimes. The eastern Arab world with its new imbalance of power, increased revisionism, intensified conflict and polarization as well as heightened domestic instability had become a much more threatening environment.

The victory of the U.S.-led coalition in the ensuing war alleviated the most immediate threats to the existing order. Considerable uncertainty remains, however, about the future of the Arab system. At the inter-state level, Iraq's overwhelming defeat, including the destruction of much of its military capability and economic infrastructure, has eliminated the serious imbalance of power among Arab Gulf states. The projected Arab security arrangements in the Gulf should help consolidate the new inter-Arab balance and deter renewed military pressures from Iraq. These commitments, together with the outcome of the entire crisis, may also serve to reduce the future offensive use of large-scale force in the heart of the Arab system. Beyond this the position of the three principal Arab members of the anti-Iraq coalition will undoubtedly also be strengthened, at least in the short run. The key role played by Egypt in organizing an Arab response to the Iraqi invasion as well as its substantial contribution to the new security arrangements should enhance its status and influence, particularly with respect to Saudi Arabia and the smaller Gulf states. The crisis should also lead to a consolidation of Saudi Arabia's leadership within a more tightly knit Gulf Cooperation Council. Syria, for its part, has emerged strengthened, having escaped its previous isolation and improved its position in its immediate region, particularly in Lebanon.

The Iraqi invasion of Kuwait generated sharp divisions within the Arab world that are likely to persist and hamper the cohesiveness of the system. These separations resulted not only from the dominant conflict between Iraq and the other major Arab powers but also from antagonisms between these same powers and the states that favored Iraq. These political divisions are unlikely to be eased by efforts to address the problem of economic disparities between Arab states, at least not in the immediate future. For one thing, increases in aid are likely to be limited by the soft condition of the world oil market. Moreover, divisions may very well be exacerbated, because aid flows are likely to be directed heavily to have-not former coalition partners (Egypt, Syria) rather than to countries that sympathized with Iraq. The latter are likely to be in worse shape economically, because they stand to lose most of their previous aid as well as significant amounts in worker remittances. Economic tensions are likely to lead to increased political tensions between the parties involved.

At the same time, the conflict contributed to a significant shift in alignments and the possible emergence of a new core coalition of leading powers. Egypt split with its former partners in the Arab Cooperation Council to join with Saudi Arabia and the Gulf states in opposing Iraq. Syria, which had previously been the odd man out, now emerged from its relative isolation to join Egypt and Saudi Arabia in the common front against Iraq. The question now is whether this anti-Iraqi front, composed of the eastern Arab world's leading powers, will persist or even be transformed into an effective coalition that provides leadership and direction to the Arab system. More generally, will the states of the eastern Arab world overcome their usual fragmentation and forge common fronts to deal effectively with the challengers on their eastern and western flanks? Or will multipolarity reassert itself? The Egyptian-Saudi connection appears relatively solid, but the Syrian link is more questionable. Problems could arise if Egypt and Saudi Arabia are unable to secure progress toward an honorable settlement on the Syrian-Israeli front or if some form of alignment develops between Iran and Iraq—in the event of a regime change in the latter. Some skepticism is thus in order in assessing the prospects for Arab cooperation.

At another level, the crisis revived the issue of the permeability of Arab state units. Saddam Hussein enjoyed significant success in his campaign of transnational political mobilization. The themes he raised struck a responsive chord among important segments of the population in many Arab states. This response reflected both the underlying frustrations at various features of the existing regional order and the shared resentments toward certain common opponents, rather than any strong attraction to the Iraqi leadership itself. Nevertheless, it did produce substantial outpourings of support in much of the Arab world. At the same time the crisis demonstrated that there were important limits to such transnational political mobilization. The responsiveness to Saddam Hussein's appeals was not as widespread, intense, or undiluted as the response Nasser received in his day. The governments of several key states were able to contain the spillover effect through tight control of the media, prevention of mass demonstrations, and strong internal security measures. At the societal level, various immunizing or countervailing factors were operative in several states. In Egypt, awareness of the unfortunate outcome of earlier Egyptian adventurous behavior, together with the maltreatment of many Egyptians who had worked in Iraq, served to weaken the appeal of Saddam Hussein's message. In Saudi Arabia, Kuwait, and other Gulf states, the immediacy of the Iraqi threat and the ruthlessness of Iraqi behavior appeared to generate a greater sense of identification with the individual state units and their interests. Hence the evidence with regard to permeability is mixed. Although in recent decades there have been tendencies toward a hardening of Arab state units, it is clearly too early to talk of an end to permeability and a consequent consolidation of the Arab state system along the lines of the post-Westphalia European system. Important common concerns and frustrations remain among the populations of many Arab countries. Moreover, the appeal of Islam remains potent and could result in regimes strongly influenced by Islamic revivalism coming to power. Any of these factors could lead to a new round of transnational political warfare and renewed state permeability in the Arab system.

Apart from its impact on inter-state politics, the conflict between Iraq and the U.S.-led coalition threatened to generate considerable domestic instability within the Arab world. Although there were significant manifestations of support for Saddam Hussein during the crisis, no major changes in regimes have occurred or seem likely to occur in the near future, except possibly in Iraq itself or, to a lesser extent, in Kuwait. Nevertheless, the crisis clearly raised political consciousness and mobilized popular opinion in many countries around the issues of Arab nationalism, the role of Islam, economic disparities, and political liberalization. By raising troubling questions among the population at large about the basic direction and policies pursued by their governments, it may have served to undermine the legitimacy and support for Arab regimes. This process of questioning could lead to substantial pressures for change and eventual political turbulence in some Arab countries. It is thus ultimately in the domestic political arena that the effects of the Gulf crisis will be felt and the patterns of inter-Arab politics will be shaped.

The uncertain prospects for the Arab system are compounded by the renewed challenges facing Arab states in the larger regional sphere. On the eastern front, the pronounced weakening of Iraq may generate a whole new set of problems in the area. Foremost among these would be a new imbalance of power, this time in Iran's favor, and a greatly increased permeability of the Iraqi state, particularly to Iranian transnational political activity and influence. The latter problem would be especially serious in the event that a regime transformation in Iraq brought about substantial enhancement of Shi'ite influence. Such a change could lead to accommodation and even a partial entente between a new Iraqi regime and Iran, posing significant new challenges to other members of the Arab system. On the western front the situation appears more difficult than ever, with Israel enjoying a stronger position, militarily, demographically, and politically, vis-à-vis the other front-line states. Its ultranationalist government is also more uncompromising regarding procedures and terms for a settlement of the conflict and indeed is overtly rejectionist in regard to the Palestinian issue. Finally, recent developments have not only underscored the preeminence of the United States in the Middle East but have also heightened the sense of vulnerability, whether military, political, or economic, of many Arab states. This vulnerability is likely to intensify their dependence on the United States and the western powers generally.

From an Arab viewpoint, therefore, it is highly debatable how much better, if any, the new regional order will be. Indeed, the question of whether the Arab system and the Middle East generally will be characterized by order or turbulence in the coming decade remains.

NOTES

The author thanks the Social Sciences and Humanities Research Council of Canada for its financial assistance in carrying out the research on which this chapter is based.

1. Michael Brecher, *The Foreign Policy System of Israel* (London and New York: Oxford University Press, 1972), pp. 1–7.

2. For a discussion of the impact of systemic characteristics on state behavior, see Kenneth Waltz, *Theory of International Politics* (Reading, Mass.: Addison-Wesley, 1979), Chs. 4, 5; and Richard Rosecrance, *International Politics: Peace and War* (New York: McGraw-Hill, 1973), Ch. 4.

3. The eastern Arab world includes Egypt, Syria, Lebanon, Jordan, the Palestinian community, Iraq, Saudi Arabia, and the remaining states of the Arabian peninsula. Previous studies include Leonard Binder, "The Middle East as a Subordinate International System," *World Politics* 10, 3 (1958); Michael Brecher, "The Middle East Subordinate System," *International Studies Quarterly* 15, 2 (1969); Paul Noble, *Regionalism and Conflict-Management: The Case of the Arab System* (Ph.D. diss., McGill University, 1971); and Ali Dessouki, "The New Arab Political Order: Implications for the 1980s," in Malcolm Kerr and El Sayed

Yassin (eds.), *Rich and Poor States in the Middle East: Egypt and the New Arab Order* (Boulder, Colo.: Westview Press, 1982).

4. Daniel Lerner, *The Passing of Traditional Society* (Glencoe, Ill.: Free Press, 1958). See also Michael Hudson, *Arab Politics* (New Haven, Conn.: Yale University Press, 1977), pp. 4–5, 11–13, 126–162.

5. Manfred Halpern, *The Politics of Social Change in the Middle East and North Africa* (Princeton, N.J.: Princeton University Press, 1963).

6. For details on the opposition in Saudi Arabia see Helen Lackner, *A House Built on Sand* (London: Ithaca Press, 1978), pp. 93–105; and David Holden and Richard Johns, *The House of Saud* (New York: Holt, Rinehart and Winston, 1982), Chs. 13–15. On Jordan, see Benjamin Shwadran, *Jordan, A State of Tension* (New York: Council for Middle Eastern Affairs Press, 1959); and A.H. Abidi, *Jordan, A Political Study* (Bombay: Asia Publishing House, 1965).

7. Patrick Seale, *The Struggle for Syria*, 2nd ed. (London: Tauris, 1986); Tabitha Petran, *Syria* (London: Ernest Benn, 1972); Itamar Rabinovitch, *Syria Under the Ba'th, 1963–66* (New York: Halsted Press, 1972); Majid Khadduri, *Republican Iraq* (London: Oxford University, 1969).

8. For domestic developments in Egypt see Robert Stephens, *Nasser* (New York: Allen Lane, dist. Penguin Press, 1971); Raymond W. Baker, *Egypt's Uncertain Revolution under Nasser and Sadat* (Cambridge, Mass.: Harvard University Press, 1978).

9. For a discussion of the main ideological currents during the 1950s and 1960s, see Majid Khadduri, *Political Trends in the Arab World* (Baltimore, Md.: Johns Hopkins University Press, 1970); Leonard Binder, *The Ideological Revolution in the Middle East* (New York: Wiley, 1964); Chs. 6, 7; Sami Hanna and George Gardner, *Arab Socialism* (Leiden, Netherlands: Brill, 1969); R. Stephen Humphreys, "Islam and Political Values in Saudi Arabia, Egypt and Syria," *Middle East Journal* 57, 2 (1978).

10. Shwadran, *op. cit.*, pp. 312–344; Abidi, *op. cit.*, pp. 129–141; *New York Times*, March 29 and April 24, 1963, and January 13, 1964 (Jordan); Holden and Johns, *op. cit.*, pp. 196–197, 204 (Saudi Arabia); Fahim Qubain, *Crisis in Lebanon* (Washington, D.C.: Middle East Institute, 1961), Ch. 10; Michael Hudson, *The Precarious Republic* (New York: Random House, 1968), pp. 42–46, 93–101; and Kamal Salibi, *Crossroads to Civil War* (Delmar, N.Y.: Caravan Books, 1976), pp. 11–12, 14–16 (Lebanon).

11. The leadership tended to be assertive toward the Western powers and periodically toward Israel as well. The Syrian government adopted a very strong stance during the Jordan waters conflict, partly because of its shaky domestic position; Edouard Saab, *La Syrie on la révolution dans la rancoeur* (Paris: Julliard, 1968), pp. 171–172. Iraq's more assertive posture on the Palestinian question as well as its claims on Kuwait may have been shaped by similar concerns. Khadduri, *Republican Iraq*, pp. 168–187.

12. This was evident in the late 1950s and the 1960s, after Nasser's espousal of socialism and the advent to power of the Ba'th in Syria. See Malcolm Kerr, *The Arab Cold War*, 3rd ed. (London: Oxford University Press, 1965), pp. 5–7, 26–33; Petran, *op. cit.*, pp. 172–184, 195–196.

13. Moshe Ma'oz and Avner Yaniv (eds.), *Syria Under Assad* (London: Croom Helm, 1988), Ch. 2; Patrick Seale, *Asad* (London: Taurus, 1988).

14. Majid Khadduri, *Socialist Iraq* (Washington, D.C.: Middle East Institute, 1978), pp. 69–76, 97–101, 177–179.

15. For domestic developments in Jordan, see Marc Yared, "Les institutions consacrent la suprématie de la monarchie Hachémite," *Le Monde Diplomatique,*

November 1977; Samir Kassir, "Jordanie: Le moindre mal," *Le Monde Diplomatique*, May 1982.

16. For an analysis of the deteriorating situation in Lebanon and the subsequent civil war, see Salibi, *op. cit.*, and Walid Khalidi, *Conflict and Violence in Lebanon* (Cambridge, Mass.: Harvard Center for International Affairs, 1979).

17. Hudson, *Arab Politics*, pp. 175–181; William Quandt, *Saudi Arabia in the 1980s* (Washington, D.C.: Brookings Institution, 1981), p. 106.

18. See infra; notes 79, 81, 82, 97, 114.

19. Robert Owen, "The Arab Economies in the 1970s," *MERIP Reports* 100–101 (1981); Malcolm Kerr, "Rich and Poor in the New Arab Order," *Journal of Arab Affairs* 1 (1981), pp. 6, 8–9; Adeed I. Dawisha, *Saudi Arabia's Search for Security*, Adelphi Paper No. 158 (London: Institute of Strategic Studies, 1979), pp. 1, 6–8, 10.

20. Dessouki, *op. cit.*, pp. 326–327.

21. For analyses of the role of Islam in contemporary Arab society, both generally and in particular Arab countries, see Ali Dessouki (ed.), *Islamic Resurgence in the Arab World* (New York: Praeger Publishers, 1982); and J. Esposito (ed.), *Islam and Development* (Syracuse, N.Y.: Syracuse University Press, 1980).

22. See Saad Eddin Ibrahim, *The New Arab Social Order: A Study of the Social Impact of Oil Wealth* (Boulder, Colo.: Westview Press, 1982), Ch. 7, for a discussion of socioeconomic factors contributing to instability in the Arab world.

23. For the growth of domestic opposition in Syria in the late 1970s, see Stanley F. Reed III, "Dateline Syria: Fin de Regime?" *Foreign Policy* 39 (1980); Alasdair Drysdale, "The Asad Regime and Its Troubles," *MERIP Reports*, 110 (1982); P. Seale, *Asad*, Ch. 19. See also Umar Abd-Allah, *The Islamic Struggle in Syria* (Berkeley, Calif.: Mizan Press, 1983).

24. Hanna Batatu, "Iraq's Underground Shi'a Movements," *Middle East Journal* 34, 4 (1981); A. Faroughy, "Laicité et théocratie au Proche-Orient," *Le Monde Diplomatique*, November 1980; Christine Helms, *Iraq: Eastern Flank of the Arab World* (Washington, D.C.: The Brookings Institution, 1984), pp. 151–162.

25. Saad Eddin Ibrahim, "An Islamic Alternative in Egypt: The Muslim Brotherhood and Sadat," *Arab Studies Quarterly* 4, 1–2 (1982); "Egypt's Islamic Militants," *MERIP Reports* February 1982; A. Ansari, "The Islamic Militants in Egyptian Politics," *International Journal of Middle East Studies*, 16 (1984).

26. For a discussion of the religiously based opposition to the Saudi regime and the Mecca uprising, see Holden and Johns, *op. cit.*, pp. 511–532; W. Ochsenwald, "Saudi Arabia and the Islamic Revival," *International Journal of Middle East Studies* 13, 3 (1981); J. Paul, "Insurrection at Mecca," *MERIP Reports* 91 (1980).

27. Samih K. Farsoun, "Oil, State, and Social Structure in the Middle East," *Arab Studies Quarterly*, 10, 2 (1989); Gad G. Gilbar, "The Middle East Oil Decade in Perspective," *Middle East Contemporary Survey: 1986* (Boulder, Colo.: Westview, 1988).

28. Juan R.I. Cole and Nikki R. Keddie (eds.), *Shi'ism and Social Protest* (New Haven, Conn.: Yale, 1986), Chs. 1, 5, 6, 7, 9.

29. Shireen T. Hunter, "The Gulf Economic Crisis and its Social and Political Consequences," *Middle East Journal* 40, 4 (1986); George T. Abed, "The Lean Years: The Political Economy of Arab Oil in the Coming Decade," in Hisham Sharabi (ed.), *The Next Arab Decade* (Boulder, Colo.: Westview, 1988).

30. Farsoun, *op. cit.*; Roger Owen, "The Arab States Under Stress," *World Policy Journal*, Fall 1986.

31. See Malcolm Kerr, "Egypt and the Arabs in the Future," in Kerr and Yassin, *op. cit.*, for a scenario based on the advent of an Islamic fundamentalist regime in Saudi Arabia.

32. Johan Galtung, "A Structural Theory of Imperialism," *Journal of Peace Research* 8 (1971), p. 89.

33. The eastern Arab world covers an area of approximately 1600 miles (north-south) by 1100 miles (east-west). Even the area of the whole Arab world is only 1600 by 3300 miles. By comparison, the area of the African system is approximately 3800 by 3100 miles, the Asian system 3000 by 4000 miles, and the Latin American system 4500 by 2500 miles; see *International Atlas* (Chicago: Rand McNally, 1969).

34. *Oxford Regional Economic Atlas: The Middle East and North Africa* (London: Oxford University Press, 1960), pp. 8–9, 56–59, 102–103; *The Cambridge Atlas of the Middle East and North Africa* (Cambridge: Cambridge University Press, 1987), pp. 84–93.

35. For economic interaction within the Arab world in the 1960s, see A. G. Musrey, *An Arab Common Market* (New York: Praeger, 1969), Appendix, Tables 2–11.

36. See Khalil Nakhleh and Elia Zureik (eds.), *The Sociology of the Palestinians* (New York: St. Martin's Press, 1980).

37. Ibrahim, *op. cit.*, Ch. 3; Fred Halliday, "Labour Migration in the Arab World," *MERIP Reports*, May 1984; *Cambridge Atlas of the Middle East and North Africa, op. cit.*, pp. 48–51.

38. The foremost example of this was Egypt's "Voice of the Arabs" in the 1950s and 1960s. See Lackner, *op. cit.*, pp. 85–86, for an indication of its audience in Saudi Arabia during this period. For more recent developments, see Hamdi Kandil, "The Media and Arab Integration" in G. Luciani and G. Salamé, *The Politics of Arab Integration* (London: Croom Helm, 1988).

39. Charles Cremeans, *The Arabs and the World* (New York: Praeger, 1963), pp. 84–85.

40. Peter Mansfield, *Nasser's Egypt* (Harmondsworth, England: Penguin Books, 1965), pp. 55–60. See Seale, *The Struggle for Syria*, pp. 253–262, 309–315; and Hudson, *Precarious Republic*, pp. 95–96, for examples of Nasser's appeal in Syria and Lebanon respectively; see also Lackner, *op. cit.*, pp. 60–61, 99–100, 109; and Holden and Johns, *op. cit.*, pp. 188–189 on the popularity of Nasser and his ideas in Saudi Arabia.

41. See John F. Devlin, *The Ba'th Party* (Stanford, Calif.: Hoover Institution Press, 1976), Chs. 7, 10–15, on the Ba'th; Walid Kazziha, *Revolutionary Transformation in the Arab World* (London: Charles Knight and Co., 1975) on the Arab Nationalist movement; Fred Halliday, *Arabia Without Sultans* (Harmondsworth, England: Penguin Books, 1974), Ch. 11, especially pp. 386–390, on the PFLOAG.

42. Noble, *op. cit.*, pp. 272–274.

43. For a brief outline of the billiard-ball model in contrast to what is termed the cobweb model, see John Burton, *World Society* (Cambridge: Cambridge University Press, 1972), pp. 28–45.

44. K. Boals, "The Concept Subordinate International System: A Critique," in Richard Falk and Saul Mendlovitz (eds.), *Regional Politics and World Order* (San Francisco: W. H. Freeman and Co., 1973), pp. 408–410.

45. Hudson, *Arab-Politics*, pp. 5–7.

46. Fouad Ajami, "The End of Pan-Arabism," *Foreign Affairs*, 1978, pp. 355–356.

47. See the country by country statistics on aid flows in the OECD triennial publication, *Geographical Distribution of Financial Flows to Developing Countries.*

48. Judith Miller and John Kifner, "Wave of Arab Migration Ending With Oil Boom," *New York Times,* October 6, 1985.

49. For an excellent discussion of this phenomenon, see Ajami, *op. cit.,* pp. 357–369.

50. For an analysis of the development of Maronite "nationalism," see Tewfik Khalaf, "The Phalange and the Maronite Community: From Lebanonism to Maronitism," in Roger Owen (ed.), *Essays on the Crisis in Lebanon* (London: Ithaca Press, 1976).

51. Alan Taylor, *The Arab Balance of Power* (Syracuse, N.Y.: Syracuse University Press, 1982), pp. 93–94; Y. Hirschfeld, "The Odd Couple: Ba'athist Syria and Khomeini's Iran," in Ma'oz and Yaniv, *op. cit.*

52. For a concise analysis of the economic and military relationship between Saudi Arabia and the United States, see Joe Stork, "Saudi Arabia and the US," *MERIP Reports* 91 (1980); William Quandt, *Saudi Arabia in the 1980s* (Washington, D.C.: Brookings Institution, 1981), Chs. 4, 8, 9; Fred Halliday, "A Curious and Close Liaison: Saudi Arabia's Relations with the United States," in T. Niblock (ed.), *State, Society and Economy in Saudi Arabia* (New York: St. Martin's Press, 1982).

53. Rex Brynen, "Palestine and the Arab State System: Permeability, State Consolidation, and the Intifada," *Canadian Journal of Political Science* 24, 2 (June 1991).

54. Citing opinion surveys taken in various Arab countries, Ibrahim maintains that the sense of Arab identity remains strong in the Arab world, *op. cit.,* pp. 123–125. Ajami contends, however, that an opinion survey taken among students from various Arab countries studying at Kuwait University reveals a predominance of Islamic sentiment and of patriotism associated with independent Arab states, Ajami, "The End of Pan-Arabism," p. 364.

55. This was particularly true of any military move against Jordan; see Shwadran, *op. cit.,* pp. 339–340; Abidi, *op. cit.,* p. 167; John Marlowe, *Arab Nationalism and British Imperialism* (London: Cresset Press, 1963), pp. 175–176.

56. On actual and potential Western intervention in the event of military moves, or even internal upheaval, affecting these states during this period, see Shwadran, *op. cit.,* p. 355; Nadav Safran, *From War to War* (New York: Pegasus, 1969), pp. 117–118; Humphrey Trevelyan, *The Middle East in Revolution* (London: Macmillan, 1970), pp. 190–194; Dana Adams Schmidt, *Yemen: The Unknown War* (London: Bodley Head, 1969), pp. 167–168, 186, 192.

57. For the importance of propaganda as a technique of statecraft in the 1950s and 1960s, see Adeed I. Dawisha, *Egypt in the Arab World* (London: Macmillan, 1976), pp. 88–89; Seale, *The Struggle for Syria,* pp. 196–198, 203–211.

58. Demographic resources were one form of soft material capability. Although these are not a direct instrument of influence, they are the basis of most other forms of material capability. Cultural and communications resources were another soft material capability. Although these factors are not normally included in analyses of power, certain features of the Arab setting rendered them particularly important. The homogeneity that made possible the strong links between Arab societies ensured that states with developed cultural facilities would be attractive to educated elements of the population in other Arab countries. Similarly, the permeability of Arab societies and their reliance on political capabilities made

98 Paul C. Noble

communications a valuable instrument of influence. Egypt's prominence in the cultural and communications spheres was striking, amounting to an overwhelming one-power pattern.

59. Kerr, "Egypt and the Arabs," p. 2; Ibrahim, *op. cit.*, pp. 154–159; Samir Makdisi, "Economic Interdependence and National Sovereignty," in Luciani and Salamé, *op. cit.*

60. Ajami, "End of Arabism," pp. 359, 368.

61. Dessouki, "New Arab Order," p. 329; Kerr, "Rich and Poor," p. 23.

62. For an analysis of Saudi Arabia's rising status in the global system, see Bahgat Korany, "Petro-puissance et système mondial. Le cas de l'Arabie Saoudite," *Etudes Internationales*, 10, 4 (1979); Nadav Safran, *Saudi Arabia: The Ceaseless Quest for Security* (Cambridge, Mass.: Harvard University Press, 1985), pp. 220–227, Ch. 17. See, however, Ali Dessouki's warning about the "fragility" of Saudi Arabian power, "New Arab Order," p. 330.

63. Mà'oz and Yaniv, *op. cit.*, especially Chs. 2–4.

64. For an original and perceptive treatment of stratification in the Arab system, see Ibrahim, *op. cit.*, pp. 132–148.

65. For a discussion of Saudi Arabian activities and influence within the Arabian peninsula during this period, see Dawisha, *Saudi Arabia's Search*, pp. 19–21; Quandt, *op. cit.*, pp. 23–28, 34; and Holden and Johns, *op. cit.*, pp. 426–427, 446–448, 474–476.

66. For an outline of Syria's efforts to create a sphere of influence in geographic Syria during the mid-1970s, see Daniel Dishon, "The Web of Inter-Arab Relations," *Jerusalem Quarterly* 2 (Winter 1977).

67. Claudia Wright, "Iraq, New Power in the Middle East," *Foreign Affairs*, 58 (1979–80).

68. Dawisha, *Saudi Arabia's Search*; Quandt, *op. cit.*, Ch. 1, 2, 3; Safran, *op. cit.*, Ch. 8, Conclusion.

69. Eliyahu Kanovsky, "Saudi Arabia's Dismal Economic Future: Regional and Global Implications," in *Middle East Contemporary Survey, 1984–85* (Tel Aviv: Tel Aviv University, 1987).

70. Helms, *op. cit.*, Ch. 6.

71. Itamar Rabinovich, "Is Syria Declining as a Power?" *New York Times*, August 17, 1989; G. H. Jansen, "Syria and the USSR," *Middle East International*, June 24, 1988.

72. William R. Thompson, "Center-Periphery Interaction Patterns: The Case of Arab Visits, 1946–1975," *International Organization* 35, 2 (1981).

73. Binder, "The Middle East as a Subordinate International System."

74. For a fuller explanation of the concepts and events, see Noble, *op. cit.*, Chs. 7–8.

75. See *ibid.*, pp. 315–324, on the techniques of statecraft.

76. Dessouki, "The New Arab Order," pp. 326–327; Taylor, *op. cit.*, pp. 51–53.

77. Quandt, *op. cit.*, pp. 66–67.

78. For a discussion of changes in the Egyptian economic system and the decline of socialist ideology under Sadat, see John Waterbury, *Egypt: Burdens of the Past, Options for the Future* (Hanover, N.H.: American Universities Field Staff), Part 3, Chs. 1, 2, 5; Mark Cooper, *The Transformation of Egypt* (Baltimore: Johns Hopkins University Press, 1982), pp. 88–125; For economic liberalization in Syria and its attendant problems, see Elisabeth Picard, "Le Syrie des Militaires,"

Le Monde Diplomatique, April 1978; and Elisabeth Longuenesse, "The Class Nature of the State of Syria," *MERIP Reports* 77 (1979), pp. 7–8.

79. See Holden and Johns, *op. cit.*, pp. 291–297, for a discussion of the Saudi-Egyptian rapprochement and of Saudi activities as an intermediary between Egypt and the United States in the eary 1970s.

80. For an outline of Egypt's developing political relations with the United States, see Anwar Sadat, *In Search of Identity* (New York: Harper and Row, 1977), pp. 276–305. For the development of military relations, see Joe Stork, "The Carter Doctrine and U.S. Bases in the Middle East," *MERIP Reports* 90 (1980), pp. 7–9.

81. Galia Golan and Itamar Rabinovitch, "The Soviet Union and Syria: The Limits of Cooperation," in Yaacov Ro'i (ed.), *The Limits of Power* (New York: St. Martin's Press, 1979), pp. 216, 220–223.

82. Adeed I. Dawisha, "Iraq Changes Course," *Middle East International*, May 23, 1980; Barry Rubin, "United States–Iraq Relations: A Spring Thaw?" in T. Niblock (ed.), *Iraq: The Contemporary State* (London: Croom Helm, 1982).

83. Yair Evron, "Washington, Damascus and the Lebanon Crisis," in Ma'oz and Yaniv, *op. cit.*, Ch. 12; Seale, *Asad*, Chs. 18, 23.

84. Safran, *op. cit.*, Chs. 14, 16; Quandt, *op. cit.*, pp. 4–71.

85. Robert O. Freedman, "Is Gorbachev Changing Soviet-Israeli Relations?" *Middle East International*, July 25, 1987; Jim Muir, "Shevardnadze's Tour—Doing What the Americans Couldn't," *Middle East International*, March 3, 1989; *New York Times*, December 12, 1989.

86. This can be seen in the opening of an official dialogue between the United States and PLO in December 1988 as well as in the attempts to accommodate Syrian interests in Lebanon.

87. Dishon, *op. cit.*, p. 46; L. Snider, "Inter-Arab Relations," in Haley and Snider, *op. cit.*, pp. 192–193.

88. William Quandt, *Decade of Decisions* (Berkeley: University of California Press, 1977), pp. 200–286; Harvey Sicherman, *Broker or Advocate* (Philadelphia: Foreign Policy Research Institute, 1978).

89. In February 1971, Sadat indicated his willingness to conclude a peace agreement with Israel without any indications that Israel was prepared to return Egyptian territory captured in the 1967 war. In June 1975, he announced his willingness to reopen the Suez Canal even though the proposed second-stage disengagement agreement had fallen through in March. In November 1977 he took the dramatic initiative of visiting Jerusalem and thus effectively recognizing Israel before any satisfactory peace agreement had been worked out. See Joe Stork, "Sadat's Desperate Mission," *MERIP Reports* 64 (1978), and Sadat, *op. cit.*, pp. 273–274, 279–280, 302–312.

90. Asad had stated as early as March 1973 that he was prepared to accept UN Resolution 242 with the proviso that Palestinian rights be recognized, Ma'oz, *Syria Under Hafiz al-Asad*, p. 15; for a further analysis of Syrian policy toward Israel, see Seale, *Asad*, Chs. 15, 16, 18, 22. For the evolution of PLO policy toward Israel see Alain Gresh, *The PLO: The Struggle Within* (London: Zed Press, 1985), Parts IV, V, VI; and Sameer Abraham, "The PLO at the Crossroads," *MERIP Reports* 80 (1979).

91. For an extended discussion of the PLO-Jordanian rapprochement and its impact on relationships among Arab front-line actors, see Emile F. Sahliyeh, *The PLO After the Lebanon War* (Boulder, Colo.: Westview Press, 1986), Part 2.

92. Ajami, "End of Pan-Arabism," p. 365. Dawisha emphasizes the prevalence of territorial issues in the Arab system, Adeed I. Dawisha, "The Middle East," in Christopher Clapham (ed.), *Foreign-Policy Making in Developing States* (New York: Praeger, 1977), pp. 52–53. This point would seem to be primarily applicable to the 1950s and 1960s.

93. In the early 1970s, Iraq renewed certain claims to Kuwait but these amounted to a border issue rather than a challenge to Kuwait's independence. The dispute soon faded into the background; Khadduri, *Socialist Iraq*, pp. 153–159. Fears about the viability of other small Gulf states also proved unfounded as they took steps to consolidate their position. In the course of the Lebanese conflict (from 1970 onwards), questions were raised about Syria's objectives regarding Lebanon but no moves toward annexation ensued. For a discussion of Syria's objectives in Lebanon, see Khalidi, *op. cit.*, pp. 82–84, 110, 116–117, 150–152; and Rabinovitch in Haley and Snyder, *op. cit.*, pp. 56–60, 67–73.

94. O.A.G. Harb, "The GCC and Regional Security in the Gulf," in Mohammed Ayoob (ed.), *Regional Security in the Third World* (Boulder, Colo.: Westview, 1986); E. Peterson, *The Gulf Cooperation Council: Search for Unity in a Dynamic Region* (Boulder, Colo.: Westview, 1988). For the ACC, see infra, note 125. For the Maghreb Union, see David Bamford, "What Does Union Mean?" *Middle East International*, February 3, 1989; and "The Dream Comes True," *Middle East International*, March 3, 1989.

95. Adeed I. Dawisha, *Syria and the Lebanese Crisis* (New York: St. Martin's Press, 1980), pp. 109, 124–139, 157–166, 185–193. For PLO-Syrian conflict see Sahliyeh, *op. cit.*, Ch. 6. and M. Ma'oz and A. Yaniv, "On a Short Leash: Syria and the PLO," in Ma'oz and Yaniv, *op. cit.* For Syrian-Jordanian conflict, see Adeed I. Dawisha, "Much Smoke, Little Fire," *Middle East International*, February 27, 1981; and Joseph Nevo, "Syria and Jordan: The Politics of Subversion," in Ma'oz and Yaniv, *op. cit.*

96. Holden and Johns, *op. cit.*, pp. 272–282, 487–488, 501–502.

97. For the rapprochement between Iraq and Saudi Arabia since 1978, see *ibid.*, pp. 488–489; Taylor, *op. cit.*, pp. 81–88; T. Niblock, *Iraq: The Contemporary State*, Ch. 10.

98. W. J. Olson, "Iraqi Policy and the Impact of the Iran-Iraq War," in Robert O. Freedman, *The Middle East After the Israeli Invasion of Lebanon* (Syracuse: Syracuse University Press, 1986).

99. Jim Muir, "Lebanon Set to Plunge over the Brink," *Middle East International*, September 23, 1988; Godfrey Jansen, "Cats-Paws in the Iraq-Syria Tussle," *Middle East International*, June 23, 1989.

100. See Kerr, "Rich and Poor," pp. 28–30; and Dawisha, *Egypt*, pp. 146–147 for the distinction between the two approaches. See Dawisha, p. 250, note 69, for the "deradicalization" of Egyptian foreign policy.

101. Nadaf Safran, *Saudi Arabia: The Ceaseless Quest for Security* (Cambridge, Mass.: Harvard University Press, 1985), pp. 126–127, 138–150, 229–230.

102. Seale, *Asad*, pp. 261–264, Ch. 17.

103. *Ibid.*, Ch. 26.

104. R. K. Ramazani, *Revolutionary Iran* (Baltimore: Johns Hopkins University Press, 1986), Ch. 4. For a brief analysis of the evolution of the war and its impact on Iran and the Arab Gulf states, see Helms, *op. cit.*, Chs. 5, 6, 7; and Gary Sick, "Trial by Error: Reflections on the Iran-Iraq War," *Middle East Journal*, 43, 2 (1989).

105. Lamris Andoni, "The Gains and Losses for the PLO," *Middle East International*, November 21, 1987; Thomas L. Freedman, "Arab Talks: Topic is Iran," *New York Times*, November 10, 1987.

106. Joe Stork and Jim Paul, "Arms Sales and the Militarization of the Middle East," *MERIP Reports*, February 1983; Anthony Cordesman, *The Gulf and the Search for Strategic Stability* (Boulder, Colo.: Westview, 1984); Anthony Cordesman, "The Middle East and the Cost of the Politics of Force," *Middle East Journal*, 40, 1 (1986).

107. For an insightful theoretical analysis of alliances and alignments in the Middle East including those within the Arab system, see Stephen M. Walt, *The Origins of Alliances* (Ithaca, N.Y.: Cornell University Press, 1987).

108. Kerr, *Arab Cold War, op. cit.,* pp. 5–6, 25–33, 40, 106, 100–117, 126.

109. This was true first of all of Abdel Karim Qasem's Iraq (1958–1963) and then of Ba'thist Syria (1963 on), *ibid.,* pp. 17–18, 85–91, 102.

110. *Ibid.,* pp. 117, 121–125.

111. On the developing entente between Egypt and Saudi Arabia in the early 1970s, see Holden and Johns, *op. cit.* pp. 291–297. On the improvement in Saudi Arabian–Syrian relations in the same period, see *ibid.,* pp. 298–299, and Petran, *op. cit.,* pp. 252–253.

112. Quandt, *op. cit.,* pp. 23–29; Safran, *op. cit.* See also Holden and Johns, *op. cit.*

113. Paul Jabber, "Oil, Arms and Regional Diplomacy," in Kerr and Yassin, *op. cit.,* pp. 430–439.

114. Fouad Ajami, "Stress in the Arab Triangle," *Foreign Policy* 29 (1977/78), pp. 92–99.

115. For an account of the growing rift between Syria and Egypt from a Syrian viewpoint, see Seale, *Asad*, Chs. 13, 14, 15, 18.

116. For Saudi attempts to reconcile Egypt and Syria, see M. Graeme Bannerman, "Saudi Arabia," in Haley and Snider, *op. cit.,* pp. 119–129.

117. Taylor, *op. cit.,* pp. 55, 59.

118. Holden and Johns, *op. cit.,* pp. 481–506; Quandt, *Saudi Arabia,* pp. 16–17, 113–116; and Taylor, *op. cit.,* pp. 73–81.

119. Taylor, *op. cit.,* pp. 73–81.

120. For PLO-Jordanian and PLO-Syrian relations, see Sahliyeh, *op. cit.,* Part 2. See also infra, note 95.

121. A. Baram, "Ideology and Power in Syrian-Iraqi Relations," in Ma'oz and Yaniv, *op. cit.*

122. See infra, note 98.

123. Jim Muir, "Traditional Preoccupations Beckon the Arab World," *Middle East International*, August 5, 1988. Godfrey Jansen, "Self-Inflicted Wounds," *Middle East International*, October 21, 1988; Fida Nasrallah, "Syria Pays the Price of Isolation," *Middle East International*, March 21, 1989.

124. Lamis Andoni, "Arab Cooperation Council," *Middle East International*, February 17, 1989.

125. Jim Muir, "In Solid Support of the PLO," *Middle East International*, December 2, 1988; Jim Muir, "The Attempts to Break the Vicious Circle," *Middle East International*, February 17, 1989; Godfrey Jansen, "The Pressures on King Fahd," *Middle East International*, March 31, 1989; Fida Nasrallah, "The Inter-

national and Regional Dimensions of the Lebanese Crisis," *Middle East International*, May 12, 1989.

126. Fred Axelgard, "Saudi Arabia Looks Ahead," *Middle East International*, March 17, 1989; Max Rodenbeck, "Egypt and Saudi Arabia," *Middle East International*, March 31, 1989.

4

From Revolution
to Domestication:
The Foreign Policy of Algeria

Bahgat Korany

The term "foreign policy domestication" has a double meaning. It means aligning foreign policy with internal or domestic policy or, alternatively, domesticating (taming and especially deradicalizing) foreign policy. Both meanings are applicable to the evolution of Algeria's foreign policy from the 1970s to the 1980s and into the 1990s.

Though less well known, Algeria's perestroika has been going on longer than Gorbachev's. At first gradual in the early 1980s, it was pressured to go faster by the end of the decade when the country made important changes concerning the basic principles of the economy and the political system. The socialist model is no longer the untouchable scared cow, and indeed laws to encourage privatization and investment have been in existence for more than five years now. A new constitution was approved by popular vote in February 1989, a constitution that transformed the country from a one-party state based on the FLN (Front de liberation nationale) to a multiparty one. Are these changes merely "conjonctural" or rather structural? If they affect foreign policy, in what direction and at what level? Do they lead to a change in orientation (role-conception) or only in behavior (role-performance)?

The experience of those writing on Eastern Europe and Gorbachev's perestroika shows the hazards of analyzing a system in flux, as Algeria certainly is at present. In the five-month period from October 1988 to February 1989, Algerians voted three times. In 1988, President Chadli Bendjedid declared that the country could not be ready for multipartism for some years to come. Yet, less than a year later, the 1989 constitution instituted this principle, and by the end of the year as many as fourteen political parties were legally constituted. They ranged from Communists to Islamic fundamentalists.

Certainly, some bases of foreign policy—such as geography or history—do not change that quickly or to such a great degree. But other bases actually did change quickly and with a great impact: population (Algeria's rate of increase is about 3.5%, among the highest in the world), resources (drastic decline of oil revenues and change in balance of payments from a surplus to a deficit), and bases of legitimacy (questioning of the one-party system and the socialist ideology). The result has been that the principles guiding the political structure and the process of policy-making at the beginning of the 1990s differ from those of the 1970s.

If one single clue to the magnitude and direction of change were isolated and traced, it would be the economy, specifically the hydrocarbon sector. In a speech to the congress of the National Union of Algerian Women (UNFA) on March 8, 1986, Bendjedid warned that the drop in world petroleum prices could well result in a loss of up to 80% of the country's revenues. This was an exaggeration, for the actual loss for that year was 40%, but still a huge amount given the fact that hydrocarbons constituted 90% of Algeria's export revenue.

This big financial loss separates the 1970s, the Boumedienne state, from the present decade and is at the basis of increasing "Deboume-dienization." This financial loss eliminated Alberia's financial cushion. For instance, between 1980 and 1985, the annual trade surplus was between $3 billion and $4 billion, but in 1986 Algeria's current trade account has a $3 billion deficit. As a political consequence, the state is increasingly unable to satisfy the population's immediate demands. Moreover, sufficient resources are no longer available to buy off opponents and contesters and hence the state's authoritarianism is less subtle. It is the end of the strong-state and the increasing affirmation of Algerian civil society. Such an affirmation raises the important question of the impact of domestic restructuring on foreign policy.

As a foreign policy actor, Algeria holds a key diplomatic position. It is located at the crossroads of Europe, Africa, and the Arab world. For many Third World countries, it represents a model national liberation movement. It paid "one million martyrs" to gain real independence whereas other countries in French-speaking Africa were "granted so-called independence." Indeed, when Frantz Fanon, the psychoanalyst from Martinique and the "Third World Marx," aimed at elaborating a theory of Third World national liberation, he took Algeria as his frame of reference.[1]

Algeria's revolutionary élan continued after independence not only with the ideology of its first president, Ahmed Ben Bella (1962–1965), but also the pragmatic revolutionism of President Boumedienne (1965–1978). It was, after all, in Boumedienne's Algeria that the Group of 77 first met (October 1967) and established the charter that governs the Third World position in North/South negotiations. When the nonaligned movement seemed in disarray, its fourth summit (Algiers, September 1973) marked its renewal and its reorientation. It was Boumedienne, as the mandated head of the Third World, who addressed the 1974 special session of the UN General Assembly, the assembly that enunciated the concept of the New International Economic Order. One could cite from the limited literature on Algeria's foreign policy[2] many other examples of Algeria as "la montreure de conduite" (the exemplar of behavior) in its desire to restructure international relations.

The first section of this chapter deals with the bases of foreign policy, emphasizing the impact of the colonial legacy on social structure and exploring the linkage between developmental needs and foreign policy. Section 2 concentrates on Algeria's critique of the contemporary global system and its demand for international restructuring through Third World coalition-building. The third section focuses on the decision-making process, analyzing the participation of both institutions and elites. The fourth examines Algeria's practice of foreign policy at the superpower, Third World, and regional Arab-African levels. The chapter concludes with an investigation of the principles and the actual conduct of foreign policy in the bid to free U.S. hostages in Iran in January 1981 and from the hijacked Kuwaiti airliner in April 1988.

THE DOMESTIC ENVIRONMENT

The political aspects of the domestic environment are changing drastically since the first edition of this book was written more than six years ago. Other factors like geography change hardly at all, whereas population and social structure fall in between.

Geography, Population, and Social Structure

For the Algerians, the formation of foreign policy has been first and foremost linked to Algeria's very special colonial legacy. For France, Algeria was not a colony, but a part of France, another *département* or province. Geography played an important role in this special colonial relationship. The relative proximity of Algeria and France had two major effects: it incited France to frenchify Algeria, and it encouraged hundreds of thousands of Algerians to seek jobs in France. After independence, these workers became an element of contention and heated negotiations between France and Algeria. Not only were these migrant workers a source of needed foreign currency for Algeria's gigantic development program, but the Algerian economy could not have absorbed their massive repatriation.

Of the 2.4 million square kilometers that constitute Algeria's surface, four-fifths is desert. The result is that 90% of Algeria's 24 million people are concentrated in the fertile and narrow littoral of hills and plains in the north by the Mediterranean. The Mitidja Plains, which extend 100 km westwards from Algiers, are highly urbanized and are under increasing pressure from immigrants from the rural areas and the hinterland.

The Sahara, however, provides Algeria with its natural resources. It was on the question of the Sahara that the last stages of Algerian-French negotiations for independence were broken off in 1961. France wanted a special status for the Sahara, a status that the Algerian negotiators adamantly refused. The Sahara, moreover, gives Algeria its African depth. Extending 1,500 km to its common frontiers with Niger and Mali, the Sahara puts Algeria in direct contact with Black Africa. Rather than accept that this vast stretch constituted a barrier between "Black" and "White" Africa, Algeria has made of the Sahara an African bridge by developing the trans-Saharan route and other means of transport. In this way, Algeria's role on the African political scene is facilitated.[3]

Proximity to France and the Saharan stretch have both left their imprint on Algeria's population and social structure. The pre-1830 Ottoman Algerian society was typical of other precolonial societies. It possessed a marked segmentation between Arabs and Berbers, nomadic herdsmen and subsistence farmers; its social organization—especially in the rural areas—reflected kinship ties. The influx of European settlers brought a new element to the existing social diversity.[4] Given the big differences in economic status and social values between the colonists and the local populations, the most important distinction in Algeria became that between "Europeans" and "Moslems." The discrimination and disabilities that Moslems suffered in France's drive to Europeanize Algeria created a strong bond of unity within the local population.

In relative terms, however, the 132 years of colonization were not as cataclysmic for Algeria's basic social organization as the eight-year War of Independence (1954–1962). For despite efforts at Europeanization and economic disruption, the rural inhabitants had managed to keep intact most of their social values, kinship organization, and traditional family ties. The War of Independence was to strike at precisely these elements:

> Individuals developed new perceptions of themselves, their abilities, and their roles through wartime activities. Women, accustomed to the sheltered and segregated life traditional in Muslim countries, found themselves suddenly thrown into revolutionary militancy. . . . Many young people struck out independently of their families and elders, and new leaders emerged, chosen more for personal traits than for social position.[5]

France's policy of resettlement of 2 to 3 million Algerians during the war (the regroupment centers) further disrupted traditonal ties and created instead bonds and solidarity networks based on shared identity as Moslems and Algerians. Three results followed from the situation of fast social change initiated by the War of Independence.

First, efforts to redress the disruptions and inequities of the colonial structure took up a large proportion of government resources and permeated educational and cultural life. Even though segregated schooling of French and Moslem children had been abolished in 1949, Moslem schools were still in an inferior position on the eve of independence in 1962. The Europe-oriented curricula were taught excusively in French; less than 30% of Moslem children were enrolled in the primary schools; and less than 10% of Moslem students reached the university level. Immediately after independence, the massive European exodus added to the problems. The education system was in disarray and enrollment in schools at all levels fell to 850,000. A big push was needed: teachers were hastily recruited and trained, expatriate teachers were brought back, and classrooms were improvised in the homes vacated by French residents who had left. By 1967, school attendance had climbed to 1.5 million; in 1975 it reached nearly 3 million.[6] Between 1960 and 1979, the number of students enrolled in primary schools (expressed as a percentage of the age group) rose from 46% to 98%, secondary schools enrollment jumped from 8% to 31%; and the adult literacy rate rose from 10% to 31%.[7]

Even though this crisis is over, developing and putting the educational system in order is still a priority for Algeria. Between 1973 and 1977, Algeria contracted three education loans from the World Bank totaling $101.5 million. Of the 36,000 university students in 1975, some 25,000 were recipients of government fellowships, and an additional 1,800 fellowships were awarded for study abroad.[8] In 1978, 27% of the total budget was allocated to education. The task includes the development and the revision of the educational system, which, Moslem religion schools apart, had been conducted in a foreign language by foreign teachers. The revision of curricula and the development of new textbooks was necessary for the expression of Algeria's Arab-Moslem identity.

Second, the mobilization of the people during the war released mass energies and whetted rising expectations that were not completely satisfied with the advent of independence. Because the nascent political system was incapable of meeting these expectations in toto and immediately, dissatisfaction developed among the population. This dissatisfaction is ready raw material for political conflict and domestic turmoil. In such a context, social issues (e.g., neofundamentalist movements and Berber cultural demands) are quickly politicized.

For instance, though very few doubt the finality of the arabization program, its application has caused conflict among elites and social groups representing diverse cultural backgrounds. One the one hand are those educated in the French cultural tradition, who are in some cases more familiar with the French than the classical Arabic heritage. Indeed, many prominent leaders of the War of Independence found it easier to speak in French, and many are still active in FLN (Front de liberation nationale) cultural and party activities. On the other hand are the religious scholars who enjoy great prestige from their knowledge of Islam's sacred texts. With them are graduates of prestigious centers of Islamic learning, and other elements of the population increasingly familiar with, or interested in, the contemporary Arab renaissance.

What makes these issues central to Algeria's social scene is that even the discussion of technicalities takes place within the context of a focus on cultural identity, the status of the French language, and the place of Islamic principles in a fast-moving, industrializing society. These issues are of course related to the status and role of the social groups espousing the different positions. Thus in his speech of November 29, 1971, in the conference of the nation's cadres, Boumedienne tried to reassure those whose position might be hurt by arabization: "After all," he said, "people are not responsible for their exclusive French formation."[9]

The third major concern of the government is reducing the effects of social cleavages and promoting the society's integration. Algeria's political orientation and behavior—domestic and international—has to satisfy "basic needs," both material and spiritual.

Algeria has one of the highest birthrates (3.5%). As a result, the population is growing by 800,000 every ten months. Consequently, the government is continuously facing a younger population dependent on it for education, health care, and jobs. Problems like accommodation and food consumption are thus aggravated and the pressure mounts on the state to "deliver the goods." In an atmosphere of bureaucratic procrastination, Berber unrest, and increasing radicalization of political Islam, frustration leads to riots.

The warning lights of the early 1980s have now become an immediate danger to political stability, ethnically or economically based. For instance, in 1980, the University of Tizi Ouzou was shut down to avert Berber disturbances; in 1985, the inhabitants of the Casbah (traditional district) of Algiers demonstrated against insecurity, insalubrity, and lack of water; then it was the turn of Gharaia (600 km from Algiers) two months later (in June 1985), where two were killed and as many as fifty-six hurt; and 1986 saw the raging disturbances in Setife and Constantine. The October 1988 events (that left 176 dead by official count and made big headlines in the foreign press) were neither the first nor exceptional. This spectrum of instability raises the problem of governability, even in what is deemed to be the most solid of Third World states, in fact, a showcase. This brings us to the characteristics of Algeria's political structure.

Political Structure

Ultimate political authority used to reside in the FLN, Algeria's only official political party (established in 1954), and the National Assembly. For the major period of Algeria's independence, the assembly's function was assumed by the Council of the Revolution (1965–1977), which Boumedienne established following the "Adjustment Revolution" that overthrew Ben Bella in June 1965. However, the description of this formal structure in no way reveals how the Algerian state actually works. To understand the system's functioning, one must keep in mind, first, Algeria's colonial legacy and the effects of the War of Independence on the structure of political elites, and second, the primacy of development and its problems.

As a result of the national liberation war, the government, the party, and the parliament of Algeria were created before the state itself was established. In 1956, a seventeen-member protoparliament—the National Council of the Algerian Revolution[10] (CNRA: Conseil national de la révolution algérienne)—was established as the ultimate wartime authority of the party, the FLN. In 1958, the National Council established in its turn Algeria's Provisional Government (GPRA: Gouvernement provisoire de la république algérienne).[11] What made the creation of these institutions both necessary and credible was the launching of the liberation war by the guerrilla army—the *maquisards*—in November 1954. This institutional development explains both the status and the role of the different social groups—especially the army—in the postindependence period.

Following the conclusion of the 1962 Evian Agreements, elections were to take place for the first time in independent Algeria in August 1962, but the elections were put off because of infighting among the Algerian leaders. There were two major divisions in this power struggle.

The first division was between the politicians and the military. Members of the Provisional Government felt they had the legitimacy to run the country; the military felt that as they had won the war that made independence possible, they deserved political recognition of their primary role. However, neither the politicans nor the military represented a neatly demarcated or monolithic group. Consequently, there was a second cleavage, between internals and externals. Within the military were two groups: the rurally oriented *wilaya* guerrillas (the internal army), and the professional army, concentrated in neighboring countries during the war (the external army). The internal army was disbanded as a distinct entity after independence, whereas the external army became the basis of the ANP (Armée nationale populaire).

To constitute the first postindependence government, the prestigious leader Ahmed Ben Bella (a politician external), supported by Colonel Boumedienne (also an external), urged the FLN to replace the Provisional Government by the Political Bureau,[12] where he was strong.

> Although never formally approved by the CNRA [the National Council], the Political Bureau soon eclipsed the authority of the GPRA. By September [1962] dissident regional guerrilla commanders had also accepted the authority of the Political Bureau, which then prepared electoral lists for the National Assembly envisioned in the Evian Agreements. It drew heavily from Ben Bella's supporters and political unknowns in the process.[13]

On September 26, 1962, the assembly—itself elected only six days earlier—gave its legitimizing stamp to the de facto power of the Ben Bella–Boumedienne team. Ben Bella became the head of the first post-independence government[14] and Boumedienne became minister of defense.

This victory, however, did not put an end to the elite infighting. The drafting of the constitution and its approval a year after independence caused further dissension. A small group of the Political Bureau drafted the document and presented it first to the FLN conference. In protest against being bypassed, National Assemby president and ex-head of the GPRA Ferhat Abbas resigned in August 1963.

The constitution (approved in a referendum on September 8, 1963) instituted the *formal* supremacy of the FLN, which became the only political organization in Algeria. In reality, however the constitution legitimized the political role of the army and consolidated the role of the president as both head of state and government and commander of the armed forces. The president appointed all high civil and military officials, and had almost no legislative check on his authority. Moreover, he could dissolve the National Assembly, but the assembly could not dislodge the president, whose mandate came to an end only through death or voluntary resignation.[15]

President Ben Bella was, however, removed in June 1965 by a military coup headed by his minister of defense and former ally, Colonel Boumedienne. Ben Bella was accused of monopolizing power, of manipulating divisions to reinforce the party against the army, and within the army itself of attempting to turn "internals" against "externals" so as to exclude Boumedienne and his supporters. For a transitional period— which in fact continued for almost twelve years and ended a year before Boumedienne's death—the new leader eliminated the Political Bureau and the National Assembly, thus further weakening the FLN. Instead, the country was run by two institutions: the twenty-six-member, all-powerful CNR,[16] which was the real policy-making body, composed mainly of the military plus some members of the defunct Political Bureau; and the Council of Ministers,[17] an executive body that ran the daily affairs of the country. Though the 1963 constitution was never formally abolished, the decree of July 10, 1965, transferred its power to the CNRA, "the depository of sovereign authority." Thus Boumedienne's 1965 "Correction" or "Adjustment Revolution" enhanced further the power of both the president and the military.

The 199 articles of the 1976 constitution, which was based on the National Charter of 1976, did not change these two characteristics of the political system.[18] As the single candidate nominated, Boumedienne was elected president on December 10, 1976, by 95.8% of the registered electorate, including emigrants abroad. Up until his death two years later, Boumedienne had no vice-president and he continued as both prime minister and minister of defense. When he fell seriously ill, effective and legal rule was transferred, on November 22, 1978, to colonels Chadli Bendjedid and Abdallah Belhouchet, commanders of the second and first military regions respectively.

With Boumedienne's death in December 1978, there were serious attempts to modify the one-man presidential pattern, but in retrospect it appears that the system was not drastically changed. With the support of the 640 army delegates Bendjedid emerged from the February 1979 FLN congress as the winner against his two rivals, Abdel-Aziz Bouteflika and Mohamed Yahiaoui, to replace Boumedienne. The party congress, however, favored the principle of collective leadership, and its redistributed the five posts previously concentrated in Boumedienne's hands. Thus, Colonel Mohamed Abdelghani—former military commander of Oran and Constantine and former member of the CNR—was appointed prime minister and also interior minister. Constitutional amendments passed on June 30, 1979, and January 7, 1980, aimed at reducing the president's powers, stating that the president must appoint a prime minister and has the right to appoint a vice-president. Moreover, the National Assembly was given the power to remove the president in the case of incapacitation due to ill health. These are, however, minor changes compared to those following the October 1988 disturbances. In fact, a new constitution was voted in February 1989 that departs from basic principles of the 1976 constitution.

In comparison with the 1976 constitution, the 1989 constitution is far more explicit about the bases and characteristics of Algeria's perestroika. The very first article, which in the old constitution stipulated that the Algerian state was socialist, now omits the word completely. Nowhere does it appear in the new text.

A second major difference concerns fundamental freedoms and rights. In the new text, they are those of the "man and citizen." The old one had emphasized the collective aspect: fundamental freedoms and rights of the people as distinct from—and even opposed to—individualism, deemed petit bourgeois and even Western. In this sense the 1989 constitution marks a great step by "recognizing the right to create associations of a political character" (Article 40). This is the germ of multipartism that is emerging in Algeria.

The third important difference concerns the role of the army. In the old constitution, it was the focus of a whole chapter (4) whereas in the new one it is only part of Chapter 3 entitled "Of the State." Previously, the army's task was to participate in "the country's development and the construction of socialism." In the new text (Article 24), its role is technical: "to safeguard national independence, defend national sovereignty, the country's unity and territorial integrity." The new constitution accelerates the depoliticization and professionalization of the army by confining it to the barracks.

There are other differences (e.g., concerning the emphasis on the role of Islam in that state), but the three mentioned above do indeed indicate that a new era has started in Algeria. Of the three basic poles of Algeria's political power—the army, the party, and the presidency—only the presidency is left intact and stronger after the February 1989 referendum.

However, the debate about governability is not ending, but starting, and in this situation of institutional flux different groups and clans are positioning themselves to influence the outcome. Details of this positioning will be discussed in the section dealing with decision-making. For understanding the working of present political structure, though, it is important to mention some leading groups that are the basis of the changing political landscape and to define their present morphology and evolution. Two especially need to be emphasized: the Islamists and an FLN changing from being the only political party ('parti-Etat' or state party) to just one—the leading one, perhaps, but still one—of fourteen political parties.

Islamists[19] emerged as a grass-roots political force in the 1980s. Indeed, both the 1986 enriched National Charter and the 1989 constitution acknowledge this new political influence by emphasizing the role of Islam in Algeria's society and state-formation. During the 1988 riots, the Islamists were in the forefront of protest forces showing their mobilization capacity, marshalling tens of thousands of demonstrators, clashing with the army, and thus having glory of dozens of "martyrs" as precious political capital. In fact, immediately after the riots President Bendjedid personally received three leaders of the Islamic movement, offered condolences, and listened to the Islamists' complaints against the provocation of the army.

Such a high-level meeting could not but confirm the emergence of Islamists as a very visible grass-roots opposition party. In fact, Algeria is the only Arab country to have permitted—following the new constitution—the formation of a religious-based or Islamic party. In this respect, two movements compete to speak in the name of a political Islam: The Ligue de la Da'awa islamique (LDI: League of the Islamic Call) and the more radical Front islamique du salut (FIS: Islamic Salvation Front). They have different followings; the FIS appeals generally to younger radicals who at present express themselves on the streets and in campus conflicts. But violent confrontations with the government (as the one in October 1988, for instance) polarize public opinion, and hence the different followings combine ranks to constitute an impressive antigovernment protest force. With massive street demonstrations using appealing slogans that call for the introduction of single-sex schools, application of *Shari'a* law, or solutions to the ever-growing problems poisoning the daily lives of the great majority of the population, the Islamists constitute an increasing threat to the presidency's political control.

The other potentially formidable contender is the newly regenerated FLN. This FLN is no longer an arm of the state, an official mobilization ministry as it was before the institution of multipartism in early 1989, but rather a political party. The November 1989 extra-ordinary FLN congress could indicate what lies ahead in the 1990s. This congress

> was intended to emphasize the former single party's transition into a
> mass-based unit able to compete effectively in Algeria's evolving multiparty
> democracy and support the government's reform program. It ended with

the FLN's membership giving its approval to Chadli's democratic experiment but only qualified support to the radical economic reform program being put in place by government.[20]

This extra-ordinary congress showed the presence of at least four tendencies.

> There are two blocs within the grass roots, one supportive of reform, the other anti-Chadli and anxious to guard traditional prerogatives. The FLN's cadres—who in the new political environment could find their jobs in jeopardy—form another distinct group; and Islamic supporters the fourth. Added to these factions backing individuals.[21]

Indeed,

> Most striking was the use of the congress not as a springboard for implementing reforms but to welcome back FLN members of the older generation. . . . The reintegration of old guard elements and concessions on sensitive social issues were essential to unify a deeply divided and recalcitrant party.[22]

To attain this goal of the unification of opposition ranks the FLN is increasingly including in its speeches Islamic symbols and demands by the different Islamic groups. This growing emphasis on religious credentials has alarmed some secular reformers and pushed one to lament, "We are now sounding more FIS than the FIS itself."[23]

Though the political situation is still very much in flux, the presidential center has managed to keep control by barring serious opponents from being elected to the fifteen-member politburo. What will determine the evolution of the political structure is the capacity of the government to diffuse protest by dealing with the ever-growing socioeconomic problems. The impact of these problems explains why so much of the present policy discussion concerns Algeria's economic orientation and the overhaul of the development model.

Economic Capabilities and the Increasing Economization of Foreign Policy

During Algeria's twenty-five years of independence, its economic policy has influenced its foreign policy in two major ways. Increasing state interventionism has caused the swelling of a technocratic or managerial elite with a policy-making role; and the increasing role of the hydrocarbons sector in the development plans enhanced Algeria's need both to find foreign economic partners and to develop sufficient credibility to borrow easily on international markets.

Though Algeria inherited a relatively good infrastructure (roads, airports), its economy at the time of independence was heavily distorted; it had been organized to function as part of France's economy and not as the economy of an independent country. An example is the concentration on vineyards and wine in a Moslem country. Economic dependence on the French market[24] put Algeria in a difficult position during the negotiations for independence and in the early years of the new state.

During those early years, the economy was also burdened with problems resulting from the War of Independence: considerable internal migration, the destruction of crops, the havoc wreaked on roads and transportation, the reduction in investments, and the deterioration of manufacturing and agricultural equipment. Moreover, the sudden departure of many French and European managers and owners[25] at the time of independence resulting in much waste and inefficiency. These conditions explain why Boumedienne's 1965 Adjustment Revolution turned inward to emphasize a nationalist form of socialism, accelerated industrialization, and hence growing state interventionism.

Development planning started in earnest with the three-year plan for 1967–1969, but the state had already been active in the economic sector. The departure of Europeans caused more than 700 factories to fall by default to the state[26] and to worker self-management. In 1966, the government nationalized major portions of the mining sector; in 1968, the large-scale manufacturing firms, and in 1970 and 1971, the hydrocarbon industry. Moreover, some private firms that either had difficulty with their workers or did not see eye to eye with the government were also nationalized. Though adequate compensation was paid, these nationalizations affected Algeria's foreign relations, particularly relations with France in 1970 and 1971.[27]

This last case is important for the economic capabilitites–foreign policy linkage. Given the legacy of relations with a colonizing power and the need for nationalization and economic restructuring, Algerian-French relations were bound to suffer. Algerian policy-makers had to find other economic partners in order to increase their overall bargaining power and to pursue their development objectives much more freely: hence the rising importance of the United States in Algeria's economic relations. This aspect of the linkage between economic capabilities and foreign policy becomes even clearer when we consider the hydrocarbon sector.

Compared to many developing countries, Algeria had a piece of good luck at the time of independence: its hydrocarbon sector had been developed by private French firms with the help of the French government. As a result, Algeria escaped the hardship of immediate postindependence balance-of-payment deficits. On the negative side, however, this sector was not under Algeria's control and hence could not be properly integrated into the development plans. To remedy this situation, a national corporation was established in the last days of 1963: SONATRACH (Société nationale de transport et de commercialisation des hydrocarbures). By 1965, SONATRACH had redefined relations with foreign oil companies and made concessions subject to review every five years.

By the time of the first review, two new developments had occurred: the rise of OPEC and the acceleration of Algeria's socialist transformation.

Thus, in February and April 1971, the Algerian government nationalized up to 51% of every petroleum exploration and production facility, and 100% of all natural gas and oil pipelines and other transport facilities. Foreign interests were to operate as junior partners or on a contract basis with SONATRACH. Thus between 1966 and 1972 the government considerably increased its control over the hydrocarbon sector: in exploitation areas, from 12% to 100%; in oil production, from 11.5% to 77%; in natural gas reserves, from 18% to 100%; in pipeline transport, from 38% to 100%; in refining, from 20.4% to 100%; and in distribution within Algeria, from 0 to 100%.[28] By 1978, SONATRACH had become the tenth largest oil company in the world.[29] Its managers are bound to influence the economic policy/foreign policy linkage in the future because of the primacy of industrial development and the vital role played by hydrocarbons in attaining this objective.

In 1978, a joint study by SONATRACH and the huge multinational Bechtel Corporation, entitled "Hydrocarbon Development Plan of Algeria, Financial Projects 1976–2005," was made public. This plan set the background for future development in the country.[30] As Chadli Bendjedid put it in an interview with *Le Monde* on November 1, 1979: "We have a global development strategy based on industrialization. . . . There is no question of going back on this path. . . . On the contrary, we have to maintain and improve the implementation of our policies while correcting inadequacies."[31] The sale of a large portion of the hydrocarbon reserves was the means of creating Algeria's large and integrated industrial base.

Indeed, reviewing Algeria's economic performance during the 1970s, one sees that it has been closely correlated with performance in the hydrocarbon sector. The revenue of this sector has risen considerably, from $1 million in 1958 to $1,050 million in 1973 and $4,100 million in 1974. The economy's growth rate followed closely. Thus when the value added in the export-oriented hydrocarbon sector was at an annual average of 4.9% during the 1973–1978 period, the gross domestic product (GDP) growth rate for 1974–1977 was 6.4%. When the hydrocarbon growth rate accelerated to 10% in 1978, the GDP growth rate increased as well, reaching the high point of 10.8% in 1978.[32]

Both the GDP and the hydrocarbon sector growth rates are crucial for Algeria's international status and its credibility in world financial markets. In early 1980, the Banque nationale d'Algérie was able to sign the best deal ever for an Algerian borrower on the international money markets: $200 million for ten years with five years' grace at an annual interest rate of 0.875% above LIBOR (London Interbank Offered Rate). Earlier deals had averaged spreads of more than 1% above LIBOR.

This standing in international financial markets is important because Algeria borrows heavily to meet investment and development needs. In 1978, SONATRACH's international borrowing reached more than $3,200 million in loans and bonds. Algeria's external debt had reached just under $20 billion by early 1980. However, increased (hydrocarbon) revenue had allowed the debt-service ratio to decrease from 25% to 22.7% of the total debt by the beginning of 1980.[33] The world oil glut of the early 1980s and Algeria's efforts at oil conservation are expected to reduce revenue and increase borrowing if the 1980–1984 development plan (whose projected investments total four times those of the 1974–1977 plan) is to be respected.

The linkage between the state of the economy and foreign policy involves the impact of the SONATRACH-Bechtel Hydrocarbon Development Plan in another way—in the extension of pipelines to Europe, pipelines that have to go through the territories of neighboring countries. The pipelines to Italy must run through Tunisia, and the project was nearly abandoned in early 1977 because of Tunisian reluctance to have the pipeline cross its territory. But in 1977, Italy—not Algeria—signed the agreement for the construction of the Tunisian section, and on June 16, 1979, Bendjedid officially inaugurated work for the 2,498-km gas pipeline, Transmed.[34] This effect of petroleum on foreign policy is not unrelated to the 1982–1983 Algerian-Tunisian high-level visits that led to the conclusion of the twenty-year "Treaty of Brotherhood and Concord" between the two countries.[35] Similarly, the route of the planned gas pipeline to Spain was changed in June 1979. Instead of the planned Oued-Al-Malah/Almeria route, it will now be moved further from the Moroccan border, running from Oran to Cartagena.[36] The February 1983 meeting between King Hassan II and President Bendjedid at the Algerian-Moroccan border was arranged not only to stop the escalation toward direct military confrontation over the Western Sahara question, but also to discuss each country's economic considerations.[37]

Military Capabilities

The record is ambiguous on Algeria's military capabilities at the time of independence. Some elements of military training were provided during the period of colonization. For instance, Algerian recruits were used within French "pacification forces" during the 132-year colonial domination. Similarly, during World War II 200,000 Algerians provided needed military manpower for the French army, and they fought with valor against the Germans from France's trenches.

The army formed after independence was completely different in outlook, for it was based on the militants who launched the 1954 revolution. Boumedienne's task was to convert the guerrilla force into a modern military institution. To attain this objective, he had to find the means to acquire sophisticated weapons, train personnel, and build sectors such as the air force and the navy from scratch.

Given the heterogeneity of the ALN (Armée de liberation nationale), the task of putting an end to factionalism and of building the professional ANP proved difficult. From 1962 to 1968, factionalism led to abortive rebellions or *wilayism* (narrow *wilaya* or province-oriented power) every year except in 1966.[38] In 1967, the ANP squashed an attempted coup d'état. By the end of the 1960s, however, the task of building an army seemed to have been successful. Boumedienne stated in October 1969:

> The edification of the state, in its broadest sense, requires the simultaneous constitution of an armed force. This operation has proceeded according to our plans. The army of peasants and workers, the army of the poor, is each being transformed into a modern army equipped with the most recent techniques and composed of dozens, if not hundreds, of engineers and technicians. Although carried out in silence, without vain publicity, this action has nonetheless met our expectations.[39]

What type of individuals is this army composed of, and what are the soldier's patterns of political socialization, their political beliefs, their values? According to a study published by the American University in Washington, D.C., this was the prototype of the Algerian career soldier in 1978:

> [He] was the son of a peasant or an urban laborer. He had the reputation of being tough, hardy, and amenable to discipline. He had a strong sense of national pride and military loyalty deriving from the accomplishments of the country's revolutionary fighters, some of whom were still in the ranks with him or among his senior officers. Moreover, he had been thoroughly indoctrinated in the nationalist and socialist goals of the continuing revolution.[40]

The army—whether the external professional group or the internal *mujahiddin* (warriors) group—has been the basis of the nationalist policy of Arab-Moslem Algeria. Did not Boumedienne say to Mohamed Heikal, *Al-Ahram*'s editor-in-chief, "We are above all militants"?[41] Thus when the third Arab-Israeli war erupted in June 1967, Algeria immediately sent to Egypt a battalion-size combat team of infantry and artillery and about 100 MiG planes; on June 25, 1967, Algeria made conscription compulsory. But this involvement was not allowed to divert funds from the development sector toward the army. From 1965 to 1973 the military budget grew by only a third, and in relation to the overall budget, its share declined from 15% to only 8%.[42]

The worsening of the Western Sahara conflict with Morocco from the mid-1970s on revived bad memories of the earlier 1963–1964 military conflict, when the Algerian army did not fare well. The pattern of Algerian troop concentrations was altered, and a sixth military region, centered on Tindouf near the Moroccan frontier, was mentioned for the first time in the press in January 1976. Military expenditure also rose: from 1 billion Algerian dinars ($285 million) in 1975 to 3.9 billion ($856.8 million) in 1982, an increase of just under 400%, compared to a 40% rise between 1965 and 1973, from 484 million to 611 million Algerian dinars. As for arms purchases, the Stockholm International Peace Research Institute (SIPRI) has shown only five agreements for the period 1970–1975, whereas the period 1976–1981 produced fifteen agreements.[43]

Moreover, the evidence suggests that Algeria's military expenditures have exceeded budget figures substantially in some years, with funds being allocated from other accounts in the national fiscal plan.[44] The difference is usually drawn from Soviet credits for armaments (as was the case in both 1967 and 1974 to make up for the arms Algeria sent to the battlefront in the Mashreq). This brings us to the effects of arms purchases on foreign policy.

As early as 1967, and despite the continued use of some French material by the rural gendarmerie, the bulk of Algeria's equipment inventory was Soviet material, and the proportion had increased by 1980. Moreover, the army has internalized the Soviet liking for large numbers and size in both equipment and organization. Indeed, the closest relations between Algeria and the Eastern bloc members and other "radical" regimes are in the military field.[45]

In the 1980s, the pattern of dependence on military supplies from Eastern European countries continued but also reflected a sustained attempt to purchase arms from Western countries and diversify supplies. Supplies were sought not only from France but also from the United States, and in 1985 Algeria's name was removed from the list of countries not eligible for purchase of U.S. arms. The possible settlement of the Western Sahara question would remove one big obstacle between Algeria and Western countries in this respect.

In fact, the Algerian-Moroccan rapprochement and the lull in the Western Sahara conflict have been associated—either as a cause or an effect—with a quasi-stationary defense budget from the mid-1980s until 1989. This budget has ranged from 4.6 billion dinar in 1984 to 4.8 billion in 1985 to 5.5 billion in 1986 to 5.8 billion in 1987 to 6.2 billion in 1988 and 6.6 billion in 1989. Given the rate of world inflation and the decline in the rate of exchange of the Algerian dinar (from $1 : 4.9 in 1984 to $1 : 6.9 dinar in 1989), the average yearly defense budget has remained the same if not declined, especially in 1989.

The army's political influence also seems to be changing. As mentioned above, Bendjedid won the contest for the presidency thanks to the army vote that tipped the balance. He was later, however, to insist on the professionalization of the army, and hence to diminish—if not to exclude— its political tutelage. The emphasis is on a technocratic army. Increasingly, reformers replace old guards in senior posts within the military establishment. Thus the newly appointed political commissar in the army, colonel Yahia Rahal, announced the army's withdrawal from politics. He was backed by other top brass among the military, such as the commander of the first military region, and also by the chief of staff.[46] To compensate the army for the relative decline of its *direct* political influence, the presidency will continue sophisticated arms purchases, especially from Western sources. However, if the economic situation continues to worsen and the austerity program affects the army too much, the army's political docility and neutrality would not be permanently guaranteed.

FOREIGN POLICY ORIENTATION: INTERNATIONAL RESTRUCTURING AND THE THIRD WORLD

In an analysis of 175 speeches delivered by Boumedienne between June 1965 and June 1970 both inside and outside Algeria, the concept "revolution" ranked first and occurred 1,698 times; the concept "national" ranked second and occurred less than half as often, only 757 times.[47] This insistence on political change—both national and international— is consistently expressed in Algeria's foreign policy objectives and strategy.

In 1975, on the occasion of the tenth anniversary of Boumedienne's Adjustment Revolution, a book published by the army specified Algeria's foreign policy objectives. Put succinctly, they are: defense of national independence; restoration of national identity; refusal of any form of foreign intervention; elimination of foreign bases and refusal of the policy of blocs and military alliances; active solidarity with national liberation movements and democratic and progressive forces; effective participation in the struggle against underdevelopment and foreign economic exploitation and domination.[48]

Although the degree of emphasis and phraseology vary, all of Algeria's official documents—from those of the GPRA to those of the postindependence governments—have been consistent in upholding these objectives. As ambassador to the UN, Algerian scholar Mohamed Bedjaoui described his country's policy orientation as "a fixation on national independence and worship of [Third World] cooperation."[49] *El-Moudjahid*—Algeria's major newspaper—put this in a wider historical context: "Algeria's attachment to its national independence is proportionate to the heavy price it paid to get it. In this sense, one can say that colonialism has constituted for Algeria's independence a strong driving force."[50] The preindependence Tripoli declaration, the 1976 National Charter, and Algeria's three constitutions, of 1963, 1976, and 1989, all go in the same direction.

In this respect, the National Charter is the culmination of the different official documents enunciating the country's foreign policy objectives. The whole of Chapter 5 of the charter is devoted to foreign policy. The single concept that dominates this chapter is at the core of the charter's spirit, and it acts as a link between its different parts. This is the concept of political change, national and international: "The great progress of the world economy, the continued expansion of the technological-scientific revolution, the irresistible developments of movements of national and social liberation, create all the time new situations, new ways of thinking, unknown imbalances, and processes in constant evolution."[51]

Concerning the international system, the underlying idea is that its structure is outdated. Article 86 of the 1976 constitution (which codifies the principles of the National Charter) is quite remarkable in its un-conventional formulation. The article affirms Algeria's respect for "the principles and objectives of the charters of the UN, of the Organization of African Unity [OAU] and of the Arab League." This original formulation was preferred, after some discussion among Algerian legislators, to the more standard one of respect for "the general rules of international law." The reason for this change in formulation was the Algerian legislators' view that the present corpus of international law preceded the emergence of Third World states and was thus elaborated without their participation. Consequently, it is neither progressive enough nor adapted to the present international context. As Bedjaoui, in his new capacity as Algeria's representative in the International Court of Justice, put it:

> International law has remained oligarchic. It has been dictated to the whole world by one or two groups of dominant states, especially the European powers who historically projected on the international level their pattern of domination and their own norms. This is why Algeria prefers the international law of participation, *i.e.*, the set of international norms based on the participation of all states.[52]

Boumedienne emphasized the same idea in his opening speech to the Fourth Summit of Nonaligned Countries (Algiers, September 1973). He asked rhetorically: "Isn't it time to restructure the rules of international law in order to reflect the new realities of the contemporary world?"

The need for international change was occasioned by the rise of the Third World, whose members have the prime responsibility in realizing the international restructuring. This restructuring is not primarily con-cerned with relations among the great powers, but rather between great powers and the small ones, for the basic international incompatibility is between small and big powers. This is the global system's number one defeat.

This scale of priorities colors Algeria's judgment of East-West détente. Although welcome in principle, this détente is criticized as being con-cerned with a few actors and dimensions of international relations: "Algeria is not ready to accept a restrictive interpretation of détente which will limit it to relations between developed countries, while leaving the rest of the world, *i.e.*, the overwhelming majority of mankind, to suffer under the yoke of exploitation, insecurity and war."[53]

As a result, East-West détente, which was motivated by a desire for nuclear balance, has not been correlated with peace and security in the rest of the global system. Yet, as Algeria's charter explicitly states, "it is increasingly in Africa, Asia and Latin America that the wars, the plots and the coups d'état organized from the outside take place, and where the battle is raging to guarantee hegemony at the level of the planet."[54] If détente is to be worthwhile, it has to be global. Global détente cannot reflect only the wishes of the closed club of a few great powers. On the contrary, it implies "a democratization of international relations and presupposes a sincere desire of real and equitable adjustment of relations between industrialized and Third World countries."[55]

The prime responsibility for bringing about this international restructuring falls on the Third World, whose members must protect their national independence and work together to overcome resistance to change. The first five pages of Chapter 5 of the charter use the expression "Third World" or an equivalent (not counting labels of partial conglomerations such as Africa or the Arab world) twenty-seven times—more than five times per page. This fixation on the Third World underlies Algeria's belief that Third World unity is a prerequisite for international change: "Imperialism uses formidable and varied means of pressure to subject to its own interests and strategic vision the newly emancipated countries. This is why these latter have to elaborate a platform of appropriate action and promote their soidarity in order to frustrate all attempts at domination."[56]

This Third World unity is to be based on a policy of nonalignment: "Third World solidarity constitutes an essential component of our foreign policy of nonalignment."[57] But nonalignment is not at all a policy of fence-sitting or the equivalent of Swiss-type neutrality. Nonalignment is not limited to political independence, but goes beyond it to insist on "the exercise of full and complete sovereignty over natural resources"[58] and the elaboration of a new international order.

To achieve this general level of Third World unity for international restructuring, Algeria's world view insists on some areas of special interest: the Maghreb, the Arab world, and Africa. These three foci of attention are an integral part of general Third World unity, and they are linked among themselves by mutual interests. For instance, the Maghreb is a part of the Arab nation, and consequently its unity is a first step on the road to pan-Arab unity. Similarly, African and Arab countries overlap, not only geographically, but also in their common objectives and interests. Moreover, Algeria's integration in all three areas is not a matter of choice or of a passing context: on the contrary, it is based on the "solidarity of struggle between all the peoples"[59] of these areas.

The word and concept "peoples" is basic for Algeria's policy-makers. When dealing with Maghrebi or Arab unity, official documents emphasize the primacy of "peoples' unity" over "states' unity."[60] To be durable, unity is not to be the simple result of agreements between governments and still less a product of a passing political context. If "peoples' unity" is not followed, the cause of Arab unity will not advance, and the end result will be a serious disappointment. This is why social and economic transformations, with their political concomitants at the mass level, are crucial for the realization of this "historical endeavor."

Algeria still supports the existing "pan" institutions, whether they be the OAU or the Arab League. However, its attitude differs toward each. Algeria emphasizes its role in the creation of the OAU and the elaboration of its charter. Concerning the Arab League, the emphasis is much more on the league's lagging behind. For this institution to be effective, its charter has to be adapted to the present regional and global context: "Only the revision of its Charter and the remaking of its structures would permit the Arab League to be in keeping with the present international context and play at the same time a more effective role in the realization of the aspirations of the Arab peoples toward unity and progress."[61]

Thus, whether at the macro level of the global system, at the level of Third World politics, or at the much more specific regional level, Algeria's world view shows consistency among its various components:

1. The emphasis all along is on the primacy of political change and international restructuring. Repeatedly and insistently, Algeria preaches the democratization of international relations, an "international law of participation."
2. If a bipolarity does exist, it is primarily between "imperialist" and Third World states, between developed and developing countries. The latter have to work together incessantly, inside and outside the UN, to stop the process of exploitation and bring about international restructuring.
3. Blueprints for unity (Maghrebi or all-Arab) have to be between peoples rather than between governments. Prior social and economic transformation within these countries would put them on the right political path and make the "unity of peoples" more easily attainable.

It is not at this level of foreign policy principles and vision of the global system that Algerian foreign policy–makers feel the necessity of revising their ideas. Whether in the 1976 National Charter and constitution, the 1986 "Enriched Charter," or the 1989 constitution, consistency is maintained.

Thus in the 1986 charter, the basic principles—what Algeria calls the foundations of its foreign policy—have not changed. However, the priorities seem to be more clearly set (with the use of subtitles) and the tone of the document is less combative. After enunciating the prime principle of the preservation of national independence and absolute rejection of international subordination, the charter's Part I—whose Chapter 5 is devoted to foreign policy—deals with the struggle for the establishment of NIEO (New International Economic Order) and South-South cooperation. Next comes the Arab world as part of the South. The same necessity of revising the Arab League's charter is insisted upon, and there is more emphasis on avoiding improvisation and short-term maneuverability in building Arab unity. More emphasis is noticeable too concerning the natural link between the Arab world and the Islamic *umma*. The chapter then deals with the Maghreb as an integral part of these Arab, Islamic, and Third World agglomerations.

Beyond the general solidarity and affinities uniting the South, the chapter actually divides the Third World into different regions of varying priorities. Thus, after the Arab world comes Sub-Saharan Africa (Section V) then in Section VII, Asia and Latin America. (Section VI discusses a region that, though not Third World, is of immediate geopolitical importance to Algeria: the Mediterranean. Sections VIII and IX deal with socialist countries and the Organization for Economic Cooperation and Development (OECD) group in this order.

Regarding socialist countries, the first sentence insists on the relations of friendship that go back to the period of the national liberation struggle. The charter insists on the highly positive aspects of this cooperation and adds the reminder that there is still a potential in this sector of relations that has not been exploited. Regarding relations with the OECD countries, the charter's tone is much more reclamatory and almost wary. Cooperation is, of course, insisted upon and has to be "based on the strict respect of sovereignty, non-intervention in internal affairs and the balance of interests." The final section (X) is devoted to Algeria's relations with the UN.

Ideological continuity of orientation—rather than change—characterizes the charter's two versions. The word revolution, for instance, still occurs 232 times followed by (national) development at 205 times. However, the points of emphasis differ slightly. Moreover, the language is modified, and the tone of the charter's second version is more functional than confrontational or revolutionary. For instance, in the 1986 version, the following paragraph has been dropped: "One of the basic characteristics of our epoch is the fundamental contradiction between, on the one hand, the aggressive forces of imperialism and, on the other, the liberation movement of Third World peoples" (page 108 in the original version).

Though general verbal consistency is maintained in the charters between the 1970s and the 1980s it may very well be exaggerated intentionally. Indeed, this apparent consistency may not reflect the change (incremental rather than sudden) in both pragmatic action and among the governing elite. This brings us to the working of the decision-making process.

THE DECISION-MAKING PROCESS

The interaction between different factors, and its impact on foreign policy, is best revealed in the decision-making process. The analysis of this process must take into account the role of both participant institutions and the persons that represent them. Institutions are the official and—in principle—enduring participants. The persons that act as representatives of their will and interests change much more rapidly. This duality is reflected in Algeria's pattern of decision-making, which has exhibited three major characteristics: the dominance of the presidential center: the president, his staff, and his trusted companions; the primacy of the military; and the growing importance of the managerial or technocratic elite.

Institutional Flux

At the institutional level, the period before Boumedienne's 1965 Adjustment Revolution contrasts sharply with the period of his presidency (1965–1978). The pre-Boumedienne regime was characterized by plurality and rapid change in the decision-making organs. There were the various political leaders (*les chefs historiques*) who had decided to launch the revolution on November 1, 1954. Once the revolution had begun, military leaders had to be consulted as they were in direct contact with the situation on the terrain. This nascent influence of the military was, however, balanced by the decision-making organs that enjoyed political legitimacy and autonomy: the 1956–National Council of the Algerian Revolution and the 1958–GPRA. The Provisional Government was the organ that planned and conducted Algeria's foreign relations through the equivalent of ministries of foreign affairs, information, economy, and defense. The GPRA was also in charge of offices in foreign countries, the equivalent of embassies, which sent periodic reports and waited for guidelines.

During this period the decision-making pattern involved different levels and issue areas, a multiplicity of organs, and dozens of persons in different fields of specialization. Because of this decentralization, the decision-making pattern did not conform to the psychologistic hypothesis or the "great men" theory of history so dominant among theoretical approaches to Third World decision-making. Indeed, at the time, Algeria's decision-making pattern came nearest to the bureaucratic politics model with its emphasis on a multiplicity of participants and their bargaining.[62] All participants, however, rallied behind the objective of political independence and the FLN as the most legitimate vehicle to attain it.

With independence, the FLN's objective was attained, but the party found it difficult to adapt to the postindependence context. Moreover, during the Ben Bella era (1962–1965) there was a concerted attempt to make the decision-making process more centralized. In retrospect, this period appears as a transition phase toward the presidentialism and primacy of the military so evident in the Boumedienne and Bendjedid eras.

Ben Bella, the first president and prime minister of independent Algeria, had little say in the decision-making of the preceding GPRA,[63] whose power he defeated with the help of Boumedienne and the army. As early as August 1962, Ben Bella was pushing for more centralized decision-making by strengthening the FLN's Political Bureau (in which his supporters were concentrated), which eclipsed, in practice if not in theory, the other decision-making organs: the CNRA and the GPRA. In the National Assembly elected on September 20, 1962, the military—

still Ben Bella's ally at this time—got the highest number of votes (18%).[64] Ironically enough, it was the military that finally put an end to Ben Bella's drive toward a monopoly over decision-making by overthrowing him.

By launching his 1965 Adjustment Revolution from a strong military base, Boumedienne found it easier to accelerate the centralization of power. All decision-making organs except the Council of Ministers were put to sleep. The focus of power was transferred to the new Council of the Revolution, composed of trustees under Boumedienne's direct command. The 1963 constitution was abolished in practice, if not officially, and its jurisdiction was transferred to the newly established council, which legislated by decree. Moreover, the already disorganized FLN was further weakened; it functioned only at the subnational level through the *wilayat*, which did not play a direct role in "high politics" or foreign policy.

To fill this institutional vacuum, Boumedienne announced in his June 1975 speech (commemorating the tenth anniversary of his Adjustment Revolution) plans for the National Charter (published and debated in 1976), for a new constitution (also in 1976), and for the election of a new Popular National Assembly (convened in 1977). In April 1977, the newly elected president for a five-year term, Boumedienne carried out the first major reshuffle of the Council of Ministers since he had come to power twelve years earlier. Over half of the council was replaced by members who came from the military, internal security, or from Boumedienne's personal staff.[65] The new constitution and new assembly notwithstanding, this change in the Council of Ministers was interpreted as a further consolidation of power by Boumedienne. The acutal decision-making pattern, based on presidentialism and the primacy of the military, remained intact despite institutional modification.

This pattern was confirmed with the president's death the following year. When Boumedienne went into a coma in November 1978 from a rare blood disease, the responsibilities of the president were transferred—not to Rabih Bitat, the head of the Popular National Assembly, as the constitution decreed—but rather to colonels Bendjedid and Belhouchet.

Moreover, the votes of the 640 army delegates to the February 1979 FLN congress were the prerequisite for Bendjedid's election as president. Attempts at collective leadership notwithstanding, Bendjedid emerged—after a short transition period—as *the* leader, combining the posts of president, defense minister, and FLN secretary-general, and eliminating from power his earlier rivals to the presidency, Bouteflika and Yahiaoui. The foreign minister, Ahmed Taleb Ibrahimi, a close collaborator of Bendjedid, came to the Foreign Ministry directly from the presidential staff.

Thus since independence, the decision-making process has become increasingly centralized, notwithstanding the reactivation of institutions a year before Boumedienne's death.

Elite Clusters

In terms of the *elite*, centralization is less pronounced, but the structural characteristics of the primacy of presidentialism and of the military are clear. At this level too, the pattern follows the institutional evolution of the four Algerian regimes.

The GPRA (1958–1962). This phase was dominated by the "historic chiefs" (*chefs historiques*) who were old hands at political action (e.g., Ferhat Abbas),[66] or had the prestige of having launched the November 1954 revolution. Their average age at the time of independence was around forty, and they represented, par excellence, the liberally oriented, Western-educated political elites so prevalent in Third World regimes at the time of independence. At the time of Boumedienne's death in 1978, one member of this generation—Rabih Bitat (born 1925)—was the head of the Popular National Assembly.

The Ben Bella Period (1962–1965). This was the transition stage toward the centralized and personalized decision-making pattern that developed after Ben Bella was overthrown. Ben Bella (born 1919) was one of the nine historic chiefs, but he allied himself with the army and overthrew the GPRA. During his presidency he attempted to centralize decision-making around the presidency and its intellectuals by curtailing the influence of the military and their supporters within his government, and by seeking to reinforce the FLN. He was overthrown by Boumedienne and the army before he could succeed.

The Boumedienne Era (1965–1978). The arrival of Boumedienne marked a change in the elite and in the pattern of decision-making. Instead of the factionalism that had characterized the GPRA and Ben Bella regimes, Boumedienne (born 1932) pushed toward centralization under his control. Under his leadership, the primacy of presidentialism and the military were combined. The military supplied the direct decision-makers in the only decision-making organ, the 1965 Council of the Revolution. Of the twenty-six council members, twelve held military positions under Ben Bella, another three were members of the General Staff (Etat Major General) under Boumedienne just prior to independence, and yet another three were members of the famous Oujda group.

The creation of the Oujda group and of the General Staff dates back to the late 1950s and early 1960s. They were initiated by Mohamed Bou Kharouba, whose war name was Boumedienne. A graduate of the most prestigious Islamic university, Cairo's Al-Azhar, Boumedienne joined the ALN after the start of the hostilities. He was promoted colonel of the Wilaya V in 1957, then commander of the western region (Oujda, on the frontiers with Morocco) in April 1958, and then head of the General Staff of the frontier army (the "externals" of the western and eastern regions) in 1960.

One of Boumedienne's aspirations was to form a military core and shape the army according to his specific views. With the support of the Oujda group (Bouteflika, Cherif Belkacem, and Mohamed Medeghri) guaranteed, he formed another military core in the eastern region (Ghardimaou, frontier command with Tunisia) around Ali Mendjli and Ahmed Kaid, with whom he formed the Ghardimaou Triumvirate. When the army was restructured and the General Staff was formed after the constitution of the GPRA was established, Boumedienne was already in a strong position to eliminate his rivals and separate the army from the "politicians," thus keeping the army tightly under his control.

On the basis of his consolidated authority and dedicated supporters, Boumedienne started to transform the lower levels of the military. He established a sort of military academy that not only taught soldiers how to harass the enemy, but also provided political education and thus trained the political cadre of tomorrow's Algeria. A few trustworthy and competent officers who had received training in the French army (e.g., Abdallah Belhouchet, Mohamed Bencherif, Bensalem, Moulay Abdel Kader named Chabou, and Souffi, who later all became members of the Council of the Revolution) were responsible for the army's technical reorganization. The reorganized military provided Boumedienne with a strong base from which to exercise pressure on the GPRA "politicians" even before independence was achieved.

During the negotiations for the 1962 Evian Agreements, the General Staff criticized the GPRA's "soft" position and its negotiating strategy. When Mohamed Ben Khedda, head of the GPRA, went to discuss the Evian Agreements with the ALN personnel in Morocco, he was met by determined protestors. ALN spokesman Bouteflika, who was then only twenty-five years old, denounced the future agreements as "a compromise paving the way for neo-colonial manoeuvers" and "a deliberate attempt to freeze the Revolution."[67] Bouteflika went so far as to threaten to impose the army's will "by military means" against the GPRA "embourgeoisie." These differences with the GPRA convinced the highest echelons of the army to throw their weight behind the Ben Bella team to unseat the GPRA.

While factionalism and intra-elite cleavages continued during the Ben Bella presidency, Boumedienne concentrated on the army to achieve some of his objectives. He resisted attempts to involve the army in the politicians' clans, worked hard to dispense with the *wilayat's* former guerrillas, the "internal" army, by either disbanding them or bringing them under his control, and generally pushed toward the consolidation of a strong, modern army.

During the 1964 FLN congress, Boumedienne came out strongly and publicly in favor of a political role for the army, and defended the army's autonomy and his own sovereignty against interference by the "Marxist Ben Bellists" and their attempts to exploit divisions between "internals" and "externals" within the army. Bouteflika—then a civilian minister in the Ben Bella government—defended his old friends and colleagues in the army and joined the 200 army delegates who constituted a solid bloc among the 1,500 civilian participants. When Ben Bella (on the eve of the Afro-Asian conference to be convened in Algiers) planned to get rid of Bouteflika, the latter's former army colleagues, headed by Boumedienne, overthrew him.

The military thus assumed direct decision-making power through the Council of the Revolution, whose members included old army colleagues of Oujda or of the General Staff. The council members who had already left the army and become "civilianized" as minister or FLN Political Bureau participants under Ben Bella still kept close contacts and maintained a solid coalition based on their common experience in the army.

In 1968, the military were joined as top decision-makers by a rising elite: the managers or technocrats. They came from government or state-run companies such as SONATRACH (oil and gas), SNS (iron and steel), SONAREM (mining), SONACOME (heavy industry), SN METAL (metallurgy), SONEL-GAZ (gas and electricity), SNIC (chemicals), SONITEX (textiles), SNMC (building industries), SNCF (railroads), CNAN (shipping), and Air Algerie.[68]

This administrative and technocratic elite did not have the same decision-making power as the military or their spokesmen, who remained the top decision-makers. But with Boumedienne's increasing emphasis on accelerated development and the growing role of gas and oil in the functioning of the economy, the administrative-technocratic elite were implementing major national decisions. They wielded significant power in their own areas of administrative and economic decision-making, and they increasingly made their influence felt on the top policy-makers, as the previously cited data on economic capabilities indicate. Consequently, "as a group the technocrats were second only to the military in power and influence, and in social status they may have been the most prestigious."[69]

The Bendjedid Presidency (1979–   ). The end of the Boumedienne era and the succession in 1979 of Chadli Bendjedid (born 1929) do not seem to have affected the established threefold pattern of decision-making (presidentialism, primacy of the military, and growing importance of the administrative-technocratic elite). Boumedienne was replaced by another active military man, an old associate, who was in fact the most senior man in the army.[70] Presidentialism and the military continue as close partners in the top decision-making.

The average age of this group at the end of the 1980s was about fifty-five years. Three-quarters are between fifty and sixty years old. When the revolution started in 1954 the members were between seventeen and twenty-seven years old and between twenty-five and thirty-five years old when Algeria won its independence. The presence of this nationalist generation[71] explains the prevalence of the kind of language, symbols, and references used in Algerian discourse. Even when behavior is showing signs of change, the "enriched" charter still maintains a remarkable continuity in language and concepts.

More importantly, the members of the present governing group also represent a geographical concentration. They come usually from the president's region, the Algerian east, and/or have been in service with him in Oran. In more than one sense then, Boumedienne's Oujda group has been replaced by Bendjedid's Annaba group. It has between seven and ten members who are strategically situated. They control the presidency, of course, the Ministry of Defense (the post of the general secretary, since Bendjedid never gave up the post of the Minister of Defense), Information, the FLN's political bureau, military security, and the gendarmerie or police. But persons occupying these posts could be easily replaced if they are not deemed sure allies of the president or firm supporters of the liberalization reforms.

The presidential center, thus, still occupies the dominant position despite the 1989 constitutional change giving more power to the Popular National Assembly and instituting multipartism. Even with the present multiplicity of players and their relative autonomy, the president keeps his power by acting as the final arbiter. The presidency thus stays supreme.

An example is the last cabinet change (September 1989). The president summarily dismissed Prime Minister Kasdi Merbah whom he had put in place a year earlier (following the October 1988 riots) to carry out the needed reforms. He was replaced by Mouloud Hamrouche, a close associate of the president and then secretary-general of the presidency. Hamrouche, as he promptly pledged, is committed to continue the regime's program of economic and political reform. The twenty-two-minister cabinet contained only eight holdovers from the previous cabinet, especially longtime allies of the president such as Hedi Khediri and Ali Benflis, in addition to some veterans like Sid Ahmed Ghozali, the present foreign minister.

The maintenance of presidential preeminence should not be confused with the preeminence of one man and hence emphasis on his idiosyncracy, i.e., a return to "the great man theory of history." Though the president as principal decision-maker is certainly important and the kind of person he is counts very much, the emphasis here is on the primacy of a group that has a certain institution at its command. This institutional privilege is cleverly used to maintain the group's control of the system. Thus as previously explained, Bendjedid was chosen among three presidential candidates, members of the FLN Political Bureau, but he soon excluded them. They were even—like some other veterans—criminally pursued for real or fabricated offenses. In fact, many Algerians called the tribunal dealing with these political quarrels, not "la cour de comptes," but "la cour de *règlement* de comptes." Others have been pushed toward early retirement and tempted with privileges. Many Algerians have dubbed this pattern chomalux or luxury unemployment. Consequently, only six of the ministers included in Boumedienne's last cabinet in 1977 figured among the forty-four ministers and ministers of state in place in 1984.

This tussle at the top could increase with the relative democratization of the political structure. Thus with the legalization of opposition parties (for example, the former Communist party, PAG or Parti de l'avant-garde socialiste—Socialist Vanguard Party), the presidency has to contend with duly constituted and institutionalized political opponents. As the part on political structure above meant to show, these opponents, whether Islamic groups or FLN historical *chefs*, have grass roots in society and are now supported by basic laws and the 1989 constitution.

For instance, the November 1989 extra-ordinary FLN congress used the occasion to reassert traditional values and reintegrate old-guard elements who were previously thought consigned to history.[72] These include Abdessalam Boulaid, the architect of Boumedienne's program for socialist development, Tahar Zbiri, former chief of staff (1963–1967) and ex-member of Boumedienne's Revolutionary Council (1965–1967) who attempted a coup d'état in 1967, many former ministers and other veterans who still carry a lot of historical weight. Included also among the newly elected members are Mohamed Yahiaoui and Abdel-Aziz Bouteflika, the two presidential candidates competing with Bendjedid after Boumedienne's death. Many took the floor and received warm ovations.

It is conceivable in this case that with the increasing flux at the top of the political pyramid the army might be tempted or pulled to join. After all the army cannot be disinterested in the debate about development models, budget allocations, and the role of Islam in society. Moreover, many members of the existing elite sprang from the army and still maintain connections with it. We should not forget what a very well informed Tunisian journalist and ex-minister said more than twenty-five years ago, "Tomorrow's Algeria will be what the ALN would really like it to be." As if to confirm Bechir Ben Yahmed, the Algerian historian Mohamed Harbi is supposed to have said: "Every state has its army but in Algeria, the army also has its state."

The Role of the Foreign Ministry

According to the constitution, the president is responsible for foreign policy, and he is to be assisted by the foreign minister, whom he appoints. The foreign minister himself is assisted by the secretary-general of the Ministry of Foreign Affairs. The ministry itself was reorganized in March 1977. As a result, the special French Directorate, which had heretofore reflected the importance of Algeria's relations with France, was integrated into the Directorate of Western Europe and North America. The structure of the ministry is pyramidal, going from the five general directorates of the ten regional directorates, to the multiple subdirectorates and bureaus.[73]

In the conduct of foreign relations, Algerian diplomats are professional, competent, and well-respected at the international level. They usually arrive at meetings with well-prepared position papers and thus guarantee Algeria's success in Third World coalition-building. That does not mean that the Foreign Ministry personnel are among the top decision-makers, yet they are essential for the conduct of the country's international behavior and thus belong to the 500 to 600 members of the general political elite. This elite includes the Central Committee members of the FLN, the 31 *wilaya* governors, the 261 members of the National Assembly, the general secretaries of ministries, presidents and directors of the fifteen or so major state-owned industries, the presidents and executive councils of the five national organizations (of workers, peasants, students or youth, women, and veterans), and heads of the numerous professional associations (lawyers, doctors, teachers, etc.).[74] The influence of the top ambassadorial and diplomatic corps varies, of course, according to the issue area and also according to the personnel's connections with the top decision-makers, the core elite. This is even more so in the case of the foreign minister.

The minister's influence, however, is much less a function of his administrative position as head of the Foreign Ministry than it is the result of his connection with the very top decision-maker, the president. Nothing illustrates this better than the position of Abdel-Aziz Bouteflika, who probably had the longest term as foreign minister in any Third World country. In a system plagued by factionalism and rivalry, Bouteflika was foreign minister from the second Ben Bella government (September 1963) until Boumedienne's death in December 1978.

Bouteflika had the reputation of being one of the youngest foreign ministers in the Third World. He was born in March 1937 in Tlemcen, in the western part of Algeria near the Moroccan frontier.[75] In the 1950s he became an activist within the "Morocco section" of the General Union of Algerian Moslem Students in France, an organization that worked closely with the FLN. After finishing his secondary school education, Bouteflika joined the ALN rather than pursue a university education. He was sent to the western region at Oujda, where Boumedienne was the commander. Their ensuing friendship meant that with the rise of Boumedienne, Bouteflika's responsibilities and influence also grew, and he was entrusted with delicate missions. An example was his selection for a three-man delegation to study the possibilities of opening a southern front against the French army and of contacting Algeria's neighbors to the south, Guinea and Mali. Along with his military experience Bouteflika was thus initiated into political-diplomatic activities.

In the last stages of the Evian negotiations, the French government permitted contacts with the FLN "historic chiefs" detained in France, the *prisonniers d'honneur*, Ben Bella and his colleagues, who were kept at the Chateau d'Aulnoy. As one of the GPRA delegates to these consultations, Bouteflika impressed Ben Bella. When Ben Bella was in conflict with the GPRA, Bouteflika served as a privileged link between him and the Oujda group whose support assured Ben Bella's political victory. In the first Ben Bella government Bouteflika became minister of youth and sports (at the age of twenty-five); a year later he became foreign minister, replacing the assassinated Khemisti, a close Ben Bella ally.

Soon, however, differences arose concerning jurisdiction in decision-making. Ben Bella and Boumedienne differed on the army's role in decision-making, and Bouteflika took Boumedienne's side. Then Ben Bella, who followed a Gaullist concept of the state and foreign policy-making, clashed with Bouteflika, who refused to play a subordinate role in foreign policy decision-making. This conflict ended in Ben Bella's overthrow.

From the beginning of the Boumedienne era, Bouteflika was a pillar of the regime. He sat on the twenty-six member Council of the Revolution and continued as foreign minister. His influence over foreign policy increased as Boumedienne devoted most of this time in the early years to the domestic front. From the late 1960s and early 1970s, however, Boumedienne and the presidential center became increasingly active in foreign affairs, and rumor revealed a latent tension between the president and the foreign minister. Friction between the two men did not, however, lead to a public break, as both agreed on the bases of Algerian foreign policy orientation and behavior. When Boumedienne died, Bouteflika was among the three candidates to the presidency. He lost to Bendjedid, the army man. He also lost his position as foreign minister and after a few months, his membership in the FLN Political Bureau.

Former finance minister Mohamed Benyahia replaced Bouteflika as foreign minister. When Benyahia died in 1981 in a plane crash while on a mission to mediate the Iraq-Iran war, Ahmed Taleb Ibrahimi, a presidential aide to Bendjedid, replaced him.

The career of the present foreign minister,[76] Sid Ahmed Ghozali (fifty-two years old), is revealing in many respects. It provides a contrast with Bouteflika and hence can reveal the change in emphasis in foreign policy as well as the pattern in elite turnover.

An engineer by training, he had his greatest hour of glory under Boumedienne in the 1960s and 1970s. In 1966, when he was not yet thirty years old, he was appointed director-general of the SONATRACH—the then-growing empire that often frightened other members of the elite by its increasing influence. Ghozali consolidated its strength for eleven years before his appointment as minister of energy and petro-chemical industries in April 1977. Less than two years later, on March 8, 1979—not even three months after Bendjedid's arrival to power—he was transferred to the Hydraulics Ministry before being sacked altogether in 1981 from both the cabinet and the FLN's central committee. He was almost in disgrace.

He remained for three years without any official position before being appointed in September 1984 extra-ordinary ambassador to both Belgium and the EEC (European Economic Community) in Brussels. His reintegration into the top political elite took place officially in November 1988. He was then appointed minister of finance in the new government of Kasdi Merbah following the October 1988 riots. This was then and is still a very delicate post in Algeria's tense economic context. But without being too self-assertive toward his colleagues in the government, he managed to control the state of finance. Moreover, he capitalized on his earlier post and connections in Brussels, maintained contact with different international organs and thus saved Algeria the humiliation of going before the Paris Club to ask for rescheduling of its debt and accept the dictates of international financial orthodoxy. In September 1989, he was transferred to the Foreign Ministry and thus became number one in government after the prime minister.[77]

Between Bouteflika and Ghozali, there is a change from the ideologue-revolutionary to the reformist financial technocrat. Such a transition might seem logical given the change in the mix of Algeria's assets and liabilities and in its new global context. Equally important in respect of this elite turnover is its present fluidity. People do not seem to be permanently in favor or out of favor, as was the case during the Boumedienne era. However, the continuity of the 1980s with the 1970s is manifest in the maintenance of the authority of the presidential center. This center permits people to be "in" or "out." Indeed, being close physically to the president seems to indicate rising influence. The career of the present prime minister confirms this pattern of elite-recruitment and mobility.

Mouloud Hamrouche joined the ALN in 1958 at the age of fifteen, and then years later he was appointed director of protocol in the cabinet. When Bendjedid succeeded Boumedienne in 1979, Hamrouche entered the FLN's central committee (as a substitute member first, then in 1984 as a regular member). In February 1986 he was moved to the presidency where he became its secretary-general—a very influential post at the top of the decision-making apparatus, a gatekeeper very close to the principal decision-maker.

This institutional continuity in the presidential preeminence notwithstanding, Hamrouche's appointment as a prime minister shows a change at the personal level. It is the arrival of a new elite generation. Indeed, the majority of the 1989 cabinet are new ministers (technocrats) whereas many of the *chefs historiques* are at present in the opposition. How does this elite change influence foreign policy behavior?

FOREIGN POLICY BEHAVIOR

If a shorthand description of the behavioral patterns of the 1970s and 1980s is desired, we can emphasize their contrast. The 1970s were a period for Algeria of accumulating petrodollars, Third Worldism, and ideological leadership. The 1980s were, on the other hand, one of rising economic hardship and hence international debt, increased attention to the Maghreb and acceleration of a cooperative pattern, and a tendency to political domestication generally.

Thus without abandoning its affinities with "radicals" like Cuba, Iran, or Libya, and still maintaining solid relations with the USSR, the 1980s were characterized by more cooperative political relations with yesterday's ideological enemies: for example, France, the ex–colonial power; the United States, "leader of world imperialism"; and Morocco, "a monarchical reactionary regime."

Nonalignment and Relations with the Superpowers

The United States. Given the two countries' diametrically opposed views of the international system, one might expect Algeria's relations with the United States to be pure conflict. Conflict does exist, but so does cooperation, especially in the gas and oil sector and in the education of Algerian students at U.S. universities.

Washington recognized Algeria on September 29, 1962, and William Porter, the U.S. consul, was promoted to the rank of ambassador in Algiers in December of the same year.[78] Algeria's ambassador to Washington, however, did not arrive until almost a year later, in September 1963. Diplomatic relations were cut off in August 1967 following the Six-Day War and were not reestablished until November 1974. Strangely enough, it was during this absence of diplomatic relations that Algeria's relations with Washington developed quickly. U.S. consulates in Oran and Constantine remained open, Kissinger stopped in Algiers in October and December 1973 during the initial stages of his Middle East shuttle diplomacy, and Boumedienne met Nixon on April 11, 1974, during the UN Special Session on Primary Products.

It was relations in the petrol and gas sector that reinforced Algeria's connections with the United States. By the end of the 1970s, the United States became Algeria's foremost partner in this sector. Boumedienne himself had to intervene publicly by early 1971 to explain this "anomaly of relations with the biggest imperialist power," and to insist that Algeria was determined to follow its own militant foreign policy and did not need lessons from anybody in its business or political relations.[79] Thus Algeria continued to sign contracts with U.S. companies—especially with El-Paso, committing itself to deliver between 35 and 40 billion cubic meters of gas in a twenty-year period beginning in 1969. By the late 1970s, 50% of Algerian petrol and gas went to the United States, comprising about 9% of U.S. imports of crude. The big refining complex at Arzwo port, built with direct U.S. participation in 1978, is evidence of the intensity of these relations.

Algeria developed its economic relations with other Western countries, too. SONATRACH signed several agreements with both the Federal Republic of Germany and Belgium. Between 1973 and 1979, the percentage of Algeria's trade with the West (or with developed market economies, according to UN usage) rose from 87.1% to 88.9%, and the percentage with the East (the centrally planned economies) declined from 6.2% to 4.7%.[80]

But the Bendjedid team seemed interested in intensifying relations with the United States following Algeria's successful mediation in the hostage crisis between Washington and Teheran. Despite ups and downs concerning the haggling over the price of Algerian petroleum, as well as U.S. arms supplies to Morocco, relations were consolidated quickly until by 1985 Bendjedid was the first Algerian president to pay an official visit to Washington. During this visit Bendjedid encouraged U.S. investment in Algeria and negotiated Algeria's removal from the list of countries that the U.S. administration had declared "ineligible" to purchase some U.S. military equipment.

The Soviet Union. One could easily imagine that Algeria's relations with the USSR would be close in all fields. The two countries share an anti-imperialist ideology and an emphasis on socialist transformation as the road to development. Other elements, however—divergent views on the solution of the Middle East conflict and on the place of Israel in the region, and different perceptions of East-West détente—intervene to disrupt the image of complete political concordance.

Despite its ideological commitment to the anti-imperialist struggle, Moscow's support for Algeria's independence in the 1950s and early 1960s was influenced by Soviet involvement in the East-West conflict and especially by Moscow's interest in President Charles de Gaulle's disengagement policies toward the North Atlantic Treaty Organization (NATO). Consequently, the USSR initially seemed favorable to an Algerian-French rapprochement. Moreover, although the GPRA representatives were received in Moscow in September 1960, Soviet de jure recognition came only in March 1962, *after* the Evian Agreements.[81]

As for Algeria, its development pattern is indeed based on a rejection of the capitalist model, but its socialism—as the charter and other declarations repeat—is very specific in its linkage to Islam[82] and its maintenance of "nonexploitive" private property. Nevertheless, the general ideological affinities of anti-imperialism and anticapitalism drew the two countries together, especially in the fields of economic cooperation, economic organization, and military collaboration and arms purchases. Three years after Algeria's independence, there were 3,500 Soviet technicians in Algeria, and by 1972 Soviet economic aid had reached $421 million.[83] Soviet arms transfers between 1966 and 1974, worth $248 million, constituted 90% of Algeria's arms purchases.[84]

From 1974 to 1981, however, Algeria varied its military relations. The twenty arms purchase agreements[85] made during this period are equally divided between the USSR and Western countries (with the United States signing five agreements). This diversity of arms sources at the quantitative level notwithstanding, agreements with Moscow were more expensive, more varied, and included real combat weaponry—MiG-23s and even MiG-25s, T-72 tanks, and ship-to-ship and ground-to-air missiles. In its weaponry and training, then, the Algerian army is Soviet-oriented.

There is, however, no Algerian infatuation with Moscow. On the contrary, political differences loom large. First, at the global level, Soviet priorities are East-West détente and the prevention of a "nuclear accident." As we have seen, Algeria's priorities are system change and the conflict between the South and the North (which includes the USSR), as Boumedienne's opening speech to the fourth nonaligned summit illustrated.[86] Secondly, Algeria and the USSR have different perceptions of Israel's place in the Middle East. These differences collided head on following the 1967 Six-Day War. The minutes of Boumedienne's Moscow meeting with Soviet leaders to discuss the Arab-Israeli conflict reveal mutual accusations, the exchange of hard words, and finally a "dialogue de sourds."[87]

During the 1980s, Algeria aimed to maintain balance in relations with the superpowers. Bendjedid's 1985 visit to the United States was part of attaining this aim. Then in 1986 he paid a visit to Moscow. In 1987 the two countries signed a draft cooperation agreement on the occasion of the visit of the Soviet chairman of the State Committee for Foreign Economic Relations in September.

Relations with *France* were not dealt with here because of space reasons and also because of the abundance of literature available on this subject.[88] But the noticeable improvement of relations between the two countries in the 1980s needs to be emphasized. Such an improvement was impossible for a long time because of the bitter historical legacy on both sides and the presence of problems that plagued their bilateral relations (for example, freezing of assets of ex-colonial settlers, immigration, illegal immigration and necessity of repatriation, mixed marriages, the status of children of separated parents, and so on). In the 1980s many of these problems were tackled. In 1982, Presidents Mitterrand and Bendjedid exchanged official visits (Bendjedid's was the first ever by an Algerian president to France). The changes of government in France following the two elections during the late 1980s (from "left" to "right" wing in 1986 then back to "left" in 1988) did not adversely affect the improvement of relations with Algeria, and Prime Minister Jacques Chirac visited the country in 1986 to discuss cooperation.

This high-level bilateral contact brought results. In 1987 Algeria unfroze assets of former French settlers, allowed them to sell their land to the Algerian state, and permitted French workers in Algeria to transfer their income to France. France reacted by providing financial assistance to Algeria for three years. Improvement continued to the extent that France increasingly suppressed Algerian opposition movements' publications in France (especially by the Algerian Democratic Movement), keeping a close eye on opposition groups, harassing and arresting their members for "illegal possession of arms," and even expelling many of them. Algeria was mediating between Iran and France for the mutual lifting of the blockade on each other's embassies in Paris and Teheran and even negotiating with Islamic groups in Lebanon for the release of French hostages.

The change in government following the 1988 French elections did not reverse this improvement trend, though some tension appeared in late 1988 following the October riots and police brutality in Algeria. In fact, the French press—including the very balanced *Le Monde*—was full of harsh criticism, and many important French personalities participated in massive street demonstrations to protest against the Algerian government's repressive actions. But in January 1989, the long-standing dispute about gas prices was settled by an agreement backdated to January 1987. Two months later (March 1989), Mitterrand visited Algeria and declared his public support for Bendjedid's reforms since "the country was entering a new era."[89]

Third Worldism

Algerian policy behavior has involved three Third World arenas:[90] (1) the Afro-Asian group, in which Algeria's activities were short-lived because of the problems inherent in the movement itself and because of Boumedienne's coup d'état on the eve of the convening of the second Afro-Asian summit in Algiers; (2) the economic development group centered around the Group of 77: Algeria hosted the Group of 77's first meeting in October 1967 and worked toward the publication of its charter; and (3) the nonaligned group. Algeria was a founding member of this group even before its independence, and it worked to promote a militant anticolonial and economically oriented interpretation of nonalignment instead of the interpretation associated with Nehru and Tito, which emphasized mediation in the East-West conflict. Three examples can be cited to demonstrate Algeria's behavioral involvement at this Third World level: the 1973 nonaligned conference in Algiers, the 1974 call for the New International Economic Order, and work within OPEC to heighten Third World unity and to restructure relations between developing and developed countries.

The choice of Algiers as a site for the fourth nonaligned summit was a recognition of Algeria's international status and a consolidation of its views of the concept of nonalignment. Algeria made the conference a success both for the movement and for itself.[91] In the summer of 1973, Algeria established an organizational committee to guarantee the largest participation. In July a few ambassadors were sent around the world to encourage attendance at the highest level. A month later, Algeria's ministers were sent on similar missions throughout the nonaligned group. As a result, seventy-five countries attended (compared to fifty-four at the third summit at Lusaka three years earlier) and as many as sixty delegations were led by their heads of state.[92]

With characteristic vigor, Algeria also summoned the 1974 UN special session that issued the Declaration on the Establishment of a New International Economic Order. As chairman of the nonaligned group and as an active link with the deliberations of the 1973 Algiers summit, Boumedienne delivered the opening speech on April 10, 1974.[93] A comparison between Boumedienne's speech and the UN declaration indicates Algeria's success: text of the UN document reflected Algeria's views as expressed in the opening speech (see Table 4.1).

Algeria profited from the global context of the mid-1970s and the rise of OPEC power in implementing its integrated and coherent approach to development, the "priority of priorities," as Boumedienne put it in his UN speech. This resulted in a confrontation with the United States, which following the panic of the 1973 oil embargo wanted to limit discussions to the problems between consumers and producers of oil.[94] Algeria objected to the 1975 Washington conference on the grounds that it attempted to form a bloc of developed countries against oil producers. Instead, Algeria insisted on dealing with oil as yet another raw material and discussing it within the general context of North-South economic relations. Algeria deployed its efforts to overcome hesitation among pro-Western oil producers, convening an OPEC summit in Algiers in March 1975. Boumedienne's opening speech set the criteria of an OPEC united front. Moreover, the OPEC summit referred explicitly on three occasions to the sixth special UN session and its resolutions as the relevant framework for coming to grips with the problems of the international economy. Nobody needed reminding that Algeria was the leading actor in both initiatives.

After abortive attempts to hold a conference on energy problems alone (thereby dividing the Third World between oil producers and oil consumers), Kissinger had to give in. He declared in Paris in May 1975 that "the dialogue between the producers and consumers will not progress unless it is broadened to include the general issue of the relationship between developing and developed countries."[95] As Bouteflika said jubilantly on another occasion, "the Third World is finally being heard"— that is, the Third World as represented by Algeria. The election of Bouteflika as president of the 1974 session of the UN General Assembly was further confirmation of Algeria's leading position.

The 1975 Paris conference on international cooperation (attended by nineteen developing and eight developed countries) set up committees on raw materials, energy, development, and financial issues to deal with the world economic situation. Each committee was cochaired by a developing and a developed country—a manifestation of Algeria's success in insisting on "effective participation" by the Third World at the decision-making level. Algeria participated in the committees on energy and on development, acting as cochair (with the EEC) of the latter committee.[96]

Algeria's Behavior at the Regional Level:
Africa and the Arab World

Algeria is an active and full member of both Africa and the Arab world,[97] but does one region take precedence for the policy-makers? The preindependence Tripoli declaration and the National Charter, written fourteen years later, talk of the Arab world (of which Algeria is an "integral

TABLE 4.1 Boumedienne's Speech to the April 1974 UN Special Session and the May 1974 UN Declaration on the Establishment of a New International Economic Order

Boumedienne's Speech	The UN NIEO Document
The present world system is as "unjust and outmoded as the colonial order from which it originated."	"The gap between the developed and the developing countries continues to widen in a system which was established at a time when most of the developing countries did not even exist as independent states and which perpetuates inequality."
"The prevailing system on international power relations" is condemned for reducing to "a passive role . . . the immense majority of peoples."	Measures should be taken to insure "more effective participation by developing countries . . . in the decision-making process" in the competent international organs "through the establishment of a more equitable pattern of voting rights.
The measures needed to promote a world development strategy are:	
"Mastery by the developing country over natural resources and control of their price mechanism."	"All efforts should be made . . . to defeat attempts to prevent the free and effective exercise of the rights of every State to full and permanent sovereignty over its natural resources.
"An integrated and coherent development is based on the exploitation of the agricultural and industrial potential of the developing country and the transformation of mineral or agricultural resources on the spot."	"All efforts should be made by the international community to . . . encourage the industrialization of the developing countries, and to this end . . . contribute to setting up new industrial capacities including raw materials and commodity-transforming facilities as a matter of priority in developing countries that produce those raw materials and commodities."
"Mobilization of international sources of financial, technological, and commercial aid from rich and developed countries to developing countries."	"Extension of active assistance . . . free of any political or military conditions; increase in the official component of the net amount of financial resource transfers. All efforts should be made" to carry out seven specific measures that assure "transfer of technology."
"Elaboration and implementation of a special program to guarantee more aid for peoples considered by the UN community as most seriously affected by unfavorable economic conditions."	"The General Assembly adopts the following Specific Program, including particularly emergency measures to mitigate the difficulties of the developing countries most seriously affected by economic crisis, bearing in mind the particular problem of the least developed and land-locked countries."

Sources: The text of Boumedienne's speech (in French) can be found in Paul Balta and Claudine Rulleau, *La Stratégie de Boumediene* (Paris: Sindbad, 1978), pp. 316–329. This translation is by Bahgat Korany. The text of the UN NIEO document is taken from Edwin Reubens (ed.), *The Challenge of the New International Economic Order* (Boulder, Colorado: Westview Press, 1981), pp. 19–37.

part"), the Maghreb, and Africa, in that order of importance. The amount of space the charter devotes to each region confirms this ranking: they merit ten, eight, and five paragraphs respectively.

These admittedly convenient indicators should be interpreted with caution for three reasons. First, Algerian policy-makers refuse to accept a clearcut separation between the three regions; they point out that the Maghreb is both Arab and African, and that 70% of all Arabs live in Africa, where they constitute 25% of the continent's total population. Second, although Algeria is tied to the Arab world by common culture and language, pan-Arab ideology has traditionally evolved in the Mashreq through Nasserism and Ba'thism, and thus Algeria's chances to lead or even to make its influence effectively felt on the main front more than a thousand miles away are slim. Other indicators of behavior show, finally, that Algeria has been heavily involved in Sub-Saharan Africa.

As both Etienne[98] and Algerian scholar Chikh[99] affirm, Africa constitutes the base of Algeria's Third World policy[100] and its prime field of action. Algeria was one of the very few African countries to carry out the 1965–OAU ministerial resolution to break off diplomatic relations with London following Rhodesia's unilateral declaration of independence. Algeria has hosted several OAU summits and ministerial meetings, as well as pan-African nongovernmental conferences such as the First Pan-African Cultural Festival, held in 1969. It has been an active member of the OAU Liberation Committee since its establishment, and has been the headquarters of a dozen liberation movements. Indeed, the Algerian government established a special section—the Department of International Studies—to coordinate aid to these movements. This section, in principle part of the FLN, is in fact directly linked to the presidency. Relations between Algiers and many of the African governments were thus established well ahead of their independence.

After independence, bilateral agreements were concluded to consolidate cooperation. Thus the total of Algeria's bilateral agreements with Sub-Saharan African countries for the sample years 1970, 1973, 1975, 1977, and 1978 amounts to thirty-seven agreements (twenty-five in the economic area, eleven in the cultural-technical area, and one—with Mali—in the diplomatic sphere).[101] Moreover, even though Algeria's trade with Sub-Saharan Africa is less than 1% of its total trade (with the trade balance usually against Algeria), Algeria still signs agreements to maintain direct contact. Between 1972 and 1976, fifteen agreements for air and maritime communication were concluded with ten African countries.[102] In contrast to communication lines with Europe or with the Arab world, the ones with Sub-Saharan Africa were run at a financial loss.

With the aim of reconciling its Arab character and its African involvement, Algeria attempted the institutionalization of the Arab-African dialogue.[103] To initiate an institutional structure, the sixth session of the Arab summit (Algiers, November 26–28, 1973) invited non-Arab Africa to send representatives, and President Mobutu of Zaire attended. The

Arab summit decided on the convening of an Afro-Arab summit (which took place in the Arab League headquarters in March 1977)[104] and on the creation of a number of basic institutions: the Arab Bank for Economic Development in Africa, with capital amounting to $738 million in 1977; the Arab Special Fund for Africa, with an initial fund of $210 million; and the Arab Fund for Technical Assistance to Arab and African Countries, with a modest initial capital of $15 million, later increased to $25 million.[105]

The most spectacular movement, however, at this level is the impressive improvement of Maghrebi relations that culminated in early 1989 with the declaration of UMA (Union du Maghreb Arabe) among Algeria, Morocco, Tunisia, Libya, and Mauritania. This union was preceded by sustained Algerian efforts to improve relations with its neighbors, notably Morocco. In this respect the 1980s of Bendjedid differ from the 1970s of Boumedienne. Contrary to Boumedienne's ideological purity and his fight for what he perceived as Polisario's[106] just cause, Bendjedid was increasingly flexible toward Morocco.

Thus a few months after the 1983 summit between Bendjedid and Moroccan King Hassan II, which diffused a lot of mistrust, restrictions were lifted on movement across the frontier of Moroccans resident in Algeria and Algerians resident in Morocco. In May 1987, Saudi King Fahd's mediation to accelerate rapprochement between the two countries led to another tête-à-tête between Hassan II and Bendjedid on the Algerian-Moroccan border. Less than a month later, the Algerian government released 150 Moroccan soldiers in exchange for 102 Algerian prisoners.

With this improvement in Algerian-Moroccan relations, the movement for the Maghrebi Union was gaining greater momentum. While resisting Libyan leader Muammer Al-Qaddafi's insistence for complete merger, Bendjedid preferred signing with Tunisia the Maghreb Fraternity and Co-operation Treaty (March 1983), which provided the framework for the creation of the Great Arab Maghreb. And Moroccan-Algerian relations continued their improvement:

In Nov. 1987 Chadli received the Moroccan Minister of Foreign Affairs, and they discussed means of accelerating the edification of the Great Arab Maghreb and of resolving the Western Sahara conflict. Maghreb unity also formed the agenda of a meeting in December between the Foreign Ministers of Algeria, Mauritania and Tunisia, when hopes were again expressed that Libya might sign the Maghreb Fraternity and Co-operation Treaty. The restoration of diplomatic relations between Tunisia and Libya in the same month was viewed as a success for Algerian diplomacy. . . . At a tripartite meeting in Tunis in February, [Chadli, Tunisia's Ben Ali, and Qaddaffi] . . . all expressed their determination to encourage cooperation between Maghreb countries and to work towards the creation of the Great Arab Maghreb.[107]

In May 1988, M. Messaadia, the FLN's secretary-general went to Morocco to invite Hassan II to the upcoming Arab summit in Algiers in June. On May 16 diplomatic relations between the two countries were resumed and borders reopened.

After the 1988 June Arab summit in Algiers, the five Maghrebi leaders announced, in a joint communiqué, the creation of a Maghreb commission of their representatives to focus on the establishment of a "semi-legislative, semi-consultative Council to align legislation in the region and prepare joint economic projects." The major steps in the successful conclusion of this Union were as follows:

1. "In July Algeria signed a co-operation agreement with Morocco, and the two countries announced plans to synchronize their railway, postal and telecommunications systems . . . ;
2. . . . At the end of August, Morocco and the Polisario Front accepted a U.N. peace plan to settle the Western Sahara Conflict, thus signalling the removal of the last major obstacle to Maghreb Unity. . . ."
3. On 17 Feb. 1989 the treaty creating the Arab Maghreb Union was signed in Marrakesh, Morocco, "between the five countries."[108]

However, this progress should not be conceived as linear. A big obstacle to the permanent settlement of the conflict between Morocco and Polisario might bring Algeria back on the side of the latter. And with the return of some *chefs historiques* within the FLN, the government will be pressed not to simply drop the Polisario and concentrate on collaboration with the multinationals and the "forces of reaction and imperialism."

The debate on Algeria's foreign policy is not yet over. For in joining the UMA, did not Algeria join a union of states rather than wait (eternally?) for the desirable union of peoples? Though without changing foreign policy orientation (i.e., role-conception or what the charter calls foreign policy principles), the order of priorities seems to be changing at the behavioral or role-performance level. The change is incremental rather than sudden and gives more weight to concrete economic calculations. Two quantitative indicators of international cooperation confirm this gradual change of priorities.

The first indicator is the number of agreements that Algeria signed with foreign governments in four issue-areas (diplomatic, military, economic, and cultural) during the twelve-year period from 1975 to 1986 (the last year for which complete data could be collected). The most important pattern of change these statistics reveal is the rise in the 1980s in the number of agreements with other Maghrebi countries (see Table 4.2). In the first half of this period—the six years between 1975 and 1980—there were eighteen agreements. This number rose in the second half of the period (1981–1986) to forty-six, an increase of more

TABLE 4.2 Algeria's Intergovernmental Agreements in Four Issue Areas: 1975–1986

REGION	1975	1976	1977	1978	1979	1980	1981	1982	1983	1984	1985	1986	Total
Maghreb	3	1	3	5	1	5	8	4	5	7	7	15	64
Mashreq	2	3	2	4	7	4	3	1	6	3	6	3	44
Sub-Saharan Africa	13	15	1	7	4	8	8	10	11	5	–	6	88
Other Third World	5	–	5	4	4	5	5	4	6	5	6	2	51
Socialist countries	13	13	15	10	20	12	10	5	8	8	4	9	127
Western countries	75	38	55	45	44	15	20	27	25	15	15	29	403
Total	111	70	81	75	80	49	54	51	61	43	38	64	777

Source: Data collected by the author from Annuaire de l'Afrique du Nord, Middle East Journal, Maghreb-Mashreq, and Le Monde for the period 1975 through 1986.

than 250%. The second indicator is that of both the frequency and rank of visits for the fourteen-year-period 1975–1988 based on the following scale: Head of state or equivalent–4 points; vice-president, prime minister, or equivalent–3 points; foreign, defense, finance minister, or equivalent–2 points; any other minister or top official–1 point.

If we compare the first four years (1975–1978) of this period with the last four (1985–1988), the most important behavioral change is the continuous rise in visits within the Maghreb, decline of visits with socialist countries, and increase of visits with Western (capitalist) countries (see Table 4.3). The change in foreign policy behavior is most noticeable concerning the latter two factors. During the first four years (until Boumedienne's death in 1978), the total visits to socialist countries was 164 points compared to 64 points for Western countries: a yearly average of 41 and 16 points respectively. This is a ratio of just less than 3:1 in favor of socialist countries.

The four-year period of 1985–1988 tells a different story: 71 points for socialist countries, 122 points for Western countries, i.e., a yearly average of 17.8 for the former and 30.5 for the latter. This is a ratio. of almost 1 : 2 in favor of Western countries. The behavioral pattern at this level was simply reversed.

CONCLUSION: MAKING THE BEST OF GLOBAL ODDS

Despite its success, an analyst can still pinpoint some incoherent aspects in Algeria's foreign policy projects. Although it insists on international system change, Algeria's business dealings are most advanced with the United States—the stronghold of the status quo. Moreover, while adopting an economically oriented concept of international relations, emphasizing the transnational dimension, and preaching the necessity of a new system, Algeria's policy and declarations still adhere to the nineteenth-century concept of an international system based on the outdated notion of state sovereignty.

The Algerian policy-maker might consider these criticisms rather academic. They do not allow for Algeria's particular dilemmas nor for the necessary limits of a Third World country's foreign policy. A Third World country comes to independent statehood burdened with a historical legacy of societal disorganization and economic underdevelopment. It faces a hegemonic system that has developed across centuries and cannot be changed overnight. Even when a country challenges the system, it has to be ready to pay the price. It must therefore sort out secondary policy objectives, which can be sacrificed if necessary, from those that must be defended at all costs.

The 1980s brought home especially the effect of the widening resource/ demand gap: decline of oil revenues coupled with rising domestic demands. Thus between 1984 and 1988 population rose from 22 million to more than 24.5 million. The great majority of this population is young

TABLE 4.3 Algeria's Intergovernmental Visits (Sent and Received): 1975–1988

REGION	1975	1976	1977	1978	1979	1980	1981	1982	1983	1984	1985	1986	1987	1988	TOTAL
Maghreb	35	32	32	21	41	20	46	14	38	27	24	29	33	40	432
Mashreq	22	21	32	24	41	59	13	22	18	32	22	13	32	15	366
Sub-Saharan Africa	50	111	49	81	75	42	66	63	48	30	59	26	34	16	750
Other Third World	6	16	8	15	12	19	6	15	7	9	20	18	9	5	165
Socialist countries	28	41	30	65	40	34	26	28	11	33	29	24	15	3	407
Western countries	25	10	9	20	14	21	32	40	53	32	30	36	45	11	378
Total	166	231	160	226	223	195	189	182	175	163	184	146	168	90	2,498

Source: Data collected by the author from Annuaire de l'Afrique du Nord, Middle East Journal, Maghreb-Mashreq, and Le Monde for the period 1975 through 1988.

and hence not yet productive. On the contrary, it is dependent on the state for education, health care, accommodation, and—later—employment. At the same time, gross domestic product continued declining from $69.9 billion in 1986 to only $54.1 billion in 1988, i.e., a decrease of over 22% in just a two-year period. The result has been a growth rate of −2.0% in 1988 and the continuation of severe austerity measures. Moreover, international debt continued rising: from $15.8 billion in 1984 to $21.5 billion in 1988, i.e., an increase of more than 30%. Consequently, political confrontation—at the military and verbal levels (e.g., over Western Sahara)—had to be muted and international accommodation was to be preferred to save existing resources for use at home.

Yet because of Algeria's historical legacy, state-formation, and elite-socialization, inherited ideological stands and radical foreign policy orientation were not to be given up. To reduce this role-conflict (i.e., incompatibility between this role-conception and accommodative role-performance or behavior), Algeria practiced international mediation. A good example is its successful mediation to free the U.S. hostages in Iran in January 1981. This mediation[109] provides a microcosm of Algeria's foreign policy orientation and behavior, and gives a glimpse of the actual daily conduct of its diplomatic personnel.

U.S. relations with the former shah, the absence of diplomatic relations between the United States and Iran, the revolutionary orientation of the new Iranian elite and the problems it faced in establishing control: all of these factors seriously complicated the hostage issue. The outbreak of the Iran-Iraq war in September 1980 only added to the problems.

In the United States, the hostage issue became the dominant daily question, and the U.S. government was hard pressed to find a way out. As no direct official channels existed with the new Iranian regime, Washington had no choice but to work through third parties. When attempts to work through Germany (September 9–16, 1980) failed, Washington seized the opportunity of the Iranian prime minister's October 1980 visit to the UN in New York (to defend Iran's case against Iraq) to ask for the good offices of both the UN secretary-general and the Algerian delegation in New York. On November 2, 1980, Iran's Majlis stated conditions for the diplomats' release and solicited Algeria's help in reaching an agreement. Algeria was thus the only third party accepted by the two opponents.[110]

The United States preferred Algeria for three reasons: (1) despite "philosophical divergences," relations were good between the two countries and communication was smooth; (2) Algeria had kept a posture of neutrality during the hostage crisis. Without condemning anyone publicly, it showed in a semiofficial way that it did not condone what had happened; and (3) Algeria's humanitarian and diplomatic behavior since the beginning of the crisis in November 1979 was appreciated by the United States. At the human level, A. Gheraieb, Algeria's ambassador to Teheran, was the first diplomat to meet the American hostages;

Cardinal Duval, archbishop of Algiers, was one of three religious figures to meet the hostages in March 1980. At the diplomatic level, Mohamed Bedjaoui, Algeria's UN representative, was a member of the UN mission sent to Teheran to mediate the crisis.

The Islamic Republic of Iran also had three reasons to favor Algeria's mediation: (1) both Algeria and the new Iran had similar international sensibilities and believed in an active Third World role; (2) the two countries were linked by a common Islamic ethos; and (3) despite the different sources of their revolutionary orientation, both countries opposed the "ancien régime" nationally and internationally, and sought authentic development based on independent identity. These affinities motivated Iran's new regime to ask Algeria to represent Iranian interests in Washington when diplomatic relations were broken off with the United States. Contacts between Algeria and Iran had been intense since the arrival of the new regime. In February 1979, Bendjedid sent a personal message to Ayatollah Khomeini; in March, Algeria sent an official delegation to Iran; and in July Algeria's first ambassador to the Islamic Republic of Iran presented his credentials. In November 1979, Iran sent an official delegation to participate in the celebrations of the twenty-fifth anniversary of the Algerian Revolution.

If Algeria's policy *orientation* ensured its acceptance as mediator by both opponents, Algeria's foreign policy *behavior* in conducting the negotiations guaranteed the successful denouement of the hostage crisis. Three personalities in Algeria's negotiating team were directly responsible for the conduct of this complicated process of international bargaining: A. Gheraieb, Algeria's ambassador to Teheran; Reda Malek, ambassador to the United States; and Mostefaï, director of Algeria's Central Bank. In addition, the Ministry of Foreign Affairs acted as an efficient clearinghouse throughout the negotiations, collecting and transmitting information for both sides. Because continuous residence in Algiers of high-level representatives of the two countries was not possible for an extended period, and because a continual shuttle was not feasible either, most of the basic work fell on the shoulders of the Algerians. The team of experts constituted by the Algerian government traveled to Teheran and Washington whenever necessary. Between November 1980 and January 1981, the Algerian team received the head of the U.S. delegation, Christopher Warren, three times, but made a total of five trips themselves, to Washington and Teheran.

The two phases (from moderator to mediator) of Algeria's behavior in the negotiations are also significant. Starting as merely a moderator, Algeria did not produce a full-fledged plan to be implemented by both sides. Instead, Algeria aimed at this stage to overcome obstacles and keep the negotiations from breaking down. At times, it used its influence to eliminate stumbling blocks and to help each of the parties reformulate propositions in terms more acceptable to the other side.

Algeria began by making an inventory of points of agreement and disagreement and sorting out "easy" and "difficult" points to be negotiated. A study was made of Iran's four conditions for the release of the hostages as expressed in Khomeini's September 1980 speech: U.S. nonintervention in Iran's internal affairs; unfreezing of Iranian assets in the United States; withdrawal of claims before U.S. courts; and return of royal assets. The first two demands were accepted by the United States. Hence real negotiations were to center on the last two, and to prevent breakdown in negotiating these difficult issues, Algeria helped each party to see the constraints of the other and to reformulate its demands in such a way as to avoid a categorical refusal.

For instance, the U.S. government did not know how much the royal assets amounted to or where they were located. Even if it had known, it could not simply return them without due process of U.S. law. Algerian negotiators helped the Iranians to see these constraints and thus reformulate their demand differently. Iran than asked for an inventory of the assets and their sequestration until they could be returned according to correct legal procedure.

When stalemate risked driving the two sides even further apart, Algeria saved the negotiations by carrying out the second, mediatory phase of its third-party role. On December 20, 1980, Teheran declared that the assets to be returned by the United States amounted to $24 billion. This figure had a disastrous effect on Washington, and some people started talking about blackmail.[111] In agreement with the United States the Algerians thus left the exact figure aside and worked instead on a procedure to assess the sum. It was in this context that the Algerians offered for the first time to issue an "Algerian declaration" instead of a bilateral agreement between Washington and Algiers. The Iranians were very receptive to this idea and a few days later their claims had been reduced to a total of $9 billion.

When the Air Algerie plane had finally transferred the hostages from Teheran, some people remarked that this was the greatest deal ever negotiated without direct contact between the parties. According to the head of the U.S. negotiating team, Christopher Warren, its success could not have been achieved without "the Algerian government, its Foreign Ministry, its negotiating team, and its diplomats." It was Warren who likened the Iranian and U.S. negotiators to two tennis players playing a match in two different courts.[112] The Algerians brought the players to the same court and umpired the match through to the end.

Algeria continued the same pattern in the late 1980s and succeeded in freeing on April 20, 1988, a Kuwaiti airline hijacked on April 5. Though two Kuwaiti passengers were killed by the hijackers during this fifteen-day crisis, it is argued that without Algeria's good offices more of the ninety-seven passengers and fifteen crew of the Kuwait Airways Boeing 747 could have perished.

The group of eight hijackers, reportedly linked with pro-Shi'i Moslem groups in Lebanon, took possession of the plane over the Arabian Sea and ordered it to fly to Iran. After refuelling it went to Cyprus, then to Algiers where the remaining hostages were finally freed. The hijackers' main demand was the release of seventeen Shi'i Moslems convicted and imprisoned in Kuwait. During the two-week crisis, they repeatedly threatened to blow up the plane if their demands were not met. They were refused landing in many countries' airports. For example, at the Syrian-controlled Beirut airport:

> Syrian troops . . . fired warning shots in the direction of the circling airliner, turned off the airport lights and blocked the runway with tanks to prevent a possible landing. For almost four hours Beirut airport control tower remained firm in its refusal to give the airliner permission to land, despite desperate pleading by the airliner's pilot.[113]

Larnaca airport, Cyprus, reopened and permitted the airliner to land to prevent its crashing into the sea. It was the amir of Kuwait, Sheikh Jaber Ahmed Al-Sabah, who asked the Algerian president to receive the hijacked airliner. Once in Algeria, Hedi Khediri, Minister of the Interior, reasoned with the hijackers on April 13, but no agreement could be concluded. On April 19, it was the turn of Dr. Ahmed Taleb Ibrahimi—Algeria's foreign minister who had just returned to the country—to negotiate with the hijackers. This second round of negotiations was successful. The hijackers dropped their demands, released the plane, and were taken to a secret location before being safely flown to a country of their choice (they ended in West Beirut).

This Algerian action of international mediation did not bring the country the unanimous praise it had received during the hostage crisis. Kuwait, as well as the other Arab countries, commended Algeria's role, which avoided massacre of the passengers following Kuwait's refusal to make any concessions. "However, the U.K., the U.S.A. and various civil aviation bodies all issued statements that were highly critical of the Algerian government's apparent decision to guarantee the hijackers safe passage to a friendly country."[114] The French president, however, went public to record his praise for Algeria's behavior during the crisis.

Thus despite the deteriorating economic situation and a certain restructuring of foreign policy behavior, Algeria continued to occupy center stage at the international level. The Arab summit was held in Algiers in June 1988. Following the 1989 Arab summit in Casablanca, Bendjedid was elected, together with Kings Fahd and Hassan II, to form a committee of sages to supervise the carrying out of the summit's resolutions, especially concerning Lebanon. In 1989, an Egyptian foreign minister visited Algiers for the first time in eleven years. Algeria continued to sign agreements with both Iran and Iraq; it acquired a nuclear reactor with Argentina's help and was elected a nonpermanent member in the UN Security Council in 1987.

But precisely because of Algeria's foreign policy domestication (in the first above-mentioned sense of internalization), mediation can be sometimes hard to practice. The Gulf crisis brought to the fore this difficulty for a polity in the process of pluralization, if not yet quite democratization. Due to Algeria's colonial history and especially its bloody war of independence, the Gulf crisis became the occasion for the surfacing of an anti-colonial or anti-Western ethos, especially by the growing Islamic groups.

With the imminence of the June 1991 legislative elections, all political parties tried during the Gulf crisis to increase their political influence by organizing campaigns and demonstrations against the presence of "foreign" troops on Arab soil. The FIS benefited most by mustering huge crowds, some 30,000 strong. The governing FLN could not afford to be left out in the cold, but when it organized an alternative dem- onstration, only 8,000 participants turned up. When the FIS intensified its campaign against government policy and asked Bendjedid to step down in order to establish an Islamic state, the FLN reacted by forming— with thirteen opposition parties—an anti–Gulf war front. In addition the FLN called on all Arab states to ignore the UN boycott of Iraq. Moreover, the government press adopted an increasingly anti-Western tone (especially expressing disappointment with the position of France), emphasizing the growing number of civilian casualties resulting from the allies' massive bombings of Iraq's "non-military" targets. State-owned television also ran pictures of injured babies and children. The government managed—with difficulty—to stop the setting up of training camps for volunteers to help "brotherly Iraq" but could not stop the establishment of FIS "physical fitness camps."

Through "radical" Islam—in addition to some old radical elements— civil society was asserting itself in force, increasingly pushing the government to either support Iraq or face "unrepresentativeness" of popular sentiment, that is, delegitimization. The emphasis, then, was not on detachment and mediation but rather on giving support to Arab- Islamic brothers against the new American-dominated attempt to impose a new colonialism. In this specific Gulf case, the process of pluralism and democratization was pushing the Algerian government to return to its radical roots, albeit in Islamic garb.

Depending on the results of the imminent legislative elections, once the Gulf crisis is over, it is not sure that Algeria's foreign policy will return to what it was in the 1960s and 1970s. But Algeria's foreign policy domestication (still in the sense of internalization) raises an important conceptual question: How does the process of political de- mocratization and economic privatization—so rampant in many Arab and other Third World countries—affect the pattern of their foreign policies? How different would the effects of these internal political- economic processes be from those in, for instance, East and Central Europe?

NOTES

1. Frantz Fanon, *Les damnés de la terre* (Paris: Maspero, 1964). Fanon was appointed Algeria's first ambassador to Ghana.

2. The review covered eleven articles published in well-known periodicals such as *Foreign Policy* (1972, pp. 108–131), *International Affairs* (1967, pp. 678–698), *Polity* (1973, pp. 477–488), *Revue Française de Science Politique* (1972, pp. 1276–1307), and *Chronique de Politique Etrangère* (1972, pp. 199–212). The article in the last-mentioned journal is by A. Bouteflika—a close companion of President Boumedienne since preindependence days who headed the Ministry of Foreign Affairs from 1963 until Boumedienne's death in 1978.

3. Slimane Chikh, "La politique africaine de l'Algérie," in Chikh et al. (ed.), *Le Maghreb et l'Afrique subsaharienne* (Paris: Fondation National de Recherche Scientifique, 1980), pp. 1–54.

4. "In the late 1970s, the Roman Catholic population had been reduced to about 45,000. In addition there were a few thousand Protestants, including members of Protestant missions. . . . The Jewish community had numbered well in excess of 100,000 before the Algerian revolutionary period, but at independence in 1962 their number had been reduced to 4,000 and to about 1,000 by 1967. Because the Cremieux Decrees of 1870 had granted them French citizenship, most of the Jews went to France." *Algeria: A Country Study* (Washington, D.C.: American University, Foreign Area Studies, 1979), p. 116.

5. *Ibid.*, p. 92.

6. *Ibid.*, p. 117.

7. World Bank, *World Development Report 1982* (New York: Oxford University Press for the World Bank, 1982), p. 111.

8. Algeria, *op. cit.*, p. 118.

9. *El-Moudjahid*, December 1, 1971, as quoted in Bernard Cubertafond, "Reflexions sur la pratique politique Algérienne" *Maghreb-Mashreq* 69 (1975), p. 31.

10. For the names, see William Quandt, *Revolution and Political Leadership: Algeria 1954–1968* (Cambridge, Mass.: MIT Press, 1969), p. 288.

11. For the names of members in the three cabinet shuffles, see *ibid.*, p. 289.

12. The number of Political Bureau members rose from five in August 1962 to sixteen in April 1964. For names and characteristics, see *ibid.*, pp. 227, 293.

13. Algeria, *op. cit.*, p. 192.

14. For names, and data on Ben Bella's three cabinets, see Quandt, *op. cit.*, pp. 232, 291–292; and Lhachmi Berrady et al., *La formation des élites politiques Maghrebines* (Paris: Librairie Générale de Droit et de Jurisprudence, 1973), pp. 109–111.

15. Jean Leca and Jean-Claude Vatin, "Le système politique Algérien 1976–1978: Idéologie, institutions et changement social," in Jean Leca et al., *Développements politiques au Maghreb* (Paris: Centre National de la Recherche Scientifique, 1979), pp. 19–31.

16. Mohamed Dahmani, *L'Algérie: Légitimité historique et continuité politique* (Paris: Le Sycomore, 1979), p. 83.

17. For the names and characteristics of council members, see *ibid.*, p. 247, and Berrady et al., *op. cit.*, p. 113.

18. For more details, see *Algeria*, p. 196.

19. François Burgat, *L'Islamisme au Maghreb: La voix du sud* (Paris: Karthala, 1988), pp. 143–170.

20. *Middle East Economic Digest*, Dec. 15, 1989.

21. *Ibid.*

22. *Ibid.*

23. *El-Moudjahid*, November 22, 1989.

24. So important is this phenomenon for understanding the present policies of Algeria that a standard book on Arab economies begins its chapter on Algeria by linking the country's economy to the historical colonial relationship. See Yusif A. Sayigh, *The Economies of the Arab World* (London: Croom Helm, 1978), pp. 514, 521.

25. *Ibid.,* p. 532; and Robert Merle, *Ahmed Ben Bella* (Paris: Gallimard, 1965), pp. 161–184.

26. *Algeria,* p. 149.

27. Paul Balta and Claudine Rulleau (with the collaboration of Mureille Duteuil), *L'Algérie des Algériens: Vingt ans après* (Paris: Les Editions Ouvrières, 1981), pp. 202–214.

28. Sayigh, *op. cit.,* p. 553.

29. *Algeria,* p. 152.

30. *Ibid.,* p. 157.

31. "Algeria" in Colin Legum (ed.), *Africa Contemporary Record 1979–1980* (London: Holmes and Meier, 1981), p. B17. (Hereafter referred to as *Africa Record.*)

32. *Africa Record,* 1980–1981, p. B13.

33. *Ibid.*

34. *Africa Record,* 1979–1980, p. B21.

35. For the text of the treaty, see *Le Lien* (Algerian Embassy, Ottawa) 5 (March 1983).

36. *Africa Record,* 1979–1980, p. B21.

37. *Le Monde,* March 1, 1983. The state of the economy/foreign policy linkage can work the other way, too, with foreign policy influencing domestic economic choices. Following the 1973 oil embargo, some developed countries talked of using the "food weapon." In order to avoid "starvation," some Third World countries worked to develop their agricultural sectors. In April 1979, at a meeting with the national secretary of the Peasants Union (UNPA), Bendjedid reiterated that the government's objective was "the realization of the highest level of self-sufficiency possible in terms of food and agricultural products and, in consequence, the consolidation of national independence." Food imports in 1978 represented a third of domestic consumption and cost $750 million. *Africa Record,* 1979–1980, pp. 19–20.

38. *Algeria,* p. 264.

39. *Ibid.,* p. 260.

40. *Ibid.,* p. 269.

41. I. William Zartman, "The Algerian Army in Politics," in I. William Zartman (ed.), *Man, State and Society in the Contemporary Maghreb* (New York: Praeger Publishers, 1973), p. 217.

42. *Algeria,* p. 272.

43. *SIPRI Yearbook,* 1980–1981 (London: Taylor and Francis for SIPRI, 1981).

44. *Algeria,* p. 272.

45. See *ibid.,* for figures, p. 284.

46. *Africa Confidential,* 30 (26 May 1989).

47. Josiano Criscuelo, *Armée et nation dans les discours du Colonel Boumedienne* (Doctoral diss., Université Paul Valéry, 1975), Figure VIII.

48. *Dix ans d'efforts* (Alger: Les Presses des Éditions Populaires de l'Armée, 1975), p. 57.

49. Mohamed Bedjaoui, "Aspects internationaux de la constitution Algérienne," *Annuaire Français du Droit International* 23 (1977), pp. 75–94.

50. As quoted in *ibid.*, pp. 75–94.

51. Charte Nationale du Peuple Algérien (hereafter referred to as Charte), edited and presented in Robert Lambotte, *Algérie, naissance d'une société nouvelle* (Paris: Éditions Sociales, 1976), p. 225.

52. Bedjaoui, *op. cit.*

53. Charte, in Lambotte, *op. cit.*, pp. 213–227.

54. *Ibid.*, p. 214.

55. *Ibid.*, p. 215.

56. *Ibid.*, pp. 216–217.

57. *Ibid.*, p. 217.

58. *Ibid.*, p. 215.

59. *Ibid.*, p. 225.

60. Paul Balta and Claudine Rulleau, *La stratégie de Boumedienne* (Paris: Sindbad, 1978), p. 226.

61. Charte, in Lambotte, *op. cit.*, p. 218.

62. The standard application of this approach in foreign policy decision-making analysis is in Graham T. Allison, *Essence of Decision: Explaining the Cuban Missile Crisis* (Boston: Little, Brown and Co., 1972).

63. Ben Bella describes his meeting with GPRA members after his release from prison in 1962 as "a bitter experience." For details, see Merle, *op. cit.*, p. 133.

64. Quandt, *op. cit.*, p. 180.

65. *Algeria*, p. 198.

66. Ferhat Abbas, *Autopsie d'une guerre* (Paris: Garnier, 1980), pp. 271–294.

67. Ali Haouchine, *L'Etat et les travailleurs*, M.S. diss., University of Montreal, 1983, p. 218.

68. John P. Entelis, "Algeria: Technocratic Rule, Military Power," in I. William Zartman et al., *Political Elites in Arab North Africa* (New York and London: Longman, 1981), p. 108.

69. *Algeria*, p. 127.

70. Jean-Louis Buchet, "Qui est réellement le nouveau président?" *Jeune Afrique* 945 (February 14, 1979), pp. 28; Balta and Rulleau, *L'Algérie*, pp. 48–51, for a synthesis of information available on Bendjedid.

71. William Zartman, "L'élite algérienne sous la présidence de Chadli Bendjedid," *Maghreb-Mashreq*, 1984. Most of the information in this part is extracted from current issues of magazines and other data sources like *Africa Confidential, Jeune Afrique, Jeune Afrique Economie, Middle East Magazine, Arabia, Middle East Economic Digest*, and *Middle East Economic Survey*.

72. *Middle East Economic Digest*, Dec. 15, 1989, p. 6.

73. For a chart on the ministry's organizational structure, see *Algeria*, pp. 234–236; Nicole Grimaud: *La politique extérieure de l'Algérie* (Paris, Karthala, 1984) pp. 435–437.

74. Entelis, *op. cit.*, pp. 101–102.

75. Albert-Paul Lentin, "Les hommes: Abdelaziz Bouteflika," *Maghreb-Mashreq* 52 (July-August 1972), pp. 7–10.

76. Jean-Pierre Béjiot, "Algérie: Passé et Présent Face à l'Avenir," *Jeune Afrique Economie*, October 1989, pp. 32–34.

77. *Jeune Afrique Economie*, 124 (October 1989).

78. Claude Roosens, "L'Algérie entre les deux grands," *Studia Diplomatica*, 34 (1981), pp. 591–608.

79. See Balta and Rulleau, *La stratégie*, pp. 255–256, for the text of his speech.

80. United Nations, *Yearbook of International Trade Statistics 1980* (New York: United Nations, 1981), p. 66.

81. Roosens, *op. cit.*, France reacted to this by reducing its diplomatic representation in Moscow to the level of chargé d'affaires from March 25 to July 26, 1962.

82. The National Charter affirms that Algeria's socialism "does not emanate from any materialist metaphysics, and is not attached to any dogmatic conception alien to our national genius." It is a socialism "in accordance with the fulfillment of our Islamic values." Charte, in Lambotte, *op. cit.*, pp. 86–87. Of the 412 submissions to Al-Moudjahid on the National Charter during the public debate in May and June of 1976, 13 insisted on the protection of Islam, and emphasized compatibility between Islam and socialism. See the excellent paper by John Nellis, *The Algerian National Charter of 1976*, Center for Contemporary Studies Occasional Paper No. 2, 1980, pp. 25–27.

83. Roosens, *op. cit.*, p. 603.

84. *The Middle East and North Africa, 1977–1978* (London: Europa Publications, 1978).

85. Data are extracted from *The Military Balance 1979–1981* (London: International Institute of Strategic Studies) and SIPRI Yearbook, 1970–1981.

86. Robert A. Mortimer, "Algeria and the Politics of International Economic Reform," *Orbis* 21 (1977), pp. 671–700.

87. Abdel-Majid Farid, *From the Minutes of Nasser's Meetings* (Beirut: Institution of Arab Research, 1979), pp. 46–78 (in Arabic).

88. In this respect, the most complete coverage in book form is still Grimaud, *op. cit.* The study ends with the Boumedienne period in 1978.

89. *The Middle East and North Africa*, 1990.

90. For greater detail, see Mortimer, op. cit.

91. For more details on the "economization of nonalignment as a movement," see Bahgat Kornay, "From the Politics to the Economics of Nonalignment," Paper presented to the Twelfth Congress of the International Political Science Association, Rio de Janeiro, Brazil, August 1982.

92. Mortimer, *op. cit.*; and Peter Willetts, *The Nonaligned Movement* (London: Frances Pinter, 1979), pp. 254–259.

93. For the text, see Balta and Rulleau, *La stratégie*, pp. 315–330.

94. Henry Kissinger, *Years of Upheaval* (Boston: Little, Brown and Co., 1982), pp. 911–920.

95. Mortimer, *op. cit.*

96. For a detailed analysis of the Paris conference by an Algerian scholar who also represented his country in North-South and OPEC meetings, see Abdelkader Sid-Ahmed, *Nord-Sud: Les enjeux* (Paris: Publisud, 1981), pp. 99–141.

97. For a treatment of relations between these two regions in the context of inter-Arab relations, see Nicole Grimaud: "Maghreb et péninsule arabe: de la réserve à la rivalité ou à la coopération," *Defense Nationale* 37 (1981), pp. 95–110; for a preliminary but rigorous attempt to compare the foreign policies of Algeria and Saudi Arabia, see Bocar E. Dia, "Etude comparative du comportement international de l'Algérie et de l'Arabie Saoudite de 1970 à 1977," M.S. thesis, University of Montreal, 1980.

98. Bruno Etienne, *L'Algérie, culture et révolution* (Paris: Seuil, 1977), p. 227.

99. Chikh, *op. cit.*, p. 4.

100. Balta and Rulleau also adopt this view in *La stratégie*, their excellent collection and classification of Boumedienne's speeches. They deal with "The Arab Homeland" in Chapter 10, and Chapter 11, entitled "From Africa to the Three Continents," includes speeches related to both Africa and the Third World in general.

101. Based on data in the excellent *Annuaire de l'Afrique du Nord*, 1970–1981 (Aix en Provence: Centre de recherche et d'étude sur les sociétés méditerranéennes) [CRESM]. For different data and years, see Chikh, *op. cit.* Both sources, however, confirm Algeria's concentration on French-speaking Africa.

102. Adapted from Chikh, *op. cit.*, p. 35.

103. For a reconstruction and analysis of the different phases of this dialogue, see Magdi Hamad, "The Role of the Arab League in the Arab-African Dialogue," in *The Arab League: Reality and Ambition* (Beirut: Center for Arab Unity Studies, 1983), pp. 509–574 (in Arabic).

104. For documents of this conference and other relevant material, see the white paper published by Egypt's Ministry of Foreign Affairs, *Afro-Arab Cooperation 1977–1978* (Cairo: State Information Service, 1980).

105. *The Arab League*, pp. 509–574.

106. "Polisario" is the name used by the People's Liberation Front for Sagui El Hamra and Rio de Oro. The group seeks to establish an independent state—the Sahrawi Arab Democratic Republic—in what was formerly Spanish Sahara.

107. *The Middle East and North Africa*, 1990, p. 307.

108. *Ibid.*, pp. 307–308.

109. Warren Christopher et al., *American Hostages in Iran: The Conduct of a Crisis* (New Haven & London: Yale University Press, 1985).

110. Algeria had its own "national interest" reasons for accepting this mediatory role. The new regime was eager to retain international credibility after Boumedienne's death, and also to promote Algeria's style of conflict resolution, as demonstrated during the 1975 mediation between Iran and Iraq. Some analyses emphasize Algeria's expectations of a "U.S. sympathetic understanding" concerning the Western Sahara conflict or the economic deals with El-Paso. See Jonathan C. Randal, "Algerians Angered by U.S. Moves Since Hostage Deal," *International Herald Tribune*, March 27, 1981, p. 4.

111. It is interesting that the Algerian team did not communicate the Iranian calculations to Washington in person, but just sent the document through their embassy, either to dissociate themselves from Teheran's figure or to spare their efforts for another round on a more workable basis.

112. As quoted in Juillard, *op. cit.*

113. *Keesings Record of World Events*, 1988: pp. 35916–35917.

114. *Ibid.*

5

The Primacy of Economics:
The Foreign Policy of Egypt

Ali E. Hillal Dessouki

In the 1970s, Egypt restructured its foreign policy orientation, and this restructuring reflected a trade-off between economic and political objectives as perceived by Egypt's primary decision-maker, President Anwar Al-Sadat. Foreign policy restructuring entails a major alteration or breakup in the orientation of an actor in *favor of* establishing a new set of commitments and alliances. It is more than a change in tactics or instruments of policy implementation; it also goes beyond the fluctuations and oscillations of foreign policy behavior of developing countries. It involves a basic reconsideration of an actor's perceptions of the global or regional system and of the country's role within that framework. Indicators of the restructuring of foreign policy orientation include patterns of diplomatic, commercial, military, and cultural relations between the country and the outside world.[1]

In the 1970s Sadat managed to change the name of Egypt (from the United Arab Republic to the Arab Republic of Egypt), its flag, and its national anthem. Economically, Egypt moved away from Nasser's Arab socialism and toward liberalization of the economy and the encouragement of private capital. Egypt's one-party political system, which had existed since 1953, was gradually replaced by a form of controlled political pluralism. At the regional level, the country changed its alliances in 1971–1973 and forged a close relation with pro-Western, moderate oil-producing states, particularly Saudi Arabia. As a result of Sadat's visit to Jerusalem in November 1977, Egypt was expelled from all Arab and Islamic councils. At the global level, Egypt moved from an essentially pro-Soviet position that included the granting of naval and air facilities to a virtual strategic alliance with the United States.

Mohamed Hosni Mubarak, Sadat's successor, initially did not make fundamental changes in this foreign policy orientation. He maintained close ties with the United States and arrangements with Israel. At the same time, he adopted low-profile measures, to redress the imbalances that resulted from this orientation during the Sadat years. In marked and deliberate contrast to Sadat, Mubarak followed a nonsensationalist and nonconfrontational style in pursuing his foreign policy objectives. These objectives centered around mending the breach with the Arab and Islamic countries, closer cooperation with the nonaligned movement, the Eastern bloc countries and the Soviet Union, as well as keeping close ties with the countries of Western Europe and Japan.

Mubarak succeeded in achieving most of his objectives. By December 1989, Egypt had restored diplomatic relations with all Arab countries except Libya. Egypt was also welcomed back into the Arab League and had become active in the nonaligned movement as well as in the Organization of African Unity (OAU). Thus it can be said that Mubarak created his own vision of Egypt's foreign policy, which in effect did not replace Sadat's but worked parallel to it, with the aim of balancing the side effects of his predecessor's policies.

This chapter examines the sources, dynamics, and contradictions of Egypt's restructuring of its foreign policy orientation. The analysis underlines issues such as the role of domestic economic factors in foreign policy change, the perception of foreign policy as a resource mobilization activity, the strain resulting from the divergence between role conceptions developed in the 1950s and 1960s and the new environment that Egypt had to deal with, and the dilemma of maintaining a balance between reliance on foreign aid and assistance and protection of the country's independence.[2]

Comparative studies of foreign policy restructuring or alliance switching show that change occurs for various reasons: security considerations, perceptions of gross external dependency and asymmetrical vulnerabilities, ideological disputes, and nationalism. In Egypt's case, there are three crucial variables to be considered.[3] The first concerns relations between the superpowers. In breaking with one superpower, the timing is essential. The alternate superpower has to be both able and willing to assume the role instead. Thus, alliance switching is more easily accomplished in a cold war situation or at least in a situation of strong competition between the superpowers.

A second variable is the personality traits of the leadership. This variable is particularly important in Third World countries characterized by low political institutionalization. We should not, however, overstate the importance of personal attributes, for leaders do not act in a vacuum, and they are not entirely free to indulge their biases and idiosyncrasies. On the contrary, structural conditions—global, regional, and domestic— determine the environment in which individual leaders must operate. Domestic conditions, including the internal balance of political groups and the degree of political stability or instability, are particularly important for their impact on foreign policy.

The third variable is the dialectical interaction of any close relationship or alliance involving unequal states in the global stratification system.

For a while, a small state may feel profound gratitude for the military and economic help coming from a superpower, but soon it may also resent the dependent relationship. The breakup of this patron-client type of relationship is to a certain extent predictable. The necessary conditions form a pattern: sufficient motivation (feeling of dependence), the existence of an alternative (the other superpower), and perception of potential benefits from a breakup.

THE DOMESTIC ENVIRONMENT

Geography

Some authors treat the geography of Egypt as an independent variable, postulating a sort of geographic determinism. In a two-volume book of more than 1,500 pages, the eminent Egyptian geographer Gamal Hamdan views the history of Egypt as an interaction between the Nile and the desert, and draws from this a number of conclusions about Egypt's national interest and policy.[4] The problem with this perspective is its static bias, its assumption of certain unchanging geographic effects of foreign policy. As was explained in Chapter 1, the effects of geography depend upon the *interaction* between geographic factors and how a particular elite or leader perceives their significance.

Egypt, a land of broad cultural and social homogeneity, is a distinct geographical and historical entity. Egypt's geographical data are simple but extremely significant. The country occupies the northeastern corner of Africa with an extension across the Gulf of Suez into the Sinai Peninsula in Asia. It is bordered by the Mediterranean Sea to the north, the Sudan to the south, the Red Sea to the east, and Libya to the west. Egypt consists of three regions: (1) the Nile Valley and Nile Delta (a little less than 4% of the total area), which extend from the Sudan northward to the Mediterranean; (2) the eastern desert and the eastern gate to Egypt—the Sinai Peninsula (28%), which extends from the Nile Valley to the Red Sea east of the Suez Canal; and (3) the western desert (68%), which stretches from the Nile Valley westwards to Libya. Briefly stated, Egypt is a line of water and verdure that runs between two deserts and widens near the Mediterranean Sea.

Two important conclusions emerge from this description. First, Egypt's geographic position made it an easy country to control and to rule. Two main features of the Egyptian society and polity are centralized rule and the absence of long-standing regional allegiances. Dependence on the Nile for irrigation called for central administration and enabled the government to extend its authority to the distant parts of the land. Because the territory is mostly desert, 96% of Egyptians live on less than 4% of the total area of their country.

Egypt's geographic position lends itself to two different perceptions and therefore, two different foreign policy objectives. Some view the relative physical isolation of the valley as the most important factor in Egypt's situation: it sets the country apart from its neighbors. In the twentieth century, this perception gave rise to tendencies toward isolationism, Swiss-type neutrality, and the advocacy of an "Egypt first" policy. Others see Egypt's geographic position primarily as a bridgehead, a linking point, a crossroads between Africa and Asia and between the eastern and western parts of the Arab world. Adherents of this school advocate an active foreign policy in the Arab world and Africa. Egypt's eastern, Arab policy is justified in terms of Arab nationalism and security; its southern, African policy rests on the need to protect the Nile waters, the lifeline of Egypt. Nasser embraced the activist view throughout most of his rule, but Sadat gradually emphasized Egyptian patriotism and the urgency of concentrating on Egypt's domestic economic problems. In the war of words that followed the Camp David Accords Sadat openly accused the Arabs of being dwarfs, uncivilized and unfit to understand the complexities of the modern world. Because of its wars with Israel, Egypt had become the poorest Arab state, Sadat frequently reminded the Egyptians.

During the 1980s, Mubarak once more revived Egypt's active role in both Africa and the Arab world. His understanding was that Egypt could not hope to fulfill its economic security, dependent on external aid, or its strategic security, without positioning itself as a regional leader. His view of Egypt's geographical position therefore emphasized the bridgehead and linking point interpretation.

Population and Social Structure

Egypt's population is characterized by social cohesiveness and since the 1950s, a baby boom. Historically, Egypt is one of the oldest continuously settled communities in the world. Egyptians long ago acquired the sense of being one people. All Egyptians speak Arabic, with the exception of the Nubians (less than 1%) and an insignificant number of isolated Berber-speaking groups in the western desert. More than 90% of the population are Moslems, and Islam is the state religion. The indigenous Copts form the largest of the other religious groups. Estimates of their numbers vary between 2.3 and 4 million. The Copts speak Arabic, and hardly any racial or ethnic differences exist between them and the Moslems. In 1983, the population of Egypt reached 45 million, and was increasing by 1 million every ten months. The population growth rate between 1966 and 1976 was about 65,000 persons each month, or 2,141 every day and one every 41 seconds.[5]

A direct consequence of the population explosion is the youthfulness of Egypt's population. Almost one-half of Egyptians are under twenty years of age; two-thirds are under thirty. Another consequence is the high dependency ratio, or the large number of dependents supported by working adults, a situation that put severe constraints on the economy in the 1970s. The government is increasingly incapable of meeting the demands for food, education, and work opportunities. A third consequence is the migration of some 3 million Egyptians in search of work to other Arab countries, particularly the oil-producing states.

In contrast to the situation in most developing countries, the population in Egypt shows a high degree of social and national integration. Nasser, Sadat, and Mubarak spoke proudly of Egypt's national unity. There are no fundamental minority cleavages to constrain foreign policy–makers and limit their options. The one major area of anxiety is the Copts' concern about the implementing of Islamic law in Egypt and the status of Copts in an Islamic state. Sadat used to contrast Egypt's deep-seated unity with the sectarian, familial, and communal fragmentation of most Arab countries. According to Sadat, this unity allowed Egypt to pursue a purposeful foreign policy and to make hard decisions (e.g., peace with Israel) impossible for most Arab countries because of their domestic fragmentation. The population of Egypt constitutes a relatively large human resource pool. It allowed the government to mobilize an army of about 1 million in 1973. Egyptians working abroad provide another positive resource: Their remittances reached $3.3 billion in 1983[6] and constituted a major source of Egypt's hard currency.

Notwithstanding these positive aspects, population growth has had an adverse impact and has limited Egypt's developmental efforts. The population explosion has aggravated unemployment problems, increased the dependency ratio, augmented rural migration to urban centers, and led to the diversion of resources from investment to consumption needs.[7] Egypt is a prime example of structural imbalance between population and material resources. Population is increasing at a rate far beyond the growth in arable cropped land, far beyond educational and industrial development. The per capita cropped area declined from 0.73 feddans per person in 1882 to 0.33 feddans per person in 1970 (a feddan equals 0.42 ha or 1.04 acres). Thus, despite the fact that the cropped area almost doubled during this period, population growth absorbed and surpassed the increase. In the 1970s Egypt had to use its limited hard currency to import foodstuffs. This made the country more dependent on the outside world and more vulnerable to the fluctuations of world food market prices. This is especially true of the wheat shortage. Egypt's wheat and flour production decreased by 3.4% between 1974 and 1980, while its requirements rose by 63%. Although some increase in wheat production took place by 1984 (1% in comparison to 1980), Egypt's imports of wheat increased by 21.7% between 1980 and 1984. This placed a severe burden on Egypt's supply of foreign currency. The extent and consequences of food dependency are likely to be major policy concerns in Egypt for years to come.[8]

Economic Capability

In the 1970s economic factors played a crucial role in the determination of Egypt's foreign policy objectives. By 1980, inflation was running at nearly 30% a year, debts reached a total of $17 billion, and the GNP per capita was $580. Sadat's decision to visit Israel was largely motivated by economic considerations: the reduction of defense expenditures (37% of the GNP in 1977), the encouragement of foreign private capital, and the need for more U.S. aid. Even before this step, Sadat's Arab policy and his forging of a Cairo-Riyadh alliance had also been predicated on expected economic gains.

Since the Second World War, Egypt has had a balance-of-payments deficit that had had to be filled from other sources. From 1948 to 1958 it was filled from existing Egyptian reserves; from 1958 to 1964 Egypt received foreign aid from Eastern and Western sources; from 1965 to 1971 the USSR shouldered most of the deficit; from 1971 to 1977 the aid was Arab money; and since 1978 it has been U.S. money. In 1981 Egypt received $2.2 billion in Western aid, of which half came from the United States. In the 1970s Egyptian debts increased by a yearly average of 28%, compared with the 13% in the 1960s.

Thus, Egyptian foreign policy has faced the important task of mobilizing external resources to ease the growing population-resources gap. Because of its important strategic-political position and role, Egypt has successfully managed to find aid to bail the country out, but this is a tragic success, as it proves the failure of Egypt's developmental plans.

The Egyptian record in the 1970s demonstrates the tensions resulting from a limited resource base, the pursuit of an activist foreign policy, and increasing economic troubles at home. Economic difficulties contributed to the evolution of a more inward-looking and less activist foreign policy. The failure of the government's development efforts to meet the needs of the country's population resulted in growing numbers of shantytowns and the potential for political instability. This led the Egyptian leadership increasingly to seek external help to resolve the country's difficult economic situation. The era of revolutionary zeal and enthusiasm (1955–1965), which had witnessed the ascendency of Egypt and a number of other Third World states in international politics, was gradually replaced by more sober behavior in the 1970s. One important factor was the limited success of development plans in these countries and the subsequent surfacing of serious internal social and economic problems. In Egypt, ideological and political considerations were overshadowed by more immediate economic concerns, and as John Waterbury wrote, "the primacy of economics has become undisputed in Egypt of 1975."[9] Thus, the balance between external and domestic concerns was greatly affected by Egypt's poor economic performance in the face of an ever-expanding population.

In 1974 Sadat inaugurated *Al-Infitah*, the open door economic policy (ODEP), to lure foreign investment into Egypt. He justified the *Infitah* on the following grounds: (1) the failure of Nasser's socialist experience; (2) the availability of Arab capital from the oil-producing countries; and (3) the international context of détente. From an economic standpoint, the two essential purposes of ODEP were, first, to attract export-oriented foreign enterprises by the establishment of duty-free zones, and second, to attract foreign capital through a liberal investment policy. However, the ultimate goal of the policy was to set the stage for the development of the Egyptian economy through joint ventures and projects bringing together Egyptian labor, Arab capital, and Western technology and management expertise.[10]

A full analysis of ODEP is beyond the scope of this chapter. What is of interest to us here is how ODEP was motivated by foreign policy considerations and what its impact on them was. Divorcing the analysis of policy-making processes in developing countries from their foreign environment can only lead to erroneous and misleading conclusions. Given their low degree of political institutionalization, their high level of political and social instability, the general structure of their international economic relations, and most importantly, their dependence upon the outside world for almost everything from food to armaments, developing countries are highly susceptible to external influences.

Little has been written on the role of external factors in the formulation of ODEP; yet these factors greatly influenced Egyptian officials, and they may become ingrained in the logic of any "open door" policy. When a ruling elite decides to pursue a development strategy based on foreign aid and capital, it follows that all necessary steps will be taken to attract and reassure its creditors. And the more dependent it is on others, the more vulnerable a country becomes to their pressure. This is especially true in developing countries whose leadership fails to produce coherent development strategies. In the case of Egypt, the initial vagueness of ODEP's goals, and the lack of consensus on its content among the ruling elite, allowed external factors to play a more crucial role.

The World Bank, the International Monetary Fund (IMF), private financial institutions, and the oil-producing Arab states have all played a role in influencing Egypt's economic policy.[11] The crux of the matter is that for two years (1975 and 1976) international financial institutions and Arab and Western creditors pressured Egypt to make its economy more acceptable and accessible to the world capitalist market by curbing subsidies and devaluing the Egyptian pound. For two years Egyptian officials resisted, mainly because the subsidies and the currency supports were what allowed the lower middle and lower classes to maintain an already low standard of living. By the fall of 1976, oil-producing Arab states joined the United States and the IMF in pressing Egypt for additional fundamental changes. They refused to give Egypt more than a limited amount of money until the government agreed to the "reforms" proposed by the IMF. Egypt's requests for loans from the IMF and United States banks were delayed in the face of a $1.25 billion deficit for the second half of 1976. Western countries provided short-term loans to finance their exports to Egypt, but the big money needed to meet debt obligations and the balance-of-payment deficit was not forthcoming.

In January 1977 the government announced price increases for a number of basic commodities such as rice, sugar, gas, cigarettes, and household cooking gas. Almost immediately, violent demonstrations erupted in major cities, leaving an official death toll of about 70. An estimated 800 people were injured, and 1,270 were arrested. Economic decisions were suspended, a curfew was imposed, and the army was called in to maintain law and order. The January riots underlined the political explosiveness of the subsidy issue. Immediately after the riots, the United States and the oil-producing Arab states came to the rescue.

The economic situation did not improve much under Mubarak. Inflation continued to rise, estimated between 25 and 40% in 1988–1989. The budget deficit increased in 1988–1989 by 46% over the previous year. Government expenditure grew by 24.6%, as opposed to a mere 18.7% increase in its revenues. The Egyptian regime found it increasingly difficult to introduce the reforms requested by the IMF, in the face of worsening economic conditions for large sectors of the population. At the same time, the external debt was placing a severe burden on the economy. Egypt had to reschedule payment on debts due in 1987–1988 and was unable to meet payments of $4 billion in the first half of 1988–1989.[12]

Thus, the impact of economic factors can be summarized as follows: Egypt's limited resources put a constraint on its government and made Egypt more dependent on foreign aid and therefore more vulnerable to external influence.

Military Capability

In the 1970s, Egypt's arms arsenal was considerably weakened by (1) the failure of the Soviet Union to resupply the army adequately after the war of 1973 and the eventual severance of the Soviet military link in 1976; (2) the time needed to shift procurement needs from the Soviet Union to the West and to forge a new link with the United States; and (3) the economic costs of massive rearmament. From 1967 to 1975, according to official estimates, Egypt spent $25 billion for military purposes, and this was matched by an equal amount in war-related losses. During the same period, Egypt received less than $900 million from Arab states.[13]

Of particular interest in this regard is the experience of the Arab military armaments organization (AMIO), founded in 1975 as a joint venture by Egypt, Saudi Arabia, the United Arab Emirates, and Qatar. AMIO was endowed with more than $1.4 billion in an effort to combine oil money with Egypt's skilled labor force. By 1978 the groundwork was laid for the establishment of a basic Arab defense industry located mainly in Egypt. Contacts were initiated with American Motors Corporation to assemble jeeps, with the Ryan Teledyne Corporation to produce high-altitude Drones (pilotless planes equipped with light and infrared sensors), and with Lockheed Aircraft Industries to build C-130 military transports.[14]

Contacts were also made with Westland of Britain to construct 50 Lynx helicopters and the Swingfire antitank missile.[15] This project was reduced by half in May 1979 in protest over the Egyptian-Israeli treaty, and the other three Arab partners decided to terminate the venture as of July 1, 1979. Egypt rejected the decision and instead transformed AMIO into a fully Egyptian enterprise. In 1981, Egypt produced $40 million worth of arms, and in 1983 it assembled the new French Alpha jets. Increasingly, Egyptian arms deals are made on the basis of coproduction, with an Egyptian role in assembly and parts production.[16]

Egypt has one of the best-trained and most highly skilled armies in the region. Egyptian armed forces number well over 300,000 making it one of the largest in the Arab world and Africa. Throughout the 1980s, Egypt embarked on an ambitious program of military industrialization, with the aim of establishing a credible indigenous arms capability. One of the major aspects of this project was the Iraqi-Egyptian collaboration to produce ballistic missile Badr 2000, modelled on the Argentinian missile, Condor 2. This incited a heated political controversy over the proliferation of unconventional weapons in the region. In 1989, due to intense pressure from the United States, Egypt declared its abandonment of this project. It is also worth mentioning that during the same year, 1989, the United States accused Egypt of obtaining a chemical weapons capability. This accusation was strongly denied by President Mubarak.

Egyptian decision-makers emphasize the readiness of their country to help other Arab states' military. Egypt provided arms, ammunition, and logistical aid to Iraq in its war with Iran. In fact, Egypt appears as one of the most active weapons exporting countries in the Third World. Moreover, despite Camp David, military expenditure did not decline in Egypt. During the period between 1984 and 1988 Egypt ranked third as importer of armaments in the Third World.

Political Structure

From 1952 to 1970 the basic characteristics of the political regime in Egypt were absence of political competitiveness, centralization of power, emphasis on mobilization rather than participation, supremacy of the executive over the legislative branch, and repression of political dissent. A clear imbalance existed between politics and administration; output institutions (bureaucracy, police, and army) far outgrew input institutions (interest groups and political organizations). Whenever possible, the government attempted to penetrate and dominate intermediary associations and groups such as trade unions, professional associations, religious institutions, and universities, bringing them under its legal and financial control. The political system gave its leaders an almost free hand in the conduct of foreign policy. The leader was not accountable to either a free press, opposition parties, or an independent strong parliament. The regime controlled both the mass media and the legislature and could mobilize their support for its objectives.

In the 1970s two important processes took place: increasing civilianization of the ruling elite and the development of a limited political pluralism. Sadat followed a policy of professionalizing the army, disengaging it from current political affairs and placing more reliance on civilians in high posts. For the first time since 1952, civilians assumed the posts of vice-president (Mahmoud Fawzi) and prime minister (Aziz Sidky, Fawzi, Abdel-Aziz Hegazi, and Mustafa Khalil). In the realm of foreign policy, Ismail Fahmy, a career diplomat, became the minister of foreign affairs for five years, 1973–1977, till his resignation in protest over Sadat's Jerusalem visit. In 1977, Boutros Ghali, a professor of political science at Cairo University, became the state minister for foreign affairs. He retained this post under Mubarak. In the 1980s, the Ministry of Foreign Affairs was held by two men, Kamal Hassan Ali, of military background, and Dr. Esmat Abdel Meguid, a career diplomat.

The second development was the gradual democratization of the political structure, leading in 1976–1977 to the establishment of a controlled multiparty system. The democratization process was inspired in part by foreign policy considerations: Sadat's rapprochement with the United States and his desire to project the image of a stable, democratic Egypt. In 1980, opposition political parties included the Labor Socialist party (LSP), led by Ibrahim Shukry; the National Progressive Unionist party (NPUP), led by Khaled Mohie Al-Din, and the Liberal Socialist party, led by Mustafa Kamel Murad. The opposition had a weak parliamentary following (20 seats out of 390), but they exercised a far greater influence through their newspapers and publications. Foreign policy was a major bone of contention between the regime and the opposition. The LSP and the NPUP attacked Sadat's pro-Western policy, Egypt's increasing dependency on the United States, Sadat's policy toward Israel, and the break with Arab countries. The Moslem Brotherhood's journal, the monthly *Al-Da'wa* (The Call), also voiced most of these concerns, and its writers condemned governmental policies.

The government could have viewed these criticisms as a justification for stiffening its negotiating position toward Israel. Sadat, however, perceived them as signs of vulnerability, weakness, and the erosion of his personal stature, an interpretation that led to political polarization and the confrontation of September–October 1981, the arrest of 1,963 persons in September, and Sadat's assassination in October.

Mubarak, characteristically, followed a more conciliatory policy towards the opposition. He released the persons arrested in 1981 and met with leaders of the opposition on a number of occasions. The democratic process became more entrenched in Egyptian society during the 1980s. Although the ruling National Democratic Party (NDP) was still in control, opposition groups and parties gained in strength. In the 1987 elections, the opposition got 100 seats in parliament, and some forces hitherto deprived of political participation found their way, though indirectly, into the democratic process, such as the Moslem Brotherhood.[17] Some constraints remained however. The Moslem Brotherhoods' journal *Al-Da'wa*, suspended during the Sadat years, was not allowed to reappear and permission was not granted for the establishment of a Nasserist party.

FOREIGN POLICY ORIENTATION

Egyptian general foreign policy objectives in the 1970s, as articulated and acted upon by Sadat, were as follows: (1) the restoration, preferably by negotiation, of Egyptian territories occupied by Israel since 1967 (As a consequence, when Sadat's February 1971 peace plan failed, the only option left was war.); (2) the termination of the war with Israel, as the economic costs had become unbearable; (3) the improvement of relations with Washington, as the United States was the only country that could influence Israel; (4) the rejuvenation and modernization of the economy through the import of modern Western technology and private capital; and finally (5) the modification of Egypt's global and regional policies in order to better pursue these objectives.

Sadat's decision to seek better relations with the United States was influenced by his mistrust of and political hostility toward the Soviets and by his belief that the United States would help solve Egypt's pressing economic problems. Sadat was a pragmatist, a realist with little attachment to grand theories and ideologies. He was essentially anti-Communist and anti-Soviet. East-West détente gave him the chance of a lifetime. Sadat saw détente and explained it to the Egyptians as the alliance between the two superpowers and their agreement on international issues. The Arabic word used to describe détente, *wifaq*, is actually the equivalent of "entente."

Sadat's attitude toward the Soviet Union was primarily one of mistrust and hostility. In his speeches on the Soviet Union one detects a feeling of humiliation, frustration, and violated dignity. Sadat spoke of the many promises that were given and never fulfilled, the many messages from Cairo that went unanswered. He once described the Soviets as "crude and tasteless people."[18] By the late 1970s, Sadat became a publicly avowed anti-Soviet; he cautioned the United States against underestimating the Soviet threat and pointed out that U.S. influence in the region was on the wane.[19] Sadat volunteered the services of the Egyptian army and territory to combat the Soviet threat. Egyptian officials spoke of the Soviet encirclement of the Middle East through surrogate states with the objective of destabilizing and overthrowing moderate pro-Western Arab regimes, particularly Egypt. In September 1981, Egypt's minister of defense stated: "Egypt is now in a very critical situation because of the threat surrounding it on the West and from the South."[20]

Sadat's strategy concerning the United States was designed to achieve three objectives: first, to outbid Israel and secure U.S. support in the peace negotiations; second, to obtain U.S. military and economic aid at an increasing rate; and third, to assure pro-Western Arab governments that their opposition to Egypt's relationship with Israel would lead nowhere and that Egypt remained the centerpiece in U.S. strategy in the region.

Sadat believed in the importance of close economic and strategic links with Western countries, particularly with the United States. Anti-imperialism, Afro-Asian solidarity, and similar clichés were out of date and no longer useful to Egypt. Sadat was attracted to the American way of life, the consumer society, and the capitalist path of development. Politically, the United States held "the key to peace" in the area, "99% of the cards of the game," he frequently stated. This was because the United States was the only country that could exert influence on Israel. Sadat's view of the superpowers was reinforced by his desire to cement his relations with oil-rich conservative Arab countries whom he perceived as a vital source of economic aid.

Contrary to Nasser, who saw the Arab world as Egypt's natural sphere of influence and leadership and as the main arena for an active foreign policy, Sadat saw Egypt's leadership position as a structural property, not a behavioral attribute, as a property that could not be challenged or taken away. Consequently, he did not feel the need to pursue an activist Arab policy to maintain this leadership. For instance, as early as 1974–1975 Egypt dismantled its apparatus of influence in Lebanon, which had included financial support to friendly political groups, subsidies for newspapers, strong intelligence presence, and close contacts with local politicians. In Sadat's mind, the costs of that leadership style overshadowed its dividends.

Upon assuming office in 1981, Mubarak developed his own interpretation of the international system and Egypt's position in it. In contrast to Sadat's American-centric world, Mubarak held a view of a multipolar world, in which Egypt's success depended on opening its channels with all powers and organizations. This vision was translated into a series of foreign policy objectives that Mubarak and Egyptian diplomats set out to achieve without resorting to shock treatments or confrontational tactics.

One of the first objectives the Mubarak regime pursued was the restoration of Egypt's relations with the Arab world. To do so, it was necessary for Egypt to distance itself to some extent from the United States and from Israeli practices in the occupied territories. This required some skill, as Egypt, for economic and political reasons, needed to maintain its close ties with the United States. Through quiet and constant diplomacy Egypt was successful in achieving this objective. Relations with almost all Arab states were reestablished by 1989, and Egypt resumed its membership in the Arab League.

Mubarak recognized that Egypt's success in obtaining international aid and successfully dealing with its enormous debt problem was related to establishing its importance as an Arab and Third World leader. The regime therefore pursued an active foreign policy in Africa as well as the Arab world. Mubarak regularly attended summit meetings of the Organization of African Unity. The Egyptian Ministry of Foreign Affairs hosted, in 1986, an international conference commemorating the twenty-fifth anniversary of the organization. Egyptian diplomatic efforts were also exerted on behalf of solving a number of African issues, such as the situation in Namibia, and the Senegal-Mauritania dispute.[21]

Egypt's role in the nonaligned movement was also revived. It called for the revitalization of the movement, for it to play a meaningful role in today's international system. The Egyptian Ministry of Foreign Affairs hosted a number of roundtable discussions with experts from India, Yugoslavia, and Zimbabwe, to discuss the means of achieving this revitalization. Mubarak also attended the nonaligned meetings in New Delhi in 1983, in Kuwait in 1987, and in Belgrade in 1988.

On the global level, Egypt continued to have close relations with the United States, despite strains resulting from a number of incidents, such as the *Achille Lauro* affair (1985) and disagreement over Egypt's debts to the United States. While the United States continued to be the primary source of economic and military aid to Egypt, relations were improved with the Soviet Union. Relations were officially resumed in July 1984, and a number of trade and other agreements followed. Egypt and the Soviet Union announced their agreement on the international conference as the means to reach a settlement of the Arab-Israeli dispute.

THE DECISION-MAKING PROCESS

Under Nasser, Sadat, and Mubarak, foreign policy was the *domaine privé* of the president and his close associates. Although the three leaders differed in their styles and orientations, all centralized and personalized the foreign policy–making process, limiting the role of institutions. The influence of different individuals upon the process depended not on their position in the cabinet or the bureaucracy but rather on their personal relations and access to the president. Thus, for instance, when the responsibilities of Ismail Fahmy, minister of foreign affairs from 1973 to 1977, were increased, it reflected Sadat's confidence in Fahmy and not a change in the functions of the ministry as an institution. Similarly, the privileged position of Dr. Osama Al-Baz under Mubarak does not derive from his position as first undersecretary of the Ministry of Foreign Affairs but from his position as an advisor on the president's own staff.

Although this picture is essentially accurate, the dynamics of the decision-making process are more complex. Presidents and kings, however authoritarian and unaccountable, do not make decisions in a vacuum but rather in a specific institutional context. The context affects the behavior of individuals, the formulation of options, and the way choices are made. Compared with other Arab countries, Egypt is an organizationally developed and intellectually diversified society. Consequently the leader, notwithstanding his immense power, has to assume the various roles of arbiter, mediator, and lobbyist at one time or another.

Egypt's foreign policy decision-making process comes closest to the "leader-staff group" or the "presidential center" type.[22] This type of process involves an authoritative decision-maker who can act alone, with little or no consultation with other people or institutions except for a small group of subordinate advisors. These advisors are appointed by the leader and have no autonomous power base.

The leader-staff type of decision-making results in a highly personalized diplomacy. It is also characterized by the ability to respond quickly and to adopt nontraditional behavior. For example, on July 8, 1972, upon the receipt of an unsatisfactory message from the Soviet Union, Sadat informed the Soviet ambassador immediately of his decision to dismiss Soviet advisors. He announced the decision ten days later. To understand leader-staff policy-making, we must take a closer look at the leader, President Mubarak.

President Hosni Mubarak represents the career officer par excellence. He had no political affiliations before being chosen by Sadat, in 1975, to be his vice-president. He had not even joined the Free Officers Association before 1952 but maintained a strict adherence to his military career, rising to the position of director of the Air Force College, then to commander-in-chief of the Egyptian air force. He held this position in October 1973 when the air force led the initial attack on Israel in what came to be called the October War. Despite this strictly military background, Mubarak demonstrated great flexibility and moderation as a political leader. He revealed himself to be a compromiser of the first order, being highly consultative, respecting expert opinion, and not seeking to impose his own.

Presidential Staff

Contrary to both Nasser and Sadat, who surrounded themselves with many functionaries in the realm of foreign policy, Mubarak relied on a small number of aides and on the machinery of the foreign ministry. Mubarak's two primary aides are Dr. Osama Al-Baz and Dr. Mostafa Al-Feky. Dr. Al-Baz is a career diplomat. His background includes the study of law (Cairo and Harvard Universities). He is a survivalist par excellence. He worked closely with Sadat as an insider on the Camp David negotiations but was able to survive the transition to the Mubarak regime, emerging as the president's chief foreign policy confidante. He holds the position of first undersecretary to the Ministry of Foreign Affairs in addition to his position on the president's staff. Dr. Mostafa Al-Feky is the president's secretary for information and supervision. He is the liaison officer between the Ministry of Foreign Affairs and the president. Both Al-Baz and Al-Feky usually travel with the president as members of the official delegation. One of them is usually present at any meeting discussing foreign policy issues.

Presidential Assistants

During the 1980s, two senior politicians assumed the position of assistant to the president: Mamduh Salem (now deceased) was sent on a goodwill trip to African countries, and ex–Field Marshal Abdel Hakem Abu Ghazalla, who was sent to France on a special mission to seek French support in solving Egypt's debt problem.

National Security Council

The National Security Council, established in 1969, is the highest organ for strategic planning and national security issues. Its membership includes, among others, the president, the vice-president, the ministers of foreign affairs and defense, and the head of intelligence. The council has no definite jurisdiction and meets upon the invitation of the president. Under Mubarak, the council hardly met.

Ministry of Foreign Affairs

Egypt's Foreign Ministry has a history that goes as far back as 1837, when it was established as a *diwan* (department) during Mohamed Ali's reign. It was abolished on December 17, 1914, with the proclamation of Egypt as a British protectorate, and it was reinstated in 1922 after independence. During the 1980s, two men assumed the position of foreign minister: Kamal Hassan Ali (of military background) and Dr. Esmat Abdel Meguid (a career diplomat). Boutros Ghali continued to hold the position of minister of state for foreign affairs.

Under Sadat, the role of the ministry was naturally overshadowed by the presidency, and the foreign minister acted mainly as a presidential advisor. He did not attend all the president's meetings with foreign officials. For example, some of the most crucial sessions in the Egyptian-Israeli negotiations were confined to Sadat. In his visits to Egypt in November 1973 and January 1974, Kissinger primarily conferred with Sadat alone. Messages were exchanged directly between the president and other countries without the knowledge of the ministry, and Egyptian ambassadors to Arab capitals were not informed about the many visits Ashraf Marwan made to these countries in the early 1970s.[23]

In contrast to Hermann's notion of "positive reinforcement," according to which staff members tend to sympathize with their leader's wishes and demands,[24] in 1977–1978 three successive Egyptian foreign ministers resigned in protest over presidential policy. When the stakes are high and the dangers great, even staff members who are totally dependent on the president may take independent positions.

Under Mubarak, the role of the ministry has significantly increased. For the first time, the president made a point of meeting all new Egyptian ambassadors before they assumed their posts. Moreover, also for the first time, heads of departments in the ministry were sent as presidential envoys.

Other Ministries

These include the Ministries of Defense (formerly called the War Ministry), Economy, and Investment. They maintain official representation in key capitals of the world.

FOREIGN POLICY BEHAVIOR

In this section we will deal primarily with Egypt's changing relationship with the two superpowers and with regional Arab policy.

Egyptian-Soviet Relations

For a long time Egypt was the cornerstone of Soviet Arab and Middle Eastern policy, and Egyptian-Soviet relations were thought of as a model of cooperation between the Soviet Union and a non-Communist Third World country. Ironically, since 1967 Soviet influence and prestige have correlated adversely with the fortunes of Egypt. The 1967 defeat greatly enhanced the Soviet presence, and the success of 1973 contributed to its waning. In the post-1973 era, relations were primarily characterized by mutual mistrust and hostility. Disagreement between the two countries covered a broad range of issues: political-diplomatic (renewed relations with the United States as a means of resolving the Arab-Israeli conflict); military (armament, compensation for weapons lost in the war, and Egypt's decision in 1975 to diversify its sources of supply); and economic (rescheduling the debt).[25]

Sadat's relations with the Soviet Union were strained most of the time. In May 1971 he removed from office the group that was perceived as pro-Moscow. The Soviets were so worried that they rushed a high-level delegation headed by Podgornyi to sign a friendship and cooperation treaty with Egypt. Sadat found the timing inappropriate because the treaty would appear to be a reaction of the purge of "Soviet friends." He suggested postponing it till the celebrations of July two months later, but the Soviets insisted, and the treaty was signed on May 27, 1971, less than two weeks after the purge of this group.

On July 19, a Communist coup in Sudan was crushed with Egyptian help. Against Soviet advice to recognize the new regime, Sadat ordered the Egyptian air force to transport back to Khartoum a Sudanese paratroop brigade that was stationed in Egypt. The brigade was instrumental in the countercoup of July 22–23.[26] The Soviet Union also obviously mistrusted Sadat's intentions and his attempts to build bridges with Saudi Arabia and the United States. Military, economic, and political issues were bones of contention between the two countries.

When Mubarak came to power in 1981, he had the choice of leaving relations with the Soviets as they stood or trying to improve them. Consistent with Mubarak's overall strategy of opening channels with various world powers, Mubarak sought to improve relations. This had to be achieved through gradual and incremental efforts, as Egypt's close ties with the United States did not allow for any dramatic steps.

Political-Diplomatic Relations. As early as November 1973, it seemed that Sadat was ready to put the U.S. option into effect. He saw what limited help the Soviet Union could provide in a peaceful resolution of the Arab-Israeli conflict. The Soviets officially cochaired the Geneva conference held in December with the United States, but Heikal reports that "they were relegated to the role of spectators."[27]

The Soviets felt uneasy about the developing Egyptian-U.S. relations. They did not like Kissinger's monopoly, with Egyptian consent, of the negotiation process, which resulted in the first disengagement agreement between Egyptian and Israeli forces on January 20, 1974. Diplomatic relations between Egypt and the United States were resumed in March, followed by Richard Nixon's visit in June. The Soviet Union expressed grave concern and Egypt's foreign minister, Ismail Fahmy, was dispatched to Moscow to discuss Soviet-Egyptian relations.

The culmination of these events was on March 14, 1976, when Sadat, in a speech to the Parliament, unilaterally abrogated the Soviet-Egyptian treaty of 1971. He gave five reasons for his action: (1) the Soviet Union showed no desire for peace in the Middle East; (2) the Soviet Union opposed Egypt's new economic policy; (3) the Soviet Union refused to reschedule Egypt's debts and demanded interest on military debts; (4) the Soviet Union not only refused to overhaul Egyptian aircraft and provide spare parts—a clear violation of Article 8 of the treaty—it also forbade other countries (India) to do so; and finally (5) the Soviet Union had a hand in Ali Sabri's plot to overthrow Sadat.

Egyptian-Soviet relations suffered another setback in August 1976, when the Soviet Union supported Libya in its dispute with Egypt. In July 1977 three Soviet technicians were reportedly killed during an Egyptian bombing raid on a Libyan radar station. This resulted in condemnation from Moscow and Egyptian countercharges of Soviet involvement in Libya. In December 1977, in the aftermath of Sadat's visit to Israel, the Soviet consulates in Alexandria, Port Said, and Aswan were closed. Egyptian-Soviet relations came almost to a complete halt. The Soviet Union opposed Egypt's policy toward Israel on the basis that it would not lead to a comprehensive peace in the area. Sadat escalated his anti-Soviet and anti-Communist remarks; he also criticized the U.S. "Vietnam complex" and asked for a more active U.S. role.

In September 1981 the Soviet embassy in Cairo was accused of being involved in harmful spying activities and the Soviet ambassador and a number of diplomats were asked to leave the country.

As a result of the Mubarak regime's diplomatic efforts, official relations between Egypt and the Soviet Union were restored, and the countries exchanged ambassadors in July 1984. Relations began to improve gradually, although no major breakthrough immediately followed. Letters were exchanged between the leaders of the two countries on a number of occasions. Mubarak also received the Soviet ambassador to Cairo after the Reykjavik summit conference, who briefed him on discussions concerning the Middle East.

Several visits by Soviet officials to Cairo and Egyptian officials to Moscow took place between 1984 and 1988. In May of 1988, Egypt's foreign minister, Esmat Abdel Meguid, visited Moscow. This was considered a significant sign of improved relations, as the first such visit in twelve years and the first high-level official visit since Gorbachev came to power. Abdel Meguid received a warm welcome and met with the Soviet leader for over an hour in an indication of the Soviet Union's interest in improving relations.[28]

Further indications of improved relations came from Cairo. The Soviet cultural center in Cairo was reopened in March 1988, and restrictions imposed on the size of the Soviet diplomatic mission in Cairo were lifted. In December of the same year, the speaker of the parliament, Dr. Rifaat Al-Mahgaub, visited Moscow, and in 1989 the Soviet foreign minister met PLO chairman Yasser Arafat and Israeli Foreign Minister Moshe Arens in Cairo.[29] In 1990 Mubarak himself visited Moscow.

Military Relations. The military dimension of the Egyptian-Soviet rift is complex. It includes problems of arms supplies, economic costs of the weapons, and interpersonal conflicts between Egyptian and Soviet officers. First there was the problem of Soviet reluctance to respond to Egyptian demands for arms.

In the aftermath of October 1973, the problem surfaced again. Egypt requested Soviet compensation for the arms lost in the war, just as the United States had compensated Israel and the Soviet Union had done for Syria. For months to follow Egypt's requests met with rejection. In June 1975, Sadat declared that if the Soviet Union continued to ignore Egypt's demands and took no notice of its economic situation, he would have to do something about it. In particular, Sadat was critical of the Soviet massive armament of Libya, whose relations with Egypt were deteriorating. He perceived this as an avenue of Soviet penetration in the area and a potential threat to Egypt.

Another dimension of the military rift was the result of interpersonal conflicts between Egyptian and Soviet officers before 1972, which left a legacy throughout the 1970s. Shazly, who worked closely with senior Soviet officers, says: "The Russians have many qualities, but concern for human feelings is not among them. They are brusque, harsh, frequently arrogant and usually unwilling to believe that anyone has anything to teach them."[30]

Soviet facilities in Egypt presented another touchy issue for the Egyptian military. The Soviets had exclusive control over a number of airfields that provided air cover for the Soviet fleet. Soviet ships obtained facilities in several ports—Alexandria, Port Said, and Al-Salloum.[31] During the years 1974 to 1976 Sadat continually reminded his people of the Soviet legacy in Egypt. He played on the sentiments of the military by reminding them that Soviet "bases" were a breach of Egyptian sovereignty, and commentators emphasized the theme of liberating Egypt from Soviet influence and domination.

A third dimension of military relations was financial. Although the famous 1955 arms deal was largely a barter agreement, hard currency was increasingly the required medium of payment for Soviet weapons and personnel. In a December 1971 interview, Sadat told Arnaud de Borchgrave of *Newsweek* that "all the Soviet officers and men [are] paid in hard currency, not Egyptian money. We are paying through the nose for the maintenance of these Soviet Sam crews in Egypt."[32] By 1972, Shazly reports that the Soviet Union "was demanding payment in full and hard currency" for all new equipment.[33] Sadat was to cite this frequently in his speeches to show that the Soviets were not the true friends they claimed to be. This situation changed somewhat with the improved relations under Mubarak. Talks concerning the rescheduling of Egypt's military debts were started soon after relations were resumed. In March 1987, an agreement was reached whereby Egypt could repay its debts over a period of twenty-five years, with a six-year period of grace and with no interest charged.[34] No military cooperation took place during this period between the two countries, although the Soviet Union is reported to have expressed its willingness to consider this.[35]

Economic Relations. In December 1975 Egypt's nonmilitary debt to the Soviet Union was $4 billion; its military debt totalled $7 billion. Despite repeated requests, the Soviet Union refused to reschedule the debt, and on December 14, 1975, Sadat announced that Egypt would not sign the trade protocol with the Soviet Union for 1976. When Egypt was ready to sign in January 1976, the Soviets postponed the signing. The protocol was finally signed on April 28, 1976, but at $640 million, it provided for $160 million less in trade than the figure negotiated the previous December.[36] In August 1977 Sadat suspended cotton exports to the Soviet Union and two months later announced that debt repayments would be suspended for ten years beginning January 1978.

Economic and trade relations decreased during this period. Economic aid agreements with Egypt declined from $1 billion in 1955–1964 to $440 million in 1965–1975, and then to zero in 1975–1979.[37] Trade relations also declined after the cotton embargo and Egypt's refusal to maintain the large trade surplus used to service its debt. The Soviet share of Egyptian exports fell from 50% in 1970–1975 to less than 15% in 1975. Egyptian imports from the Soviet Union also dropped from about 25% of Egypt's total imports to around 10%. Soviet exports to Egypt dwindled from 301 million rubles in 1974 (about $4 million) to 200 million rubles in 1976, to 148 million in 1978, and to 127 million in 1979. Soviet imports from Egypt decreased as well, from 427 million rubles in 1974, to 331 million in 1976, and to 198 million in 1978 and 1979.[38] By 1979 a few Soviet technicians and a limited volume of trade were the remnants of a once flourishing relationship. In the political crisis of September 1981, when the Soviet embassy in Cairo was accused of helping some communist elements and indulging in spying activities, most of those technicians were ordered to leave the country.

Once relations improved during the Mubarak period, one of the first talks that took place concerned the maintenance of certain factories built in Egypt through Soviet assistance in the 1960s. The Soviet Union agreed to provide the technical assistance necessary. During 1986 and 1987, talks centered around trade and economic relations. A short-term trade agreement was signed in 1987, while talks continued over the settlement of Egyptian debts to the Soviet Union. Agreement on this issue was finally reached in February 1988, and a long-term trade agreement was signed, as well as the first tourism agreement between the two countries. In the same year, 1988, an agreement of economic and trade cooperation was signed.

Egyptian-U.S. Relations

In the 1970s, the United States made a dramatic return to Egypt and the Arab world. U.S. diplomacy could contain, outmaneuver, and sometimes expel Soviet influence from the area. Even with "radical" Arab states such as Algeria or Syria, the United States maintained flourishing commercial and economic relations. The big success story, however, is that of U.S.-Egyptian relations. In 1970 there were no diplomatic relations between the two countries; they were resumed in March 1974. Within four to five years, Egypt developed special relations with the United States. Since 1978, the United States has become a "partner" in Egyptian-Israeli relations, the major supplier of arms, and the primary donor of economic assistance to Egypt. This left the Egyptian regime open to criticisms, domestic and Arab, of being a client of the United States. A study of U.S.-Egyptian relations during the 1980s showed a significant degree of independence from the United States displayed by the Mubarak regime. Egypt would seem to fall into the category of client-prevalent and client-centric.[39] This is a category of relations, described by Christopher Shoemaker and John Spanier, in which the client has a substantial degree of independence and maneuverability in the conduct of foreign policy. This independence was not exploited or displayed under the Sadat regime, because it was essentially a period of creating and consolidating relations with the United States. Once relations became more routine under Mubarak, the regime, motivated by the personal inclinations of the leader as well as internal criticism of Egyptian-U.S. relations, began to exert this independence on a number of issues. For example, the Mubarak regime resisted pressures from the United States for military facilities in the Ras Banas base. The Egyptian press was allowed to criticize U.S. positions on a number of issues. The regime was keen on enhancing Egypt's image as an independent regional and Third World leader to bolster both its domestic legitimacy and its bargaining position at the international level.

Political-Diplomatic Relations. In the first three years of Sadat's rule, 1970–1973, the United States continued its policy of total support to Israel. The Israeli occupation seemed stable and the Arab states appeared incapable of launching a new war. The United States, on the other hand, was busy ending its Vietnam involvement, opening new inroads to China, and inaugurating a decade of détente.

In February 1971, Sadat proposed opening the Suez Canal and signing a peace treaty with Israel, but nothing much came from this proposal. The expulsion of Soviet advisors from Egypt in July 1972 provided a new opportunity for the United States. It seems that Egyptian-U.S. contacts were initiated at that time. Heikal reports that talks were conducted through two channels, the diplomatic channel of foreign ministries and also a quiet one suggested by Nixon—the U.S. Central Intelligence Agency (CIA).[40] In addition, a third avenue was provided by Saudi Arabia, whose dignitaries communicated messages between Washington and Cairo. All efforts, however, including National Security Advisor Hafez Ismail's visit to the United States in 1973, led nowhere. It took the war of 1973 to finally bring the seriousness of the situation to Washington's attention. It became clear that Egypt and the Arabs could act and take the initiative; they could coordinate an attack and harm Israel. The use of oil as a weapon showed that U.S. interests in the area could be threatened.

Through his famous "shuttle diplomacy," Kissinger monopolized the indirect negotiation process that took place after the war, resulting in the first disengagement agreements between Egypt, Syria, and Israel in 1974. The oil embargo was lifted, and in June 1975 the Suez Canal was opened. Egypt signed the second Sinai agreement in September 1975, a step that created a rift in the Arab world because of the failure of Syria and Israel to achieve a similar agreement. In 1977–1978 Sadat became more emphatic about the importance of the U.S. role. The United States was not just a mediator, but a full partner in the peace process. Thus, Sadat concentrated on American public opinion, he spent endless hours with media people, senators and congressmen, and leaders of the Jewish community. And he did make an impact on them. One is tempted to argue that the target of his visit to Jerusalem was not only the Israelis but equally the American people. He made the visit in front of television cameras, and well-established news stars such as Walter Cronkite and Barbara Walters accompanied him. The visit was a media event, an exercise in television diplomacy, and Sadat captured the imagination of millions in the West. He definitely improved the image of Egypt and its leadership, but his other more subtle objective—political disengagement between Israel and the United States—did not materialize, and strong U.S. pressure on Israel was not forthcoming. U.S.-Egyptian relations were closely related to the negotiations with Israel. Carter's decision to take an active role in 1978 resulted in the signing of the Camp David framework and the Egyptian-Israeli treaty in 1979. The treaty opened the door for much closer economic and military relations.

An important outcome of U.S. involvement in the peace process was that Egyptian-U.S. relations could no longer be viewed in purely bilateral terms. Israel constantly figures as an important factor in what are, for all intents and purposes, triangular relations. Many Egyptians feel that relations between Egypt and the United States are influenced not only by Egyptian policies toward the United States but also by its policies toward Israel. This situation gives Israel added leverage over Egypt and adds tension to the relationship as a whole. Egypt perceives itself as the weaker partner in the Israeli-U.S.-Egyptian triangle and is aware that the United States is more sensitive to Israeli demands. This is clear in relation to the question of a comprehensive settlement of conflict in the area. The main failure of the Camp David accords was in the collapse of negotiations concerning Palestinian autonomy in the West Bank and Gaza. The Mubarak regime is anxious to resume efforts toward such a settlement. Mubarak argues that an international conference would be the best means, but the United States stands closer to the Israeli position. This disagreement was evident in the Mubarak visits to Washington in 1985 and again in 1988.

During this period, the relationship was severely tested by the events of the 1985 *Achille Lauro* affair and the interception of an Egyptian plane by U.S. military planes. There was widespread official and popular condemnation of this incident in Egypt. There were attempts by the U.S. government to overcome this strain, through a message from President Reagan and a special envoy to the area, but the event left a shadow on relations for some time. This strain was compounded by the Israeli attack on the PLO headquarters in Tunisia, which reemphasized U.S. support of Israeli actions.

The strength of Egyptian-U.S. relations becomes clear, however, by their ability to withstand these and other strains. During the 1970s, Sadat conducted the relationship with a higher degree of visibility, using the U.S. media and visits by presidents and foreign ministers as his tools for demonstrating the strength of the relationship. Under Mubarak, however, relations became more regularized and institutionalized. The day-to-day relationship is no longer a visible political matter. Even when the regime seeks to establish its independence from the United States, this is done with no attempt at sensationalism. Thus when Egypt withstood U.S. pressures to enter into confrontation with Libya in 1988, this was done in a quiet, restrained, and diplomatic fashion. This characterizes Mubarak's style in conducting the relationship as a whole.

Military Relations. Military cooperation between the two countries has taken various forms: arms supplies, transfer of military technology, provision of military facilities, and joint training and maneuvers. In 1975, Sadat emphasized the need to diversify Egypt's sources of arms. Egypt acquired some British and French jet fighters, helicopters, and air-to-surface missiles, and U.S. arms came slowly and gradually. In 1975, after the signature of the second disengagement agreement, Egypt was offered U.S. military credits, making the United States Egypt's major arms supplier.

Military relations between Egypt and the United States also included the licensing and coproduction of arms. After the collapse of AMIO in October 1979, Egypt and the United States agreed to cooperate in the manufacturing and assembling of armored vehicles and electronic equipment. As another form of cooperation, Egypt offered the U.S. "temporary limited access" to airfields near Cairo (Cairo West) and in Ras Banas on the Red Sea. Though separated from the Gulf by Saudi Arabia, Ras Banas is still a strategic point in relation to the Suez Canal and the Mediterranean. It is all the more important as more oil is shipped through Saudi Arabia by pipeline and up to the Red Sea, through the Suez Canal to the Mediterranean.[41]

The United States hoped to convince Sadat to sign an agreement making the Ras Banas base available to the U.S. Army. Secretary Alexander Haig discussed this during his visit to the region in April 1981, but with no success. Egypt resisted the idea of signing a formal agreement with the United States guaranteeing access to military facilities.[42] Sadat's formal position was that Egypt would make the facilities available to the United States in response to a request by any member of the Arab League. This commitment was reiterated by President Mubarak.

The United States and Egypt also collaborated in joint training and maneuvers. In 1980 U.S. troops began conducting exercises in Egypt under the name "Bright Star." These were conducted every two years during the early 1980s but were suspended in 1985 due to Egyptian discontent over the *Achille Lauro* affair.[43] The exercises took place in 1987 and in 1989. In April 1988, U.S. and Egyptian ministers of defense signed a memorandum of understanding that established the principle of cooperation between the two countries and enhanced their military-strategic relations.[44] This dealt primarily with military industrialization and transfer of technology. An agreement was also reached concerning production of the U.S. M-1 tank in Egypt.

Economic Relations. In the last three decades, Egypt has been a major recipient of foreign aid in the Third World. Thirty-seven percent of total investments in development and 36% of total imports between 1952 and 1975 were financed by foreign aid. As for the United States, between 1946 and 1980 U.S. economic aid totaled $7.2 billion, most of which ($6.8 billion or 94%) was given in the late 1970s. The increase in economic aid coincided with the shift in Egypt's domestic and foreign policies. The political underpinnings of the aid were articulated in a 1981 AID (Agency for International Development) document as follows: "Our high level of aid to Egypt is premised on the belief that President Sadat's peace initiatives are crucial to that objective and that these efforts will be supported and enhanced by a vigorous and growing economy."[45]

The aid covers a broad range of needs: food, infrastructure improvement, the upgrading of social services, technical assistance, agricultural and industrial projects, and loans to help Egypt's balance of payments. This last item, called general economic support, is the largest single item of aid.

The size and nature of U.S. aid to Egypt became a major issue in the 1980s. In 1985, for the first time since relations were restored in 1974, Egypt officially requested an increase in economic and military aid.[46] Over the following years, Egypt pressed the United States on several occasions to increase the aid, to restructure it, and to give Egypt the same terms as Israel. The United States was not cooperative in this respect, although it continued to supply Egypt with large amounts of aid. In 1986, the United States released $110 million in cash and granted Egypt a total of $2.12 billion in 1987.[47] This included a $1.3 billion military grant, $115 million of it in cash. It also granted Egypt $195 million in food aid. The United States stipulated, however, that the cash be used to improve Egypt's balance of payments and that Egypt undertake a program of economic reform. These stipulations were not made the previous year and illustrate a growing concern over Egypt's debt situation.

Bilateral talks over the issue in the mid- and late 1980s revealed differences of opinion over the nature of U.S. aid to Egypt, particularly its military aspect. Egypt views this aid in terms of a political commitment by the United States, linked to U.S. strategic interests as well as to the peace process with Israel. The United States was not responsive to this argument and intensive efforts were made by the Egyptians to achieve at least a rescheduling of debts. As a result of visits by Mubarak, Abu Ghazala, and a number of other high officials to Washington, in 1988 Egypt secured $1.3 billion in military assistance and $815 million in economic assistance.[48] Although Egypt was second in amount of U.S. aid received (Israel was first), the United States refused to increase the cash component of its assistance.

U.S.-Egyptian relations have thus changed drastically since 1973, from no diplomatic relations to very close political and military relations. The new pattern of relations does have its problems and contradictions. Egyptians have grown wary of the increasing dependence of their country on the United States and the decline of Egypt's image as a nonaligned country.

Egyptian-PLO Relations

As mentioned earlier, one of Mubarak's first foreign policy objectives was the restoration of relations with the Arab world. To achieve this, it was necessary for Egypt to demonstrate its continued commitment to Arab causes, despite the signing of the Camp David accords. The Palestinian issue presented itself as the obvious means by which the Mubarak regime could demonstrate this. Paradoxically, while Egypt was ostracized in the late 1970s because of its alleged abandonment of the Palestinians, it emerged in the 1980s as one of the main supporters of the PLO and its political leadership.

The Mubarak regime held frequent and close consultations with the PLO leadership in an attempt to revive the search for a comprehensive peace settlement in the region. Egypt mediated between the PLO and Jordan to reach an agreement on the delegation representing the Palestinians in an international conference. Mubarak also strove to improve the PLO's international image. During the Achille Lauro crisis, he tried to give the PLO the chance to disassociate itself from terrorism by trying the hijackers. (This attempt was foiled by U.S. intervention.) The Mubarak regime announced its recognition and support of the Palestinian state announced by the Palestinian National Congress in Algiers in 1988. Furthermore, Mubarak tried to find a compromise to the deadlock over the future of the occupied territories through his 10-point plan put forward in the summer of 1989.

The PLO, in turn, was appreciative of Egypt's efforts. The PLO leadership was instrumental in achieving Egypt's return to the Arab fold. Yasser Arafat even addressed the Arab League summit in Casablanca in June 1989, welcoming Egypt back to the Arab League.

Egyptian-Israeli Relations

While Egypt's relations with the Arab world improved during the 1980s, its relations with Israel came to be characterized as a "cold peace." From the beginning there was a fundamental difference between Egypt's and Israel's understanding of the peace process. Peace to Egypt was basically a solution to its economic and social problems; a means of creating stability and allocating resources back to development. To Mubarak, as to Sadat, this meant the end of hostilities and the establishment of proper relations with a neighbor state. This did not mean a privileged position for Israel in Egypt. The Israelis, on the other hand, had a broader understanding, which took concrete shape as the process of "normalization," a complex web of economic, social, athletic, tourist, and other relations.

A number of issues stood in the way of completing this normalization of relations between the two countries. One important factor was Israel's policies toward the Palestinians and the neighboring Arab countries. Israel's bombing of the Iraqi nuclear reactor, its invasion of Lebanon and implication in the Sabra and Shatilla massacres, as well as its raid on the PLO headquarters in Tunisia and its suppression of the *Intifada* (uprising) in the occupied territories, all have forced Egypt to distance itself from Israel and to freeze the normalization process. Egypt was forced to withdraw its ambassador from Israel by the shock and outrage of Egyptians over the Sabra and Shatilla massacres. A new ambassador was not named until after agreement concerning the Taba issue. Israel's policy of continuing the settlements in the West Bank and of declaring Jerusalem as its capital forced Mubarak to refuse to visit Israel, as Egypt still considers the future of the West Bank as subject to negotiation.

Egypt continues to call for an international conference as a means of settling the issue, but Israel persists in refusing.

Another bone of contention during the 1980s was the Taba issue, a small area in Sinai where Israel raised doubts about the exact demarcation of the border line. Despite overwhelming evidence from the Egyptian side, Israel contested the issue. Egypt eventually conceded to accept arbitration, and the agreement concerning the return of Taba was signed in September 1989, after which Egypt named its ambassador to Israel. There was also the question of Deir Al-Sultan, an Egyptian Coptic monastery in Jerusalem. Israeli military authorities had forced the Egyptians to evacuate in 1970 and then turned over the monastery to Ethiopian Coptic monks. In 1982 the Egyptian church prevented Copts from making pilgrimages until it was returned.

More "sensationalist" sources of strain in the relationship came from a series of attacks from 1984 to 1986 on Israeli diplomats by a group that called itself "Egypt's Revolution," and the attack, in 1985, on some Israeli tourists by an Egyptian draftee, claimed to have been imbalanced. The group behind the assassination attempts was arrested in 1987 and brought to trial in 1988. The Egyptian draftee, Sulaiman Khater, was also tried and was found dead in his cell a few days later, supposedly having committed suicide. The most important issue in Egyptian-Israeli relations in the late 1980s was disagreement over Palestinian rights and autonomy in the occupied territories. The Mubarak regime is making concentrated efforts on reaching some means of breaking this deadlock. The Israeli response in this respect will determine the prospects of bilateral relations in the near future.

The Arab World

Egypt's Arab policy has been primarily motivated by two objectives: the need for a good Arab consensus to reach a comprehensive solution of the Arab-Israeli conflict, and the need to generate massive economic and financial aid. Egyptian tactics and positions have changed over time in pursuing these two objectives.

In the early 1970s Sadat ridiculed the distinction between revolutionary and conservative Arab states; the real criterion should be a country's position toward the Arab effort against Israel. "Egypt measures each Arab country by its relation and orientation to the Palestinian resistance," Sadat stated on October 15, 1972. He started to build a broad Arab front by reconciling differences between Arab regimes, advocating non-intervention in each other's internal affairs, and emphasizing the need for Arab solidarity. To achieve this, Sadat paid many visits to various Arab countries; he was the first Egyptian head of state ever to visit Iraq or Kuwait.

Sadat demonstrated his ability for swift action; in most cases he could outbid and outmaneuver his critics. The ups and downs of Egypt's relations with other Arab countries must be seen in the context of its search for an end to the Arab-Israeli conflict. Thus, for instance, the first public rift between Egypt and Syria centered around Egypt's second disengagement treaty and its acceptance of Kissinger's step-by-step approach. The major developments, however, took place after Sadat's visit to Israel in November 1977.

The decision to go to Israel was motivated by a number of factors: Sadat's frustration with Arab disunity, the feeling that Syria was not enthusiastic about an early resumption of the Geneva conference, increasing economic problems at home (the January food riots), and U.S. impatience with the push and pull of Arab politics.

The reactions of Arab states to the visit differed markedly. Morocco, Sudan, Somalia, and Oman supported the move; Algeria, Libya, Syria, Iraq, South Yemen, and the PLO condemned it in a meeting they held in Tripoli in December 1977. Sadat responded by severing diplomatic relations with the five Arab states. In the middle, Saudi Arabia, Jordan, and the Gulf states were neutral, giving Sadat the benefit of the doubt.

The Camp David Accords (1978) and the ensuing Egyptian-Israeli treaty (1979) were met by almost universal Arab rejection. In an Arab summit meeting in Baghdad, Arab states decided to break off diplomatic relations with Cairo, suspend Egypt's membership in the League of Arab States, transfer the headquarters of the league from Cairo to Tunis, and boycott any Egyptian company that would do business with Israel.

Certain Arab countries were engaged in special relations with Egypt. Chief among them was Saudi Arabia. As mentioned earlier, in the early 1970s there was a close alliance between the two countries. Egypt needed Saudi Arabian financial help and Faisal needed Sadat to sustain stability in the Arab East. He expected Sadat to diminish Nasser's revolutionary model of development, cut close relations with the Soviet Union and restrain radicals in Syria, Iraq, and the PLO. One story relates that President Richard Nixon urged Saudi Arabia in mid-June 1972 to pressure Egypt to get rid of the Soviet presence as a precondition to an active U.S. role.[49] Relations between the two countries were not affected by the visit to Israel. Indeed, Saudi Arabia agreed to represent Egyptian interests in Iraq, Syria, and South Yemen after the severing of diplomatic relations. Later Saudi Arabia went along with other Arab countries, breaking off diplomatic relations with Egypt and refusing to pay for the fifty U.S.-made F-5E fighter jets ordered by Egypt earlier.

Thus, at the time of Sadat's death in October 1981, Egypt was virtually isolated in the Arab world. One of Mubarak's primary foreign policy objectives was to restore Egyptian-Arab relations, while reassuring the United States and Israel of Egypt's respect for its Camp David commitments. Propaganda campaigns against the Arabs were halted. Mubarak seized every opportunity to demonstrate that Camp David did not tie Egypt's hands regarding its Arab commitments. Thus Mubarak condemned the Israeli invasion of Lebanon in 1982, withdrew the Egyptian ambassador from Tel Aviv after the Sabra and Shatilla massacres, and refused to visit Jerusalem.

In a more positive assertion of Egypt's Arab ties, Mubarak extended military support to Iraq in its war with Iran and coordinated efforts with Jordan to move negotiations on the future of the West Bank and Gaza. Mubarak also extended recognition and support to the new Palestinian state and consulted frequently with the PLO political leadership. It can be argued that although the Iran-Iraq war created the suitable environment for the return of relations between Egypt and the Arab countries—with Iraq and Gulf states seeking Egyptian support— it was in fact Egypt's efforts on behalf of the Palestinians that undermined the opposition to Egypt in the Arab world. With the support and endorsement extended by the Palestinians to Egypt and its regime, states like Algeria and Syria could no longer condemn Egypt for betraying the Palestinian cause. Mubarak's diplomatic efforts therefore succeeded and relations with Arab countries improved markedly. Jordan was the first Arab country to resume relations with Egypt in September 1984. The intensification of the Gulf war reflected on Arab foreign policy. At the Arab summit in Amman in 1987, the Arab League decided it had no jurisdiction over bilateral relations between Arab countries. This opened the way for several Arab countries to resume relations with Egypt. In the span of three months, relations were resumed with all Arab countries except Algeria, Libya, and Syria.

In 1989, Egypt's situation in the Arab world improved further. At an Arab summit in Casablanca in June 1989, Egypt was officially welcomed back into the Arab League. Relations with Algeria had already been restored, and by December relations with Syria were resumed. In October of the same year talks were held between President Mubarak and Libya's Qaddafi in a bid to improve relations strained for well over a decade. Last but not least, Egypt entered into an agreement of cooperation with Jordan, Iraq, and North Yemen. The Arab Cooperation Council, in February 1989, expressed its aims mainly in economic terms, but the political implications of such a gathering obviously cannot be ignored. However, with the Kuwait crisis, the cooperation council seemed in jeopardy, and in the summer of 1990 the Arab world seemed divided again with Egypt and Iraq in different camps. Egypt felt threatened by the Iraqi invasion of Kuwait, which seemed to be a challenge to Egypt's regional role. The Iraqi army occupied Kuwait less than ten days after Saddam Hussein had promised Mubarak not to use force. The fact that the two countries were partners in the Arab Cooperation Council was a further complicating factor; Iraq should have consulted with Egypt about such a decision or should bear the consequences alone, Egyptian officials felt. This explains Egypt's firm position throughout the crisis. Mubarak called for an Arab summit meeting, endorsed its resolutions, and sent Egyptian troops to Saudi Arabia. Despite the fears of potential Israeli participation in the war and the agonies people felt during the massive bombardment of Iraq, Cairo did not waver.

The war and its aftermath provided an opportunity for Egypt to reassert its regional position. It led to the rise of a new grouping consisting of the GCC countries, Syria, and Egypt. Gulf states relinquished Egyptian debt and promised more development aid. Whether these trends are transient or will prove stable and long lasting remains to be seen.

NOTES

1. On the concept of foreign policy restructuring see K. J. Holsti, *Why Nations Realign: Foreign Policy Restructuring in the Post-War World* (London: George Allen and Unwin, 1982).

2. This issue was discussed in Franklin Weinstein, *Indonesian Foreign Policy and the Dilemma of Dependence* (Ithaca, N.Y.: Cornell University Press, 1976).

3. Ali E. Hillal Dessouki, *Egypt and the Great Powers 1973–1981* (Tokyo: Institute for Developing Economies, 1983).

4. Gamal Hamdan, *The Character of Egypt*, 2 vols. (Cairo: Maktabat Alam Al-Kutub, 1980 and 1982) (in Arabic).

5. *Al-Ahram Al-Iktisadi* [The Economist], May 1, 1977, pp. 8–9.

6. *The Arab Strategic Yearbook, 1986* (Cairo: The Al Ahram Centre for Political and Strategic Studies, 1987), p. 338.

7. Robert Mabro and Samir Radwan, *The Industrialization of Egypt* (Oxford: Clarendon Press, 1976), p. 32.

8. *The Arab Strategic Yearbook, 1985*, pp. 354, 355.

9. John Waterbury, "Egypt: The Wages of Dependency," in A. L. Udovitch (ed.), *The Middle East: Oil, Politics and Hope* (Lexington, Mass.: Lexington Books, 1976), p. 293.

10. Ali E. Hillal Dessouki, "The Politics of Income Distribution in Egypt," in Gouda Abdel-Khalek and Robert Tignor (eds.), *The Political Economy of Income Distribution in Egypt* (New York: Holmes and Meier, 1982), pp. 55–87.

11. Ali E. Hillal Dessouki, "Policy-Making in Egypt: A Case Study of the Open Door Economic Policy," *Social Problems* 28, 4 (1981), pp. 410–416.

12. *The Arab Strategic Yearbook, 1988*, pp. 610–611.

13. Interview with Egypt's Minister of Planning, *New York Times*, April 9, 1975.

14. *Christian Science Monitor*, February 8, 1978.

15. *Arabia and the Gulf*, September 18, 1978, p. 10.

16. Jim Paul, "The Egyptian Arms Industry," *Merip Reports* 112 (February 1983), pp. 26–28.

17. *The Arab Strategic Yearbook, 1987*, pp. 332, 333, 334, 338.

18. *Time*, January 2, 1978, p. 19.

19. Interview with Joseph Kraft in the *Los Angeles Times*, April 14, 1980.

20. Interview with Field Marshal Abu Gazala in *Armed Forces Journal International*, September 1981, p. 49.

21. *The Arab Strategic Yearbook, 1988*, pp. 657, 658, 659, 660.

22. Charles Hermann, "Decision Structure and Process Influences on Foreign Policy," in Maurice A. East, S. Salmore, and C. Hermann (eds.), *Why Nations Act* (Beverly Hills, Calif.: Sage Publications, 1978), pp. 69–102.

23. Hamdi Al-Taheri, *Five Years of Politics* (Cairo: Publisher not identified, 1982), pp. 21–23 (in Arabic).

24. Hermann, *op. cit.*

25. For a general survey of Soviet-Egyptian relations, see Karen Dawisha, *Soviet Foreign Policy Towards Egypt* (New York: St. Martin's Press, 1979), pp. 54–82.

26. Jon D. Glassman, *Arms for the Arabs: The Soviet Union and War in the Middle East* (Baltimore, Md.: Johns Hopkins University Press, 1975), p. 90.

27. Mohamed H. Heikal, *The Sphinx and the Commissar* (New York: Harper & Row, 1978), p. 219.

28. *The Arab Strategic Yearbook, 1988*, p. 671.

29. *Ibid.*, p. 670.

30. Saad Al-Shazly, *The Crossing of the Suez* (San Francisco: American Mideast Research, 1980), p. 50.

31. Ammon Sella, *Soviet Political and Military Conduct in the Middle East* (London: Macmillan, 1981), p. 31.

32. *Newsweek*, December 13, 1971, p. 43.

33. Shazly, *op. cit.*, p. 70.

34. *The Arab Strategic Yearbook, 1988*, p. 670.

35. *Ibid.*, p. 671.

36. K. Dawisha, *op. cit.*, p. 76.

37. *Communist Aid Activities in Non-Communist Less Developed Countries, 1979* (Washington, D.C.: Foreign National Center, 1980), p. 7.

38. Alan H. Smith, "The Influence of Trade on Soviet Relations with the Middle East," in A. Dawisha and Karen Dawisha (eds.), *The Soviet Union and the Middle East* (London: Heinemann Educational Books, 1982), pp. 110–111.

39. Christopher C. Shoemaker and John Spanier, *Patron-Client State Relationships: Multilateral Crises in the Nuclear Age* (New York: Praeger Publishers, 1984), pp. 26–44.

40. Mohamed H. Heikal, *The Road to Ramadan* (Glasgow: William Collins and Co., 1975), p. 202.

41. Christopher Madison, "U.S. Reducing Act in the Middle East," *National Journal* 28 (November 1981), p. 2107.

42. *Newsweek*, March 23, 1981, p. 35.

43. *The Arab Strategic Yearbook, 1988*, p. 667.

44. Quoted in Saad Eddin Ibrahim, "Superpowers in the Arab World," *Washington Quarterly* 4, 3 (Summer 1981), pp. 88–89.

45. *The Arab Strategic Yearbook, 1985*, p. 379.

46. *The Arab Strategic Yearbook, 1986*, pp. 465, 466.

47. *The Arab Strategic Yearbook, 1988*, p. 666.

48. A detailed treatment is found in Ann Mosely Lesch, *Irritants in the Egyptian-Israeli Relationship*, Universities Field Staff International, no. 34 (Indianapolis: UFSI, 1986).

49. *New York Times*, July 24, 1972.

6

The Dialectics of Domestic Environment and Role Performance: The Foreign Policy of Iraq

Ahmad Yousef Ahmad

Analyzing Iraqi foreign policy is important for a number of reasons. First of all, Iraq has played a significant role in inter-Arab politics. Second, in the 1970s Iraq adhered to a Ba'thist, pan-Arabist socialist ideology and projected itself as a model for Arab revolutionary countries. Third, Iraq is an active member of the nonaligned countries. And finally, Iraq has played a significant role as an oil-producing country advocating producers' demands.

Iraq provides a prime example of the salience of domestic factors as influences on foreign policy orientation and behavior. As we shall see, geography and population structure are crucial variables in the determination of Iraqi policies. Iraq also provides an example of the "unfulfilled leadership role." Although it possesses most of the ingredients of national power, circumstances have always diluted this potentiality; a gap has always existed between possibility and performance, between role conception and role enactment.

DOMESTIC ENVIRONMENT

This analysis of Iraq's domestic environment will deal with geography, population and social structure, economic and military capabilities, and political structure. Emphasis will be placed on the population and social structure variable because of its significance in Iraq's foreign policy.

Geography

The geography of Iraq presents more constraints than opportunities for the country's foreign policy. Located in the Gulf area, and possessing elements of national power such as population and wealth, Iraq has always been a potential leader in the area. Ironically, throughout history not only has Iraq been unable to fulfill that role, it has also suffered from the invasion of great powers and their overbearing influence. In fact, Iraq never achieved the capabilities inherent in its geographic position.

The geography of Iraq is distinguished by the number and identity of adjacent countries. Iraq is bounded by six countries: on the north by Turkey, on the east by Iran, on the south by Kuwait, on the southwest by Saudi Arabia and Jordan, and on the northwest by Syria. This maximizes Iraq's national security problems, particularly in the light of population structures and resource availability in the area. Bordered by deserts in the south and a multitude of passes in the north, Iraq is virtually without defense against invasion.[1]

Two examples of vulnerability are Iraq's borders with Iran and its sources of surface water supply. The southern portion of the frontier with Iran, below Basra, follows the course of the Shatt Al-Arab waterway and has been a subject of conflict between the two states for a long time. From 1936 to 1975 Iraq controlled the whole waterway, a situation that became increasingly unacceptable to Iran. In March 1975 the two countries signed an agreement in Algiers by which the border was restored to the pre-1936 Thalweg line, dividing the countries in the middle of the deepest shipping channel in the waterway.[2] For a variety of reasons to be discussed in the analysis of the Iraq-Iran war, Iraq unilaterally abrogated that agreement in September 1980, and the border dispute came to the fore again. The two countries were engaged in a war that lasted for eight years, and the border dispute is still a primary source of conflict.

The other example concerns the water supply. Unlike the situation in other Arab oil-producing countries, the pivotal role played by oil in the Iraqi economy has not diminished the importance of the agricultural sector. The central region around Baghdad and the southern area of Iraq constitute the principal agricultural zone of the country. Its two rivers, the Euphrates and the Tigris, are the only sources of water. The Euphrates, like the Tigris, rises in the Armenian mountains of Turkey, but unlike the Tigris (1,850 km), which enters Iraq directly from Turkey, the Euphrates (2,333 km) flows first through Syria (675 km) and then Iraq (1,200 km) till it joins the Tigris.[3] In this context, geography has been relatively unkind to Iraq in the sense that the country's political frontiers have left its vital sources of surface water supply in the hands of neighboring, and not always friendly states.[4]

Population and Social Structure

There is every evidence to suggest that understanding Iraqi foreign policy through population and social structure is a promising perspective. The Iraqi population was estimated in mid-1986 at 16.5 million.[5] On the whole Iraq is underpopulated and could support a larger number of inhabitants.[6] The loss of lives resulting from the eight years of war obviously did not improve this situation. This explains President Saddam Hussein's opposition to campaigns of birth control or any attempts to reduce the annual growth rate, estimated at 3.6% in the years 1980–1986.[7]

A relevant feature of Iraq's population composition is its age structure. The Iraqis are an exceptionally young people; by the late 1970s one in five was under ten years old, and two in three were under 25.[8] Another feature is the lack of skilled labor and managerial personnel. Particularly in the 1970s, there was a shortage of skilled labor required to implement the vast schemes of agricultural and industrial development that were contemplated or in the process of execution.[9] The Iraq-Iran war aggravated the situation. More important, however, is the ethnic composition of the population. Steeped in the tradition of confessionalism and communal politics, Iraqi society remains a mosaic of religious, linguistic, and regional groups.[10]

From an ethnic perspective, in addition to the Arabs and the Kurds who together constitute about 95% of the population, there are other ethnic groups such as the Turkomans, the Persians, the Lurs, and the Armenians. With the exception of the Kurds and to a lesser degree the Persians, it could be said that these minority groups have practically no relevance to foreign policy.[11] The Kurds, who speak a language of Indo-European origin, account for about 15 to 20% of Iraq's population. They number over 1.5 million and may be approaching 3 million. Most Iraqi Kurds live in the north and northeast of Iraq—the region contiguous with the Kurdish zones of Turkey and Iran.[12]

Religiously speaking, Iraq has both Christian and Jewish minorities. However, the most politically relevant division is to be found within Iraq's Islamic majority itself. Since the days of Caliph Ali (656–661 A.D.) Moslems in general, and Iraqi Moslems in particular, have been divided into Shi'ites (the followers of Ali) and Sunnites (the followers of orthodox Islamic law). Iraqi Shi'ites make up 55 to 60% of the population.[13] In geographical terms, northern Iraq is largely Sunni; Baghdad itself is divided between Sunni and Shi'i Islam; and southern Iraq is under strong Shi'i influence.[14]

The main cleavages in Iraqi population structure (i.e., the ethnic division between Arabs and Kurds, and the religious one between Sunnis and Shi'ites) are not mutually exclusive. Apart from some different religious practices from Sunni Arabs, Iraqi Kurds are Sunnis.[15] The Sunni-Shi'i division has some economic and social implications. Sunni Moslems are in general wealthier than the Shi'ites.[16]

The Kurdish issue represents one of the most important linkages between population structure and Iraq's foreign policy, especially at the regional level. Before World War I, the Kurds lived under two regimes, the Ottoman Empire and the Qajar dynasty of Iran. After the fall of the Ottoman Empire, and as a result of their cordial relations with the victorious European power, the Kurds were promised under the Treaty of Sèvres an autonomous Kurdistan and, "if they should show that they wanted it," the right to independence.[17] However, their hopes were short-lived and in 1923 the Treaty of Lausanne, which replaced that of Sèvres, divided Kurdistan between Turkey, Iran, Iraq, Syria, and the Soviet Union.[18]

The change of heart was dictated in large measure by international oil interests. The British and French were interested in seeing Iraq acquire the Mosul region because of their joint control of the Iraqi-based Turkish Petroleum Company. The United States also sided with the British and French because of the inclusion of United States oil interests in the Turkish Petroleum Company.[19]

Not only did oil interests directly cause the splintering of Kurdistan and the resultant Kurdish problem for Iraq; they continued to be a main source of conflict in the years to come. Among the few bonds that kept the Iraqi Kurds united were their continuous demands for an autonomous region including the oil-rich province of Kirkuk (which produces approximately 70% of Iraq's oil), and sharing of oil revenues.[20]

Between 1919 and 1932 many tribal uprisings took place in Iraqi Kurdistan.[21] During the 1930s and 1940s, the Kurds, under the leadership of Mullah Mustafa Barzani, engaged the government forces in intermittent guerrilla warfare. In the mid-1940s, the situation took a rather dramatic turn. With Soviet encouragement and military support by troops stationed in northern Iran (1941–1946), the Kurds in Iran declared their independence and the establishment of the Republic of Mahabad. Barzani moved several thousand of his tribal troops from Iraq into the new republic, where he fought against the Iranian army. After the Soviets had withdrawn their troops from Iran, the republic came to an end. Barzani and the remnant of his army crossed over to the Soviet Union, where he stayed until 1959 when he was allowed to return to Iraq.[22]

Between the mid-1940s and the overthrow of the monarchy in Iraq in 1958, there were no major disturbances in the Kurdish area of Iraq. The Kurds hailed the 1958 revolution in the hope that the new regime would be more sympathetic to their cause. Indeed the revolutionary regime responded positively. Constitutionally, the Arabs and the Kurds were considered partners in the Iraqi fatherland and their national rights within the unity of Iraq were acknowledged. One of the three members of the "Sovereignty Council" established to undertake the responsibilities of the president was a Kurd, and another Kurd was included in the first cabinet. Moreover, all Kurdish political prisoners were released and Barzani and his followers were permitted to return from the Soviet Union.

A phase of cooperative relations between the government and the Kurds followed. This was best manifested when the Kurds formed for a while an important element of the power base of Abdel Karim Qasem's regime. In fact, the main reason for the cooperation between Qasem and the Kurds was their common opposition to Arab nationalist forces in Iraq. When the Kurds made demands that Qasem perceived as secessionist, he turned against them and in the spring of 1961, the Kurds renewed their revolt against the regime.[23]

Between 1961 and 1975 a pattern of stalemated civil war persisted despite several temporary truces, negotiations, and a number of changes in the regime. In 1975, however, the Iraqi army was able to achieve a major military victory over the Kurds. Although there were reports afterwards of renewed skirmishing, it was not serious enough to challenge the government's military achievement of 1975.[24]

It is not true, however, that the Kurdish conflict was stabilized only by military means. The revolt of 1961, which lasted fourteen years, and the military resistance of the Kurds made it inevitable to seek a political solution and to respond to Kurdish demands. Apart from the above-mentioned "oil demands," the Kurds pressed for a free hand in handling their own affairs. They argued that in order to preserve this freedom as well as their national identity, the Kurdish area should be granted autonomy, Kurdish should be made the official language, and only Kurds should be given government appointments in these areas.[25] Because of the high cost of the long war, both parties showed a readiness for compromise. The government moved gradually toward recognition of the national rights of the Kurds, and the Kurds were ready on more than one occasion to accept a formula that did not completely satisfy their demands.[26]

In March 1970, the Iraqi government reached an agreement with the Kurds. The agreement satisfied almost all apart from "oil demands."[27] The war continued after the agreement, and it was through a combination of diplomacy and force that the conflict was considerably stabilized in 1975. The crucial factor in terminating the war was Iraq's agreement with Iran whereby the latter, the Kurds' main source of supply and support, agreed to abandon that role.

The Kurdish problem has a negative impact on the economic and military capabilities of Iraq. It also influenced Iraqi policy toward the issue of Arab unity. Over the years the government of Iraq entered into a series of political and military agreements to achieve unity with several Arab states. However, the Kurdish issue acted as a constraint and this explains in part Iraq's failure to pursue an active unionist policy even when pro-union groups were in power.[28]

Kurdish opposition to Iraqi union with other Arab countries was both ideological and political. As early as 1960, the Kurds categorically rejected the idea that Iraq was part of the Arab world on the ground that historically, Kurdistan was never considered part of Arab lands. The

Kurdish stance in this respect was that the "Iraqi Republic consists of a part of the Kurdish nation, whose country is Kurdistan, and a part of the Arab nation, whose country is the great Arab homeland." This Kurdish ideological opposition continued even after the 1970 agreement. In other words, the autonomy promised the Kurds according to the agreement was not enough to make them abandon their ideological stance.[29]

The relevance of the Kurdish conflict to an understanding of Iraq's foreign policy was not limited to the Iraqi position in Arab affairs. It was also felt in the broader regional context. As in other civil war situations, the war against the Kurds created an environment for external intervention.[30] For its part, the Kurdish leadership saw increasing foreign involvement in the conflict as instrumental in forcing the Iraqi government to give more concessions. Most prominent as an interventionist power was Iran, which had more than one reason to involve itself. One was the Shatt Al-Arab issue. Another was the struggle for influence in the Gulf area. A third was to check Iraq's radical and revolutionary regional policies and to divert the attention of its leadership toward domestic issues. In the 1980s, the Iranians aimed at undermining the Iraqi war effort through intervening in the Kurdish issue.

Economic Capability

Oil is the principal source of wealth in Iraq. By the end of the 1970s, output from the oil sector (entirely owned by the state) was estimated to constitute about 60% of Iraq's GNP, and oil revenues accounted for four-fifths of the country's foreign exchange receipts. Income remained stable in the early 1960s at 120–135 million Iraqi dinars* (ID), but in the fiscal year ending March 31, 1972, oil revenues had risen to ID 354 million as a result of increased production and revised agreements with the oil companies. The improvement was halted for a short time by the nationalization of the Iraq Petroleum Company (IPC) in 1972, which led to a temporary loss of production. As a result of price increases since 1973, the volume of oil revenues[31] has increased correspondingly (see Table 6.1).

The future of Iraqi oil seems promising. A favorable factor was the discovery in 1975 of major new oil fields.[32] In terms of both proven and probable reserves, the published 1978 CIA estimate for Iraq was 36 billion barrels, a fraction of Saudi Arabia's 150 billion, and behind Kuwait's 71 billion, Iran's 60 billion, the Soviet Union's 40 billion, and the United States' 39 billion. However, in both Saudi Arabia and Iran

---

*From September 1949 to August 1971 an Iraqi dinar equalled $2.80; between December 1971 and February 1973 it was worth $3.04; between 1974 and 1980, $3.38. During the war with Iran, its value had considerably deteriorated. From 1986 to 1988 an Iraqi dinar was worth $0.31.

TABLE 6.1 Iraq's Oil Revenues, 1970–1985 (in millions US$)

Year	1970	1971	1972	1973	1974	1975	1976	1977	1978	1979	1980	1981	1982	1983	1984	1985
Revenue	521	840	575	1,843	5,700	7,500	8,500	9,631	10,200	21,291	25,981	10,400	10,100	9,700	11,200	11,900

Source: Figures for 1970 through 1980, *Middle East Economic Survey* 25, 1 (October 19, 1981), supplement, p. 7; figures for 1981 through 1985, the Arab League, *Arab Unified Economic Report, 1986*, Supplement 6-13 (in Arabic).

old oil has been pumped faster than new oil has been found, whereas exploration activities in Iraq since 1977 have steadily expanded proven reserves and sustainable capacity levels. The latest estimates of proven Iraqi oil reserves (end of 1987) is 100 billion barrels.[33] In February 1981, an Iraqi diplomat stated that "The world is approaching a period of time when dependence on oil will increase. . . . If we recall that we have established the fact that Iraq is considered to be one of the strongest countries in terms of oil reserves, then we can conclude that the role of Iraq will increase in importance in the next two decades."[34]

One of the positive features of the Iraqi economy is the fact that Iraq is one of the few Arab countries with the potential for a balanced economic development. Roughly half of Iraq's 443,000 square kilometers is arable, and of this, only about one-fourth is under cultivation. If the agricultural sector were fully developed, it could feed twice the present population.[35] The Iraqi leadership has shown considerable awareness of the necessity to build a self-sustained economy. In 1978 Saddam Hussein stated that Iraqi strategy was to ensure that when oil lost its importance as a source of energy, or when it was exhausted, the Iraqi economy would be able to sustain the planned growth rate.[36] The relation between a balanced economy and an active foreign policy is clear in the mind of Saddam Hussein.[37]

Oil has provided Iraq with a considerable capability, especially since 1973. Oil revenue has made heavy increases in military expenditure possible and enhanced Iraqi bargaining power in arms purchases. The Iraqi government has been able to use grants and loans as instruments of foreign policy. The main source of weakness in the Iraqi economic situation is, of course, its dependence on oil, a dependence that Iraq had plans to ease through an ambitious program of economic diversification.

Unfortunately, the war with Iran drastically affected those plans. As Adeed Dawisha put it, "The Iranian bombing of Iraq's oil industry and infrastructure is bound to slow Iraq's massive efforts at industrialization and modernization. Given the damage to Iraq's oil industry, national income will be reduced drastically, and what is left will have to be used to re-equip the armed forces."[38] A senior official of the Iraqi Ministry of Planning admitted the government's inability to initiate new economic projects under the circumstances. He also admitted that the oil sector has been affected because of the halt in oil exports through the Gulf and Syria (as a result of the latter's support of Iran in the war).[39] Saddam Hussein stated in 1983 that the first two years of the war went without economic hardships. However, it was natural, according to Hussein, to make some adjustments in the third year of the war. All Iraqis were asked to adopt certain patterns of rational economic behavior with a view to protecting the national economy and coping with the requirements of war.[40] Despite these measures, Iraq's prewar financial reserves of over $30 billion were replaced by a $60 billion debt.[41]

To promote productivity and conserve foreign exchange, in early 1987 the government initiated a series of steps aimed at promoting private investment and reducing the bureaucracy that regulates economic activity.[42] Such a process of privatization is expected, according to its advocates, to have clear economic benefits. It is too early to evaluate the final outcome, but if economic liberalization works, it will have repercussions on Iraq's domestic and international affairs.

Military Capability

The two main resources for Iraq's military capability are its large population and its oil revenues. In terms of population, Iraq ranks fifth in the Arab world (after Egypt, Morocco, Algeria, and Sudan) and seventh in the Middle East (if one adds Turkey and Iran). In 1980 Iraq had the third largest army in the Arab world (242,500 soldiers after Egypt's 367,000 and Syria's 247,500) and the fifth in the Middle East (if one adds Israel's 629,600 and Turkey's 567,000).[43] During most of the 1970s, oil revenues enabled Iraq to be third in military expenditures in the Arab world (after Egypt and Saudi Arabia) and sixth in the Middle East.

According to 1987 figures, however, Iraq now has the largest army in the Arab world and the Middle East (one million soldiers) with Iran coming second (654,500). In terms of military expenditure, Iraq ranks second to Saudi Arabia ($13,996 million and $16,235 million respectively).[44]

Although such figures in the Middle East do not necessarily reflect real military power, the Iraqi experience in the Iran-Iraq war should not be ignored. In fact, the Iraqi army has emerged from it as one of the most powerful armies in the Middle East. At the very least, it is the largest and most experienced one.

The war revealed the use of a number of new capabilities on the part of Iraq. It is widely believed that Iraq used chemical weapons on a number of occasions. Iraq was also able to modify the Soviet Scud missiles, successfully increasing their range to reach Teheran. This was probably achieved by reducing the weight of explosives carried by the missile. Reports indicate that Iraq may be cooperating with Egypt and Argentina to produce a 700-km-range missile.[45]

An important aspect of Iraq's military power is the government's plan to establish a nuclear capability. Using the leverage of oil in 1976, an agreement with France was signed to supply Iraq with a nuclear research center containing two reactors and three years' supply of enriched uranium. Iraq also signed agreements with Brazil and Italy for the supply of uranium and nuclear technology. Although Iraqi leaders consistently denied any intention of using the nuclear reactors for military purposes,[46] Israel was unconvinced. On June 7, 1981, the Israeli air force destroyed the Iraqi nuclear reactor near Baghdad only three months before it was due to begin operations.[47] Although President Saddam Hussein has emphasized that Iraq will continue to pursue plans for its own nuclear capability,[48] it is unlikely that the country will be able to do so in view of the economic hardships resulting from the war with Iran.

The bombing of the Iraqi nuclear reactor raises the issue of constraints on Iraq's military capability. Israel is not the only constraint or even the most important one in this respect. An analysis of the regional use of the Iraqi army in the 1960s and the 1970s shows that both geography and population structure are unfavorable factors that seriously limit military strength.

For two decades the Kurdish conflict severely limited the use of the military as a means of conducting Iraqi foreign policy. For example, an anti-Kurdish general offensive in 1965 was estimated to include 40,000 to 50,000 troops. In 1974, the government dispatched—for the same reason—three army divisions totaling 48,000 troops, or nearly half of its armed forces. These divisions included Iraq's best armored units. At the beginning of August 1974 the government launched its biggest offensive, involving some 100,000 troops.[49]

Geography and population structure have been sources of conflict with Iran over the disputed Shatt Al-Arab, the Kurdish problem, and Sunni-Shi'ite relations. For the first time since the Second World War, these and other sources of conflict led the two countries to a war lasting eight years. Although Iraq emerged from this war more powerful from a military point of view, the constraints on its military capabilities must not be underestimated. The cease-fire did not bring about a final resolution to the conflict, and Iraq still has to deal with the heavy economic burden the war left behind.

Political Structure

According to the 1970 Iraqi constitution and its 1973 amendments, the Revolutionary Command Council (RCC) is the supreme political organ and the highest legislative body. It oversees all foreign and domestic policies and elects (by two-thirds vote) one of its members as president of the RCC and the republic and another as vice-president. The RCC has the right to relieve any of its members or add new ones up to a maximum of twelve. Although the president is theoretically responsible to the RCC, the constitution makes no reference to his term of office or to the procedure for unseating him, except by resignation. The president is the chief executive and the commander-in-chief of the armed forces. He nominates members of the council of ministers.

The constitution also calls for a national assembly representing all political, economic, and social groups in the country. The assembly is responsible for considering bills proposed by the RCC or by one-fourth of the assembly members. In initiating legislation, the assembly may not deal with military matters or with issues of internal security. According to the constitution, when a difference of opinion takes place between the RCC and the National Assembly, it is resolved through a joint meeting of the two councils.[50] In actuality, the National Assembly was not even formed until July 1980. In that month, more than 7 million Iraqis elected 250 assembly members. This number included an over-whelming majority from the Ba'th party, 75%, and all the members of the RCC who had decided to stand. The exercise was repeated in October 1984 with more or less the same results.[51] The assembly did not play a significant role in Iraqi politics, hampered as it was by its restricted powers and the war situation.

Since 1970, the Iraqi political system has been dominated by the socialist Arab Ba'th party. In theory, the Iraqi Ba'th party is a branch of the same party that rules Syria, but because of strong ideological and political differences, the two regimes are at odds with each other. In an attempt to broaden its political base in November 1971, the Ba'th party issued a National Action Charter and initiated negotiations with other political parties. In 1973 the Ba'th and the Communist party formed the National Progressive Front.[52]

President Saddam Hussein considered the front to be a first in the sense that the Ba'th had launched a revolution alone, assumed political power successfully, and then voluntarily invited other revolutionary political powers to share that responsibility.[53] However, the emphasis on the special role of the Ba'th in the front was a source of tension. The Ba'th leaders tended to minimize the role and strength of other political forces in the country, including their single partner in the front. In 1978, a group of Communists were executed after being convicted of conducting political activities inside the army, an act prohibited by law and by the front documents. The execution invited severe criticism by Communist countries, and Hussein took issue with this criticism.[54] In 1980 President Hussein acknowledged the problems within the front.[55] In reality, the Ba'th remained the sole governing party in Iraq.

During the second half of the 1970s Saddam Hussein had been the strongman of Iraq behind ex-president Hassan Al-Bakr. For several years he maintained a low profile as vice-president of the RCC; then, on July 17, 1979, Saddam Hussein assumed the presidency when Al-Bakr, on grounds of ill health, handed in his resignation.[56]

Until the eruption of war with Iran in 1980, there was strong evidence that Saddam Hussein had achieved a considerable degree of stability in Iraq. Although the internal security apparatus must have played an important role in this respect, the economic and social policies of the regime contributed a great deal as well. The war was a serious challenge, to the Iraqi regime. The improved Iraqi performance since late 1987, however, appears to have enhanced the regime's legitimacy. Although activities by some opposition groups have been reported since the cease-fire, there are no indications that they pose any real threat to the regime.

In November 1988, a few months after the cease-fire, President Saddam Hussein unveiled a program of political reforms allowing the establish-ment of political parties in opposition to the Ba'th. The official rationale for this was that all the Iraqis, of different ethnic, ideological, and religious backgrounds, had participated in the war and therefore had earned the right to play an institutionalized role in the decision-making process.

In fact, the third National Assembly, elected in April 1989, is charged with enacting the necessary laws legalizing new political parties. No one is expecting the emergence of a Western-style liberal democracy. The Iraqi president has referred to the fact that because Iraqi society is different from Western societies, different practices are to be expected. However, Egypt's similar experiment with liberalization since the mid-1970s has led to a decline in the regime's control over the political process, even though a Western-type democracy has not emerged. Similar developments could take place in Iraq in the coming years if the political system follows its normal course.

FOREIGN POLICY ORIENTATION

In this section, Iraqi foreign policy orientation is presented through an analysis of Ba'th party ideology and the views of Saddam Hussein. Hussein's speeches reflect definite views on the global and regional systems and of Iraq's role in the world. Without underestimating the impact of the global system, Hussein maintains that the crucial factors in the making of Iraq's policies and priorities are primarily domestic and regional.[57] His writings and speeches reveal his awareness of a distinct Iraqi role in regional and global politics.

The Global System

The Iraqi president holds a consistent view of the current phase of the evolution of the global system. The two distinguishing elements in his world view are: (1) that the global order is moving from bipolarity to multipolarity, necessitating certain Iraqi and Arab roles to influence the process; and (2) that the impossibility of a direct war between the superpowers, because of its nuclear implications, had led to the proliferation of small wars by proxy between Third World countries. Saddam Hussein perceives the world as going through a process of fast and radical change, similar to the period during and immediately after the Second World War. However, current global change is more basic and more comprehensive. It will lead by the turn of the century to a multipolar world and to the emergence of new centers of global power and influence. These centers will include China, Western Europe, and Japan. This new multipolar system is perceived as a welcome development for Iraq and other Arab countries because it will increase their freedom of action. Enhancing this development requires an Iraqi and an Arab "role" to influence the process of change. Concretely, this would involve neutralizing or even securing the support of one or more of the new centers with regard to Arab strategic objectives such as achieving Arab unity and pursuing the conflict with Zionism. Arabs assume that they have a role to perform in the shaping of a new global system because, they believe, no superpower can afford to follow a policy that is opposed by a great number of small countries.[58]

Another dimension of the Iraqi president's perception of the global system is his understanding of the growing tensions and contradictions between the superpowers. Since the global balance of power does not allow direct wars between the superpowers, wars by proxy take place between pro-Eastern and pro-Western developing countries.[59] This situation does not favor the interests of Third World countries. There are no reliable sources on President Hussein's perception of the new Soviet-American détente, which has appeared since the mid-1980s.

In addition to these two characteristic views, Hussein shares most of the views of revolutionary Third World leaders on colonialism, equality between nations, national liberation movements, and the need for a new international economic order. He also shares the view that the developed, industrialized countries are to be blamed for failing to establish that new order.[60]

For Saddam Hussein, the core of Iraq's foreign policy is nonalignment, considered to be the best strategy to deal with the changing global system. First of all, as an Arab nationalist, Hussein is not inclined to favor either of the two superpowers, and in his speeches he refers to them indiscriminately. Second, nonalignment was more necessary and possible in the context of mounting tension and increasing conflict between great powers than in a period of détente. Finally, the nonalignment movement has a special role and responsibility in building the New International Economic Order.[61]

The Regional System

The ideology of the Ba'th party is primarily a nationalist ideology based on the concept of the oneness of the Arab nation, a nation that has a glorious past and a mission to fulfill in the future. The Ba'th ideology underlines three historical goals for the Arab nation: (1) unification of the existing, artificially created Arab states into a larger Arab political entity; (2) freedom from all foreign influence and hegemony; and (3) socialism. Although Ba'thist writers do not dwell much on the implications of their ideology for foreign policy in general, they do direct their attention into inter-Arab and regional issues. To be a Ba'thist means that you hold an ideology perceived as valid for all Arab countries. It does not accept the legitimacy of existing political divisions and frontiers and seeks to change them. Thus, it is inherently a change-oriented ideology. Other implications follow. The order of priority given to Ba'thist objectives (unity, freedom, socialism) opens the way, for example, for collaboration with conservative Arab regimes. Adherence to the concept of the Arab nation leads Ba'thist leaders to sympathize with, if not directly support, the demands of groups of Arab origin living in non-Arab states—groups such as the Eritreans in Ethiopia.

Saddam Hussein's statements advocate an Iraqi regional role very similar to that of Nasser's Egypt in the 1950s and the 1960s. In June 1975 he openly espoused such a role, stating: "In brief, we want Iraq to play a leading role in the area and especially in the Arab homeland. We want Iraq to play a leading role in the consolidation of anti-imperialist policy at the international level."[62] In October 1979, a few months after assuming the presidency, he spoke of a historical role for Iraq. According to Hussein, for centuries Iraq and the Arab nation had been denied the congruent elements of national power: wealth, leadership, ideology, and organization. Arab states possessing one of these elements were sadly bereft of the others. Now, for the first time, Iraq had all of them; it had the credentials for a historical Arab role.[63]

This perception of Iraq's historical and regional role was obviously altered by the experience of the war. The regional and global constraints on Iraq were made abundantly clear to the Iraqi president. His efforts at rebuilding the country reveal a more pragmatic approach in this respect.

FOREIGN POLICY DECISION-MAKING

As in many other Third World countries, sufficient and accurate data on the details of foreign policy decision-making in Iraq are simply not available. The existing literature on Iraq is confusing, gives contradictory information, and in many cases is obsolete.

We have already seen that according to the constitution, the RCC oversees all matters of foreign policy. It declares general mobilization and war, accepts armistice, and concludes peace (Article 43-B). It ratifies treaties and international agreements (Article 43-D). We have also seen that the president is entrusted with the responsibility of preserving the independence of the country and its territorial integrity (Articles 58-A and 58-G). The president appoints Iraq's diplomatic representatives abroad (Article 58-E). Although the constitutional amendment of 1973 created a council of ministers as a separate institution, this council is headed by the president (Article 60) and is primarily concerned with domestic issues (Article 61). Finally, our analysis has already disclosed the limited powers of the National Assembly and the unfavorable circumstances that followed its formation in June 1980. The assembly is headed by a member of the RCC.

We may conclude that foreign policy decision-making in Iraq is influenced by a very limited group. The president, Saddam Hussein, is the principal decision-maker because of his powerful constitutional position and because of his personality and style. In this context, three questions are in order: What is the role of the Ba'th party; what is the role of political institutions other than the RCC and the presidency; and what, if any, are the political and institutional constraints on the president?

As to the party: all members of the RCC, with the exception of the Kurdish vice-president, must belong to the Ba'th leadership.[64] However, there is no evidence that the party plays an influential role in foreign policy–making. Indeed, President Saddam made the point that it was not necessary to have total congruence between the party's positions and those of the state. Of course, both follow the same strategy, but the state has to adapt to changing circumstances and conduct day-to-day affairs; the party does not. Saddam illustrated this distinction with examples drawn from the foreign policy field, pointing out the need for the state to tolerate and deal with reactionary Arab regimes that are condemned by the party.[65]

As regards the role of political institutions, the decision-making process is without a doubt dominated by the RCC and the president. However, at a meeting with Iraqi ambassadors in Western Europe and Japan, Saddam Hussein emphasized the importance of accurate information for correct decision-making:

> One of the most essential conditions for a successful decision is the availability of accurate information. Hence, when headquarters or rear command wants to make a decision, it must rely on the data supplied by the front lines or the observation posts, as they say in the armed forces . . . ambassadors will be expected not only to transmit information but also to make a preliminary analysis. . . . Don't hesitate because of any thought that your information, opinions and analysis may not be needed by the center which has better information. The mind of the command and headquarters cannot function without the eyes and the minds of those in the front lines.[66]

Thus, Iraq, as does Egypt, comes closest to the leader-staff style of decision-making. The president is the center of the process, and other individuals and institutions participate as advisors.

In the matter of constraints, we have to distinguish between institutional-legal and social-political constraints. Although Saddam Hussein may be relatively free from institutional constraints, he is subject to a variety of internal constraints, determined by geography and population structure, that severely limit his freedom of action. Iraqi leaders cannot afford to take a serious step toward unity with another Arab country without taking the Kurdish reaction into account. The Shi'ites constitute another constraint. Saddam's decision to go to war was partly a reaction to revolutionary Islamic appeals to Iraqi Shi'ites.

There are no indications of a significant change in foreign policy decision-making. Despite some changes in Iraqi internal politics, the unresolved conflict with Iran and the leadership style of Saddam Hussein do not point to any liberalization of decision-making in this area.

FOREIGN POLICY BEHAVIOR

In this section, we review Iraq's foreign policy behavior at the global and regional levels. From a global standpoint, our analysis includes

Iraq's relations with the superpowers, Western Europe, and Japan; its non-aligned status; and its oil policies. From a regional standpoint we will deal primarily with Iraq's policy toward other Arab countries and Iran.

The Global Level

Relations with the United States. Iraq's Ba'thist ideology creates a potential for conflict rather than cooperation with the United States because of U.S. support for Israel and because of the nature of U.S. interests in the Arab world, especially in oil. Iraqi-U.S. relations were mainly influenced by ideological considerations in the late 1960s and early 1970s, but practical necessities have affected these relations since the late 1970s.

Because of the United States' pro-Israeli policy in the war of 1967, a number of Arab countries, including Iraq, severed diplomatic relations with the United States. According to a senior Iraqi diplomat, the Carter administration initiated contacts with Iraq to restore the relationship, and a number of emissaries were sent to that effect. In Baghdad they were told that as the United States had not changed its unconditional support of Israel, Iraq could find no adequate reason to restore diplomatic relations between the two countries.[67]

From the mid-1970s the deterioration of Soviet-Iraqi relations and the Iraqi rapprochement with prerevolutionary Iran created a new context for U.S.-Iraqi relations. Despite Iraq's leading role in mobilizing Arab states against the Camp David Accords and the Egyptian-Israeli treaty, Iraq and the United States later found common ground, albeit for different reasons, in their desire to contain, if not undermine, the impact of Khomeini's revolutionary Iran.

In the 1980s there was a gradual Iraqi rapprochement with the West. On April 14, 1980, National Security Advisor Zbigniew Brzezinski stated: "We see no fundamental incompatibility of interests between the United States and Iraq. . . . We do not feel that American-Iraqi relations need to be frozen in antagonism."[68] In 1981 President Saddam Hussein announced that Washington had submitted certain suggestions through its representative in Baghdad to strengthen the relations between the two countries. The Iraqi government approved some of these suggestions, granting the U.S. representative in Baghdad a sort of diplomatic status (the right to be informed of Iraqi positions and to meet Iraqi officials for consultations) and opening the possibility of exchanging visits or holding meetings between representatives of the two countries. The Iraqi government also allowed U.S. representatives in Baghdad to have communications facilities similar to those of other embassies.[69]

This changing environment led to more consultations, including two meetings between the U.S. and Iraqi foreign ministers in 1983. Iraq's attitude toward restoring diplomatic relations became ambivalent. In 1982 Iraqi officials, including President Saddam Hussein, referred to having diplomatic relations with the United States as natural.[70] Iraqi statements no longer made a direct link between restoring the relations and U.S. support to Israel. In July 1983 Tarek Aziz, deputy prime minister and minister of foreign affairs, stated that "we have clearly informed the American side that the Iraqi leadership does not think well of restoring diplomatic relations while the war with Iran is still going on."[71] No reference to U.S. policy toward the Arab-Israeli conflict was mentioned in this context.

As the war continued, however, Iraq's need for support from the international community led it to alter its position on several issues, including relations with the United States. In October 1983, Saddam Hussein indicated that Iraq might possibly resume relations with the United States regardless of its position toward the Arab-Israeli conflict. A year later, in October 1984, he stated that the right time for Iraq to consider the best means of conducting relations with the United States may be after the U.S. elections. Six weeks later, in November 1984, full diplomatic relations were restored between the two countries.[72]

From the American point of view, Iraq's foreign policy had begun to display significant changes, taking more moderate stands on such key issues as the Arab-Israeli conflict and international terrorism. In addition, the deterioration in Iraqi-Soviet relations in the 1980s was probably a catalyst in creating the Iraqi-U.S. rapprochement.

Relations with the Soviet Union. Since the mid-1950s the Soviet Union has emerged as a global ally of Arab nationalist regimes. However, the nature of pan-Arabist ideologies has limited Soviet-Arab relations. One source of tension stemmed from differing views of the role of Arab Communists in the politics of their countries. This led to a rift with Egypt in the late 1950s and with Iraq in the 1970s. When the Ba'th party assumed power in July 1968, Iraqi-Soviet cooperation was already established, particularly in the economic field through Soviet participation in the development of the Iraqi oil industry. Relations reached a new height by the conclusion in April 1972 of a treaty of friendship and cooperation between the two countries. The treaty provided for full cooperation in political, economic, commercial, technical, cultural, and other fields, including regular consultations, defense support, and military cooperation.[73]

Thus Iraq was broadly perceived in the West as a Soviet satellite. In fact, sources of tension were gradually mounting. Internally, problems created by the Ba'thist-Communist front led in 1978 to the execution of some Iraqi Communists. At the regional level, there was considerable Iraqi dissatisfaction with the Soviet policy permitting Soviet Jews to emigrate to Israel,[74] and with the Soviet pro-Ethiopian policy against both Somalia and the Eritreans.[75] Since early 1980, Soviet intervention in Afghanistan has been officially condemned at the highest levels.[76]

However, the above symptoms of tension in Soviet-Iraqi relations appear minor when compared with their differing evaluations of the

Iranian revolution. The Iraqi leadership perceives it as a "reactionary" movement; the Soviets view the Iranian revolution as essentially anti-imperialist. This perception has affected Soviet policy toward the war between Iraq and Iran, delaying the delivery of Soviet arms purchased by Iraq. From the second half of 1981 there were signs of easing tension and calculated improvement in the relations. The Iraqi president declared at the press conference held after the bombing of the Iraqi nuclear reactor in June 1981 that the Soviets had expressed a desire to continue and to develop relations with Iraq. Military cooperation was resumed in 1982. In July 1983, Foreign Minister Aziz related the improvement in relations to an increasing Soviet understanding of the Iraqi view of the conflict with Iran.[77]

The tension in Iraqi-Soviet relations, however, did not entirely disappear. It became evident once more in 1987, as Soviet positions regarding the war became increasingly pro-Iranian. In 1989, the tension reached a new peak following the successful visit by the Iranian leader Rafsanjani to Moscow. The Iraqis were especially angered by the public commitment made by the Soviets during this visit to bolster Iranian defensive capabilities.

Relations with Western Europe and Japan. In our analysis of Iraq's foreign policy orientation, we have seen that the Iraqi leadership expects the evolution of a multipolar world and that the new centers of power will include Western Europe and Japan. We have also seen that President Saddam Hussein referred to the need for an Iraqi and Arab role to influence this process.

This attitude was encouraged in the case of France by the French policy adopted, especially since de Gaulle, toward the Arab-Israeli conflict. This led from the early 1970s to a pattern of close cooperation between Iraq and France in economic and military fields. According to Iraqi figures, in 1978 France was Iraq's fourth largest trading partner.[78] Increasingly, France became a major arms exporter to Iraq and was crucial in building Iraq's nuclear facilities. Cooperation in the field of oil will be dealt with later in this chapter.

The Federal Republic of Germany also has special relations with Iraq. West Germany was Iraq's second largest trading partner in 1978 and its first in 1977. In both years Western Europe came first as a region.[79] Iraq has a positive attitude toward Euro-Arab dialogue. Even when the third economic agreement was concluded between the European Economic Community (EEC) and Israel in 1975, Saddam Hussein called for a "calculated" Arab reaction. He criticized those who proposed an end to the Euro-Arab dialogue. He implied that such an attitude would, in the final analysis, serve U.S. interests.[80]

Iraq's relations with West European countries have also encountered difficulties. Saddam Hussein once accused West German officials of trying to impose unequal relations and accused the German mass media of being hostile to Iraq.[81] He was also dissatisfied with the French reaction to the Israeli bombing of the French-built Iraqi nuclear reactor in June 1981.[82]

As for Japan, it became Iraq's number one trading partner in 1978.[83] In that year, the value of Iraqi-Japanese trade alone exceeded the value of Iraq's trade with all other Asian or socialist countries.

Iraq continued the policy of close cooperation with Western Europe and Japan during the war years. These relations became an important means of avoiding a recurrence of the isolation Iraq found itself in in the early 1980s through its strained relations with both superpowers.

Nonalignment. Analysis of the Iraqi leadership's perception of the global system reveals the central position of nonalignment. Iraq played a distinctive role in nonaligned summit meetings in the 1970s, and especially at the Havana conference in 1979. At that conference, Iraq called for more institutionalization of the movement and for the establishment of an international fund to help Third World countries offset the effects of inflation.[84] This fund was to have been financed by industrially developed countries and Third World oil-producing countries. Iraq was to host the 1982 summit meeting in Baghdad and Saddam Hussein was to become the spokesman of the nonaligned movement for the following three years. Because of the war, the meeting was postponed for a year and moved to New Delhi. Nevertheless, in a world of "increasing alignments," Iraq's foreign policy still reveals a substantial commitment to nonalignment. This is especially true with respect to its behavior toward the two superpowers as described earlier.

Oil Policy. Traditionally, Iraq has been opposed to the foreign oil concessions awarded by the British to the Iraq Petroleum Company in 1925. However, the Qasem regime (1958–1963) rejected nationalization as impractical, pressing instead for higher shares of oil profits. This led in 1961 to serious strains in relations with oil companies, which were unable to reach a settlement with the regime. Consequently, the Iraqi government expropriated all IPC concessionary areas not yet under production (i.e., 99.5% of the area for which it held prospecting rights). The government then enacted a law that authorized a state-owned Iraqi National Oil Company (INOC) to exploit all resources throughout the country except in the areas already being developed by the IPC and its associates.

Iraqi oil policy worked as a catalyst in improving relations with some countries, especially the Soviet Union and France. Both a French state-owned group of companies and the Soviet Union expressed willingness to enter into agreements with INOC for oil prospecting and exploration. The French group became a contractor under INOC, which held all proprietary rights pertaining to oil and installations to be constructed in Iraq. However, it was agreed that the French agency would receive from INOC 50% of the oil discovered in commercial quantities. On the other hand, INOC acquired Soviet loans totaling $72 million to develop the North Rumeila oil fields. In addition, Iraq received promises of technical cooperation from the Soviet Union and East European countries.

Notwithstanding these developments, the Iraqi government still received a major proportion of its oil income from the Western oil companies operating in the country. In early 1972, either for purely commercial reasons (as the IPC and its affiliates claimed) or to put pressure on the government (as the Iraqi regime perceived it), the Western oil companies reduced oil production in Iraq. The Iraqi government reacted on June 1, 1972, by nationalizing all IPC assets in Iraq. Again, this was a catalyst in promoting relations with the USSR and France (among other countries). To overcome the difficulties related to oil transportation and distribution, the Soviet Union had agreed to lease tankers to INOC. On the other hand, Iraq concluded an agreement with France for the sale of oil from the nationalized fields. Contracts were also made with Spain, Italy, Greece, India, Japan, and Brazil. By the end of 1972, it was clear that Iraq was coping with the marketing problem.[85]

From 1973 onwards, Iraq became an influential "hawk" in pushing for higher prices at the meetings of OPEC. President Saddam Hussein viewed raising oil prices as a reaction to the rising inflation in industrialized countries.[86] Iraq has developed a policy of relating production to its developmental needs and also to the oil needs of friendly countries.[87] Here again, the war had its dramatic effect on Iraqi policies. While Teheran consistently pressed for high prices even when it was clear that the market would not support them, Baghdad virtually ignored OPEC production restraints that were supposed to increase prices. High production served to maximize revenues needed for the war effort. Moreover, Iraq's oil reserves being larger than Iran's, it benefitted in the long run by keeping prices low enough to preserve its market share.[88]

The Regional Level

Inter-Arab Politics. In retrospect, the 1970s may be viewed as the decade most favorable to the fulfillment of Iraq's Arab role since the Second World War. This decade witnessed increasing political stability in Iraq and enhanced economic capability because of oil. The 1975 success in resolving the Kurdish problem and the signing of a new agreement with Iran concerning the Shatt Al-Arab were added favorable factors. With all these developments, the stage was set in the second half of the 1970s for an active Iraqi role in the Arab world. President Sadat provided the opportunity for Iraq to act by his conclusion of the Camp David Accords in September 1978. Traditionally, Iraq had followed an extremist line toward the Arab-Israeli conflict, and the Ba'thist regime opposed any kind of peaceful settlement. Iraq rejected Resolution 242, adopted in 1967, and all diplomatic initiatives based on it. Militarily, Iraq participated in the 1973 October War in support of Syria. The Camp David Accords were thus perceived by the Iraqi leadership as primarily serving the interests of Israel and diluting the potential for the Arab struggle against Israel in the next twenty years. With the emergence of more centers of global power and better Arab management of the conflict with Israel, Arabs would be able to achieve their goals, felt the Iraqi leaders. Hence the Camp David policy had to be contained and discredited.[89]

Opposition to the Camp David Accords took priority over all other Iraqi concerns. The Iraqis insisted that the Arabs unite against this grave threat, and Iraq led the formation of this united front. At the Baghdad Arab summit (November 1978), called to discuss concerted Arab action against Egypt, Iraq performed successfully in its new diplomatic role.[90] One outcome of the Baghdad summit was the improvement of Iraqi-Syrian relations. Iraq and Syria had been at odds with each other for a number of reasons. The first was a long-standing dispute over the distribution of the Euphrates water.[91] Then there was the Iraqi dependence on the transit routes across Syrian territory to the eastern Mediterranean terminals and disagreements over oil royalties.[92] In the 1970s, the alleged manipulation of Iraq's Shi'ites by the Syrian Alawite rulers was another source of tension.[93]

This Iraqi-Syrian rapprochement at the Baghdad summit was perceived by many Arabs as a promising development in the inter-Arab politics. It was hoped that through an Iraqi-Syrian alliance the strategic imbalance created by the Egyptian withdrawal from the military front with Israel would be redressed. However, relations soon became strained. Iraq accused Syria of supporting dissident elements and of following a policy that threatened Iraqi security and national integrity. Thus, it is not surprising that Syria chose to support Iran in its war with Iraq. Bearing out Iraqi accusations that Syria was involved indirectly in the war,[94] the Syrian government stopped the flow of Iraqi oil across its territory, inflicting considerable losses on Iraq. Thus, as soon as a cease-fire was arranged, Iraq turned its attention toward "punishing" Syria. It called for Syria's expulsion from the Arab League. Moreover, it involved itself in the Lebanese situation, throwing its weight into backing the Christian Lebanese forces with arms and money.[95]

It is interesting to observe the process of adaptation and change in Iraqi policy toward the Arab-Israeli conflict both during the Baghdad summit and afterwards. As Dawisha puts it:

> Iraq had a great stake in insuring the success of the Conference, but realized at an early stage the difficulties involved in reaching a position acceptable to all Arab states. . . . The Iraquis themselves were forced to temper their hitherto rigid revolutionary position. The Baghdad Summit appears to have given the Iraqi leaders a taste for diplomacy, as well as a greater awareness that moderate and pragmatic positions could prove far more effective than revolutionary orthodoxy in influencing Arab attitudes and policies.[96]

Saddam Hussein's proclamation, in February 1980, of an Arab National Charter emphasizing the strategy of national consensus was another sign of the new Iraqi moderation.[97] This strategy was suggested as the best way to deal with the Arab-Israeli conflict because no individual Arab country, regardless of its capabilities, could liberate Palestine alone.[98] Iraq accepted King Fahd's Fez formula, which provided a peaceful approach toward the settlement of the conflict with Israel and does not refer to the concept of a "secular, democratic Palestine." (The Fez formula is Fahd's Middle East plan, accepted in the Arab summit held in Fez in 1982.)

Iraq now accepts the Palestinian National Council (PNC) resolutions of November 1988, which recognized UN Security Council Resolutions 242 and 338 as one basis for settling the Palestinian issue, on condition that the right of self-determination be guaranteed to the Palestinian people. The PNC resolutions also declared an independent Palestinian state, based on the UN General Assembly Resolution 181, which had formerly endorsed the creation of a Jewish state in Palestine. Accordingly, it is believed that Iraq will support any consensus solution to the Palestinian question based on the previous principles.

The moderating influence of the war on Iraq's foreign policy was nowhere clearer than in the case of its relations with Egypt. The war situation made Iraq dependent on Egyptian military support in terms of arms and ammunition. Under Sadat and Mubarak, Egypt took a position of unreserved support of Iraq. The Iraqi leadership came to view the Egyptian absence from the Arab family as creating a strategic imbalance reflected in all Arab issues. It perceived that by 1983 circumstances in the Arab world were no longer what they had been in 1978. Two new factors were the Iranian challenge and the threat of further balkanization. The situation in Egypt was also different under Mubarak.[99] These developments led to the reestablishment of contracts with Egypt, the restoration of economic relations, the exchange of official visits, and finally the restoration of full diplomatic relations after the Amman Summit Conference in November 1987.

Moreover, in February 1989 Iraq founded with Egypt, North Yemen, and Jordan the Arab Cooperation Council. Since the council includes Egypt, Israel's only Arab peace partner, it may be interpreted as an indirect recognition by Iraq of the possibility of peaceful coexistence with Israel. The ostensible goals of the council have been expressed in economic terms, but political aspects are inevitably involved.

Conflict with Iran. Sources of conflict in Iraqi-Iranian relations were discussed earlier: geography, the contest for influence in the Gulf area, and population structure. Before 1958, these issues were overshadowed by a similarity in monarchical political regimes and by their common alignment with the West. The Iraqi revolution of 1958 brought the sources of conflict to the fore.

Iranian intervention in support of the Iraqi Kurds began soon after 1958 and continued in varying degrees, depending on the political climate. By the end of 1965, fighting occurred close to the Iraq-Iran border, leading to a number of frontier violations that engendered sharp tension between the two states during the first half of 1965. The Iranian army was even engaged on some occasions in actual combat against the Iraqi army.[100] When open hostilities between the Iraqi army and the Kurds broke out in October 1968, the Iraqi government claimed that the rebels were receiving aid from Iran. With the new round of fighting in March 1974, the shah of Iran, Mohamed Reza Pahlavi, escalated his assistance to the Iraqi Kurds. Not only did he begin to supply artillery, sophisticated antitank weapons, and ammunition: he also facilitated the flow of other foreign aid to the rebels.[101] In all, it seems that Iranian intervention was so effective that terminating it became a necessary condition for the Iraqi government to end the fighting. Unable to put an end to Iran's intervention militarily, the Iraqi regime was forced to reach a compromise with the Shah.

On March 6, 1975, at the OPEC meeting in Algeria, both countries agreed to end any infiltration of "subversive character." The price Iraq paid for this was its acceptance of the Iranian proposal that the Shatt Al-Arab waterway border be drawn down the center of the estuary, dividing it equally. As a consequence of this détente, the Iranian government ceased its financial and military help to the Kurds.

Iraqi-Iranian relations remained more or less cordial until the success of the Iranian Islamic revolution in 1979. From the very beginning, the Iraqi leadership perceived this as a "reactionary" development and did not see progress prospects for the situation in Iran. The revolution was not led by workers or even the middle class. Its religious leaders represented the industrial, agricultural, and commercial bourgeoisie in Iran.[102] Later on, the Iraqi leadership accused the Iranian revolutionary regime of being faithful to the expansionist tradition of the "Persians" against the Arabs. In the perception of the Iraqi leadership, the Iranian threat is not confined to Iraq, but extends to the whole Gulf area. Iraq has a special role in defending the Gulf countries against this threat.[103]

Despite this perception, the Iraqi leadership initially maintained cordial relations with Iran. On more than one occasion Iraq expressed its sympathy toward the Iranian people in their struggle, its desire for close friendship with them, and its support of Iran's desire to join the nonalignment movement. However, traditional sources of conflict as well as the revolutionary zeal of the new leaders in Iran became paramount in influencing the relations between the two countries. The deterioration began with a war of words that soon developed into subversive activities, border clashes, and eventually total war.[104]

On September 17, 1980, President Saddam Hussein unilaterally abrogated the 1975 agreement. At the time, all indications suggested that Iranians were increasingly disillusioned with the factionalism and incompetence of the revolutionary government in Teheran, that the Iranian armed forces were demoralized, and that because of Iran's almost total international isolation, its army was lacking in essential spare parts. The Iraqi leadership concluded that militarily, the Iranians were no match for the Iraqi army.[105]

On September 22, the Iraqi army launched a full-fledged war against Iran. Quick and impressive victories were achieved by the Iraqis at the beginning.[106] However, the Iranians showed unexpectedly stiff resistance, and Iranian counterattacks eventually forced Iraqi troops to withdraw to Iraq's international borders with Iran. By 1983, the Iraqi leadership was ready for a peaceful settlement based on a cease-fire and direct or indirect negotiations. Mutual nonintervention in internal affairs, respect by both parties of the sovereignty and territorial integrity of each country, and the exclusion of the use of force in relations between them must be the basis for any future settlement.[107]

The war continued for another five years due to Iran's rejection of these terms and to the inability of either side to gain a decisive victory. However, on July 18, 1988, Iran accepted a cease-fire. This dramatic change was mainly due to Iraq's increasingly effective use of air power against Iranian shipping, oil facilities, and economic infrastructure, as well as to the major Iranian military setbacks on the battlefield in the first half of 1988.[108]

CONCLUSION

One underlying theme of this chapter has been the influence of Iraq's domestic environment on its foreign policy. Although Iraqi policies were largely influenced in the 1970s by the preferences of Saddam Hussein, his choices were affected by the structural characteristics of Iraq's situation. This is not to suggest that external variables are irrelevant to Iraq's foreign policy. However, the most crucial external variables have exercised influence through domestic variables (the Kurdish conflict and the war with Iran).

Throughout the 1970s, it seemed that the Iraqi leadership had successfully managed Iraq's domestic environment and brought together the elements of national power to fulfill Iraq's potential as a regional leader. Iraq's economy was enhanced through a distinctive oil policy; oil revenues were skillfully used to diversify the economy and develop the military; the Kurdish conflict was resolved; and for the first time since the Second World War, Iraq enjoyed political stability. Iraq's relations with Iran improved considerably after 1975, and the Iraqi role against Egypt's peace with Israel led to a more pragmatic political line. By the late 1970s it seemed that Iraq was finally ready to fill the role of regional leader. At that very moment, the Iranian revolution occurred, and the new Iranian government started its appeals to Iraqi Shi'ites. War became inevitable.

It is perhaps an ironic twist of history that Iraq had to divert its resources, political and material, to the war situation just when all other conditions seemed so favorable for it to play such a leading role. The war had its inevitable effect on Iraq's regional position. As discussed earlier, the war had a moderating effect on Iraq's foreign policy. While the "victorious" outcome of the war enhanced Iraq's position in the Arab world, its moderate foreign policy could lessen its distinctiveness as opposed to other Arab leaders such as Egypt and Saudi Arabia. More seriously, however, the situation with Iran was far from resolved by early 1990. The Iranian threat remained a serious constraint on Iraq despite the cease-fire. It appeared then that Iraq's moment of history had passed it by as a result of the war.

However, the outcome of the war represented a potential source of legitimacy for Iraq in the Arab world. It became clear that, with a victorious end of the war with Iran and a credible military capability, the Iraqi leadership would keep pursuing a leading role in the region. Nevertheless, the lesson of the war with Iran was well learned. The next target was the rich micro-state of Kuwait. And during the conflict around Kuwait, Saddam Hussein gave up almost everything to Teheran. He aimed to guarantee Iran's neutrality, if not support, for Iraq's "integration" of Kuwait.

On the second of August 1990 Iraqi troops invaded Kuwait, which was eventually declared part of Iraq on historical grounds. These dramatic developments followed a short crisis that began on July 17, 1990. On that day Saddam Hussein announced that Kuwait and the United Arab Emirates were adopting oil policies that aimed at undermining Iraq. He threatened to initiate action "to put things in their proper place" and frustrated every attempt to reach a diplomatic solution to the crisis. After the invasion Saddam Hussein insisted that Kuwait would stay an integrated part of Iraq forever. He tried to deter U.S. intervention by threatening to use all weapons at his disposal (including chemical and biological weapons) and to destroy oil fields in both Kuwait and Saudi Arabia. On the other hand, he sought to disintegrate the Arab alliance against him by linking the two issues of Kuwait and Palestine and inciting poor Arab countries against the oil-rich ones. He succeeded in mobilizing the support of significant segments of the Arab masses and some Arab regimes.

However, his fatal mistake was that he underestimated the U.S. resolve to fight a war and overestimated Arab reaction to such a recourse. In addition both Egypt and Syria stood firm against Iraqi ambitions. Thus the war became inevitable, and in this war that lasted for almost seven weeks in January and February 1991, a definite end was put to Iraq's potential as a regional power for many years to come. As a result of the destruction imposed on the country by coalition forces, Iraq would be busy in the immediate future with its own reconstruction, national unity, and even political viability.

NOTES

1. David E. Long and John A. Hearty, "Republic of Iraq," in David E. Long and Bernard Reich (eds.), *The Government and Politics of the Middle East and North Africa* (Boulder Colo.: Westview Press, 1980), p. 107.

2. W. B. Fisher, "Iraq," in *The Middle East and North Africa, 1979–1980* (London: Europa Publications, 1979), p. 386.

3. Zohurul Bari, "Syrian-Iraqi Dispute over the Euphrates Water," *International Studies* 16, 2 (1977), pp. 228–230.

4. Keith McLachlan, "Iraq, Problems of Regional Development," in Abbas Kelidar (ed.), *The Integration of Modern Iraq* (New York: St. Martin's Press, 1979), p. 137.

5. World Bank, *World Development Report 1988* (New York: Oxford University Press for the World Bank, 1988), p. 223.

6. Fisher, *op. cit.*, p. 387.

7. Saddam Hussein, *Our Own Way to Build Socialism*, 2d ed. (Baghdad: Dar Al-Horriya, 1980), p. 91 (in Arabic); *World Development Report 1988*, p. 275.

8. Claudia Wright, "Iraq, New Power in the Middle East," *Foreign Affairs* 58, 2 (1979–1980), pp. 269–270. For the implications of age distribution in calculating national power see Nazli Choucri, *Population Dynamics and International Violence* (Lexington, Mass.: Lexington Books, 1974), p. 71.

9. Fisher, *op. cit.*, p. 401. For greater detail on Iraqi population composition see Ali Fahmy, "The Basic Sociological Features of Iraq, A Simplified Sociological Map," *National Review of Social Sciences* (Cairo, Egypt) 18, 1–2 (1981), pp. 63–92.

10. R. D. McLaurin, Mohammed Mughisuddin, and Abraham Wagner, *Foreign Policy Making in the Middle East* (New York: Praeger Publishers, 1977), p. 108.

11. *Ibid.*, p. 109. There was an important Jewish community in Iraq, larger than in most Arab countries. After the establishment of Israel and Iraqi involvement in the first Arab-Israeli war, there was considerable emigration of Jews from Iraq, especially in the years 1951 and 1952. The number of Iraqi Jews was estimated in 1976 to be about 2,500 (compared with 125,000 in 1947). See Fisher, *op. cit.*, pp. 387–394, and also by Fisher, "Ethnic and Religious Minorities in Egypt, Iraq, Jordan, Lebanon and Syria," *Middle East Review* 9 (Fall 1976), p. 61.

12. McLaurin, *op. cit.*, pp. 108–109.

13. *Ibid.*, p. 108.

14. Fisher, "Iraq," p. 391.

15. *Ibid.*, p. 419; McLaurin, *op. cit.*, pp. 108–109.

16. Fisher, "Iraq," p. 387.

17. McLaurin, *op. cit.*, p. 130.

18. Sa'ad N. Jawad, "The Kurdish Problem in Iraq," in Kelidar, *op. cit.*, p. 171.

19. Theodore Richard Nash, "The Effect of International Oil Interests Upon the Fate of Autonomous Kurdish Territory: A Perspective on the Conference at Sevres, August 10, 1920," *International Problems* 15, 1–2 (1976), pp. 119–120.

20. McLaurin, *op. cit.*, p. 109; Jawad, *op. cit.*, p. 180.

21. *Ibid.*, p. 171.

22. McLaurin, *op. cit.*, p. 131.

23. Omran Yahya Feili and Arlene R. Fromchuck, "The Kurdish Struggle for Independence," *Middle East Review* 9 (1976), p. 51.

24. Jawad, *op. cit.*, pp. 177–180; and McLaurin, *op. cit.*, pp. 133–139.

25. Jawad, *op. cit.*, p. 171.

26. McLaurin, *op. cit.*, pp. 133–134; Jawad, *op. cit.*, p. 178.

27. On the oil issue, the two sides argued that Kirkuk should not be included in the Kurdish autonomous region until a plebiscite was held. However, the

plebiscite was postponed indefinitely, and the Kurds complained that the postponement was meant to give time for more Arabs to emigrate to the area. The March agreement provided for full recognition of Kurdish nationality, autonomy within a four-year period, and the appointment of a Kurdish vice-president. Kurdish was declared an official language and was to be taught, together with Arabic, all over Iraq. Moreover, Kurds were granted the right to form their own political and professional organizations, and a number of Kurdish forces were kept as border guards as part of the Iraqi armed forces. More important was the government declaration that the Kurds were part of the divided Kurdish people and Kurdistan, and that the Kurdish national movement was part of the general Iraqi national movement. See *ibid.*, pp. 179–180; and Honore M. Catudal, Jr., "The War in Kurdistan: End of Nationalist Struggle," *International Relations* 7, 3 (1976), pp. 133–134.

28. McLaurin, *op. cit.*, pp. 110–111.

29. The Sudanese experience is most relevant in this respect. See William H. Dorsey, "An Interview with Joseph Lagu, Anyana Leader," *Africa Report* 17, 9 (1972).

30. Evan Luard, "Civil Conflicts in Modern International Relations," in Evan Luard (ed.), *The International Regulation of Civil Wars* (London: Thames and Hudson, 1972), p. 7. For a full analysis of the internationalization of civil war situations, see James N. Rosenau (ed.), *International Aspects of Civil Strife* (Princeton, N.J.: Princeton University Press, 1964).

31. Fisher, "Iraq," p. 40; and McLaurin, *op. cit.*, p. 146. Also consult "Detente and the Arab Zionist Conflict," Interview of Saddam Hussein by Egyptian journalist Sakina Al-Sadat in January 1977, in Saddam Hussein, *Social and Foreign Affairs in Iraq*, trans. Khalid Kishtainy (London: Croom Helm, 1979), pp. 90–91.

32. Fisher, "Iraq," p. 387.

33. *Al Mustaqbal Al Arabi*, 123 (May 1989), p. 184 (in Arabic).

34. Salah Al-Mukhtar (press counselor of the Iraqi mission to the UN), "The Role of Iraq in the Next Two Decades," Lecture delivered in Houston, Texas, February 1, 1981, pp. 16–18. Mimeo.

35. Long and Reich, *op. cit.*, p. 130.

36. Press conference of Comrade Saddam Hussein held on July 18, 1978 (Baghdad: Dar Al-Horriya, 1978), pp. 54–55 (in Arabic).

37. "Detente," in Hussein, *Social and Foreign Affairs*, pp. 87–88.

38. A. I. Dawisha, "Iraq: The West's Opportunity," *Foreign Policy* 41 (1980–1981), p. 147.

39. Interviews with Ismail Al-Delimy, Advisor of the Iraqi Ministry for Planning, *Al-Hiswar Al-Arabi*, November 1982, pp. 108–112 (in Arabic).

40. Speech by President Saddam Hussein on the sixty-second anniversary of the establishment of the Iraqi army. Supplement, *Sout Al-Talaba Magazine* 167 (February 1983), pp. 29–32 (in Arabic).

41. Laurie Mylroie, "The Baghdad Alternative," *Orbis* (Summer 1988), p. 348. According to other estimates the debt may amount to $85 billion. However, most of it is not expected to be repaid. See *The Military Balance 1988–1989* (London: International Institute of Strategic Studies), p. 95.

42. Mylroie, *op. cit.*, p. 348.

43. "Strategic Statistics," *Arab Strategic Thought* 1 (1981), pp. 480–493 (in Arabic).

44. *The Military Balance 1988–89*, p. 225.

45. *Ibid.*, p. 94.

46. Dawisha, *op. cit.*, pp. 143–144; Wright, *op. cit.*, pp. 263–264.

47. See the excellent report by Mahmoud Azmy, "Strategic and Military Dimensions of the Bombing of the Iraqi Nuclear Reactor," in *Arab Strategic Thought* 1 (1981), pp. 399–416 (in Arabic).

48. Press conference of President Saddam Hussein held after the Israeli bombing of the Iraqi nuclear reactor (Baghdad: Dar Al-Horriya, 1981), pp. 9–12 (in Arabic).

49. Catudal, Jr., *op. cit.*, pp. 1024, 1029.

50. The provisional constitution of the Iraqi republic, issued on July 16, 1970, and amended in 1973. As Western sources on Iraq's political structure are full of inaccurate data, it is always advisable to consult Iraqi official documents.

51. Adeed Dawisha, "The Politics of War: Presidential Centrality, Party Power, Political Opposition," in Frederick W. Axelgard (ed.), *Iraq in Transition* (Boulder, Colo.: Westview Press, 1986), p. 26.

52. Long and Reich, *op. cit.*, p. 122.

53. Press conference of Comrade Saddam Hussein, held on July 18, 1978, *op. cit.*, pp. 8–9.

54. *Ibid.*, p. 11.

55. Saddam Hussein, *One Ditch or Two Ditches?* (Baghdad: Dar Al-Horriya, 1981), pp. 4–5 (in Arabic).

56. Long and Reich, *op. cit.*, p. 117.

57. Saddam Hussein's statement to the Iraqi ambassadors to Western Europe and Japan, June 12, 1975, in Hussein, *Social and Foreign Affairs*, p. 78.

58. Speech given by Comrade Saddam Hussein at the general meeting of the National Progressive Front's committees on June 7, 1975 (Baghdad: Dar Al-Horriya, 2d ed., 1980), p. 7 (in Arabic).

59. Speech given by President Saddam Hussein at Al-Najaf Province on October 17, 1979 (Baghdad: Dar Al-Horriya, 1980), pp. 31–34 (in Arabic).

60. The analysis is based on several speeches by President Saddam Hussein in the years 1975 to 1977. Saddam Hussein, *Our Struggle and International Politics*, 2d ed. (Baghdad: Dar Al-Horriya, 1980), pp. 2–19, 54–57, and 85–86 (in Arabic).

61. Speech given by President Saddam Hussein on the thirteenth anniversary of the 1968 revolution (Baghdad: Dar Al-Horriya, 1981), pp. 46–47 (in Arabic).

62. Speech given by President Saddam Hussein at the Sixth Summit Conference of the Nonaligned Movement held in Havana, September 3–7, 1979 (Baghdad: Dar Al-Horriya, 2d ed., January 1980), p. 17 (in Arabic).

63. See Article 38-C of the Iraqi constitution and the interview with President Saddam Hussein in *Al-Majalla* 167 (December 4–10, 1982), p. 19 (in Arabic).

64. *Ibid.*

65. Speech given by comrade Saddam Hussein at the meeting of the regional and Iraqi leadership of the Ba'th party on December 26, 1977 (Baghdad: Dar Al-Horriya, 1978) (in Arabic).

66. Hussein, *Social and Foreign Affairs*, pp. 65–66.

67. Al-Mukhtar, *op. cit.*, pp. 8–13.

68. Cited in Dawisha, "Iraq: The West's Opportunity," p. 149.

69. Press conference of President Saddam Hussein held after the Israeli bombing of the Iraqi nuclear reactor, *op. cit.*, pp. 83–85.

70. Interview with Hussein, *Al-Majalla, op. cit.*, p. 18.

71. Interview with Mr. Tarek Aziz, Iraqi deputy prime minister and minister for foreign affairs, in *Attadamon* 1, 14 (July 16, 1983), p. 7 (in Arabic).

72. Federick W. Axelgard, "U.S.-Iraq Relations: A Status Report," *American-Arab Affairs* (Summer 1988), pp. 2–3.

73. Edith Penrose and E. F. Penrose, *Iraq: International Relations and National Development* (London: Ernest Benn, 1978), pp. 426–434.

74. Statement of Comrade Saddam Hussein to *Der Spiegel* (Baghdad: Dar Al-Horriya, 2d ed., 1980), p. 41 (in Arabic).

75. Press conference of Comrade Saddam Hussein held on July 18, 1978, *op. cit.*, p. 92.

76. Press conference of President Saddam Hussein held after the Israeli bombing of the Iraqi nuclear reactor, *op. cit.*, pp. 87–88. See also Dawisha, *op. cit.*, p. 137.

77. Interview with Hussein in *Al-Majalla, op. cit.*, p. 18. Interview with Tarek Aziz in *Attadamon, op. cit.*, p. 8.

78. See *Statistical Handbook for 1978*, pp. 34–39.

79. *Ibid.*

80. Hussein, *Social and Foreign Affairs*, pp. 82–83.

81. Statements of Comrade Saddam Hussein to *Der Spiegel, op. cit.*, p. 45.

82. Press conference of President Saddam Hussein held after the Israeli bombing of the Iraqi nuclear reactor, *op. cit.*, pp. 98–99.

83. *Statistical Handbook for 1978*, pp. 34–39.

84. Speech given by President Saddam Hussein at the Sixth Summit Conference of the Nonaligned Movement, *op. cit.*, p. 16.

85. Fisher, *op. cit.*, p. 398; McLaurin, *op. cit.*, pp. 148–150.

86. Press conference of Comrade Saddam Hussein held on July 18, 1978, *op. cit.*, pp. 52–54.

87. Statement of Comrade Saddam Hussein to *Der Spiegel, op. cit.*, p. 36. Press conference of President Saddam Hussein held after the Israeli bombing of the Iraqi nuclear reactor, *op. cit.*, p. 107.

88. Mylroie, *op. cit.*, p. 343.

89. See statement of Comrade Saddam Hussein to *Der Spiegel, op. cit.*, pp. 15–28.

90. Dawisha, *op. cit.*, p. 140.

91. For details see Bari, *op. cit.*, pp. 234–244.

92. Fisher, *op. cit.*, pp. 396–399.

93. *Ibid.*, p. 400; Wright, *op. cit.*, pp. 265–267.

94. Speech given by President Saddam Hussein on the occasion of the Iraqi army anniversary on January 6, 1981, pp. 25–26 (in Arabic).

95. Laurie Mylroie, "Iraq's Changing Role in the Persian Gulf," *Current History* (February 1989), p. 90.

96. Dawisha, *op. cit.*, pp. 144–145.

97. Speech given by President Saddam Hussein on the thirteenth anniversary of the 1968 revolution, *op. cit.*, pp. 32–33.

98. Press conference of President Saddam Hussein held after the Israeli bombing of the Iraqi nuclear reactor, *op. cit.*, pp. 66–78.

99. Interview with Mr. Tarek Aziz, in *Attadamon* 1, 13 (July 9, 1983), pp. 6–7 (in Arabic).

100. Feili and Fromchuck, *op. cit.*, p. 53.

101. Catudal, Jr., *op. cit.*, p. 1036.

102. Interview with Mr. Tarek Aziz, *Attadamon* 1, 14 (July 16, 1983), p. 8.

103. Speech given by President Saddam Hussein on the Iraqi-Iranian dispute at the third Islamic summit, January 25–28, 1981, pp. 8–15 (in Arabic). Saddam Hussein, "Iraq: A Mobilized Army," pp. 30–31. Speech by President Saddam Hussein on the sixty-second anniversary of the establishment of the Iraqi army, *op. cit.*, pp. 9–13.

104. For a full Iraqi official record of these developments, see the speech given by President Saddam Hussein on the Iraqi-Iranian dispute, *op. cit.*, pp. 25–30.

105. Dawisha, *op. cit.*, p. 146.

106. Speech given by President Saddam Hussein on the Iraqi-Iranian dispute, *op. cit.*, pp. 35–36.

107. Interview with President Saddam Hussein in *Al-Majalla, op. cit.*, p. 16.

108. See Graham E. Fuller, "War and Revolution In Iran," *Current History* (February 1989), p. 81.

7

The Politics of
Vulnerability and Survival:
The Foreign Policy of Jordan

Ali E. Hillal Dessouki
Karen Aboul Kheir

For Jordan, as for few other states, foreign policy is the major national resource. The Hashemite Kingdom is a small and vulnerable country that has played a role in regional and international politics far exceeding its size.[1] Jordan is equipped with neither a solid demographic base, rich natural resources, nor defensible borders. Nevertheless, the Kingdom's history, and its location, have propelled it to the very center of regional conflicts. The successful manipulation of its foreign policy involvements is Jordan's indispensable means of ensuring its survival as a sovereign state.

The full dimension of the essential paradox of Jordanian foreign policy—the necessity for so weak a state to play so large a role—is best illustrated in the Jordanian involvement in the question of Palestine. Jordan's deep involvement with the Palestinian issue began even before the creation of the Jordanian state; the Hashemite cooperated with the British against the Ottoman Empire during World War I in return for a promise of self-rule to all of the Arab provinces. After the war, however, the victorious allied countries ignored this promise. The area was divided into a number of newly created states placed under the mandatory rule of Britain and France; Britain controlled Iraq and Palestine, while France took over Lebanon and Syria. These events caused a great deal of turmoil in the area, led by the Hashemites and their supporters. Resentments were further inflamed by the revelation of the British promise to support the creation of a Jewish homeland in Palestine.

Britain, in response to the discontent in the area, developed a strategy to appease the Hashemites as well as to contain the influence of its traditional rival, France. British authorities placed one Hashemite on the throne in Baghdad and created a new entity, the Emirate of the Transjordan, under the rule of another Hashemite, Prince (later King) Abdullah. Prince Abdullah was promised that this emirate, carved from British-controlled Palestine, would not be subject to the terms of the Balfour declaration. Suggestions were made that this new entity was a temporary solution, a stepping-stone to larger possibilities, including the throne in Damascus.[2] At any rate, it is clear that Prince Abdullah regarded this arrangement as temporary. Hashemite ambitions and a belief in Arab nationalism both spurred him to expand the Transjordan into a more viable entity. The opportunity presented itself in the 1948 war that followed the foundation of the State of Israel. Prince Abdullah sent his famous Arab Legion into the fight and, from his point of view, succeeded in rescuing the West Bank and the city of Jerusalem from Israeli usurpation. To many Palestinians and Arab states, Prince Abdullah's "occupation" of the West Bank was motivated purely by self-interest, an exploitation of the Palestinian plight to increase the strength of his own state. Prince Abdullah, on the other hand, argued that his actions would in fact be in the Palestinian's best interests, and therefore announced, in 1950, the establishment of the Hashemite Kingdom of Jordan, comprising both banks of the River Jordan. King Abdullah granted the Palestinian inhabitants of the West Bank, as well as those who had fled to the East Bank, full Jordanian citizenship.[3] Despite some support for this move among West Bank notables, there was violent protest as well. King Abdullah lost his life soon after at the hands of a Palestinian who believed Abdullah betrayed his nation.

The incorporation of the West Bank into Jordan was the beginning of a long and turbulent relationship between the Hashemite family and the original Transjordanian population on the one hand and the Palestinian people on the other. This act created a contradiction that influenced Jordanian politics for more than three decades. The West Bank, with its fertile land, the economic revenues and international prestige of its ancient city, Jerusalem, and its relatively sophisticated and educated population, brought a substantial enhancement to Jordan's strength and importance. At the same time, the continued attachment of the Palestinians, now full Jordanian subjects, to their own national identity and the idea of liberating their land prevented the Hashemite Kingdom of Jordan from developing as a cohesive, integrated society. The strains associated with the relationship had a seriously destabilizing impact on Jordan's domestic environment.

THE DOMESTIC ENVIRONMENT

Geography

Jordan is a small country that occupies a critical strategic position in the Middle East but enjoys neither defensible borders nor a wealth of natural resources. Therefore, while its location gives it central importance in regional affairs, its inability to protect its boundaries leaves it vulnerable to pressures from regional and international powers seeking to further their own interests in the area.

Jordan is surrounded by Syria in the north, Iraq in the northeast, Israel in the west, and the Gulf of Aqaba and the Red Sea in the south and east. With the exception of a small length of the River Jordan, there are no natural boundaries separating Jordan from its neighbors. Geographically, Jordan is divided into three regions. The first region is the eastern plateau, which rises to as much as 1,700 meters above sea level in some places and grades imperceptibly into arid uplands of Syria, Iraq, and Saudi Arabia. Extending from Irbid in the north to the Rum Mountains in the south, these heights are separated by a number of valleys, such as Wadi Al-Arab, Wadi Zarqa, and others. The second part, extending from the Gulf of Aqaba in the south to Lake Tiberius and the Syrian border in the north, is a down-faulted rift including the valley of the River Jordan. The third part consists of the highlands of the West Bank (under Israeli occupation since 1967), which run parallel to the eastern heights and are about the same altitude.[4] Jordan is landlocked except for one part on the Gulf of Aqaba, which means that Egypt, through control of navigation in that part of the Red Sea, is of central importance to Jordan's vital phosphate exports.

Jordan's ability to strengthen its economy through agricultural expansion is severely constrained by the shortage of water for irrigation. About 75% of Jordan's land is desert. Irrigation in the valley of the River Jordan and the Dead Sea is dependent mainly on water flows from the highlands to the east. The Yarmuk and Zorga are the only rivers with a permanent flow, with the exception of the River Jordan, and are the country's only real assets in terms of agricultural irrigation. This sorely needed water has been, since 1939, the subject of regional conflict. The River Jordan runs through Israel, Syria, and Lebanon as well as Jordan. Although repeated attempts have been made to develop an integrated scheme for water use in the entire river basin, they have been undermined by the repeated wars and the general atmosphere of tension in the area.[5] Jordan is particularly threatened by Israeli exploitation of the river waters. By controlling the Golan Heights as well as the West Bank, both occupied since 1967, Israel has the power not only to proceed unfettered with its own plans but also to halt joint Jordanian-Syrian plans for the development of irrigation.[6] Jordanian perceptions that Israel's water projects exploit an unfair share of the waters and will have future, irreversible effects on Jordan's share of the River Jordan, add urgency to Jordanian endeavors to reach a peaceful settlement in the area. A shortage of water for irrigation would have grave consequences for Jordan's ability to meet the growing demands of its population.[7]

Population and Social Structure

The Jordanian population, though slender (3,656,000),[8] is rendered unstable by the social and political tensions between its two major components, the original Jordanian inhabitants of the Emirate of Transjordan (the East Bank) and the Palestinian population incorporated into Jordanian society since 1948. The original inhabitants of the East Bank numbered less than 400,000 in 1948.[9] These people were mainly village dwellers and bedouins who did not enjoy high levels of education, health services, or the benefits of large and sophisticated urban centers. Through a conscious and active policy on the part of Jordan's Hashemite rulers, this population was strongly linked to the monarchy and is perceived as having a vested interest in the system and the independence of Jordan. The Palestinian population had a distinctly different background. The Palestinians were predominantly urban, educated, and Westernized, used to a relatively high degree of services and access to information media, and had almost double the population of the original Jordanians.[10]

A significant part of the Palestinian population moved from the West to the East Bank in a series of migrations as a result of regional hostilities and in search of better economic prospects. By early 1968, the Palestinian population outnumbered the original Jordanians on the East Bank, 900,000 to 581,000.[11] Thus even after the loss of the West Bank to Israel in 1967, the Palestinians remained a significant majority in Jordanian society. These Palestinians played a major role in the development and modernization of Jordan. With their superior education and skills, they earned a relatively high level of social and economic status, rousing the jealousy of the original Jordanian population.[12] The Palestinian people, for their part, remained distinct through their different cultural and social background as well as through their continued attachment to Palestinian nationalism as an expression of their identity. Furthermore, they felt alienated from the regime through their sense of being politically underrepresented and excluded from the higher levels of government positions and military rank. This situation is in marked contrast to the privileges enjoyed by Jordan's two small minority groups: the Christians, estimated to number about 78,000 people in 1979,[13] and the Circasians, non-Arab Sunni Moslems estimated to number about 12,000 people in the early 1950s.[14] Although small in number, both minorities are regularly represented in the Jordanian cabinet and form a disproportionately large percentage of government and military employees.

These conditions have had serious implications for the social and political cohesiveness of Jordanian society. The legitimacy of the Hashemite regime rests on the support of the original tribal population as well as that of the Christians and Circasians—all of whom are minorities. The majority of the population is a politically conscious Palestinian component, with strong ties to a different national identity, severely critical of the Hashemite role in regional affairs. The different political and national priorities of the two groups are a serious constraint on the ability of the monarch to maneuver in the realm of foreign policy.

Economic Capability

With limited mineral resources and a small industrial sector, agriculture remains an important economic resource for Jordan. The loss of the West Bank in 1967 deprived Jordan of some of its most fertile land and opportunities to develop its system of irrigation. Despite this setback, the regime has made a concentrated effort to expand agricultural production. In 1977, the Jordan Valley Authority took over control of rural planning, irrigation, and farming services, which resulted in an enormous increase in the production of vegetables. Wheat, barley, and animal fodder are still grown in areas dependent on rainfall and are, therefore, liable to weather fluctuations. Thus, for example, wheat production was 50,000 tons in 1950, 16,000 tons in 1979, 134,000 tons in 1980, and 50,000 tons in 1984.[15] Such fluctuations make it very difficult for Jordan to achieve self-sufficiency of these important crops and leave it even more dependent on external help.

In terms of mineral resources, Jordan is relatively poor except in phosphates, of which it is the fifth largest producer and the third largest exporter in the world. Phosphates represent the bulk of all Jordanian exports.[16] Jordan has a few industries, such as cement and potash, that also make up part of its exports. Production costs for these industries, as well as for the small sector of pharmaceuticals, cigarettes, and paper products, remain high, since Jordan relies almost totally on imported energy resources.[17]

Jordan has, in principle, a free economy, but the government plays a major economic role. The public sector contributes half of all national investments and employs almost half of the labor force.[18] This extensive public sector role gives the regime considerable domestic strength, but it also makes it the target of demands for new jobs and better living standards. Given its modest economic resources, Jordan has traditionally relied on external assistance to meet its peoples' needs and demands.

During the 1970s and early 1980s, money flowing from the oil-rich Arab countries, through direct assistance and the remittances of Jordanian workers, was the basis of a considerable economic boom. Between 1973 and 1981, Arab aid rose from $71.8 million to $1.71 billion. The expatriate workers' remittances also rose from $15 million to almost $1 billion during the same period.[19] This economic situation had a significant impact on both private and public expenditures. Between 1980 and 1987, government consumption increased at a rate of 5.3%, and private consumption grew at the rate of 7.3%. Gross domestic investment, meanwhile, grew only at a rate of 4.3%.[20] The effect of this increased consumption had a particularly disastrous impact on Jordan's balance of payments, as imports grew to almost four times the size of exports.[21]

Cereal imports alone rose from 171,000 metric tons in 1974, to 950,000 metric tons in 1987.[22]

Jordan faced a serious economic situation when this flow of oil money was significantly reduced in the mid-1980s, and it became clear that it had not made the best use of these resources. Total official development assistance to Jordan dropped from $1.065 billion in 1981 to $595 million by 1987.[23] The remittances from workers abroad also dropped to $844 million by 1987. Jordan was left with development projects it could not finance and a level of consumption it could no longer sustain. In searching for additional international aid and loans, Jordan became liable to pressure from the International Monetary Fund (IMF) to make economic reforms, such as decreasing government expenditures, reducing imports, and removing subsidies on basic consumer goods. The compliance of Jordan with some of these demands resulted in a number of violent disturbances in protest of high prices and shortages of basic commodities.[24]

The formation of the Arab Cooperation Council with Egypt, Iraq, and North Yemen in February 1989 offered some promise of economic opportunities, but it is unlikely to be an answer to Jordan's problems in the short run. Jordan's trade with Iraq, long Jordan's major export market, significantly declined during the war years and is not likely to revive soon in view of Iraq's economic troubles. Its trade with Egypt, on the other hand, was resumed after grinding to a halt with the breaking of diplomatic relations in 1979. Trade protocols set bilateral trade at $150 million in 1985 and $250 million in 1986.[25] This small volume of trade is unlikely to offset the diminished returns from Jordan's phosphate exports that resulted from a fall in world prices. Jordan's economic prospects in the 1990s are therefore generally bleak. In this weakened economic situation, Jordan is left vulnerable to pressures from international aid donors, and this limits its foreign policy options.

Military Capability

Despite its meager resources, Jordan places a high priority on its defense capabilities. Jordanian strength in the field remains almost insignificant in comparison with its strong neighbors. Jordan's defense budget for 1989 stood at $465.7 million, compared to an estimated $14.69 billion for Saudi Arabia, $2.49 billion for Syria, $6.37 billion for Israel, and an estimated $12.87 billion for Iraq in 1988. Jordan's active armed forces are also relatively small, 85,250 compared to Israel's 141,000, Saudi Arabia's 65,700, Syria's 404,000, and Iraq's million-man army.[26] These figures make it abundantly clear that the Jordanian army cannot play a decisive role in implementing Jordan's regional foreign policy objectives. While the Arab Legion under King Abdullah was considered a prestigious and powerful force, the Arab Army of Jordan, as the legion came to be called, was almost completely annihilated by the overwhelming strength of the Israeli forces in 1967. Jordan was not a partner to the 1973

October War and extended only token assistance to the Syrian army at the time.

The primary role played by the army has been the protection of the monarchy against internal threats. Hashemite rulers have consciously and deliberately developed close ties with the armed forces to ensure their loyalty and allegiance. The army has been the principal means of crushing domestic disturbances threatening the regime. The most notable incident was the willingness of the Jordanian army to engage in battle in 1970 and 1971 with the Palestinian guerrilla forces based in Jordan. This confrontation amounted to no less than a civil war, which ended only with the withdrawal of Palestinian forces from Jordan. Although this action on the part of the Jordanian army was extremely unpopular in Jordan and the Arab world, the army's loyalty to the monarchy was unshaken. The realization of the domestic as well as regional imperatives of security makes improving its military capability a constant Jordanian priority. In the face of continued U.S. insensitivity to Jordan's demands for sophisticated missiles and aircraft, King Hussein has on occasion threatened to turn to the Soviet Union for help. Jordan's close cooperation with Egypt, a major Third World producer and exporter of arms, and Iraq, a major regional military power, is clearly designed to offset Jordan's own vulnerability in this respect.

Political Structure

The Jordanian political system revolves around the strong figure of the monarch, who delegates executive authority to a cabinet that is accountable to a bicameral parliament. Jordan had a multiparty system until 1957, when regional and domestic unrest posed a serious threat to the monarchy, and King Hussein responded by declaring a state of emergency and abolishing all political parties. Several attempts were subsequently made to form a single national political organization, but they did not meet with success. The growing stature of the monarchy as an institution and King Hussein as a leader within this context is both an asset and a liability to the system. While the longevity and strength of King Hussein have a stabilizing influence on the system, his visibility also makes him the target for demands and discontent. The failure of King Hussein to respond to demands made on him would undermine his legitimacy and strength, while compliance with demands, particularly for more free and effective political participation, may well pose an even greater threat to the survival of the monarchy.

The Jordanian constitution allots great powers to the king,[27] but this is not the chief source of his strength. According to the constitution, the king appoints the cabinet and may relieve it of its duties, he calls parliament into session and may disband it and also appoints the members of its upper house. He is head of the armed forces and appoints major military personnel as well as government officials and judges. He may also promulgate and approve laws, declare war, and sign treaties. The king may also draw on any further powers he may need through declaring a state of emergency. Nevertheless, King Hussein's centrality to the system, and his legitimacy, rests on his personal abilities and prestige as well as the historical/religious significance of his family, the Hashemites.

King Hussein's personal prestige has developed through his ability to survive threats and cope with difficulties during his long reign. (He acceded to the throne in August 1953.) He is credited with personal charm and an ability to inspire the loyalty of his subjects. He has made active use of these qualities in maintaining the traditionally close ties with the tribal elements of his population, established by his grandfather, King Abdullah, as well as with the military. These strong relations provide him with a solid core of support within the political system. His familial heritage is also of great significance to these elements of society. The Hashemites are direct descendents of the prophet Mohamed and this imbues them with an element of prestige and respect. As a descendent of the leaders of the great Arab revolt, King Hussein projects a sense of historical mission to himself and his family that equally encompasses his fellow Jordanians and provides a basis for their mutual solidarity.

These sources of legitimacy, personal charisma, and tradition are not alone sufficient to persuade the growing numbers of educated and politically conscious Jordanians, particularly those of Palestinian origin. The latter perceive the monarchy to be compromised by its long and close associations with Western powers. The religious significance of the Hashemites has also been undermined through the loss of Jerusalem to the Israelis and the loss of their tradition of service to the Islamic holy places in the Hejaz (the western Arabian peninsula) to the Saudi family. Finally, even the most loyal of King Hussein's tribal followers have been negatively affected by the difficult economic situation and have displayed symptoms of discontent.

King Hussein developed a bold and decisive response to the domestic and regional pressures on the monarchy by announcing the breaking of legal and administrative ties with the West Bank in 1988 and the holding of free parliamentary elections, on the East Bank alone, in late 1989. These decisions were presented by King Hussein as a response to popular demands expressed through the continued uprising on the West Bank for an independent national entity there as well as to internal Jordanian demands for more effective political participation. A major argument used by the regime against holding open elections in Jordan while the West Bank was under Israeli occupation was that this would jeopardize the rights of its inhabitants by signalling Jordan's acceptance of the Israeli annexation. On a foreign policy level Jordan feared such an action would also be interpreted as the relinquishing of Jordanian claims to the West Bank, effectively weakening its bargaining position in any settlement negotiations. In terms of domestic politics, King Hussein clearly hoped this action would bolster his position through limiting the destabilizing impact of the uprising on the East Bank Palestinians and by strengthening their integration into the Jordanian system by responding to their demands for better political representation.

The 1989 parliamentary elections, the first in over twenty years, brought a sizeable opposition parliament (52 seats), drawn predominantly from the Islamic movement (38 seats). The unique situation of the Islamic opposition in Jordan, however, suggests that this is not as clear a break with traditional Jordanian politics as it may seem.[28] The Moslem Brothers, one of the largest organizations within the Jordanian Islamic movement, was not disbanded along with other political parties in the 1950s. The activities of the Moslem Brothers in the West as well as in the East Bank served as a means of maintaining links with the population there. The Moslem Brothers also extended support to their Syrian counterparts, and, therefore, provided Jordan with some indirect leverage on the Syrian regime.[29] On a tactical and ideological level, the Jordanian regime and the Islamic movement agree on their mutual opposition to leftist influence and activities. Thus far, King Hussein has been able to keep the Islamic opposition within bounds as much by invoking his religious prestige in support of a moderate and modernizing interpretation of Islam, as by using his political skills and powers. Nevertheless, the Islamic movement in general and the Moslem Brothers in particular have a power base independent of the king. Their open involvement in the political structure may serve to widen this base at the expense of the king's own popularity. Moreover, worsening economic conditions and increasing regional pressures may push the Islamic opposition in a more radical direction, posing a serious threat to the stability of the regime. The ability of the regime to withstand these possible consequences will rest as much on King Hussein's ability to create better conditions for his subjects as on his skill in responding to difficult situations.

FOREIGN POLICY ORIENTATION

The major thrust of Jordanian foreign policy has always been Islam and Arab nationalism. Characteristically, Jordan seeks to exert its moderating influences in these two spheres to achieve its primary foreign policy objective: Jordan's survival. Hashemite political wisdom has long recognized that Jordan's fate is influenced by factors beyond its immediate control and, yet, are subject to skillful manipulation. Their only chance of ameliorating the impact of hostile pressures has been in playing an active role in regional affairs, primarily as the mediator, or broker, between the various parties involved. The two general aims of Jordanian foreign policy activities have been the creation of regional and international links to strengthen Jordan's position and the peaceful settlement of the Arab-Israeli conflict on the best possible terms for Jordan.

The Hashemites' history of religious and Arab nationalist traditions serves as the basis of their definition of Jordan's role in regional and international affairs. The Hashemite family puts great stress on its connections with the prophet Mohamed and its role as a historical defender of the Islamic faith and its holy places. Both King Hussein and Crown Prince Hassan invoke this prestige to promote a moderate interpretation of Islam. They sponsor activities and institutions related to the protection of Islamic heritage and promotion of their own moderate religious interpretations such as *Aal-Al-beit* (the house of prophet Mohamed) and Institute for Islamic Civilization.[30] Jordan invokes this prestige to exert influence in Islamic circles. For example, Jordan made an early bid to act as mediator between Iraq and Iran, both "Islamic sisters."[31] At the same time, King Hussein was careful to overcome past animosities between the Hashemites and the Saudi family to maintain good relations with the Saudi regime. Jordan is careful not to openly challenge the Saudi bid for leadership in the Islamic world, and in its turn, Saudi Arabia has been a significant donor of aid to Jordan.

King Hussein's interpretation of Arab nationalism is also characterized by moderation and varies significantly from the Nasserist pan-Arab vision. To King Hussein, Arab nationalism means the equality, as well as brotherhood, of all Arab states.[32] He stresses the necessity of respecting the sovereignty and independence of all Arab states as well as the necessity of refraining from interference in their domestic affairs. This interpretation is in obvious accordance with Jordan's preoccupation with preserving its territorial and political integrity. Arab cooperation and harmony is equally important as a favorable environment for sustaining a secure and stable Jordanian state. King Hussein therefore strongly criticized the interventionist nature and polarizing effect of Nasser's pan-Arabism. He also harshly condemned the socialist content of this version of Arab nationalism, perceiving it as the means of introducing "Communist" influences into the area.[33] Anti-communism was, in the 1950s and 1960s, a central component in Jordan's foreign policy orientation, both as part of its close association with Western powers and in fear of communism's detrimental domestic consequences. During the past two decades, however, Jordan has tempered its attitudes toward the Soviet Union, recognizing that it may play a helpful role in reaching a Middle East peace settlement.

Dedication to the Palestinian cause and involvement in the search for a Middle East settlement through peaceful means have been central themes in Jordanian foreign policy orientation since 1948. The Hashemites have always explained their involvement in the Palestinian issue, including the incorporation of the West Bank into Jordan, as stemming from their obligation to defend the rights of their fellow Arabs. The loss of the West Bank to Israel, therefore, was a great blow to the Hashemites' self-image as protectors of Arab nationalism and of religious symbols, and their intense efforts to regain it relate to their sense of historical mission. The economic losses resulting from the Israeli occupation, the destabilizing impact of the Palestinian refugees, and the increased radicalization of the Palestinian national movement were equally strong motivations for Jordan to reach a settlement. In view of Jordan's, as well as the Arabs', relative military weakness, a political solution to the problem was the only alternative. Hashemites point out that the Palestinian problem would have taken a different direction if the Arabs had accepted this position earlier.

Jordanian efforts to reach a political settlement that would satisfy its own aspirations and security needs as well as those of the West Bank population, were not, however, met with success. In view of its regional and domestic liabilities, Jordan required the satisfaction of three conditions to conclude a settlement. These are the open support, or at least tacit agreement, of surrounding regional powers, the participation of Palestinian elements that enjoy both good relations with the Jordanian regime and the support of the West Bank population, and finally the cooperation of the United States and its willingness to exert pressure on Israel.[34] For almost four decades, one ingredient or another has been missing from this formula. In the late 1950s and early 1960s Jordan was too isolated regionally, and destabilized domestically, by the overwhelming forces of Nasserist pan-Arabism to even consider attempting a settlement. Although Arab-Jordanian relations subsequently improved, Jordan's relations with the United States were severely strained by Jordan's participation in the 1967 war. Although King Hussein was probably aware of this war's disastrous results, it was thought that Israel was likely to invade the West Bank one way or the other and that the Hashemite regime would never survive the stigma of not defending it. By participating in the war, Jordan at least salvaged its Arab connections, albeit at a high price.

Jordan's relations with its Arab neighbors, as well as the Palestinian population throughout the Arab world, was severely tested by the confrontation between the Jordanian army and Palestinian resistance forces in 1970 and 1971. Palestinian resistance forces operating out of Jordan not only exposed it to Israeli attacks but also openly challenged the Jordanian regime on its unwillingness to engage Israel in battle. The combined threats of external aggression and domestic revolt could only be met through suppressing Palestinian military strength and activity in Jordan. This action had severely negative consequences not only in terms of Jordan's domestic stability but also in terms of its credibility as a defender of Palestinian rights. The subsequent growth in Palestinian, Arab, and international recognition of the PLO as the sole representative of the Palestinians further undermined Jordan's role as a mediator for a political resolution of the conflict. Jordan continued to be a central party in the efforts to reach a Middle East settlement, however, due to the insistence of the United States on its involvement. Throughout the 1980s, therefore, Jordan maintained its ties both with the PLO and the population of the West Bank in an attempt to keep all its options open. It resisted pressure from the United States to join the Camp David

Accords between Egypt and Israel because they did not enjoy the support of other Arab countries and did not involve suitable Palestinian representation in the negotiations. Moreover, Egyptian willingness to go a long way toward implementing the U.S. understanding of peace in the area significantly undermined Jordan's influence and leverage in its relationship with the United States and increased the latter's insensitivity to Jordanian security requirements. In the early 1980s, therefore, it appeared that Jordanian foreign policy efforts had become basically ineffectual.

Changing regional conditions in the mid-1980s, however, once more provided Jordan with the opportunity to play its role as mediator. Jordanian foreign policy became focused on improving Jordan's bilateral relations with its neighboring Arab countries as well as promoting general Arab harmony. Jordan's efforts in this respect, notably its resumed relations with Egypt and Syria as well as its involvement in the foundation of the Arab Cooperation Council, signify its attempt to strengthen its position in future negotiations for a settlement in the area as well as guaranteeing itself a part in influencing regional affairs.

THE DECISION-MAKING PROCESS

In line with the importance of foreign policy to the survival of Jordan and the central role of the monarchy in the system, King Hussein is the sole decision-maker in the realm of foreign policy. His long practical experience and considerable political skills shape Jordanian foreign policy responses to regional and international pressures and are to a great extent responsible for the survival of the Jordanian state.

King Hussein ibn Talal is one of the longest-serving heads of state in the world. Born in Amman on November 14, 1935, Hussein was at the side of his grandfather, King Abdullah, when he was assassinated entering Al-Aqsa Mosque in Jerusalem in July 1951 and narrowly escaped death himself.[35] He was called on to ascend to the throne at the age of eighteen, when his father, King Talal, abdicated after a short reign. Hussein, who was a cadet at Sandhurst at the time, had no political experience but was credited with a strength of character and personal charm inherited from his grandfather. Subsequent events proved him to possess great personal and political courage as well as flexibility and a great talent for maneuvering.

During the early years of his reign, Hussein was not the uncontested decision-maker in foreign, or domestic, policy. His powers were constrained by the presence of a number of strong figures with independent bases of support. One of these figures was the British Glubb Pasha, the head of Jordan's armed forces who had been at the center of Jordanian politics for decades and of whose patronizing manner Hussein bitterly complained. Another threatening figure was that of Suleiman Al-Nabulsi, head of the National Socialist party, who rose to the premiership on the crest of the Arab nationalist wave that swept through Jordan and the region in the mid-1950s. Nabulsi took effective charge of Jordan's foreign policy, moving it out of the orbit of its traditional Western alliances and into the sphere of influence of the leader of Arab nationalism at the time, Egypt. As these developments were in complete variance with Hussein's foreign policy orientation and in view of the subsequent overthrow of the Hashemite regime in Iraq, an imminent threat to his regime, Hussein acted boldly by dismissing Nabulsi's government and cracking down on all political activities in the country. In a character-istically clever maneuver, he also dismissed Glubb Pasha and "Arabized" the army during this period, thereby appeasing the strong nationalist trends at the time and ridding himself of an undesirable strong figure in the same stroke. During the following years, King Hussein achieved a firm grip on the reins of power. It is safe to argue that subsequently, political figures with strong political backings or clear policy orientations only came into positions of power when their persuasions were useful to Hussein's foreign strategy at the time. Moreover, the influence of the prime minister or other officials on decision-making stems mainly from their personal relationship to the king.

The foreign ministry in Jordan functions as an executive organ of government and does not play a role in the making of policy. The king retains his grip on Jordan's foreign relations by personally appointing Jordanian ambassadors. Their political and professional backgrounds, as well as their proximity to the king, vary according to the importance of the country to which they are sent. Moreover, their reports are often sent directly to the king rather than the foreign ministry. The king also uses individuals from outside the ministry to act as his emissaries to other states such as, for example, the chief of the Royal Hashemite Diwan or the minister of the royal court.[36]

The major representative of the kingdom in foreign affairs is Crown Prince Hassan ibn Talal, King Hussein's younger brother. Prince Hassan was educated at Harrow, England, and obtained his M.A. degree from Oxford University in history and political science. He is credited with significant intellectual abilities, and is much in demand as a public speaker. Prince Hassan was involved in founding a number of scientific, cultural, and research institutions in Jordan, such as the Royal Scientific Society, and the Arab Thought Forum. He is also involved in a number of similar institutions outside Jordan such as the Afro-Arab Cooperation Forum in Morocco, for which he and Leopold Senghor, ex-president of Senegal, were elected co-presidents of the founding committee. He has addressed various groups and organizations throughout the world, and especially in the West, in the context of improving Arab-Western relations and urging the need for a settlement in the Middle East.[37]

The Hashemite family pays particular attention to its international image, and the selection and training of the heirs to the throne involve an exposure to Western society and culture, particularly through study at Western institutions as well as a firm grounding in Arabic and Islamic traditions and customs. In foreign policy, as in domestic affairs, the Hashemites uphold a commitment to their sense of a historical mission for themselves and their country.

FOREIGN POLICY BEHAVIOR

U.S.-Jordanian Relations

Since the 1950s, Jordan has maintained a close relationship with the United States, based on their joint espousal of anti-communism and the need for a political solution to the Middle East conflict. Jordan depends on the United States for economic aid as well as crucial military assistance. In turn, Jordan is an important regional asset for the United States able, through its central position, to exert a moderating influence in the area.[38] The United States looks to Jordan as an essential partner in any regional settlement, and one that, moreover, would assist in realizing U.S. policies in this respect.

Despite its dependence on U.S. aid, which at times was the regime's only means of survival, Jordan displayed significant independence from the United States during the late 1970s and 1980s. Jordan resisted U.S. pressures to join in the Camp David Accords signed between Egypt and Israel with U.S. sponsorship in 1978. King Hussein criticized the parts of the accords related to the West Bank and in particular the "impossible" role assigned to Jordan: that of protecting the Israelis from the West Bank population.[39] Such a situation would have set up Jordan for the disapproval of the Palestinian population both in Jordan and on the West Bank and would have caused the termination of the considerable Arab aid to Jordan. While Egypt could, with U.S. assistance, survive the Arab boycott, such an alternative was out of the question for Jordan. It would have risked the military intervention of other regional powers, such as Syria, and would have been untenable on economic, as well as domestic political grounds.

Although King Hussein described the 1982 Reagan initiative for peace in the area as encouraging, he grew increasingly critical of U.S. policy by the mid-1980s. He openly blamed the deteriorating atmosphere in the area—the Israeli invasion of Lebanon and the worsening conditions on the West Bank—on U.S. support for Israel. He accused the United States of maintaining a double standard and sharply criticized it in 1984 for failing to supply Jordan with arms it had previously promised.[40] The king announced his intention of going to the Soviet Union for the arms that are so necessary for Jordan's survival. King Hussein's statements reflected growing Jordanian frustration at U.S. insensitivity to the realities of the regional situation as he perceived them. He was strengthened in his independent behavior by the presence of abundant Arab aid to balance his dependence on U.S. assistance.

Jordan's ability to withstand U.S. pressures diminished toward the end of the 1980s as a result of worsening domestic and regional conditions. Due to the fall in oil prices, Arab aid was no longer as forthcoming, and Jordan suffered severe economic troubles. At the same time, the continued uprising on the West Bank had potentially destabilizing domestic effects on Jordan, and the declaration of the State of Palestine invited renewed expressions from Israel that "Jordan is Palestine." As U.S. pressure intensified for King Hussein to play a central role in a Middle East peace settlement that may have had serious consequences for the stability of his regime, Jordan had few viable options. Jordan turned to its regional connections for some means of enhancing its position.

Arab-Jordanian Relations

Jordan exerted marked efforts at consolidating its own position in the Arab world during the 1980s as well as improving the Arab environment in general. The aim of these activities was to strengthen the position of Jordan by reducing its regional liabilities as well as creating new assets. Jordanian foreign policy continued to be consistent with its moderate Arab nationalist and Islamic orientation.

In response to the Iran-Iraq war, Jordan at first attempted to play the role of mediator in an effort to contain the destructive regional consequences of the conflict. When these efforts failed, Jordan openly declared its support for Iraq, its close neighbor and ally. It called for the neutrality of the Gulf area and openly denounced the practices of the Iranian revolution as un-Islamic. These positions were motivated by Jordan's close ties with the Gulf states and fear of growing Iranian influence with Shi'i elements in Lebanon as well as the Gulf states.[41]

Jordan also viewed with alarm the Israeli invasion of Lebanon and subsequent developments there as a serious indication of the strength of extremist elements in Israeli society who are committed to the notion that Jordan is the state of Palestine. Jordan strongly denounced the invasion and arranged for some relief aid to the Palestinian population in Lebanon.

In 1984 and 1985, Jordan improved its relations with two major regional powers, Egypt and Syria. Jordan was the first Arab country to restore full diplomatic relations with Egypt after the achievement of an implicit Arab agreement in this respect. The return of relations was followed by close Jordanian-Egyptian cooperation, particularly in relation to peace efforts in the area. Jordan also played an important role in improving bilateral relations between Egypt and a number of Arab countries and founded, in cooperation with Egypt, Iraq, and North Yemen, the Arab Cooperation Council in 1989. In December 1985, Jordan announced the resumption of diplomatic relations with Syria following a Syrian-Jordanian summit meeting held in Damascus. The relations, cut off since 1980, were continued largely as a result of the special committee created by the extra-ordinary Arab summit held in Casablanca in September 1985 for the purpose of improving inter-Arab relations.[42] King Hussein assisted these efforts by indirectly apologizing to Syria for the support extended by Jordanian elements to the Moslem Brothers opposition to the Syrian regime. He also appointed, in April 1985, a new prime minister, Zeid Al-Rifaey, who enjoys close personal relations with Syrian officials, including the Syrian president Hafiz-Al-Asad. Points of diagreement between the two regimes, such as their positions on the Iran-Iraq war and the role of the PLO, remained unresolved and are potential sources of future discord.

PLO-Jordanian Relations

With the closing of the 1980s, a qualitative change occurred in the relationship of the Jordanian regime with the PLO, which opened the way for a new framework of mutual cooperation.[43] By 1985, Jordan and the PLO, with active Egyptian support, reached an agreement on a joint approach to the peace process that was based on the Arab Fez peace plan. Jordan was unable, however, to persuade the United States to deal with the PLO on the basis of this framework, and the agreement collapsed when the PLO refused to accept UN Resolution 242 on its own as the basis for peace negotiations.

The Jordanian policy of "open bridges" and "open doors" with the Palestinians of the West Bank continued, however, throughout the 1980s. This policy, which meant that the population of the West Bank could market its produce in Jordan as well as maintain ties with the Jordanian regime, was designed to enhance Jordan's position as a spokesman on behalf of the Palestinian refugees across the frontiers into Jordan. In accordance with this last consideration in particular, Jordan announced the adoption of a five-year development plan for the West Bank to parallel its own 1985-1990 development plan. This had little more than token significance, however, since Jordan was unable to generate enough financial support to implement it.[44]

The policy of open bridges with the West Bank became an increasing liability for Jordan with the continuation of the *intifada* and its potentially destabilizing effects within Jordanian society. It inspired a new departure in Jordanian foreign policy behavior, with the announcement of the termination of legal and administrative links between the East and West Banks of the River Jordan in 1988. This move set the stage for a new basis of Jordanian-PLO cooperation. Jordan appeared to finally concede all claims to the West Bank and to accept the PLO, and Palestinian President Yasser Arafat, as the sole representative of the Palestinian people.

This new understanding may not signify the end of all tension in Palestinian-Jordanian relations, however. The United States continues to urge Jordan to play a central role in the Palestinian question, along lines that are likely to be more consistent with Israeli notions of security than with Palestinian aspirations of independence or Jordanian concerns over domestic and regional vulnerability. This has already been indicated by the role assigned to Jordan in the Camp David Accords. King Hussein's announcement in December 1989 of his continued cooperation with the Palestinian President Yasser Arafat was also overshadowed by renewed Israeli declarations that Jordan is the real Palestinian state, invoking the dual threats of Israeli aggression against Jordan and radical domestic responses that may overwhelm the Jordanian monarchy.

CONCLUSION

Jordan has survived into the 1990s despite its extreme vulnerability by relying on the political skills of the monarch as displayed in the regional and international arenas. This pattern of reliance on foreign policy as the major resource for solving Jordan's problems has been called into question in the beginning of this new decade by a number of regional, economic, and political conditions that seriously limit Jordanian leverage in foreign affairs.

Jordan's inherent vulnerability manifests itself in a series of contradictions that continue to threaten the regime's survival. The centrality of Jordan's location is an important foreign policy resource, yet Jordan's inability to defend itself against regional threats makes it a constant liability. Jordan's need for economic assistance has never been greater, yet the fall in oil prices has deprived it of an important source of aid and has left it extremely vulnerable to pressures from the international environment. King Hussein's need to enhance the legitimacy of his regime led him to move in the direction of expanding political participation, which ultimately undermines the monarchic system.

The historical record cautions against underestimating the Hashemite regime or the Jordanian sense of commitment to the Hashemite Kingdom. Already Jordan is seeking new means of improving its situation by strengthening its regional links. The question remains of how adequate will these responses be in the face of intensifying pressures, and how skillful will King Hussein's successors be at manipulating Jordan's complex environment. "Uneasy lies the head,"[45] is indeed an apt description of the lot of every Hashemite called on to steer the course of the Jordanian state.

The 1990 Gulf crisis showed precisely the relevance of this autobiography's title. In a context of high tension Jordan became a victim of increasing cross-pressures. Despite the fact that by political orientation, social background, and education, the main decision-maker (King Hussein) is to be classified pro-Western, Jordan abstained or expressed reservations on Arab League resolutions (early August) condemning Iraq's invasion of Kuwait. Though the king declared Jordan's acceptance of UN sanctions against Iraq, the Jordanian port of Aqaba continued to channel food and other imports to Baghdad.

Jordan's uncomfortable middle position and its stalling for time are due to its delicate internal situation, Iraq's proximity, and the intertwining of these two countries' economies. A great majority of Jordanians—certainly the half of Palestinian origin—see Saddam as an Arab hero, unfairly attacked by the West at Israel's behest. By the first week of August more than 40,000 Jordanians were said to have volunteered to fight for Iraq. Political forces that were usually at odds (e.g., Muslim militants, leftists, and Arab nationalists) formed a national front against foreign intervention in what they consider an Arab affair. Instead of Jordan's boycotting Iraq as Western countries or the UN asked for, these people asked for the boycott of U.S. goods. Some even think that a boycott of U.S. goods would be less painful economically than boycotting Iraq, since the Jordanian and Iraqi economies are increasingly interdependent. For instance, in 1990 Iraq supplied Jordan with 95% of its crude oil. Baghdad bought almost a quarter of Jordanian exports in 1989. Iraq-related cargo accounts for 45% of traffic at Jordan's Red Sea port of Aqaba and fills two-thirds of the 12,000 trucks registered in the kingdom. In December 1989 when Iraq halted the oil exports it used to truck to the port of Aqaba, Iraq committed itself to importing all its grain through this port. These exports reached 300,000 barrels per day at the height of the war with Iran when other Iraqi outlets were cut. Aqaba port employs 15,000 of the 35,000 people working in the transport sector, one of the few areas to escape recession.

Having distanced himself from his natural allies in the West and in the Arab world, King Hussein's dilemma and his country's survival could not be more acute. As the king said to a CNN correspondent on August 12, 1990: "Ironically, I have Israel on the one hand and I have its strategic ally, the United States; on the other hand I have an Arab country threatened and I really would have to handle it as it comes." With the bitter defeat of Iraq, Jordan must feel vulnerable and threatened. Its options were limited, and King Hussein's plea in late February 1991 to forget the past and start a new chapter was rebuked by President Mubarak of Egypt. It seems that Jordan's reinstatement with the Gulf and Egypt must in all likelihood go via Damascus.

NOTES

1. The United Nations's definition of vulnerable states is "entities which are exceptionally small in area, population and human and economic resources, and which are emerging as independent states." Quoted in Ali Hassan Al-Ibraheem, *Kuwait and The Gulf* (Washington, D.C.: Georgetown University Center for Contemporary Arab Studies, 1984), p. 23.

For other interpretations of the question of vulnerability, see Michael Handel, *Weak States in the International System* (London: Frank Cass and Co., Ltd., 1981); and Elmer Plischke, *Microstates in World Affairs* (Washington, D.C.: American Institute for Public Policy Research, 1977).

2. James Hunt, "Jordan," in Michael Adams (ed.), *Handbook to the Modern World: The Middle East* (London: The Macmillan Press, Facts on File, 1988), pp. 410–412.

3. Subhi J. M. El Uteibi, "The Politics of Middle Ground: The Case of Jordan," Unpublished study (Cambridge, Mass.: Harvard University Center for International Affairs, 1983), pp. 31–32. Used by permission of the author.

4. Michael Adams (ed.), *Handbook to the Modern World: The Middle East* (London: The Macmillan Press, Facts on File, 1988), p. 53.

5. Uteibi, *op. cit.*, p. 73; see also Aaron Miller, "Jordan and the Arab-Israeli Conflict: The Hashemite Predicament," *Orbis*, 29, 4 (Winter 1986), p. 806.

6. Adams, *op. cit.*, p. 415; and Uteibi, *op. cit.*, pp. 34–37.

7. Adams, *op. cit.*, p. 709. See also *The Arab Strategic Yearbook, 1988* (Cairo: Al Ahram Center for Political and Strategic Studies, 1988), pp. 423–450, which includes a special study on the political economy of water resources in the Arab world and a discussion of the situation on the River Jordan (in Arabic).

8. These are United Nations estimates for 1986, quoted in "Jordan: Introductory Survey," *The Europa Yearbook, 1988: A World Survey*, Vol. 1 (London: Europa Publications Ltd., 1988), p. 1556.

9. Eliyaha Kanousky, *The Economic Impact of the Six-Day War* (New York: Praeger Publications, 1970), p. 146.

10. Shahal Michael, *West Bank/East Bank: The Palestinians in Jordan (1949–1967)* (New Haven, Conn.: Yale University Press, 1978), p. 2.

11. These calculations are based on statistics in *The Palestinian Refugees* (Beirut: The Institute of Palestinian Studies, 1970), p. 178.

12. Anne Deardon, *Jordan* (London: Robert Hale, 1985), pp. 87–88.

13. Adams, *op. cit.*, p. 54.

14. Saad Abu Deyya, *The Decision Making Process in Jordan's Foreign Policy* (Amman: Manshourat dar el Thagafa Wal Funun, 1983), p. 64 (in Arabic).

15. Adams, *op. cit.*, p. 709.

16. *The Europa Yearbook, 1988*, p. 1555.

17. Fahed El Fanak, "An Analysis of the Future of the Jordanian Economy," *Al-Ahram Al-Iktisadi*, September 22, 1986 (in Arabic).

18. *Ibid.*

19. Data taken from International Monetary Fund, *Balance of Payments Yearbook*, for the respective years, cited in Robert Satiloff, *Trouble on the East Bank: Domestic Challenges to the Stability of Jordan* (Washington, D.C.: The Center for Strategic and International Studies, Georgetown University, 1986), p. 10.

20. World Bank, *World Development Report, 1989*, p. 171.

21. El Fanak, *op. cit.*

22. World Bank, *World Development Report, 1989*, p. 171.

23. *Ibid.*, p. 203.

24. *Ibid.*, p. 199.

25. *The Europa Yearbook, 1988*, p. 1555.

26. *The Military Balance 1989–1990* (London: International Institute of Strategic Studies, 1989). Figures on Jordan, p. 104, Saudi Arabia, p. 111, Syria, p. 114, Israel, p. 102, and Iraq, p. 101.

27. M. Graeme Bannerman, "The Hashemite Kingdom of Jordan," in David E. Long and Bernard Reich (eds.), *The Government and Politics of the Middle East and North Africa* (Boulder, Colo.: Westview Press, 1980), p. 264.

28. Hala Mostafa, "Jordan and the Democratic Experiment," *Al-Ahram*, January 12, 1990 (in Arabic).

29. *Ibid.*

30. Uteibi, *op. cit.*, p. 19.

31. *Ibid.*, pp. 66–71.

32. Naseer H. Aruri, *Jordan: A Study in Political Development (1921–1965)* (The Hague: Martinus Ninjoff, 1972), p. 169.

33. King Hussein I, *Uneasy Lies the Head: An Autobiography of Hussein Iben Tallal of Jordan* (London: Bernard G. Association, 1962), p. 90.

34. Miller, *op. cit.*, pp. 816–820.

35. Hunt, in Adams, *op. cit.*, p. 414.

36. Samir A. Mutawi, *Jordan in the 1967 War* (London: Cambridge University Press, 1987), pp. 13–14.

37. Uteibi, *op. cit.*, pp. 8 and 12–16.

38. Miller, *op. cit.*, p. 816.

39. Statements by King Hussein published in the *New York Times*, April 8, 1979.

40. Hassan Abou Taleb, "Jordanian criticisms of American foreign policy," *Al-Siyassa Al-Dawliya*, July 1984, pp. 118–120 (in Arabic).

41. Uteibi, *op. cit.*, pp. 66–70.

42. Ahmad Abul Hassen Zaid, "The Syrian-Jordanian Summit," *Al-Siyassa Al-Dawliya*, April 1986, pp. 141–144.

43. Uteibi, *op. cit.*, pp. 80–82.

44. *Arab Strategic Yearbook, 1988*, p. 372.

45. King Hussein, *op. cit.*, autobiography's title.

8

Heroic Politics:
The Foreign Policy of Libya

I. William Zartman
A. G. Kluge

Since the military coup that overthrew the government of King Idris in 1969, the foreign policy of what is now formally called the Socialist People's Libyan Arab Jamahiriya has earned the country a reputation as an "Arab Prussia" and an "international gadfly."[1] Libyan leader Colonel Muammer Al-Qaddafi, generally recognized as the strongman behind the state's power, has been associated with international terrorism on a grand scale, from attempts to destabilize neighboring countries to the funding of radical groups such as the Irish Republican Army (IRA) and the Palestine Liberation Organization.[2] Libyan foreign policy, like Libya's leader, is widely perceived to be capricious. Egyptian president Anwar Al-Sadat even went so far as to call Qaddafi "crazy."[3] Such labels, however, do not serve to increase our understanding of Libya's leader or its foreign policy. It is a serious mistake to dismiss what initially may appear alien or incomprehensible. Or, as one scholar of Arab politics writes: "It is easier to judge but hard to understand the ghosts with which people and societies battle, the wounds and memories that drive them to do what they do. Even if we disagree with people's choice of allegiance, we must understand the reasons for their choice, the odds they fight against, the range of alternatives open to them."[4]

The task, then, is to convey the motives, opportunities, and constraints that influence Libyan state behavior. The unpredictability of human enterprises will not disappear, but from this perspective Libyan foreign policy emerges more clearly as a product of a particular cultural and historical context. It is against this backdrop that this chapter outlines the beginning of a framework for analyzing Libya's foreign policy as that of a rational, goal-oriented nation pursuing its professed revolutionary aims of "freedom, socialism, and unity." What makes it so controversial is not only its hostility toward the great powers of the West but also its unconventional nature, for it challenges—basically, unsuccessfully—the established rules by which foreign relations are generally conducted.

DOMESTIC ENVIRONMENT

Historical Legacy

The conception of foreign policy as the "role" of a nation has deep grounding in Arab political tradition and is a powerful tool for understanding Libyan behavior in particular.[5] The language of heroism and historical role was used by the revolutionary new Egyptian premier, Gamal Abdal Nasser, in 1955 to describe his perception of the Arab world of his time:

> For some reason it seems to me that within the Arab circle there is a role, wandering aimlessly in search of a hero. And I do not know why it seems to me that this role, exhausted by its wanderings, has at last settled down, tired and weary, near the borders of our country and is beckoning to us to move, to take up its lines, to put on its costume, since no one else is qualified to play it.[6]

With the defiant seizure of the Suez Canal from British control in 1956, Nasser's Egypt became the center and symbol of Arab unity and assertiveness. For a time, it appeared that Egypt had successfully assumed the role "to spark this tremendous power latent" in the Arab world.[7]

To Qaddafi, listening to Radio Cairo's Voice of the Arabs and plotting to depose the Libyan monarchy, Nasser was a hero and example. Even after the Arab defeat of 1967 at the hands of the Israelis revealed the illusions of Nasser's pan-Arabism, Qaddafi remained loyal to the shattered dreams of his spiritual father, and the defeat spurred his coup against the Libyan monarchy two years later.

The content and heroic form of Nasser's aims continued to have a profound influence on Qaddafi's policies. Just after the Libyan coup in 1969, Qaddafi reported to Mohamed Heikal, then Egyptian minister of information and former editor of *Al-Ahram*: "Libya represents depth. We have hundreds of miles of Mediterranean coastline; we have the airfields; we have the money; we have everything: tell President Nasser we made this revolution for him. He can take everything of ours and add it to the rest of the Arab world's resources to be used for the battle."[8] The total identification of Libya with the goals of Nasser provoked Heikal to call Qaddafi "shockingly innocent—scandalously pure."[9] The incident nevertheless gives telling insight into Qaddafi and his perception of Libya as a geopolitical hinterland for the policies of Nasser.

On the rhetorical level at least, Qaddafi's espousal of Nasser's revolutionary goals of "freedom, socialism, and unity" has been remarkably consistent. Since the 1977 proclamation of the new Libyan constitution and "Jamahiriya" or "state of the masses," neither Qaddafi nor his former Revolutionary Command Council (RCC) insurrectionists hold official posts in the government. Qaddafi nevertheless remains the de facto head of the state and the chief architect of Libyan foreign policy. Qaddafi's frequent pronouncements on foreign policy, in the press and his widely publicized *Green Book,* represent both an adherence to and a unique elaboration of Nasserism.

Qaddafi's brand of neo-Nasserism is distinctive in several respects. Nasser's view of his nation's role was shaped by the Egyptian experience; he spoke with the prestige and worldly wisdom of Cairo and with the authority of Egypt's tens of millions of people. Qaddafi's vision of his country's role shares much with that of Nasser, but it also bears the marks of Libya's different cultural traditions and socioeconomic conditions. Heikal writes of Qaddafi:

> Two people and two backgrounds combined to make Qaddafi the man he was. The people were the Prophet Mohammed and Gamal Abdel Nasser. . . . His two backgrounds were the army and the desert. . . . Qaddafi's difficulty was that he lacked the resources and the experience to enable him to digest all the conflicting influences that operated on him. But the result of this conflict was a personality of fascinating complexity.[10]

Heikal saw Qaddafi as a complicated mix of Nasserism and Islam, but he also claimed, at least in the 1970s, that Qaddafi was "a simple puritan caught up in a complicated world full of intrigue and manoeuvre."[11]

Lastly, Qaddafi's loyalty is to the dreams of the charismatic and heroic Nasser of the days of Suez, rather than to the wiser man who survived the Arabs' crushing 1967 defeat. Many of Qaddafi's policies show the characteristics of heroic politics, betraying more aesthetic appeal than political wisdom. For example, Qaddafi continues to proselytize the unimpressive "Third International Theory" of his *Green Book.* In the typical wisdom of the *Green Book,* Qaddafi advocates direct political participation of the masses, stating: "Theoretically, this is the genuine democracy. But realistically, the strong always rule, i.e., the stronger part in the society is the one that rules."[12] Qaddafi vastly overestimates the applicability and importance of the grand schemes of the *Green Book.* In 1979, Qaddafi told a Western journalist: "The Green Book is the new gospel. . . . One of its words can destroy the world. Or save it . . . the third world only needs my Green Book. My word. One word and the whole world could blow up. The value of things could change. And their weight . . . everywhere and forever."[13]

There is indeed a very Sufi-sounding tone to this and many other of Qaddafi's statements that is quite different from Nasser's language.[14] For Qaddafi is neither a copy nor an imitation of Nasser but rather is inspired by his example, expressing similar goals in different ways. Here enters a second source of Qaddafi's views and behavior, the mystic and fundamentalist reformist of the Libyan desert. Alongside of the secular neo-Nasserism is the purifying religious movement of the Senussiya, established about 1843 in Cyrenaica.[15] Although centered in Libya and later headed by Idris Al-Senussi, who became Libya's first and last monarch, the Senussiya was an international movement calling for a return to basic revitalized Islam. As a reaction against the formalism and the corruption of urban practices of the time, the Senussiya represented one of the recurring waves of desert revivalism that Ibn Khaldun identified as a feature of the Arab world.[16] In all of the characteristics, the "Qaddafiya" is similar to its predecessor, the latest wave of austere fundamentalist revivalism, seeking to create solidarity across state boundaries.

Grand schemes, dramatic and irrevocable decisions appeal to Qaddafi. During the Israeli siege of Beirut in 1982 (to cite a recent example), Qaddafi urged PLO commander Yasser Arafat "to commit suicide rather than accept disgrace." "Your suicide will immortalize the cause of Palestine for future generations. . . . It is the road to victory. . . . It is the decision to die."[17] Martyrdom may be heroic, but in the context of the Arab-Israeli dispute it is hardly the most practical course.

Geography and Population

The second element in the domestic environment from which Qaddafi's foreign policy springs is the geographic and demographic "depth" that he offered to Nasser.[18] Libya is a big country (the fourth largest in Africa) with few people (4 million, ranking thirty-third in Africa and eleventh in the Arab world). The vast land area has little value other than its geostrategic location on the Mediterranean shore and the borders of four Arab and two Sahelian countries. Little of it is arable today, even though it was the breadbasket for Rome some fifteen centuries ago. Its meager population, a twelfth the size of Egypt's, is concentrated in three areas, around Tripoli and Benghazi on the coast and along the Fezzan oases in the southwestern interior. Only Tripolitania has an urban tradition, and it is scarcely the cosmopolitan center one finds in most other Arab countries. The one thing of value the land holds is oil, in reserves estimated at the beginning of the 1990s at 20 billion barrels, enough to provide the small population with a per capita income of $9,000 at the beginning of the 1980s and $6,000 a decade later. Since Qaddafi's coup, this wealth has been used for an ambitious social welfare program (including extensive education facilities) and for equally ambitious foreign ventures (including extensive arms acquisitions far beyond Libya's own capabilities for use).[19] In sum, Libya's position is exactly the reverse of Egypt's: Libya has few people and much wealth in a peripheral position, whereas Egypt is burdened with a large population and few resources, situated in a central location in both the Arab and global strategic world.

The implications of this situation for foreign policy are straightforward. Libya has the means (oil) and the purpose (neo-Nasserism) that the Arabs need, but lacks the population and strategic location of other

Arab states. The goal of Libya policy is to unite the two, a goal that at the same time follows and leads to the neo-Nasserite purpose of Arab unity and anti-imperialism. Of course, other Arab countries have oil too, but they do not have a clear vision (or a vision at all) of the role that Qaddafi has seen, and so it becomes important to build popular Arab support and adherence to Qaddafi's policy, not just state support.[20]

Economic and Military Capabilities

Economic and military capabilities in relation to foreign policy are determined by population and geography. Except for its oil production and revenues, Libya has only a small national economy, and is highly dependent on outside sources of supply for both food and manufactured goods. Despite intensive efforts, Libyan agriculture has not given the nation the desired self-sufficiency. Nor is this likely to occur in the near future, in some measure because of poor management and planning.[21] Libya has no industrial base and no raw material to transform. There is no armaments industry and no possibility of developing self-sufficiency in armaments. Libya's military is limited by the small population and by its lack of a background in technical skills or in military traditions in general. But it is geography that fuels Libyan foreign policy through its contribution of oil revenues. Libya's policy is a perfect fit to Walter Lippman's statement that a state's foreign policy ends and means must always be in balance. Faced with a sudden windfall of oil revenues in the late 1960s and thereafter, Qaddafi responded with sweeping goals and unconventional approaches. But when the oil revenues fell off after 1985, Qaddafi pulled in his horns and became much more conventional and less disruptive in his approach, tailoring his immediate goals to his reduced means. The same logic indicates that a new rise in oil prices—as predicted for the mid-1990s—would revive the goals of military adventure, wide support for revolutionary movements, material inducements for foreign policy support, and reassertion of a hard line in Arab and African revolutionary causes.

Libya's army stands at 90,000, the seventh largest in Africa and the eighth in the Arab world, about the size of Saudi Arabia's. It has been growing steadily since the military government came to power, with the largest jump in 1978, when it increased by two-thirds over the previous year, and in 1982–1984, when it nearly doubled again. There is a high ratio of soldiers to civilians (24 : 1), much higher than other African and Arab states (except for Syria, Iraq, and UAE).[22] Qaddafi, who knows about military coups, rather scorns his army, and in 1988, on the nineteenth anniversary of his own coup and following on military dissatisfaction and reversals in Chad, he announced the dissolution of the army; however, later that year he specified only a reorganization into a regular army of "Jamahiri Guards," compulsory two-year conscripts, and part-time recruits. The army still depends on foreign training and even foreign operators, particularly in the air force. Soviets, North

Koreans, Pakistanis, and Palestinians pilot Libyan planes.[23] The results have not been outstanding: The Libyan army was beaten by the Egyptians in the border war of July 1977 and the Chadians and their allies in the fight for northern Chad in 1987, and its efforts on behalf of fallen governments in Uganda (1979) and Chad (1983) have not been successful. Libya's most impressive military activity has been its transport capability, notably demonstrated in the airlift and groundlift of tanks and troops to Chad in 1981, carried out with Soviet assistance. Libya is a party to three presumably inactive military assistance treaties, the 1975 Treaty of Hassi Mess'oud with Algeria, the 1981 Treaty of Aden with Ethiopia and South Yemen, and the 1980 unification agreement with Syria. The orientations indicated in these treaties were superseded at the end of the decade by the Marrakesh treaty of February 17, 1989 instituting the Arab Maghret Union (UMA). The treaty has only negative security implications, in that it prohibits support of any activity or alliance that would threaten the security of cosignatories but does not create collective defense obligations. It ties Libya to an economic ensemble that is planned to create a security community as much as any military treaty.[24]

Political Structure

By advocating both Islam and socialism, or social justice, Qaddafi has tried to monopolize the cultural symbols of legitimacy. In addition, Qaddafi has taken a strong stance on what is perceived to be a powerful test of Arab nations: support for the Palestinian cause.

Libya has a long tradition of rebellious and powerful religious leaders. In recognition of the power of Islam, from genuine belief, or both, Qaddafi has attempted to give an Islamic cast to the Jamahiriya (people's state) by reviving the Qur'an as the basis of Libyan legislation.[25] Qaddafi's personal and modernist interpretation of Islam has alienated more traditional members of society, yet to Qaddafi Islamic society is a radically different and important alternative to Communist and Western models.

In practice, Qaddafi and his junta have been grappling with age-old questions of governance as they search for new and satisfying answers. The repeated attempt to find appropriate institutions for the revolution has taken forms that seek to be as inventive as the neologism "jamahiriya." Qaddafi's regime has tried to combine authority and participation, giving power to the people and at the same time completely reorienting the people's notions of what to do with power. Qaddafi's attempts have been serious, but in the end, his answers have not been new, and the outcome of his effort to reconcile conflicting values has been the classical response of authoritarianism and reorientation, under the label of popular power and participation.

The first round of institutions covered the first half of the 1970s, when authority was represented by the Revolutionary Control Council of the Free Officers, with participation by the people's committees and the Arab Socialist Union, all Nasserist bodies.[26] When each body failed to do its job, the reorganization of 1975 began, leading to the second round. The institutions were embodied in the current pyramid of "people's" bodies, with the People's General Congress (PGC) as the surrogate legislature and the people's committees acting as participatory organs at all levels. Various secretaries were appointed as agents of authority and control. For further vigor and control, appointed revolutionary committees were gradually added, creating more disorder than revolutionary fervor. In 1978, a third phase of socialist austerity began, which in turn alienated the same growing middle class that the oil boom had favored. As dissatisfaction grew, so did repression. The confrontation reached its height in 1986, when an opposition movement appeared close to overthrowing the government.[27] At that time, the U.S. raid on Tripoli had the dual effect of consolidating nationalist support behind the regime (thus delegitimizing the opposition) and causing a time of uncertainty and then apparent liberalization in government. A new government introduced to the PGC in March 1987 was largely composed of technocrats, and it in turn introduced a number of measures relaxing state control of society and economy, privatizing much of production, proclaiming a human rights charter, and opening up (and even demolishing) prisons. Nonetheless, the conflict between authority and participation has not yet been resolved.

LIBYAN FOREIGN POLICY ORIENTATION: "FREEDOM AND UNITY"

In order to assess the success of Libya in playing out the neo-Nasserist role it has defined, at least rhetorically, for itself, it is necessary to examine the specifics of the state's official policy as well as its actual behavior. In the Nasserist slogan of "freedom, socialism, and unity," proclaimed in 1969 to be the guiding philosophy of the Libyan revolution, "freedom" deliberately is first. Though the definitions of the terms overlap in Libyan usage, "freedom" is closely related to "socialism" and is considered the essential means to the ultimate goal of Arab "unity."

In a speech in Tripoli shortly after the revolution, Qaddafi set forth the official interpretation of the Nasserist slogan. "Freedom . . . is the liberation of our dear land from all evil and intruders, from every imperialist and reactionary element, and also emancipation of the Arab homeland, in all its parts, from every intruder and guilty aggressor."[28] Qaddafi sees "freedom" as the elimination of imperialist and reactionary elements both from Libya and from the "Arab homeland," i.e., from the Arab states and Palestine.

From the very beginning of his regime, Qaddafi has been critical both of the "imperialist" camp (initially Israel, the United States, and the USSR; later only the first two) and of "reactionary" Arab states. Though Qaddafi asserts that Libya is an Islamic regime, he is nevertheless critical of Arab and Islamic regimes that are in his opinion reactionary.

Heikal cites an interesting Qaddafi assessment of King Hassan of Morocco at the Rabat summit in December 1969. As the chief of the royal cabinet greeted King Hassan by kissing his hand, in keeping with Moroccan tradition, Qaddafi is "horrified," Heikal writes. Heikal notes Qaddafi's outburst: "Does hand kissing still go on in the Arab world? Do we still stick to these relics of feudalism and slavery? How are we ever going to liberate Palestine if we still kiss hands?"[29]

The example points to an important and continuing strain in Qaddafi's policy—his perception that a modernist stance (albeit Islamic) is necessary for freedom. This modernist inclination is an important factor in Qaddafi's relations with the conservative Arab states and in his relations with the Soviet Union and its client nations.

"Freedom" has an additional, related meaning in official Libyan ideology. In the same 1969 Tripoli speech Qaddafi stated: "Freedom also is the liberation of the individual from poverty, illness, ignorance, and injustice."[30] This internal freedom is closely related to what Qaddafi means by "socialism." Libyan socialism is used synonymously with the phrase "social justice" to distinguish it from a Marxist-atheistic socialism deemed incompatible with Islam. "The people who have long been deprived of social justice, and whose wealth and treasures have been robbed will accept no alternative for socialism. They will impose socialism by force and will fight for it until social justice has become an accomplished fact and until this people has ensured a sufficiency in production along with just distribution.[31] Clearly, beneath the martial rhetoric is an attempt to rally the people behind Qaddafi's aim. The goal of socialism, one gathers from the phrases, means a socially just distribution (apparently based on Islamic principles) and self-sufficiency. Qaddafi's vision of self-sufficiency implies an autarkic state.

Further elaborating foreign policy goals for his country, Qaddafi delineates a progressive or dynamic sequence of policies.

> In order to preserve this great and national unity which is a distinguishing mark of Libya, the door should be closed to partisanship. Regionalism should also on no account be allowed to grow after today. We must raise the following slogans and proceed behind their banners, towards execution and application. We must raise the slogan of full evacuation, of positive neutralism and of non-alignment. We must raise the slogan of "being hostile to those who antagonize us, and being friends to those who befriend us." We must also raise the slogan of national unity as a first step along the road of all-embracing Arab unity.[32]

From this statement, we may discern important elements of Qaddafi's foreign policy.[33] First is his emphasis on Libyan unity. Second is his goal of full independence, i.e., no foreign military bases. Third are the broader goals of "positive neutralism and non-alignment" and of support for helping powers and enmity for hostile powers. And of course, true to the Nasserist tradition, Qaddafi claims his ultimate goal to be an "all-embracing Arab unity." It should be noted that the first and last goals are those of consolidation of power, perhaps Qaddafi's power.

As with most countries, one might expect to find various shifts and phases in Libyan foreign policy, perhaps corresponding to periods in Libyan domestic policy.[34] Indeed, for about the first five years of the regime, such periods can be noted: first a focus on recovering control of national assets (bases, oil prices, oil production) in 1969–1971; then (and slightly overlapping), the period of Arab unification, with Sudan, Syria, and Egypt, in 1970–1973, ending in isolation; and then a last attempt with Tunisia in 1974. Certainly, the time of isolation during the October War of 1973, corresponding with the time of domestic renewal in the Cultural Revolution, was a serious turning point in Libyan political behavior. It seems to have led to a new period of disenchantment with the Arab East and renewed attention to the Arab West and the Moslem south. The short-lived Libyan union with Tunisia was followed the next year by the Hassi Mess'oud treaty with Algeria; at the same time, Libya took on initial funding of the People's Liberation Front for Saguia Al Hamra and Rio de Oro (Polisario) in the Western Sahara, financial aid for Mauritania and then direct interference after the military coup of 1978, and growing support for dissident groups in Mali, Niger, and eventually Senegal. By the early 1980s Libya was providing support for military coups in Gambia, Ghana, and Upper Volta, and direct support for the rebellion in Chad after the conservative military coup in 1975 through the union attempt and military occupation of 1981. Close relations with the military government of Idi Amin in Uganda also covered the last half of the 1970s. After Sadat's visit to Jerusalem in 1977, Qaddafi helped found the Rejectionist Front and then the Steadfastness Front, remaining faithful to their principles (the three "no's" of the Arab summit resolution of Khartoum in 1967: "no" to direct negotiations with Israel, "no" to recognition of Israel, and "no" to peace with Israel) even after their collapse in 1982 at the Arab summit of Fez. But in the first half of the 1980s, Libya found itself increasingly isolated in its Steadfastness among the Arabs and increasingly rejected in its Chadian campaign among the Africans. Libyan foreign policy became dominated by efforts to break out of isolation at as little cost as possible to substantive goals. Libya's informal entente with Morocco in 1983 and then its formalization as the Arab-African Union in 1984 was such an effort. But the latter, the Oujda Treaty, was denounced by Morocco in 1986, and the entry into the Algerian-Tunisian-Mauritanian Friendship Treaty was blocked by Tunisia in 1987. The proposed union referendum with Algeria of the same year was vetoed within Algeria itself. The presidential succession and a more supple policy in Tunisia, economic constraints and a more accommodating policy in Algeria, and a Libyan willingness to agree to something less than absolute union as a price for rescue from isolation all combined in 1989 to produce the Arab Maghreb Union as the 1990s, or cooperative, phase of Libyan foreign policy.

A closer look at dates blurs the phases. Qaddafi's interest in Mauritania dates from his visit there in 1972, when he discovered that Mauritanians speak the same Arabic dialect as his maternal home; that same year marks the visit of President Ngarta Tombalbaye to Libya and the Chadian "secret recognition" of Libyan rights over the 'Aouzou Strip of northern Chad. Official truces with Morocco and renouncement of all disputes with the monarchy in mid-1981 and mid-1983 may show a pattern of regularity, but this pattern was interrupted by the wreckage of the OAU summit over the Saharan and Chadian issues on two occasions in 1982 and the renewed intervention in Chad in mid-1983.

It appears that Libyan foreign policy is a policy of opportunity, conducted on the basis of rather constant principles as outlined above. When an opportunity presents itself, Libya acts. When opposition is too strong, Libya effects a strategic withdrawal, but not a change in goals. Ironically, this tactical flexibility no doubt contributes to Qaddafi's reputation as opportunistic and capricious and hides the consistency of his goals.

THE DECISION-MAKING PROCESS

The personalization of Libyan policy and the interchangeable usage of the leader for the country are not merely literary devices; Qaddafi is the personal policy chief of Libya, to an even greater extent in foreign than in domestic policy. He makes specific decisions of importance and establishes the ideological context within which they are made; Qaddafi is his own chief delegate and envoy as well as the leading foreign policy authority at home. Yet, without suffering any diminution, this personal primacy does operate within an institutional framework and under some political constraints.

The agency responsible for foreign relations in Libya is the Office of External Contacts (*Maktab Al-Itisal Al-Khariji*), which replaced the Foreign Ministry in 1980. The office is chaired by the secretary of the People's Committee for External Contacts; under the Jamahiriya system the people in a branch of service form a committee and choose their own manager. Overseas, the office is represented by Fraternity Offices (*Makatib Al-Ikhiwa*) in Arab and Moslem countries and People's Offices (*Makatib Al-Sha'biya*) in others. Again in theory, it is the Libyan community in these countries that constitutes these offices and chooses its leaders. In fact, however, the various offices in Libya and abroad are run as a diplomatic service, with offices posted as decided in Tripoli and officials appointed by Qaddafi or by diplomatic officials.

The actual operations within this structure or in the political circles outside are difficult to penetrate. Qaddafi's most visible and active lieutenants are External Contacts Secretary Jadullah Azzouz Al-Tal and former foreign minister and then presidential advisor for foreign relations Abdel Salam Triki. On occasion the remaining Free Officers act as either emissaries or collegial decision-makers: Major Abdel-Salam Jallud, in charge of government affairs; General Abu Bakr Unis Jabr, in command of the army; General Mustafa Kharrubi, in charge of intelligence; and Major Khuwaildi Hamidi, in charge of the people's militia and chief of staff. Similarly, other presidential advisors besides Triki are sometimes involved in foreign affairs as they touch political matters (Omar Al-Osta) and security matters (Ahmed Keddaf Eddem).[35]

Apart from a few notable events, little is known about divisions of advice and opinion on foreign relations among these members of the foreign affairs group. The most serious of these events was the Meheishi affair in 1975, a major turning point in the direction of the junta.[36] Major Omar Al-Meheishi, one of the original Free Officers, sought to restrain the emerging radical orientation of the regime and to limit its foreign adventures and its heavy spending for Soviet arms at a time when oil revenues were in temporary decline. His planned coup was discovered and checked, and Meheishi fled to Egypt and then to Morocco, from whence he was returned to Libya during the Oujda Treaty and murdered. Earlier there had been serious disagreement over related matters: the decision in late 1970 to push for union with Egypt over closer Maghrebi relations, the decision to pursue the union with Egypt despite a cool reception in July 1972 and March 1973, and the decision to come to a "medium high" rather than a "high high" settlement with the oil companies in the second Tripoli negotiations of March 1971.[37] On the Egyptian decisions, Qaddafi won, in the latter instances by threatening the opposing majority with his resignation; in the 1970 case, Free Officer Mohamed Najm was forced to resign as foreign minister. In the petroleum case, Jallud prevailed over Qaddafi in collegial decision-making. Since the Meheishi affair, however, decision-making has been less collegial among the military colleagues, the original junta has been reduced in size, and specific sectors of politics have been assigned. Even Jallud had a falling out in the mid-1980s over Chadian policy and went abroad to Syria when the Chadian offensive failed in 1986 before returning to favor a year later. The members of the foreign affairs group are advisors, not lieutenants, to Qaddafi.

FOREIGN POLICY BEHAVIOR

The Third International Theory of Qaddafi's *Green Book* suggests an alternative model of political, economic, and cultural development to those advocated by the Communist and Western blocs.

> The Third International Theory is offered as a substitute for communist and capitalist ideology, applicable specifically to Islamic countries but also offering useful principles to non-Islamic Third World states. Libya advocates nonalignment in general and positive neutrality in particular as alternatives to alignment with either East or West. Whereas nonalignment is based on merely the avoidance of ties with either of the two blocs, positive neutrality

involves the aggressive pursuit of foreign policy goals that may include bilateral relations short of alignment with the East and West.[38]

It is clear that Qaddafi does not pursue nonalignment as defined here, "the avoidance of ties with either bloc." As we have seen, however, Qaddafi does endorse the goal of Libyan self-sufficiency. He is especially concerned with agricultural self-sufficiency, which is a high priority of the regime: "There is no independence for those who secure their food from abroad."[39]

Libya and the West

Rhetoric aside, Libya has fairly stable commercial relations with the West and continues to be dependent on the West for food, manufactured goods, and even some skilled labor. With the notable exception of military purchases, the pattern of Libyan imports has changed little from before the 1969 revolution to the present. A former Italian colony, in 1979 Libya imported approximately 26.4% of its general purchases from Italy (up from 21.6% in 1970). Germany (14.3%), France (8.2%), and Japan (8.9%) followed just behind Italy as sources of imports in 1979; this ranking has remained constant since 1971 through the 1980s.[40]

Moreover, Libya continues to export far more heavily to Western Europe (and from 1975 to 1982, the United States) than to the Soviet bloc nations or other developing nations. In 1979 the United States was the Jamahiriya's single largest export recipient (36.1%, up from 2.7% in 1970). Italy followed, receiving 18% of Libyan exports (down from 25.9% in 1970).[41]

Ironically, until President Reagan's embargo on the U.S. purchase of Libyan crude in 1982, Libyan exports to the United States showed an inverse relation to the deteriorating political relations between the two countries. Libya succeeded in the early 1970s in taking majority control of most foreign oil companies on its soil.[42] Libya is still dependent on foreign technicians, however, to operate the petroleum plants. Since the exodus of U.S. workers in 1982, Libya has been successful in recruiting engineers from Canada, Iran, Algeria, Kuwait, and the United Arab Emirates.[43] In all sectors including the oil industry, Libya had 467,000 foreign workers at the end of 1981, a figure approaching half the native Libyan labor force.

Libya's foreign debts were reported to be $10 billion in 1983, "of which $2.3 [billion] is owed to foreign companies exporting to Libya and $6–7 [billion] to construction firms operating there."[44] Libya is reportedly making attempts to step up exports to Soviet bloc nations, in order to relieve international debts and to pay for arms purchases. With the world recession, the U.S. embargo is affecting Libyan development plans as well as Libyan military activity:

> The world oil glut, coupled with the U.S. embargo, has greatly hampered the implementation of the $62.5bn five-year plan for 1981–1985, which

was announced at the General People's Congress in January 1981. Libya's production of oil had fallen to 0.5m bpd, and income from oil exports was well below current expenditure. As a result, Colonel Qaddafi was forced to withdraw his troops from neighboring Chad, and sought to settle debts with trading partners such as Turkey, Greece, Sweden and East European countries.[45]

Despite the American embargo and the world oil glut, Libya still maintains an unusually large economy for a Third World country—tied with Saudi Arabia for the fourth highest per capita Arab GNP and the highest per capita African GNP—and one that is closely tied to the West. European policies of business-as-usual with Libya often leave the United States isolated in its attempts to create a common Western policy toward Libya. Even a decade and more later, a 1979 financial report is still relevant:

> Through the Libyan Arab Foreign Bank (LAFB), millions of petrodollars are being funneled to such economically weak and politically unstable European nations as Italy, Turkey, Spain, and Greece. No one knows how much money Libya has invested abroad, but in the last two years it has bought nearly 10% of Italy's Fiat, for $415 million; given a $300 million loan to Turkey to curb its slide into political chaos; and sent hundreds of millions of dollars to Spain, Greece, Tunisia, and Morocco.[46]

Libya's dependence on, and investment in, Western nations (not to mention Libya's significant dependence on the skilled labor of pro-Western allies, such as Egypt and Tunisia, in the Libyan work force) form one element in Libya's ambivalent relation with the West. "Despite its huge Soviet-supplied arsenal and an ideology vaguely evocative of Marxism, the country still leans economically toward the West, selling oil to the United States and its European allies and purchasing their technology. Libyan students go to universities in the United States, not the Soviet Union."[47] Another primary element of Libya's relation to the West is Qaddafi's opposition to Western "imperialism," which is responsible for his alliance with the Soviet Union and his support of international terrorism.

Qaddafi is alleged to be associated with international terrorism and national liberation movements of every sort. Terrorist organizations tend to be secretive about supporters and funding, hence Libyan backing is often difficult to prove. Qaddafi admits backing Uganda's dictator Idi Amin, the Italian Red Brigades, the IRA, and radical "rejectionist" factions of the PLO. Less clear is Qaddafi's involvement in several hijackings and the 1972 Munich Olympics massacre of Israeli athletes.[48] One scholar of Libyan politics, John Wright, asserts that there is evidence that Qaddafi pursues foreign adventures for the sake of international prestige or notoriety and that his actual monetary contributions are correspondingly exaggerated.[49] If this is true, then U.S. hysteria about Libyan threats to U.S. security and purported assassination attempts on U.S. figures only contributes to his power.[50] Similarly, the gunboat diplomacy of the Reagan administration, including the 1986 raid on Tripoli and the last-gasp dogfight and mooted chemical plant raid of early 1989, both raises Qaddafi's prestige and shows him to be a symbolic surrogate for more dangerous radicals of the Middle East who are beyond the range of U.S. power.

Libya and the Soviet Union

Though Libya is no more "free" in 1990 of dependency on Western goods and services than it was before the coup, Qaddafi has succeeded in changing the orientation of Libyan foreign policy. Under the Senussi monarchy of King Idris, Libya was timid and Western-oriented.[51] Under pressure from Qaddafi, the British and Americans agreed to evacuate their military bases in Libya. The withdrawals were complete in 1970.[52] In the years since, Qaddafi has given Libyan foreign policy a strident pan-Arabist voice and has shifted its primary military alliance to the Soviet Union.

At present, Libya's most important military ally is the Soviet Union. Although in 1978 Qaddafi threatened to join the Warsaw Pact, he has thus far been neither invited nor accepted. A friendship treaty was agreed on "in principle" in March 1983 but not signed. Qaddafi has overcome his initial antipathy to the atheistic Communism of the Soviet Union and to what he criticized in the early 1970s as Soviet "imperialist designs" in the Indo-Pakistani war.[53] From limited initial arms deals with France, Qaddafi turned to the Soviets to supply a new increase in armaments purchases. Until about 1973, the new Libyan regime purchased a generally balanced array of military supplies, but in 1974–1975, the Libyan regime began to purchase arms for apparent stockpile rather than use.[54] Purchases rose over the following decade, then dropped after 1983 to about a third of the previous highs of 1979 and 1982. It should be noted, however, that Libya has been only about 50% dependent on Soviet arms. The other 50% is almost equally shared by Western Europe, Eastern Europe, China, and new Third World suppliers.

Like everything else in the clandestine world of strategy and arms transfers, specific rationales for arms acquisitions seldom appear uncloaked in the press. Since the early 1970s Libya has acquired more weaponry than is warranted for the purpose of national defense:

> Libya, with fewer than 3,000,000 people and such unthreatening neighbours as Tunisia, Niger, Chad and Sudan, has the tenth largest force of medium tanks in the world. With the exception of Israel and Syria, all the other members of this select group with over 2,000 tanks have at least ten times Libya's population. Libya is the limiting case in that class of oil-rich, population-poor states whose defence expenditure is neither constrained by circumstances nor directed against recognisable military threats. Nor does it seem bound by an unimaginative adherence to traditional military percepts: the ratio of tanks to artillery pieces in the Libyan army is of the order of 13 to 1.[55]

The Soviet Union is not forthcoming about its motives in supplying such massive arms to the Libyans. Soviet academician Anatoly Gromyko states, "the USSR and Africa's independent countries are closely cooperating to eliminate the vestiges of racism and colonialism and fight against neocolonialism, and that brings notable results and promotes closer relations between this country and the young African states."[56] At the same time, Gromyko asserts that the Soviet Union opposes the export of any kind of revolution and that it offers aid only to legitimate governments. Official Soviet statements about the provision of aid or arms to Africa are cloaked in the rhetoric of trade, cooperation, and of course, anti-imperialist liberation. Other analysts, however, offer more mundane reasons for the Soviet provision of arms to Africa and to Libya.

Analysts have pointed out that the Soviets began shipping arms to Libya in the mid-1970s not only because they were annoyed at being expelled from Egypt, but because they were seeking the hard currency that the Libyan oil revenues provide: "Particularly noteworthy among Soviet objectives is a familiar capitalist imperative—to acquire hard currency in order to meet balance of payments deficits resulting from trade with the United States and Western Europe. Interestingly, Soviet agreements with oil producing countries have almost always been concluded on a cash (hard currency) basis."[57] While giving lip service to common causes, the Soviets have always been wary of too close an association with Qaddafi's enterprises. As he moved into the 1980s, Qaddafi sought ever closer Soviet protection against ever more aggressive U.S. pressure; yet his remaining notions of nonalignment kept him from providing the one element that the Soviets wanted: naval bases. By 1986, at the time of the U.S. raid, the USSR was counseling Libya to avoid adventuresome provocation of the United States, and with the new regime of Mikhail Gorbachev, Soviet-Libyan ties have been distanced considerably. Short on cash and troublesome for U.S.-Soviet relations, Qaddafi is no longer of much use to the USSR.

On Libya's side, the rationales for armament are expressed in terms of the broadest foreign policy aims. In fact, Libyan press statements deal more often with mobilization against the Israeli and U.S. enemy than against Libya's more immediate neighbors. An example of the official Libyan preoccupation with Israel and the United States as military opponents, the following Libyan broadcast calls for the arming of the Libyan people.

> The leader [Qaddafi] explained that the transformation of the schools, institutions and colleges into military barracks will hasten the creation of an armed people as soon as possible, confirming that this was the real popular mobilization of the masses to confront the aggression to which the Arab nation is being subjected these days and to face the siege which imperialism is trying to lay around Libya.[58]

This illustrates the general tone of Qaddafi's foreign policy, that of militant anti-American pan-Arabism. Qaddafi clearly envisions Libya as surrounded by hostile "imperialist" nations bent on aggression.

Officially, Libyan military acquisitions and modernization are aimed primarily at the United States and "Zionist imperialism." One military analyst writes:

> The armaments which the Libyan regime has been buying in ever-increasing amounts since 1970 are intended for the modernization of the armed forces, which in turn are officially stated to be intended for the sole purpose of destroying the Israeli presence in the Middle East. . . . In recent years these equipment acquisitions have clearly exceeded the ability of the Libyan armed forces to operate them even in terms of sheer manpower availability, and it must be assumed that a large proportion are destined for other Arab nations when they finally see the light and join Libya in one last victorious *jihad* against Israel.[59]

Even beyond its capability to absorb such weapons, Libya is buying and stockpiling arms for a holy war against Israel and U.S. imperialism. There is a more ominous note, however, in Libya's neo-Nasserist rhetoric. In October 1980, Libya's Qaddafi urged the "Arab people" to "embark on a counterattack, ignoring all regimes and boundaries." He continued: "We urge the Arab people from the Ocean to the Gulf to embark on counter-attacking U.S. bases, the U.S. presence and its main base in Palestine. Should the Arab regimes obstruct the counterattack of the Arab people, they must pay the price for this; they will be treated like the United States and the Israelis."[60] Qaddafi's inflammatory rhetoric has serious implications for the use of Libyan arms in the Middle East and North Africa. Under the cover of attacking "imperialism," Libyan equipment is to be directed against local regimes perceived to be sympathetic to the U.S. cause, or rather, obstructionist of the Libyan cause.

Despite the overlap of Libyan and Soviet interests, specifically anti-Americanism, the overlap is more apparent than real. Qaddafi sees regional and international issues as related, but for Qaddafi the cause of Arab unity is paramount. In 1979 Qaddafi told a Western journalist: "The Soviet Union is on the side of the Arabs against Israel. This we consider an anti-imperialist position. . . . I know that there are two great powers. . . . I also know the Soviets are our friends."[61] Because he needs Soviet training and arms, Qaddafi is willing to cooperate with them, so long as it suits his purpose.[62] Neither country is an agent of the other, neither agrees to the other's basic philosophy, but both are frequently on parallel courses and encourage, benefit from, and try to influence the other's foreign policy behavior, with little success in the 1980s and less likely in the 1990s.

Regional Goals

Officially, the Qaddafi regime echoes the Nasserist conceptions of three circles of concern: the Arab circle, the continent of Africa, and the worldwide Islamic circle.[63] In practice, these circles overlap, and Qaddafi divides his interest between the Moslem Arab Mashreq, the Moslem Arab Maghreb, and the rest of the African continent. Although Qaddafi depends both on the West (for food, goods, and services) and on the Soviet Union (for arms and training), his main interests are regional.

Qaddafi sports a checkered history both in the Maghreb, the Mashreq, and in Black Africa. In the early 1970s, Qaddafi sought to expand his territorial base and his prestige through unity with Egypt, Syria, Sudan, and later with Tunisia. These aborted attempts marked in each case deterioration of relations with Libya. In the 1980s, Libya made overtures to Chad, again to Syria, to Mauritania, to the Polisario Front in the Western Sahara, and to Algeria. These too left worsened relations. The only unity attempt that reached any fruition was the Arab-African Union—in reality, an alliance—with Morocco, which served its limited purposes for two years, 1984–1986. The challenge of the 1990s is to see whether the other members of the Arab Maghreb Union—Mauritania, Morocco, Algeria, and Tunisia—will breathe life into their economic cooperation agreement and whether Libya too will contain its energies within the more conventional confines of the UMA.

In all of these cases, Qaddafi ostensibly sought the Nasserist goal of unity. Unlike his earlier successes in evacuating Western military bases, Qaddafi's attempts at unity failed miserably. Qaddafi's relations with Egypt soured in 1973, when Egyptian President Anwar Al-Sadat ordered an attack on Israel without the slightest consultation of his Libyan ally, and worsened in subsequent years as Libya turned toward the USSR as Sadat turned to the United States for support. Following bomb explosions in Cairo in 1975 and 1976, for which Egypt accused Libya, the two neighbors fought an intense five-day border war in July 1977.[64] Sadat's trip to Jerusalem and the ensuing Camp David agreements and Washington treaty completed the policy differences between the two states and brought Libya to play a major role in the Steadfastness and Rejectionist Fronts and the expulsion of Egypt from the Arab League. Qaddafi's insistence on unity and policy alignment on his terms brought only disunity and discord. It took a full shift in Arab politics a decade after the Camp David agreements to bring the two countries back together. In May 1989, Qaddafi met with Sadat's successor, Hosni Mubarak, at the Rabat Arab summit, and in October the two leaders exchanged personal visits on the Egyptian-Libyan border. The rapprochement was part of Qaddafi's new policy of gaining respectability and emerging from isolation, a policy that mirrored Egypt's own needs as it completed its return to Arab councils.

After the collapse of Tunisian-Libyan unity talks, their relations deteriorated, and in 1980 Libyan guerrillas raided the Tunisian mining town of Gafsa; in 1982, the town of Kasserine; and in 1984, the pipeline at Henchir Al-Bassassa. The two nations have long disagreed over the ownership of oil in the Gulf of Gabès[65] until an International Court of Justice decision in 1986 and a reconciliation with the new Tunisian government in 1988. In the Hassi Mess'oud treaty, Libya agreed with Algeria to give material support to the Polisario against Morocco; in the Oujda Treaty, Libya agreed with Morocco to oppose the Polisario and the Algeria friendship treaty which excluded both states. Yet behind such shifts and slights, Libyan policy is often doggedly principled: Libya refused to recognize the government in exile of the Polisario (which it supported) because it opposed new Arab states, and it refused to join the Algerian friendship treaty (with which it otherwise agreed) because it did not abolish boundaries.

Libya offended Black Africa by its occupation of Chad's northern 'Aouzou Strip in 1973, by its announced intention to unite with Chad in 1981, and by its invasion of Chad in 1983. Libya supported the Transitional National Union Government (GUNT) under Goukouni Weddei, whom it helped bring to power, and continued to support Goukouni— to the point of blocking an OAU summit in 1982—even after he had lost control of Chad and had been evicted. Libya's policy in Chad was one of the reasons why Qaddafi was deprived by African states of his opportunity to be president of the OAU in 1982–1983.[66] Libya finally declared an end to its war with Chad, under heavy OAU pressure, in May 1988 but did not renounce its claims or its hold on the northern 'Aouzou Strip, despite OAU pressure to take the issue to the International Court of Justice.

Unfortunately, examining the Libyan trail of violence and instability in its three circles of operation is a larger task than can be completed here. Qaddafi's Nasserist goal of unity has thus far eluded him. In fact, Qaddafi's actual role in regional relations is destabilizing. An Israeli general assessed the effectiveness of Qaddafi in uniting the Arabs against Israel thus:

Look, in the long run, of course we have to take Qaddafi seriously. He is a man with a single purpose: the destruction of Israel. In the long run, he has the money, the arms, and the means to cause us all serious harm, including you in the West. In the medium and short runs, it's a different story. You might even say that for Israel, Qaddafi can be a kind of asset. Who else, in all his frantic attempts to unite the Arabs, is keeping them divided to the extent Qaddafi is? He is a strategic threat, but perhaps a tactical asset; an agent of division in the Arab World.[67]

Qaddafi has achieved his goal of pursuing "positive neutrality" to a large extent. Libya has no military bases of either the Western or Soviet bloc on its territory. The heavy military purchases from the Soviets are offset by Libya's close economic ties with the West. But Libya has failed miserably at attaining the most important goal of Arab unity. We may speculate that the difficulties lie more in the policy than in Qaddafi's particular personality, however "capricious" some may deem him. Writes George M. Haddad:

> Egypt nevertheless had its conspiracies and purges. . . . Moreover, while Nasser's Egypt kept its people and its officers under control, it was largely responsible for the instability of the other Arab countries by its revolutionary propaganda, its incitement to violence, its direct intervention and its subsidies to the dissident and mercenary elements. The mere example of the changes imposed by the officers in Egypt accompanied by the initial success of Nasser's challenges to the great powers and their Arab allies also produced an unsettling effect on the various Arab states.[68]

Thus, it is an irony of Arab history that in so closely emulating the revolutionary goals of freedom, socialism, and unity, Qaddafi has recreated the actual Nasserist role of a destabilizer, a catalyst of disunity.

CONCLUSIONS

Internally and externally, Qaddafi has tried to impose heroic politics of military mobilization for the Nasserist goal of Arab unity. Internally, Libya faces a double-edged legacy of violent reform. Qaddafi has tried to generate mass support, and to the extent that he has raised the standard of living of Libya's poor, he may well have succeeded. But as in every society, reforms engender resistance, and the severest threat comes from those with access to the means of violence, the military. Writes Ruth First:

> The coup is becoming conventional wisdom not only among Africa's army men, but among her young intellectuals. . . . Young aspirants for power, or social change, consider the making or unmaking of African governments in terms of their contacts within the Army. . . . Power lies in the hands of those who control the means of violence. It lies in the barrel of a gun, fired or silent.[69]

Resistance within the dissatisfied military, in liaison with civilian groups inside and outside the country, rose until 1986, when it was both delegitimized and dismantled. It is the ultimate irony of Qaddafi's regime that by the end of the decade it had so squeezed politics out of society that it could attract neither support nor opposition as participation, only quiescence.

External, it is likely Qaddafi will continue his policy of seeking unity through destabilization and force. Qaddafi's Nasserist dreams appear to be unrealizable visions for the aggrandizement of Libya and Qaddafi. Abdullah Al-Qusaymi writes: "The story of the big state and the big empire has never been the story or idea or hope of the masses. It has always been the story of men who wanted to be great men or tyrants by diminishing others."[70] Qaddafi's violent methods, and the difficulty of the quest itself, will likely continue to make his vision of Arab unity unattainable, for Qaddafi preaches pan-Arab dreams and ideological designs to an Arab world that knows their failure all too well. It is the ultimate irony of Qaddafi's foreign policy that the Arab reconciliation of the late 1980s came about through moderate rather than revolutionary goals and that the latest form of unity occurred in the Maghreb, not in the Mashreq, and was used to tame, not unleash, Libya's energies and resources. The time of Nasser is past, and in trying to perform a Nasserist role in the international theater, Qaddafi's Libya finds itself in the embarassing position of playing to an audience that is not paying attention. The charismatic nation, like the charismatic figure, needs a following. Or, as Weber writes: "[The] charismatic claim breaks down if [the] mission is not recognized by those to whom [the bearer] feels [it] has been sent."[71]

There is another side to heroic foreign policy that students of heroes often miss. In seeking simple interpretations, in rejecting the ultrasophisticated conventions of the urbane diplomatic world, in denouncing imperialism and other perceived evils of the world, in acting like the Jeha or the Asterix or the Popeye of his world, Qaddafi often gets applause as a wily common-man folk hero, doing things people who know better would love to do (if they didn't know better), taking a poke at the big boys and getting away with it. This kind of behavior will not gather followers, but it does attract grudging admirers. In its language and goals, Libya only expresses—sometimes in extreme terms— ideas that are common to many parts of state and society in the Middle East. His style may be uncouth and his tactics may be ones less revisionist states avoid, but Qaddafi often expresses themes that are widely felt, and in ways regarded as daring. Sometimes the tactics draw disapproval, to be sure. But like a student revolt that turns passive onlookers into sympathizers when it can claim police brutality, Qaddafi can gather more sympathy for his ill treatment at the hands of the West than he can for his claim to leadership. In this sense, Libya has found a different role—not that of charismatic leadership, the man on a white horse, but that of the free-lance outlaw, the folk hero, the desert raider admired for his exploits but having no seat at court. To his admirers, Qaddafi is not King Richard the Lion-Hearted or Salah Al-Din, but Robin Hood.

NOTES

1. John K. Cooley, *Libyan Sandstorm* (New York: Holt, Rinehart and Winston, 1982), p. 265. See also Robert Rinehart, "Historical Setting," *Libya: A Country Study*, Area Handbook Series (Washington, D.C.: American University, 1979), p. 50.

2. *Ibid.*, p. 186.

3. *Ibid.*, p. 115. See also Fouad Ajami, *The Arab Predicament* (Cambridge: Cambridge University Press, 1981), p. 126.

4. Ajami, *Predicament*, p. 198.

5. See for example Nadav Safran, *Egypt in Search of Political Community* (Cambridge, Mass.: Harvard University Press, 1961).

6. Gamal Abdel Nasser, *Egypt's Liberation: The Philosophy of the Revolution* (Washington, D.C.: Public Affairs Press, 1955), pp. 87–88.

7. *Ibid.*, p. 88.

8. Mohamed Heikal, *The Road to Ramadan* (New York: Times Book Co., 1975), p. 70.

9. *Ibid.*, p. 71.

10. *Ibid.*, p. 185.

11. *Ibid.*, p. 189.

12. Muammar Al-Qaddafi, *The Green Book*, 3 vols. (London: Martin Brian & O'Keeffe: 1976), 1:41.

13. Oriana Fallaci, "Iranians Are Our Brothers," *New York Times Magazine* (December 16, 1979), p. 123.

14. Cf. Martin Lings, *A Muslim Saint of the Twentieth Century* (New York: Macmillan, 1961), notably p. 156.

15. E. E. Evans-Pritchard, *The Senussi of Cyrenaica* (New York: Oxford University Press, 1963).

16. Ibn Khaldun, *The Muqaddimah*, trans. E. Rosenthal (Princeton, N.J.: Princeton University Press, 1958); see also A. G. Kluge, "The 'Objective' of Ibn Khaldun and Max Weber," Senior Honors Thesis in Social Studies, Harvard University, 1981.

17. Muammar Al-Qaddafi (Tripoli Voice of the Arab Homeland, July 3, 1982), quoted in Karen Dawisha, "The U.S.S.R. in the Middle East: Superpower in Eclipse?" *Foreign Affairs*, Winter 1982/1983, p. 438.

18. The best overall book on Libya is John Wright's *Libya: A Modern History* (Baltimore, Md.: John Hopkins University Press, 1982).

19. On the economy, see Yves Gazzo, "L'Economie Libyenne," *Maghreb-Mashreq* 93 (July 1981), pp. 56–57. On arms, see I. William Zartman, "Arms Imports: The Libya Experience," in *World Military Expenditures and Arms Transfers 1971–1980* (Washington, D.C.: U.S. Arms Control and Disarmament Agency, 1983), pp. 15–22.

20. Said Qaddafi in an interview with *Le Monde*, February 11, 1976, "Regimes don't interest me anymore; I address myself to the Arab masses." Cited in Wright, *Libya*, p. 206.

21. J. A. Allani, "Management of Agricultural Resources in Coastal Libya," *Maghreb Review*, September-December 1980, p. 113.

22. Figures from *World Military Expenditures 1989*.

23. John Keegan, *World Armies* (London: Macmillan Press, 1979), p. 446; Michael Martin et al., "Les armées et la défense," *Annuaire de l'Afrique et du Moyen Orient* (Paris: Editions Jeune Afrique, 1981), p. 255.

24. Mary Jane Deeb, "The Arab Maghrib Union," *Middle East Insight* 6, (Spring 1989), pp. 42–46.

25. See Ann Elizabeth Mayer, "Le droit musulman en Libye à l'age du livre vert"; Hervé Bleuchot, "Le livre vert: Contexte et signification," *Maghreb-Mashreq* 93 (July 1981), pp. 5–38; Lisa Anderson, "Qaddafi's Islam," in John Esposito (ed.), *Voices of Resurgent Islam* (New York: Oxford University Press, 1983); and François Burgat, *L'islamisme au Maghreb* (Paris: Karthala, 1988) and F. Burgat, "Kadhafi et le Maghreb," in Alain Claisse and Gerard Conac (eds.), *Le grand Maghreb* (Paris: Economica, 1988), pp. 182–201.

26. On Libyan domestic governance, see Raymond A. Hinnebusch, "Libya: Personalistic Leadership of a Populist Revolution," in I. William Zartman et al., *Political Elites in Arab North Africa* (New York: Longman, 1981), pp. 177–222; Remy Leveau, "Le système politique libyen," in Maurice Flory (ed.), *La Libye nouvelle* (Paris: CNRS, 1975), pp. 83–100; Wright, *Libya;* Omar Fathaly, Monte Palmer, and Richard Chakerian, *Political Development and Bureaucracy in Libya* Lexington, Mass.: D. C. Heath & Co., 1977); Omar Fathaly and Monte Palmer, *Political Development and Social Change in Libya* (Lexington, Mass.: D. C. Heath & Co., 1978); Marius Deeb and Mary Jane Deeb, *Libya Since the Revolution* (New York: Praeger Publishers, 1982); Ruth First, *Libya: The Elusive Revolution* (Baltimore, Md.: Penguin Books, 1974); Jacques Roumani, "From Republic to Jamahiriya: Libya's Search for Political Community," *Middle East Journal* 37, 2 (Spring 1983), pp. 151–168; *Maghreb-Mashreq* 93, Special issue, *Libye 1978–81* (July 1981); E.G.H. Joffe and K. S. McLachlan (eds.), *Social and Economic Development of Libya* (Boulder, Colo.: Westview Press, 1983).

27. Lisa Anderson, "A Coup Will Topple Qaddafi if We Just Keep Our Hands Off," *Washington Post*, April 13, 1986; and Mary-Jane Deeb, *Libya's Foreign Policy in North Africa* (Boulder, Colo.: Westview Press, 1991), p. 172.

28. Muammar Al-Qaddafi (Tripoli Radio, October 16, 1969), cited by Meredith O. Ansell and Ibrahim Massaud Al-Arif, *The Libyan Revolution: A Sourcebook of Legal and Historical Documents* (New York: Oleander Press, 1972), p. 88.

29. Heikal, *Ramadan*, p. 79.

30. Qaddafi, Tripoli Radio, October 16, 1969.

31. *Ibid.*, p. 89.

32. *Ibid.*, p. 92.

33. See "The Libyan Revolution in the Words of Its Leaders," *Middle East Journal* 24, 2 (Spring 1970), pp. 203–219.

34. On Libyan foreign policy, see I. William Zartman and Aureniano Buendia, "La politique étrangère Libyenne," in Flory, *La Libye;* Lisa Anderson, "Libya and American Foreign Policy," *Middle East Journal* 36, 4 (Autumn 1982); Nathan Alexander [pseud.], "The Foreign Policy of Libya," *Orbis* 24, 4 (Winter 1981), pp. 819–846; René Otavek, "La Libye révolutionnaire au sud du Sahara," *Maghreb-Mashreq* 94 (October 1981), pp. 5–35; Mary Jane Deeb, "Qaddafi's Calculated Risks," *SAIS Review* 6, 2 (Spring 1986), pp. 151–162; and M. J. Deeb, *Qaddafi's Foreign Policy* (Boulder, Colo.: Westview, 1990).

35. See *Jeune Afrique* 1110 (April 4, 1982), p. 32.

36. On the Meheishi affair, see *Libya*, pp. 186, 196, 252, 276; Cooley, *Sandstorm*, p. 166; and *Jeune Afrique* 770 (October 10, 1975), pp. 26–27.

37. On these various events, see Leveau, "Le système politique," p. 93; Wright, *Libya*, p. 187; G. Henry M. Schuler, "The International Oil Negotiations," in I. William Zartman (ed.), *The 50% Solution* (New York: Doubleday & Co., 1976, and New Haven, Conn.: Yale University Press, 1987), pp. 124–207.

38. William A. Mussen, Jr., "Government and Politics," in *Libya: A Country Study*, p. 214.

39. Muammar Al-Qaddafi, cited in Allani, "Agricultural Resources," p. 108.

40. "Libyan Arab Jamahiriya," *1980 Yearbook of International Trade Statistics* (New York: United Nations, 1981), 1:592. See also Zartman and Buendia, "La politique," p. 108.

41. "Libyan Arab Jamahiriya."

42. Cooley, *Sandstorm*, p. 75.

43. *Al-Fajr Al-Jadid,* October 28, 1981; see also *Maghreb-Mashreq* 95 (January 1982), p. 79; *Jeune Afrique* 1105 (March 10, 1982), p. 23; *Arabia,* April 1983.

44. *Arabia,* April 1983.

45. *Ibid.*

46. "Libya's Quiet Investments in NATO Countries," *Business Week,* March 26, 1979.

47. Christopher S. Wren, "Libya's Identity Blurred by Ties with East, West and Terrorism," *New York Times,* October 14, 1979.

48. Cooley, *Sandstorm,* p. 186.

49. Wright, *Libya,* p. 173.

50. "Washington Steps up Pressures on Qaddafi," *Arabia: The Islamic World Review,* April 1982.

51. Alexander, "Foreign Policy of Libya," p. 823.

52. Zartman and Buendia, "La Politique," p. 105.

53. On Libya and the Soviet Union, see Lisa Anderson, "Qaddafi and the Kremlin," *Problems of Communism* 24, 5 (September 1985), pp. 29–44; Carol Saivetz, "The Soviet Union in North Africa," in Mark Habeeb and I. William Zartman (eds.), *State and Society in the Modern Maghrib* (Boulder, Colo.: Westview, 1990); I. William Zartman, "Soviet-Maghribi Relations," in Edward Kolodziej & Roger Kanet (eds.), *The Limits of Soviet Power in the Developing World* (Baltimore: Johns Hopkins, 1989), pp. 301–331; and "Choices in Northeast and Northwest Africa," in Kolodziej & Kanet (eds.), *Prospects for East-West Cooperation in the Third World* (forthcoming).

54. Keegan, *Armies,* p. 441.

55. *Ibid.,* p. 437.

56. Anatoly Gromyko, "Soviet Foreign Policy and Africa," *International Affairs,* February 1982, p. 33.

57. William H. Lewis, "Arms Transfers and the Third World," in *World Military Expenditures, 1970–1979,* p. 31.

58. Muammar Al-Qaddafi, Foreign Broadcast Information Service (FBIS), November 13, 1980.

59. Keegan, *Armies,* p. 439.

60. Muammar Al-Qaddafi, FBIS, October 8, 1980.

61. Fallaci, "Iranians."

62. Zartman, "Arms Imports."

63. Nasser, *Egypt's Liberation,* pp. 109–111.

64. Cooley, *Sandstorm,* p. 118.

65. Alexander, "Foreign Policy of Libya," p. 835; *Jeune Afrique* 1105 (March 10, 1982), pp. 24–25.

66. "Libya," *Middle East Journal* 36, 2 (Spring 1982), p. 230. See also I. William Zartman and Yassin El-Ayouti (eds.), *O.A.U. After 20 Years* (New York: Praeger Publishers, 1984).

67. Cooley, *Sandstorm,* p. 100.

68. George M. Haddad, *Revolutions and Military Rule in the Middle East: The Arab States, Part II: Egypt, the Sudan, Yemen and Libya* (New York: Robert Speller and Sons, 1973), p. 392.

69. Ruth First, *The Barrel of a Gun* (London: Penguin Press, 1970), p. 6.

70. Abdullah Al-Qusaymi, "So that Harun al Rashid Would Not Return," *Mawaqif* 1 (October-November 1968), pp. 24–40, as cited in Ajami, *Predicament*, p. 38.

71. Max Weber, *From Max Weber*, translated, edited, and with an introduction by H. H. Gerth and C. Wright Mills (New York: Oxford University Press, 1946; reprint 1975), p. 246.

9

The Survival of a Nonstate Actor: The Foreign Policy of the Palestine Liberation Organization

Mohamed E. Selim

Among all foreign policy actors analyzed in this book, the Palestine Liberation Organization (PLO) is the only nonstate actor. Foreign policy analysts have traditionally excluded nonstate actors from their studies. For them, a foreign policy actor must possess the legal quality of sovereignty; consequently, only states qualify for this role. However, the new realities of international politics, especially the emergence of powerful transnational and transgovernmental organizations and the obvious structural weakness of some states, have led growing numbers of foreign policy analysts to shift away from this state-centric paradigm. In the new view, the defining characteristic of a foreign policy actor is the behavioral attribute of autonomy. Autonomy in this sense means the ability to behave in ways that have consequences in international politics and cannot be predicted entirely by reference to other actors.[1] According to this definition, a wide variety of nonstate actors can be classified as foreign policy actors, including multinational business enterprises, revolutionary movements, trade unions and scientific networks, international organizations, and powerful domestic groups.[2] By virtue of its undeniable impact upon the international politics of the Middle East, its international status, its elaborate linkages with the Palestinian people, and finally, its internal dynamics, the PLO, though not a state, is a major Arab actor.

When they formulate foreign policies and operate in the international system, nonstate actors confront certain problems that state actors do not usually experience. Nonstate actors, especially when they take the form of a regional revolutionary movement aspiring to alter the territorial status quo, lack territorial political symbols to draw upon as a basis for defining foreign policy. They confront problems of control and legitimacy, factionalism, visibility, durability, and maneuverability.[3] Lacking a territorial base and the conventional means of conferring legitimacy, these actors find the legitimacy of their representation to be always in question. They must be concerned with the issue of being heard, perceived, and recognized by nation-states and international organizations. The visibility of nonstate actors brings to the forefront the issues of durability and maneuverability. As the nonstate actors become more visible and draw more international support, they run the risk of being portrayed by their adversaries as mavericks threatening international legitimacy. Allies may also become a source of threat. Supporters of nonstate actors expect a higher level of compliance from them than they expect from their state clients.

In this chapter, we will analyze the interplay of these problems in the making of the foreign policy of the PLO. The choice of the PLO as the actor representing the Palestinian dimension in Arab politics is justified by the PLO's status as the only representative acceptable to the Palestinian people. At the inter-Arab level, according to a resolution issued by the Arab summit held in Rabat in 1974, the PLO is recognized by all Arab countries as the sole legitimate representative of the Palestinian people. The PLO represents Palestine in the League of Arab States, and the United Nations has granted the PLO an observer status. The PLO is also recognized by 112 countries as the representative of the Palestinian people, sometimes with full diplomatic status, and maintains official bureaus in almost 90 countries. Since 1976, the PLO is a full member of the nonaligned group.

DOMESTIC ENVIRONMENT

Historical Legacy: The Origins of the PLO

The establishment of the PLO in 1964 was a function of two converging trends: the resurgence of Palestinian national feelings in the 1960s and the inter-Arab consensus to draft a common strategy against Israel. The breakup of the Egyptian-Syrian union in 1961 and the failure of the 1963 unity talks between Egypt, Syria, and Iraq shook the faith of the Palestinians in the eventual realization of Arab unity, earlier viewed as a prerequisite for the restoration of Palestine. The 1962 victory of the Algerian revolution convinced the Palestinians that self-reliance would be a more viable strategy for achieving their goals. As a result, they began to form their own organizations. By 1965, about forty such organizations existed.[4] In response to this increasing Palestinian militancy, the first Arab summit, held in Cairo in January 1964, decided inter alia to organize the Palestinians to enable them to carry out their role in liberating their homeland. The summit further asked Ahmed Al-Shukairy, the representative of Palestine in the League of Arab States at the time, to study the feasibility of establishing a Palestinian entity.[5]

The idea of a Palestinian entity received mixed reactions in the Arab world.[6] Reservations came from Jordan, Saudi Arabia, Syria, and some Palestinian resistance organizations. On the other hand, this proposal was fully supported by most radical Arab regimes, especially Egypt, Iraq, and Algeria.

Shukairy invited 422 Palestinians representing the various Palestinian groups (excluding Palestinians who lived in Israel) to attend the first Palestine National Council (PNC) in May 1964. It was at this meeting that the PLO was proclaimed. The council drew up a national charter and a fundamental law as the basic constitution of the PLO. The second Arab summit, held in Alexandria in September 1964, endorsed the establishment of the PLO and gave it the pan-Arab stamp of legitimacy.

An examination of the subsequent evolution of the PLO reveals certain elements of change and continuity that have played a crucial role in PLO foreign policy. The PLO underwent three basic changes: the shift of its leadership from traditionalism to radicalism, the shift from individual membership to organizational representation, and the shift from a leader-staff pattern of decision-making to a collective pattern of interorganizational bargaining.

During the first five years of its existence, the PLO was dominated by traditional Palestinian elements, especially local notables, businessmen, bankers, and mayors. This resulted in a pattern of membership that was heavily traditional and strictly individual. Individuals sat on the various political structures of the PLO in their own capacity and not as representatives of other organizations. Further, the PLO failed to set its own program of military and political action to achieve its objectives. Its leadership attempted to duplicate the operations of Palestinian resistance organizations that had declined to enter the PLO. This tarnished the PLO image and incited an increasing number of members to call for a change. In December 1967, the Executive Committee of the PLO (EXCOM) forced Shukairy to resign; Yehia Hammouda replaced him.

The new chairman approached resistance organizations to coordinate their activities with PLO actions. This policy resulted in the convening of a new session of the Palestinian National Council in Cairo in July 1968; the session was attended by resistance organizations for the first time. From this point on, PLO membership counted an increasing number of representatives from various organizations. It was only a matter of time before formal PLO leadership was transferred to commando organizations as well. In the next session of the PNC, held in February 1969, Yasser Arafat, the leader of the Palestine National Liberation Movement (Fateh), was elected chairman of the PLO. The membership of commando organizations in the PLO required the adoption of a new

Palestinian Patriotic Charter in 1968. This replaced the Palestinian National Charter of 1964.[7] Since then, the PLO has emerged as the focal point for Palestinian loyalties and actions. It has developed an overall strategy of political and military action, established extensive political links with the Palestinians living in Palestine, and begun to play a mediating role between various Palestinian organizations. Finally, when the guerrilla organizations joined the PLO this caused a shift in the decision-making process. Under Shukairy (chairman from 1964 to 1967), the PLO chairman enjoyed tremendous powers. He chaired both the Executive Committee and the Palestine National Council and chose the members of the Executive Committee at his own discretion. Subsequently, the EXCOM and PNC chairmanships were separated, and the powers of the PLO chairman were reduced to brokerage between various PLO commando organizations.

Two basic elements of the PLO historical legacy continued to influence it functioning, namely intra-Palestinian rivalries and the intervention of Arab governments. Shukairy recalls that during his consultations to establish the PLO, he rarely found two Palestinians agreeing on anything.[8] Once the PLO accepted organizational membership, interorganizational conflicts and differences in strategies and ideologies between Palestinian resistance groups were indelibly imprinted on PLO politics. The problem of organizational unity became one of the nagging issues that has plagued the PLO ever since.

By virtue of the very nature of its creation, the PLO was highly vulnerable to the manipulation and intervention of Arab governments. As soon as the PLO was established, it became embroiled in the Arab cold war of the 1960s. The PLO aligned itself with Arab radicals, especially with Nasser's regime. Jordan and Saudi Arabia almost forbade PLO mobilizational activities within their territories. In the early 1970s, the PLO aligned itself with the Egyptian-Syrian-Saudi axis, and by the end of the decade it became part of the "Steadfastness Front" that set out to reject the Egyptian-Israeli treaty. Moreover, Arab governments established their own individual guerrilla organizations. As these organizations entered the PLO, they injected into its politics the policies of their respective patrons. In a sense, the PLO became a microcosm of inter-Arab politics.

The Geographical Dispersion of the Palestinians

The total population of Palestine is almost 4.5 million. The Palestinians do not live in a single territory under the control of one political authority. They are geographically dispersed in various countries and territories, as Table 9.1 indicates. Almost 58% of the Palestinians live outside the territory of mandatory Palestine. According to the 1948 statistics, the total number of the Palestinians was 1,474,500; almost 20.2% of them became refugees in the West Bank, Gaza, and various Arab countries. In the wake of the June 1967 war and by the end of 1967, about 178,000

TABLE 9.1   Geographical Distribution of the Palestinian People in 1970 and 1981

Location	1970		1981	
	Population	%	Population	%
West Bank	670,000	22.7	833,000	18.7
Gaza Strip	364,000	12.4	451,400	10.0
Israel	340,000	11.5	550,800	12.4
Jordan	900,000	30.5	1,148,334	25.9
Lebanon	240,000	8.1	358,207	8.0
Kuwait	140,000	4.8	299,710	6.7
Syria	180,000	6.1	222,525	5.0
Saudi Arabia	20,000	0.7	136,779	3.0
Egypt	33,000	1.1	45,605	1.2
Gulf States	15,000	0.5	60,737	1.4
Libya	5,000	0.2	23,769	0.6
Iraq	14,000	0.5	20,604	0.5
Other Arab countries			50,706	1.1
United States	7,000	0.2	104,856	2.3
Other countries	20,000	0.7	140,116	3.1
Total	2,948,000	100.0	4,447,148	100.0

Sources: The 1970 statistics are taken from Ibrahim Abu-Lughod, "Educating a Community in Exile: The Palestinian Experience," *Journal of Palestine Studies* 2, 3 (1973), p. 97. The 1981 statistics are taken from *Compendium of Palestinian Statistics for 1981* (Damascus: Central Statistics Office of the PLO, 1982), p. 30 (in Arabic).

West Bank Palestinians and almost 127,000 Gaza residents had been forced to leave their homes.[9] The geographical dispersal of the Palestinians set in motion four basic processes affecting the Arab-Israeli conflict and PLO policy.

The Demographic Shift. The dispersal of the Palestinians tilted the Palestinian-Israeli demographic balance in favor of Israel. If one projects the Arab population of the West Bank and Gaza in 1952, which was about 1.06 million, at an estimated natural growth rate of 3.3%, one would expect it to have reached 2.76 million. If one adds the Palestinians who live in Israel (550,800), the figure comes to 3.3 million. The total number of Palestinians who reside within the boundaries of mandatory Palestine is only 56% of this figure and these figures can change in favor of Israel with the influx of Soviet Jews.

Social Mobilization and National Identity. The fragmentation of the Palestinians triggered a process of social mobilization and led to the development of a well-defined Palestinian national identity. The Palestinians underwent three basic processes: depeasantization and semi-proletarianization, increased education, and the emergence of a new national leadership. A 1973 study of the West Bank and Gaza revealed that almost 50% of the active population were wage workers, almost 77% of them were employed in industry, and only 23% were in agriculture.[10] Parallel to the shift in the work force, the Palestinians' educational status improved remarkably. According to the 1975 statistics, almost 22% of the Palestinians are enrolled in educational institutions, with almost 1.2% in institutes of higher education. This ratio goes as high as 3% among West Bankers and 5.5% among Palestinians in the Diaspora.[11] Mar'i attributes this "Palestinian phenomenon" to the dispersion of the Palestinian community,[12] and Davies cites the value of education for a displaced community as the major factor behind this phenomenon. For Palestinians, education has proven to be a means of survival and insurance against future uncertainties. For these uprooted, displaced, and dispossessed people, education is a portable and transferable commodity.[13]

Finally, the geographical fragmentation of the Palestinians resulted in the decline of the old family groups and parties that had dominated the political and social life of Palestinian society during the British mandate. As a result of urbanization and increased education, a new and modern professional and nationalist leadership emerged. It is this leadership that controls the PLO and other member resistance organizations. The new Palestinian is more educated, revolutionary, and ideologically inclined.[14] The influence of the new leadership on the Palestinian community surpasses that of the old traditional one. In a survey study of the Palestinian refugees living in Lebanon, Bassam Sirhan found that the influence of the old feudal leadership has declined considerably. He also concluded that the political leadership among camp refugees rests firmly in the hands of the vanguard of the resistance movement.[15]

The interplay of these factors led inter alia to the social and political mobilization of the Palestinians and to the sharpening of their national consciousness and sense of identity.[16] The basic components of this identity can be summarized as follows: (1) the theme of resistance, and the refusal to accept expulsion and statelessness, (2) emphasis on the land of Palestine as a potent symbol of Palestinian identity, (3) emphasis on the common origins of the Palestinians and on Palestinian traditions as intrinsically good, (4) distinction between the specific Palestinian identity and the general Arab identity, and (5) emphasis on the ability of sustained struggle to restore Palestine.[17] A sample survey of the Palestinians who live in the Shatilla refugee camp in Lebanon came to several conclusions concerning the components of the Palestinian national identity.[18] At the cognitive level, almost 69% of the respondents were aware of the history, geography, national leaders, and other national symbols of Palestine. Almost 80% of the respondents identified themselves as Palestinian Arabs or Arab Palestinians, whereas 3.5% identified themselves as just Arabs. At the affective level, almost 88% displayed a strong feeling of belonging to Palestine and 94% preferred to marry only fellow Palestinians. At the behavioral level, almost 80% of the respondents expressed willingness to let their children join resistance organizations in the future. One of the most revealing findings is that these conclusions apply to the 1948 exodus generation as well as to the post-1948 generation. The only exception was that the new generation is more militant than the old generation. Whereas only 49% of the old generation rejected the 1947 Partition Resolution, almost 71% of the new generation rejected it.[19]

Various factors account for the tenacity and intensification of Palestinian identity. Social mobilization was found to be a crucial factor in the process of national differentiation.[20] The conditions in which the Palestinians lived, whether in Palestine or in the Diaspora, inadvertently led to the same outcome. Prominent among these conditions are the limited socioeconomic absorptive capacity of Arab countries and the discrimination directed against the refugees by governing authorities.[21]

The emergence of the new Palestinian leadership and the PLO was both a source and an outcome of the emergence of the Palestinian identity. The PLO helped to reinforce and crystallize this process through various mobilizational mechanisms, and the rise of the PLO to international prominence also sharpened the Palestinian feeling of national pride and identity. On the other hand, the emergence of a strong Palestinian identity was the base from which the PLO drew its resources, according to Rosemary Sayigh.[22]

The Ideological Fragmentation of the Palestinian Elite. The geographical dispersion and the social mobilization of the Palestinians contributed to the ideological fragmentation of the Palestinian political elite, including the PLO leadership. The absence of a well-defined territorial framework and the extraterritoriality of the bulk of the Palestinian leadership have resulted in the absence of agreed upon reference points of political-cum-territorial definitions.[23]

Penetration of the PLO by Arab Regimes. The dispersion of the Palestinians in various Arab countries inevitably involved them in the politics of these countries, and enmeshed them in broader Arab rivalries. The Palestinians became involved in Arab politics either by acquiring citizenship in these countries (Jordan) or through participating in various Arab political movements. This sometimes led to confrontations between them and the host Arab countries,[24] and made the Palestinians highly vulnerable to Arab manipulation. Some Arab regimes used them to bolster legitimacy claims, sometimes to the detriment of the Palestinian cause. Consequently, Palestinian politics often involved a form of "pawn politics."[25]

Social Structure

In addition to the Diaspora and its implications, one can identify certain social-historical factors that have characterized the evolution of Palestinian society and influenced the functioning of the PLO. These relate to historical social cleavages in the Palestinian society, the Palestinian cognitive conceptions of authority, and the Palestinian class structure.

The Palestinian society that evolved under Ottoman rule was characterized by a bifurcation of political power among the Ottoman bureaucracy and the local nobility. Sources of power, instruments of rule, and bases of legitimacy were separate. Moreover, Palestinian society was divided by various social cleavages, most prominently between the urban notables and the rural sheikhs, between various antagonistic segments of the urban notables (e.g., the Hussaini and the Nashashabi families), and between Moslems and Christians.[26] After the 1948 exodus a new cleavage developed between the old notables and the emerging middle-class leadership.

This legacy is reflected in PLO politics in various subtle ways. The evolution of the PLO before and after 1969 reflects the cleavage between the old notables and the leaders of the new middle class. During its first five years, the PLO was dominated by Palestinian notables who almost alienated broad middle-class sectors from the newborn organization. Consequently, when the new leadership took over in 1969 it eliminated the notables from key policy-making organs of the PLO. The formation of various commando organizations can be likened to the politics of the old family cleavages. For example, it has been argued that some resistance organizations are extensions of the old family networks or reflections of some religious-political traditions.[27]

These divisions are further reinforced by the tendency of the Palestinians to personify authority. Palestinians tend to identify authority with the personalities of their leaders, which helps to produce a spectrum of clique-like coalitions around certain leaders and fosters organizational fragmentation.[28] Some resistance organizations have evolved mainly around certain key personalities. This tendency limited the cohesiveness of the PLO.

However, the structural evolution of Palestinian society over the last thirty years has influenced Palestinian politics in a different way. After the 1948 exodus, Palestinian society developed a broad middle class and a relatively broader proletariat of workers. These two classes constitute the social power base of the PLO. Most of the PLO's financial and human resources, as well as its leadership, are essentially drawn from these two classes.

One of the major areas of sociopolitical change in the Palestinian community during the last decade is the *intifada* (uprising), which broke out in the West Bank and Gaza Strip in December 1987 and is still going on. The *intifada* is the result of the convergence of certain variables, namely: (1) the maturation of a new Palestinian generation that became convinced, thanks to the October 1973 War and the Israel-PLO War of 1982, that Israel is not invincible; (2) the rapid growth of education in the West Bank and Gaza where schools and universities became centers for civil resistance; (3) the mobilizational activities of the PLO and some resistance organizations and the apparent failure of the Arab summit held in Jordan in 1987 to address itself to the Palestinian question, which convinced the Palestinians in the occupied territories that they have only themselves to rely upon. The murder of two Beirzeit University students on December 15, 1987, triggered mass protests that soon developed into a series of resistance processes, such as strikes, demonstrations, civil disobedience, stone-throwing, in addition to certain activities aimed at disengagement from the Israeli economy. In all cases, the protestors avoided resort to armed violence.[29]

Although the *intifada* was partly encouraged and developed by the PLO as a pressure strategy against Israel, it did influence the PLO's foreign policy as well. The *intifada* provided the PLO leadership with a sense of power and dignity, which, in turn, "emboldened us to publicize our peace initiatives," Arafat said.[30]

Economic and Military Capabilities

As a transnational revolutionary movement lacking a territorial base of its own, the PLO is mostly dependent upon external economic support. PLO financial resources are drawn in large measure from three sources. The first source is the "liberation tax" levied on Palestinian workers by some Arab governments. These governments usually deduct 5% of salaries paid to Palestinian employees and channel the total taxes collected to the PLO. Cash outlays by Arab governments constitute the second source. According to a resolution passed by the second Arab summit in 1964, Arab governments are committed to pay certain annual financial contributions to the PLO. The actual amount and breakdown of these contributions varies from year to year. For example, the Arab summit held in Rabat in 1974 granted the PLO a subsidy of $50 million, mostly paid by the Arab oil-producing countries. The Arab summit held in Baghdad in 1978, in the wake of the signing of the Camp David agreements, allotted the PLO $300 million annually for the ensuing ten years.[31] Most Arab governments have not honored their commitments to the PLO either because of financial hardships or to show their displeasure with the PLO's policies. Between 1964 and 1971, Sudan, Morocco, and Yemen failed to pay their shares. Iraq and Tunisia paid only for one year and the rest of the Arab governments paid only for two years. According to Shukairy, during this period Arab governments owed the PLO 19 million Egyptian pounds (about $44 million) in arrears.[32] Also, Arafat revealed that in 1982, Libya confiscated the taxes collected from the Palestinians.[33] Contributions from friendly individuals and governments are the third source of support. For example, Dubai imposed taxes on hotel bills, cables, and air tickets for the benefit of the PLO. Kuwait deducts 1% of the salaries of Kuwaiti teachers for the PLO. The Jordanian Chamber of Commerce also pays financial contributions to the PLO. These are drawn from levies on merchants based on the amount of their registered capital, and from a fixed fee paid for every business transaction.[34]

The reliance of the PLO on Arab financial support limits its political options. It created a dilemma for PLO leaders who attempted to strike a balance between the necessities of compliance, especially in relation to major contributors, and the quest of autonomy, prestige among the Palestinian population, and progress toward its goals. In fact, Arafat admitted that the PLO's reliance on Arab financial support has made it a "hostage" to Arab regimes.[35]

The PLO also attempted to create an income-generating mechanism of its own through an industrial infrastructure known as Samid (literally, the "steadfast"). Samid was originally established in Jordan in 1970 as a rehabilitation center for the children of martyrs. In 1971, Samid was forced out of Jordan, as a result of the PLO-Jordan confrontation. But Samid was reestablished in Lebanon to provide jobs for Palestinians barred from employment according to Lebanese laws. In Lebanon, Samid established thirty-five industries employing some 5,000 Palestinian workers. During the course of the Israeli invasion of Lebanon in 1982, Samid's infrastructure was virtually destroyed, and it was forced to move its headquarters once again to Jordan. Samid rebuilt most of its industries in Lebanon and evolved into an international enterprise managing a huge network of economic activities in Arab and Third World countries. Samid's activities vary from land reclamation to motion picture production.[36]

The total financial revenues of the PLO are secret, but have been estimated at approximately $500 million annually.[37] This is perhaps an inflated figure. The financial report submitted to the Palestine National Council in June 1970 listed the total expenses of the PLO during the fiscal year 1969-1970 at $3.9 million, 68% of which was allocated to the armed forces.

Militarily, the PLO has a broad base of human resources for recruitment, almost half a million. The PLO has established across-the-board conscription for all Palestinian men between the ages of eighteen and thirty. As a result, the PLO is able to maintain three military forces: a regular force known as the Palestine Liberation Army (PLA), guerrilla forces, and a people's militia.

The PLA consists of three basic formations: (1) the Ain Jalut Brigade of about 1,000 men, stationed in Egypt until the late 1970s; (2) the Qadissiya Brigade of almost 1,500 men, deployed in Iraq until 1971; and (3) the Hittin Brigade of almost 1,500 men, stationed in Syria and Lebanon. Most of these forces are now deployed in Syria and Lebanon. The PLA is mainly an infantry army equipped with Soviet-made infantry weapons such as assault rifles, machine guns, light and heavy mortars, light and medium field artillery, recoilless rifles, armored cars, and some T-34 tanks.[38] The army is controlled by a Palestinian chief of staff, whose headquarters are situated in Damascus. He is directly accountable to the PLO Executive Committee, on which he sits as a permanent member.

The PLA is to a large extent controlled by the Arab governments in whose territories it operates. Arab governments, including the staunchest allies of the PLO, have traditionally insisted on controlling the PLA units stationed on their territories. This applied in particular to Egypt in the 1960s and Syria in the 1970s. Consequently, the PLA actually became a separate body from the PLO, sometimes serving the interests of the sponsoring Arab regimes rather than those of the PLO. Syria used the Hittin Brigade against the PLO commando forces during the Lebanese civil war in 1976, and in the course of the war, PLO commando forces took the chief of staff of the PLA as a prisoner of war.

In addition to the PLA, each PLO member organization maintains its own guerrilla forces. These forces are organized as relatively self-sustained cells and equipped with light arms. Some groups, such as Fateh, possessed heavy weapons such as armored cars, 106-mm field guns, and antiaircraft guns. Most of this equipment was lost in the PLO-Israel war in 1982. It is difficult to give an accurate estimate of the exact manpower strength of the PLO, especially after the 1982 war. Prewar estimates for Fateh, the largest group, varied between 8,000 and 12,000 men with another 15,000 in the militia, which could be mobilized within forty-eight hours. Add to this an additional few thousands for each of the handful of resistance organizations.[39] These forces are under the direct control of their sponsoring organizations, with the PLO performing a coordinating function.

Finally, the PLO maintains an auxiliary people's militia. The PLO militia operate as a rear guard to the resistance forces. They are also trained to master urban guerrilla tactics including first aid, morale raising, and supply operations.[40]

PLO military forces are strategically controlled by the military departments of the PLO through the General Command of the Forces of the Revolution (GCFR). The Executive Committee of the PLO appoints the commander general of the GCFR and his chief of staff. The commander general, in turn, appoints the Supreme Military Council (SMC) under his chairmanship. The SMC consists of the top military leaders of the resistance organizations. The GCFR formulates the military plans of the PLO, coordinates the military activities of all PLO forces, drafts the budget, and administers the PLO court martial.[41] The military department also supervises the "War College of the Palestine Revolution," which trains officers to serve in the PLO forces.

The PLO forces are plagued by certain structural weaknesses that limit their effectiveness. Most of these forces operate from outside Palestine. They have not been able to build a network of cells in the occupied territories or to mobilize the Palestinians living in these territories. This has made them highly vulnerable to Israeli incursion and to Arab manipulation. Israel has exploited this vulnerability by attacking military and civilian targets of the PLO in Arab host countries, putting a strain on PLO relations with these countries that finally forced

Arafat in July 1981 to halt all military operations against Israel. The extraterritoriality of the PLO put it on a collision course with most Arab host countries (notably Jordan and Lebanon) and forced it to resort to commando actions rather than guerrilla warfare.[42] Further, after the 1970 PLO-Jordan confrontation, the PLO forces underwent a process of "regularization" as a result of the absorption of large numbers of regulars from the Jordanian army. Heavy equipment was bought and military ranks were introduced. The fedayeen were transformed "from a guerrilla organization—invincible because it was elusive—into a regular army bogged down with heavy weaponry and structures that made it an easy target for the Israeli army."[43] Finally, organizational fragmentation and dissension in the PLO ranks has severely limited the military effectiveness of its forces.

In the course of the PLO-Israeli war of 1982, the second major PLO-Israeli direct confrontation since the Karama battle of March 1968, the PLO forces suffered tremendous casualties. The PLO lost its heavy equipment and a sizable portion of its military forces.[44] The rest of the forces have been dispersed over seven Arab countries, especially Tunisia, where PLO headquarters is presently situated.

The PLO has managed to rebuild its fighting forces. China compensated the PLO for all its losses in armament.[45] Yugoslavia has also helped the PLO to acquire a limited air force based in the Red Sea.[46] Further, the PLO has been able to restation some of its forces in southern Lebanon and to stage some guerrilla attacks on Israeli forces from therein.[47] However, the PLO has not been able to regain its credibility as a factor in the military equation in the Middle East.

Political Structure

Unlike the Palestinian nationalist movement of the 1930s and 1940s, the PLO created an elaborate set of political institutions. Together, these institutions form an integrated political regime that, by virtue of its composition, influences the PLO's foreign policy. The PLO political structure consists of the following basic institutions:

The Palestinian National Council. The PNC is the highest policy-making institution of the PLO. It formulates basic policies, issues instructions and guidelines to the Executive Committee and nominates its members and has the power to create or abolish any PLO institution. Membership in the PNC varies from one session to another. At present it is around 400 strong. Members representing resistance groups, trade unions, and professional organizations are nominated by their respective organizations on a quota basis. Independent members are chosen by a committee of the preceding council. In 1983, eight resistance organizations were represented in the PNC: the Palestinian National Liberation Movement (Fateh), the Popular Front for the Liberation of Palestine (PFLP), the Democratic Front for the Liberation of Palestine (DFLP), Al-Sa'iqa, the Arab Liberation Front (ALF), the Popular Front General Command (GC), the Palestine Liberation Front (PLF), and the Palestine Popular Struggle Front (PPSF). Ten Palestinian unions and syndicates, e.g., the General Union of Writers and Journalists and the General Union of Palestine Workers, were also represented. The PNC has a three-year term; it meets every year or meets in extra-ordinary sessions upon the request of the Executive Committee or 25% of its members. The PNC also has a chairman, who is directly elected by the membership at the beginning of each term.

The Executive Committee. The Executive Committee (EXCOM) is the highest executive body in the PLO. It has full operational authority over all the institutions of the PLO within the policy set up by the PNC. According to the PLO's basic statute, the EXCOM represents the Palestinian people, supervises all the formations of the PLO, issues instructions and takes decisions regulating PLO actions within the policy, implements the fiscal policy of the PLO, and prepares the budget. The committee consists of twelve members elected by the PNC from among its members. In electing members of the EXCOM, the PNC ensures the representation of major resistance groups and independents. Committee members, in turn, elect the chairman of EXCOM. In the seventeenth session of the PNC, it was decided that the PNC would elect the chairman of the EXCOM. The committee is in permanent session and its members work on a full-time basis. Each EXCOM member has his own portfolio (e.g., foreign affairs, education, and culture).

The Central Council. The Central Council (CC) is an intermediary advisory institution between the PNC and the EXCOM. It consists of sixty members, representing various resistance organizations, who meet every three months under the chairmanship of the head of the PNC to review the activities of the EXCOM and plan for future activities.[48]

The PLO Departments. In addition to these three institutions, the PLO maintains nine functional departments that resemble the ministries of state governments. The activities of these departments are supervised by the EXCOM. Each department has its own head except the military department, which is directly headed by the chairman of the EXCOM. Whereas the PNC, the EXCOM, and the CC are staffed so as to ensure the representation of various Palestinian groups, these departments are organized on a professional basis.

Chief among these are the political and military departments and the Palestine National Fund. The political department represents the PLO at international conferences, supervises its offices abroad, and undertakes various diplomatic activities on its behalf. The military department's basic function is to coordinate the activities of the PLO military forces in collaboration with the GCFR. The chairman of the EXCOM is ex officio head of this department. Finally, the Palestine National Fund (PNF) resembles a finance ministry. It supervises all the financial activities of the PLO, handling all financial donations and supervising spending and investing within the framework of the budget approved by the

PNC. The PNF administers Samid and supervises the Institute for Social Affairs and Welfare and its affiliate institutions—the Palestinian Society for the Blind, Social Care for the Wounded, and Social Care for Martyrs' Families, among others. The PNF director is elected by the PNC from among its members and is also ex officio a member of the EXCOM.

Other departments include the education department, which administers the educational affairs of Palestinians living in Arab countries; the health department, which supervises the Palestine Red Crescent Society; the Department of Popular Organizations, which acts as coordinator between the PLO and the Palestinian professional associations, syndicates, and input groups; the information and national guidance department, which conducts all information activities of the PLO; the Department of National Relations, which represents the PLO in Arab governments, especially regarding the status of the Palestinians; and the Department of the Occupied Homeland's Affairs, which deals with the Palestinians under Israeli control.

Generally, a political structure can influence the direction of foreign policy in a number of ways. It can provide policy-makers with social and political resources, and it can also act as a constraint on the policy-making process. The resources provided by a political structure depend upon the scope of societal activities under its control, the degree of political institutionalization, and the level of public support.[49] Judging from the scope and domain of the PLO political structure, one may argue that it provides the PLO with ample resources.

The extent and intensity of the PLO's political and social activities deserve further attention. The scope of the PLO political structure may be illustrated by several examples:

1. The PLO has been able to exercise what amounts to sovereign powers over the Palestinians in war situations. The PLO represented the Palestinians in war situations with Jordan and Lebanon and during various incursions into Israel.
2. The PLO exercises extradition powers over the Palestinian people. On many occasions Arab governments have turned over to the PLO Palestinians charged with criminal activities. They were tried and sentenced by the PLO judicial system.
3. The PLO exercises taxation powers over the Palestinians through Arab governments.
4. The PLO exercises judicial powers. It established a revolutionary court, a revolutionary penal code, a revolutionary code of criminal procedures, and a revolutionary rehabilitation code. These codes apply to all sections of the Palestinian people.[50]
5. The PLO sponsors various social, economic, and educational activities, which provide the Palestinians with basic services.
6. The PLO plays a crucial political role in inter-Palestinian conflict resolution, especially among various resistance organizations. For

example, when the conflict between the PFLP and DFLP escalated in 1969 to the point of armed clashes, the PLO Executive Committee intervened to mediate between the two organizations.

The PLO has established both a cohesive set of structural arrangements to regulate its many activities and a well-defined set of decision-making rules, which operate within the context of an elaborate bureaucracy.[51] It is the consensus of the foreign policy literature that all of these dimensions and resources increase an actor's capacity to act in the arena of foreign policy. On the other hand, the political structure can limit the capacity of an actor to conduct foreign policy. The constraining role of the political structure depends upon the degree of coherence and unity both within the regime itself and between the regime and other institutions, the nature and extent of its accountability, and the degree to which the regime represents the wider society.[52] An examination of the PLO political structure reveals that these three variables have tremendously limited the PLO's capacity to make and implement a well-defined foreign policy.

By its nature as an umbrella organization, the PLO comprises a number of resistance organizations. These organizations entered the PLO as groups retaining their ideological and organizational identity. Consequently, PLO institutions are structured to reflect proportional representation of each organization in addition to the few independent members. This has turned PLO politics into coalition politics. Furthermore, these organizations are not a homogeneous set. They differ in their conception of Israeli-Arab conflict (moderates vs. rejectionists), their ideological orientation (Islamic nationalists, Arab nationalists, and Marxist-Leninists), and in the strength of their linkage with Arab regimes (universalists vs. subservients).

An examination of the ideologies of some of the leading organizations may be in order. Fateh adopts an instrumental definition of the conflict that guarantees the mobilization of all resources regardless of ideologies. It perceives the Arab-Israeli conflict as essentially a Palestinian-Israeli conflict, with Arabs and national liberation movements on one side and Zionists and imperialists on the other. The PFLP and DFLP reject Fateh's nationalist approach and advocate a class analysis of the conflict. According to these two organizations, the social dimension of the conflict cannot be ignored because the establishment of Israel was a result of an alliance between various Arab and Jewish bourgeois classes. Consequently, the PFLP and the DFLP include Arab reactionaries among the prime adversaries of the Palestinian revolution, and emphasize the revolution's proletarian nature.

The PLO resistance organizations also differ in the nature and scope of their connections with Arab governments. Some of them are highly institutionalized; others maintain a universalist orientation. The institutionalized or subservient organizations are organically linked with specific Arab regimes; they reflect the ideology and implement the strategy of their patron regime. Prominent among these institutionalized organizations are Al-Sa'iqa (affiliated with the Syrian Ba'th party), and the ALF (affiliated with the Iraqi Ba'th party). The universalists, such as Fateh and the PFLP, reject control by or affiliation with any Arab government. They fear that affiliation with any Arab government will reduce their freedom of action.[53] The representation of these conflicting organizations in the PLO political structure (the PNC, the CC, and the EXCOM) tends to hamper its ability to formulate policies. This has sometimes resulted in inaction. For example, in the fourteenth session of the PNC, Fateh and other resistance organizations became polarized over the issue of their representation in the new EXCOM, with the result that the old EXCOM was retained. The constraining impact of these competing organizations has been further exacerbated by the inability of the PLO to make dissent disadvantageous for these organizations. Resistance organizations that disagreed with the PLO foreign policy did not encounter substantial costs for departing from the umbrella structure. Arab governments also tend to protect and support client dissenting groups.[54]

The negative consequences of the coalitional structure of the PLO for its foreign policy are nowhere more exemplified than in the developments the PLO witnessed in 1983–1986. In May 1983, an armed mutiny, supported by Syria, broke out within the ranks of Fateh forces stationed in northern Lebanon. The main issues were Arafat's "dictatorial" leadership style, his "peer" management of the PLO-Israeli 1982 war, his "challenge" of the Syrian leading role and tilt toward Egypt and Jordan. Other resistance organizations polarized around these issues into two groups: the "Patriotic Alliance," compromising the GC, Al-Sa'iqa, and the PPSF, and the "Democratic Alliance" consisting of the PFLP, the DFLP, and the ALF. Whereas the first group supported Fateh mutineers, the second group adopted a middle-of-the-road approach, which led to the near paralysis of the PLO. This forced Arafat to slow down his talks with Jordan concerning future PLO-Jordan diplomatic moves. Despite the mediation efforts of Algeria and South Yemen, the Patriotic Alliance boycotted the seventeenth session of the PNC held in Jordan in 1984. Further, it formed "The Palestine Patriotic Salvation Front," in Damascus in 1985 as an alternative to the PLO. The front coalesced with certain Lebanese Shi'ite forces to remove the remnants of the PLO's forces in Lebanon.

As a result of the contending views between these factions, when Arafat finally reached an agreement with Jordan in 1985 concerning future strategy, he insisted that the agreement be secret. Furthermore, the agreement turned out to be a vague document designed to satisfy all the factions. If this were not enough, Jordan publicized the agreement, which put Arafat in an awkward position with the PLO extremists, especially the Democratic Alliance, and forced him to demand the amendment of the agreement to accomodate their viewpoints. As a result, Jordan "froze" the agreement in 1986. Immediately after the Jordanian decision, another mutiny broke out, this time within the ranks of the PLA command. General Alalla (Abu Al-Zaim) led a group of almost 400 PLA officers in protest of the PLO's failure to honor its agreement with Jordan. This led to their expulsion from the PLA.[55]

FOREIGN POLICY ORIENTATION

Evidence of the PLO's foreign policy orientation can be found in the PLO Patriotic Charter issued in 1968, the resolutions and programs of the sessions of the PNC, and the statements by the successive chairmen of the EXCOM: Shukairy, Hammouda, and Arafat. Although these sources differ in the depth of commitment expressed, they articulate a well-integrated foreign policy belief system whose elements can be outlined as follows:

The Global System

The PLO leadership views international politics at the global level as fundamentally anarchic and conflict-ridden. It views the global system as characterized by wars, arms races, and imperialist conspiracies. Structurally, the system is perceived as a loose bipolar system, consisting of two basic contending global powers with a group of Third World actors endeavoring to reduce the threat of a global war. The basic stances of the two superpowers are viewed as intrinsically irreconcilable.[56]

The global system is also viewed as highly unstable. The basic interactions of the system are undergoing a process of fundamental transformation. The crux of this process is the collapse of the old world order of imperialism, colonialism, and racism, and the emergence of a new order whose basic features have not yet been specified.[57]

Within the present global system, the PLO perceives Western imperialism led by the United States and Great Britain as the major adversary of all national liberation movements, including the PLO.

> World imperialism under the leadership of the United States of America is the foremost adversary of all peoples. It is also responsible for various forms of aggression against the liberty and independence of peoples and the usurpation of their resources. This has been clearly manifested in the creation and support to the Zionist entity in our Palestine.[58]

The Soviet Union, the People's Republic of China, and other socialist countries are viewed as major supporters whose collaboration is always appreciated.[59] In an interview with the *New Times* of Moscow, Arafat said "The USSR and its communist party have always supported the just struggle of the Palestine people."[60] Furthermore, because of its geographic location, the PLO considers itself a part of the Third World in general and of the national liberation and nonalignment movements in particular.[61] In this respect, the PLO strives to unify the forces of global revolution and at the same time benefit from the lessons and advice of other liberation movements.[62] The PLO considers itself to be part of the militant group within the nonalignment movement. For the PLO, nonalignment does not mean equidistance towards the global powers, because one of them (the United States) is a mortal adversary. It means active support of national liberation movements against global imperialism, racism, and Zionism.[63] As a result of this global identity, the PLO views itself as playing a particular global role: that of a global anti-imperialist agent and a liberator-supporter of all national liberation movements in Africa, Asia, and Latin America.[64]

The Regional System

The foreign policy domain of the PLO is essentially the Middle East region. The basic issues, interactions, and conflicts of the PLO's foreign policy are located in this region. In fact, the PLO's global orientation is mostly shaped by its view of the basic issues of the regional system. The PLO views the Middle East regional system as containing elements of harmony and conflict. There is a harmony of interests among the Arab peoples; the conflict is between the Arabs and Israel.

The PLO leadership believes that the Arab peoples enjoy a fundamental harmony of interests by virtue of their common language, culture, and history. Conflict in inter-Arab politics is viewed as an aberration. Accordingly, Arab unity is seen as an inevitable historical process. The liberation of Palestine and Arab unity are viewed as complementary and mutually supportive values. The Palestinian charter states that "Each one paves the way for the realization of the other. Arab unity leads to the liberation of Palestine and the liberation of Palestine leads to Arab unity. Working for both goes hand in hand."[65] The organic link between the Palestinians and the rest of the Arabs places the Palestinian cause at the heart of the Arab integrative process and puts special responsibilities upon all Arabs to liberate Palestine.[66] Further, the PLO considers Arab territories surrounding Israel as hinterlands for resistance action. Any attempt to restrict Palestinian resistance in any Arab country is tantamount to betrayal of the goals of the Arab nation.[67]

However, such complementarity does not mean the subservience of the Palestinian struggle to Arab regimes, or the minimization of the Palestinian dimension in the Arab-Israeli conflict. The PLO rejects all forms of "official" Arab intervention in its own affairs. Meanwhile, it does not interfere in the domestic affairs of Arab regimes "except when" these affairs affect the Palestinian cause.[68]

The PLO views the Middle East system as essentially a revolutionary Arab regional system, characterized by sociopolitical conflicts between the forces of Arab national liberation and the forces of imperialism and social exploitation. The PLO maintains that underlying the Arab regional system is a pan-Arab liberation movement that is going through the state of national democratic revolution. According to the PLO, the basic tasks of this revolution are: (1) the realization of full political and economic independence; (2) the destruction of all forms of imperialism and its local subordinate forces; (3) the liberation of Palestine; (4) the liberation of the Arab masses from all forms of exploitation practiced by foreign and local counterrevolutionary forces; and (5) the mobilization of Arab resources in order to achieve pan-Arab socioeconomic development and Arab integration.[69] The PLO clearly identifies with the Arab revolution against Arab "reactionary" forces. Arab revolutionaries are considered the strategic allies of the PLO, and Arab reactionaries are perceived as adversaries even if they provide the Palestinian struggle with limited support in order to protect themselves.[70]

However, the main conflict defining the basic system of interactions in the region is still the Arab-Israeli conflict. The PLO views this conflict as containing core and peripheral actors. The core actors are the PLO, Western imperialism, and Israel. The PLO is supported by an outer circle of Arab and global national liberation movements and regimes.

The national liberationist self-image has led the PLO to de-emphasize the role of social ideology in its program. The PLO adopts an instrumental self-image that guarantees the mobilization of all resources regardless of ideology. Social contradictions among various Palestinian classes are considered secondary to the basic national contradiction with Israel and Zionism. Liberation requires the unity of all forces regardless of ideology.[71] Arafat succinctly stated this conception as follows: "Is this the proper time to stipulate a social content (of the revolution)? We are still in the stage of national liberation. How could I then deprive some classes of the Palestinian people from taking part in the nationalist struggle?"[72]

Image of the Opponent

The PLO perceives Israel as a political adversary whose basic goal is the annihilation of the Palestinian people. Israel is also viewed as a Zionist state that espouses expansionist aspirations in the Arab territories and racist views toward the Arabs.[73] It is not interested in any compromise with the Palestinians; as Arafat states: "Israel insists on and wants only one thing, the non-existence of the Palestinian revolution."[74] The PLO further believes that Israel is pursuing a maximalist policy in its dealings with the Arabs. A resolution of the Palestine National Council stated: "The Zionist invasion of Palestine was and still is a prelude for the occupation of other parts of the Arab land and converting it into a Zionist colony which serves imperialist interests."[75] The PLO also likens Israel to the apartheid regime of South Africa. By virtue of its Zionist ideology, Israel views Arabs as inferior subjects. The Israeli-Zionist racist image of the Arabs, the PLO maintains, is clearly exhibited in the structure of the Israeli state and its laws, which discriminate against the Palestinians. "Settler colonialism in Southern Africa and Zionist settler colonialism in Palestine are not only phenomena that resemble each other from a distance. They are also strategically and organically linked,"[76] Arafat stated. The PLO interprets Israeli expansionist and racist policies as emanating from the Zionist character of the state. Expansionism and racism are intrinsic to the Zionist ideology. Consequently, as long as Israel remains a Zionist state there is no hope of changing its present goals.

The PLO's dispositional attribution of Israel's goals is further reinforced by a perception of Israel as an imperialist agent. Israel is viewed by the PLO as a part of a system designed and coordinated by imperialism. Israel plays a crucial role in safeguarding imperialist interests, dividing the Arab land, and destabilizing Arab regimes.[77]

Article 22 of the PLO Patriotic Charter summarizes these perceptions of Israel as follows:

> Zionism is a political movement organically related to world imperialism and hostile to all movements of liberation and progress in the world. It is a racist and fanatical movement in its formation; aggressive, expansionist and colonialist in its aims; Fascist and Nazi in its means. Israel is the tool of the Zionist movement and a human and geographical base for world imperialism. It is a center and a jumping-off point for imperialism in the heart of the Arab homeland, to strike at the hopes of the Arab nation for liberation, unity and progress. Israel is a constant threat to peace in the Middle East and the entire world.[78]

One of the major areas of change in the PLO's image of Israel is its view of the homogeneity of the Israeli society and elite. Initially, the PLO saw Israel as a monolithic actor. Policy differences among various segments of the Israeli society or political elite were considered to be negligible and not likely to bring about any radical change in the character of the Israeli society.[79] By the early 1980s, however, the PLO began to view Israel as composed of various political groups espousing different policies toward the Arabs. Although the Israeli political establishment remains fundamentally united on major policies, there are new democratic and progressive forces in Israel, such as the Peace Now Movement, the Shelli party, and the Rakah party, which oppose Israeli aggression. Arafat believes the PLO ought to accommodate these forces as the basis for Palestinian-Israeli coexistence.[80]

Goal Selection and Goal Definition

The PLO believes that it should select optimal goals for political action. Settling for the most feasible goals or compromising on maximalist goals, the PLO argues, means losing the battle before it begins. The task of goal selection ought to be approached within this historical paradigm of politics, regardless of the short-term prospects of success or failure. Once the optimal goal has been defined it should not be modified or abandoned, and any tactical goal must represent a step toward the realization of that optimal goal.

The PLO's approach to goal selection is based on its conception of the Arab-Israeli conflict. Arafat argues that history is an inevitable and circular process. History repeats itself, and contemporary and future events are basically replays of past scenarios. Consequently, one can predict the outcome of present policies by analyzing past trends, and one can also choose political goals according to the nature of previous historical patterns.

An analysis of these patterns, Arafat maintains, reveals that the PLO's goal of liberating Palestine will be achieved eventually. The history of the Crusades points to this inevitable outcome. "One who reads history will realize that the logic and inevitability of history support this."[81] If this is the basic pattern of Arab history, then it is only logical to subscribe to the optimal goal of liberating the entire territory of Palestine. This goal may not seem to be feasible today, yet in the long run it will be achieved, Arafat asserts. "Our generation is the generation of suffering, the generation of pain and hardships; it is the next generation that will win, that will reap the harvest of this harsh and wearisome struggle. We have never claimed that we should liberate our territory in a year or two or three. We believe in the necessity of a long-term people's war of liberation."[82]

The PLO's approach to goal selection is reflected in its goal definition. For the PLO, Palestine is the territory of mandatory Palestine. This territory is an indivisible unit and belongs to the Palestinian people.[83] The PLO's basic objective is to establish a democratic state in the territory of mandatory Palestine. This objective was first articulated by Fateh in 1968 and later adopted by the PLO in the sixth session of the PNC in September 1969, which resolved that, "The Palestinian struggle aims at terminating the Zionist entity in Palestine, the return of the Palestinian people to their homeland and the establishment of the democratic Palestinian state on the entire Palestinian territory without any form of racial discrimination or religious fanaticism."[84]

The democratic state is to replace the present political structures in the territory of mandatory Palestine. As a result the PLO initially rejected the establishment of a Palestinian state on a part of the territory of Palestine.[85] In this sense, the notion of the democratic state represents a reaffirmation of the view of the old PLO leadership, which called for the eradication of Israel. As Ahmed Al-Shukairy phrased it: "We believe that the existence of Israel is fundamentally null and must be eradicated as the imperialist existence has been eradicated from many Afro-Asian and Latin-American countries. Israel has no place amidst us. These who want Israel must carry it on their shoulders and plant it in their own territories."[86]

However, the notion of a democratic state does represent a shift from the PLO policy as stated in the 1968 charter. Whereas the charter would permit only Jews who lived in Palestine before 1948 to live in the future Palestinian state, the democratic state would incorporate all Jews who presently live in Israel, provided that they renounce Zionism. This was made clear in a 1970 document, which stated that "All Jews, Moslems and Christians living in Palestine or forcibly exiled from it will have the right to Palestinian citizenship. . . . Equally, this means that all Jewish Palestinians—at present Israelis—have the same right provided, of course, they reject Zionist racist chauvinism and fully accept to live as Palestinians in new Palestine."[87]

According to the PLO, the future democratic state will embrace secularism, democracy, and social justice. The state will assure the adherents of all religions an equal civic status. Popular participation, protection of basic liberties, and political accountability will also be ensured. Socially, the future state, dedicated to a high degree of social justice, will attempt to end all forms of social exploitation.

The PLO-Jordanian confrontation in 1970 and the ensuing expulsion of resistance groups from Jordan forced the PLO to rethink its options and to assess the tactical feasibility of the democratic state proposal. By early 1972, the PLO Research Center initiated studies on the feasibility of a Palestinian state in the West Bank and Gaza.[88] The international legitimacy bestowed upon the PLO after the 1973 October War encouraged it to shift its emphasis from the democratic state goal to the goal of a Palestinian state in the West Bank and Gaza, especially when the former was subjected to severe criticism in Israel and the West. Consequently, the PNC resolved in its Transitional Political Program, issued in June 1974, to accept a separate Palestinian state in a part of Palestine: "The PLO is fighting by every means, primarily by armed struggle, to liberate the Palestinian land and to establish a national independent and fighting authority in every part of the Palestinian soil which can be liberated."[89]

This shift was reinforced by the outbreak of the Lebanese civil war in 1976. The war helped to discredit the notion of a secular state and underlined the urgency for the Palestinians to obtain some sort of a sovereign state. In January 1978, Arafat emphasized that he would be content with a West Bank–Gaza state and would welcome protection from United Nations forces.[90] He reiterated this objective in May 1978, maintaining that the "only possible solution" is for a Palestinian state and Israel to coexist under the joint guarantee of the superpowers.[91]

The PLO quest for a Palestinian state is explicitly for a state alongside Israel in the West Bank and Gaza. However, the PLO is prepared to establish this state on any part of the Palestinian land that can be liberated. Regarding the relations between the new Palestinian state and Jordan, the PLO proposes a confederal connection between the two countries on the basis of sovereignty[92] and the enactment of international guarantees.

The PLO's conception of the goal of the creation of a Palestinian state underwent a fundamental change. Initially, the PLO considered the

Palestinian state as an interim solution to the Arab-Israeli conflict and emphasized that such state does not imply the abandonment of the democratic state objective. The Transitional Political Program of the twelfth session of the PNC issued in June 1974 stipulated that the Palestinian state is a step toward the democratic state.[93] Arafat gave certain signals that he was prepared to consider the Palestinian state as a final solution, and that once such a state had been established, it will not press for further territorial aggrandizement. However, he refused to make public such an obligation arguing that the PLO prefers to be the last actor to define its final stand.[94] Further, Arafat linked the recognition of Israel to the latter's recognition of a Palestinian state.[95] The Declaration and Political Program of the nineteenth session of the PNC held in Algeria in November 1988 heralded the beginning of a fundamental change in this conception. The PNC declared in the Declaration and Political Program the establishment of a Palestinian state according to the United Nations Partition Resolution of 1947 and the recognition of UN Security Council Resolutions 242 and 338 within the framework of security guarantees for all states in the Middle East. In a press statement, Arafat declared that although the Palestinian state derives its legitimacy from the UN Partition Resolution, it will be established within the June 1967 borders, namely in the West Bank and Gaza Strip. In December 1988, Arafat, in collaboration with representatives of American Jews, issued the Stockholm Declaration, in which he publicly recognized the existence of Israel. In the same month, Arafat addressed the UN General Assembly held in Geneva. In his speech, Arafat called for co-existence between the Palestinian and Israeli states according to Security Council Resolutions 242 and 338. Immediately after his speech, Arafat held a press conference in which he announced unequivocally his recognition of Israel's right to exist and recognition of Security Council Resolutions 242 and 338 as a basis for future negotiations.[96] Finally, during his visit to France in May 1989, Arafat declared that the documents of the nineteenth session of the PNC have made the Patriotic Charter of the PLO (which rejects the legitimacy of Israel) *caduque* (decrepit).[97] Accordingly, the PLO, at present, views the Palestinian state within the 1967 borders as a final solution to the Arab-Israeli conflict.

Foreign Policy Strategies

The PLO's conception of the Arab-Israeli conflict as a historical process necessarily entails a long-term strategy of goal implementation. Foreign policy goals will not be decided by a single action, but by a series of strategies that will inevitably culminate in the realization of goals.

The PLO follows two interrelated strategies: the popular war of liberation and mass political mobilization. A war of liberation launched by a revolutionary vanguard creates the right atmosphere for mobilization of the masses, which in turn provides the war of liberation with new momentum. In theory, the strategy goes as follows: A long series of small attacks on virtually all Israeli targets is to be launched. During these attacks, the resistance movement will avoid direct military engagements with the adversary in order to neutralize the latter's technological superiority. By persisting in this process regardless of short-term setbacks, the resistance movement will finally achieve its ultimate goal. For the PLO, the popular war of liberation has many advantages. It prevents Israel from enjoying the fruits of a peaceful occupation, continues the spirit of resistance, wears Israel down, and keeps the problem on the agenda of the world community.[98]

A companion strategy to the popular war of liberation is the mobilization of the Palestinian masses. The PLO considers "the Palestinians both inside or outside the occupied lands as the instrument of the revolution."[99] These masses ought to be activated and involved in the various functions of the Palestinian revolution. The mobilization of the masses is a sine qua non for the success of the popular war of liberation.

According to the PLO, military force plays a crucial role in implementing the strategy of the popular war of liberation and in cementing the mobilization and unity of the masses. This has been a consistent line in the PLO's definition of strategy. However, one may distinguish between three phases in the PLO's conception of the role of military force in goal attainment. During the Shukairy phase, military force was perceived as the only instrument to liberate Palestine. This line of thinking continued to characterize the PLO's conception of military force after the resistance organizations came to power in the PLO. Military force was perceived as a *foco* strategy, as advocated by Ché Guevara.

By the early 1970s, the PLO's view of military force became more complex. Although the PLO continued to value it as the major instrument, it argued that military force ought to be supplemented by other forms of political struggle. International negotiations and diplomatic contacts would help the PLO to reap the fruits of armed struggle, the PLO asserted.[100] Arafat articulated this view after the PLO departure from Beirut as follows: "The struggle is a political and military one. Armed struggle is one form of political struggle which has a loud voice. The Palestinians have the right to struggle by all military, political, diplomatic and information means."[101]

Accordingly, the PLO at present pursues two interrelated foreign policy strategies: the first is of a political-international nature and the second is mainly military-mobilizational. The PLO believes that an international conference held under the auspices of the United Nations and attended by all permanent members of the Security Council and all concerned parties including the PLO, is the best strategy to resolve the Arab-Israeli conflict. The conference will strive to make arrangements for the withdrawal of Israeli forces from the territories occupied in 1967 and the eventual establishment of a Palestinian state in these territories and provide security guarantees for all concerned states in the conflict.[102]

The PLO strongly believes that Israel will not attend the proposed international conference unless it is forced to do so through the military-mobilizational activities of the Palestinians. Consequently, the PLO maintains that military force should not be abandoned as a foreign policy strategy. However, military force ought to be used only inside the occupied territories and against Israeli military targets. This view was clearly reflected in the Cairo Declaration announced by Arafat on November 7, 1985. In this declaration, the PLO denounced all terrorist activities and vowed to halt attacks against Israeli targets outside the occupied territories.[103] The *intifada* in the West Bank and Gaza Strip represents the PLO's embodiment of this strategy. The PLO played an active role in formulating the strategy of the *intifada* in collaboration with local communities in the West Bank and Gaza Strip. The leaders of the *intifada* resorted mainly to tactics of civil disobedience and stone-throwing on Israeli forces.

THE DECISION-MAKING PROCESS

In analyzing the foreign policy decision-making process in the PLO, one must differentiate between the formulation of general foreign policy objectives and the making of foreign policy decisions. This is because the structures involved in the two areas are not the same. Whereas the PNC is the supreme foreign policy–making unit in the PLO, the Executive Committee is entrusted with the task of making specific foreign policy decisions. Following the Hermann model, the structural characteristics of the two units may be compared in terms of their size, power distribution, and the role of members.[104]

The PNC is a general assembly that represents various Palestinian groups. It elects the EXCOM, which is a small group of 12 members who take care of the day-to-day decision-making tasks. However, the two units converge as far as the power distribution and the role of members are concerned. Power is more or less evenly distributed in the two units. There is no authoritative leader who can commit either of the units to decisions against the majority opposition of the members. The chairman of the EXCOM does not enjoy the autocratic powers traditionally exercised by most Third World leaders.

This balance of power is a change from the Shukairy years. Shukairy used to nominate members of the EXCOM himself, and as a result he enjoyed tremendous power in deciding PLO policy. For example, the PLO-Tunisian conflict in 1966 was completely handled by Shukairy himself without any input from other members of the EXCOM, Shukairy recalls in his memoirs.[105] After Shukairy was ousted in 1968, the PNC limited the powers of the committee chairman and subjected him to continuous scrutiny by the EXCOM and the PNC. However, since the fifteenth session of the PNC in 1981, Fateh has increasingly played a major role in the decision-making process by virtue of its ever-increasing majority in the PNC and the EXCOM. Finally, the majority of the members of the PNC and the EXCOM are representatives of resistance groups. As a result, they are constrained in their deliberations by the policies advocated by their parent organizations. Using Hermann's terminology, the PNC and the EXCOM may be labeled as a delegate assembly and delegate group respectively.

Foreign policy–making in the PNC is a collegial process. Policies are formed by all members of the council through a process of public debate and majority voting. As a result, the foreign policy–making process is essentially a process of ideological conflict. Delegates advocate policies that reflect the ideology of their parent organizations. Because of the constitutional equal power distribution and the public debate and majority voting system, representatives enter into political skirmishes trying to prove to other delegates the righteousness of their advocated policy or to convert undecided independents to their side. As a result, ideological alignments dominate the deliberation process, and ideological compromise becomes the basic foreign policy–making mechanism. Bilal Al-Hassan, a member of the PNC, outlines the deliberation process in the PNC as follows:

> The members of the National Council have become accustomed, at every session, to witness dialogue and conflict about a number of questions or about a single central question that polarizes attention in the debate. They have also become accustomed to finding themselves aligned with or opposed to a certain view, with the Council automatically dividing up into two conflicting trends, so that argument is heated, impetuous and stormy, and quiet does not return to the hall until the democratic process acts as umpire in any disagreement and settles it in its own way.[106]

The PNC's response to the Brezhnev Middle East initiative in 1981 was typical of its policy-making process. The PNC's fifteenth session witnessed a heated debate over the initiative with members polarized into three alignments: those who rejected the initiative because it referred to the right of Israel to exist, those who unreservedly accepted the initiative because it emphasized the PLO's role in the final settlement, and those who advocated reserved support of the initiative. The final outcome was a compromise through which the PNC welcomed the Brezhnev initiative, emphasizing those points which affirmed the role of the PLO and the rights of the Palestinians.[107]

A similar debate occurred in the sixteenth session of the PNC over the Arab summit Fez Plan. Some members welcomed certain elements of the plan. Others, such as the PFLP and the PFLP-GC strongly rejected the plan, especially its provisions concerning Israel. As a result the PNC resolved that the plan represents "the minimum basis for Arab political action which must complement military action."[108] Another controversy occurred in the nineteenth session of the PNC over the Security Council's Resolutions 242 and 338. Members were extremely polarized around the acceptance or rejection of those resolutions. The conflict was resolved through formal voting, with 84% of the members accepting the resolutions.

The primary decision-making process in the EXCOM is one of collegial incremental bargaining. It is collegial because all members take part in deliberating the issue before any decision is taken. For example, the decision to leave Beirut in 1982 was made by all the members of the EXCOM.[109] The process is incremental because the EXCOM is accountable to the CC and the PNC and because of the need of some participants to confer with parent organizations. The EXCOM cannot take major decisions without at least checking with the CC. It must also justify its decisions to the PNC. Members of the EXCOM, including its chairman, must adapt their views to the needs of other members if a decision is to be taken.

The chairman of the EXCOM plays a coalescent role in the decision-making process. He manages the proceedings of the deliberation process, reviews all important considerations and expedient alternatives, attempts to narrow the gaps between various delegates, and channels the deliberation process toward the options he perceives as consistent with the policy set by the PNC.

FOREIGN POLICY BEHAVIOR

During its two decades of existence, the PLO has developed stable patterns of dyadic, regional, and global behavior. These patterns are influenced by Palestinian national attributes and the PLO's political structure, and also by other systemic, relational, and situational variables in the global and regional systems. The patterns are directly determined by the PLO's orientations toward its external environment.

In order to describe the basic patterns of the PLO's foreign policy behavior, we have followed the international events approach,[110] making use of the data set of the Conflict and Peace Data Bank (COPDAB). The bank is an extensive, computer-based, longitudinal collection of daily international and domestic events between 1948 and 1978 of almost 135 international actors. An event is defined in the COPDAB data set as an official, newsworthy communication. It must be articulated or undertaken by an official representative of the government involved and reported in the press. An event involves (1) an actor, (2) a target, (3) a time period, (4) an activity, and (5) an issue. Each event record contains variables describing the actions, reactions, and interactions of the actors listed in it, in terms of the activity (the verbal or physical act that an actor initiated), the scale value of the event (the degree of cooperation or conflict), and the issue involved.

We compiled all the events in which the PLO was an actor between 1964 and 1978, which gave us the 102,727 events listed in Table 9.2. The events are tabulated according to the dyad of actors (e.g., PLO behavior toward the United States and U.S. behavior toward the PLO). The behavior of each actor in a dyad is divided into two types of behaviors—cooperation and conflict—and each type is broken down by period: 1964–1967, 1968–1973, and 1974–1978. Finally the behavior is aggregated by type of interaction and by period. The data set forth in Table 9.2 reveal certain basic patterns in the PLO's foreign policy behavior:

First, the total amount of foreign policy activities generated by the PLO has been increasing over time. If we divide the total number of events initiated by the PLO in each period by the number of years included, we find that the average annual foreign policy activity has increased from 720 incidents in the first period to 4,307 and 4,698 in the second and third periods. This reflects the PLO's increased capacity to act in the international system due to the growing availability of resources and skills necessary for the conduct of foreign policy behavior.

Second, the initiation of contact is divided equally between the PLO and other actors. Almost 51% of foreign interactions are initiated by the PLO; 49% are initiated by external actors. This is a consistent pattern that cuts across the two types of behavior and the three time periods. It reflects world awareness of the importance of the PLO in Middle East politics.

Third, most PLO foreign policy actions (almost 75%) involve conflict. This is a function of the liberationist role and change-oriented goals of the PLO. We have seen that the PLO perceives its global and regional role as that of an anti-imperialist liberator. Its behavior, therefore, challenges the global and regional status quo and creates a conflict relationship with most political regimes. This explains why almost 54% of the PLO's negative interactions involve countries that defend the status quo in the Middle East, namely Israel and the United States; whereas only 0.2% of its conflicts involve countries that reject the status quo, namely the USSR and the People's Republic of China.

However, the prominence of conflict in the interactions of the PLO has changed over time. Whereas conflict characterized 87% and 90% of the total interactions during periods 1 and 2 respectively, the percentage declined to 57% during the latest period. This decline corresponds to the shift of the PLO toward accepting a limited Palestinian state in the West Bank and Gaza Strip, and to the PLO's emergence to assert its international legitimacy. Obviously, the more the PLO becomes integrated into the international system, the more it shifts toward cooperation rather than conflict.

Fourth, the PLO seems to be locked in a complex process of reciprocal interactions. When it initiates a great deal of conflict, it inspires other actors to do the same. Almost 71% of actions initiated toward the PLO by other international actors are conflictive. Israel and the United States account for 56% of the total conflict actions initiated toward the PLO.

This pattern of reciprocity holds for both positive and negative interactions. Changes in behavior by the PLO were accompanied by

TABLE 9.2   International Interactions of the PLO, 1964–1978

	Cooperation			Conflict		
Dyad[a]	1964–67	1968–73	1974–78	1964–67	1968–73	1974–78
PLO-West[b]	12	125	136	72	1,543	674
West-PLO	6	163	218	50	1,054	215
PLO-U.S.	–	7	25	5	43	57
U.S.-PLO	–	4	25	1	48	30
PLO-UK	12	37	18	56	132	144
UK-PLO	6	30	22	50	76	–
PLO-France	–	12	42	–	94	222
France-PLO	–	6	88	–	157	85
PLO-East[c]	62	242	588	–	180	–
East-PLO	140	208	230	–	272	73
PLO-USSR	–	112	372	–	60	–
USSR-PLO	–	107	–	–	32	–
PLO-PRC	62	94	30	–	–	–
PRC-PLO	124	30	36	–	–	–
PLO–Third World	–	26	3,001	–	422	218
Third World–PLO	70	152	2,931	–	385	226
PLO-Israel	6	58	108	1,922	10,941	8,273
Israel-PLO	65	175	285	1,875	11,107	6,974
PLO-Arabs	289	2,143	6,269	519	10,160	4,223
Arabs-PLO	500	3,415	6,275	284	9,463	3,704
PLO-Jordan	61	561	417	503	6,938	403
Jordan-PLO	96	733	471	243	5,524	356
PLO-Lebanon	–	534	851	–	2,295	1,474
Lebanon-PLO	16	432	674	6	2,387	1,559
PLO-Syria	65	170	1,078	–	152	1,205
Syria-PLO	154	363	1,028	–	224	1,073
PLO-Egypt	56	198	732	–	132	710
Egypt-PLO	132	346	842	–	117	243
PLO–Saudi Arabia	–	86	419	16	204	6
Saudi Arabia–PLO	22	243	370	6	200	–
PLO-Iraq	67	102	227	–	110	239
Iraq-PLO	50	305	229	29	47	224
PLO-Libya	–	78	563	–	99	6
Libya-PLO	–	443	480	–	185	90
PLO-Algeria	20	76	308	–	6	–
Algeria-PLO	10	149	275	–	6	–
PLO-World[d]	369	2,594	10,102	2,513	23,246	13,388
World-PLO	781	4,113	9,939	2,209	22,281	11,192

[a]Order of listing indicates which party initiated event. PLO-U.S. interactions are those initiated by the PLO.
[b]All Western countries including the United States, Great Britain, and France
[c]All Communist countries including the USSR and the People's Republic of China
[d]Total interactions with the West, the East, the Third World, Israel, and Arab countries

| Total by Type of Interaction | | Total by Period | | | Total |
Co-op	Conflict	1964–1967	1968–1973	1974–1978	Interactions
273	2,289	84	1,668	810	2,562
387	1,319	56	1,217	433	1,706
32	105	5	50	82	137
29	79	1	52	55	108
67	332	68	169	162	399
58	126	56	106	22	184
54	316	–	106	264	370
94	242	–	163	173	336
892	180	62	422	588	1,072
578	345	140	480	303	923
484	60	–	172	372	544
107	32	–	139	–	139
186	–	62	94	30	186
170	–	124	30	16	170
3,027	640	–	488	3,219	3,667
3,153	611	70	537	3,157	3,764
172	21,136	1,928	10,999	8,381	21,308
525	19,956	1,940	11,282	7,259	20,481
8,701	14,902	808	12,303	10,492	23,603
10,190	13,451	784	12,878	9,979	23,641
1,039	7,844	564	7,499	820	8,883
1,300	6,123	339	6,257	827	7,423
1,385	3,769	–	2,829	2,325	5,154
1,122	3,952	22	2,819	2,233	5,074
1,313	1,357	65	322	2,283	2,670
1,545	1,297	154	587	2,101	2,842
986	842	56	330	1,442	1,828
1,320	360	132	463	1,085	1,680
505	226	16	290	425	731
635	206	28	443	370	841
396	349	67	212	466	745
584	300	79	352	453	884
641	105	–	177	569	746
923	275	–	628	570	1,198
404	6	20	82	308	410
434	6	10	155	275	440
13,065	39,147	2,882	25,840	23,490	52,212
14,833	35,682	2,990	26,394	21,131	50,515

Source: Based on data taken, with thanks, from Edward Azar's COPDAB, formerly at the University of North Carolina, Chapel Hill, and now at the University of Maryland. An event is a statement in a public source about who does or says what to whom when and about what issues. Edward E. Azar and Thomas J. Sloan, *Dimensions of Interaction,* International Studies Association Occasional Paper No. 8.

similar changes in the behavior of other international actors toward the PLO. As the PLO annual average for conflict changed from 628 to 3,874 to 2,678 in the three successive periods, international actions against the PLO went from 552 to 3,714 to 2,238. As the annual average cooperative behavior by the PLO increased from 92 to 432 to 2,020, international cooperative actions toward the PLO increased correspondingly, 195 to 686 to 1,988.

Finally, the basic domain of PLO foreign policy is the Middle East region. Almost 87% of the total foreign policy interactions of the PLO occur in this region, especially with Arab countries (46%) and Israel (41%). Israel and the PLO have the most active relationship (41%), followed by PLO-Jordanian relations (16%). At the global level, PLO international interactions are basically with the Third World (7%), the West (4%), and the Communist East (2%).

Having identified some basic patterns in the PLO's foreign policy behavior, we will illustrate them by looking at specific international actors. At the global level, we will focus upon PLO policy toward the United States, the USSR, and the PRC; at the regional level, we will review PLO policy toward Israel, Jordan, Egypt, Lebanon, and Syria.

The PLO and the United States

Although the United States does not occupy a prominent place in the PLO's interactions with the West, PLO-U.S. interactions have markedly increased since 1964, with almost 75% of interactions characterized by conflict. This holds equally for PLO behavior toward the United States (77%) and U.S. behavior toward the PLO (72%). Relations between the PLO and the United States have become increasingly more complex and differentiated over the years. This is reflected in the relative decline of conflictive interactions and a modest increase in cooperative contacts. For the PLO it went from 86% conflict between 1968 and 1973 to 70% conflict from 1974 to 1978. Comparable percentages for the United States were 92% and 55%.

The United States attempted to discourage the establishment of the PLO in 1964. It sent secret aides-mémoires to moderate Arab regimes warning against the establishment of the new organization and promising a settlement through the UN.[111] This was partly a response to Shukairy's anti-American posturing when he was Syria's representative to the UN. The PLO-U.S. pattern of conflict continued after 1967. The PLO rejected the 1970 Rogers Plan. It charged that the plan conceded part of Palestine to Israel, recognized Israel's legitimacy, and consolidated imperialist influence in the Middle East.[112] The PLO also accused the United States of orchestrating the Jordanian attack on the PLO in September 1970.

With the signing on September 1, 1975, of an Egyptian-Israeli interim agreement mediated by Kissinger, the United States made a commitment to Israel that it would neither recognize the PLO nor negotiate with it as long as the PLO refused to recognize Israel's right to exist and refused to accept Security Council resolutions 242 and 338. The commitment has since been reaffirmed many times by the Ford, Carter, and Reagan administrations. The PLO rejected Resolution 242 outright because it dealt with the Palestinian question as a refugee issue only. It demanded an amendment to the resolution that would add a reference to Palestinian national rights; a demand that the United States opposed. Furthermore, the PLO welcomed, with some reservations, the Soviet-U.S. statement of October 1977, which referred to the rights of the Palestinians. However, under Israeli and Egyptian pressure the United States shelved the statement a few days later.[113]

Despite its outright denunciation of the Camp David agreements and the Egyptian-Israeli treaty in 1979, and despite its refusal to join the autonomy talks, the PLO began to make some approaches to Washington. In July 1979, Arafat declared that he was prepared to send a PLO delegation to Washington to begin a dialogue with the United States for a new framework for peace.[114] The United States insisted on the PLO's unilateral recognition of Israel as a precondition for such a dialogue.

The PLO-U.S. impasse deepened with the Israeli invasion of Lebanon in June 1982. The PLO charged that the United States had played a major role in the Israeli operation. "The USA took part with Israel in the Lebanese war. It gave Israel military, political, financial, and diplomatic support. The USA made a record out of using its veto power to block any Security Council action,"[115] said Arafat. The PLO also charged that the United States had broken promises given to the PLO to protect Palestinian refugees in Lebanon after the PLO's departure from Beirut. The PLO, Arafat asserted, had protected U.S. civilians and diplomats during the Lebanese civil war, but Washington did not honor its promise.[116] The PLO adopted a middle-of-the-road approach toward the Reagan Plan of September 1982. Various prominent PLO leaders declared that the plan contained some positive points but fell short of the minimum demand of the PLO for a West Bank and Gaza state.[117]

The U.S.-PLO pattern of conflictual interaction continued from 1982 to 1988. The United States charged that the PLO was condoning terrorism by some of its member organizations and insisted on its outright recognition of Israel and Security Council Resolutions 242 and 338 as preconditions for dealing with the PLO. President Reagan threatened to boycott the 1985 General Assembly if Arafat attended. In 1987, the United States closed down the PLO's Information Office in Washington, D.C., began to take steps toward the expulsion of the PLO's Permanent Mission to the UN in New York, and declined to grant Arafat an entry visa to address the 1988 UN General Assembly. On the other hand, the PLO charged that the United States took an active role in the Israeli raid on its headquarters in Tunis that aimed to kill Arafat.

The resolutions of the nineteenth session of the PNC and Arafat's speech before the UN General Assembly in Geneva paved the road for intensive behind-the-scenes negotiations with Sweden acting as an intermediary. The result was a PLO-U.S. agreement according to which the PLO would recognize Israel and Security Council Resolutions 242 and 338, and pledge that the future Palestinian state would co-exist peacefully with its neighbors. The United States in turn, would deal publicly with the PLO and support the idea of an international conference. On December 15, 1988, Arafat publicly honored his part of the agreement, and immediately after the United States declared its decision to enter into direct dialogue with the PLO.

The PLO and the Soviet Union

PLO-Soviet interactions—unlike the PLO-U.S. interactions—are predominately positive (87%). About 80% of them are initiated by the PLO. When the PLO was established in 1964, Shukairy took the initiative in contacting the USSR and requesting arms supplies. The Soviets politely rebuffed him, pleading for more time to assess the situation.[118] As a result, Shukairy turned to the People's Republic of China, which was quite willing to replace the Soviets. The Arab defeat in 1967, the change in the PLO leadership, and the PLO's adoption of a new Arab-Israeli strategy created new opportunities for a closer relationship with the Soviet Union. The PLO-Soviet rapprochement was slowed down because of sharp criticism by the PLO of the Soviet endorsement of the Security Council Resolution 242.

The turning point in the relationship came in 1968, following Arafat's secret visit to Moscow as part of an Egyptian delegation.[119] The visit marked the beginning of Soviet recognition of the Palestinian resistance movements. This was clearly articulated by Kosygin in December 1969 when he affirmed Soviet support of the Palestinian struggle.[120] In February 1970, Arafat visited Moscow in his capacity as chairman of the PLO Executive Committee. Although the Soviets expressed their support of the PLO, they remained noncommittal regarding Arafat's request for military aid. It was not until July 1972 that the Soviets agreed to provide the PLO with arms, which began arriving in September 1972. The Soviets began to view the PLO as a genuine national liberation movement that truly represents the Palestinian people. However, they took issue with the PLO's emphasis upon armed struggle as the basic means for goal attainment. They criticized the PLO for not recognizing the possibility of a political resolution of the conflict with Israel.

The PLO-Soviet rapprochement deepened after the October War of 1973. Four basic issues dominated relations during this period: PLO and Soviet participation in the Arab-Israeli negotiations, recognition of the PLO, the Lebanese civil war, and the Israeli invasion of Lebanon. The PLO demanded Soviet participation in the Arab-Israeli negotiations as a safeguard against a U.S.-imposed settlement. The Soviet Union insisted in turn on the PLO's active role in the negotiations. In July-August 1974, Arafat visited Moscow. During this visit the Soviet Union endorsed the Arab summit's decision to recognize the PLO as the sole legitimate representative of the Palestinian people and agreed to open a PLO office in Moscow. The Soviet Union further supported the PLO stand during the Lebanese civil war in 1976. It openly denounced the Syrian intervention in Lebanon, risking the loss of its valuable Syrian connection.[121] Soviet support of the PLO increased in the wake of President Sadat's visit to Israel. Both the PLO and the Soviet Union condemned the Camp David agreements and the Egyptian-Israeli treaty of 1979.

Because of several factors that go beyond the PLO-Soviet relationship, the Soviet Union adopted a cautious approach toward the PLO-Israeli war in Lebanon in 1982. The Soviet Union restricted its response to verbal condemnations of Israel and the United States and the shipment of limited quantities of arms to the PLO, which were seized by Syria.[122] This muted response led to the disenchantment of some PLO leaders with the Soviet Union. Hawatema, the leader of the DFLP, criticized the Soviet policy as ineffective. Salah Khalaf, one of the prominent leaders of Fateh, accused the Soviet Union of collusion in the Israeli invasions.[123] However, Arafat moved quickly to patch up the disagreements. In January 1983, Arafat conferred in Moscow with Yuri Andropov. After the talks, he announced that Andropov supported the PLO plan for a confederal link between Jordan and the Palestinian state.[124]

PLO-Soviet relations deteriorated once more as a result of the PLO's conflict with Syria, one of the Soviet Union's closest allies. "The Soviet Union preferred to side with the Syrian ally rather than the Palestinian friend," Arafat charged.[125] This was reflected in the Soviet boycott of the seventeenth session of the PNC. However, Gorbachev's emphasis on restrengthening Soviet-U.S. détente and the PLO's move toward opening a dialogue with the United States has led to a limited improvement in PLO-Soviet relations. Arafat was officially received in Moscow in April 1988, but the Soviet Union refrained from recognizing the newly declared Palestinian state.

The PLO and the People's Republic of China

The People's Republic of China is the only international actor whose interactions with the PLO have been cooperative ever since 1965.[126] It was the first non-Arab state to establish ties with the PLO and remains the only great power that has consistently supported it. In March 1965, a PLO delegation headed by Shukairy was warmly received in Peking. A PLO office was opened in Peking and de facto diplomatic recognition was accorded. China provided the PLO with arms and ammunition and some PLO cadres were trained in the PRC. PLO-PRC relations seemed to have cooled in the wake of the Great Cultural Revolution and the removal of Shukairy from the leadership of the PLO, but the new PLO leadership moved to recement its Chinese connection. In March 1970, Arafat paid a visit to Peking during which he secured the continuous flow of arms to the PLO. On the eve of the September 1970 PLO-

Jordanian war, the PLO was heavily influenced by Chinese thought and tactics on the utility of military force and guerrilla warfare.[127]

After the 1970 war, PLO-PRC relations continued at a different level. China concentrated upon behind-the-scenes pressuring of various PLO groups to unite. PLO-PRC communications continued but the Chinese restricted their PLO connection to the level of verbal support. A 1977 visit by Arafat to Peking did not result in any noticeable change in this stand. This was essentially because of the growing connection between the PLO and the Soviet Union, the PRC's major adversary.

President Sadat's peace initiatives in 1977 threatened the PLO-PRC relationship. China had an interest in strengthening Sadat's anti-Soviet role, which ran counter to the PLO's anti-Sadat policy. In October-November 1978, a PLO delegation visited Peking with an aim of persuading Chinese leaders to oppose Sadat's Middle Eastern policy. The Chinese were ready to express support for the PLO and to condemn Israel, but refused to criticize Egypt.[128] Since then, PLO-PRC interactions have been kept at this low-key but cooperative level. China compensated the PLO for all its losses in armament during the PLO-Israeli war of 1982 and recognized the Palestinian state declared by the PNC in 1988.

The PLO and Israel

The PLO and Israel are engaged in a relationship of pure conflict, and there has been no change in this pattern since the two actors began interacting in 1964. The two actors initiate about the same amount of negative interactions toward each other. This pattern of interaction is a reflection of the issues at stake in the conflict and of the two actors' views of each other. The PLO and Israel both claim an exclusive historical right to the same territory. Neither envisages the possibility of a long-range mutual accommodation, and each denies the legitimacy of the other.

During the first five years of its existence, the PLO's reaction toward Israel was mainly restricted to verbal condemnations and military preparations for the future. After 1969, the PLO emerged as a coordinator of resistance operations against Israel and as a sponsor of the organized Palestinian resistance in the West Bank and Gaza. The 1969–1979 period witnessed the greatest volume of PLO-sponsored guerrilla operations against Israel. Israel responded by attacking various PLO targets.

After the expulsion of the PLO forces from Jordan, guerrilla operations declined considerably, but by 1973 operations began to escalate again from new Lebanese sanctuaries. The Lebanese civil war and Israeli reprisals forced the PLO in April 1982 to offer to sign a nonaggression pact. Israel refused.[129] Shortly after the PLO offer, Israel initiated a large-scale invasion of Lebanon (in June 1982) in order to destroy the PLO's infrastructure. The ensuing three months of fighting between the PLO and Israeli forces resulted in the eviction of most of the PLO guerrilla forces from Lebanon.

After the PLO-Israel confrontation in 1982, the PLO concentrated on three areas of interaction with Israel: rapprochement with the Israeli peace groups, rejection of unilateral recognition, and escalation of military operations. For the first time, PLO leaders openly met with leaders of various peace groups in Israel, as a sign of the possibility of Palestinian-Israeli coexistence.[130] However, the PLO insisted on mutual Israeli-Palestinian recognition rather than the unilateral recognition envisaged by the United States. Arafat justified this policy on three grounds: (1) unilateral recognition would result in increased Israeli intransigence; (2) recognition is a major bargaining card for the PLO, and it ought not be abandoned without a guaranteed gain; and (3) the political platform of the Likud coalition negates the independent existence of the Palestinians and it ought to be amended along with the PLO position.[131] Finally, the PLO began to regroup its forces and to stage guerrilla operations against Israel. The PLO leadership claims that between September and December of 1982 it staged 361 military operations against Israeli positions in southern Lebanon.[132] Meanwhile, the Israeli government has repeatedly asserted that it rejects any compromise with the PLO even if the latter recognizes its existence. Israel clung to this assertion after Arafat's recognition of Israel's right to exist in the fall of 1988.

Relations with the Arab Countries

The PLO interacts most frequently with Arab countries. One would normally expect this interaction to be mostly cooperative, but this is not the case. Almost 60% of PLO-Arab interactions are conflictive. During the last period considered (1974–1978), however, a new pattern of cooperative behavior did emerge and the percentage of conflict behavior dropped. As a general rule, the PLO initiates more negative interactions with the Arab world than the latter initiates toward the PLO. This holds equally true for the three periods of interaction.

By virtue of its character as a nonstate actor, the PLO is vulnerable to the manipulations of Arab regimes. The PLO's efforts to create a "Palestinian Hanoi" in Jordan in the 1960s and in Lebanon in the 1970s, and the subsequent damage inflicted upon these countries by the Israelis, caused constant tension between the PLO and the governments of these countries. The existence of a majority of the Palestinians under the control of various Arab regimes also caused a PLO-Arab conflict over the loyalty of these Palestinians. The PLO's attempt to ensure its autonomy and establish a direct relationship with the Palestinians inevitably engulfed it in conflict with most Arab regimes.[133] Differences of opinion between the PLO and the Arab governments over the appropriate solution to the Arab-Israeli conflict exacerbated this underlying tension. Finally, the difference in decision-making style between the PLO and other Arab countries complicated their conflicts. Arab regimes viewed the PLO's more democratic decision-making style as a potentially destabilizing force in their own countries.[134]

PLO-Arab interactions are also cooperative, however. The Arab countries recognize the PLO as the sole legitimate representative of the Palestinian people. The emergence of the PLO to international prominence after 1973 was basically an outcome of a collective Arab effort. Furthermore, the PLO has played the role of interlocutor in inter-Arab disputes such as the Algerian-Moroccan dispute in 1976 and the Egyptian-Libyan war in 1977.

In order to review the interplay of all these factors in the making of the PLO's foreign policy toward Arab countries, we will briefly outline PLO foreign policy behavior toward interacting countries: Jordan, Lebanon, Egypt, and Syria.

The PLO and Jordan. By virtue of the geographic and demographic connections between Jordan and the Palestinians, Jordan has the most active relationship with the PLO of any Arab country. PLO-Jordanian interactions represent almost 35% of total PLO-Arab interactions, and almost 85% of these interactions involve conflict.

The conflict between the PLO and Jordan in the mid-1960s was in essence a fight for the loyalty of the Palestinians living in Jordan and a struggle over territorial control of the West Bank. King Hussein did not permit the PLO to solicit support among the Palestinians until the PLO assured him it did not aspire to control the West Bank. The PLO also demanded the militarization of the Palestinians in Jordan under its partial supervision, a demand which the king rejected.

After the 1967 defeat, resistance organizations began to operate from Jordanian bases. The Egyptian-Jordanian post-1967 rapprochement helped them to consolidate their military presence in Jordan. After the Karama battle in March 1968 and the ensuing upsurge in the popularity of the resistance organization, King Hussein opted for a closer cooperation with the organizations. However, clashes escalated between the Jordanian army and the resistance organizations because of the latter's undisciplined behavior. The spark that lit the civil war in September 1970 was provided by the PFLP when it hijacked civilian airplanes and blew them up on Jordanian territory. The defeat of the PLO was completed by the end of 1971, when the Jordanian army eliminated PLO strongholds in northwest Jordan.[135]

PLO-Jordanian relations began to improve again after the 1973 war, and after Hussein agreed at the Arab summit of October 1974 to recognize the PLO as the sole legitimate representative of the Palestinian people. In April 1978, a PLO-Jordanian joint National Consultative Council was established. The thaw of enmity between the PLO and Jordan was accelerated by their common opposition to the Camp David agreements. In December 1978, Arafat visited Jordan. A "working charter" was signed to coordinate future relationships. The two parties also formed the "PLO-Jordan Joint Coordinating Committee for the Support of Steadfastness" as the mechanism for joint action supporting the Palestinians of the West Bank and Gaza.[136]

For the PLO, the harvest of the 1978–1980 rapprochement with Jordan was dismal. The PLO wanted a political dialogue that would lead to the return of its former military bases in Jordan, but Jordan restricted the dialogue to economic issues pertaining to the support of the Palestinians under Israeli occupation. The report of the EXCOM to the fifteenth session of the PNC in 1981 was rather pessimistic in its assessment of the record of the new PLO-Jordanian dialogue.

The PLO rapprochement with Jordan gained a new momentum after the PLO's departure from Beirut in 1982. The PLO entered into extensive negotiations with King Hussein through which the two sides agreed to establish a confederal connection between Jordan and the suggested Palestinian state. However, the PLO refused to authorize King Hussein to negotiate on its behalf with the United States or Israel.[137]

On February 11, 1985, the PLO and Jordan announced that they had reached an agreement concerning the framework for their future diplomatic moves. The Amman Agreement, as it was called, was supposed to be a secret document. However, King Hussein declared the provisions of the agreement in order to get the PLO to publicly commit itself to it. This infuriated the PLO leadership which found itself in an awkward position with its own extremist organizations. The PLO began to demand certain amendments to the Amman Agreement in order to accommodate the criticisms of the extremists who accused Arafat of abandoning the representational role of the PLO to the Palestinians. The PLO's hesitation led King Hussein to freeze the Amman Agreement on February 19, 1986 and to shut down some of the PLO offices in Jordan. In a lengthy public speech, King Hussein charged that the PLO is more interested in practicing power than in restoring the occupied territories. As attempts to patch up the PLO-Jordan rift failed, and the Arab summit held in Algiers reaffirmed that the PLO is the sole legitimate representative of the Palestinians, on July 31, 1988, King Hussein decided to sever all the legal and administrative links between Jordan and the West Bank. King Hussein's decision put the responsibility of restoring the West Bank solely on the shoulders of the PLO.

The PLO and Lebanon. Relations between the PLO and Lebanon resemble PLO-Jordanian relations in their intensity and in the issues at stake. The PLO became active in Lebanon as early as May 1968. Lebanon offered the PLO a center of communications and accessibility to northern Israel. As Israeli strikes against guerrilla bases became more frequent and as their electrified barrier along the Jordan River went up, PLO forces moved increasingly into Lebanon. As PLO activities in Lebanon increased, Lebanese politicians became apprehensive. They feared Israeli retaliatory measures against Lebanese targets and the disruptive impact of Palestinian militancy on the delicate Lebanese communal balance. This led to military clashes between PLO forces and the Lebanese army in April and October 1969. Through Egyptian mediation, the PLO and Lebanon signed the November 1969 Cairo agreement, which set certain guidelines for their future relations. It recognized the right of the Palestinians to work, reside, circulate, and participate in the armed struggle within the framework of Lebanese sovereignty and security.

The Cairo agreement pacified PLO-Lebanese relations temporarily. Later, army units and right-wing militia members, especially Phalangists, began to clash with resistance members more often. Matters worsened as PLO forces moved into Lebanon after their defeat in Jordan. Israeli retaliatory measures forced Lebanese policy-makers to demand the evacuation of the PLO units from southern Lebanon, and the PLO leadership agreed.[138] The situation in southern Lebanon returned to normal until the Israelis reactivated their military operations against the PLO in early 1973. This led to a new round of fighting between the PLO forces and the Lebanese army.

The involvement of the PLO in the Lebanese civil war and incessant Israeli incursions against PLO targets finally forced the PLO in 1979 to halt all military operations against Israel from Lebanese territories. Further, as the Lebanese felt the brunt of the Israel all-out invasion in June 1982, virtually all Lebanese factions, including the pro-PLO leftists, asked the PLO to evacuate Beirut in order to save Lebanon from total destruction. In September 1982, the bulk of the PLO leadership left Beirut.

In 1983, Arafat managed to redeploy some of his forces in northern Lebanon under his leadership. But pro-Syrian groups forced him to withdraw under Egyptian protection. Since then, the PLO has only been successful in stationing some of its forces in the Palestinian refugee camps in southern Lebanon in order to protect the refugees from the wrath of the Amal party Shi'ite forces and to launch limited commando attacks on Israeli forces in southern Lebanon and northern Israel.

The PLO and Syria. The dilemma of Arab regimes in dealing with the PLO is nowhere more pronounced than in Syria. Although the Syrians are among the most outspoken supporters of the Palestinian cause, they have always kept the PLO presence in Syria under firm control and have helped to weaken the authority of the PLO by creating their own organization, Al-Sa'iqa.

Initially, the Ba'thist regime of Amin Al-Hafez was not enthusiastic about the creation of the PLO in 1964. It was already involved with Fateh, which was launching military operations against Israel. The Syrian regime considered the PLO to be a reactionary organization and a facade for Nasser. Consequently, it rejected the integration of Fateh forces with the PLO units and insisted upon Ba'thist control of the PLO units in Syria.

It was not until the chairmanship of Arafat that the PLO began to make a breakthrough with Syria. This new connection was further cemented during the PLO struggle against the Jordanian regime in 1969–1970. During the September 1970 clashes, Syria pushed some PLA units to intervene in Jordan on the side of the PLO.

In November 1970, Hafiz Al-Asad took over as president of Syria. The Asad regime imposed new restrictions on the PLO. When the PLO criticized the Asad-Sadat agreement of September 1973, Syria closed down the PLO's radio station in Damascus. Badly in need of Syrian support, the PLO had very limited options indeed. In March 1975, the PLO agreed to set up a joint political-military command at the suggestion of President Asad, but by early 1976, relations had deteriorated sharply. The catalyst was the Lebanese civil war. When the PLO rejected Syria's conceptions of a Lebanese settlement, the Syrian army intervened in Lebanon in June 1976 to prevent the victory of the alliance between the PLO and the Lebanese leftist forces and to reassert its primacy over the PLO.

The Sadat peace efforts in 1977–1978 brought the PLO closer to Syria once again. The enemies who had bitterly fought each other in Lebanon both became members in the Steadfastness Front. Syria's dismal performance during the Israeli invasion of Lebanon in 1982 revived the underlying sources of tension between the PLO and Syria, and this was reflected in the PLO's decision to move its headquarters to Tunis from Damascus. As the PLO began to adopt a more conciliatory tone and to break away from Syrian guardianship, the Syrians began to criticize the PLO leadership and to challenge Arafat's right to speak on behalf of the PLO. In June 1983, relations came to the breaking point. Arafat accused Syria of supporting the mutiny within Fateh's military ranks and Asad reacted by expelling Arafat from Damascus.

PLO-Syria relations have been deteriorating ever since Syria supported the Fateh mutineers to expel Arafat from his newly formed military headquarters in northern Lebanon in 1983. Syria also backed the Patriotic Alliance to remove Arafat from the PLO leadership and attempted to block the convening of the seventeenth session of the PNC by persuading members of the Patriotic Alliance to abstain. In response to the Amman Agreement between Jordan and the PLO, Syria sponsored the Palestinian National Salvation Front, as a supposedly alternative organization to the PLO. Moreover, it orchestrated the War of the Camps, a war launched by pro-Syrian organizations in Lebanon to destroy the remnants of the pro-Arafat Fateh forces there.

The main nagging issue in the PLO-Syria relationship has always been Syria's attempt to control the PLO. "Asad wants the Palestinian card in his own pocket," Arafat asserted.[139] He also charged that the Asad regime has secret links with Israel and wants to turn the Middle East into communal cantons.[140] Relations between the PLO and Syria remain extremely tense.

The PLO and Egypt. The PLO's interactions with Egypt are significantly different from its relations with other Arab actors. Because of the absence of a substantial Palestinian community in Egypt or a territorial base for anti-Israeli operations, the issues in PLO-Egyptian relations have been basically restricted to different approaches toward the resolution of the

Arab-Israeli conflict. In formulating its Palestinian policy, Egypt has been able to perform without significant PLO pressure.

Only 34% of PLO-Egyptian interactions involve conflict. The PLO tends to initiate more negative behavior toward Egypt than does Egypt toward the PLO. During the three periods under consideration, 46% of the PLO's total behavior was conflictive; the corresponding percentage for Egypt was 21%. A brief review of the evolution of PLO interactions with Egypt will clarify this pattern.

Nasser played a major role in the establishment of the PLO. As a result, the PLO was widely perceived, especially by Syria and Saudi Arabia, as a tool of Nasser's policy. However, PLO-Egyptian relations were not as smooth as might have been expected. Nasser insisted on full Egyptian control of PLA units stationed in Egypt and refused any PLO participation in their military affairs. He also became displeased with PLO leadership when Shukairy agreed with the Chinese to ship light arms to Alexandria without Nasser's prior permission. Moreover, Egypt did not pay its contributions to the PLO and charged the PLO heavily for the various services it used.[141]

After June 1967, Egypt helped in training and arming PLA units, building the PLO intelligence network, and strengthening its broadcasting facilities.[142] However, relations deteriorated after Nasser's acceptance of the Rogers Plan in 1970. The PLO severely criticized the Egyptian move and Nasser, in turn, closed down the PLO radio facilities in Cairo.

Under Sadat, PLO-Egyptian relations were more conflictive than cooperative. Sadat implied that PLO leadership was involved in the student demonstrations against his regime in 1972. However, Sadat managed to calm his tense relations with the PLO after severing his relations with Jordan in protest over the United Arab Kingdom proposal. As a goodwill gesture to the PLO, the assassins of Wasfi-Al-Tall, former prime minister of Jordan, were never brought to trial. The PLO politely turned down Sadat's suggestion to establish a Palestinian government in exile.

After October 1973, the PLO severely criticized the Sinai I and Sinai II Egyptian-Israeli interim agreements. The two sides managed to patch up their relations when Sadat sided with the PLO in its conflict with Syria during the Lebanese civil war. Arafat played a role in the mediation efforts between Egypt and Libya in July 1977. The uneasy alliance between Sadat and the PLO finally broke down when Sadat, in a parliamentary meeting at which Arafat was present, announced his decision to visit Israel in November 1977. From then on Sadat became the archenemy of the PLO. Relations deteriorated further when Sadat accused the PLO of being involved in the assassination of Yusuf Al-Siba'i, the editor-in-chief of *Al-Ahram*, in Cyprus in February 1978. In July 1979, an unknown Palestinian organization called the "Eagles of the Revolution" attacked the Egyptian embassy in Turkey.

After the PLO's departure from Beirut, a new pattern of PLO-Egyptian rapprochement emerged. The catalyst for this rapprochement was President Mubarak's condemnation of the Israeli invasion and his decision to withdraw the Egyptian ambassador in Israel. Arafat responded by cabling Mubarak to hail his decision. After his departure, Arafat appealed to Mubarak to shoulder Egypt's historical responsibility toward the Palestinians. No Arab country, he said, had been able to fill the gap created after Egypt opted out of the Arab system.[143] Relations deteriorated very briefly after the announcement of the resolutions of the sixteenth session of the PNC, which seemed to snub the Egyptian government by hailing the opposition as representing the true patriotic Egyptian sentiments. Mubarak viewed the resolution as an unacceptable interference in Egypt's domestic affairs.

Relations between the PLO and Egypt began to improve as Syria mounted its pressure on the PLO leadership. In 1983, the Egyptian navy protected the vessels carrying Arafat and his forces retreating from Lebanon under Syrian military pressure. Further, Egypt played a crucial behind-the-scenes role in reaching the Amman Agreement between the PLO and Jordan in February 1985 and announcing the Cairo Declaration in November 1985, a document in which Arafat renounced terrorism and which was supposed to form a basis for a dialogue between the PLO and the United States. The PLO's perception of Egypt's role was summed up by Hami Al-Hasan, Arafat counsel, as follows: "The battle for inheriting Egypt's role in the Arab arena has proven that there are no heirs."[144] The PLO, in turn, played a crucial role in the summit of the Organization of the Islamic Conference in 1984 and the summit of the League of Arab States in 1989 for the resumption of Egypt's membership in both organizations. When the PNC declared the establishment of a Palestinian state in November 1988, Egypt recognized it after some hesitation.

CONCLUSION

The analysis of PLO foreign policy illustrates the dilemmas that revolutionary nonstate actors confront when they formulate foreign policy. Lacking a secure power potential or a territorial base, such actors face a real dilemma: to guarantee external support even at the expense of their goal pursuit or to sacrifice the former for the latter. In the case of the PLO, this is further complicated by the dispersion of its population, which is controlled by often conflicting regimes. This engulfs the PLO in the domestic affairs of these regimes and in the various conflicts between them. The difference in legal definitions and perceptions of appropriate strategies between a revolutionary organization that challenges the status quo and established political regimes also adds to the perplexity of the foreign policy-making process. Once established regimes envisage an opportunity for the attainment of their limited goals, they are tempted to crack down upon the maximalist actor. All of this leads to a decentralized foreign policy process, mostly uncontrolled by a

302   *Mohamed E. Selim*

sufficient degree of executive authority. It also leads to a foreign policy behavior characterized by incessant conflicts with the state actors who strive to control the behavior of the PLO.

The interplay of all these variables has led to certain miscalculations that impeded the effectiveness of PLO foreign policy. The PLO used to articulate goals that went beyond its capabilities as a nonstate actor. The gap between the articulated goals and the actual capabilities created another credibility gap for the PLO in the international arena. Consequently, the course of PLO foreign policy has been mostly centered around the attempt to articulate "feasible" goals. Further, the PLO has not always been successful in timing its foreign policy initiatives or arranging its foreign policy priorities. Most of the PLO's foreign policy initiatives have been declared after the regional balance of power and the international arena have drastically moved to new horizons that make such initiatives almost obsolete. The PLO also has not been able to schedule two foreign policy priorities: the restoration of the occupied territories and the rule of these territories once restored. This has been the main issue in the PLO-Jordan relationship.

The most recent changes in PLO foreign policy appear to be an attempt to overcome these problems. Yasser Arafat's statements concerning the acceptance of Israel's right to exist, as well as the new stress on the establishment of the Palestinian state in the West Bank and the Gaza Strip as a solution to the problem, represent qualitative changes in this respect. There is still a long way to go, however, before this new PLO foreign policy goal, the Palestinian state, takes concrete form.

The problems of the PLO's foreign policy and its adjustment continue. The 1990–1991 Gulf crisis has drastically reduced the fortunes of the PLO. During the crisis the PLO sided with Iraq and insisted on linking the withdrawal of Iraqi forces from Kuwait with the withdrawal of Israeli forces from the West Bank and Gaza Strip. The argument was that international legality is indivisible and that Middle Eastern problems should be tackled simultaneously. In the Arab summit held in Cairo in the wake of the Iraqi invasion of Kuwait, Arafat voted against the resolutions calling for the withdrawal of the Iraqi forces. As the crisis escalated, members of the PLO leadership moved to fight alongside Iraqi forces against the coalition forces.

One could account for the PLO pro-Iraqi stance in the light of the collapse of the dialogue between the PLO and the United States and the slowdown of the diplomatic activities to resolve the PLO-Israeli conflict. The PLO estimated that Iraq's capture of Kuwait with its rich oil fields and Iraq's emergence as a powerful ally of the PLO could create a number of bargaining possibilities with the United States.

Regardless of the motives of the PLO pro-Iraqi stance, the PLO emerged from the Gulf crisis as a likely loser. Arafat's stance antagonized a number of Arab states who had formerly been solid allies of the PLO, namely Egypt and the Gulf states. Those states are likely to suspend their financial and diplomatic support of the PLO as long as the present PLO leadership is in power. Further, the outcome of the Gulf crisis seems to have absolved the United States and European countries from any commitment to deal with the PLO. They are likely to search for an alternative Palestinian leadership to negotiate with Israel.

However, the Gulf crisis has created a new momentum for the resolution of the Arab-Israeli conflict and the resumption of the Arab-Israeli negotiations. This could create new possibilities for reintegration of the PLO into these negotiations, at least in their final stages, depending on two factors: (1) the ability of the PLO to close ranks with the Arab pro-coalition states, especially Egypt and Saudi Arabia—something the PLO has been able to manage in the past, and (2) the ability of the PLO to maintain its representational nature of the Palestinians, just as the PLO pro-Iraqi stance reflected the feelings of the majority of the Palestinians.

In all cases, the PLO's capacity to act will be constrained in the short run.

NOTES

1. Raymond Hopkins and Richard Mansbach, *Structure and Process in International Politics* (New York: Harper & Row, 1973), p. 4; Howard Lentner, *Foreign Policy Analysis* (Columbus, Ohio: Charles Merril, 1974), pp. 17–19; and Oran Young, "Actors in World Politics," in James Rosenau, V. Davis, and M. East (eds.), *The Analysis of International Politics* (New York: Free Press, 1972), pp. 125–144.

2. For recent works analyzing the foreign policies of various nonstate actors see Judy Bertelson (ed.), *Non-State Nations in International Politics: Comparative System Analyses* (New York: Praeger Publishers, 1977), Stanley Thames, "The Multi-national Corporation as a Foreign Policy Maker," Paper presented at the seventeenth meeting of the International Studies Association, Toronto, 1976; Samuel Huntington, "Transnational Organizations in World Politics," *World Politics* 15, 3 (1973), pp. 333–368; and Nassif Hitti, "The League of Arab States: Toward an Independent Foreign Policy," *Arab Affairs* (Tunis), December 1981, pp. 76–86 (in Arabic).

3. Ernest Haas, *Beyond the Nation-State, Functionalism and International Organization* (Stanford, Calif.: Stanford University Press, 1964), pp. 469–475; Judy Bertelson, *The Palestinian Arabs: A Non-State Nation System Analysis* (Beverly Hills, Calif.: Sage, 1976), pp. 11–12; and Ronald Macintyre, "The Palestine Liberation Organization: Tactics, Strategies and Options Towards the Geneva Peace Conference," *Journal of Palestine Studies* 4, 4 (1976), pp. 76–79.

4. Rashid Hamid, "What Is the PLO?" *Journal of Palestine Studies* 3, 4 (1975), p. 4. For a review of these organizations see Ass'ad Abdel-Rahman (ed.), *The Palestinian Liberation Organization: Its Roots, Establishment, and Activities* (Nicosia: Published for the Research Center of the PLO by Al-Abhath Publishing Co., 1987), pp. 29–60.

5. *Compendium of Palestine Documents* (Cairo: State Information Service, 1970), Part 2, p. 1273.

6. Ahmed Al-Shukairy, *From the Summit to the Defeat with the Arab Kings and Presidents* (Beirut: Dal Al-Awada, 1971), pp. 60–62 (in Arabic).

7. Abdel-Moniem Al-Sa'adoun, "The Palestine Liberation Organization," Diploma diss., Institute of Arab Studies and Research, Cairo, 1976, pp. 180–211 (in Arabic).

8. Al-Shukairy, *op. cit.*, p. 112.

9. George Kossaifi, "Demographic Characteristics of the Arab Palestinian People," in Khalil Nakhleh and Elia Zureik (eds.), *The Sociology of the Palestinians* (London: Croom Helm, 1980), p. 25; and Edward Hagopian and Antoine Zahlan, "Palestine's Arab Population: The Demography of the Palestinians," *Journal of Palestine Studies* 3, 4 (1974), p. 61.

10. Gamil Hilal, "Class Transformation in the West Bank and Gaza," *Journal of Palestine Studies* 6, 2 (1977), pp. 172–173; and Pamela Ann Smith, "Aspects of Class Structure in the Palestinian Society, 1948–1967," in Uri Davis, A. Mack, and N. Yuval-Davis (eds.), *Israel and the Palestinians* (London: Ithaca Press, 1975), pp. 98–112.

11. Sammy Mar'i, "Higher Education Among Palestinians with Special Reference to the West Bank," in Gabriel Ben-Dor (ed.), *The Palestinians and the Middle East Conflict* (Ramat Gan, Israel: Turtledove, 1978), pp. 181–182; and Nabil Shaath, "High Level Palestinian Manpower," *Journal of Palestine Studies* 1 (1972), pp. 80–97.

12. Mar'i, *op. cit.*, p. 441.

13. Philip Davies, "The Educated West Bank Palestinians," *Journal of Palestine Studies* 8, 3 (1979), p. 65.

14. Muhsin Yusuf, "The Potential Impact of Palestinian Education on a Palestinian State," *Journal of Palestine Studies* 8, 4 (1979), pp. 70–93; and Michael Hudson, "The Palestinian Resistance Movement Since 1967," in Willard A. Beling (ed.), *The Middle East: Quest for an American Policy* (Albany: State University of New York, 1973), p. 109.

15. Bassam Sirhan, "Palestinian Refugee Camp Life in Lebanon," *Journal of Palestine Studies* 4, 2 (1975), p. 107.

16. Rosemary Sayigh, *Palestinians: From Peasants to Revolutionaries* (London: Zed Press, 1979), p. 125.

17. Rosemary Sayigh, "Sources of Palestinian Nationalism: A Study of a Palestinian Camp in Lebanon," *Journal of Palestine Studies* 6, 4 (1977), pp. 22–23.

18. Abdel-Meguid Amer, *The Patriotic Identity of the Palestinian People: A Field Study of a Camp*, M.A. diss., University of Cairo, 1982, pp. 93–94, 117–118, 129, 136 (in Arabic).

19. *Ibid.*, p. 167.

20. Karl Deutsch, *Nationalism and Social Communication, An Inquiry into the Foundations of Nationality* (Cambridge, Mass.: MIT Press, 1962).

21. Hamid Ansari, "Palestinian National Identity: Challenges and Continuity," Working Paper No. 32, Comparative Interdisciplinary Studies section of the International Studies Association, 1975, pp. 3–8.

22. Rosemary Sayigh, "The Palestinian Identity Among Camp Residents," *Journal of Palestine Studies* 5, 3 (1977), pp. 11–12.

23. John Amos II, *Palestinian Resistance: Organization of a National Movement* (New York: Pergamon Press, 1980), p. 150.

24. Ibrahim Abu-Lughod, "The Palestinians Today," in Hatem Hussaini and F. El-Boghdady (eds.), *The Palestinians* (Washington, D.C.: Arab Information Center, 1976), p. 30.

25. Fawaz Turki, *The Disinherited, Journal of Palestinian Exile* (New York: Monthly Review Press, 1974), pp. 37–38.

26. Donna Robinson Divine, "The Dialectics of Palestinian Politics," in Joel Migdal (ed.), *Palestinian Society and Politics* (Princeton, N.J.: Princeton University Press, 1980), pp. 212–229.

27. *Ibid.*

28. William Quandt, Fuad Jabber, and Ann Lesch, *The Politics of Palestinian Nationalism* (Berkeley: University of California Press, 1973), pp. 80–82.

29. Abdel-Wahab El Messeri, *The Palestinian Uprising and the Zionist Dilemma* (Cairo: Commercial Press, 1989) (in Arabic); *The Arab Strategic Yearbook, 1988* (Cairo: Al-Ahram Center for Strategic Studies, 1989), pp. 340–358 (in Arabic).

30. Arafat's interview in *Shu'un Filistinia*, 194, May 1989, pp. 143–144.

31. Amos, *op. cit.*, pp. 163–164.

32. Al-Shukairy, *op. cit.*, pp. 192–194.

33. Arafat's statement in *Fikr* 2, 6 (June 1985), p. 31.

34. Amos, *op. cit.*, p. 16.

35. Arafat's statement in *Fikr, op. cit.*

36. For a review of Samid's history and activities see "An interview with the Director of Samid," *Samid Al Iktisadi* 6, 47 (February 1984), pp. 10–42, and 7, 53 (February 1985), pp. 16–39; Cheryl Rubenberg, "The Civilian Infrastructure of the Palestine Liberation Organization," *Journal of Palestine Studies* 12, 3 (Spring 1983), pp. 66–69; "The Reality of Arafat's Financial Empire," *Al-Mijalla*, December 24, 1985, pp. 17–18.

37. Amos, *op. cit.*, pp. 158–159.

38. Sara Bar-Haim, "The Palestine Liberation Army, Stooge or Actor," in Gabriel Ben-Dor, *op. cit.*, pp. 181–182.

39. *Ibid.*, pp. 58, 61, 71, 205.

40. *Ibid.*, pp. 167–168.

41. Resolutions of the thirteenth session of the Palestine National Council, held in March 1977, *Journal of Palestine Studies* 5, 3 (1977), pp. 194–195.

42. Y. Harkabi, "The Weakness of the Fedayeen," in Y. Harkabi, *Palestinians and Israel* (New Brunswick, N.J.: Transaction Books, 1975), pp. 102–114.

43. Eric Rouleau, "The Future of the PLO," *Foreign Affairs* 62, 1 (Fall 1983), pp. 140–141. Also for a similar viewpoint see Yezid Sayigh, "Palestinian Military Performance in the 1982 War," *Journal of Palestine Studies* 12, 4 (Summer 1983), p. 8.

44. From an interview with Salah Khalaf, member of the Palestine National Council, *Al-Mussawar* (Cairo) 3025 (October 1, 1982).

45. Arafat's statement in *Fikr, op. cit.*, p. 58.

46. Arafat revealed that the PLO air force has been used to support the Sandinista regime in Nicaragua. Arafat's interview with *Al-Mussawar*, July 19, 1985.

47. According to Arafat, the PLO launched some 863 military operations from southern Lebanon in 1985. His interview with *Al-Ahram*, February 19, 1986.

48. Al-Sa'adoun, *op. cit.*, pp. 127–130.

49. Barbara Salmore and S. Salmore, "Political Regimes and Foreign Policy," in Maurice East, S. Salmore, and C. Hermann (eds.), *Why Nations Act: Theoretical Perspectives for Comparative Foreign Policy Studies* (Beverly Hills, Calif.: Sage, 1978), p. 111.

50. Anis Kassim, "The Palestine Liberation Organization's Claim to Status: A Juridical Analysis Under International Law," *Journal of Palestine Studies* 10,4 (1981), pp. 142–153.

51. Amos, *op. cit.*, p. 176.

52. Salmore and Salmore, *op. cit.*, pp. 111–113.

53. For a full review of the programs of all Palestinian guerrilla organizations, see Ghazi Khorsheid, *A Handbook of the Palestinian Resistance Movement* (Beirut: PLO Research Center, 1971) (in Arabic). For further analyses of these programs see Muhammad Muslih, "Moderates and Rejectionists Within the Palestine Liberation Organization," *Middle East Journal* 30, 2 (1976), pp. 127–140; Paul Jureidini and W. Hazen, *The Palestinian Movement in Politics* (Lexington, Mass.: D. C. Heath and Co., 1976), pp. 19–40; Fouad Moughrabi, "The Palestine Resistance Movement, Evolution of a Strategy," Paper presented at the seventeenth annual convention of the International Studies Association, Toronto, 1976; and Fawaz Hamed Al-Sharkawy, "Palestinian National Liberation Movement, Fateh," M.A. diss., University of Cairo, 1974; Helena Cobban, *The Palestinian Liberation Organization: People, Power, and Politics* (Cambridge: Cambridge University Press, 1984), pp. 139–167; Aaron David Miller, *The PLO and Politics of Survival* (New York: Praeger, 1983, Washington Papers series No. 99), pp. 40–64.

54. Bruce Stanley, "Fragmentation and National Liberation Movements: The PLO," *Orbis* 22, 4 (1979), pp. 1053–1054.

55. For a review of these developments see *The Arab Strategic Yearbook, 1985* (Cairo: Al-Ahram Center for Strategic Studies, 1986), pp. 301–304 (in Arabic). *The Arab Strategic Yearbook, 1986* (Cairo: Al-Ahram Center for Strategic Studies, 1986), pp. 304–307 (in Arabic).

56. Yasser Arafat's speech in the United Nations on November 13, 1974. Text printed in *Journal of Palestine Studies* 4, 2 (1975), pp. 181–192.

57. Arafat's interview with *Al-Muharrer* (Beirut), April 27, 1972.

58. Arafat's interview with *Al-Hawadess* (Beirut), August 2, 1974.

59. Resolutions of the second session of the PNC in *ibid.*, p. 75, and of the third session of the PNC in Rashid Hamid (ed.), *Resolutions of the Palestine National Council, 1964–1974* (Beirut: PLO Research Center, 1975), p. 94.

60. Arafat's interview with the *New Times* (Moscow), November 1973. In *Palestinian Arab Documents for 1973* (Beirut: Institute for Palestine Studies, 1976), p. 497.

61. Arafat's speech at the OAU meeting in Kampala on July 29, 1975. Text in *Journal of Palestine Studies* 5, 1 (1975 and Winter 1976), p. 258.

62. Resolutions of the fourth session of the PNC, in Hamid, *Resolutions*, p. 111.

63. Arafat's speech at the Fourth Summit of the Nonaligned Movement, held in Algeria in 1973. Text of speech is in George Nasrallah (ed.), *The Palestinian and Arab Documents for 1973* (Beirut: Institute for Palestine Studies, 1976), pp. 279–280. Resolutions of the fifteenth session of the PNC are in the *Journal of Palestine Studies* 10, 4 (1981), p. 187.

64. Resolutions of the fifteenth session, *ibid.*

65. Article 13 of the Palestinian Patriotic Charter, in Hamid, *Resolutions*, p. 123.

66. Article 15 of the Palestinian Patriotic Charter, in *ibid.*, p. 123.

67. Resolutions of the seventh session of the PNC, in *ibid.*, p. 166.

68. Resolutions of the sixth session of the PNC, in *ibid.*, p. 152.

69. The political program of the tenth session of the PNC held in April 1972, in *ibid.*, p. 218.

70. *Ibid.*

71. Article 9 of the Palestinian Patriotic Charter, in *ibid.*

72. Arafat interview with Talal Salman, "With Fateh and the Fedayeen" (Beirut: Dar Al-Awda, 1969), p. 10.

73. Resolutions of the tenth session of the PNC, in Hamid, *Resolutions*, p. 199.

74. Arafat's interview with *Al-Hawadess*, August 2, 1974.

75. Resolutions of the fifth session of the PNC, in Hamid, *Resolutions*, p. 137.

76. Speech by Arafat at the OAU meeting in Kampala, July 29,1975, *op. cit.*, p. 259.

77. Resolutions of the fourth session of the PNC, in Hamid, *Resolutions*, p. 111.

78. In *ibid.*, p. 124.

79. Resolutions of the seventh session of the PNC, in *ibid.*, p. 166.

80. This has been clearly articulated in Arafat's interviews with Professor Kelman: Herbert Kelman, "Talk with Arafat," *Foreign Policy* 49 (Winter 1982–1983), pp. 126–127.

81. Arafat's interview with *Filastine Al-Thawra* on January 1, 1973, in *Journal of Palestine Studies* 2, 3 (1973), p. 168.

82. *Ibid.*, p. 167.

83. Articles 1 and 2 of the Palestinian Patriotic Charter, in Hamid, *Resolutions*, p. 122.

84. *Ibid.*, p. 151.

85. Resolutions of the fifth session of the PNC, in *ibid.*, p. 138.

86. Ahmed Al-Shukairy, *Decisive Situations in the Palestine Issue* (Cairo: PLO Office, n.d.), p. 79 (in Arabic).

87. "Towards a Democratic State in Palestine," Paper submitted to the Second World Conference on Palestine, held in Amman in September 1970. Reprinted by the Arab Information Centre, Ottawa, Canada, n.d., pp. 15–16.

88. Ann Lesch, "Palestinian Politics and the Future of Arab-Israeli Relations," in Robert Freedman (ed.), *World Politics and the Arab-Israeli Conflict* (New York: Pergamon Press, 1979), p. 225.

89. In Hamid, *Resolutions*, p. 247.

90. Quoted in Lesch, *op. cit.*, p. 230.

91. Arafat's interview with the *New York Times*, May 4, 1978.

92. The official spokesman of the PLO, as quoted in *Al-Akhbar* (Cairo), October 13, 1982.

93. Resolutions of the twelfth session of the PNC, in Hamid, *Resolutions*, p. 247.

94. Arafat's interview with *Rose Al-Youssef* (Cairo), October 21, 1974, and with *Al Akhbar*, November 28, 1973.

95. Arafat's interview with *Al-Mussawar*, December 31, 1982.

96. *The Arab Strategic Yearbook, 1988* (Cairo: Al-Ahram Center for Strategic Studies, 1986), pp. 364–367 (in Arabic).

97. *Al-Ahram*, May 4, 1989.

98. Resolutions of the fourth session of the PNC, in Hamid, *Resolutions*, p. 103.

99. Resolutions of the fourth session of the PNC, in Hamid, *Resolutions*, p. 105.

100. Resolutions of the thirteenth session of the PNC, in *Journal of Palestine Studies* 5, 3 (1977), p. 188.

101. Arafat's interview with *Al-Hawadess*, January 7, 1983.

102. Statement of Farouk Kaddoumi, the head of the PLO's Political Department in *Al-Ahram*, May 28, 1986, and Arafat's speech at the UN General Assembly held in 1988, text of speech in *Al-Ahram*, December 14, 1988.

103. The text of the Cairo Declaration in *Al-Ahram*, November 8, 1985.

104. Charles Hermann, "Decision Structure and Process Influences on Foreign Policy," in East, Salmore, and Hermann, *op. cit.*, pp. 77–78.

105. Al-Shukairy, *Summit to Defeat*, p. 211.

106. *Journal of Palestine Studies* 11, 1 (1981), p. 172.

107. *Ibid.*, p. 177.

108. Ibrahim Abu-Lughod, "Flexible Militancy: A Report on the Sixteenth Session of the Palestine National Council, Algiers, February 14–22, 1983," *Journal of Palestine Studies* 12, 4 (Summer 1983), pp. 37–38.

109. Arafat's interview with *Al-Majallah* (London), October 9, 1982, pp. 2, 5; see also Rashid el Khalidi, *The PLO Under Siege: Decision Making During the 1982 War* (New York: Columbia University Press, 1986).

110. For a review of the international events approach, see Charles W. Kegley, Jr., et al. (eds.), *International Events and the Comparative Analysis of Foreign Policy* (Columbia: University of South Carolina Press, 1975).

111. Al-Shukairy, *Summit to Defeat*, pp. 93, 118, 122.

112. Resolutions of the sixth session of the PNC, in Hamid, *Resolutions*, p. 169.

113. Raymond Cohen, "Israel and the Soviet-American Statement of October 1977: The Limits of Patron-Client Influence," *Orbis* 22, 3 (1978), pp. 613–634.

114. Arafat's interview with *Al-Safir*, July 23, 1979.

115. Arafat's interview with *Al-Majallah*, September 17, 1982.

116. Arafat's interview with *Al-Siyassa* (Kuwait), January 8, 1983, and with Saad Ibrahim, "With Yasser Arafat."

117. Arafat's statement in *Al-Akhbar*, October 14, 1982; statement of Khalil Al-Wazir in *Al-Ahram*, October 16, 1982; statement of Nabil Shaath in *Al-Akhbar*, October 13, 1982.

118. Al-Shukairy, *Summit to Defeat*, pp. 216–217.

119. It is important to note that Arafat visited Moscow in his capacity as leader of Fateh.

120. Galia Golan, *The Soviet Union and the Palestine Liberation Organization* (New York: Praeger Publishers, 1981), p. 11.

121. *Ibid.*, pp. 11–28, 123–125, 232–233.

122. As revealed by Arafat in his interview with Saad Ibrahim, "With Yasser Arafat."

123. Mohamed Selim, "The Soviet Union and the Palestinian-Israeli War," *Al-Siyassa Al-Dawliya* (Cairo) 18 (1982), p. 152.

124. *Al-Ahram*, January 14, 1983.

125. Arafat's interview with *Al-Mussawar*, July 19, 1985, p. 13.

126. For a full review of the PLO-PRC relations, see the following: Yitzhak Shichor, *The Middle East in China's Foreign Policy: 1949–1977* (Cambridge: Cambridge University Press, 1979), pp. 114–119; Hashim Behbahani, *China's Foreign Policy in the Arab World, 1955–1975* (London: Routledge and Kegan Paul, 1981),

pp. 20–133; Yitzhak Shichor, "The Palestinians and China's Foreign Policy," in Chun-tu Hsueh (ed.), *Dimensions of China's Foreign Relations* (New York: Praeger Publishers, 1977), pp. 156–190; Mohamed Selim, "The People's Republic of China and the Palestine Question," *Al-Siyassa Al-Dawliya* 7, 25 (July 1971), pp. 58–83; John Cooley, "China and the Palestinians," *Journal of Palestine Studies* 1, 2 (1972), pp. 19–34; and Moshe Maoz, "Soviet and Chinese Influence on the Palestinian Guerrilla Movement," in Alvin Rubinstein (ed.), *Soviet and Chinese Influence in the Third World* (New York: Praeger Publishers, 1975), pp. 109–130.

127. Lillian Craig Harris, "China's Relations with the PLO," *Journal of Palestine Studies* 7 (1977), pp. 142–145.

128. Aryeh Yodfat and Y. Arnon-Ohanna, *PLO Strategy and Politics* (London: Croom Helm, 1981), p. 80.

129. Statement of the Israeli minister of tourism, *Al-Ahram*, January 15, 1983.

130. *Al-Ahram*, January 22, 1983.

131. Arafat's interview with *Al-Mussawar* (Cairo), December 31, 1982.

132. Arafat's interview with *Rose Al-Youssef*, January 3, 1983.

133. For a review of the linkages between the PLO and the Arab system, see Gabriel Ben-Dor, "Nationalism Without Sovereignty and Nationalism with Multiple Sovereignties: The Palestinians and Inter-Arab Relations," in Ben-Dor, *op. cit.*, pp. 143–172; and Walid Kazziha, *Palestine in the Arab Dilemma* (London: Croom Helm, 1979).

134. Alan Taylor, *The Arab Balance of Power* (Syracuse, N.Y.: Syracuse University Press, 1982), pp. 57–58.

135. P. J. Vatikiotis, *Conflict in the Middle East* (London: George Allen and Unwin, 1971), pp. 168–179; Mahmood Hussain, *The Palestine Liberation Organization* (Delhi: University Publishers, 1975), pp. 56–64; and Riad El-Rayyes and Dunia Nahas, *Guerrillas for Palestine* (London: Croom Helm, 1976), pp. 89–91.

136. Yodfat and Arnon-Ohanna, *op. cit.*, pp. 12–14.

137. Arafat's interview with *Al-Mussawar*, December 31, 1982.

138. Vatikiotis, *op. cit.*, pp. 180–181; and Jureidini and Hazen, *The Palestinian Movement*, pp. 67–70.

139. Arafat's interview with *Al-Mijalla*, March 19, 1985, p. 9.

140. Arafat's interviews with *Al-Watan Al-Arabi*, October 17, 1985, and with *October*, October 19, 1986.

141. Al-Shukairy, *Summit to Defeat*, pp. 152, 277.

142. Amin Hewaidi, *Abdel-Nasser's Wars* (Cairo: Dar Al-Mawkef Al-Arabi, 1982).

143. Arafat's interview with *Al-Mussawar*, December 13, 1982; with *Al-Hawadess*, January 7, 1983; and with *Rose Al-Youssef*, January 3, 1983.

144. Al Hassan's statement in *October*, September 8, 1985, p. 18.

10

Defending the Faith amid Change: The Foreign Policy of Saudi Arabia

Bahgat Korany

DIZZYING CHANGE AND THE CONTINUING MIX OF ASSETS AND LIABILITIES

One of the contemporary popular stereotypes about Saudi Arabia is that it is a land of miracles. Though two-thirds the size of India, its land is barren, a huge sandbox including the enormous desert of Al-Rub Al-Khali or empty quarter, never traversed by man before 1930. Yet in the 1970s the country planted wheat in the desert (with subsidies five times the world price) and in the 1980s, produced enough wheat to meet its needs and also to export. During this decade too, it initiated a tense negotiating debate with European countries to convince them to lower protective barriers against Saudi exports of petrochemicals.[1]

This quick change in Saudi Arabia's newsworthiness is mirrored by the change in academic coverage of the country. Before the early 1970s, no books and only a handful of articles had been published on this country's foreign policy. Other aspects of Saudi Arabia were only slightly better analyzed. After a survey of 120 books and 5,500 articles in eleven U.S. scholarly journals, Braibanti and Farsy emphasize "the scholarly aridity comparable to Al-Rub Al-Khali, that vast empty quarter of the Arabian Desert rarely traversed by man."[2]

Scarcity of information also characterized newspapers and other nonscholarly sources. Malcolm Peck puts it succinctly:

In 1968, the *New York Times Index* revealed twice as much reporting on Albania as on Saudi Arabia, five or six times as much on Malaysia in

1969 and four times as much on Burma in 1970. *Time* had only one story relating to Saudi Arabia in 1969, reporting the death of King Saud and commenting on his physical ailments and the size of his harem. No mention was made of Faisal's visit to Washington in 1971. *US News and World Report* did not mention Saudi Arabia in 1969 or 1971 . . . [For] the duration of the 90th and 91st Congresses, 1969–72, the index to the Congressional Record reveals that no reference was made to Saudi Arabia.[3]

The quality of resources was equally poor. The information provided was frequently careless, shallow, erroneous, or stereotyped. For instance, in covering the fourth nonaligned summit in Algeria (September 1973), the *New York Times* mentioned that Saudi Arabia did not attend, although the country's delegation was headed by King Faisal in person. A month later the oil embargo and price rises followed. The quantity of reporting on Saudi Arabia increased greatly, but its quality did not improve.

> To earlier shortcomings was added a new distorting factor—a compound of fear and hostility in face of the threat which the oil weapon and visions of endlessly accumulating petro-dollars conjured up. While a *Washington Post* editorial of April 1973 dismissed the first Saudi warning linking oil and politics, it suggested that the "more important oil becomes, the less important the Arab-Israeli dispute." An editorial of 2 January 1974, in the same newspaper, noted the threat of a reduction in Saudi oil production and attacked the "feudal government and its aging monarch" over the King's position on terms of a settlement.[4]

This change in coverage—at least at the quantitative level—reflects the change in the kingdom's situation. Whether measured by accumulation of oil revenues, increase in number of schools, number of students inside and abroad, acquisition of arms, change in international status (from neglected to center stage), Saudi Arabia came to the forefront of international and regional politics in a matter of a few years (the equivalent of days in the multimillenial history of this old region).

Though change can bring advantage, rapid change may bring liabilities if a country does not have the basic skilled manpower and organizational capacity to master—or at least to cope with—this change. Continuity of leadership could be a conservation factor amid this change. Since its unification and declaration as a nation-state in 1932, the country has passed from the founder Abdel-Aziz Ibn Saud (1932–1953) to his four sons (Saud, 1953–1964; Faisal, 1964–1975; Khaled, 1973–1982; and Fahd 1982–). Certainly the qualities of leadership make a difference but do not cancel out structural factors—assets or liabilities. A comparison between Kings Saud and Faisal shows this point.

Saud mismanaged the country's then meagre financial resources. He oscillated—externally—between siding with the nationalist Arab trend and keeping the U.S. connection and—internally—between counting on traditional tribal elements and the emerging middle class as well as "radical" young princes. After a brief period of power struggle, the kingdom's notables (influential members of the royal family, tribal heads, and religious establishment) helped the able Faisal to replace him.

Faisal's reign saw the apogee of Saudi Arabia's foreign policy. He took over power in 1964 when the country was divided (even within its ruling royal family), engaged in a war against Egypt by proxy (during Yemen's civil war 1962–1969), and in deep financial trouble. But Faisal established his leadership and achieved consensus of government around his style, coped with the departure of (protective) British troops from Aden, and imposed the 1973 oil embargo against the United States. At the time of his assassination in 1975, he left Saudi Arabia as a petropower and a financial giant. But did this exceptional quality of personal leadership change the structural elements shaping Saudi foreign policy or establish an identifiable objective pattern of coping with change, internal and/ or external?

Formidable handicaps thus exist to the analysis of the country's foreign policy decision-making. But available data on social structure, the economy, development plans, and oil policy are increasing, data that can be used to reveal the workings of the political system. In few countries is the relationship between foreign policy and the pattern of state formation and state structure so close.

The second section of this chapter discusses this matrix of foreign policy. The third section deals with how elements of the domestic environment (geography, population, social structure, and the basis of political authority) affect foreign policy. The fourth section concentrates on foreign policy orientation, discusses Saudi Arabia's "Islamic theory of international relations," and examines whether the different components of Saudi Arabia's world view are consistent. The fifth section concentrates on decision-making and the role of different social groups. The sixth section uses several indicators to measure the tilt of Saudi international behavior toward the West and examines how political-strategic interests determine its policy in the Arab system, in its own backyard (the Gulf region), and on the issue of oil within OPEC. The last section touches on the policy-maker's dilemma in the face of vertiginous social change and the limits of attempting to carry out a regional and world role through one-dimensional financial power. It emphasizes the importance of planning and managing foreign policy. Saudi foreign policy is the result of an interplay between Islam's legitimizing function, geostrategic determinants, oil power, and the use of "riyal politik"[5] as a privileged instrument of both diplomacy and war (as Saudi financing for the coalition forces during the 1990–1991 Gulf crisis showed).

THE FOREIGN POLICY MATRIX

On the surface, important assets seem to define Saudi Arabia's status in the global system and give it a great deal of influence and freedom of maneuverability. At the spiritual level, it is the birthplace of Islam and Arabness, and Saudi Arabia can justifiably pride itself on keeping both of them "uncontaminated" since it has never been colonized. It is to Mecca that the billion Moslem faithful of this world turn five times a day for their prayers. Thus what Saudi religious authorities say and do can have a huge mobilizational effect on these masses, even above the heads of their governments.

At the material level, Saudi Arabia's impact is different but no less influential. It is by all standards an oil giant, first international exporter and largest possessor of world oil reserves. The so-called Seven Sisters of the multinational oil companies are now reduced to four stepsisters of which Saudi Arabia is one[6] (the other three being Kuwait—sometimes called Kuwait Inc. because of its international assets of about $100 billion—Shell, and Exxon). Islam and oil, then, are two bases of the country's foreign policy. Many countries would like to be in Saudi Arabia's position, combining the power of the word (Islam) and physical power (since a barrel of oil can easily be transformed into the power of a gun). But there is another side to the coin.

Once a country is so much at center stage, it is envied, can be contested and even overpowered if it does not have the necessary means—internally and externally—to deter covetousness. Thus revolutionary Islam (for example, Khomeini's Iran, Lebanon's Hizbullah, Egypt's Jihad) contests Saudi Arabia's right to speak in the name of Islam or even to represent "the right Islam," an attack against the kingdom's very basis of legitimacy. Since the 1987 Mecca riots by Iranian pilgrims, the question of Hajj, or pilgrimage, has become a huge security headache for Saudi authorities. Iraq's invasion of Kuwait impressed on Saudi decision-makers the immediacy of external dangers by "big brothers."

Petrol as an asset has not meant smooth sailing either because of the difficulty for many OPEC members to respect their oil production quotas and thus prevent gluts and price declines on the world market. Saudi Arabia during most of the 1980s had to act as the swing producer, the balancer. Though a balancer is usually in a position of influence, it is also vulnerable to challenges and accusations of collusion with buyers ("Western imperialists" and/or "Israel's allies").

This hypersensitivity to the world market reveals a structural liability. The country's economy is absolutely dependent on this one commodity for its functioning and even for the state's survival. Yet both the demand and price levels for this commodity are beyond the kingdom's control, as the experiences of the 1980s amply show. The result is an acute Saudi vulnerability increased—rather than reduced—by being too influential to be ignored and by being pressed to offer concessions and/or give aid to help weaker actors.

Saudi Arabia's immediate geopolitical situation adds to this feeling of vulnerability. It is terribly close to Iran and shares borders with Iraq. These two ambitious regional powers profess historical missions, whether Islamic revolution or pan-Arab unification, and thus have adopted messianic foreign policies. Saudi Arabia's behavior or budget allocations (whether for aid or defense) cannot be explained without reference to this foreign policy matrix and its main components: cradle of Islam, oil giant, poor in non-oil resources, absolutely dependent on the vagaries of the world market, and the geopolitical characteristics of its immediate environment.

Some of these components can fluctuate but do not radically change or disappear. This explains the continuity of Saudi Arabia's foreign policy from the 1970s to the 1990s. For instance, the 1970s were dominated by the rise of oil prices and revenues but also by Egypt's "defection" to sign a separate peace with Israel. The 1980s were dominated by the decline in oil prices and especially the Iran-Iraq war. The end of the decade witnessed the return of Egypt to the Arab fold and the cease-fire between Iran and Iraq, which eliminated the extension of high-level hostilities to Saudi Arabia itself. On the other hand, this cease-fire freed its two Gulf rivals to extend their political or military influence into Saudi Arabia's backyard or arouse its big Shi'i minority. This brings us to the domestic environment.

THE DOMESTIC ENVIRONMENT

Geography and Population

The dominant historiographical trend accounting for the rise of the Saudi state is highly personalized and romanticized. An alternative thesis could emphasize the role of "objective" or ecological factors such as geography. These factors provide the parameters, the context, which limit the range of individual decisions.

The land of Saudi Arabia is barren, and its climatic conditions are harsh. Because of the aridity and relatively cloudless skies, the extremes of temperature range from 50°C in the summer to severe frosts and even weeks of snow in winter. Near the coast (the Gulf and the Red Sea), high atmospheric humidity makes living conditions extremely unpleasant. Several sociopolitical consequences follow from these geographical "givens."

First, in an age of colonial scramble, geographical hardships acted as a protective shield. To the south of Najd (the headquarters of the Al-Saud family) lies what is commonly known in Saudi Arabia as *Al-Ramla* or *El-Rimal*, literally "the Sands," commonly known in the West as Al-Rub-Al-Khali or the Empty Quarter. The first European to enter it was Bertram Thomas in 1930, and information about this region was gathered only after oil was discovered. Rainfall is rare at best, and sometimes stops altogether for as long as ten years, which explains why even local tribes only skirted its fringes. Ibn Saud realized this protective dimension of his country's geography when he said: "My kingdom will survive only as far as it remains a country of difficult access, where the foreigner will have no other aim with his task fulfilled, but to get out."[7]

Al-Badya, the bedouins or nomads, still made up 25% of the population in the 1970s.[8] Their society—least tarnished by foreign penetration or population settlement—is highly segmented. The nomadic social organization determines this population's skills and political culture (i.e., the basic values and beliefs governing political organization and practice), and makes accurate estimates of their number difficult.

Estimates of Saudi Arabia's total population also vary.[9] On January 1, 1956, the estimate was 6,036,400. A census was held in 1962-1963, but the results were officially repudiated. In preparation for the Second Development Plan (1975–1980), a census was conducted in 1974, but the results were unclear. First reports put the census total at 4.3 million, but later, a figure of 7,012,642 was announced. In 1975, Saudi officials were still quoting the figure of 5 to 6 million. The UN estimates that total Saudi population rose from 7,251,000 in 1975 to 8,960,000 in 1980, and official estimates put them at 14 million in 1988.

Whatever their number, no ambiguity exists about the level of skills of the general population. According to World Bank statistics, adult literacy did not exceed 16% in 1977.[10] This lack of basic skills has been a major handicap in the country's rush to development following the huge oil revenues of the 1970s. The First Development Plan (1970–1975) and the Second (1975–1980) spent as much as 31.1% and 25.2% respectively on human resource development.[11] However, the Saudi government still depended on foreign manpower to carry out the country's development projects. In 1980, foreign manpower—especially at the high managerial level—still outnumbered Saudis.[12] Saudi Arabia is thus dependent on the outside world not only for revenue but also for manpower, and with the influx of foreigners come foreign values and social practices. One dilemma of the Saudi policy-maker is how to maintain the development drive while keeping the society "untarnished."

The ruling elite's political culture[13] is still the "untarnished" heritage of geography. The bedouin population is significant beyond mere numbers; its sociopolitical import is considerable. Helms reports that over 80% of the population of the Najd—the northeastern region of the Arabian Peninsula—presently identify themselves with some tribal group.[14] "Moreover, the present ruling elite . . . the Al-Saud, descends from one of the major Bedouin tribal confederations of Najd, the Anazah, a kinship affinity of which they are conscious and proud. The moral fabric, the social order, and the value system of Saudi society today cannot be fully comprehended without an understanding of its Bedouin component."[15]

Social Structure, Political Authority, and the Legitimizing Role of Islam

Two elements underline Saudi Arabia's social organization and political authority: the tribal system based on kinship and *asabiya* (sense of tribal solidarity) and Islam (of the strict Hanbali type). Whereas tribal organization constituted a formidable barrier to the constitution of a centralized state, Islam was the raison d'être of the impressive army, Al-Ikhwan (literally Moslem Brethren), who fought until central political authority was achieved in the late 1920s.

The inspiration for both Al-Ikhwan and the present Saudi state was a 1745 alliance between Sheikh Mohamed Abdel-Wahab (a strict Islamic revivalist who preached *Tawhid*, the unity of God, and aimed to purify Islam from innovation) and the Al-Saud (rulers of Dar'iyah in Najd in the center of Arabia). This first Saudi state came to an end in 1818, when Egyptian troops (in the name of the Ottoman caliph) and the Al-Rashid, forced the Al-Wahab–Al-Saud dynasty to take refuge in Kuwait. In 1901, Abdel-Aziz Al-Saud, with a handful of tribesmen, left their refuge to recapture Riyadh in 1902 and thus revive a kingdom based on the Al-Wahab–Al-Saud alliance. This was the second Saudi state. It took Abdel-Aziz thirty years and the help of Al-Ikhwan to establish his political control and declare the unified kingdom of Saudi Arabia in 1932.[16]

Saudi Arabia is modeled on the original Islamic state of the seventh century. It has no legal political parties. Its constitution is the Qur'an and its source of laws and regulations is the *Shari'a* or Islamic law. In March 1980, Crown Prince Fahd appointed a small committee of ministers, religious leaders, and judges. Under the chairmanship of his brother and minister of the interior, Prince Nayef, the committee drew up a basic system of government and prepared a formula for the establishment of a consultative council. Saudi government is based on Islamic principles, a direct result of the pattern of Saudi state formation and the role of Al-Ikhwan in this process.

The Ikhwan were bedouin warriors who left their nomadic life to settle down and lead a life consonant with Islamic teachings and practice.[17] Between the year of their establishment in 1913 and their demise in 1929 after their conflict with Abdel-Aziz Al-Saud, the Ikhwan were able to win for Abdel-Aziz every battle they fought.[18] The Ikhwan replaced tribal segmentation, eternal shifting balances, and *razzias* (tribal raids) with Islam as a unifying element, and thus transformed tribesmen from undisciplined warriors into an army. They achieved this task without losing the fervor and dedication typical of earlier intertribal wars. The political control scheme used to weaken the tribal bands was the establishment from 1912 to 1913 of *hijras*,[19] cooperative, agriculturally oriented colonies that recognized the Al-Saud as the holder of the lawful Islamic leadership, or imamate.[20] These *hijras*, which numbered between 200[21] and 222,[22] gave Abdel-Aziz in 1926 a formidable Ikhwan army of 150,000.[23]

Colonel Dickson, a British agent in Bahrain, described Abdel-Aziz's control scheme in 1920:

[Abdel-Aziz] would send for the Shaikh and tell him in blunt terms that his tribe had no religion and they were all "Juhl" [ignorant, like in pre-

Islamic days]. He next ordered the Shaikh to attend the local school of ulama [religious scholars], which was attached to the great mosque in Riyadh, and there undergo a course of instruction in religion. At the same time half a dozen ulama, attended by some genuinely fanatical Akhwan . . . were sent off to the tribe itself. These held daily classes teaching the people all about Islam in its original simplicity. . . . When the Shaikh of the tribe was supposed to have received sufficient religious instruction, he was invited to build a house in Riyadh and remain in attendance on the Imam.[24]

In a rare letter dated January 17, 1928, Abdel-Aziz Al-Saud revealed to Dickson his acute awareness of the problems of political centralization in a segmented tribal society and the importance of Islam in coping with these problems. "The Government . . . has been established in this wide desert . . . by the virtue of the social teachings of religion . . . [which] made all the desert tribes within the lands under our control."[25]

FOREIGN POLICY ORIENTATION: AN ISLAMIC BELIEF SYSTEM

The analyst is indeed struck by the prevalence of Islamic symbols in social values, political culture, state apparatus, and leadership declarations. Does domestic Islamism extend to the international scene through Saudi foreign policy? If so, to what degree, and in what form? This question touches on one of the basic debates in foreign policy analysis: the importance of ideology or religion versus national political interest in determining a country's foreign policy.

Even though the Qur'an contains no explicit theory of international relations, there is an Islamic view of the international system. This view developed with the establishment of the first Islamic state and its transformation into an empire. The basis of this Islamic world view was the dichotomy between *Dar Al-Islam* and *Dar Al-Harb* (territory of Islam versus territory of war). By propagating Islam through *jihad* (holy war), Moslems were to increase their *umma* (Islamic community) at the expense of *Dar Al-Harb*, the non-Moslem territory.

The fragmentation of the Islamic empire and the realities of international politics led to the decline of this classical Islamic view of the world. Even in the heart of the Arab world, many countries replaced the concept of *umma*, with its emphasis on religious identification, with the secular concept of "people," with its emphasis on citizenship. The latter was the basis of the Arab nationalist ideology of both Nasserism and Ba'thism. The Saudis reacted to this trend by emphasizing its foreignness to the Arab-Islamic tradition and by promoting even more ardently a pan-Islamic view of the world. In the heat of the confrontation between Nasserist pan-Arabism and Saudi pan-Islam in 1963, King Faisal expressed the inherent opposition between these two world views:

"We do not need to import foreign traditions. We have a history and a glorious past. We led the Arabs and the World. With what did we lead them—the word of God and the Shariah [Islamic law] of His Prophet."[26]

Saudi ulamas joined in. They published articles to stress the foreign character and divisive function of secular Arab nationalism. One of those ulamas was Sheikh Abdel-Aziz Ibn Al-Baz, who in his *Critique of Arab Nationalism Based on Islam and Reality,* wrote:

> If advocates of Arab nationalism desire to raise the banner of Islam and rally the Arabs behind it, they would have advised the Arabs and urged them to follow Islamic principles and implement them. . . . Arab nationalism . . . was introduced by Christian Westers to fight Islam. . . . Many Arabs, opponents of Islam, adopted this call and were followed by ignorants . . . [Thus Arab nationalism] is an assault against Islam and its followers. A number of reasons can be given: the call to Arab nationalism differentiates between Moslems; it separates the non-Arab Moslem from his Arab brother; it divides the Arabs among themselves, because not all of them accept it; any idea that creates divisions in the ranks of Moslems is rejected, because Islam calls for unity, solidarity and cooperation to help the poor and enforce the word of God.[27]

Does this then mean that the kingdom's policy-makers give priority to the Moslem world[28] rather than the Arab region?[29] For many Saudis, no such distinction is feasible, since Arabs are part of the *umma.* Geography and history play a part in determining this world view, for Arabia was both the cradle of Islam and of the Arabs, and thus the two are hardly separable or even distinguishable. Consequently we can redraw the basics of the Saudi world view as shown in Figure 10.1.

As for the non-Moslem world, it is seen as a potential threat to the essence of *umma* and its norms. The West, however, was preferred to the erstwhile Communist East, more out of necessity than moral choice. Close cooperation with the West and not the East is justified on the grounds that the East's Communist, revolutionary doctrine, its materialist theory of history, and its atheism are more morally abhorrent and dangerous to the kingdom's policy-makers.

How does Zionism, the West's stepchild and its ally, fit into the Saudi world view? The three main sources of tension according to the Saudi world view are Zionism, radical Islamic regimes such as Qaddafi's Libya and Khomeini's Iran, and the Soviet bloc. The Saudi policy-makers have faced each in such a way as to emphasize harmony and consistency in their world view.

Zionism

Israel has been the privileged ally of the West, especially of the United States. It is with the United States that Saudi Arabia maintains the highest level of cooperation, and hence Saudi Arabia and Israel end up

FIGURE 10.1 The Structure and Components of the Saudi World View

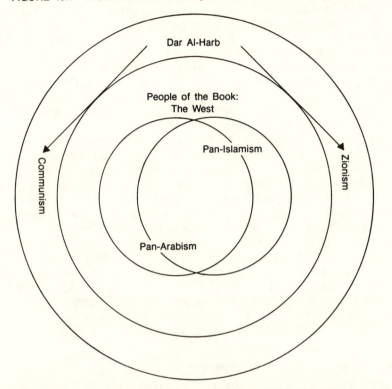

Source: Adapted from David Long, "King Faisal's World View," in Willard
Beling (ed.), *King Faisal and the Modernization of Saudi Arabia* (Boulder, Colo.:
Westview Press, 1980), p. 176.

being *objectively* in the same camp. Saudi policy-makers have reacted
to this dilemma by emphasizing Zionism's early association with socialist
ideology and the Communist political backing it received in the initial
stages of Israel's creation. Moreover, to show that they are not soft on
Israel, Saudis emphasize the pan-Islamic dimension of the Arab-Israeli
conflict. The 1967 occupation of Jerusalem—the third holiest city in
Islam—helped them to promote this pan-Islamic dimension and thus
put Saudi Arabia at the forefront of the anti-Israel coalition. In 1969,
following the fire in Al-Aqsa Mosque, Saudi efforts succeeded in convening
the First Pan-Islamic Conference, in Rabat, Morocco. Moreover, King
Faisal had talked repeatedly of his desire to pray at Al-Aqsa Mosque.
After his assassination in 1975, his successors continued the attempt to
mobilize all Moslems and Arabs behind this demand and thus behind
Saudi policy. Saudi leaders have also seized the opportunity of the
annual pilgrimage to Mecca to emphasize, as King Khaled did during

the 1977 pilgrimage ceremonies, "the regaining of the third holiest mosque in Jerusalem, and noble Jerusalem itself, and for clearing them of all the impurities."[30] To emphasize this pan-Islamic context of the conflict with Israel, the Saudi foreign minister stated in May 1977 his opposition to Israel's attempt to transform the "Jerusalem problem from a religious to a political one."[31] Several statements by Saudi officials refer to jihad as the only means of confronting Israel, but these statements make clear that jihad does not mean outright war, but rather the mobilization of all resources for a concentrated effort in the political, diplomatic, economic, and military fields.[32]

It is in this context that Saudis tend to defend their close relations with the West, Israel's prime backers. Not only is the West the privileged source of sophisticated technology and necessary arms, it can also be pressured to reduce its support for Israel or at least moderate its policies. In this respect, they emphasize to their Western partners—especially the United States—Zionism's destabilizing effects in the region. They argue, for instance, that the 1947–1948 defeat of traditional Arab regimes encouraged the rise of a radical Arab order and brought Soviet influence into the region—both unwelcome risks to stability. As late as 1981, Sheikh Zaki Yamani, the Saudi oil minister, used this argument with Western journalists. "When the United States, due to internal political pressures, refrains from performing its duty in bringing peace to the area, it thereby serves the Russian interests, to the detriment of its own interests and perhaps those of Israel itself."[33]

The Soviet Bloc and Saudi Nonalignment

One of the basic components of Saudi foreign policy orientation is nonalignment. Saudi Arabia is a founder-member of the nonaligned movement and has participated in seven out of the nine summit conferences (1961–1989), yet until 1990 Saudi Arabia had no diplomatic relations with the Soviet bloc; all its relations were with the West. The Soviet Union was, however, one of the very first countries to recognize Abdel-Aziz Al-Saud's new authority and to establish diplomatic relations in the 1930s. Moreover, the Soviet bloc has been in the forefront in supporting the Arab cause, whether against the old colonial empires or against Israel since 1954. Did not these countries (with the exception of Rumania) break off diplomatic relations with Israel following its initiation of the 1967 Six-Day War?

This absence of Saudi-Soviet relations is not due to a lack of Soviet overtures. On January 30, 1979, Igor Bilayev, one of the leading Soviet specialists on the Arab world, stated in an article in *Literaturnaya Gazeta* that Saudi Arabia and the USSR "had never fought each other" and had never had "any insoluble conflict." Instead of continuing the earlier Soviet practice of labeling the kingdom "reactionary," "feudalist," the "Kingdom of Darkness," the article portrayed the country in sympathetic terms and stressed common positions, such as the rejection of the Camp

David Accords.[34] Although he adopted a conciliatory tone in the context of U.S. support of Camp David and its "inaction" in the face of Khomeini's threatening regime, Prince Fahd continued to talk about "ideological differences" with the Soviet Union and stated that "the question of diplomatic relations is . . . premature."[35]

The Saudis feared the Soviet military threat,[36] the revolutionary ethos of its doctrine, and the radicalism of its regional allies, but they couch their distrust in terms of inherent opposition between spiritual Islam and atheist, materialist Communism. When Soviet troops entered Afghanistan in late 1979, the Saudis capitalized on this action to defend their position. The Saudis emphasized the strategic-political dangers of the Soviet move as well as the threat against Moslem peoples as a whole. Oil Minister Yamani warned that the main motive "of the Soviets was the oil fields and the Soviets' future oil needs."[37] In the same spirit, Foreign Minister Saud Al-Faisal suggested that the Soviet presence so close to the Straits of Hormuz was merely "a step in the direction of the sources of oil in the Gulf."[38]

In addition, most Saudi statements carried strong Islamic overtones, claiming that "the hour of confrontation between Islam and Communism had begun violently," and that "the atheist threat" had to be checked.[39] Consequently, the Saudi newspaper *Al-Bilad* called on January 1, 1980, for a meeting of heads of state to lay down a common strategy on "the Soviet threat . . . [which] is pointed directly at the Islamic faith."[40] The Saudi government played a leading role in convening the Islamic conference in Islamabad (Pakistan) in late January. In his speech to the conference, Saud Al-Faisal described the Soviet action as a "flagrant challenge to the Islamic world, a gross disregard for Moslems and Islam."[41] The conference ended by supporting the Saudi position. It condemned "Soviet military aggression against the Afghan people," called for the "immediate and unconditional withdrawal of all Soviet troops," and urged the Soviets to "refrain from acts of oppression and tyranny against the Afghan people and their struggling sons." The conference suspended Afghanistan's membership in the Organization of the Islamic Conference, discouraged recognition of, and recommended severing diplomatic relations with, "the illegal regime in Afghanistan," affirming "solidarity with the Afghan people in their just struggle to safeguard their faith, national independence and territorial integrity." Stating its "complete solidarity with the Islamic countries neighbouring Afghanistan," the conference called for the collection of "contributions from member states, organizations, and individuals" in support of the rebels, and for "nonparticipation in Olympic Games being held in Moscow in July 1980."[42]

The speedy collapse of the Soviet bloc and the declining pace of Communism as a global trend were bound to encourage Riyad to restructure its relations with Moscow and Eastern Europe (e.g., establishment of diplomatic relations). This restructuring would in effect be accelerated by developments near home and Soviet reactions toward them (e.g., Soviet support of all Security Council resolutions condemning Iraq during the 1990–1991 Gulf Crisis). However, the Saudi leadership's perception of, and reaction to, any "radical" movement, whether communist or otherwise, would be the same: hostile and resistant. In this respect, basics of Saudi foreign policy stay relatively consistent.

In their "anti-radicalism" reactions,[43] Saudi policy-makers attempt to reconcile the kingdom's immediate strategic interests and its inherent Islamic beliefs. Consistency among the different components of the Saudi world view is important to reinforce the regime's legitimacy. This brings us to regional dynamics and the kingdom's relations with other Islamic regimes.

Regional Dynamics

Conflicts with the radical Islamic regimes are the most serious for Saudi Arabia since they strike at the very basis of the Saudi state and its legitimacy. Consequently each side has tended to put up a die-hard defense of its concept of Islam, even though the conflicts have had other sources. During the 1970s and early 1980s, the Saudi kingdom faced serious challenges from two activist and radical Islamic regimes almost on its doorstep: Qaddafi's Libya (1969–) and Khomeini's Iran (1979–1989).

The incompatibility of Saudi Arabia and the Islamic radicals is not limited to the doctrinal debate about the interpretation of political Islam and its translation into specific policies. For instance, there have been cleavages concerning oil prices and production levels in OPEC, relations with the dominant hegemonic power (the United States), the war between Iran and Iraq, the yearly pilgrimage to Mecca, and even (for Iran) the status of the Shi'i within the Gulf and in Saudi Arabia itself. The general pattern reveals that in the 1970s the conflict with Qaddafi's Libya was dominant, while in the 1980s, the confrontation with Qaddafi declined, but conflict at various levels—including military—with Khomeini's Iran heightened. Concrete cases will be discussed in the section on foreign policy behavior.

DECISION-MAKING:
INSTITUTIONS, NORMS, AND GROUPS

Three institutions govern the making of decisions in the kingdom. They are, in descending order of importance, *Majlis Al-Shura* (the Consultative Council), *Ahl al-Hal wa al-Akd* (those who solve and bind), and the cabinet. At the heart of all three are the royal family and its tribal-religious partners by marriage and/or social alliance. At the top of the pyramid is the king.

It is not the king's idiosyncratic characteristics that are important, as the psychological approach overemphasizes, but rather, his social position at the head of the three institutions and his capacity to achieve consensus. For the system is based—with rare exceptions—on the Islamic concept of *ijma'a* or consensus, and hence the status of the chief, rather than his idiosyncrasies, is the important factor at this individual level. Indeed, Ibn Saud, the founder of the present kingdom, frequently quoted to Philby[44] what the Qur'an said in this respect: "Take counsel among yourselves, and if they agree with you, well and good: but if otherwise, then put your trust in God and do that which you deem best." The king's influence then is felt in the case of dissension in the decision-making group. But if he does not manage to put an end to this dissension or build consensus around his person and policies, he loses—as in systems of basic tribal democracy—this legitimacy of his position and is deposed forthwith, as King Saud learned the hard way in 1964.

Thus, rather than being based on one individual, the decision-making process is hierarchical. The hierarchy is a reflection of the social structure, with its tribal organization and political culture, and a direct consequence of Saudi state-formation. At the extreme top of the pyramid are the members of the royal family (between 4,000 and 7,000, with 700 direct descendants of Ibn Saud). The influential members of this family continue to monopolize the highest positions of internal and external security, for example, Ministries of Defense, Interior, Foreign Affairs, and of course the National Guard. Beyond the monopoly of these crucial institutions, the royal family is helped by members of the influential families or tribes with whom they intermarried and/or contracted alliances such as Al-Shaikh and the Sudairis—the powerful bedouin dynasty from northern Najd that intermarried with all branches of Al-Saud and to which belong King Fahd and Princes Sultan and Nayef, ministers of Defense and the Interior respectively. These influentials number about 20,000 people. If we add nonroyal partners, like members of the religious establishment, the top elite can be as much as 100,000.[45] Only a fraction of them are in the three decision-making institutions mentioned above.

Except for the cabinet, no precise information is known about the identity of or even the number of members of the two other institutions. The membership of *Ahl al-Hal wa al-Akd* is supposed to be between 100 and 160, of whom the majority are said to be descendants of Abdel-Aziz. For instance, there were sixty-eight signatories of the document deposing Saud and putting Faisal in his place of whom thirty-eight were Ibn Saud's sons and twelve were distinguished ulama.[46]

When a group of Islamic fundamentalists attacked and occupied the Great Mosque in Mecca and challenged the very legitimacy of the regime to govern, the *fatwa* or religious verdict to permit the Saudi authorities to attack the Mosque and dislodge the rebels was signed by twenty-nine ulama. The text of this *fatwa* is quoted in detail because it not only indicates a collective pattern of decision-making but also reveals some of its underpinnings.

On Tuesday [November 20, 1979], his Majesty King Khalid Ibn Abd Al-Aziz Al-Saud called us . . . and we met in his majesty's office. . . . He informed us that at dawn that day, immediately following the dawn prayers, an armed group had entered the Holy Mosque, closed the doors of the Holy Place [Haram] and placed armed guards at the doors. They then asked for a declaration of allegiance [*bay'a*] to what they called the Mahdi. They started to declare their allegiance to him. They prevented people from leaving the Haram, fighting those who opposed them. They opened fire on people inside and outside the Mosque. They killed some government men, injured others, and continued to fire on people outside the Mosque. King Khalid asked our opinion of them and what should be done with them.

We told him it is incumbent to call on them to surrender and lay down their arms. If they did, their surrender would be accepted and they would be imprisoned until their case was considered according to the Shari'a. If they refused, all measures would be taken to seize them and to kill those who were not arrested or had not surrendered, in accordance with what the Almighty says: 'But fight them not at the Holy Mosque unless they first fight you there. But if they fight you, slay them. Such is the reward of those who suppress the faith.'

The Prophet, may the blessings and peace of God be upon him, said: 'He who comes to you while you are unanimous in your opinion and wants to divide you and disperse you, strike off his neck'. . . . Chapters of the Qur'an and the Hadith are abundant in this connection. We ask the Almighty to put his word, render his faith triumphant and send failure to those who want evil for Islam and Muslims.[47]

As for the cabinet, though its membership is clear, its importance lies in being the locus—par excellence—of the rise of the new middle class and their participation in decision-making. Though embryonic structures of the Ministries of Foreign Affairs, Defense, Interior, and Finance evolved slowly in the 1930s and 1940s, the decision to establish a cabinet was taken in 1953 (apparently before Ibn Saud's death). The formal decree to establish the cabinet was issued only on 17 March 1954 after Ibn Saud's son Saud had acceded to power. The twenty-four articles of this decree emphasize the preeminence of the royal family as represented by the king, who presides over the Council of Ministers or delegates the viceroy and crown prince. The king's advisors or those designated by him can also attend the council. What strikes the observer of the Saudi cabinet is its relative longevity and stability: The cabinets that have governed the country for the last two decades or so are extremely few in number and the system works by cabinet reshuffle.[48]

What is important to emphasize is the close link between foreign policy and state/society dialectics. Quandt alluded to this aspect when he said that Saudi Arabia

is a monarchy, but the King is only one among several key personalities who participate in most important decisions. It is a family enterprise, but the family itself is not united and commoners are anxious to gain power. It is an Islamic state, but secular influences are everywhere present. It is an authoritarian government, but access to rulers is comparatively easy and citizens' demands for individual redress of grievances are often met. It is a society avidly seeking the comforts of the modern world, but traditional elements such as tribes remain influential. It is a country in which unbelievable wealth coexists alongside pockets of subsistence-level poverty.[49]

Thus the locus of foreign policy decision-making is not limited to the foreign ministry, with its prestigious, Princeton-educated young minister and its growing number of diplomats.[50] Even at the technical level, jurisdiction does not seem to be clear. Rather, the decision-making process has the following four characteristics:

First, there is an organic link between domestic and foreign policies because of the historical legacy of the state. As a result, foreign policy decision-making is not limited to the ministers of defence, oil, or the head of intelligence, but includes other members of the elite (the royal family or religious establishment) whose primary concern might be domestic. Second, although the power of the Al-Saud family is paramount, other groups do participate and wield differing degrees of influence depending on the issue area. For instance, in the field of relations with foreign Islamic groups, the role of the ulama is substantial.

The third characteristic of Saudi decision-making is that much bargaining occurs before an important decision is announced. In some cases, there can be an "ambiguous" decision or a "nondecision" because of the necessities of compromise or the need to avoid serious dissension. The tendency is to defer and delay issues, especially when they are unduly divisive or difficult to cope with. Quandt gives an example:

> Many foreigners have been concerned about the vulnerability of Saudi oil-fields to sabotage or attack. When asked, most Saudis will avoid the issue. In private they may acknowledge that they are worried, but since no easy solution can be found, a public stance of denial is adopted. This has the virtue, perhaps, of not advertising one's vulnerability . . . but it may also have the effect of preventing serious discussion of the issue altogether.[51]

This points up the fourth characteristic of the slow and improvised process of Saudi decision-making. The Saudi leadership often feels "lost" in crisis situations (e.g., the 1979 Mecca incident, the Iran-Iraq war). Unable to cope, the leadership usually turns to outside powers to settle the problem. French expertise in "counterterrorist" activities was sought during the Mecca incident, and U.S. AWACS planes were invited in at the beginning of the Iran-Iraq war. In brief, Sadat's style of "electric shock diplomacy" is inconceivable in Saudi decision-making. Despite the consistency of the different elements of the Saudi world view, Saudi

Arabia's foreign policy behavior is plagued with delays and a failure to follow through.

These four characteristics are influenced by the increasing complexity of Saudi Arabia's regional and global environment, and by the growing demand on the country to perform an active role. More importantly, these characteristics reflect the multiplicity of groups participating in the decision-making process.

The Royal Family and the Foreign Ministry

The country's name—Saudi Arabia—indicates to whom belongs, in theory and practice, the final power to decide. No one seems to know the exact number of the royal family's male members. Estimates range from 3,000 to 5,000, a figure equivalent to the number of dedicated members in an effective political party in most Third World countries. This is why an analysis of Saudi decision-making cannot be based on the role of one man or his psychological traits. To understand Saudi decision-making, one must understand Al-Saud family politics: the structure of relations between brothers from different mothers, between senior and junior princes, and between traditional and Western-educated family members; and the techniques of consensus-building that ensure the family's survival.

This structure of family politics is the direct result of the formation of the Saudi state. Very few leadership patterns in the Arab world mirror the state of their society as well as that of the Al-Saud of the Najd region. As mentioned earlier, to achieve primacy Abdel-Aziz Al-Saud formed an alliance with Sheikh Abdel-Wahab and used religion to offset tribal affiliation and social segmentation. To consolidate Al-Saud's overall and hereditary control, Abdel-Aziz formed strong alliances through marriage with the Sudairi, Ibn Jelawi, and Shammar tribes. Estimates put the number of Abdel-Aziz's legal wives at fifteen, producing thirty-seven to forty-five sons, 150 grandsons, and 500 great-grandsons.[52] If his 10 brothers produced the same number of progeny, the majority of the country's settled inhabitants could easily be Al-Saud family members.

Though intertribal marriage guaranteed allegiance, it also created disunity and tension among royal family members with different maternal/tribal affiliations.[53] Competition and tension increased when seniority was not followed as the basis of accession to the throne. For instance, Abdel-Aziz's fourth son, Mohamed, gave up his claim to the throne in favor of the fifth son, Khaled (1975–1982). Tension within the family is also created when a strong individual or clan attempts to accumulate maximum power and hence threaten the share of the others. The death of Khaled (a Jelawi) could have created fears and opened the succession issue within the family. With the accession of Fahd (the head of the strong "Sudairi Seven") to the throne, and the presence of his two full brothers at the head of crucial ministries (Sultan for defense, and Nayef for the interior), the balance of power among the different clans was threatened. Thus, it was mandatory that Abdallah become the crown prince. Though he has no full brothers to assist him in the contest for power, his mother belongs to the strong Shammar tribe of the North, a tribe which has traditionally been hostile to the authority of Al-Saud. In addition, Abdallah has been the head of the dedicated National Guard since 1962.

Whether a member of the royal family will belong to the inner circle of decision-makers depends on several factors: age, clan affiliation, and the balance of power within the family.[54] In 1958, when Saud was endangering the family's rule by his mismanagement of the country's resources and his inability to cope with the Nasserist tide, the senior princes limited his powers and finally forced him to abdicate in favor of his half-brother, Faisal.

Very few leaders have had such long and direct association with foreign policy as Faisal.[55] In 1919, at the age of thirteen, he was appointed by his father to head the Saudi delegation to the Paris peace conference, after which he met King George in London. In 1930, four years after the establishment of the foreign ministry structure, Faisal was put in charge of it. From the age of twenty-four until his death in 1975 at the age of sixty-nine (with the exception of the December 1960–March 1962 period of conflict with Saud), Faisal was almost supreme in foreign policy.[56] He was the king's representative in Hejaz from 1925 until his father's death in 1953. Hejaz held a very distinct international status because of the annual arrival there of the Moslem world's dignitaries to perform the pilgrimage to Mecca. Faisal's repeated involvement in world politics, as well as the autonomous budget he handled, reinforced his position within the royal family. He brought the country's international relations under his own jurisdiction. Even when he became the official head of state, Faisal retained the post of foreign minister and appointed only a deputy foreign minister and some advisors.

Since the establishment of the Saudi kingdom, the foreign ministry has evolved very slowly. When first established in 1926, it was called the Directorate of Foreign Affairs, and consisted of four departments (legal, political, administrative, and consular). The royal decree stipulated that Abdel-Aziz would be responsible for the first two departments and Faisal for the others. When the directorate became a ministry and Faisal minister, he was assisted by a director-general and fifteen civil servants. The 1930 decree stipulated, though, that the king was still in charge, and it limited the authority of the minister. In 1954, a year after Abdel-Aziz's death, the ministry was reorganized, following Western models, and Faisal was put completely in charge. This coincided with Faisal's official nomination as president of the council of ministers, after becoming its de facto head a few months earlier.[57]

The work of the ministry increased in scope and complexity. At the *bureaucratic level*, it grew from a few departments into a complicated structure with a permanent undersecretary and deputy and assistant deputy ministers to head the six major departments and desks: diplomatic missions abroad, Western affairs, Afro-Asian, Islamic, petroleum, and Arab affairs. Additional functional, or technical, desks were established to deal with commercial, financial, and cultural affairs.[58] Supporting these departments are the offices of protocol, consular affairs, administration, cables and wireless, and public relations and press.[59] The technical nondiplomatic support staff for this bureaucratic structure numbered about 500 civil servants in 1982.[60] A diplomatic institute on the model of institutions such as Vienna's Diplomatic Academy or Cairo's Diplomatic Institute was established in the late 1970s to give young diplomats the proper training.[61]

At the *diplomatic representations* level, the ministry's work expanded to keep pace with Saudi Arabia's increasing international status. In 1937, the kingdom had but three delegations (in Cairo, London, and Baghdad) and two consulates. In mid-1983, the ministry organized a general consultation and evaluation meeting for its seventy ambassadors.[62]

Given the increasing complexity of the kingdom's international relations, even Faisal had to delegate authority. In April 1968 a royal decree instituted the post of minister of state for foreign affairs and entrusted it to Omar Al-Saqqaf. The position was filled by Mohamed Masood after Saqqaf's death, and passed to Faisal's son Saud in March 1975 after Faisal's assassination. Saud was then instituted as foreign minister.

The product of "inherited" and "achieved" social status, Saud Al-Faisal is typical of the new generation of young royal technocrats. Born in 1941 to Faisal's most favored wife (Iffat Bint Ahmed Al-Thunayyan), he was tutored by his father and by Kamal Adham, King Faisal's Turkish-born brother-in-law and his intelligence chief. But Saud is also the prototype of the bright, ambitious, college-educated second generation of Saudi princes. A graduate in economics from Princeton, he is particularly skillful in addressing the U.S. public, and has done well in international conferences. Saud attended the 1980 Islamic conference in Pakistan, which condemned the Soviet intervention in Afghanistan.[63] In January 1983, he was the first Saudi foreign minister to visit Beijing (Saudi Arabia has diplomatic relations only with Taiwan) as a member of the Arab summit's delegation on the Palestinian question. Saud emphasizes the centrality of the Palestinian issue in the Arab-Israeli conflict, and believes in linking oil politics to this conflict.

As foreign minister, Saud Al-Faisal has worked with two kings: Khaled and Fahd. Khaled was very different from his predecessor, King Faisal. Frequently described as a "man of the desert," he was interested in the society's traditional groups and in practicing the time-honored sport of falconry. Khaled's poor health forced him to delegate authority, and consequently the number of participants in decision-making increased. Press reports talked about the Khaled-Fahd "duarchy"[64] as a decision-making system. Other influential princes were also increasingly involved in the decision-making process. Sultan, the defence minister; Nayef, the interior minister; and Abdallah, head of the National Guard, negotiated agreements of international cooperation or arms deals. Abdallah intensified his Arab contacts, and in 1980 he capitalized upon his close relations with Syria's president Asad and the president's brother and intelligence chief, Rifa'at Al-Asad, to successfully mediate the rising tension between Syria and Jordan. Even nonmembers of the royal family, like Faisal's protégé Zaki Yamani, accrued influence. Yamani, in conjunction with Fahd, had great freedom in oil affairs. This attenuation, after Faisal's death in 1975, of the one-man primacy in foreign affairs did not change the structural characteristics of decision-making. Senior princes still had their word, and secrecy in visits, payments, and agreements was still the order of the day.[65]

In terms of foreign policy decision-making, King Fahd is bound to follow the Faisal pattern more closely than Khaled. Before Khaled's death, Fahd was already the kingdom's strong man, described by an informed scholar as being "the single most important figure in shaping Saudi foreign policy."[66] Some consider him more pro-American and less anti-Egyptian than many of the other influential senior princes, such as Crown Prince Abdallah. Abdallah, a harsh critic of U.S. foreign policy on the Palestinian question, told a *Time*-sponsored delegation of businessmen and editors visiting Saudi Arabia in 1981 that the most dangerous threat to the Middle East was not the USSR, as the Reagan administration had argued, but the United States. He explained: "I say this because of your total alliance with Israel, which makes the mass of our people take it for granted that Americans are anti-Arab, and makes it convenient for the Arab people to look to the Soviet Union as a friend, since they feel they have been abandoned by the Americans."[67]

This difference in view between the two top men of the kingdom helps to balance the different factions of the royal family's power system. Abdallah's influence, together with that of Saud Al-Faisal, prevents a monopoly of the Sudairi Seven over decision-making and keeps foreign policy from being Fahd's show alone.

The Religious Establishment: The Ulama

Due to its historical legacy, Saudi Arabia considers itself the guardian of Islam and Islamic values throughout the world. Islam is more than a religion; it is a way of life in the kingdom. As a result, the ulama's influence is all-pervasive.[68] They participate directly in decision-making, but more importantly, they shape the social values and the frame of reference of those who judge issues, determine political priorities, decree legal practices, and interpret behavioral results. The views of the ulama are at the basis of the social fabric and the regime's legitimacy. Are they not called "*Ahl al-hal wa al-akd*," the final arbiters and definitive decision-makers?

The ulama's direct influence in decision-making follows three channels: (1) direct and privileged access to the highest locus of decision-making, (2) monopoly over some ministries and areas of policy, and (3) popular mobilization.

Through Wahabism, the religious establishment was a partner in both the establishment and management of the Saudi state. The Al-Shaikh family of Abdel-Wahab enjoyed continuous prestige and intermarried with the Al-Saud family. King Faisal's mother was from the Al-Shaikh family. Even prominent ulama who were not members of the Al-Shaikh family enjoyed influence, for Abdel-Aziz permitted them direct access to the Majlis, the council that directed the state's affairs. In addition, the ulama had a regular weekly meeting with the king on Thursday afternoons, during which views were exchanged and policy coordinated.[69] Subsequent kings followed the tradition of the Thursday meeting.[70]

Traditionally, the religious establishment has monopolized the Ministries of Education, Justice, Pilgrimage Affairs, and *Awqaf* (religious endowments); the Departments of Missionary Activities, Religious Research, and *Ifta* (verdicts); and the Committee for Commanding the Good and Forbidding the Evil.[71] The influence and activities of these institutions far exceed that of their secular counterparts. If the ulama have not managed to monopolize the Saudi government, they have at least created a parallel one.

Through the regular Friday sermon, usually well attended, the ulama have a public forum to question or support not only religious issues, but also social values and political and economic practices. As a result, their views on Arab and Moslem affairs are very influential. Historically, the ulama have arbitrated intra-elite conflicts. In 1929, Abdel-Aziz had to separate from his formidable army of Al-Ikhwan, but first he needed to secure his continuing legitimacy with the ulama, through a *fatwa* (a religious verdict) that he had not deviated from the right Islamic path. Abdel-Aziz was also willing to delay the introduction of Western mechanical equipment—wireless communications, telegraph, and automobiles—until the ulama were persuaded to give their sanction. In 1950, when the ulama objected to the king's plans to celebrate a golden jubilee marking the fiftieth anniversary (in lunar years) of the capture of Riyadh from the Al-Rashid, the project was duly abandoned.[72] In 1958, when conflict raged within the royal family, the ulama's pressure was crucial in allowing Faisal to take Saud's place. When Faisal himself was assassinated in 1975, the designation of Khaled as his successor had to be approved by the ulama. Last but not least, when the Al-Saud dynasty faced its most serious challenge during the 1979 Mecca incident, even military necessities were subordinated to the ulama's verdict: the counterattack to dislodge the rebels had to await the ulama's green light.

The Military

The Al-Saud family has ambiguous feelings about the armed forces. On the one hand, increased covetousness and threats from the outside are factors pushing the government to strengthen the armed forces. On the other hand, Third World and Arab experience shows that the armed forces are usually serious contenders for political power: Syria had three coups d'état in 1949; the military took power in Egypt in 1952, in neighboring North Yemen in 1962, in Algeria in 1965, and in Libya and the Sudan in 1969. Even in countries where the military are not *formally* in power, a few violent attempts have occurred (e.g., Morocco in 1970–1971). Is it coincidence that in 1934, after the brief war with Yemen, and Saudi Arabia's acquisition of Najran, the army was disbanded entirely?[73]

The 1962–1967 Yemen war greatly revived interest in the army. As a result, in the mid-1960s a huge program of military modernization was begun. The 1967 Arab defeat at the hands of Israel made the Saudi government realize that for both domestic and regional political reasons, it was dangerous not to have at least token military participation in the Arab-Israeli conflict. The 1968 British announcement of its intention to withdraw from the Gulf then stripped the region of its permanent foreign military protection.

With the oil boom of the 1970s, the military modernization program progressed rapidly, at least in terms of hardware. The military sector, like the civil sector, suffers from a chronic manpower shortage, especially of skilled personnel. From 1979 to 1981, despite huge investments in training, incentives, and the building of facilities,[74] the armed forces only rose from 36,000 to 47,000 men. Because of the manpower shortage, there has been a conscious effort to create a capital-intensive military force. Defense expenditures rose from $387 million in 1969 to $24.4 billion in 1981, and was to be $28 billion, or 25% of GNP, in 1982.[75] Defense has been the largest expense in the three development plans. At least 105 arms purchase agreements were made between 1970 and 1982.[76]

To counterbalance any potential danger from the military to the present structure of decision-making in the kingdom, the royal family adopted three "insurance policies."

The first is the presence of members of the royal family within the army, not only at the top but also at lower levels of command. Sultan, King Fahd's full brother, has been minister of defense since 1962. Fahd Ibn Abdallah is head of air force operations, Turki Al-Faisal heads intelligence, and Bandar Ben Sultan (recently appointed ambassador to the United States) has been a practicing and influential pilot.

Second, the training of military personnel has been entrusted to "safe" hands. In the 1950s, Saudi Arabia was in conflict with Britain over the Buraimi Oasis on the frontiers with Kuwait, and so sent Saudi military cadets to Egypt's military training schools. But in the late 1950s, long before the 1962 Yemen revolution, the royal family stopped this practice to eliminate any risk of socialization in Nasserist ideology. This left the United States, which now enjoys a virtual monopoly in the training of Saudi army personnel. Between 1973 and 1977, no less than 4,300[77] upcoming officers of the army, navy, and air force were sent for varying periods of training in the United States. Additional cadets were sent to the U.S. base in Bahrain. Moreover, the armed forces are supervised by the U.S. government or its companies at the structural level. The U.S.-Saudi Joint Commission on Security and Cooperation was established in the 1970s. Bendix Corporation is very involved in the army, Lockheed in the air force,[78] and Northrop in the development of military personnel. In addition, prior to the 1991 war there were about 40,000 U.S. military men and women in different parts of Saudi Arabia.[79]

As a final protection, the government maintains other autonomous military institutions. Prominent among these are the National Guard, the Royal Guard, and to a lesser extent, the Coast Guard and Frontier Force, but most important is the National Guard. Estimates of its strength vary from 20,000 to 35,000 men.[80] The National Guard developed out of the White Army (composed of swordsmen), which in turn was a later version of the old Ikhwan army of the 1920s. The National Guard is composed of loyal tribesmen, who receive the same incentives (land and cash) as the personnel of the regular army. Since 1962 they have been under the direct command of Crown Prince Abdallah, Fahd's half-brother. In 1975, serious efforts were made to modernize the National Guard and provide it with armored cars and other mechanized weaponry. In 1975, a $77 million contract was awarded to the U.S. Vinnell Corporation to train the guard and modernize its methods.[81] At present, the guard is becoming computerized. It was the National Guard's responsibility to flush out the attackers who took the Ka'aba Mosque in Mecca in November 1979.[82]

The Technocrats

Technocrats are the representatives par excellence of what M. Halpern[83] dubbed "the new middle class." The influence of this class does not depend on family origin, tribal convictions, religious support, or other traditional qualifications. The influence and upward mobility of technocrats depend, above all, on education, training, expertise, skill, and talent. These qualifications have been in demand since the establishment of the kingdom's first Council of Ministers in 1953 and the subsequent establishment of technical ministries. Abdallah Tariki was oil minister until 1965,[84] followed by Zaki Yamani. The influence of this class was increasingly felt with the rush to development that followed the 1970s oil boom.

Technocrats complete most of their studies and training outside the kingdom, in secular, mainly Western, universities. Egyptian universities used to receive many Saudi students, but to avoid contamination by Nasserist ideology they were increasingly sent during the 1960s to U.S. universities. In 1971-1972, Saudi students were the twenty-seventh largest group of foreign students in U.S. universities. Five years later, they were the twelfth largest. By 1977, about 30,000 Saudis had finished their studies in the United States.[85] According to the Saudi newspaper *Al-Jazirah*, by 1980 there were more than 11,000 Saudi[86] students studying at U.S. universities. Of the sixty-four ministers and deputy ministers in the Saudi government in 1979, nineteen had Ph.D.s, mostly from U.S. universities.[87]

Though they are not a homogeneous group and lack the institutional base of the ulama or the military, Saudi technocrats "nonetheless represent a serious group with an impact on economic and financial decisions," if not yet on "high politics" across the board.[88] Their political hopes were raised during the 1958–1960 period of fighting within the royal family between King Saud and his brother Faisal. To regain his influence, Saud used the technocrats' support and established a cabinet where they made up the majority. However, this was a short-lived tactical move on Saud's part.

However, their participation in government has continued and accelerated. In 1965, the Saudi Council of Ministers was composed of fourteen ministers: five princes, three representatives of the Al-Shaikh family, and six technocrats (in the fields of oil, agriculture, communications, information, health, and labor). After the shuffle in 1975, the number of cabinet members rose to twenty-five. The representatives of the Al-Shaikh family remained at three; the number of princes rose to eight; and that of technocrats to fourteen. After Khaled's death and Fahd's accession to power in June 1982, the number of cabinet members was increased to twenty-seven, and the two new members were technocrats. On foreign policy issues members of this group are generally nationalistic, insisting on an "evenhanded" U.S. foreign policy in the Arab-Israeli conflict. Cooperation will grow between them and young royal family members such as Saud Al-Faisal, the foreign minister. Moreover, their resistance to waste and undisciplined consumerism could appeal to some members of the religious establishment. Even without an independent institutional base, the impact of Saudi technocrats will be increasingly felt in the different sectors of decision-making.

Their impact is much greater in its potential, especially with the increasing pace of industrialization and bureaucratization of the system. In addition, the technocrats are still subordinate in the highest echelons of decision-making. At present they lose when they come into conflict with the religious establishment and especially with the royal family. Thus in 1983 and 1984 three ministers resigned or were dismissed: Abdel-Aziz Al-Qurayshi, the head of SAMA (Saudi Arabia's Monetary Agency); Mohamed Abdu Yamani, minister of information; Dr. Ghazi Al-Gosaybi, minister of health.

Al-Gosaybi's case is notable because he is regarded as the leader of the Saudi intelligentsia. Contrary to many of the technocrats who came from the relatively open Hejaz, Al-Gosaybi came from a merchant family in Najd associated with Ibn Saud since his conquest of the rest of

Arabia. But Al-Gosaybi clashed with Sultan, defense minister, and dared to express his views in a poem published in a Saudi daily. He was dismissed and exiled as ambassador to neighboring Bahrain. The consequences for Al-Gosaybi were not harsher probably because he supported Fahd's modernization policy and thus could still be protected by him.[89]

The most publicized dismissal, however, was that of Zaki Yamani, made petroleum minister in 1962. His was a household name worldwide thanks to television, and he was often dubbed "Mr. Oil" because of his capacity to drive oil prices—and the world economy—up or down. Such centrality at the world stage certainly aroused jealousies among his fellow technocrats and even among royal family members.

> Throughout the post-1973 period, an increasing number of Princes developed an antipathy towards Yamani. They resented his over-exposure, high profile and star role in the foreign media, which often portrayed him wrongly as the sole arbiter of Saudi oil policy. They especially disliked the fact that he exceeded the limits of his exposition as a technocrat and behaved as if he were part of the inner core of the Royal Family. Some of his opponents included conservative, influential figures who resented Yamani's overtly Westernized patterns of conduct, style and three-piece European-tailored suits. There were other opponents who questioned the economic, financial and political costs of his policies. This coalition of rivals waited for the opportunity to press for his removal.[90]

The opportunity was provided by the decline of oil prices from the early 1980s onwards and especially their extreme fluctuations within a very short span of time—a situation that jeopardized not only the kingdom's revenue but also its economy. Thus in 1984, for instance, Saudi Arabia based its economic policy on 6 million barrels per day (m bpd) at a fixed price. But "price declined, and when OPEC ministers met, Yamani—to raise the price—accepted a lower production quota of 4.5 m bpd for Saudi Arabia. But the world oil market takes some time to react. As a result there was that year a decline of as much as 80% in production and revenues, which resulted in budgetary deficits, depletion of financial reserves, and recession and criticism at home."[91] Yamani was accused of not knowing how to stand up to OPEC's cheating and deception and of subordinating Saudi national interest to this organization. In 1986, a similar crisis occurred when there was an overproduction of oil, due mainly to some members not respecting their quotas. Yamani this time increased production, the price plunged from $25 to $8 a barrel within months, and the stage was set to regulate production quotas to respect a price that King Fahd insisted upon: $18.

> In October [1986], before and during OPEC's session in Geneva, Yamani made it clear that demand for OPEC oil would not increase at a price above $15. As a result, during the 17-day OPEC meeting, King Fahd repeatedly intervened from Riyadh and contradicted Yamani on several key issues. Finally, the King sent a message to the OPEC meeting em-

powering Yamani to agree to a two-month extension of the August agreement but only on condition that the per barrel price should be set at no less than $18 and that everyone should adhere to this price. Although Yamani accepted a final resolution that extended the August agreement, he flouted the King's orders by making no reference to the $18 figure. Yamani was dismissed ten days later.[92]

Though some members of the royal family were interested in the job, he was replaced by another member of the technocratic elite: Hisham Nazer, then minister of central planning, and who in fact was Yamani's deputy from 1962 to 1968.

The Commercial Class

Even though it is generally accepted that Saudi Arabia is a bedouin state par excellence, some specialists attach great importance to the role of commercial interests as the basis of the state.[93] Put succinctly, this thesis holds that commercial interests provided revenue to the Al-Saud and linked the whole area to the world economic system, thus making the major powers of the period concerned for the survival of the Al-Saud.

Of the ten biggest family businesses in the Gulf region in 1981, five were situated in Jeddah on the Red Sea and one in Riyadh. But the commercial basis of society goes deeper than that.[94] Were not the prophet and his first wife Khadija in commerce? In fact, before the oil boom, the royal family counted on financial help from this group to run the state and maintain power.

The present context, however, is quite different, for the rise of the oil economy has led to less dependence by the Al-Saud on the financial support of the commercial class. This does not mean that the partnership between the ruling family and the commercial class has ended, but the partnership has changed form. Despite the fact that large traditional families continue to dominate commerce in the kingdom, their composition, orientation, and relationship with the ruling family has changed. The influx of oil revenues has led to the rise of a new class of businessmen, a second generation of naturalized Saudis like billionaires Adnan Khashoggi and Ghaith Pharaon.[95] This second generation capitalizes on its international business connections and partnership with Najdi aristocrats or members of the royal family. With so many government contracts going around, and with the government policy of prohibiting wholly foreign firms and banks from engaging in business, a bonanza of joint ventures has linked the royal family and the commercial class.[96] The commercial class thus has effective supporters at the highest echelons of the decision-making process, and as long as the commercial class is receiving windfall profits from the oil wealth, it is supportive of both the system and its foreign policy.

Both Yassini[97] and Shaw and Long[98] confirm this transformation of the commercial class and its relationship of mutual benefit with the ruling dynasty. The Rajhis of Riyadh and Jeddah have their money exchange offices throughout the kingdom. The Ali Rizaz family of Jeddah, who founded an import-export company in 1862, now has holdings that include engineering and construction firms, heavy equipment importing, and a petroleum exploration company. Another case is that of Mohamed Ben Laden, formerly a mason at Aramco, "who through construction contracts for the royal family and the government, became the biggest contractor in the country."[99]

Whether it affects decision-making directly or by proxy, this commercial class is in favor of the present economic policy, the free market mechanism, and the consolidation of the private sector. It supports resistance to any "socialist" contagion and continuation of relations with Western and "moderate" countries, even at the expense of a militant nationalist line. This brings us to the analysis of the country's foreign policy behavior.

FOREIGN POLICY BEHAVIOR

Although the Saudi kingdom's foreign policy orientation may suffer from internal inconsistencies, no such discrepancy exists between this orientation and its translation into specific behavior. At the global level, almost all Saudi interactions have been with the West, especially the United States. At the regional level, the majority of the country's relations are with Arab-Moslem countries, with a preference for those considered "moderate." The watershed of the 1973 oil embargo did not change this pattern; it only helped the country to pursue it more effectively. In short, Saudi international behavior emphasizes the primacy of Islam, pursues a close strategic alliance with the dominant Western power, and promotes "moderate" or pro-Western regimes in the Arab-Islamic world.

Though Saudi foreign policy behavior manifested some noticeable changes in the 1980s, especially in relation to the Eastern bloc, the pattern was still guided by the three constants: (1) emphasis on the primacy of Islam (Jeddah is still the headquarters of the Organization of the Islamic Conference), (2) close strategic alliance with the dominant Western powers, and (3) promotion of moderate or pro-Western regimes in the Arab-Islamic world.

The Global Pattern

Indicators such as the exchange of visits, the pattern of diplomatic representation, trade transactions, or arms purchases do confirm these behavioral characteristics. Formal diplomatic representation with Moscow and other members of the Eastern bloc remained nonexistent at the end of the 1980s, visits (despite some notable signs of change that we will mention soon) were highly skewed in favor of the West, and the five top trading partners were still the United States, Japan, the United Kingdom, West Germany, Italy, and France (about $51 billion and $43 billion for 1985 and 1986 respectively).[100]

It is in the field of arms purchases that confrontation intensified between the kingdom and its major Western partner, the United States, threatening their "special relationship." Between 1970 and 1982, the kingdom concluded 105 arms agreements, sixty-one of which were with the United States. The value of these Saudi purchases of U.S. arms and equipment for the eight-year period 1973–1980 was $34 billion (compared to $1.2 billion for 1950–1972).[101] This $34 billion does not include the $9 billion 1981 AWACS deal that caused so much uproar and friction between the U.S. administration and the pro-Israeli lobby in Congress.

The public debate between Congress and the U.S. administration, the questioning of Saudi motives, and attempts to control its policies continued. Thus the *Washington Post* revealed on October 10, 1987, that after two weeks of negotiations, the Reagan administration and the U.S. Senate had reached a compromise agreement on a proposed $1 billion arms sale to the kingdom. The contents of the compromise became known when the administration submitted the arms deal formally to Congress at the end of October. The compromise eliminated the much-disputed 1,600 Maverick anti-tank missiles from the sale.[102] Yet by December the U.S. Senate voted to forbid the sale of F-1SE jets and other fighter planes that can launch ground attacks. The vote also placed a limit of sixty on the number of F-15s the kingdom could possess. In addition some congressmen went on to emphasize the failure of the Royal Saudi Arabian Air Force to come to the assistance of the USS *Stark* when it was mistakenly attacked by an Iraqi aircraft in the Gulf in May 1987.

It was in anticipation of such public censorship and unreliability of U.S. arms sources that the kingdom started in the early 1980s its diversification efforts, first buying arms from France then in September 1985 from Britain. This last deal centered on Tornado fighters together with a support and training system, at the cost of $8,275 million, the biggest single arms deal signed by Britain. But the 1987 blocking of U.S. arms purchases by the U.S. Senate pushed the kingdom to adopt one of its most sensational foreign policy moves: the 1988 deal with China for the purchase of CSS2 medium-range ballistic missiles. Significantly, it was Prince Bandar, the kingdom's ambassador in Washington, who effected a surprise flight to Beijing to finalize the deal. In July 1988, Fahd, speaking to Saudi armed forces, confirmed that the kingdom would continue its arms diversification efforts (according to the *New York Times*, July 9 and 11, 1986, a British/Saudi memorandum of understanding for $30 billion was signed). If diversification efforts continue at this rate, the United States is bound to be displaced as the kingdom's first arms supplier. The objective of such sustained effort at diversification is to save Saudi arms acquisitions "from extortion of any kind."

Intensification and formalization of relations with "socialist" countries continued. In November 1988 Prince Bandar and the Chinese ambassador to the United States signed a memorandum of understanding in Washington for the establishment of trade offices in each other's capitals. And contacts with Moscow were not far behind. Already in 1986, the kingdom did not prevent the establishment of diplomatic relations between Moscow and Oman and the UAE, Riyadh's Gulf Cooperation Council co-members. Then–oil minister Zaki Yamani also paid a visit to Moscow in 1986. Moscow's overtures intensified for the establishment of diplomatic relations with Riyadh. But Saudi Arabia insisted that there should first be "a non-belligerent Soviet attitude towards Islam," meaning, as Defense Minister Sultan made it clear later, the withdrawal of Soviet troops from Afghanistan. In 1987, Foreign Minister Saud Al-Faisal was invited to visit Moscow, a visit he carried out in January 1988. He discussed with Soviet Foreign Minister Shevardnadze the Gulf war, the occupied territories, and resumption of diplomatic relations between the two countries. Though the reestablishment of diplomatic relations was not declared by the end of the 1980s, the 1989 Soviet troop withdrawal from Afghanistan was certainly helped by Saudi good offices. Thus in December 1988 talks were held in Ta'if between representatives of the Afghan guerrillas— Mujahidin—and the USSR. These talks were followed by an exceptional gesture on the part of Riyadh: King Fahd in person received on December 5 Soviet Deputy Foreign Minister Yuli Voronstov. Consequently, Saudi Arabia's basic Islamic belief system guiding its foreign policy behavior is becoming complex in comparison with the previous one guiding its foreign policy orientation, as Figure 10.2 shows.

Regional Diplomacy

The focus on the West at the global level is matched by Saudi opposition to "radical" regimes at the regional level. Saudi Arabia countered the radical wave of Ba'thist-Nasserist Arab nationalism by insisting on pan-Islamism. In May 1962, an international Islamic conference in Mecca, sponsored by Saudi Arabia, declared that "those who disavow Islam and distort its call under the guise of nationalism are actually the most bitter enemies of the Arabs whose glories are inseparable from the glories of Islam."[103] The conference established the World Moslem League, with headquarters in Mecca. Its objective is to counter "all alien ideologies and habits inconsistent with Islam, and to coordinate the effort of Islamic organizations around the world."[104] In 1965, King Faisal toured Moslem countries such as Jordan, Malaysia, and Pakistan to regroup them in a pan-Islamic coalition to counter the radical nationalist trend. The Egyptian-Syrian humiliating defeat in the 1967 war with Israel facilitated the rise of the Saudi trend. In 1969, the first pan-Islamic summit was held in Rabat, Morocco.

Following Nasser's death on September 28, 1970, Saudi Arabia intensified its efforts to deradicalize Egypt and to get rid of the 20,000 Soviet advisors invited in by Nasser. In November 1970, King Faisal sent Adham, his personal advisor and intelligence chief, to meet Sadat discreetly. His mission was to persuade Sadat to get rid of the Soviets

FIGURE 10.2 International Practice and an Evolving Islamic Belief System

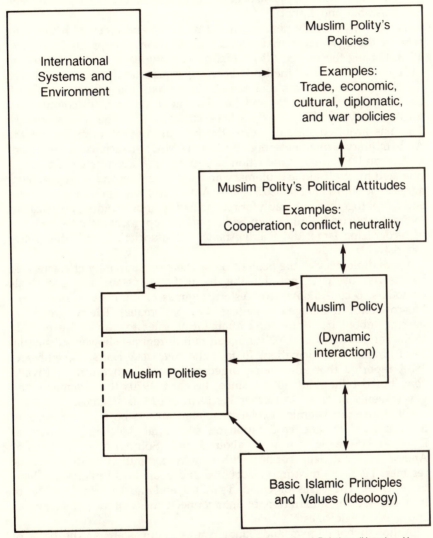

Source: 'AbdulHamīd AbūSulaymān, *The Islamic Theory of International Relations* (Herndon, Va.: The International Institute of Islamic Thought, 1987), p. 132.

so that relations might improve with the United States,[105] whose help might then be enlisted in solving the Arab-Israeli conflict. When Sadat expressed his readiness to work along these lines, Adham passed the word to Washington. The Saudi role of go-between for Egypt and the United States was just one aspect of the increasing coordination between Saudi Arabia and Egypt.

Faisal was the only person trusted by Sadat and Asad with the exact time of the Egyptian-Syrian attack against Israeli troops on October 6, 1973. During the war Saudi Arabia, overcoming earlier hesitation to use the oil weapon against the United States,[106] was crucial in the oil embargo decision. After the war, the Riyadh-Cairo axis (based on a trade-off between Egyptian muscle and Saudi money) aimed to discourage any revolutionary ideology or "practices subversive of the status quo."[107] The axis acquired military teeth through the official formation of the Arab military armaments organization (AMIO), which combined Gulf money and Egyptian production capabilities.[108] Even when Sadat accelerated his go-it-alone diplomacy and signed the second disengagement agreement with Israel in 1975, Saudi Arabia still managed to bring Syria and Egypt together in Riyadh for reconciliation, thus avoiding polarization in the Arab world. Only when Sadat pushed rapprochement to the point of recognizing Israel did Saudi Arabia find association with this policy too risky.

Saudi diplomacy of the post-1973 era was predominantly characterized by the rise of "riyal politik," the use of Saudi petropower and riyals or dollars to consolidate pro-Western regimes or induce previously pro-Moscow ones to change course (e.g., Egypt, Somalia). The congressional hearings about the Iran-contra affair (arms sales to Iran and especially to the contras fighting the Nicaraguan radical regime) showed substantial Saudi financial participation. In fact, the *New York Times*, December 6, 1987, reported that after being urged by the U.S. government, Riyadh contributed billions of dollars since the early 1970s to movements and governments in order to further Western anti-Marxist goals.

Of course, an Islamic "explanation" can always be found to account for Saudi aid to, and co-optation of, such Arab Moslem countries as Egypt and Somalia, but what about Kenya, South Korea, or Taiwan? And what about deep conflict with equally committed Arab or Islamic regimes? Here the mixture of doctrinal and geopolitical interests is hard to separate. The cases of Qaddafi's Libya and the Islamic Republic of Iran provide an illustration of interconnectedness of doctrinal factors and geostrategic ones.

Although both Libya and Saudi Arabia claim Islam as the basis of their regimes, the gap between the Saudis' conservative version of Islam and Libya's radical one has kept the two countries' world views far apart. They tend to disagree strongly on everything from military relations with their respective patrons to oil policy. For instance, in October 1980 the Saudi government invited the United States to send four AWACS planes to use Saudi airfields as a base for observing the evolution of the Iran-Iraq war to detect any potential threats to oil lines or to the kingdom itself. This was the occasion for a diatribe by Qaddafi against Saudi leaders. On October 19, 1980, he urged Moslem pilgrims not to make the traditional trip to Mecca that year because Saudi Arabia and its Moslem holy places were "under U.S. occupation," and he urged jihad to liberate them.[109] King Khaled replied in person to Qaddafi, "It is regretful to see you join Israel, the enemy of Islam and the Moslems, in opposing our request [for the AWACS's visit]. You have proved that you have become a spearhead against Islam and its sanctities."[110] Three days later the Saudi foreign ministry announced the country's decision to break off diplomatic relations with Libya because Qaddafi "was disparaging Islam and sowing discord among the Moslem people."[111] Though Islam seemed to be at the center of the controversy, Libya's siding with Iran was the immediate cause of this Saudi-Libyan name calling.

Seventeen months later, there was another verbal flare-up between the two governments. The immediate cause was their divergent oil policies. Radio Tripoli quoted Qaddafi as saying that Saudi "overproduction" was deliberate "in order to serve the imperialist interests of the U.S. and to undercut oil producers." Typically, the controversy spilled over to the two countries' policy orientations. At the beginning of March 1982, Qaddafi called for a revolt in the Saudi kingdom and said that "the Saudi oil income of more than $100 billion a year is shared by 5,000 princes of the royal family."[112] The Saudi mass media counterattacked. The Saudi daily *Al-Madina* stated that Qaddafi "has afflicted the Arabs like the plague."[113] *Al-Nadwah* accused him of using Libyan oil income to serve the cause of world Communism "by helping international terrorists" instead of helping his own people.[114] *Al-Jazirah*, in an editorial quoted by Radio Riyadh, continued the same theme. Colonel Qaddafi, it said, "is a perfect example of a communist agent." It charged that he had been financing "terrorist movements" in the world, and that he "murdered" Imam Musa Al-Sadr, the spiritual head of Lebanon's Shi'ite Moslems.[115] On March 11, Saudi Arabia called for Libya's expulsion from the Arab League and from the Organization of African Unity. A week later, the Saudi-based Council of High Ulamas described Colonel Qaddafi as a heretic and "a devout servant of evil," who had publicly ridiculed the teachings of Islam, urged pilgrims not to go to Mecca, and dedicated himself to spreading anarchy and dissension.[116]

On December 31, 1982, however, diplomatic relations were resumed. A joint statement issued simultaneously in Riyadh and Tripoli on December 30, 1982, emphasized the need to insure unity of Arab ranks to face the common enemy, an allusion to Israel and its invasion of Lebanon. This resumption of relations, however, did not change the divergence in the two countries' world views.

But during the 1980s the two countries tried to keep this basic divergence from spilling over into open conflict. Saudi Arabia did not want to fight an ideological war on two fronts at the same time, with Libya and Iran, and did not want to help their alliance against the kingdom. Qaddafi's Libya was increasingly on the defensive and isolated because of a U.S.-instigated campaign against "international terrorism," and naturally sought to obtain Saudi political-diplomatic support, especially after the 1986 U.S. attack on Libya. Initially, Libya was disappointed in the lack of "positive action." This lack, however, characterized not only Saudi Arabia but also almost all Arab countries, and hence escalation with Saudi Arabia or creating disturbances during the pilgrimage season were averted. On the contrary, Saudi Arabia approved Libya's demand for an Arab meeting to study the U.S. attack against Libya *as well as* "all external attacks directed at the Arab nation" (the reference is to Iran's continuing war against Iraq), and thus it was Syria that blocked the convening of such a summit. While Libya and Saudi Arabia continued to differ on oil policies, exchange continued between them, with ten messages exchanged between Fahd and Qaddafi in 1986.[117] Visits even were made, though not at the summit level, such as that by Libya's Foreign Minister Al-Talhi to Riyadh one year after the U.S. invasion.

Khomeini's Iran, though not Arab, is a major power in the Gulf, Saudi Arabia's strategic underbelly. Before Khomeini's rise to power, Saudi relations with Iran followed contradictory lines. On the one hand, there was competition and mutual fear, as shown by the arms flowing to the two countries. On the other hand, they had a common interest in preventing the political upheavals of radical ideologies (from Iraq or South Yemen) from upsetting either their traditional domestic political structure, or the balance within the peninsula and the Gulf region. This mutual interest led to routine relations conducted on a friendly basis and an unwritten agreement during King Faisal's reign (1964–1975) regarding "areas of influence." The Saudis were apparently allowed a relatively free hand within the peninsula, while Iran was allowed preponderance in the Gulf waters.[118]

When serious resistance developed against the shah's regime in 1978–1979, the official Saudi reaction was that the events were an "internal Iranian affair."[119] Nevertheless, official Saudi statements tilted in favor of the shah's regime "based on legitimacy." Several Saudi commentators denounced the alliance between "religious extremists in favor of the subversive ideologies" and the "Communist Tudeh party" that undermined the rule of the "legitimate authority." As for Khomeini, they condemned him and his "clique" for advocating "these wrong subversive ideologies" and criticized Khomeini's "involvement" with and "trust" of the Communists.[120] Once the shah's demise and Khomeini's rise were accomplished, the serious threat to the kingdom became more concrete and immediate.

First, repeated calls to overthrow the Saudi regime made by Tehran were combined with propaganda campaigns among Shi'ites in Hasa and pilgrims in Mecca. Secondly, Iran's radical posture was viewed by the Saudis as considerably increasing uncertainty about the security of the Gulf in general, and that of the Straits of Hormuz in particular. Thirdly, there were Iranian threats against some of the Gulf principalities, considered to be the Saudi "soft underbelly," and above all, there was a revival of the Iranian claim for ownership over Bahrain on historical and religious grounds.[121]

Yet when the war broke out between Iran and Iraq in September 1980, Riyadh had difficulty choosing between two radicals. Instead, it maintained adherence to the principle of Islamic solidarity. In an interview in New York on October 5, 1980, Saudi foreign minister Saud Al-Faisal affirmed his government's neutral stand. Al-Faisal insisted that "the conflict between two brother Muslim countries . . . has to be brought speedily to termination. It is not a conflict [in which] we want to support one side against the other in order to gain advantage. . . . It is a fratricidal war."[122]

However, by December 1981, Saudi policy-makers emphasized the threat from Khomeini's regime to the Gulf countries and to the legitimacy of these regimes. Relations between the two countries started to deteriorate. On December 1, 1981, the Saudi newspaper *Okaz* countered Khomeini's attack on Fahd's eight-point Middle East peace plan (issued on August 8, 1981). The editorial accused the ayatollah of cooperating with Israel in draining Iraq's energy away from the conflict with Israel.[123] In the same month, and after an attempted coup in Bahrain (allegedly backed by Iran), the Saudi minister of the interior, Prince Nayef, signed a security accord with Bahrain. Nayef accused Iran of training, arming, and financing terrorists with the aim of undermining stability throughout the Gulf.[124] He declared that "the Iranians, who said after their revolution that they did not want to be the policemen of the Gulf, have become the terrorists of the Gulf."[125] Consequently, Saudi Arabia "placed its entire potential in the service of Bahrain's security."[126] As for the Iran-Iraq war, it was no longer considered a fratricidal war. Nayef believed that Iraq's war against Iran was "not in defense of its lands and sovereignty alone, but also of the whole Arab nation" and that "Saudi Arabia stands with Iraq in the same position . . . in facing the dangers confronting the Arabs."[127] Consequently, on December 26, 1981, Saudi Arabia and Iraq signed an agreement ending a border dispute nearly sixty years old amid signs of growing cooperation between the two countries against Iran.[128]

Disturbances by Iranian pilgrims against the Saudi regime and Khomeini's repeated declarations that monarchy is incompatible with the Qur'an's basic tenets show the degree of divergence between the two countries in the politics of Islam. This is the main reason Saudi Arabia and the other Gulf regimes bailed Iraq out, enabling it to continue the war.

Saudi Arabia's siding with Iraq in the continuing Gulf war was facilitated by what appeared to be an Iranian threat. Khomeini repeatedly declared the Islamic Republic's intention to export its revolutionary model and to extend the war to the conservative Gulf states. Iran even seemed to back up such threats by isolated instances of military confrontation in the Gulf (various Iranian attacks against Kuwaiti and Saudi vessels). In 1984, a Royal Saudi Air Force fighter shot down an Iranian jet. But there was no break as yet. On the contrary, in December 1986 Saudi Arabia made a concession in OPEC concerning an oil price and output strategy that not only pleased Iran but paved the way for the recovery in the fortunes of all OPEC countries in 1987.

This would not, however, put an end to the continuing doctrinal debates nor especially to the escalation of confrontational behavior to support them. For instance, the increasingly large number of Iranian pilgrims to Mecca used the occasion to post Khomeini's picture and sing the glory of revolutionary Islam. Naturally, clashes with Saudi police followed. On one such occasion (July 1987), as many as 400 people were killed in rioting, including 275 Iranians. While on the Gulf front, military threats, especially against Kuwait, were increasingly supported by action, which finally provoked direct U.S. intervention in the Gulf and confrontation with Iran. At the same time Saudi Arabia and other Gulf countries continued their financial support to Iraq (by 1987 about $40 billion, including $25 billion cash) to help this latter offset the huge decline in its oil revenues. By 1988—just before the Iraq-Iran cease-fire—Saudi Arabia had decided to impose quotas on the number of pilgrims, especially Iranians, and finally broke off diplomatic relations with Teheran in April. The official Saudi communiqué laconically said that "the Iranian policy toward the kingdom has been at variance with diplomatic rules and contrary to mutual respect and good neighbourliness including attempts to smuggle explosives in the kingdom."[129]

The 1988 cease-fire and Khomeini's death in June 1989 might revive attempts to improve relations, since Saudi Arabia still wants to project itself as a neutral peacemaker between Iran and Iraq and a consensus builder generally (e.g., Fahd's 1987 mediation between Algeria and Morocco). However, given the relatively large number of Shi'i minorities living in the Gulf countries, this possible de-escalation of confrontation would not put an end to doctrinal debates or even mutual accusations of subversive activities. But a geopolitical earthquake event in the Gulf could change the pattern of alliances and conflict.

The Gulf region is Saudi Arabia's soft underbelly, and present relations among Gulf countries have their historical origins in tribal and dynastic relations. When the Al-Rashid defeated the Al-Saud in the nineteenth century, the Al-Saud found refuge at Al-Sabah, in what is now Kuwait, and it was from Kuwait that Abdel-Aziz departed to regain Al-Saud power in 1902. However, the impetus for interstate institutionalization in the 1970s and 1980s was the rise of petropower. As the secretary-general of the Gulf council, Abdallah Bishara, reminds us, the proposal officially came in May 1976 from A. G. Al-Sabah, the amir of Kuwait.[130] The project at the time included both Iraq and Iran, whose ministers attended a preliminary meeting in Muscat (Oman) in 1977. With Iran's revolution and the Iran-Iraq war, the idea of a Gulf council changed. By excluding the two warring countries—Iran and Iraq—the new council proposal gave Saudi Arabia the chance to be the sole regional power present in the projected institution. Consequently, Saudi Arabia overcame its hesitation about collective security pacts and on February 4, 1981, convened the foreign ministers of the five small Gulf states (Bahrain, Kuwait, Oman, Qatar, and the United Arab Emirates) to meet in Riyadh. The meeting established the Gulf council machinery, with headquarters in Riyadh. During the eighteen months that followed the First Gulf Council Summit (Abu Dhabi, May 25, 1981), no less than thirty-four meetings of ministers and specialized committees were held.[131] The council works to integrate the members' economic, defense, and foreign policies in the interest of the "stability of the Gulf region," as the communiqué of the first summit affirmed. But the establishment and functioning of this council goes beyond the regional objectives of Saudi diplomacy.[132] The council's aims—as a professor[133] at the United Arab Emirates University took pains to emphasize—have to be situated within the global strategic context and Saudi oil policy. Saudi behavior during the 1982–1983 glut in the world oil market is a good illustration of this policy.

OPEC and Oil Policy

Faced with the crisis of a world oil glut and lower prices in the 1980s, OPEC's thirteen members were in danger of undercutting each other on the world market. Increasing oil supplies (from the North Sea, Alaska, and Mexico) led to the decline of OPEC's world share from 68% in 1976 to only 46% at the end of 1982, and a decline in its financial resources from a peak of $109 billion in 1980 to a deficit of $18 billion two years later.[134] An OPEC meeting in late January 1983 ended in disagreement, and some observers started talking about the end of OPEC.

It was in this context that Saudi Arabia convened the oil ministers of the Gulf council in Riyadh (February 20–23, 1983). Together, these countries hold the major share of both oil production and petrodollars; consequently, they can adjust more easily to fluctuations in the world oil market. Did not Saudi oil minister Yamani affirm in autumn 1975 that to ruin the other countries of OPEC, all that his country need do was to produce oil to its full capacity?[135] In conjunction with the other members of the Gulf council, Saudi Arabia was certainly in a good position to shape OPEC's decision on production and price levels.

Confident of the crucial influence of its own coalition, Saudi Arabia conducted its diplomacy in a typical velvet-fist style. The Riyadh Gulf council meeting of oil ministers agreed on a lower price, but Riyadh would not declare this price on the world market before a "last chance" OPEC meeting to agree on a common price and level of production. The suggestion was then made to reconvene an OPEC meeting. A month or so before the OPEC meeting, Dr. Oteiba, the oil minister of the United Arab Emirates (and also the president of OPEC at that time), declared that his country had decided to increase its production by 45% to meet a swelling budget deficit.[136] The message was clear: the Gulf states are ready to flood the market. In this context, OPEC members had to choose between accepting a version of the decision of the Saudi-led coalition, or provoking a price war on the world market with the probability of being beaten and blamed for OPEC's demise. Consequently, when OPEC members met in London in March 1983 an agreement was reached: reduce production to 17.25 million bpd, and reduce the official price from $34 to $29 per barrel. In this way, Saudi Arabia managed to restore a measure of "stability" to the world oil market.

The pattern of acting as a "swing producer" was also practiced during the much more serious crisis of 1986. OPEC's production and share in the world market has been declining (and the share of non-OPEC producers like Britain, Mexico, and Egypt has been increasing). Moreover, price has been fluctuating (from as high as $25 a barrel in December 1985 to $10 within a few months to rise again to $18 by the end of 1986). One reason for these fluctuations was the difficulty OPEC members had in reaching an agreement on their oil production quotas (most of them were finding their oil revenues seriously declining with resulting unbearable budget deficits). Hence there was occasional "cheating" by some members who went beyond their production quotas. Saudi Arabia reacted very strongly.[137] Its finance minister, M. Aba Al-Khayl, declared that the kingdom "has always sought to restore stability to oil prices at its own expense. We have learned our lesson. . . . We will not make any more sacrifices by cutting our oil output in order to prop up world oil prices." And Yamani affirmed, "We abandoned forever the role of a swing producer; we just want to get more money into the Treasury because we are facing an intolerable recession." Consequently, Saudi oil production shot up from 2 million barrels per day to over 6 million, and the price dropped from $25 to $10 per barrel. Other oil members found themselves in an extremely difficult financial position, and Iran's reaction was the clearest. Finding Saudi action a threat as fatal as Iraq's military action, a senior Iranian official considered "unrestrained oil production that leads to lower oil prices as a hostile act, a declaration of war against us, aimed at reducing our ability to carry on the war against Iraq."[138] After repeated OPEC meetings, some stability was brought to oil production quotas, though countries like Kuwait and the United Arab Emirates exceeded their limits, and Iraq refused to be part of the quota agreement unless it had the same quota as Iran. By March 1988 petroleum prices were $15 per barrel, and non-OPEC members offered to reduce their production by 5% on condition that OPEC members did the same, but Saudi Arabia insisted that quotas should be respected first. When by October prices fell to $12 per barrel, a November OPEC meeting lowered production and gave equal quotas to both Iran and Iraq. By June 1989 oil prices had gone up to $18 per barrel, and it was time to increase OPEC's production limit from 18.5 million barrels per day to 19.5 million as world oil market conditions were getting better. Saudi Arabia seems to have weathered, nationally and regionally, one of its worst crises that could have had dire consequences for its economy and geopolitics.

CONCLUSION: COPING WITH CHANGE

The matrix of Saudi foreign policy—the elements shaping Saudi international orientation and behavior—is closely related to the Saudi pattern of state-formation, geopolitical context, and the dialectics of its state-society relations.

Despite the magnitude of its assets, both spiritual and material, Saudi Arabia is a very vulnerable country according to both the perception of its policy-makers and also to "objective" criteria. In the 1970s much of this vulnerability was concealed because the kingdom's rise to world prominence in the global economy was so fast and impressive. In the span of nine years, its revenue rose thirty-eight times (from $2.7 billion in 1972 to $102 billion in 1981). But this seeming richness is also part of the problem, for it is dependent on the sale of one product, oil, and hence the kingdom's economy and daily life become mortgaged to the vagaries of elements beyond its control: the fluctuations of the world market and the action of other producers, even non-OPEC members like Britain, Mexico, or Egypt who could contribute to the world oil glut. The lessons of the 1980s were very clear in this respect.

If financial resources are absolutely necessary to keep friends and deter enemies, not only outside but also inside Saudi Arabia's segmented society, their decline increases vulnerability, both perceptual and real. Such declines and fluctuations reduce the possibility of planning and budgeting. The 1986–1987 budget was available five months late, and monthly government spending then was one-twelfth of what it was one year earlier. The result is the stalling of needed government projects in a country that still has to develop its basic infrastructure:

> In 1978, the Commonwealth of Massachusetts, which is about one hundredth the size of Saudi Arabia, had some 33,000 miles of paved roads or 50 percent more than the kingdom at that time. . . . Israel, which is also one hundredth the size of Saudi Arabia, had proportionally about forty times as many miles of paved roads as the kingdom.[139]

Certainly, a lot has been done at this level since then, but these figures show the starting point and the distance to be covered to attain the development objective. In the 1980s, as it was in the 1970s, this developmental objective was to be attained through the hiring of both foreign qualified personnel and manpower. Added to all these liabilities (extreme dependence on one export commodity and a few partners, the need for infrastructure and human capital development) are the constantly changing environment, both regional and global, and the necessity for the kingdom to react and cope with them.

Events at the end of the 1980s may have relieved the pressure on the Saudi decision-maker. Soviet troops left Afghanistan in 1988, the Iran-Iraq cease-fire took effect in the same year, Egypt has been reintegrated formally into the different organs of the Arab system in 1989, and the crisis of oil glut and price decline seems to be reversing itself. In the 1980s, the kingdom survived many problems. This experience should consolidate its learning capacity to cope with other crises in the 1990s. And they are sure to come.

Indeed, these crises were not long in coming. The summer of 1990 was certainly a hot one, for it brought a political earthquake with the Iraqi capture of Kuwait city on the night of August 2. For Saudi policy-makers, a member of the GCC has politically disappeared. Moreover, Iraq's justification for its action and its mass-media attack on the Al-Sabah regime was couched in terms that could equally be applied to Saudi Arabia: a rich oil-producing country governed by a royal family of tribal origin. Though Baghdad declared that its troops would not cross the frontiers into Saudi Arabia, Iraqi attacks against Kuwait's ancien régime (its fabulous wealth and "Club Med" life-style in an ocean of poverty and frustration) were an indirect attack against the same pattern of living characteristic of Saudi Arabia and other Gulf states. Consequently, Saudi legitimacy could be construed as being equally in jeopardy.

Moreover, despite its huge defense expenditure the kingdom did not seem capable of standing up to a potential Iraqi threat. In an unusually quick move Saudi Arabia accepted the stationing on its territory of massive numbers of U.S. and coalition troops with their huge arsenals.

Contrary to Saudi Arabia's habitual dithering, this time the decision was fast and unambiguous. The satellite photos that the U.S. defense secretary brought with him concerning the concentration of Iraqi troops seem to have been compelling for the Saudi governing elite. But so was the influence of younger princes, especially Prince Bandar, the kingdom's energetic ambassador in Washington (as mentioned previously, Bandar was the key figure in the Saudi-Chinese secret deal of Chinese missiles).

Though in this present situation of constant and dizzying flux, it is hard to reach permanent conclusions about the evolution of Saudi Arabia's foreign policy, it seems that in the face of a serious threat to Saudi territoriality, the second generation of princes can act in an energetic and decisive way. Saudi Arabia is at present at a crucial crossroad, and this crisis is bound to leave a clear impact on its geopolitical thinking, decision-making pattern, and even political evolution.

NOTES

1. Standard yearbooks as well as good journalistic accounts emphasize these aspects. See, for instance, *The Middle East and North Africa, 1982–1983* (London: Europa Publications, 1982), pp. 677–705. David Holden and Richard Johns, *The*

House of Saud (London: Pan Books, 1982); Robert Lacey, *The Kingdom* (New York: Avon Books, 1982).

2. Malcolm C. Peck, "The Saudi-American Relationship and King Faisal," in Willard A. Beling (ed.), *King Faisal and the Modernisation of Saudi Arabia* (Boulder, Colo.: Westview Press, 1980), pp. 235–236.

3. *Ibid.*, pp. 238–239.

4. *Ibid.*

5. Concerning the Saudi currency—the riyal—see Lacey, *op. cit.*, pp. 445–457.

6. *South*, July 1988, pp. 9–12.

7. Holden and Johns, *op. cit.*, p. 385. Helms confirms: "the absence of a peasant class bound to the land and incorporated into the urban structure . . . meant that the Ottomans and later the British found the prospect of establishing their control in Najd very daunting." Christine M. Helms, *The Cohesion of Saudi Arabia* (Baltimore, Md.: Johns Hopkins University Press, 1981), p. 58.

8. Saad E. Ibrahim and Donald P. Cole, "Saudi Arabian Bedouin," *Cairo Papers in Social Science*, 1, 5 (1978), p. 3. In his in-depth analysis of the Saudi economy, El-Mallakh estimated the agricultural share of the GDP as 5.8% for the same period. Ragaei El-Mallakh, *Saudi Arabia: Rush to Development* (London: Croom Helm, 1982), p. 85.

9. *Middle East and North Africa, 1982–1983*, pp. 677–705.

10. The World Bank, *World Development Report 1982* (London and New York: Oxford University Press, 1982), p. 110.

11. El-Mallakh, *op. cit.*, p. 169.

12. *Ibid.*, p. 116.

13. A recent attempt to deal with this aspect is Summer Scott Huyette, *Political Adaptation in Saudi Arabia* (Boulder, Colo.: Westview Press, 1985).

14. Helms, *op. cit.*, p. 60.

15. Ibrahim and Cole, *op. cit.*, p. 3.

16. Abdel-Aziz, known as Ibn Saud, governed for more than fifty years (1902–1953). He was followed by his sons Saud (1953–1964), Faisal (1964–1975), Khaled (1975–1982), and Fahd (1982–).

17. John S. Habib, *Ibn Saud's Warriors of Islam* (Leiden, Netherlands: E. J. Brill, 1978), p. 19.

18. Ayman Al-Yassini, "Saudi Arabia: The Kingdom of Islam," in Carlo Caldarola (ed.), *Religions and Societies: Asia and the Middle East* (The Hague, Netherlands: Mouton, forthcoming), p. 6. I am grateful to Dr. Al-Yassini for making available to me, before publication, both this excellent paper and another one on Islam and Saudi foreign policy.

19. Literally, *hijra* means immigration and was first used to label the prophet Mohamed's move from Mecca to Medina to establish the first Islamic state. The word is thus pregnant with important religious and emotional associations.

20. Helms, *op. cit.*, p. 130.

21. Al-Yassini, *op. cit.*, p. 6.

22. "Although this number may not be definitive . . . [this] writer has been able to identity 222." Habib, *op. cit.*, p. 58.

23. Helms, *op. cit.*, p. 138.

24. Habib, *op. cit.*, p. 30.

25. Helms, *op. cit.*, p. 78.

26. David E. Long, "King Faisal's World View," in Beling, *op. cit.*, pp. 177–178. On April 20, 1963, at the height of the Arab cold war and the conflict in Yemen, King Faisal reiterated: "We stretch out our hands . . . [and] open our breasts to our Arab brethren. . . . We are prepared to reach the goal set before us, which is complete Arab unity, but we cannot forget in any situation that this country has . . . her geographical location and the presence of the holy places . . . [which] distinguish her from other Arab countries. . . . We support Islam above all things; and we look upon Islam as our solid foundation." Ayman Al-Yassini, "Islam and Foreign Policy in Saudi Arabia," Center for Developing Area Studies Paper, McGill University, Montreal, 1983, p. 12.

27. Al-Yassini, "Islam and Foreign Policy," pp. 10–11.

28. Long, *op. cit.*, p. 176.

29. William Quandt, who appears to follow the Saudi position, emphasizes the Arab world and the Palestinians over the Islamic world. See his lucid book, *Saudi Arabia in the 1980s* (Washington, D.C.: Brookings Institution, 1981).

30. Haim Shaked and Tamar Yegnes, "Saudi Arabia," in Colin Legum, Haim Shaked, and Daniel Dishon (eds.), *Middle East Contemporary Survey, 1976–1977* (London: Holmes and Meier, 1978), pp. 565–585. (Hereafter referred to as *Middle East Survey*).

31. *Ibid.*

32. Jacob Goldberg, "The Saudi Arabian Kingdom," in Legum, Shaked, and Dishon, *Middle East Survey, 1979–1980*, pp. 681–721.

33. *New York Times*, April 24, 1981, pp. A1 and A7.

34. Quandt, *op. cit.*, p. 145. On the death of King Khaled in June 1982, Brezhnev sent a message of "profound condolences" to King Fahd, the Soviet press agency Tass reported. *New York Times*, June 15, 1982.

35. Goldberg, *op. cit.*, p. 755.

36. For the views of Prince Bandar Ben Sultan, expressed to me during a meeting at Harvard University of September 19, 1979, see Bahgat Korany, "Petropuissance et système mondial: le cas de l'Arabie Saoudtie," *Etudes Internationales*, 10, 4 (1979), pp. 797–819.

37. Goldberg, 1979–1980.

38. *Ibid.*

39. *Ibid.*

40. *Ibid.*

41. *Ibid.*

42. See the *New York Times*, January 30, 1980, p. A13, for the complete text.

43. For other cases, see Quandt, *op. cit.*, p. 44.

44. H. St. John Philby, *Saudi Arabia* (Beirut: 1968), p. 292, as quoted in Mordechai Abir, *Saudi Arabia in the Oil Era* (Boulder, Colo.: Westview Press, 1988), p. 100.

45. Abir, *op. cit.*, pp. 9–14.

46. *Ibid.*, p. 17.

47. Joseph Kechichian, "The Role of the Ulama in the Politics of an Islamic State: The Case of Saudi Arabia," *International Journal of Middle East Studies*, 18, 1 (February 1986), pp. 53–71.

48. For details see Huyette, *op. cit.*, especially pp. 49–103, 139–171.

49. Quandt, *op. cit.*, p. 76.

50. Talk with Mr. Ziyad Al-Shawaf, Saudi Arabia's ambassador to Canada, Ottawa, July 5, 1983.

51. Quandt, *op. cit.*, p. 109.

52. Ghassan Salama, *The Foreign Policy of Saudi Arabia Since 1945* (Beirut: Institute of Arab Development, 1980), p. 47 (in Arabic). This Arabic edition is based on Dr. Salama's well-researched Ph.D. dissertation, University of Paris, Sorbonne. For more data on the royal family see also *Time*, June 28, 1982.

53. Helen Lackner, *A House Built on Sand* (London: Ithaca Press, 1978), pp. 57–58.

54. Some foreigners have also participated in decision-making. Dr. Rashad Pharaon, Abdel-Aziz's Syrian physician, also became his personal advisor; and Turkish-born Kamal Adham was both King Faisal's brother-in-law and the kingdom's intelligence chief. Lacey, *op. cit.*, pp. 169, 358–359, 393, 447–448; Holden and Johns, *op. cit.*, pp. 102, 139, 179, 364–365.

55. This information is from Salama, *op. cit.*, pp. 47–84.

56. The one exception was relations with the Gulf principalities, which Abdel-Aziz handled himself because of his relations with the different tribal chiefs.

57. Charles Harrington, "The Saudi Arabian Council of Ministers," *Middle East Journal* 12, 1 (1958), pp. 1–20.

58. Conversation with Ambassador Al-Shawaf, *op. cit.*

59. Richard Nyrop et al., *Area Handbook for Saudi Arabia*, 3d ed. (Washington, D.C.: American University, 1977), pp. 216–217. Among the ten political departments no less than six are devoted to Arab & Islamic Affairs. See Fouad Al-Farsy, *Saudi Arabia: A Case Study in Development* (London and Boston: Kegan Paul International, 1982), p. 100.

60. Conversation with Ambassador Al-Shawaf, *op. cit.*

61. *Ibid.*

62. *Ibid.*

63. Quandt, *op. cit.*, p. 84.

64. *Time*, June 28, 1982.

65. Salama, *op. cit.*, pp. 47–83.

66. Quandt, *op. cit.*, pp. 81–82.

67. *Time*, June 28, 1982, p. 23.

68. For a different view, see Alexander Bligh, "The Saudi Religious Elite (Ulama) as Party in the Political System of the Kingdom," *International Journal of Middle East Studies*, 17, 1 (February 1985), pp. 37–50.

69. Tim Niblock, "Social Structure and the Development of the Saudi Arabian Political System," in Niblick (ed.), *State, Society and Economy in Saudi Arabia* (New York: St. Martin's Press, 1982), p. 92.

70. Al-Yassini, "Saudi Arabia," *op. cit.*, p. 15.

71. *Ibid.*

72. Niblock, *op. cit.*, p. 92.

73. John A. Shaw and David E. Long, *Saudi Arabian Modernization* (Washington, D.C.: Center for Strategic and International Studies, 1982), pp. 67–74.

74. *The Military Balance* (London: International Institute of Strategic Studies), data on Saudi Arabia in the different volumes from 1970–1971 to 1982–1983.

75. "Facts and Figures on Defense: Saudi Arabia," *Military Technology* 5, 28 (1981), pp. 69–73.

76. For Saudi policy-makers, Saudi defense expenditures are too important to be affected by decline in oil revenues. For instance, in 1975–1976 oil revenues declined by 2.4% over the previous year but total defense and security expenditures rose by 155% in the same period. In 1978–1979 oil revenues declined again by 11.3% over 1977, but total defense and security expenditure rose by 9.5%. For extensive data, see Nadav Safran, *Saudi Arabia: The Ceaseless Quest*

for Security (Cambridge, Mass.: The Belknap Press of Harvard University Press, 1985), pp. 70, 108, 182, 423.

77. Data calculated from the information provided by Salama, *op. cit.*, pp. 319–328. Salama draws upon Congress reports on U.S. arms policies in the Gulf and the Red Sea Area.

78. Jean-Louis Soulié and Lucien Champenois, *Le royaume d'Arabie Saoudite à l'épreuve des temps modernes* (Paris: Albin Michel, 1978), pp. 201–202.

79. *Middle East Intelligence Survey* 7, 17 (December 1–15, 1979), p. 129; "Facts and Figures on Defense," *op. cit.*

80. "Facts and Figures on Defense," *op. cit.*

81. Nyrop et al., *op. cit.*, p. 323.

82. *Middle East Intelligence Survey* 7, 17 (December 1–15, 1979), p. 129.

83. Manfred Halpern, *The Politics of Social Change in the Middle East and North Africa* (Princeton, N.J.: Princeton University Press, 1963), Chapter 4.

84. For a detailed analysis of this group as represented by Tariki, see Stephen Duguid, "A Biographical Approach to the Study of Social Change in the Middle East: Abdallah Tariki as a New Man," *International Journal of Middle East Studies* I (1970), pp. 195–220.

85. Peck, *op. cit.*, p. 240.

86. Al-Yassini, "Saudi Arabia," *op. cit.*, p. 20.

87. Niblock, *op. cit.*, p. 101.

88. Quandt, *op. cit.*, p. 87.

89. Abir, *op. cit.*, pp. 201–202.

90. Jacob Goldberg, "The Saudi Arabian Kingdom," *Middle East Survey*, 1986, pp. 543–573.

91. *Ibid.*

92. *Ibid.*

93. Niblock, *op. cit.*, p. 76–77.

94. Michael Field, *The Merchants: The Big Business Families of Saudi Arabia and the Gulf States* (Woodstock, N.Y.: The Overlook Press, 1984).

95. Holden and Johns, *op. cit.*, pp. 244–245, 359–366; Lacey, *op. cit.*, pp. 464–470, 507.

96. David B. Ottaway, "Sudden Drop in Oil Wealth May Give Saudis Severe Jolt," *Montreal Gazette*, June 11, 1983.

97. Al-Yassini, "Saudi Arabia," *op. cit.*, p. 23.

98. Shaw and Long, *op. cit.*, pp. 78–81.

99. Al-Yassini, "Saudi Arabia," *op. cit.*, p. 23.

100. "Saudi Arabia," *Middle East Economic Digest*, a Special Report, June 1986.

101. Shirin Tahir-Kheli and William O. Staudenmaier, "The Saudi-Pakistani Military Relationship," *Orbis* 26, 1 (1982), pp. 155–171.

102. *New York Times*, October 30, 1987.

103. Al-Yassini, "Islam and Foreign Policy," p. 13.

104. *Ibid.*

105. This information is confirmed by diverse sources, for instance: Holden and Johns, *op. cit.*, p. 392; Lacey, *op. cit.*, p. 393, Mohamed Heikal, *The Road to Ramadan* (New York: Ballantine Books, 1976), p. 118; David Hirst and Irene Beeson, *Sadat* (London: Faber and Faber, 1981), p. 97.

106. King Faisal said as late as August 1972: "The use of the oil weapon against the USA should be ruled out," *Middle East Journal* 26, 3 (1972).

107. Paul Jabber, "Oil, Arms, and Regional Diplomacy," in Malcolm H. Kerr and El Sayed Yassin (eds.), *Rich and Poor States in the Middle East: Egypt and the New Arab Order* (Boulder, Colo.: Westview Press, 1982), pp. 415–447.
108. *Ibid.*
109. *New York Times*, October 25, 1980.
110. *Ibid.*
111. *Keesings Contemporary Archives*, August 7, 1981, p. 31011.
112. *New York Times*, March 7, 1982.
113. *Ibid.*
114. *Ibid.*
115. *Ibid.*
116. *Keesings Contemporary Archives*, September 3, 1982, p. 31682.
117. Goldberg, in *Middle East Survey*, 1986.
118. Shaked and Yegnes, *op. cit.*, p. 574.
119. Jacob Goldberg, "The Saudi Arabian Kingdom," in Legum, Shaked, and Dishon, *Middle East Survey*, 1978–1979, pp. 736–769.
120. *Ibid.*
121. Goldberg, in *Middle East Survey*, 1979–1980.
122. Ami Ayalon, "The Iran-Iraq War," in *Middle East Survey*, 1979–1980, p. 23.
123. *Keesings Contemporary Archives*, June 4, 1982, p. 31523.
124. *New York Times*, December 21, 1981.
125. *Keesings Contemporary Archives*, June 4, 1982, p. 31523.
126. *New York Times*, December 21, 1981.
127. *Keesings Contemporary Archives*, June 4, 1982, p. 31523.
128. *New York Times*, December 28, 1981.
129. *Keesings Contemporary Archives*, 1988, p. 36056.
130. Abdallah Bishara, "The Gulf Cooperation Council," Paper submitted to the Symposium on "The Domestic and International Framework of Cooperation in the Arab Gulf Region," sponsored by Kuwait University and the Economic Society of Kuwait, Kuwait, April 18–20, 1982 (in Arabic).
131. *Middle East Magazine* (London), December 1982, p. 8.
132. Interview with A. Bishara in *Middle East Magazine*, September 1981.
133. Abdullah El-Nefissi, "The Gulf Cooperation Council: The Politico-Strategic Framework," Paper submitted to the Symposium on "The Domestic and International Framework of Cooperation," *op. cit.* (in Arabic).
134. *Time*, February 7, 1983, pp. 34–38.
135. Saudi Arabia produced 40% of OPEC's world production in 1981. *Middle East and North Africa*, 1982–1983, pp. 677–705.
136. *Time*, February 7, 1983.
137. Goldberg, in *Middle East Survey*, 1986, pp. 543–573.
138. *Ibid.*, p. 545.
139. Safran, *op. cit.*, p. 223.

11

The Foreign Policy of a Fragmented Polity: The Case of Sudan

Gehad Auda

Sudan is conspicuous among Arab countries because of its distinct structural characteristics. The first characteristic is extensive plurality of socioeconomic, demographic, and geographic realities. The second is an enduring but segmented civic society with politico-religious transnational links. The third is the overlapping of domestic issues of poverty, civil war, mass migration, and political instability with foreign issues of regional conflict, external intervention, and economic aid. In a nutshell, Sudan is a fragmented polity par excellence.

For the first time in its history, political and administrative central-ization came to Sudan with the Egyptian invasion in 1821. Before that time, Sudan was divided into a number of kingdoms in Darfur, Nuba, and the hinterland. Feudalism was prevalent; the economy was pastoral; Sufi affiliations were the main social institutions; and the population was dispersed.[1] In the period from 1821 to 1956, the year of independence, Sudanese political history was characterized by British domination, revolutions, conflicting political-ethnic-religious affiliations, and the ad-ministrative division into North and South. Sudan was underdeveloped and impoverished.[2]

As a foreign policy actor, Sudan, since independence, has been largely constrained by its fragmentation. Its socioeconomic and political structures consist of disjointed units, whose behavior indicates limited social reconcilability and a tendency for conflict. Moreover, in addition to the "official" orientation and behavior, analysis of Sudan's foreign policy should include other informal orientations and behaviors of political forces and civic groups.

This chapter investigates the foreign policy orientation, decision-making, and behavior of Sudan during the 1980s, particularly from the fall of Ja'far Numieri's military regime in 1985 to the fall of Sadiq Al-Mahdi's civilian regime in 1989. The chapter also places the analysis within the larger context of Sudanese foreign policy since independence in January 1956. The main research questions are: How have conditions of societal fragmentation induced domestic instability, and how has foreign policy orientation and behavior been affected?

Fragmentation of the Sudanese polity suggests the primacy of environmental factors. Three crucial elements are considered here. The first element is political regime type, which is critical to foreign policy-making because it indicates the degree of control over resource mobilization and allocation. Since the 1970s, Sudan witnessed three political regimes: Numieri's military regime (1969–1985), Al-Mahdi's civilian government (1986–June 1989), and Omar Hassan Al-Beshir's military regime since then. The second element is regional alliances and balances that show the pattern of borrowed resources and projected threats. As a consequence of the rising internal opposition to Numieri's regime since the mid-1970s, both the regime and the opposition forces forged alliances with regional powers. Since then, regional alliances continued as assets to different Sudanese political forces. The third factor is natural changes of desertification, drought, hunger, and decay that had an impact on internal social fragmentation and foreign policy behavior.

THE DOMESTIC ENVIRONMENT

Geography

Sudan is the largest country in Africa and the Arab world. Its total area is over two million square kilometers. Geography in Sudan functions as a compounding factor. Societal cleavages in terms of ethnic, linguistic, tribal, and religious affiliation are heightened and perpetuated through the dialectics of geographic concentration and natural diversity.

Sudan is divided into two geographic regions. The first is the North where agriculture depends on the Nile. It extends from south of Khartoum to the border with Egypt. This region encompasses the three most arable pieces of land in Sudan, namely Gezirah Delta, Al-Qash Delta, and Tuqar Delta. It is populated by Arab, Nubian, and Beja tribes. The most arid areas are found to the north of Darfur, north of Kassal in the east, and virtually all the area of the northwest, adjacent to the Egyptian border. The second region is the South where most of the land is covered by swamps and savanna grass. The main activity is cattle herding. This region is populated by two main tribal groups: Nilotic and Niger. Dinka, Nuer, and Shilluk tribes are examples of the Nilotic group and Azande is representative of the Niger.

The impact of the geographic separation of North and South is compounded by the international boundaries of Sudan. Sudan is surrounded by eight countries: Egypt and Libya in the north, Chad, Central

African Republic, and Zaire in the west, Ethiopia in the east and southeast, and Uganda and Kenya in the south. These boundaries constitute potential sources of conflict with neighboring countries. Boundaries with Ethiopia,[3] for example, were settled by long negotiations between England and Ethiopia. The boundaries were demarcated along the natural divides of the rivers Baro, Pibor, Akobo, and Melile and with the supplement of the use of topographical lines. The results were the spread of the Ethiopian empire into the Sudan's natural terrain, and the partition of Al-Anwak and Al-Beja tribes. (Al-Anwak, whose main groups reside in the Al-Subat basin, is a part of the Dinka-Nuer ethnic group in the southern region, and Bani-Amer tribes with their connections to Eritrea are part of the Al-Beja ethnic group in the northern region in the east.) Other boundary settlement cases with Libya, Zaire, Uganda, and Kenya have fragmented the unity of tribes, interfered with their migration cycles, and provided means for external intervention. Libyan, Chadian, and Central African borders with Sudan remain until now either undecided, as in the case of Libyan-Sudanese borders,[4] or a mere topographical delineation, as in the case with Chad and the Republic of Central Africa. A large number of tribes at Darfur and Kordofan, such as Al-Zaghawa, Al-Kababish, and Al-Bedaiat not only have ancestral ties in Libya, Chad, and the Republic of Central Africa but also travel seasonally across their boundaries.

Five of the surrounding countries—Libya, Chad, the Republic of Central Africa, Egypt, and Ethiopia—share the same drought region with Sudan. The drought area in Sudan covers half of the country, including Darfur, Kordofan, the Blue Nile, part of northern Khartoum, and the northern part of the South.[5] Most of the tribes of this area are pastoral tribes and live on routine migration for water. Drought intensifies migration for water across borders and keeps the ethnic composition around the peripheries in constant change.

Thus, Sudan is a country of multiple geographic fragmentation. Geography, in other words, has mitigated against the ability of the central government to dominate and control. The size of the country, its topography, boundaries with eight surrounding states, and tribal affinities across borders helped restrict the authority of the central government over the peripheries. The geographic division into North and South has cultivated measures of autonomy that ultimately handicapped governmental ability to penetrate and mobilize resources.

Social Structure and Population

The Sudanese social structure consists of multiple disjointed units. It encompasses more than the adverse impacts of ethnicity and religion. The land ownership and social dislocation matrix reveal additional dimensions.

Religious affiliations have interacted within the framework of ethnic plurality to leave the Sudanese with a limited sense of territorial and national integration. There are in Sudan 567 tribes and five linguistic groups. Interaction across ethnic and communal lines has been hampered by the religious contentions of Islam, Christianity, and African traditional religions. Islam is widespread in the North, while in the South Christianity mixed with African beliefs and manners is dominant.

Personal mobility and communications as means of social integration have been limited. Poor transportation has kept communities and regions virtually isolated. Travel from Juba, the capital of the southern region, to the North is only possible by air. Travel through the Nile is difficult during winter and war times. Furthermore, in the far west of Sudan, no paved roads exist between Darfur and the rest of the country.

Other integrative forces have also been limited in transcending diversity. For instance, Sudanese nationalism has been the torch of many of the northern leaders for national unity and independence. But it created new cleavages between those advocating the independence of Sudan and those wishing for unity with Egypt. More importantly, the rise of the Sudanese nationalist movement was a "northern" phenomenon in which the South did not participate due to disparities of social development and the isolation imposed by the British administration.[6]

Sufism, naturally, proved integrative among Muslim tribes only. In the case of Al-Hadendowa tribes, in the east, Sufi areas functioned as a medium for Islamic education and socialization. There are two major Sufi *tariqa* in Sudan, Al-Mahdiyya and Al-Khatmiyya, each of which represent a major social and political force. Paradoxically, sufism has been instrumental in enforcing fragmentation and transnational culture in Sudan: A substantial number of Sufi orders in Sudan find followers in neighboring countries and regions.

Modes of land ownership function to reinforce social fragmentation. In Sudan there are three modes of land ownership each reflecting a specific mix of social factors. Private ownership, widespread in the northern cultivated area around the Nile, indicates a market economy, agriculture settlement, and government intervention.[7] Village ownership, dominant in the western part, stands for a subsistence economy, nomadic semi-settlement, and social autonomy from the government.[8] Tribal ownership, mainly in the South, signifies an economy of cattle rearing, tribal feuds, and antagonism against government.[9] In short, modes of land ownership correspond highly to differences in self-perception and relations to the government. Still more significantly, they dilute the impact of nationalism and sufism.

Social dislocation has been another major source of social fragmentation. The magnitude of social dislocation caused by urbanization and modern education increased during the 1970s. In the 1980s migration and human dislocation were a further source of social fragmentation. The need for agricultural labor in the Gizerah area brought workers from Darfur, Kordofan, and neighboring countries, particularly Chad. One expert estimated the number of foreign workers in the Gizerah during the 1980s ranged from 2 to 4 million.[10] Desertification, drought, and the renewed war in the South since 1983 led to more migration into urban centers.[11] These developments led to the proliferation of subloyalties in urban centers and increasing demands upon the government.

Political Structure

Since independence on the first of January of 1956, Sudan changed back and forth from civilian rule (1956–1958, 1964–1969, and 1984–1989) to military rule (1958–1964, 1969–1984, and 1989). Civilian rule was identified with traditional parties' dominance of political life,[12] while the military governments coincided with either no-party or one-party systems.[13] From May 1986 to June 1989 Sudan was ruled by a coalition government headed by the Umma party and its leader Sadiq Al-Mahdi. In June 1989, the military intervened and initiated a new chapter in Sudanese politics.

After the fall of Numieri's military regime a new constitutional document was issued in October 1985, according to which the system was remodelled along parliamentary lines. Formal political power was distributed between three institutions: the Constitutional Assembly, the Council of Ministers, and the Council of the Head of the State. The Council of Ministers consists of the majority party in the assembly. The Council of the Head of the State had nominal political power. Political participation was organized in a multiparty system and over sixty-four political parties and organizations became active.

Competition politics in a fragmented social environment strengthened the ability of small political parties and organizations to exert pressures and create a climate of crisis. Thus, executive power-sharing and political coalitions were the main characteristics of the government of Al-Mahdi. This resulted in four cabinet changes in the span of two years. The first change, on June 3, 1987, entailed a redistribution of ministerial seats between the Umma party and the Democratic Unionist party (DUP), the largest partners in the coalition. The second change, on May 16, 1988, widened the coalition to include the National Islamic Front. The third change, on December 28, 1988, was caused by the withdrawal of the DUP because of disagreement on the South issue as will be explained later. The fourth change, on March 26, 1989, reinstated the DUP in cabinet. Three factors underlay this changing structure: a fragmented party system, unsettled civil-military relations, and the continued war in the South.

Political parties resurfaced after sixteen years of disbanding and represented different fragments of the sociopolitical structure. They include traditional parties such as Al-Umma and the DUP whose main base of support is rooted in Sufi orders. The Umma party is affiliated with the Al-Mahdiyya sect and the DUP with Al-Khatmiyya sect. Other types of parties and organizations included ideological, racial, ethnic, and separatist parties and organizations such as the southern parties of the African-Sudanese Conference, Political Federation of the South of Sudan, the National People's party. Other ethnic parties included Al-Beja Conference, the Darfur Front, the National Sudanese party (representing the southern Nuba Mountains) and the Federation of Bahr Al-Gazal. There are also religious parties such as the Muslim Brothers and the National Islamic Front led by Hassan Al-Turabi. Other nationalistic parties and organizations include the Unionist Federation, the Communist, Nasserist, and Ba'thist parties.

The parliamentary election of 1986 demonstrated the power and influence of the traditional parties. Out of 264 seats, Al-Umma party won 100, the Democratic Unionist party sixty-three, the National Islamic Front fifty-one, and the Communist party one seat. The remaining forty-nine seats were won by racial and ethnic parties and independents. Al-Mahdi formed a coalition government with DUP. Modern political parties and organizations were left without parliamentary representation. Consequently, they were involved in agitational politics.

The unsettled civil-military relations have been a major dilemma for the government in Sudan.[14] Political and social divisions are reflected in recruits for the military. Senior officers were recruited from the North, particularly from Al-Ansar and Al-Khatmiyya sects. The rank and file has been drawn from ethnic minorities such as Al-Beja tribe of the east and Al-Messeriyya tribe from the west. Junior commanders were penetrated by different radical ideologies such as Nasserism, Ba'thism, Islamism, and communism. For instance, Numieri's coup of 1969 was launched by junior officers in collaboration with forces of the left. Many abortive coups since 1969 involved ethnic and ideological elements.

Support of the military high command for the return of democracy in 1964 and 1984 was a sufficient condition for the military regimes of 1958 of General Aboud and 1969 of Numieri to fall. After the return of democratic institutions in 1985, some parties, namely the Umma and National Islamic Front sponsored a policy of establishing their own militia. A memorandum presented by the general commander of the army to the head of the Council of the Head of the State in February 1989 warned that these militias represented a major threat to Sudanese national security. The warning induced some sixty-four party and union federations (after a long political crisis) to agree upon a new government program focused upon preserving the unity of the armed forces, achieving peace in the South, solving the economic crisis, and keeping a balanced foreign policy stand. The fourth cabinet change was consequently the final outcome where the National Islamic Front did not participate.

The war in the South has been fought between the Sudanese People's Liberation Movement and its adjunct army (SPLM/SPLA) led by Colonel Dr. John Garang de Mabior and the central government. The war was renewed ten years after the signing of the Addis Ababa Agreement in 1972 as a direct consequence of Numieri's abolition of the administrative division of the South into three governorates, which was a violation of the accord. Numieri's consequent implementation of Islamic *Shar'ia* deepened the southern antagonism. Colonel Garang was a senior commander in the Sudanese army who deserted and declared war against the government.

SPLM/SPLA projects itself as an integrationist and nationalist Sudanese movement.[15] The movement demands redistribution of political power to accommodate the different political and social forces, construction of true plural democratic institutions, and a Sudanese assertion of its autonomy versus surrounding countries. The movement includes some prominent figures from the North like Dr. Mansour Khalid, a Muslim, former foreign minister under Numieri, and a leading assistant to Numieri before his resignation in 1978. Dr. Khalid is the spokesman of the movement.

Militarily, the war in the South is not likely to be won by the central government. Moreover, the political competition between the Umma party and the DUP created governmental vacillation in dealing with SPLM/SPLA. On November 16, 1988, the DUP signed a document with Garang outlining a framework for peace. The Umma party initially approved the agreement but later refused to abide by it. The National Islamic Front, the junior partner of the government, denounced the agreement. In protest the DUP withdrew from the government. A political crisis ensued that led to the intervention of the high command of the army in February 1989 and the reinstitution of the DUP.

In this context, the military suffered from low fighting capability and feared the threat of disintegration of its unity. From its perspective, it was victimized by the civilian politicians and wanted to maintain its cohesiveness against the impact of a fragmented political system. Thus, it was not surprising that Al-Beshir moved in June 1989 to seize power and abolish political parties.

Basically, Sudanese democracy failed to create a balance between articulation and aggregation of interests. Extensive interest articulation with little institutional capacity to aggregate left the government vulnerable to the adverse impact of societal fragmentation. Conversely, societal fragmentation as evidenced by the rifts between the Umma and the DUP hindered the ability of the government to forge consensus over the main political issues. Government decisions, consequently, came in most part in the interest of perpetuating clientelism.

Economic Capability

Sudan has a significantly low level of economic capability. During the period 1979–1982, Sudan produced 67% of the average world production rate per country in cotton lint, 33% in groundnuts, 16% in sorghum, and 30% in wheat.[16] During the same period, the annual economic growth rate was negative, the exchange rate was devalued four times, and by 1981–1982 the deficit on the current account was twenty-eight times its level in 1970–1971.[17] The average annual growth of total domestic investment declined from 6.5% during the period 1965–1980 to −5.2% during the period 1980–1986.[18]

Living on borrowed resources has been the result of such a deteriorating economic situation. Public and publicly guaranteed debt increased from US$5.165 billion in 1982 to US$7.876 billion in 1987.[19] Short-term debt jumped from $582 million in 1980 to $2.019 billion in 1987.[20] In this context, International Monetary Fund (IMF) credit to Sudan increased from $342 million in 1980 to $859 million in 1987.[21] Arrears climbed from $300 million in May 1986 to $600 million by mid-1987.[22] The development dilemma in Sudan is represented in the disparity between its development potential in terms of natural resources and the capability of development investment. Lacking means of investment such as finances and management aggravated Sudan's staggering needs for borrowed resources.

Sudan's major economic problems are the result of the policies followed in the later years of the Numieri regime. The economy worsened under the civilian government. Major economic reform decisions since 1985 were compromised as a result of political instability and government indecision. Failing to impose economic and social discipline has rendered the government soft in dealing with economic problems.

Defense Capability

Sudan's defense capability is weak. Conscription is legislated but not implemented because of the government's limited control of the society. The military suffered handicaps under Numieri. Although the central government funds allocated for defense and security increased from 13.4% in 1978–1979 to 21% in 1981–1982,[23] the modernization of organization and weaponry was virtually nonexistent. The reasons were: (1) most of these funds went to upgrading the internal security apparatus; (2) Numieri's dismissal of the chief-of-staff in 1987 and leaving the position vacant for some time caused a distortion of the military communication chain and coordination network; and (3) military involvement in functions related to internal security and export-import business hampered military professionalism.

Sudanese weaponry procurement and deployment capacities have been insignificant. Sudanese weaponry is generally a collection of outmoded pieces, mostly from Western sources. In terms of sophisticated fighting machinery, in 1988–1989 Sudan had two MiG-23 aircraft, one SA-7 missile, and two Falcon-20 helicopters.[24] Serviceability of weapons is at best questionable.[25]

Reliance on regional defense alliances, with Egypt under Numieri and occasionally Libya under the civilian government, has been the national security policy for defense. During the period 1976–1989, Sudan had a mutual defense treaty with Egypt, which continued only nominally after the 1985 overthrow of Numieri. Many Sudanese officers were trained in Egypt, Egypt supplied Sudan with emergency parcels of weapons when needed, and Egyptian-Sudanese regional security aims, to a great extent, coincided. The changes in regional alliances did not significantly enhance the military's fighting power against the SPLA in the South. The Sudanese army experienced heavy losses from 1987 to 1989 and important cities, Al-Nasr, Karmk, and Pibor, fell into the hands of SPLA for long periods.

Al-Beshir's coup came in the context of the military's need to increase its defense capability. It was not unexpected, hence, to publicly blame the parties and the civilian government of Al-Mahdi for weakening the country's capability to defend itself. In short, Sudan's defense capability was based upon borrowed resources that fluctuated according to changing of bilateral relations with Egypt and Libya.

FOREIGN POLICY ORIENTATION

The problem with analyzing foreign policy orientation in Sudan is that parties in power tend to have two positions; they express themselves as partners in the government bound by a common program and as independent parties with independent positions. During the democratic phase, 1986–1989, the concept of "good neighborhood" was stressed on the official level in the speeches of Al-Mahdi, the prime minister. However, this concept in most cases was not adopted by most major political forces. The Democratic Unionist party, the National Islamic Front, Umma party and other smaller parties and professional unions preferred Sudan to have some special relations with some regional states. Hence, Sudan had two articulated orientations on foreign policy: the official or formal orientation as expressed by the prime minister and government statements and the informal orientation as found in speeches of politicians as party leaders, including those who were in power.

In an analysis of 122 speeches delivered by Sadiq Al-Mahdi from May 6, 1986, to December 31, 1988,[26] internal fragmentation and regional concerns were found to shape his foreign policy orientation. This orientation was framed in the concept of "good neighborhood." Good neighborhood was a complex concept that linked internal political and socioeconomic problems with the regional balance of power. Its core idea aimed at achieving the national sovereignty, securing territorial integrity, preserving the society against foreign penetration, and enhancing democracy and living conditions in general.[27] The orientation was against regional alignments, involvement in armed conflicts, external clientelism, and foreign ideological or economic influence.

Good neighborhood was an orientation of self-assertion, not through mobilization of resources and confrontation, but through cutting ties between foreign actors and domestic groups. Within this context, the perception of the war in the South and external military intervention in Darfur was formulated. War in the South, although Al-Mahdi recognized its internal reasons, would be settled when Ethiopia could restrain itself from supporting the SPLM/SPLA.[28] Darfur's problem was a by-product of Chad's internal political conflict during the 1970s and Libyan and French military involvement during the 1980s.[29] Desertification, drought, and undelineated boundaries intensified the impact of Chadian problems upon Darfur. For Al-Mahdi, the solution was to increase the administrative resources in the region, to mediate between the fighting parties in Chad, to forge an understanding between Sudan and Chad, and to settle boundaries with the Republic of Central Africa.

Good neighborhood had a developmental dimension as well. In a reception for Fikry Silasy, the Ethiopian prime minister, in Khartoum on December 16, 1988, Sadiq Al-Mahdi asserted the relationship between development and noninvolvement in wars and conflicts.[30] On the other hand, financial assistance from governmental and nongovernmental international organizations was welcomed as long as it was channeled through the government and did not imply favors to certain political factions or social groups. This developmental aspect was perhaps the justification for Al-Mahdi to maintain good relations with Libya and Iran.

This concept implied a potential mediating role for Sudan and reflected an element of continuity in the Sudanese foreign policy. In 1966 and 1967, Sudan mediated between Nasser's Egypt and King Faisal's Saudi Arabia over the war in Yemen. Also, since the establishment of the Organization of African Unity (OAU) in 1963 Sudan involved itself in its mediation efforts. However, Al-Mahdi's perception of playing a mediating role was more articulate. Mediation was to become one of the main functions of Sudanese foreign policy; it was to be a part of the solution of the Sudanese internal problems; and it was to enhance the independence of the Sudan. Al-Mahdi proposed mediation between Libya and Egypt, Iran and Iraq, and Libya and Chad. Most of his mediating efforts were not successful for reasons inherent in the very concept of good neighborhood. The concept entailed restrictions of the influence of some powers such as Egypt, Ethiopia, and Iraq in Sudanese domestic politics. These countries, consequently, perceived the concept and its adjunct mediating role as antagonistic to their foreign policy interests in Sudan.

Further, this orientation was not based on a consensus inside Sudan. Good neighborhood policy stood against one of the most enduring characteristics in Sudanese politics: transnational links and clientelism. It ran against the transnational links that the Umma party of Sadiq Al-Mahdi himself cultivated with Libya during Numieri's regime and with the long-standing relations of the DUP with Egypt.

The informal foreign policy orientation was significant due to three sources. The first source was the fragmentation of boundaries between Sudan and the surrounding countries as was explained. The second reason was the historical legacy of the formation of the modern Sudanese state, which emerged as a result of the Egyptian occupation of 1821–1822. From that time until 1956 the Egyptian and Sudanese political histories had great affinities. As with Ethiopia, geography and ethnicity tied the two countries together. The third was the war in the South (1955–1972 and 1982 until the present) during which relations between the political parties and the southern rebels and regional states such as Egypt, Ethiopia, and Kenya were paramount in making war or peace.

With the ascendancy of Al-Beshir to power, the concept of good neighborhood has been of little influence in shaping Sudanese foreign policy. Al-Beshir asserted from the very beginning that the relationship with Egypt is a strategic and special one. He adopted a different perception to the solution of the South problem. In July 1989, Sudan and Ethiopia, with the encouragement of Egypt, agreed to link the settlement of the war in the South to the termination of the war in Eritrea. That was a radical departure from Al-Mahdi's views, which did not link the two issues. If these tendencies continue, the Sudanese foreign policy orientation may change from restricting the impact of social fragmentation upon foreign policy to manipulating fragmentation for foreign policy purposes.

THE DECISION-MAKING PROCESS

Under Al-Mahdi, Sudan's foreign policy was made by four actors: the prime minister and his office, minister of foreign affairs, the Council of the Head of the State, and the Defense Council. The primary actor was the prime minister, followed by the minister of foreign affairs. The Defense Council was responsible for issues of Sudanese national security. The Council of the Head of the State (headed by Ahmed Al-Mirghani, a core member of the Democratic Unionist party), exercised, constitutionally, nominal executive powers as those of the head of state in the parliamentary system. Al-Mahdi displayed heavy personal interest in foreign policy issues and on important issues ran the day-to-day foreign policy affairs. As for Al-Mirghani, he enjoyed great room for informal influence on the decision-making process for two reasons. The first reason was his personal status as a member of the leading family in the Al-Khatmiyya sect. The second reason was his strong and sympathetic relations with Egypt.

In many cases Al-Mahdi conducted himself in foreign policy through personal assistants for special missions and as emissaries. One example was retired Lt. Gen. Fadlala Borma whom Al-Mahdi sent to Libya to mediate between Libya and Chad.[31] (Borma, a state minister for defense from February 1987 to April 1987, was from the Al-Messeriyya tribe and had an affiliation to Al-Ansar sect.) Ibrahim Al-Amin was sent to Cairo on many occasions to help improve relations. (Al-Amin, confidant of Al-Mahdi, a medical doctor, was head of the Umma Cairo office when the Umma party was in the opposition to Numieri, a governor of Khartoum from 1985 to 1986, a member of the Political Bureau of the Umma party, and a minister of expatriate affairs in the last cabinet before the coup.) From the available data, it is doubtful that Al-Mahdi's assistants operated in coordination with the foreign ministry.

Six ministers assumed the portfolio of foreign ministry during the period from April 1986 to June 1989. They were Al-Sharif Zien Al-Abdien Al-Hendi, Muhamed Tawfiq Ahmed, Ma'mon Senada, Hussein Suliman Abu-Salah, Hassan Al-Turabi, and Said Ahmed Al-Hussein. All but Al-Turabi were leading members of DUP, which believed in Sudan's special relationship with Egypt. But it appears that this specific view of the five foreign ministers did not constrain Sadiq Al-Mahdi from lowering the level of cooperation with Egypt. The limited power of the foreign minister revealed the declining institutional role of the ministry. The prime ministerial monopoly of foreign policy reflected the presidential legacy inherited from the long period of military presidentialism of Numieri, 1969–1985.

The role of the foreign ministry expanded after 1985 only on two occasions: during the uprising against the Numieri regime in 1985 and during the military-civilian transitional government from 1985 to 1986. In the first case, the foreign ministry succeeded in influencing the uprising leadership to issue Declaration No. 3 on April 10, 1985,[32] in which there was an emphasis on the need for reconciliation with the surrounding countries and for solving regional problems through negotiation and diplomatic means. The second case was the signing of the Koka Dam Accord on March 24, 1986, between a delegation of the political forces that championed the uprising against Numieri, and SPLM/SPLA. The accord laid out for the first time since the renewal of the war in the South a framework for peace that was influenced by the foreign ministry's experts' opinions. The Umma party signed the accord but later when Al-Mahdi assumed the prime ministership he rejected it.

Little is known of the Defense Council's membership and activities. Headed by Al-Mahdi, the council included a few of Al-Mahdi's selected officers. One of the demands of the memorandum by the general commander of the army in 1989 was the enlargement of the membership to include senior active officers. According to available sources of data, the Defense Council was involved in making decisions concerning the military intervention in Darfur.

In general, although the prime minister was the trump card in the foreign policy decision-making process, his power was somewhat limited by the enduring transnational links of many important forces in Sudan as well as by the protracted war in the South. Further, his personal indecision and inability to commit himself on vital issues created an atmosphere of ambivalence in foreign policy.

Under Al-Beshir's military rule, there has been a revival of presidential legacy in foreign policy–making. The status of the foreign ministry continued to deteriorate. Furthermore, he has shown signs of ambivalence with regard to problems in the South.

FOREIGN POLICY BEHAVIOR

This section deals with Sudan's foreign policy behavior at the global and regional levels, particularly under Al-Mahdi. Foreign policy behavior under Al-Beshir is mentioned to indicate elements of continuity and change. Behavior vis-à-vis five main regional states—Egypt, Libya, Saudi Arabia, Chad, and Ethiopia—is given special attention.

The Global Level

Sudanese global relations are governed by its relations with the surrounding countries. The position of Sudan as the gate to the Horn of Africa, a bridge between the Arab world and Africa, and an important backdoor to Middle East politics shapes Sudan's relations on the global level.

The United States. After the fall of Numieri in April 1985, Sudan's primary objective was to rationalize relations with the United States. U.S.-Sudanese relations under Numieri, particularly during the last three years of his regime, were special yet inconsistent. The United States considered Sudan an important security asset and perceived it as a barrier against the spread of Libyan-Ethiopian-Soviet radicalism. The United States consequently raised the level of strategic cooperation with Sudan in terms of intelligence activities, diplomatic and strategic support, and financial assistance. Conversely, the United States grew dissatisfied with Numieri's unstable domestic politics, particularly over the South issue, the implementation of *Shari'a* law, and economic mismanagement. The United States had to freeze $194 million of economic aid to pressure Numieri into reforming his domestic politics.

The United States continued pressuring Sudan through economic aid during the transitional period (1985–1986). That came as the result of the transitional government's refusal to take part in the joint military maneuvers with the United States and Egypt (Bright Star maneuvers) and the failure to reach an agreement with the IMF on economic refrm. Political instability-cum-fragmentation, Libyan intervention in Sue politics, and the transitional government's efforts to normalize relations with Libya intensified tension in U.S.-Sudanese relations.

The main concern of Al-Mahdi after April 1986 was how to renew U.S. economic assistance to Sudan and at the same time pursue his policy of good neighborhood, which entailed mending relations with countries perceived as hostile by the United States. Although he succeeded in securing economic aid from the United States, the relations remained intense and unsettled.

Al-Mahdi's behavior toward the peace settlement in the South and relations with Libya and Iran antagonized the United States. As for the South issue, although the United States shared Sudan's position of strategic hostility toward Ethiopia, the United States encouraged direct negotiation between the government and SPLM/SPLA. In December

1987, a high-ranking U.S. military delegation visited Sudan and concluded successful negotiations with the general commander of the army. Tension between the United States and Al-Mahdi ensued over the relative distance between Garang's position and Ethiopian policies. In March 1989, a U.S. congressional delegation visited the South and met with Garang. Later on in May 1989 the United States officially invited him for a state visit. Although Al-Mahdi strongly objected to the visit and the invitation, he continued close strategic-military cooperation with the United States. The United States was able to bring Al-Mahdi to conclude a successful round of negotiations with Garang on June 10–11, 1989.

As for Sudanese-Libyan relations, the United States had to exert pressures to restrict Sudanese tolerance of the Libyan military and political encroachment in Sudan. In September 1986, Al-Mahdi's government offered to mediate between the United States and Libya, but nothing was concluded. However, Al-Mahdi's government was responsive in curtailing Libyan territorial threats against U.S. interests in Sudan.

The coming of Al-Beshir through a military coup invited some U.S. reservations. The U.S. government publicly regretted the fall of democratic institutions in Sudan. Three days after the coup, Al-Beshir openly asked the U.S. government to recognize the new government. Until the end of August 1989, the U.S. administration did not give an official answer. However, the Bush administration continued contacts with Al-Beshir's government particularly on the issues of humanitarian aid and peace in the South.

The Soviet Union. One goal of Sudanese foreign policy after the fall of Numieri was to normalize relations with the Soviets. The transitional government made certain to assert in November 1985 that the U.S. Rapid Deployment Force was not stationed in Sudan. The new government asked the United States to evacuate its military equipment that was left behind in Port Sudan after joint military maneuvers in 1982.

Al-Mahdi's visit to the Soviet Union in August 1986 brought to an end fifteen years of estrangement between the two countries. During the Numieri era relations with the Soviets deteriorated as a consequence of the failure of the Communist coup of July 1971, which Numieri accused the USSR of supporting. He withdrew the Sudanese ambassador from Moscow. In 1977, he asked the Soviets to withdraw ninety of their experts and to reduce the size of their diplomatic mission.

Al-Mahdi was successful and secured Soviet military spare parts. The Soviets were responsive though cautious to Sudanese rapprochement efforts. The Soviet Union activated trade and cultural relations with Sudan but was restrained in mediating between Sudan and Ethiopia or SPLM/SPLA. The Soviet-Sudanese relations under Al-Mahdi were moderate, without political or strategic overtone.

Maintaining normal relations with the Soviets has been one of Al-Beshir's prime concerns. Two weeks after the coup, he emphasized Sudan's need for Soviet technical help in renovating Soviet-built factories and maintaining Soviet weaponry in Sudan.

China. Sudan's relations with China were excellent under Numieri. Numieri visited China three times in 1970, 1977, and 1984. Sudan aimed to counter Soviet hostility with close relations with China. Under the transitional government, the army chief of staff visited China in January 1986. Agreements of technical assistance, trade, and supply of military spare parts were concluded.

Iran. The relations with Iran before 1974 were greatly constrained by the position of the Shah's support of Israel. In the mid- and late 1970s, relations between the two countries improved as a result of the Egyptian-Iranian rapprochement during the 1973 war, the beginning of the Egyptian-Israeli peace process, the severing of Sudanese-Iraqi relations in July 1971 (because of Iraqi support of the coup against Numieri), and the growing affinities of the Egyptian-Sudanese relations within the general context of Western alliances and interests. In this context, Numieri visited Iran in February 1974. (It was the first visit by a Sudanese president.) Furthermore, Numieri initially approved the dispatching of Sudanese armed forces to replace Iranian forces in Oman.

After the Iranian Islamic revolution in 1979, Sudan's foreign policy followed the steps of Egypt in expressing hostility toward Iran. Moreover, Sudan severed diplomatic relations with Iran and sent military forces to fight by the side of Iraq in the Gulf war, and Numieri accused Iran of trying to destabilize Sudan.

Under the transitional government, Sudanese behavior, in divergence with that of Egypt, changed to resume close relations with Iran. Diplomatic relations were renewed in August 1985 and Al-Mahdi paid an official visit to Iran in December 1986, following two visits of high-ranking Iranian foreign ministry officials in August 1985 and in June 1986.

The growing closeness of the Sudanese-Iranian relations after 1986 owed much to Sudan's need for oil and financial aid and the Sudanese ambition to play a mediating role between the Arab Gulf states and Iran. In the joint Sudanese-Iranian communiqué after the visit of the Sudanese minister of energy to Teheran in September 1986, Iran made an explicit commitment to supply Sudan with significant portions of its oil requirements.

Sudan's foreign policy behavior vis-à-vis Iran was constrained by Iran's hostile attitude toward Saudi Arabia, Iraq, and Egypt. Sudan officially protested the Iranian involvement in the Mecca riots in August 1987. Sudan was careful not to allow Sudanese-Iranian relations to be seen as hostile to Iraq, Egypt, and Saudi Arabia.

The Regional Level

Egypt. One of the major aims of Al-Mahdi was to change the nature of Egyptian-Sudanese relations from being special to normal interstate relations. During 1986 and 1989, the transitional government and Al-Mahdi succeeded in reducing major facets of Egyptian-Sudanese relations into insignificance. In 1987, Decision No. 220 cancelled the Integration

Scheme between Egypt and Sudan. In its place, Al-Mahdi proposed a loose framework of understanding called the Charter of Fraternity. During his visit to Egypt in February 1987, Egypt and Sudan agreed upon the charter, which meant very little in practice.

Within this framework, an Egyptian-Sudanese committee was formed on the ministerial level to function as an institutional framework for cooperation. The Egyptian prime minister visited Sudan three times (November 28, 1987, April 9, 1988, and October 8, 1988). A number of Sudanese ministers and technical experts came to Cairo several times and concluded technical agreements.

Egyptian-Sudanese relations suffered from strategic divergence regarding the approach to the war in the South. Sudan viewed the war as a form of external aggression emanating from Ethiopia; Egypt perceived it as an internal problem related to Sudanese domestic politics. Egypt continued to provide Sudan with needed weapons but without making a defense commitment against Ethiopia.

It seems that Egypt's accommodating response did not resolve much of the political and security tension in the relations nor did it help to overcome the mutual mistrust between Al-Mahdi and President Hosni Mubarak of Egypt. Al-Mahdi cancelled three times a planned visit to Egypt under different pretexts. The propaganda war occasionally erupted over a number of political issues such as Egypt's support of Numieri after 1985 (Egypt granted him political asylum in 1985), Sudanese-Libyan relations, the war in the South, and Egyptian relations with Ethiopia.

On the other hand, representatives of most political forces and parties visited Egypt either to gather support for their position in Sudan or to nurse their transnational links with Egypt. Mohamed Othman Al-Mirghani, the leader of the Democratic Unionist party and Egypt's traditional political ally, visited Cairo three times in 1988 (March 5, August 3, and September 24). These visits involved coordination with Egypt of the DUP's initiative to conclude an agreement with SPLM/SPLA. The visits also signaled the steady alliance between Egypt and the DUP which was visibly demonstrated when in March 1988 Ahmed Al-Mirghani demanded—in close coordination with DUP—Al-Mahdi publicly apologize to Egypt after Al-Mahdi accused Egypt of sluggishness in supplying Sudan with weapons. Leaders of other forces also visited Egypt for negotiation with Egyptian officials. The Sudanese Communist party, southern parties, Al-Turabi, the leader of the National Islamic Front, and emissaries from SPLM all visited Egypt during the period 1986–1989.

The coming of Al-Beshir to power was welcomed by Egypt. Immediately after the coup Egypt officially recognized the new regime and sent a delegation headed by the director of intelligence to demonstrate its support. The first foreign visit by Al-Beshir was made to Egypt. Egyptian-Sudanese relations improved dramatically for some time. However, Egypt started to see some forthcoming inconveniences in relations with Sudan as a result of the growing reluctance of Al-Beshir to make commitments on vital economic and political issues.

Saudi Arabia. The general pattern of Sudanese-Saudi relations has been one of accommodation. For Sudan, Saudi Arabia has been needed for its massive influence upon important sociopolitical forces in Sudan and its financial resources. Traditional forces such as Sufi orders, modern forces such as businessmen, and sectors of professionals and religious forces such as the Muslim Brotherhood and the National Islamic Front all have connections with Saudi Arabia.

The fact that the traditional parties and the National Islamic Front controlled the parliament and formed the government greatly enhanced cooperation between the two countries. In June 1986, the Saudi foreign minister visited Sudan, and the head of the Sudanese state, Ahmed Al-Marghani, visited Saudi Arabia. Saudi-Sudanese cooperation involved the means for revitalizing the Sudanese economy and substantial humanitarian aid to Sudan. Another source of Saudi interest in Sudan was the continued implementation of the Islamic *Shar'ia.*

Sudan and Saudi Arabia shared the same strategic view of hostility toward the Ethiopian Marxist regime. Saudi Arabia backed Al-Mahdi with moral and diplomatic support in his rivalry with Ethiopia. Further, Saudi Arabia acted to punish Ethiopia for its alleged attack on Sudan. In December 1987 Saudi Arabia communicated to Sudan its refusal to receive an Ethiopian delegation seeking financial assistance. As for the Iranian threat, Sudan unsuccessfully proposed its mediation between the two countries and condemned Iranian internal destabilization of Saudi Arabia. However, this economic and strategic cooperation did not produce any formal agreement between the two countries. In February 1987, Sudan proposed a Framework of Fraternity with Saudi Arabia which the Saudis did not welcome.

Saudi Arabia was the second Arab country after Egypt that Al-Beshir visited. The visit came in the context of Al-Beshir's request for financial aid and oil. Although Saudi Arabia did not officially recognize the new regime, it continues to supply Sudan with humanitarian aid.

Libya. Relations between Libya and Sudan continued to grow during the civilian government. Under the transitional government, a military cooperation agreement was signed in July 1985. Al-Mahdi visited Libya several times. Four months after his assumption of power, Sudan signed a treaty of commercial, cultural, and labor cooperation with Libya that also included a plan for integration between Darfur region and Kufra region in Libya. Furthermore, relations developed in October 1988 to the level of conducting a formal negotiation for unification. Within this framework, Libya supplied Sudan with financial assistance, weapons, free oil, and political support against SPLM/SPLA and increased the number of Sudanese working in Libya.

The relationship, however, had three major problems. The first problem was related to Libyan military intervention into Darfur region and Libya's slow response to the Sudanese request for evacuation. The second was the activities of the Libyan Cultural Bureau in Khartoum. The third was the rejection by the DUP of the unification scheme with Libya that was encouraged by the prime minister. The three setbacks were moderated through direct contact between the two governments.

Chad. Al-Mahdi adopted a policy of neutrality vis-à-vis the conflict between the Chadian factions and Libyan involvement in the war. Through this policy Sudan reached an agreement with Chad for good neighborhood and borders security. A Chadian-Sudanese committee was formed. In December 1988 Al-Mahdi successfully concluded a deal with Chad, with Libyan consent, to shield the Sudanese territory from the impact of Libyan-Chadian conflict.

But relations with Chad deteriorated as a result of the coup attempt made by the Chadian general commander of the army in May 1989 and his escape to Sudan seeking harbor among his tribesmen in Darfur. Chadian forces pursued him and arrested him in Sudan.

Ethiopia. Sudan's relations with Ethiopia have been troubled in the last two decades especially in view of Ethiopia's support of SPLM/SPLA. In 1983 Numieri severed diplomatic relations with Ethiopia accusing it of interfering in Sudanese domestic affairs. Under the transitional government relations were restored in October 1985. But they suffered from Sudan's continuous accusations of Ethiopian support of SPLM/SPLA. In return Ethiopia complained of Sudan's support of secessionist movements in Eritrea and in the Ethiopian hinterland.

Relations with Ethiopia were pursued by Al-Mahdi in the hope of gaining its support in the South. In this context, the Sudanese-Ethiopian committee was revived in 1986. The committee met in May 1988 in Addis Ababa and emphasized the principles of mutual noninterference and respect of sovereignty between the two states.

In dealing with Ethiopia, Al-Mahdi's position was that, if peace were to be achieved in the South, it should come as a result of direct negotiation between Sudanese and Ethiopian authorities. The implication being that peace should not lead to an increase in the political power of any of the Sudanese political parties. That was why he rejected the agreement for peace reached by the southern parties with SPLM in August 1987 and the one signed by the DUP and Ethiopia in November 1988. In a nutshell, Al-Mahdi wanted the war to be settled through him as prime minister and thus be conceived as a victory for the Umma party. He was ready to dilute and frustrate other peace efforts if they promoted his political competitors.

CONCLUSION

The general pattern of a Sudanese foreign policy behavior has been shaped by the following four determinants: (1) the need for external sources of finance; (2) the detrimental impact of regional and global alliances on national security; (3) the significance of regional clientelism; and (4) the impact of societal fragmentation on political stability and the freedom of the decision-maker. This pattern took on different forms depending upon the strategic changes in the region, the nature of the Sudanese political regime, and magnitudes of social change.

The dilemma of the Sudanese foreign policy–maker stems from the specificities of Sudan as a geographically large country, economically poor, politically unstable, demographically diverse and culturally divided. In this situation, the rationality of foreign policy is not primarily to maximize benefits but rather to minimize threats and dangers.

Thus, it was surprising that Khartoum was carried away in the violent days of the Gulf crisis and took a definite position in support of Iraq. Two factors account for the Sudanese behavior. First, Iraq was the major source for cheap, almost free, oil for Sudan, and—what was even more important—Baghdad provided Sudan with arms in its war with the South. Second, in the quest to prove independence from Egypt, the ruling military junta perhaps thought of playing the Iraqi card against Egypt. If Iraq were to get away with its adventure, Sudan would have greatly improved its position. Alas, nothing of this proved true, and Sudan emerged from the crisis in a more difficult situation. In addition to its usual economic and political domestic problems, its closest ally, Libya, came closer to Cairo during the crisis. Sudan must feel isolated and threatened. It lost the financial help of the Gulf countries, the sympathy of many western states, and its source of cheap oil. Whether Iran will be interested in rescuing Sudan, which has declared the implementation of Islamic law, is yet to be seen. The prime issue will continue to be Sudan's relations with Egypt.

NOTES

1. On the premodern history of Sudan, see R. S. O'Fahey and J. L. Spaulding, *Kingdoms of the Sudan* (London: Methuen, 1974); O.G.S. Crowford, *The Funj Kingdom of Sennar* (London: John Bellows, Gloucester, 1951).

2. On the modern history of Sudan, see P. M. Holt, *A Modern History of the Sudan* (London: Weidenfeld and Nicolson, 1962); Mohamed Omer Beshir, *The Southern Sudan: Background to Conflict* (London: C. Hurst and Co., 1967).

3. On the history of the Sudanese-Ethiopian settlement of boundaries, see El-Sayed Ali Ahmed Felifel, "The Drawing of Sudanese-Ethiopian Boundaries and Its Impact on the Tribes of Watawit, Berta, Burun and Khama," Paper presented to the International Symposium of the Nile Basin, University of Cairo, Institute of African Research and Studies, March 1987 (in Arabic).

4. On Libyan-Sudanese boundaries, see Faisal Abdel-Rahman Ali Taha, "The Sudan-Libya Boundary," *Sudan Notes and Records* 58 (1977), pp. 65–72.

5. Abdel Aziz Kamel, *Studies in Human Geography of Sudan* (Cairo: Dar el-Ma'arf, 1972), p. 70.

6. On ethnicity and nation-building in Sudan, see Mohamed Omer Beshir et al., *The Sudan: Ethnicity and National Cohesion*, The Bayreuth African Studies Series (Bayreuth: University of Bayreuth, 1984).

7. The Gizerah Scheme is a case in point. See Hyder Ibrahim Ali, "On the Development and Social Change in Sudan," in *Proceedings of A Symposium on Socio-Economic Formation in the Arab Countries* (Kuwait: The Arabic Institute for Planning, 1983), pp. 434–437.

8. Villages in Kordofan are a case in point. See *ibid.*, p. 430.

9. Dinka economy is an example. See George Tombe Lako, "The Impact of the Jonglei Scheme on the Economy of the Dinka," *African Affairs* 84 (January 1985), pp. 21–33.

10. Ali, "On Development and Social Change," p. 438, fn. 1.

11. Republic of Sudan, Ministry of Social Welfare, Zakat and Displaced: Commission of Displaced, *Memorandum on Public Policy toward the Flyers*, October 29, 1988.

12. On the experience of the democracy and civilian regimes in Sudan, see Mohamed Ahmed Mahgoub, *Democracy on Trial* (London: Andre Deutsch, 1974).

13. On the dynamics of politics under the military regimes, see Tim Niblock, *Class and Power in Sudan* (London: The Macmillan Press, Ltd., 1987).

14. On civil-military relations in Sudan, see Muddathir Abdel-Rahim, *Changing Patterns of Civilian-Military Relations in the Sudan*, Research Report No. 4 (Uppsala, Sweden: The Scandinavian Institute of African Studies, 1978); and Gehad Auda, "Compradorism and Military Rule: The Case of Sudan Under Nemiri," in *Proceedings of African Latin American Dialogue: Seminar III*, Ministry of Foreign Affairs, Institute of Diplomatic Studies (Cairo: Dar el-Ma'arf, 1986), pp. 71–83.

15. Interview with Mansour Khalid in *Sudan Now* 10 (August 1985), pp. 9–10.

16. Ali Abdel Gadir Ali, *Some Aspects of the Sudan Economy*, Post-Graduate Teaching Material Series No. 1 (University of Khartoum: Development Studies and Research Center, 1984), p. 11.

17. *Ibid.*, pp. 14–15.

18. World Bank, *Report on Development in the World, 1988*, p. 260 (in Arabic).

19. World Bank, *World Debt Tables: External Debt of Developing Countries, 1988–1989*, p. 266.

20. *Ibid.*

21. *Ibid.*

22. *The Middle East and North Africa 1988* (London: Europa Publications, 1989), p. 715.

23. Gehad Auda, "Compradorism and Military Rule," p. 80.

24. *The Military Balance 1988–1989* (London: International Institute of Strategic Studies), pp. 114–115.

25. *Ibid.*

26. The General Secretary of the Council of Ministers, *Speeches of Sadiq al-Mahdi May 16, 1986–December 31, 1988*, 3 vols (Khartoum: Government Publications, n.d.). (Hereafter referred to as *Sadiq Al-Mahdi Speech.*)

27. *Sadiq Al-Mahdi Speech*, March 18, 1987, 2d vol., p. 66.

28. *Ibid.*, p. 73.

29. *Sadiq Al-Mahdi Speech*, December 12, 1988, 3d vol., pp. 241–258.

30. *Sadiq Al-Mahdi Speech*, December 16, 1988, 3d vol., p. 267.

31. Mentioned in *Sadiq Al-Mahdi Speech*, March 23, 1987, 2d vol., p. 94.

32. *The Sudanese Embassy in Cairo*, public circular, April 10, 1985.

Revisionist Dreams, Realist Strategies: The Foreign Policy of Syria

Raymond A. Hinnebusch

Syria's foreign policy is ultimately rooted in the historical frustration of Syrian nationalist aspirations by Western imperialism. In the wake of the 1917 Arab revolt, Syrians expected the creation of an independent Arab state in historic Syria (Bilad Al-Sham) linked to a wider Arab federation. Instead, betraying their promises to the Arabs, the Western powers subjugated the Arab East, dismembered historic Syria into four ministates, Syria, Jordan, Lebanon, and Palestine, and sponsored the colonization and establishment of the state of Israel in Palestine.[1] In time, Syria gained political independence, but its separation from Jordan, Lebanon, and the Arab world proved irreversible; Israel became a formidable enemy on Syria's doorstep and a permanent obstacle to its nationalist aspirations. The resulting powerful brew of anti-imperialist, anti-Zionist, pan-Arab, and pan-Syrian sentiment has imparted an enduring revisionist and irredentist thrust to Syrian foreign policy. This revisionism reached a climax in the effort of the radical wing of the Ba'th party (1966–1970) to make Damascus the bastion of a pan-Arab revolution and a war of liberation in Palestine. This, however, only brought on the 1967 defeat and the Israeli occupation of new Arab lands, including the Syrian Golan Heights. This defeat generated intense new security fears in Syria, gave new roots to revisionism, and further locked Syria into the conflict with Israel and its backers.

But a foreign policy is shaped by capabilities as well as frustrations, fears, and desires, and the truncated Syrian state provides a slim resource base for a revisionist foreign policy. The 1967 defeat brought home the high costs of messianic revisionism and provoked the rise to power of Hafiz Al-Asad, a leader who, while no less stamped by Syria's grievances and dreams, was prepared to chart a more realistic course matching

Syrian objectives and means. He scaled down Syria's objectives, focusing them on recovery of the occupied territories, defense of the Syrian state, and enhancement of its stature in the Arab world; he also greatly upgraded Syrian capabilities. Yet, as the capabilities of his adversaries and the intractability of Syria's environment simultaneously increased, the gap between goals and means has persisted and the attainment of even Syria's scaled-down goals has proved elusive. In these conditions, earlier ambitions and grievances have remained alive and Syrians have yet to be fully reconciled to the status quo state system. Thus, Syrian policy continues to be buffeted between persisting revisionist dreams and the constraints of Syria's capabilities and environment.

THE DOMESTIC ENVIRONMENT: THE SHAPING OF FOREIGN POLICY DETERMINANTS AND CAPABILITIES

Geography, Society, Economy

Syria's geographic position in the heart of the Arab East and astride a land without a historic tradition of statehood has shaped a foreign policy orientation that looks outward to the wider Arab world. This position is also highly vulnerable to external pressures, being unprotected by natural boundaries and exposed on all sides to countries that, at one time or another, have constituted threats: Jordan, Turkey, Iraq, and, above all, Israel. Syria lost the Golan Heights, its one natural defense against its main enemy, Israel, in 1967 and is also vulnerable to Israeli outflanking movements through Jordan and Lebanon. Syria's relatively small size and population provide a limited manpower base and little strategic depth or deterrence to invasion. The dominance of Syria's regional environment by threats and constraints inevitably makes security a prime preoccupation. But the country's Arab centrality and front-line position with Israel do give it an importance that can be parlayed into resources—notably Arab aid—and diplomatic support beyond its own borders.

The population has grown substantially, exceeding 10 million in the 1980s, but is still at a medium level of development, a mere step removed from the village and possessing limited modern skills and organizational capabilities. Total national mobilization is obstructed by a multitude of social and ideological cleavages, notably the antiregime animosity of the old upper classes displaced by the Ba'th and wider resentment of the disproportionate representation of sectarian minorities (notably the Alawis, 12% of the population) in the regime at the expense of the Sunni majority (75% of the population).

Syria's economy is too slim to support its foreign policy commitments. While sustained bursts of growth have widened and diversified the economic base of national power, industrial and technological capacity remains limited. State domination of the economy has, however, harnessed national resources to foreign policy goals: 15–17% of gross national product (GNP) and almost a third of public expenditures have been devoted to defense. Twenty percent of manpower serves in the armed forces.[2] But development and consumption also make claims on limited resources, and a growing resource gap has heightened Syrian dependence on external aid and loans, chiefly from the Arab oil countries, the Soviet bloc, and Western Europe. Only the diversification of this dependence eases the constraints it puts on Syria's policy options. By the 1980s the growing resource demands of the state had become a heavy burden on the economy which helped bring growth to a halt. Moreover, external aid declined (Arab aid may have fallen by one- to two-thirds of the $1.8 billion received in 1978) while the Soviet military debt burgeoned. The growing economic pressures could ultimately force a change in foreign policy.

Military Capabilities

Syria's military capabilities have continually expanded, especially under Asad, resulting in an enormous military machine for a country its size, although it has developed much less in qualitative terms. The rudimentary army at independence grew by the late 1960s into a 75,000-man force equipped with 450 tanks and 140 combat aircraft, but the quality of the politicized officer corps was limited. Asad built up the professionalism and morale of the armed forces and in the 1973 war their fighting spirit was high. The lack of experienced command was, however, manifested in an unsophisticated steamroller offensive and the failure to seize strategic points on the Golan which allowed an Israeli counterattack; but subsequently the army's stubborn dug-in defense made Israeli advances slow and costly. While Syria's air defense umbrella limited Israeli air superiority over the battlefield, the Syrian air force, with inferior planes and pilots, could not make deep offensive strikes or defend Syria from deep penetration attacks on economic targets.[3]

The military balance between Israel and Syria has historically been a component of a larger balance between Israel and a potential Arab war coalition. In 1973, the Egyptian-Syrian war coalition was the heart of this balance, though Iraq also contributed to it. But as Egypt's peace treaty and Iraq's war with Iran took them out of this coalition, Syria was left alone facing Israel and at a quantitative as well as a qualitative disadvantage. Asad therefore set out, with Soviet help, to acquire "strategic parity." Syria's late 1970s force of 230,000 men, 2,500 tanks, and 500 planes was both bigger and better equipped than in 1973 but remained inferior to Israel in leadership, organization, and training. The U.S. supply of Israel with the world's most electronically advanced weaponry also kept Syria's Soviet-equipped forces a technological step behind. In the 1982 Lebanon war the odds were stacked against Syria. Israel's force was larger and Syria allowed itself to be taken by surprise. Syria suffered dramatic losses in the air, where technology counts the most, and a neutralization of its air defense led to equipment losses on the ground, too. Syria's ground forces were often effective and stubborn, inflicting serious losses on Israel, but were forced to retreat from strategic sectors of Lebanese terrain.[4]

Nevertheless, at least in defense, the Syrian army has become a formidable force. Since 1973 it has a record of tenacity that has consistently denied Israel a knockout blow. There has been a marked improvement in the technical and tactical capacity of the Syrian soldier, although the army suffers from chronic maintenance and serviceability problems. Reequipped and expanded after the 1982 war, the armed forces had by 1986 5,000 tanks, 650 combat planes, including 200 high-performance aircraft, and 102 missile batteries. Two army corps, totalling 500,000 men, are made up of nine mechanized or armored divisions with their own artillery and air defense. A new Soviet-supplied long-range air umbrella was in place and SS-21 missiles and strike aircraft gave Syria a new capacity to hit targets in Israel itself.[5] A developing chemical weapons capability may become part of Syria's deterrent. A 500,000-man reserve force suggested Syria was approaching the total mobilization achieved by Israel. An Israeli attack on Syria, given this balance of forces, is likely to be very costly, with no guarantee that the Syrian army could be defeated.

Even less, however, does Syria, acting alone, possess a credible offensive capability against Israel. Because the ratio of forces stationed permanently on the Golan is to Syria's advantage (it has six divisions), a Syrian surprise strike might seize at least part of the heights before the rest of Israel's force mobilized; but once this happened, Syria would find itself sharply disadvantaged.[6] Moreover, Lebanon must now be included in the possible theater of operations, forcing Syria to spread its defenses too widely. Syria might still consider a Golan strike desirable if it were likely—as in 1973—to lead to an internationally imposed settlement in which Syria recovered territory. Moreover, were the Arab war coalition to be reconstructed, incorporating with Syria the large Egyptian and battle-tested Iraqi armies, the strategic balance might be decisively altered in the Arab favor. But in 1990 that did not appear to be in the cards.

FOREIGN POLICY ORIENTATION

Role-Conception

Syria has traditionally thought of itself as the "beating heart of Arabism." National identity has focused on a larger Arab nation rather than the contemporary Syrian state, long regarded as a creation of imperialism. Overcoming the fragmentation of the Arab world was seen as the historic mission of Ba'thism, the official ideology; Syria was seen not as a national unit but as a base for this mission. Indeed, Syria has been the most consistent center of Arabist sentiment and is the only Arab country to surrender its sovereignty—in the 1958 union with Egypt—in the name of pan-Arabism.

Since then, however, the gap between this ideal and foreign policy behavior has steadily widened. In 1963, the ostensibly pan-Arabist Ba'th government proved unwilling to sacrifice its power on the altar of reunion with Nasserite Egypt and in 1978 a project to unite Syria and Iraq foundered on similar rivalries between state elites. Forty years of statehood, disappointments with unity experiments, and a growing awareness of the costs of and obstacles to unionist ambitions have made pan-Arabism an ever less immediate determinant of actual Syrian policy. It has increasingly given way to a conventional policy of raison d'état which seeks the defense, power, and prestige of the Syrian state within the existing regional state system.

Nevertheless, Syrians still do not perceive the regional environment as a classical state system of distinct national entities; the Arab states are still thought to make up a nation with an overriding national interest that ought to govern their foreign policies. Syria's special identity remains Arab: It is in the Arab arena that Syria seeks to establish leadership and, indeed, Syrians view Syria as the most Arab of the Arab states and the main champion of the Arab cause. On this basis, Syrian leaders claim the right to define the higher Arab national interest and view Syria's military-security needs—as the most steadfast of the front-line states in the battle with Israel—to be virtually indistinguishable from it. From the viewpoint that what's good for Syria is good for the Arab nation, they have felt entitled to draw on the oil wealth of other Arab states, to demand the expulsion of Egypt from the Arab camp, and even to discipline the pursuit of Palestinian particularism. This view has taken on an even sharper thrust in Syria's relations with the former "fallen away" components of Bilad Al-Sham over which Syria as the "parent state" has come to presume special rights and responsibilities. While this has sometimes been depicted as a pursuit of pan-Syrianism, for most Syrians and their leaders there is not incompatibility between pan-Arabism and "Greater Syria" since the latter is an integral part of the wider Arab nation.

Whatever its pan-Arab intent and justification, Syria's insistence on the priority of its own ends, the resultant pursuit of a Syrian raison d'état, combined with the claim to special rights over the entities of Bilad Al-Sham, were bound to end in conflict with other Arab powers at the expense of Arab solidarity. Moreover, in time, the cumulative parochialism induced by this orientation has circumscribed the practical meaning of Arabism in Syrian decision-making. What, after all, can be the substance of an Arabist policy which supports Iran against other Arab states and attacks the Palestinian resistance, the very expression of the "Arab cause"?

Syria in Its Regional Environment

Israel. The conflict with Israel remains the most central and durable preoccupation of Syrian foreign policy. Syrians perceive Israel as an imperialist-linked colonial-settler state implanted in the heart of historic Syria at the expense of Syria's Palestinian cousins and a permanent obstacle to Arab unity. The two states have fought four major wars and many lesser conflicts in which Israel has typically inflicted punishment or humiliation on Syria. Since 1967 Israel has occupied a chunk of Syrian territory, the Golan Heights. To Syria, history shows Israel to be an inherently expansionist threat to its security. Thus, Syria is locked by the need to recover lost territory and to defend against new expansion into a permanent high-profile conflict with Israel.

Syrian-Israeli animosity escalated from the 1948 war onward, initially feeding on border skirmishes over Israel's encroachment on the demilitarized zones established after the armistice and its subsequent bid to divert the headwaters of the Jordan. Under the radical Ba'th, it was Syria that challenged Israel, giving support to the Palestinian fedayeen and trying to push the Arab states into preparation for a war of Palestinian liberation.[7] But the 1967 defeat forced a realization that Syria can do little to reverse the establishment of the Zionist state. Israel's legitimacy is still denied but under Asad Syria's actual Israeli policy has focused on the recovery of the territories occupied in 1967, including the return of the Golan Heights and the achievement of Palestinian national rights in the West Bank and Gaza.

Syria is prepared to accept an end to the state of war with Israel in return for evacuation of these lands; but is must be a total rollback that deprives Israel of the rewards of conquest and quenches its expansionist impulse. Although a formal peace treaty might be acceptable, Syria prefers the settlement come about through a UN accord. Demilitarized zones and peacekeeping forces are acceptable, provided they are on both sides of the Israeli-Syrian border. In practice, such a settlement would, no doubt, bury the Syrian-Israeli military conflict. But the end of belligerency would entail neither diplomatic nor trade relations which Syria considers the right of any sovereign state to pursue as it wishes. Nor would peace imply Syrian recognition of Israel's right to Palestine and indeed political struggle with Zionism over the rest of Palestine would continue, taking, for example, the form of insistence on the rights of Palestinians to return to and enjoy equal citizenship in Israel; if successful this could ultimately efface Israel's character as an exclusively Jewish state and alien bridgehead in the Arab world.

Asad, a realist, has never believed that negotiations alone could substitute for military strength in the struggle to achieve these goals. But diplomacy, if combined with military power and Arab solidarity, was an indispensable tool in the struggle with Israel. It could win international support important in preventing the isolation of Syria which had previously allowed Israel to attack with impunity. In the belief that diplomacy, exploiting global rivalries and certain conflicts of interest between the United States and Israel, might force an Israeli withdrawal to the 1967 lines, after the 1973 war Asad explored a peaceful settlement of the conflict under international and U.S. auspices. The failure of diplomacy subsequently led him to believe that such a path would be fruitless until Syria and the Arab world achieved military and political parity with Israel and, in the long interim required to achieve this, Syria has largely eschewed negotiations and sought to obstruct U.S.-sponsored ones pursued on Israel's terms. Time, Asad believed, was on the Arabs' side since modernization could only enhance their strength; in the meantime, Syria would keep the Arabs' military option open. Israel, likewise, shows little interest in a settlement with Syria which it regards as implacably hostile yet largely impotent to upset the status quo. Syria and Israel have found ways to control their rivalry, as, for example, in the exercise of mutual restraint for periods in Lebanon. Currently, they are locked in a certain deterrence relationship in which each realizes it has more to lose than to gain by resort to war.[8] This relation is, however, unstable: Syria's frustrations and the heavy burden of "no war/no peace" could tempt it to break the current stalemate. And some Israeli leaders have contemplated a preemptive strike to cut Syria down to size before it becomes an offensive threat.

Arab Actors. Under the radical Ba'thists, Syria distinguished between progressive Arab forces (e.g., Egypt, Algeria, the PLO) and reactionary ones (e.g., Jordan, Saudi Arabia) viewed as agents of Western imperialism, against which it tried to export revolution. Under Asad, Syria seeks to forge and lead a concert of all Arab states, regardless of ideology, aimed at recovering Arab rights from Israel. Syria seeks to mobilize the resources of other Arab states behind its goals in the common struggle and to prevent other Arab actors from pursuing separate tracks in the Arab-Israeli conflict which threaten its strategy and leadership in the Arab arena.

The *Syrian-Palestinian* relation is a complex mixture of alliance and conflict that exemplifies Syria's drive to both advance the Arab cause and subordinate other Arab actors to its strategy. Palestine is seen as the heart of the Arab cause; Syria regards Palestine as a lost part of itself and Palestinians as southern cousins. Championship of Palestine is regarded as an ideological imperative and essential component of regime legitimacy. Syria sees itself as the main champion of the Palestinians, having made the heaviest and most consistent sacrifices in the conflict with Israel and having played the major role in the formation and support of the Palestinian resistance, in keeping the Palestine cause on the world agenda, and in preventing any solution to the Arab-Israeli conflict that ignores it. In the 1960s, the Ba'th was committed to the liberation of all Palestine, but under Asad this evolved into the lesser demand that Palestinian rights be satisfied, defined as a Palestinian state on the West Bank and Gaza and the right of exile Palestinians to return to their homes.[9]

Yet, conflict, as much as solidarity, has marked Syro-Palestinian relations. From the moment the radical Ba'th helped put Fateh on its feet in 1966, Syria and Arafat clashed over who would lead the struggle for Palestine. Syria has claimed tutelage over the Palestinians and the PLO, insisting Palestinian interests not be pursued in conflict with the overall Arab interest the Ba'th claims to represent: Israel is a threat to the whole Arab nation and Palestine is an Arab and Syrian as much as a PLO cause. Syria has also sought to "play the Palestinian card;" Syria's bargaining leverage in the Arab-Israeli conflict would be greatly enhanced if it enjoyed the capacity to veto any settlement of the Palestininan problem that left Syria out or to "deliver" the Palestinians into an acceptable settlement. The PLO has insisted on an independent policy, regardless of Syrian interests, and has sought to preserve its autonomy from Syria by playing against Damascus the influence of Syria's rivals—Egypt, Iraq, Saudi Arabia—a practice that enrages Asad.

Many specific issues have also divided the two parties. Syria and the PLO have suspected each other's ultimate goals. Palestinians have questioned Syria's commitment to Palestinian liberation, fearing it might settle with Israel separately; they also have suspected that incorporation of liberated Palestinian territory into some larger Arab entity might better satisfy Ba'thist ideology or pan-Syrian dreams than independent Palestinian statehood. The two parties have also differed on tactics: Syria has at times challenged Palestinian rejectionism when this has diverged from its own accommodationist tactics and, more recently, Palestinian moderation as it has threatened Asad's own rejectionist tactics.[10] Syria has regarded Palestinian armed struggle against Israel as a means of demonstrating to Israel and its U.S. patron the costs of failure to accommodate Arab interests. But since Asad regards guerrilla war as subordinate in weight and efficaciousness to Syrian power and diplomacy and because it carries grave risks, he has sought to control its scope and timing and constrained it when it invited Israeli retaliation threatening to Syrian security; as this has increasingly become the case, Syria has sought to curb the Palestinian armed struggle, eliminating it on the Golan and dampening it in southern Lebanon. Finally, personal animosities between Arafat and Asad, reinforced by disputes over responsibility for the 1982 defeat in Lebanon, have lent a new durability and intensity to "normal" Syrian-Palestinian frictions.

The diverse instruments by which Syria has sought to control the PLO, ever more intrusive and heavy handed, have led to widening conflict. Damascus long tried to exert influence inside the PLO through Palestinian surrogates such as the Syrian-sponsored guerrilla movement, Al-Sa'iqa, and Syrian-based Palestinian Liberation Army (PLA) units. It has used these groups and alliances with PLO leader Yasser Arafat's rivals to challenge the legitimacy of Arafat's policies and in a drive to depose him. Arrests and armed attacks on Palestinians in the areas where the PLO is vulnerable to Syrian power have escalated from the jailings of Palestinian leaders like Arafat and George Habash in the 1960s to the 1976 armed intervention against the PLO-leftist alliance in Lebanon, to the 1983 siege of Tripoli and the War of the Camps by which Syria sought to drive Arafatists out of Lebanon. As, after 1982, Arafat pursued a negotiated settlement, Syria sponsored the formation of a rival Palestine National Salvation Front made up of various radical splinter groups, but it had limited staying power and has not become a credible alternative to Arafat's PLO.[11]

Relations with *Egypt* have been central to Syrian policy, either as the backbone of or the main weakness in resistance to Israel. Under the radical Ba'th, Syria sought and attained Nasser's acceptance of a joint progressive axis which led both into the shared disaster of 1967. In the early 1970s, a common interest in recovery of the occupied territories, attainable only in concert, cemented the war coalition that made possible the 1973 war and opened prospects for a diplomatic settlement. But Sadat's wartime tactics, which allowed Israel to concentrate its armies against Syria, his acceptance of a cease-fire without Syrian consent, and his unilateral postwar diplomacy, leaving Syria out, shattered the alliance. His separate peace with Israel left Syria vulnerable and without diplomatic leverage.[12] This led to a Syrian bid to prevent the legitimation of Egypt's separate peace and to ostracize and replace its leadership in the Arab world. But, hoping to overcome Syria's isolation and reestablish Arab solidarity, in 1990 Asad moved to reconstruct Syria's historic alliance with Cairo.

Syrian policy toward the "Eastern Front" states of Lebanon, Jordan, and Iraq illustrates both Syria's Arabist obsession with the struggle with Israel and its tendency to confuse Arab and Syrian interests. *Lebanon* is regarded as a sisterly country once a part of Syria in which it has special interests and responsibilities. Yet the radical Ba'th tried to sponsor revolution in Lebanon and turn it into a base for Palestinian fedayeen. Asad initially wished to preserve a controlled fedayeen presence while maintaining Lebanon as a buffer state against Israel for, to the extent it became a "confrontation" state, Syria would be vulnerable to an Israeli drive into Lebanon threatening its western flank. As, after 1975, the breakdown of order in Lebanon and the growing Palestinian presence led to Maronite anti-Arabism and growing Israeli interference, Syria sought hegemony in Lebanon, establishing a dominant military and diplomatic presence. It has aimed at containing security threats, at preserving the unity and Arabism of Lebanon against balkanization and Israeli penetration, and, with little success, at the reconstruction of the country under Syrian tutelage.

Iraq, Syria's militarily strong, oil-rich, Fertile Crescent twin ruled by a wing of the Ba'th party, should have been a pan-Arab partner and natural ally against Israel. Asad initially tried to build a military alliance with Iraq which, in fact, helped defend the Syrian front in the 1973 war. But interparty ideological quarrels, notably Iraq's radical "rejectionism" and its challenges to Syria's claims of Ba'thist and Arab nationalist legitimacy, later transmuted into personal animosity between Asad and Saddam Hussein, have since sharply divided the two states. Hostility was expressed in mutual subversion and in economic conflicts, e.g., over Syria's control of Euphrates water, and Iraq's downgrading of the trans-Syria oil pipeline, threatening Syrian rent from it. The threat of Camp David briefly brought them together in a 1978 unity project but it foundered on mutual leadership fears and Iraqi insistence on ascendance. Asad, seeing Iraq's invasion of an anti-Israeli Iran as a traitorous diversion from the common struggle with Israel, took the Iran-Iraq war as an opportunity to enervate his rival and struck an alliance with non-Arab Iran. The victory of a much strengthened Iraq exposes Syria to a two-front military threat. Asad's fear of Saddam Hussein's ambitions were expressed in his stand against Iraq's invasion of Kuwait.

Syria long regarded *Jordan* as an artificial state carved out of southern Syria, but under Asad Damascus gave up trying to subvert the Hashemite monarchy and sought instead to include it in its strategy against Israel. To Asad, Jordan was a military asset, important in preventing an Israeli outflanking of the Golan defenses; it was also a potential participant in negotiations over the West Bank and had to be kept from making a separate peace with Israel. Syria's growing military preponderance and its control of Jordan's overland access to the west gave Asad leverage over King Hussein. He courted the king, forging an alliance in the 1970s manifested in some economic integration, military cooperation, and Syrian success in containing unilateral Jordanian diplomacy. But Jordan, tiring of the suffocating Syrian embrace, sought a counter in Iraq, joined Iraq over the Iraq-Iran war, and permitted anti-Asad Islamic dissidents to operate from Jordan. In 1980, a period of hostile confrontation began between Jordan and Syria, superseded in the late 1980s by a wary détente. To Syria, Jordan has proven an unreliable, but indispensable partner on the Eastern Front.

Syria's orientation to *Saudi Arabia* manifests Asad's policy of all-Arab solidarity and his drive to mobilize the Arab resources needed to sustain his strategy toward Israel. His radical predecessors, regarding Riyadh as a center of reaction and Western influence that prevented the mobilization of all-Arab resources for the battle, sought without success to encourage the regime's overthrow. Asad, subordinating ideological disputes to all-Arab unity, buried the hatchet with the Saudis in exchange for financial aid. After the October War Syria felt itself entitled to a share of the Saudi oil windfall and complained that Syria had born the brunt of the fighting, while Saudi Arabia reaped the advantages in increased oil prices. But in the late 1970s, Saudi Arabia was the biggest contributor to the fund for "steadfastness" states in the wake of Camp David. To Damascus, the Saudis' stake in their U.S. connection has deterred them from using the oil weapon against the United States, but Syria recognizes their unique influence in Washington to be potentially useful in countering Israel's, whether to get U.S. restraint of or pressure on Israel for a negotiated settlement. In return, the Saudis have expected Syria to refrain from reigniting the Arab ideological war and to restrain radicals, whether leftist Palestinians or pro-Iranian extremists. The Syro-Saudi relation remains uneasy: Saudi Arabia has feared the growth of Syria's influence and deplored its alliance with Iran. The Saudis have used Syria's economic dependency to moderate its radicalism and ambition, while Syria has tried to counter Saudi leverage by raising the spectre of instability which the Saudis so fear. The dispatch of Syrian troops to bolster Saudi Arabia against Iraq is likely to initiate a new stage in Syro-Saudi relations.

Iran. The Islamic revolution, transforming Iran from an ally of Israel into a partisan of the Arab cause, set the stage for a durable, if bizarre, alliance between Syria, a radical Arab republic, and the Iranian theocracy. Syria backed Iran in the war with Iraq: In cutting off the pumping of Iraqi oil across its territory, it damaged Iraq's capacity to finance the war; in posing a certain threat to Iraq's western border and supplying arms to Iran and to Iraqi Kurds, Syria made itself a military nuisance for Iraq. Diplomatically, it prevented the mobilization of the Arab world against Iran. Besides historic animosity for the Iraqi regime, Syria's pro-Iranian policy grew out of resentment at Iraq's diversion of Arab energies from the Arab-Israeli conflict, and a drive to neutralize it in the Arab arena; a certain "Syro-Iranian pincer" could also be used to keep Saudi Arabia and the Gulf states deferent to Syrian interests. A large Iranian delivery of free or low-cost oil buttressed Syria's economy and Iranian-sponsored Shi'ite radicalism proved useful in countering Israeli and U.S. designs in Lebanon. Though Syria opposed Iranian capture of Iraqi territory, its plans for an Islamic regime in Iraq, any expansion of the Gulf war, and hegemony of Islamic radicalism in Lebanon, these strains were not allowed to jeopardize the Iranian alignment.[13]

Syria in Its International Environment

Syria's sense of national victimization at the hands of Western imperialism and the Western backers of Israel shaped an official ideology identifying it as a member of the anti-imperialist Third World camp. As the European powers withdrew from their imperial role in the Middle East, their relations with Syria correspondingly improved and, except under the radical Ba'th, Syria valued economic relations with Western countries. But the *United States*, in its support for Israel, quickly replaced classic imperialism as Syria's antagonist. The formative experience of the current political elite includes a history of U.S. support for Israel and intervention in the Middle East against Syrian interests in the 1950s: efforts to harness Syria to anti-Soviet alliances perceived as neo-imperialistic, intervention with Britain against Arab nationalists in Lebanon and Jordan, attempts to "quarantine" Syria and subvert its nationalist government. Overt acts of U.S. hostility against Syria's Ba'thist regime included Arthur

Goldberg's delay of a UN Security Council meeting allowing Israel to complete its 1967 conquest of the Golan Heights, U.S. preparations to intervene, with Israel, against Syrian forces fighting King Hussein during the 1970 "Black September," and massive U.S. arms shipments during the 1973 war that allowed Israel to reverse Syrian advances and keep its grip on the Golan Heights. Radical Ba'thist thought taught that the United States, the head of the world imperialist bloc, was organically, not accidentally, linked to Israel: Israel was a surrogate acting for U.S. interests and the United States was a vital lifeline and strategic depth without which Israel could not survive. After the 1967 war, diplomatic relations were broken with the United States.

The credible military challenge of the Arabs to Israel in the 1973 war and the subsequent rise of Arab oil power was understood by Syrian leaders as introducing a potential divergence between Israeli and U.S. interests giving new Arab leverage over the United States. Washington might be brought to consider Arab interests and pressure Israel to withdraw from the lands taken in 1967 in order to protect its own stake in the Middle East from the instability inherent in continuing Arab-Israeli conflict. At this juncture, Syria renewed diplomatic relations with the United States and accepted Kissinger's mediation in the Golan Heights disengagement negotiations. The minor Israeli rollback achieved and the brief commitment of the Carter administration to a comprehensive peace seemed to justify the new strategy. Moreover, U.S. mediation with Israel, particularly in assuaging Israeli opposition to Syria's intervention in Lebanon, more than once proved its value in keeping Syro-Israeli rivalry there from escalating out of control. But U.S.-Syrian relations soured over the continuing effort of the United States to keep Israel militarily stronger and divide the Arab world through separate settlements, as manifested in Sinai II, the massive arms shipment to Israel thereafter, and Camp David. Asad has since sought to demonstrate that a credible U.S. role in Middle East diplomacy and a peace essential to regional stability cannot succeed in disregard of Syrian interests. The Reagan administration, viewing Syria as a Soviet surrogate, largely disregarded these interests. Its 1981 intervention in the crisis over Israel's threat to destroy Syrian antiaircraft missiles in Lebanon did seem to show an American recognition of the threat of Syrian-Israeli tension to the wider peace, but Secretary of State Haig's green light to the Israeli invasion of Lebanon showed a greater interest in punishing Syrian "intransigence." The U.S.-Syrian showdown over the 1983 Lebanese-Israeli accord, in which car bombs inflicted heavy casualties on U.S. troops and U.S. guns and planes were used against Syria and its surrogates, brought the two countries to the brink of war, but the failure of U.S. military power to prevail seemed to make Asad's point that Syria cannot be ignored. Syria has also tried to use its "good offices" in obtaining the release of U.S. hostages in Lebanon to make a similar point: that with its cooperation things can be achieved in the Middle East. The United States is unlikely to abandon its reliance on Israel for the evenhanded approach needed to satisfy Syria, but the U.S. interest in stability remains a key to containing further Israeli expansionism of which Syria will continue trying to make use.[14] The passing of the Reagan administration and U.S. support for Syrian policy in Lebanon introduced greater warmth into U.S.-Syrian relations. With the decline of Soviet power, Damascus is aware that better relations with the remaining global superpower are indispensable.

The Soviet Union has been Syria's major international patron. The basis of good Syrian-Soviet relations was laid in the late 1950s when Moscow gave protection to Syria from intense Western pressures and broke a Western arms embargo of the country. Syrians quickly learned that the Soviet Union was the one country willing to supply them with significant amounts of economic and military aid without unacceptable compromise to the nationalist commitments. The leftist ideologues of the radical Ba'th forged a network of political and economic relations which made the Soviet Union Syria's main trading partner and source of development aid and technology. Despite the fall of the radicals and the subsequent relative decline of Syrian economic dependency on the Eastern bloc, the conflict with Israel and unlimited U.S. support for the latter has institutionalized the Soviet-Syrian alliance. Given the high risks of the conflict and the formidable resources of its enemy, Syria cannot do without a powerful patron-protector. While the Soviet Union did nothing to protect Syria in 1967 and the nature of subsequent guarantees is uncertain, the Soviet alliance has had an undoubted deterrent effect that checks Israel's freedom of action against Syria. Only Soviet arms supplies give Syria a credible military capability, and though these arms have typically been of lower quality than U.S. supplies to Israel, they match Syria's absorptive capacity and have arrived in formidable quantities at minimal cost. Huge deliveries made before and during the 1973 war were key to Syria's relative success and were made even at risk to détente. While there were differences between Syria and the USSR over the poor performance of Soviet weapons in the 1982 war, unprecedented postwar deliveries more than replenished Syria's capabilities. In return for its support, the USSR gets military facilities, a conduit for Soviet influence in the area, and a pivotal role in the Middle East diplomacy despite U.S. efforts to exclude it, all the more crucial after Moscow's ouster from Egypt. In essence, Syria has exploited superpower rivalries in successfully enhancing its capabilities well beyond its own slim resource base.

While the Syrian-Soviet relation is an unequal client-patron one, Syria has never allowed Soviet wishes to shape its vital decisions and has resisted Soviet pressures on several occasions. Several radical Ba'thist initiatives in the conflict with Israel, such as support for fedayeen raids on Israel and the 1970 intervention in Jordan, were taken against Soviet counsels of caution. Soviet objections to Asad's 1976 assault on the PLO and calls for cooperation with the Palestinians or Iraq have been ignored.

The key source of friction in the relation was the Syrian feeling that the Soviets were unwilling to make commitments to them comparable to those of the United States to Israel. Syria also wants to be the Soviets' main if not sole Arab partner, while the Soviets sought broader ties. In the 1970s, the Soviets feared that Syria might chuck them as Sadat did were the United States to satisfy Syrian demands, and they felt that Syria ignored their wider Middle Eastern interests. But as Syria was shut out of the U.S.-sponsored peace process, Syria's growing need for the USSR led Asad to strengthen his Soviet connection in 1980 through a formal treaty of friendship and defense which he had previously eschewed. The decline of superpower rivalry under Gorbachev and the broadening of Soviet links to other Middle East states has since reduced Syria's value to Moscow, while the declining Soviet willingness to back Syria against Israel has devalued the alliance in Damascus. Nevertheless, as Syria's nearly sole source of arms the USSR remains an irreplaceable patron.[15]

THE DECISION-MAKING PROCESS

The Syrian political structure has in many ways been shaped by its external environment: the product of a nationalist party and an army radicalized by the conflict with Israel, it developed into a huge authoritarian national security state that concentrates power at the very top. It is dominated by a powerful presidency resting on three institutional pillars, the Ba'th party, the military, and the ministerial bureaucracy; the leaders of these institutions make up a power elite that the president both leads and consults in the decision-making process.

Asad's Role

President Hafiz Al-Asad, a man of strong personality, unique authority within the elite, and possessed of wide powers of office, is clearly the dominant decision-maker. As such, Asad has left a distinct personal imprint on Syrian foreign policy. Asad is, first of all, an intense nationalist, strongly committed to the Arab cause, and unprepared to concede major principles; indeed, he would like to be viewed as an Arab nationalist leader of Nasser's stature. The Israelis calculate that as long as he is in power no settlement on their terms can be reached with Syria. But Asad is also a realist rather than an ideologue; he has, in fact, contrasted his realism with the theory of the Ba'th radicals who allowed ideology to dictate policy to the neglect of the calculus of power. No pan-Arab revolutionary, he is a man of order who respects the Arab status quo. Asad tends to think in the objective strategic terms of the military professional. He is cautious, never moving without thorough analysis of the balance of forces, and less ready to expend than to accumulate power used to influence; his harrowing experience in 1967 when, as defense minister, he saw his unprepared forces mauled in a war brought on by the recklessness of ideologically minded colleagues, no doubt helps account for these traits. He is flexible and will bargain if it can be done from a position of enough strength to win some advantage; otherwise, a man of infinite patience, he will wait. He has proven to be an audacious and tenacious bargainer. Thus, in the disengagement negotiations he conducted a tough policy of "fighting while talking"; Kissinger found that, by contrast to Sadat's impulsive tendency to make concessions, in Damascus the smallest issue was a matter of stubborn haggling. Asad also has a cool nerve, can recover from setback, and is uneasily panicked, as the Israelis and Americans, who expected his rapid retreat from Lebanon in 1982, learned to their dismay. Nor will he readily forgive a slight, no little factor in Syria's conflict with the PLO's Arafat. Asad is a shrewd practitioner of power politics, able to manipulate power balances, proxies, threats, and subversion, ruthless toward opponents, and a true Machiavellian prepared to use any means, from the bombardment of civilians to assassinations. Determined, intelligent, energetic, able to learn from mistakes, and with a keen grasp of international affairs, he has developed into a statesman of more than local stature. It is he who almost singlehandedly has turned Syria from a pawn of stronger states into a credible actor in the regional power game.[16]

The Structure of the Decision-Making Arena

While Asad enjoys unique stature inside the Syrian elite, decision-making nevertheless retains a certain collegial character and decisions are made in a relatively stable circle of top foreign policy and military elites who are Asad's colleagues, not mere staff readily dismissed or ignored. First among them is Abdel-Halim Khaddam who by virtue of loyalty to the president, sharp intellect, and his office as foreign minister and then vice-president for foreign affairs, has played a key role in decision-making, especially in presiding over policy in Lebanon. Defense Minister Mustafa Tlas, Chief of Staff Hikmet Shihabi, Deputy Chief of Staff General Ali Aslan, and, until his eclipse, General Naji Jamil, are long-time Asad stalwarts who have presided over the professional military. Security chiefs such as Muhammad Al-Khuli, Ali Duba, and, until 1984, Rifat Al-Asad, the president's brother, have also been part of the inner policy circle. Especially crucial decisions may be decided or at least approved in a wider circle of leaders including the prime minister, the two assistant secretaries of the party, various presidential advisors, and possibly even the full party leadership. Ba'th party congresses have functioned as arenas for discussing and approving the major long-range goals of policy.

While the final decision is his, Asad seems to be a relatively consensual leader who weighs the views of his subordinates. There is some evidence for collegial decision-making: Kissinger found that, by contrast to Egypt where only Sadat had to be convinced, in Syria the whole top leadership had to be collectively persuaded. Dawisha suggests a thirty-eight person consultation unit decided on the 1976 Lebanon intervention, although there are also claims that Asad forced this controversial departure from traditional policy on his reluctant colleagues.[17] There is little doubt that if Asad feels strongly about an action a coalescence of other elites against him is extremely unlikely, that the choice of those to be included in the consultation unit is his, and that he stands above and arbitrates among a typically divided elite. It appears that as his personal stature has increased over time, Asad has become more autocratic. There is certainly no evidence that any elite actor has contested his role as final arbiter and survived politically.

Foreign Policy Factions and Interest Groups

The concentration of power in the top elite permits the making and implementation of foreign policy relatively free of institutionalized constraints. Despite this, the little tolerance of pluralism by the regime and the elites' relative unity under Asad, there is some evidence of divergence in elites' views, sometimes reflective of ties to extra-elite opinion or interests, and some evidence that decision-makers have felt constrained to take account of the expectations or demands of groups below them in the power structure.

There are occasional signs of intra-elite divergences between relatively hawkish and dovish views toward Israel. Elites appear to have been divided over Kissinger's step-by-step diplomacy. Reputedly, a hawkish faction led by Khaddam rejected direct negotiations and partial agreements with Israel under U.S. auspices, believing the post-1973 shift of power to the Arabs permitted Syria to hold out for a comprehensive settlement on its own terms while U.S.-sponsored settlements would put an end to the Arab revolution. Prime Minister Mahmoud Al-Ayubi, arguing that Syrian leverage was at a maximum in the aftermath of the war but less sanguine about the future, is said to have held that negotiations were necessary to get something to show for the war. It was Asad who at the last minute closed the deal on the first disengagement and pulled his hard-line colleagues with him. Elites have also differed in their preference for alignments, for example, over a strong Soviet connection and over the depth of ties with Saudi Arabia. Thus Mustafa Tlas, supposedly speaking for Sunni military, business, and religious opinion, long had a reputation as a critic of the Soviets, especially of Soviet weapons, and for pro-Saudi views. In the late 1970s, Rifat Al-Asad stood out as an advocate of pro-bourgeois and pro-Western opinion in the regime.

The officer corps as a whole has at times had a reputation for radical nationalism; its reluctance to accept the cease-fire in the October War contributed to the Syrian decision to launch a war of attrition on the Golan and Mt. Hermon while the disengagement negotiations were going on. Elements of the military overtly or covertly resisted the 1976 intervention against the Palestinians in Lebanon. Senior professional officers like General Shihabi are thought to be chiefly concerned with the capabilities and integrity of the armed forces, and to be advocates of greater defense spending and of pressure on the USSR for more advanced weaponry. In the 1980s, some generals have reputedly advocated the use of Syria's growing military power in a bid for the Golan before the Israelis strike first, but have been reined in by a cautious Asad.

Ba'th party cadres have at times appeared to constrain the options of top decision-makers by their ideological and nationalist militancy. Prior to the October War, forces in the party remained adamant against a deal with Israel and during the Golan disengagement negotiations, their views still limited Asad's flexibility; to make it palatable he had to portray this agreement as a mere first step in Israeli withdrawal from all the conquered lands. A residue of militant socialists opposed the opening of relations with the West after the war. There has always been a faction in the party that wanted to exchange Syria's Saudi and Egyptian alliances for an Iraqi one. The intervention against Palestinians in Lebanon agitated the party, resulting in a considerable attrition of committed Ba'thists. The alliance with Iran, offensive to Arabism, was also unpopular in the party bases. That the top elite nevertheless persisted in such policies shows the extent to which it can manipulate its base, claiming broad discretion in interpreting the party policy supposedly decided at party congresses, and repressing overt challenges from within its own constituency. Cumulative purges, resignations, and new recruitment have greatly diluted the ideological intensity of the party ranks, turning the party into a patronage machine whose members are more interested in career and personal connections. Thus, broad, sustained opposition to the leadership has not crystallized.

By comparison to the party, the foreign policy professionals in the Foreign Ministry and the presidency appear to be voices of pragmatism in regime councils. Though the diplomatic establishment seems to carry little institutional weight compared to a country like Egypt, diplomats' conduits to the president give them some influence.[18]

Mass Political Control and Public Opinion

The structures of the Ba'th state are a formidable machine for harnessing society to the regime's foreign policy goals. Government control of the economy permits commitment of the country's resources to such goals. The military and security establishments, increasingly disciplined after years of unreliability, can now be largely depended upon to implement command decisions. The political apparatus—the single party and its "mass organizations"—which incorporates a large segment of the population, has mobilized indispensable support for the regime. In times of tension or war with Israel, the population tends to close ranks behind the regime. A half-literate population is vulnerable to manipulation by an elite enjoying a near monopoly of the mass media and intolerant of dissenting views and on some policy matters the public is inattentive or divided. The relative public acquiesence the government won for its Lebanese intervention against Palestinians, a policy which hitherto seemed politically unimaginable, indicates the wide latitude enjoyed by decision-makers, although the Islamic uprisings of the late 1970s may have partly been a function of the erosion of regime legitimacy from this venture.

A "public mood" does seem to define certain bounds outside which decision-makers dare not tread without risk to their legitimacy. This is no small matter in a regime where legitimacy is precarious and closely linked to nationalist issues and where, owing to the long struggle with Israel, the nationally mobilized and attentive segment of the public is considerable. This is especially so for an elite whose nationalist credentials are vulnerable to attack because of a heavily minority (Alawi) composition that permits opponents to challenge its Arabism. On several issues, public opinion has considerably narrowed regime options. Until Camp David, there was a strong pro-Egyptian public sentiment that Ba'th leaders had to try to satisfy. Because it is responsible for the loss of the Golan, the Ba'th is under special burden to recover it without compromise, and the some 100,000 Syrians expelled from the area remain a permanent constituency keeping the issue alive. Syrian opinion upholds a special obligation to the Palestinian cause, and although the regime may, it seems, challenge the PLO's leadership in the name of Syrian tutelage over this cause, opinion would probably not permit its overt abandonment.

In fact, on core issues such as the conflict with Israel and international alignments, government policy largely reflects the public mood. To be sure, there is a militant rejectionist and anti-Western element especially among students and intellectuals, but it has few mass roots. A pro-Western peace tendency, strongest among the commercial bourgeoisie, would have liked to follow Sadat's course, anticipating greater business prosperity and a lesser role for the military and government in society if the war were to end. This right wing also opposes the Soviet alliance as a threat to its religious ideals and material interests. The dominant trend in public opinion favors nonalignment, but considers the Soviet connection indispensable. Tired of years of conflict and stalemate, Syrians want a peace settlement, but not at any price: The regime position— peace in return for withdrawal from the occupied lands—reflects the mainstream view fairly accurately.[19]

FOREIGN POLICY BEHAVIOR

The Rise of Asad
and the Triumph of Realism (1970–1973)

The regime and foreign policy of Hafiz Al-Asad emerged as a reaction to the collapse of the Ba'th party's revolutionary-nationalist strategy in the 1967 war. Under the radical Ba'thists (1966–1970), Syria launched an attack on the whole regional state system, at the center of which was a challenge to Israel and its backers. Israel was the last bastion of imperialism in the heart of the Arab nation and the principal obstacle to its aspirations; it was incumbent on Arab revolutionaries to act against it before it became irreversible. The radicals argued that while Israel might be militarily superior, the Arabs could prevail in a protracted "war of popular liberation" in which the numerically superior Arab masses, the Arab armies, and Arab oil would be totally mobilized in the national struggle. Their effort to launch this war took two main forms. Syria began to train, arm, and support Palestinian fedayeen in a guerrilla campaign against Israel's borders. It also sought to stimulate revolution in the traditional pro-Western Arab states through which the Arab masses would be politically mobilized and the oil weapon enlisted in the struggle. This provocative policy helped bring on the 1967 war in which the Arab armies were defeated and new Arab land seized. The Ba'th radicals were determined to maintain their militant course and make Syria a firm obstacle to any political settlement in which the Arabs would have to accept Israel. But the loss of Syrian territory in the war had fatally compromised their legitimacy, rendering them vulnerable to challenge by a "realist" faction in the regime led by Defense Minister Hafiz Al-Asad. Asad argued that Syria could not sustain an interminable and ineffective guerrilla war with Israel, that the Syrian army was unprepared to repulse the Israeli retaliation it would bring on, and that Syria had to give the more immediate and realistic goal of recovering the occupied lands, above all the Golan, priority over the liberation of Palestine. Toward this end, the rebuilding of the shattered Syrian army had to be the first priority. This required détente with the traditional oil states who alone could finance it and alliances with Arab states whose armies could contribute to the battle. The divisive pursuit of revolution inside and outside Syria had to be subordinated to all-Arab national unity in the struggle with Israel. The radicals countered that without pan-Arab revolution all-Arab resources could never be mobilized and that deferring the liberation of Palestine meant its abandonment. The struggle between the two sides came to a head over the proper response to King Hussein's repression of the fedayeen during Black September 1970. The radicals, in spite of threats from Israel and the United States, sent forces to Jordan to save the fedayeen and if possible overthrow the monarchy, in the belief that to do nothing for the cause was worse than to suffer defeat. Asad, deterred by the threats, ever aware of the actual balance of power, and unwilling to risk his forces in this adventure, refused to commit air support. When the Syrian force was repulsed and the radicals tried to dismiss Asad, he deposed them in a coup and brought his own "realist" faction to power. This turning point in Syrian history marked an end to messianic revolutionary activism and the beginning of a policy of realpolitik.[20]

Under Asad, the regime substantially scaled down its foreign policy goals: The new aim was the mobilization of all resources for "the liberation of the occupied territories." From this flowed a whole series of alterations in strategy. The main thrust was preparation for a conventional war to retake the Golan. To acquire the necessary arms Asad maintained Syria's close alliance with the USSR and by 1972 Soviet arms, though still inferior to those of Israel, were flowing into Syria in quantities that would make a military challenge possible. The Soviets were more comfortable with the cautious Asad than his reckless predecessors, sought to reward Syria for rejecting Sadat's expulsion of Soviet advisors, and realized they could not keep their Arab allies unless they helped break the intolerable stalemate that allowed Israel to keep Arab lands. Asad also forged new alliances with the Arab oil states, repudiating the radical cold war with them, and won in return a growing subsidization of his military buildup.

He also struck a strategic alliance with Sadat's Egypt, the most militarily powerful of the Arab states, which shared Syria's interest in recovery of the occupied territories. The Egyptian partnership was a first requisite making possible the 1973 war. The outcome of Asad's efforts to create an effective Eastern Front was much more ambiguous. Personal and political rivalries prevented the military cooperation with Iraq that Asad sought, and though Iraq sent forces during the Golan war that checked a dangerous Israeli offensive, this would have been more effective if prearranged. Despite King Hussein's continuing embarrassing repression of the Palestinians, Asad sought to draw him into the military alliance essential to protect Syria's southeastern flank. Asad tried to mediate between the king and the fedayeen and prevented fedayeen operations against Jordan from Syria. When the Jordanians remained unbending, he resorted to border closings and skirmishes with them, all to no avail. Hussein liquidated the fedayeen presence and Asad not only failed, by contrast to his radical predecessors, to defend them, but also went on to forge his alliance with Hussein. He was willing to pay the political cost because for him the Jordanian army was a more important military asset than the Palestinians. In 1973 Jordan did protect Syria's flank but made no major contribution to the war.

The Palestinian resistance retained a reduced place in Asad's strategy. The Ba'th-controlled Al-Sa'iqa was expanded and Syria continued to permit, even sponsor, guerrilla raids from Syrian bases that occasionally escalated into military clashes with Israel. In 1973 Syrian-based PLA units helped thwart a Lebanese attempt to crush the PLO. It was politically important for Asad to continue Syria's patronage of the Palestinian cause and guerrilla operations that contested Israel's tightening grip on the Golan. But the fedayeen were now regarded as auxiliary forces subordinated to Syria's overall strategy rather than the cutting edge of liberation.

A new diplomacy complemented military preparations: Asad, abandoning the total rejectionism of the radical Ba'th, signaled Syria's readiness for a settlement with Israel. In Asad's view, Israel was, in the absence of a demonstrated Arab military challenge, unprepared for a settlement. But world opinion had to be satisfied that the Arabs had exhausted all peaceful options before resorting to war. Moreover, like the Egyptians, Syria went to war in 1973 anticipating that, even if the military outcome fell short, the balance of power could be shifted enough to upset the status quo and force a settlement incorporating the minimum Arab demands. Though Syria still rejected UN Resolution 242 because it clearly specified neither full Israeli withdrawal nor Palestinian rights, Syrian decision-makers must have known that in the aftermath of the war negotiations for a settlement might require they accept Israel in exchange for the conquered land.[21]

From the October War to Camp David (1973–1978)

Syria failed to recover the Golan in the October War and even yielded some additional ground before accepting a cease-fire, but the war did shift the balance of power toward the Arabs. Israel had, for the first time, been seriously challenged militarily; this, together with the oil embargo, showed the potential costs to the West of failure to accommodate Arab interests. The recovery of lost national dignity and new world recognition of Arab interests and power caused an unprecedented Arab cohesion. Syria believed that in these conditions a satisfactory comprehensive settlement might be rapidly imposed if the Arab states struck together, maintained the threat of renewed war and oil boycott in the absence of a settlement, and refrained from separate deals that settled for less than a return to the 1967 lines. Hence Syria explicitly accepted UN Resolutions 242 and 338, interpreting them to mean an end to the state of war, a total Israel evacuation, and creation of a Palestinian state on the West Bank.

Damascus's hopes for a quick overall settlement were, however, quickly dashed. The United States refused to impose such a settlement on Israel, Sadat was prepared to accept separate, partial deals, beginning with his first disengagement, and in the aftermath of the latter, Saudi Arabia lifted the oil embargo, undermining Syria's bargaining leverage. King Faisal had induced Kissinger to "do something" for Syria similar to the Egyptian disengagement, however, and Asad's immediate attention was thus focused on the need to maximize his gains in disengagement negotiations on the Syrian front. Asad's aim was to force the Israelis back as far as possible on the Golan without permitting disengagement to become a substitute for an overall settlement. He bargained tenaciously, with Israeli prisoners of war and by conducting a war of attrition on the Golan and Mt. Hermon which forced Israel to maintain a costly mobilization. Kissinger, to show the Arabs that reliance on the United States paid, pressured Israel to make concessions comparable to those in the Sinai. In the end, Asad had to settle for a partial Israeli withdrawal, recovering only the land lost in 1973 and a sliver of that lost in 1967 in return for a UN observer force between the Syrian and Israeli lines. The rollback of Israeli forces, uncomfortably close to Damascus, was a security gain, Syria had not had to negotiate directly with the Israelis, and there was the possibility, as Kissinger promised, that the Israeli pullback would set a precedent for further future ones. But the agreement reduced military pressure on Israel: The UN presence would make a future war for the Golan more difficult and Asad tacitly accepted an end to guerrilla operations on the Golan. The agreement facilitated the U.S. effort to defuse the wartime crisis as a substitute for an overall settlement and legitimized step-by-step diplomacy, an approach that weakened the Arabs' hand and especially those, Syria and the PLO, to whom the Israelis were least likely to make concessions.

After the Golan disengagement, Syria aimed to steer negotiations toward an international conference in which a united Arab delegation would settle for nothing less than total Israeli withdrawal, preventing a second unilateral deal on the Egyptian front. The USSR could balance U.S. influence and the PLO could be represented and its national demands legitimized and satisfied. Asad tried to rally an Arab consensus against separate deals at the 1974 Rabat summit, sought to forge a joint Syrian-PLO stand declaring that the two would make peace together or not at all, and worked to stiffen Jordan against separate deals. However, this did little to check movement toward Sinai II, a second separate agreement on the Egyptian front. This agreement, largely removing Egypt from the military confrontation and accompanied by a huge U.S. arms delivery to Israel and U.S. promises not to deal with the PLO or demand further concessions of Israel, greatly relieved pressure on Israel to bargain. Thereafter, both the United States and Israel believed Syria to have lost the leverage it had enjoyed from a threat of renewed war in the absence of a settlement, and since Damascus was, in any case, insisting on linkage between the Golan and West Bank, the idea of a second disengagement on the Syrian front was quickly shelved. In allowing Israel to concentrate its forces on the Syrian front, Sinai II greatly increased the threat to Syria's security. To Syria, it seemed that the United States was more interested in dividing and weakening the Arabs than settling the Middle East conflict. The Carter administration briefly offered hope of a U.S. commitment to an all-party international conference, a comprehensive settlement, and a Palestinian homeland, but under Zionist pressure, Carter retreated from the prospect of imposing a settlement on Israel. Thereafter Sadat, convinced that Israel would never agree to a comprehensive settlement, but might concede the Sinai to relieve pressures for one, embarked on his trip to Jerusalem. This brought the Syrian-Egyptian coalition, which had upset the pro-Israeli status quo, to a final break. Asad refused to join Sadat in further negotiations, having lost all confidence he could be held to a common position. To Syria, Sadat had dissipated Arab bargaining power by showing himself ready for peace at any cost and by overtly recognizing Israel and its annexation of Jerusalem beforehand.[22] As Egypt and Israel made peace, ostensibly defusing the Middle East conflict, pressures on Israel for a wider settlement and any incentive to deal with Syria or the Palestinians disappeared.

Asad's Bid for Arab Leadership (1975-1989)

Egypt's course sparked a policy transformation in Syria. Renewed war for the territories was, without Egypt, out of the question. Asad still aimed—as against the total "rejectionists"—for a comprehensive settlement through some combination of military and diplomatic pressures. But, burned by his dependence on Egypt, he now set out to mobilize the resources to go it alone, and in the next half decade a Syrian strategy for doing so emerged. Renewed priority was given to a new military buildup: The threat of an Israel rearmed and emboldened by the neutralization of its southern front had to be contained and successful peace negotiations, Asad began to insist, depended on restoration of a more favorable Arab-Israeli power balance. Equally important, Syria had to find a substitute for the Egyptian alliance and assert the leadership in the Arab arena needed to rally the Arabs behind its strategy. Thus, Asad sought to forge a new Arab concert drawing Lebanon, Jordan, and the PLO under Syrian leadership. As each shared with Syria the insecurities of a border with Israel, a stake in rolling back the Israeli occupation, and the common heritage of Bilad Al-Sham, such an alliance under the leadership of Damascus was, in Syria's view, a natural one. This alliance would both guard against military flank attacks on Syria through Lebanon and Jordan and deter attempts by any of the parties to pursue separate negotiations with Israel. Lebanon was a special danger spot, particularly vulnerable because of its civil war and the Palestinian presence, to Israeli military and political penetration. In establishing Syria as leader of a power bloc in the Arab East, Asad also sought to demonstrate to Washington that Syrian conditions would have to be satisfied if the "peace process" was to be carried further. More than that, he aimed to establish the prestige and power to replace Egypt as the one state which—under Nasser—had had the recognized right to define acceptable norms of Arab state behavior in the conflict with Israel. As it turned out, Asad had some success for limited periods in imposing Syrian leadership on his junior neighbors and in making Syria a serious political force in the Arab East. But, ultimately, the Syrian embrace generated its own counterpressures and Lebanon and the PLO, in particular, became the rocks on which Asad's vessel eventually foundered.[23]

The Struggle for Lebanon. Syria's intervention in Lebanon marked the first challenge of Asad's new strategy. The prospect that civil war and partition would open the door to Israeli penetration posed a grave security threat to Syria, but the conflict also presented an opportunity for Damascus to insert itself as arbiter and draw Lebanon under its political-security wing. Syria tried to both constrain and exploit the crisis. In its early interventions (1975–early 1976), Syria bolstered its traditional allies, the Palestinian-Muslim "left" camp, against a Maronite "right" drive of expansion and partition. It imposed an end to the fighting and sponsored reforms meant to appease each side: a mild redistribution of power in the Muslims' favor and Palestinian respect for Lebanese sovereignty. But when Syria's own allies rejected its reforms in the name of a secular radical state and appeared intent on a military defeat of the Maronites, Syria perceived potential new security threats. In 1976 Syria intervened in greater force and against its former allies to prevent a Maronite defeat. Asad was well aware of efforts on the Maronite right to draw Israel into the fighting on its behalf and feared the conflict would throw the Christians into the hands of Israel and balkanize Lebanon. As the Palestinians defied him, Asad resolved to deprive the PLO of the autonomous Lebanese stronghold from which it could evade Syria's pressures for strategic "coordination" and embark on initiatives threatening its strategy and security. In particular, Asad sought to prevent the emergence of a "rejectionist" Palestinian-dominated Lebanon, aligned with Iraq, sponsoring guerrilla war against Israel, and giving the latter an excuse to evade peace pressures and to intervene militarily. If this happened, not only might Israel realize its historic ambition to seize southern Lebanon, but an Israeli drive through the Bekaa Valley to split Syria and encircle Damascus was by no means implausible. Personal ties and animosities, fear that sectarian strife could spill across the border, and outrage at the defiance of his own allies were added motives for Asad's intervention. Syria curbed the PLO-Muslim alliance and ended the fighting with Syrian forces well entrenched on Lebanon's terrain. Syria had no intention of incorporating Lebanon but it was determined to assert an exclusive sphere of influence there.[24]

Syria briefly appeared to win hegemony in Lebanon. The Palestinians and Muslims accepted Syria's "peacekeeping" role and the Syrian army was positioned to guard Syria's western flank. Asad set out to reconstruct a reformed, less sectarian Lebanese state under Syrian tutelage and bound to his diplomacy. But if Asad expected his defense of the Maronites would win him their trust and acceptance of a lesser role in a Lebanon under Syrian influence, he miscalculated. They preferred de facto partition, resisted Syrian penetration of their domains and reconstruction of the central government, and set about forging a Christian canton in the mountains and East Beirut. They also sought a total expulsion of the PLO from Lebanon as against Syria's desire for a controlled Palestinian presence in the south. When the Maronites collaborated with Israel in carving out a southern enclave meant to seal the border, Syria threw its support to Palestinian-leftist forces resisting this project, but stood by when Israel's 1978 invasion consolidated Saad Haddad's "security zone" against Palestinian incursions. Syria's subsequent military drives to punish the Maronites pushed them back into central Lebanon, but, deterred by Israel, Syria could not bring them to heel and only drove them further into Israeli arms. Two Maronite enclaves, overtly aligned with Israel, presented stubborn obstacles to the reconstruction of a united Lebanon and threats to Syrian security. Israel, now under Menachim Begin, upgraded its alliance with the Maronites and began looking for a way to expel Syria from Lebanon. From 1979 to 1980, Syria supported Palestinian efforts to restore a southern presence and halfheartedly challenged regular Israeli incursions. In 1981, a Maronite bid to extend their control into the Syrian-held Bekaa Valley, cut Syrian access to Beirut, and draw Israel deep into Lebanon almost succeeded. Syria pushed the Maronites back, but when the Israeli air force intervened on their behalf and Syria moved antiaircraft missiles into eastern Lebanon, Israel threatened to destroy them. The United States restrained Israel and the "missile crisis" petered out. But Israel as much as Syria had become the arbiter of Lebanon. Syria's own actions—first weakening its own allies, strengthening a Maronite right whose interests were incompatible with Syria's, then pushing the Maronites into the Israeli embrace—helped bring about what it most feared.[25]

Israel's 1982 invasion of Lebanon, encouraged by growing Arab fragmentation and Syria's post–Camp David vulnerability, aimed at smashing the PLO, expelling Syria, and demolishing resistance to Camp David. Militarily, Syria took a beating, and although Syrian forces extracted a price from Israel and stubbornly refused, as Israel expected, to evacuate Lebanon, Israel inflicted large losses and pushed Syria from strategic sectors of Lebanese terrain, including the nerve center, Beirut. Moreover, it expelled the PLO from most of Lebanon and in the wake of the war a U.S.-Israeli *combinazione* tried to impose a Maronite client regime in Beirut and a virtual peace treaty on Israeli terms. This Lebanese-Israeli accord of 1982 would have opened Lebanon to Israeli influence, forces, and products, outlawed Arab forces on Lebanese soil, and effaced its Arab character. Israeli withdrawal was made contingent on Syria's, putting Syria's role on an equal footing with Israel's. The United States and Israel believed a militarily weakened and isolated Syria had no choice but to accept the Lebanese-Israeli accord and withdraw or face continued Israeli occupation of Lebanon. Yet Syria chose to defy their overwhelming military power and in a short time brought about a remarkable turnabout in the balance of forces. Syria refused to withdraw and took advantage of the growing resentment of Lebanese Muslims against Israeli and Maronite domination to strike an alliance with them. Buttressed by Syria, Muslim militias checked the Maronite Gemayel government's consolidation of power over the country and the intervention of U.S. guns and plans on its behalf could not deter them. Israel, wearied by the casualties of Lebanese occupation and aware of the risks of a renewed drive against a Syrian army much reinforced by Soviet arms and backing, began to withdraw from Lebanon. The bombing of U.S. Marine positions and the downing of U.S. bombers flying against Syrian forces demonstrated to the United States the costs of involvement and brought about its withdrawal, too. The weakened Maronite government was forced to cancel the accord with Israel. Israel, under Syrian-backed guerrilla threat, withdrew from Lebanon except for the "security zone" in the south, ending the immediate military threat to Syria. Thus, through a shrewd use of proxies, steadfastness under threat, an enhanced military capability on the ground, and Soviet backing, Asad snatched victory from the jaws of defeat.[26]

But if Syria defeated major threats to its security, it has since failed to reconstruct a stable pro-Syrian Lebanon. Syria's ascendance in the wake of Israeli disengagement was initially acknowledged by President Amin Gemayel. The defeat of the Maronite militias under the anti-Syrian Samir Ja'ja by the pro-Syrian Shi'ite and Druze forces, combined with Syria's reining in of the latter's advance, created the possibility that a chastened Maronite camp might abandon its opposition to Syrian-sponsored reform and reconstruction. But Syria could find no Maronite leader able to deliver the community. At Lausanne in 1984 the traditional Maronite politicians rejected a Syrian-sponsored national unity accord providing for a more equitable distribution of power to the Muslims, and thereafter Gemayel proved an unreliable partner. Syria then found a Maronite militia leader, Elie Hobeika, ready to strike a similar deal—the "Tripartite Agreement"—with his Shi'ite and Druze counterparts that acknowledged a Syrian "protectorate" over Lebanon. But the revolt of the Maronite community against him and the reemergence of Ja'ja showed the Maronites preferred cantonization to equalization and Syrian tutelage. Syria's position was further complicated when its post-1983 conflict with Arafat's PLO began to split the pro-Syrian Muslim camp. While Syria backed the Shi'ite Amal militia's effort to block a return of Arafatist forces to Lebanon, Lebanese leftists and the Druze backed the PLO. A new Shi'ite force, the fundamentalist Hizbullah, which challenged Syria's influence and project for a secular Lebanon, also took sides with Arafat and there were even signs of a budding PLO-Maronite alliance against the common threat from Damascus. The 1986 return of the Syrian army to West Beirut partly restored Syria's ability to control events on the ground and its own proxies in the Muslim camp. But Lebanon's growing fragmentation and armed mobilization was making it increasingly ungovernable. The failure of Syria's 1988 attempt to make election of a new Maronite president conditional on Christian acceptance of reform left Lebanon divided between two rival governments—one headed by Selim Hoss and the other by the Maronite general Michel Auon; a sign of Syria's declining control was Auon's 1989 attempt to challenge Syria's very presence in Lebanon. The Taif accord and inter-Maronite fighting seemed, however, to rescue Syria's position. The preoccupation of Auon's Iraqi and Israeli backers with the Gulf crisis gave Syria the chance to crush him and reestablish its hegemony in Lebanon.

Overall, Syria's venture in Lebanon seems to have merely dissipated its energies and tarnished its image instead of bolstering its claim to all-Arab leadership. But Syria is determined to remain in Lebanon until

Israel evaluates the south, a friendly government is in power, and Lebanese unity is restored.[27]

The Struggle for the PLO. Syria's effort, as part of its grand design for Arab hegemony, to bind the PLO to a strategic alliance was dealt a setback by the bloody 1976 conflict in Lebanon between the two parties; indeed, the mistrust created in this conflict has never been fully overcome. But in the post–Camp David period, Syrians and Palestinians shared certain interests that brought them together again. For Asad, as long as the PLO acted in concert with Syria, the Camp David attempt to "solve" the Palestinian problem and vindicate Egypt's separate peace with a cosmetic West Bank "autonomy" could be prevented and any Jordanian bargaining over the West Bank would lack the Palestinian blessing it needed to be credible. Many Palestinians thought their interests and Syria's coincided since they had an equal stake in scuttling a disposition of the West Bank which denied them a state; they, too, were vulnerable in Lebanon, the soft spot in the Arab front, where forces seeking to destroy opposition to Camp David were likely to strike. In 1981 the Palestine National Council embraced alliance with Syria as the last obstacle to Arab capitulation. While the radical PFLP and DFLP moved closer to Syria, Arafat, however, remained very wary of Asad and determined to maintain his autonomy and negotiating options; he thus undermined Syria's claim to control the "Palestinian card" at a time when this was a crucial strategic asset for Damascus. To Asad's outrage, Arafat refused to burn his bridges to Egypt, undermining Syria's drive to prevent the legitimation of Camp David. To Arafat, Syria claimed a kind of protectorate over the PLO, but failed to assume the responsibilities incumbent on this role, notably to defend the PLO in southern Lebanon. Syria's inaction during the 1978 Israeli invasion of Lebanon and especially its acceptance of a cease-fire during the 1982 invasion while the PLO was still fighting, opened all the old wounds. Arafat, deprived after 1982 of a Lebanese base except in areas under Syrian control, which he was determined to evade, became convinced the struggle had to focus on the West Bank where Zionist settlement threatened. In a major threat to Syria, Arafat and Jordan began to explore the Reagan Plan, a warmed-over version of Camp David–style autonomy which, at best, would have led to an Israeli-Jordanian condominium over the West Bank. Making no provision for the Golan, it seemed to Damascus a second prong of the Israeli-U.S. offensive developing against it in Lebanon in 1983. When rebellion broke out inside the PLO against Arafat, in good part for his flirtations with Jordan, Egypt, and the Reagan Plan, Syria saw a golden opportunity to depose him and reshape a pro-Syrian PLO. Palestinian radicals led by Abu Musa and Ahmad Jibril and at times including the PFLP and DFLP were grouped in a Damascus-based Palestine National Salvation Front (PNSF). Syrian forces supported them in expelling Arafat loyalists from the Bekaa and then in the siege that drove Arafat from Tripoli. Yet, this only rallied the majority of Palestinians to their leader and pushed him into the arms of Syria's rivals: Arafat's subsequent visit to Cairo was a first step in breaking Egypt's Arab isolation. Nor could he be stopped from exploring peace negotiations in partnership with King Hussein. In the War of the Camps Syria backed the Shi'ite Amal's drive against the PLO to punish Arafat and to check his emerging anti-Syrian alliances in Lebanon. Even though the Arafat-Hussein partnership collapsed, Asad continued the vendetta, seemingly less a rational strategy than part of a personal feud with the man most Palestinians still considered their leader. This campaign drove a wedge between the major Palestinian radical groups, the PFLP and DFLP, and Damascus, precipitated a closing of Palestinian ranks, and gradually undermined the PNSF. It was also profoundly delegitimizing: Fighting Palestinians vitiated Syria's status as the champion of the Arab national cause, the role that was the basis of Asad's claim on the support and cooperation of other Arab states. Such strange bedfellows as Iran and Iraq, Egypt and Libya, as well as Saudi Arabia were all found in opposition to Syria's support for Amal. Moreover, in 1987 and 1988, the War of the Camps threatened to be the catalyst for formation of a broad anti-Amal Lebanese coalition of Syria's former allies and enemies alike, forestalled only by Syrian troop deployments in Beirut and on-and-off cease-fires around the camps. Syria's legitimacy was also threatened by the service it and Amal seemed to be doing Israel in curbing Palestinian and Hizbullah resistance in south Lebanon. The 1987 reunification of the PLO on a hard-line basis stimulated a halfhearted reconciliation between Arafat and Damascus. But Arafatist and Syrian-backed Abu Musa forces were nevertheless soon locked in another battle over the camps. In the end, Asad largely came off the loser in the power struggle with Arafat. The PLO established Lebanese footholds, particularly in Sidon, Amal failed to take the camps, and the PLO became a part of the anti-Syrian equation in Lebanon. Worse, in 1988 Arafat's "moderate line," buoyed by the West Bank *intifadah*, prevailed within a unified PLO; most of Asad's Palestinian surrogates deserted him and his bid to play the "Palestinian card" seemed lost.[28]

Syria in the Post–Camp David Arab World. Syrian policy after Camp David was aimed at containing the threat of an Israel strengthened by the withdrawal of Egypt from the conflict, at preventing the legitimation of the "Camp David process" in the Arab world, and at claiming the support to which Syria was entitled as the only remaining front-line Arab state. Initially Egypt's move toward peace with Israel drew the Arab states together to Syria's benefit. A Steadfastness Front including the radical states of Libya, Algeria, and Democratic Yemen gave Syria diplomatic support, although they were too far from the front lines to carry much weight. An alliance struck with Jordan in 1975 helped bring King Hussein to reject Camp David and Syria's "strategic alliance" with the PLO took on a new reality in the late 1970s. Syria and Iraq seemed on the verge of burying the hatchet and reconstructing the Eastern Front; at the 1978 Baghdad Conference, they possessed the political weight to force Egypt's ostracism and major all-Arab financial support for Syria's military buildup.

But before long Syrian policy was in disarray. The Eastern Front collapsed, in good part over the Iran-Iraq war: The breakdown of Syrian-Iraqi détente was crystallized by Syria's support for Iran and the war diverted a major Arab army from the Israeli front. King Hussein, reasserting an independent foreign policy, aligned with Iraq and pursued peace initiatives over the West Bank in disregard of Syrian wishes; the Damascus-Amman entente collapsed over Syria's support for Iran and Jordan's for anti-Syrian dissidents. The threat of Iranian expansionism assumed a much higher priority than the Arab-Israeli dispute in Saudi Arabia and the Gulf states; Syria's alliance with Iran therefore alienated the oil states whose political and financial support Syria needed. Iran made up for the financial losses and Asad put the enervation of a rival Arab regime ahead of Arab solidarity, compromising his claim to championship of the Arab cause. At the same time, Syria was locked in a protracted struggle with Israeli-backed Maronite forces in Lebanon. By 1980 Syria had seldom been so isolated, so lacking in the diplomatic leverage that could flow from its leadership of a wider Arab bloc and more likely to be left to its own devices in case of Israeli attack. Bedeviled by internal rebellion as well and convinced that nothing could be expected from U.S. diplomacy, Syria sought the new arms and guarantees that went with a Soviet friendship treaty which it signed in 1980. Israel's 1981 "annexation" of the Golan, by which it seemed to irreversibly close the door to a settlement with Syria, heightened Syria's fears that further Arab-Israeli negotiations were likely to leave it out. In these conditions, the conviction stiffened in Damascus that no acceptable political settlement with Israel was possible until a balance of forces more favorable to the Arabs emerged and until Syria achieved military parity with Israel. Syrian policy in the 1980s manifested a "tactical rejectionism" that sought in the meantime to obstruct the U.S.-sponsored "peace process."[29]

Arab fragmentation and Syrian isolation invited the 1982 Israeli invasion of Lebanon which deepened capitulationist sentiment in the Arab world. Its defeat of the Israeli-U.S. *combinazione* in Lebanon briefly boosted Syria's prestige and confidence. Asad made much of the fact that Syria, in spite of Israeli superiority and the passivity of the Arab world and the Soviet Union, had nevertheless remained steadfast, inflicted casualties on the enemy, and denied him his goals. The subsequent Israeli withdrawal showed, moreover, that Israel could be made to withdraw from Arab land without unacceptable concessions. Certainly, Syria's refusal to crumble in the face of apparently overwhelming power gave some credibility to Arab resistance to Camp David.

But Syria was unable to translate this into acknowledged Arab leadership or reverse the drift of the Arab world toward negotiations with Israel. In allowing its relations with the PLO to deteriorate, Syria opened the door to the 1985 formation of a PLO-Jordanian-Egyptian axis which advanced the legitimation of the partial peace initiatives Syria so feared. But, for a period, the Syrian-backed PNSF deprived Arafat of a Palestinian consensus for negotiations and an impatient King Hussein, breaking with him, decided on a rapprochement with Syria in which he eschewed separate deals. In the various Lebanese hostage affairs, Syria sought to demonstrate its indispensability to the West; but the Hindawi affair (in which an attempt was made to plant a bomb on an Israeli airliner) isolated Damascus internationally. Lebanon was becoming ever more unmanageable, relations with Syria's major ally, Iran, were periodically strained over Hizbullah, and the PNSF was soon in disarray.

As long as Egypt and Iraq remained on the Arab peripheries, Syria's inter-Arab weight, in spite of its frequent conflicts with other Arab parties, remained formidable. But Egypt, in its patronage of the PLO (in good part against Syria) and support for Iraq and the oil states in the Gulf war, progressively inched out of its isolation. Iraq, Syria's main Arab rival, emerged unexpectedly victorious from the war and began to support Maronite defiance of Syria in Lebanon. The *intifadah* gave a tremendous boost to Arafat's fortunes, too, at Asad's expense. When Egypt and Iraq joined with Jordan in a new axis behind the PLO's 1988 declaration of a Palestinian state and call for peace negotiations while Syria remained on the sidelines, Asad seemed to forfeit to them all claim to a special protectorate over the "Arab cause"; this was unmistakable at the 1989 Casablanca summit where Asad sat silently glowering as the Arab world united behind arch-rival Arafat and a negotiations strategy which left Syria out. His Soviet ally openly backed the PLO peace bid and the United States prepared to circumvent and blunt Syrian objections to it. There seemed to have been a dramatic shift in the balance of inter-Arab power against Syria and all of Asad's efforts to build Arab leadership appeared to have backfired, leaving him isolated. One sign of this was the formation of the Arab Cooperation Council institutionalizing a block embracing Egypt, Iraq, Jordan, and North Yemen, to Syria's exclusion; another was the blame put on Syria for the conflict in Lebanon by a committee of the leaders of Algeria, Saudi Arabia, and Morocco, all formerly friendly to Asad. By 1989 Asad was being forced to make the tactical retreats, notably acceptance of Egypt's rehabilitation, necessary to make Syria a part of rather than a victim of the emerging Arab consensus.

By mid-1990, indeed, Asad's cumulative adaptation to changing conditions seemed to spell a major shift in Syrian strategy. The return of Egypt and Iraq to the Arab center required Syrian accommodation with at least one of them, and, Egypt being more amenable and Iraq the greater threat, Asad reestablished his links to Cairo. The decline of Soviet power and, hence, of the likelihood of a military solution to the conflict with Israel dictated a movement toward the moderate Arab states and better relations with the United States. Asad's stand against Iraq's invasion of Kuwait cemented this new alignment. Thus, Syria seemed headed back into the early 1970s alliance with Egypt and Saudi Arabia that had sought a U.S.-brokered settlement with Israel. But it was far from clear that a viable "peace process" necessary to sustain this course was in the cards.

CONCLUSION: THE RECORD OF SYRIAN FOREIGN POLICY UNDER ASAD

When Hafiz Al-Asad came to power he inherited an enormous gap between the goals of Syria's foreign policy—the virtual overthrow of the regional state system—and the regime's modest capabilities; pursuit of this policy in an environment of high risk had ended in the disaster of 1967 which shattered the dreams of messianic Arab nationalism. Asad set out to narrow the gap by scaling down goals and upgrading capabilities.

Asad replaced revolutionary revisionism with a new realism which made the recovery of the territories lost in 1967 the central goal of foreign policy. This meant, in effect, the reluctant acceptance of the regional state system, including Israel; this is evident in the limited objectives of the 1973 war, détente with the traditional Arab states, acceptance of UN Resolution 242, Syria's unconcern to annex Lebanon, and its stand against Iraq's invasion of Kuwait. Increasingly, the special interests of the Syrian state and the security imperatives of the regime took precedence over pan-Arab obligations; this was most evident in the repeated subordination of Palestinian wishes to Syrian strategy and security. Yet the identification of Syrian interests with the Arab cause was no mere fiction and a purely Syria-centered policy has never taken form. Had it done so, Asad could have pursued a Sadat-like settlement with Israel instead of mortgaging Syria's welfare and future to a struggle with Israel rooted chiefly in Arabist irredentism, not narrowly defined Syrian raison d'état. Syria's interests, as Asad defines them, coincide more than those of other Arab states with wider Arab national goals, and without pan-Arab solidarity those goals cannot be achieved. Thus, Syria remains the most committed of the Arab states to Arabism, the least prepared to fall back on a separate statehood apart from the Arab nation or to abandon the Arabs' minimal demands in the struggle with Israel. Nevertheless, the immediate objectives of actual foreign policy behavior under Asad were much more sharply circumscribed than hitherto.

Asad also expanded Syria's capabilities. From an unstable, readily penetrated victim of external forces, Asad forged the Syrian state into a solid power base, a powerful and central actor in the regional arena. Relative to its regional neighbors, including Israel, Syria's capabilities increased significantly.[30] Asad made the Syrian army a formidable force;

while it has come off second best in each encounter with Israel, it has suffered no strategic defeat since 1970 and in extracting a high cost from Israel, has become a significant deterrent to Israeli freedom of action. Asad's Machiavellian skill in exploiting every available resource—persuasion, rewards, threats, terrorism, stubborn patience, the mistakes of enemies, alliances, the manipulation of proxies—has allowed him to prevail against the odds in a number of undertakings, notably in his defeat of the Israeli-Lebanese accord.

Nevertheless, Syria alone could not attain its goals and only through a diplomacy able to win superpower and Arab backing could it hope to prevail. Israel can be pushed back to the 1967 lines only by the threat or action of a Soviet-backed Arab war coalition or a pan-Arab diplomacy that diluted U.S. support for Israeli occupation. Under Asad, Syria's diplomacy reached a new level of effectiveness in widening Syrian access to external support, but his overall record is nevertheless mixed.

It was Asad's ability to exploit superpower rivalries and maintain both the Soviet connection and ties to conservative Arab oil states that mobilized the resources for a huge military buildup going well beyond Syria's internal capacity to support. Asad also proved astute in exploiting certain divergences of interest between Israel and the United States in the aftermath of the October War, particularly in the Golan disengagement negotiations, the original Lebanese intervention, and generally in using links to the United States to constrain Israeli freedom of military action against Syria.

In the inter-Arab arena, Asad achieved the alliance with Egypt and Saudi Arabia necessary for the 1973 war and the brief exercise of Arab diplomacy thereafter. But though he won a small gain on the Golan he could not prevent Egypt from breaking ranks or force a more vigorous use of the oil weapon. Thereafter, Syria failed to construct a viable Eastern Front and since Camp David no Arab war coalition has been in existence. Asad made a credible bid for pan-Arab leadership after 1975 and in making Syria the major power on the front line with Israel, achieved a certain Arab nationalist legitimacy and enhanced influence in the inter-Arab arena; this was particularly manifested in his success in winning the large military subsidies and the condemnation of Camp David necessary to his policy. For certain periods, Asad seemed to harness Lebanon, Jordan, and the PLO to his strategy. His major achievement was to demonstrate that Middle East diplomacy could not advance except with Syria's cooperation and that if Syria could not impose a peace to its liking, it could prevent one that damaged its interests or Arab rights: That seemed to be the lesson of the collapse of both the Lebanese-Israeli accord and of the Hussein-Arafat collaboration over the Reagan Plan. But Asad's pan-Arab leadership proved fragile. In the end Syria failed to reconstruct Lebanon under its tutelage, failed in its bid to "play the Palestinian card," and failed to sustain its claim to define Arab strategy in the conflict with Israel.

In part, Syria's failures were due to the intractability of the environment. For instance, in Lebanon Syria went to great lengths to accommodate Maronite interests but their intense particularism, under Israeli protection, proved an impossible nut to crack. But Syria's own behavior also contributed to its failures. Syrian and Palestinian interests coincide far more than they diverge, yet Asad's insistence on subordinating Palestinian needs to Syria's immediate security interests and his heavy-handed coercion of the PLO ultimately turned natural allies into enemies. Syrian Machiavellianism, a too-cynical pursuit of narrow regime interests, was also exemplified in the support for Iran against Iraq. Both the anti-PLO and anti-Iraq policies took an extremely high toll of a crucial if intangible asset which Syria, given its slim resource base, could not dispense with if it was to exercise inter-Arab leadership: its special Arab nationalist legitimacy. These practices also led to an accumulation of resentments and old scores which fueled anti-Syrian reactions.

The root of Syria's problem is that without Arab backing for its goals it cannot achieve them, but Syria simply lacks sufficient assets to assume the role of pan-Arab leader. It has neither the wealth nor the population of rival centers of Arab power—Egypt, Iraq, Saudi Arabia. Asad lacks the personal pan-Arab charisma of a Nasser and the Arab world is in a phase of fragmentation in which immediate state and communal identities are supplanting Arabism. Thus, in overextending himself, in demanding a larger-than-realistic role in Arab politics, Asad invited the formation of the counter-coalitions that isolated him throughout much of the 1980s. But his reestablishment of inter-Arab links at the beginning of the 1990s is testimony to his ability to adapt to and salvage a bad situation.

Asad well may prove correct that, given the current balance of power, no satisfactory peace can be reached with Israel; if peace negotiations fail, Syria could yet become the linchpin of a new Arab alignment against Israel. But for the immediate future, conditions appear bleak for attaining Syria's foreign policy goals. Syria under Asad is likely to continue poised between a revisionism born of continued frustration and a cautious aversion to the risks of upsetting the status quo until the illusive conditions of success seem at hand.

NOTES

1. A. L. Tibawi, *A Modern History of Syria* (London: Macmillan, 1969); Zeine N. Zeine, *The Struggle for Arab Independence* (Beirut: Khayats, 1960).

2. Syrian Arab Republic, *Statistical Abstract*, various years, 1976–1984; *The Military Balance* (London: International Institute for Strategic Studies), various years; Zeev Ma'oz, "The Evolution of Syrian Power, 1948–1984," in Moshe Ma'oz and Avner Yaniv, *Syria Under Assad* (New York: St. Martin's Press, 1986), pp. 72–76.

3. Richard Nyrop (ed.), *Area Handbook for Syria* (Washington, D.C.: Government Printing Office, 1971), pp. 287–296; P. R. Chari, "Military Lessons of the Arab-

Israeli War of 1973," *Institute for Defense Studies and Analysis Journal*, New Delhi, April–June 1976; Riad Askar, "The Syrian and Egyptian Campaigns," *Journal of Palestine Studies*, 14, 2 (1974), pp. 15–33.

4. *The Military Balance*, various years; Geoffrey Kemp, "The Arab-Israeli Military Balance," in Colin Legum, Haim Shaked, and Daniel Dishon, *Middle East Contemporary Survey, 1976–77* (London: Holmes & Meier, 1978), pp. 74–81; Yehosha Raviv, "Arab-Israeli Military Balance," *Jerusalem Quarterly*, 18 (Winter 1981); Yezid Sayigh, "Israel's Military Performance in Lebanon," *Journal of Palestine Studies*, 13, 1 (Fall 1984), pp. 24–65; Ze'ev Schiff and Ehud Ya'ari, *Israel's Lebanon War* (New York: Simon and Schuster, 1984), pp. 151–194; R. D. McLaurin, Mohammed Mughisuddin, and Abraham Wagner, *Foreign Policy Making in the Middle East* (New York: Praeger Publishers, 1977), pp. 236–237; Mark Heller, Dov Tamari, and Zeev Eytan, *The Middle East Military Balance, 1983* (Tel Aviv: Jaffee Center for Strategic Studies, 1984).

5. Jay Kent, "War Clouds over Golan," *Middle East International*, 271, 21 (March 1986); Aharon Levran, "Syria's Military Strength and Capability," *Middle East Review*, 14, 3 (Spring 1987).

6. Raviv, *op. cit.*, p. 137.

7. Avner Yaniv, "Syria and Israel: The Politics of Escalation," in Ma'oz and Yaniv, *op. cit.*, pp. 157–178; Avraham Ben-Tsur, *The Syrian Ba'ath Party and Israel* (Givat Haviva, Israel: Center for Arab and Afro-Asian Studies, 1968); Maxime Rodinson, *Israel and the Arabs* (Harmondsworth, England: Penguin, 1968), especially pp. 167–171.

8. Itamar Rabinovich, "Controlled Conflict in the Middle East: The Syrian-Israeli Rivalry in Lebanon," in Gabriel Ben-Dor and David B. Dewitt, *Conflict Management in the Middle East* (Lexington, Mass.: Lexington Books, 1987), pp. 97–111; Avner Yaniv, "A Syrian-Israeli Detente?" *Middle East Insight*, 5, 5 (1988), pp. 27–33.

9. Rodinson, *op. cit.*, pp. 161–171; Fuad Jabber, "The Palestinian Resistance and Inter-Arab Politics," in William Quandt, *The Politics of Palestinian Nationalism* (Berkeley: University of California Press, 1973), pp. 157–175, 188–194, 201–204; Hafiz Al-Asad, "Speech Delivered by Comrade Hafiz al-Asad Before a General Plenum of Local Government Councils," Damascus, July 20, 1976; Moshe Ma'oz and Avner Yaniv, "On a Short Leash: Syria and the PLO," in Ma'oz and Yaniv, *Syria Under Assad*, pp. 192–196.

10. Aaron D. Miller, "Syria and the Palestinians," *Middle East Insight*, 4, 2 (June/July 1985), pp. 3–9.

11. Yezid Sayigh, "Understanding Palestinian-Arab Relations: The Interventionists," *Middle East International*, 297, 3 (April 1987), pp. 17–18.

12. William Brown, *The Last Crusade: A Negotiator's Middle East Handbook* (Chicago: Nelson Hall, 1980), pp. 37–53; Muhammed Hassanein Heikal, *The Road to Ramadan* (New York: Ballantine Books, 1976).

13. Yair Hirschfeld, "The Odd Couple: Baathist Syria and Khomeini's Iran," in Ma'oz and Yaniv, *op. cit.*, pp. 105–124.

14. Patrick Seale, *The Struggle for Syria* (London: Oxford University Press, 1965); "Speech by Noureddin Atasi to the UN General Assembly, June 20, 1967"; Edward Sheehan, *The Arabs, Israel and Kissinger: A Secret History of American Diplomacy in the Middle East* (New York: Reader's Digest Press, 1976); R. Bruce Ehrnman, "The United States and Syria: The Awkward Relationship," *Middle East Insight*, 4, 4–5 (1986), pp. 14–20; Kati Marton, "Peril or Possibility: America and Syria at the Crossroads," *Middle East Insight*, 4, 6 (1986); Talcott

408   *Raymond A. Hinnebusch*

W. Seelye, *US-Arab Relations: The Syrian Dimension* (Portland, Oreg.: National Council on Arab Relations, 1985).

15. Jaan Penner, "The Soviet Road to Damascus," *Mizan*, 9 (1967), pp. 23–29; Galia Golan, "Syria and the Soviet Union Since the Yom Kippur War," *Orbis*, 21, 4 (1978), pp. 777–802; Lawrence L. Whetten, "Soviet-Syrian Moves in the Middle East," *Roundtable*, 279 (1980), pp. 258–265; Robert O. Freedman, "Moscow, Damascus and the Lebanon Crisis," in Ma'oz and Yaniv, *op. cit.*, pp. 224–247; Meir Zamir, "The Emergence of Syria?" in Aurel Braun, *The Middle East in Global Strategy* (Boulder and London: Westview and Mansell, 1987), p. 59.

16. Sheehan, *op. cit.*; Matti Golan, *The Secret Conversations of Henry Kissinger* (New York: Quadrangle, 1976), pp. 179–212; Moshe Ma'oz, "Hafiz al-Asad: A Political Profile," *Jerusalem Quarterly*, 8 (1978).

17. Sheehen, *op. cit.*; A. I. Dawisha, "Syria's Intervention in Lebanon, 1975–1976," *Jerusalem Journal of International Relations*, 3, 2–3 (1978), pp. 245–267.

18. Sheehan, *op. cit.*; McLaurin et. al., *op. cit.*, pp. 243–244.

19. Reiser's survey of Syrian students studying in the United States showed 45% would accept an Israel within its 1967 boundaries while a majority rejected it. While this group is a select one, this does seem to capture the ambiguity in public opinion, a split between an emotional rejection and a pragmatic willingness to end the conflict in return for territorial concessions—the government position. They also shared the government position that only military power, not diplomacy alone, could achieve peace. Little significance should be attributed to the higher "rejectionism" among respondents from other Arab states such as the Gulf area since acceptance of Israel is, for them, a purely abstract question while Syrians must carry the actual burden of the conflict. See Stewart Reiser, "Islam, Pan-Arabism and Palestine: An Attitudinal Survey," *Journal of Arab Affairs* 3, 2 (Fall 1984), pp. 189–204.

20. Tabitha Petran, *Syria* (London: Ernest Benn, 1972), pp. 194–204, 239–249, 252–257.

21. Malcolm Kerr, "Hafiz al-Asad and the Changing Patterns of Syrian Politics," *International Journal*, 28, 4 (1975), pp. 289–306; Aryeh Yodfat, "The End of Syria's Isolation?" *The World Today*, 27, 8 (1971), pp. 335–339; Itamar Rabinovich, "The Limits of Power: Syria Under Hafiz al-Asad," *New Middle East*, March 1973, pp. 36–37.

22. See interview with Asad, *International Herald Tribune*, January 9, 1978.

23. Raymond A. Hinnebusch, "Egypt, Syria, and the Arab State System," in Yehuda Lukaus and Abdalla Battah, *The Arab-Israeli Conflict: Two Decades of Change* (Boulder, Colo.: Westview Press, 1988), pp. 182–190.

24. Asad, "Speech," 1976; Marius Deeb, *The Lebanese Civil War* (New York: Praeger, 1980), pp. 122–128; Dawisha, "Syria's Intervention," 1978; Adeed Dawisha, *Syria and the Lebanese Crisis* (London: Macmillan, 1980); Peter Heller, "The Syrian Factor in the Lebanese Civil War," *Journal of South Asian and Middle Eastern Studies*, 4, 1 (1980), pp. 56–76.

25. Adeed Dawisha, "Syria in Lebanon: Asad's Vietnam?" *Foreign Policy*, 33 (Winter 1978–1979); William Haddad, "Divided Lebanon," *Current History*, 81, 471 (January 1982); Rabinovich, "Controlled Conflict," pp. 184–185.

26. Rabinovich, "Controlled Conflict"; Schiff and Ya'ari, *op. cit.*, pp. 286–300; Tabitha Petran, *The Struggle for Lebanon* (New York: Monthly Review Press, 1987), pp. 295–334, 345–348; Adeed Dawisha, "The Motives of Syrian Involvement in Lebanon," *Middle East Journal* (Spring 1984), pp. 228–234.

27. Petran, *The Struggle for Lebanon,* pp. 345–369; William Harris, "Syria in Lebanon," *MERIP Reports,* 134 (July–August 1985), pp. 9–16.

28. Petran, *The Struggle for Lebanon,* pp. 335–344, 361–366, 370–377; Raymond A. Hinnebusch, "Syrian Policy in Lebanon and the Palestinians," *Arab Studies Quarterly,* 8, 1 (Winter 1986), pp. 1–20.

29. Karim Pakradouni, "Asad's Syria and the Politics of Change," *Middle East Insight,* 3, 6 (1984), pp. 3–8.

30. Zeev Ma'oz, in Ma'oz and Yaniv, *op. cit.,* pp. 72–81.

13

Arab Foreign Policies in a Changing Environment

Bahgat Korany
Ali E. Hillal Dessouki

Though the main objective of this book was to provide straightforward information on the foreign policies of nine developing countries, conceptual aspects of foreign policy analysis were not avoided. For in times of upheaval, which is presently the case par excellence of Arab countries in their regional and international environments, conceptual sensitivity may help us to avoid being tempted by the sensational and to sort out the accidental from the structural bases in foreign policy explanation.

Consequently, the analysis of foreign policy patterns among Arab countries and the sources or determinants of these policies cannot be separated from the three main building blocks of a potential foreign policy theory.

1. Foreign policy *outputs*. We insisted in our framework in Chapter 1 that these outputs are dual in nature. Jordan's, Egypt's, or Saudi Arabia's foreign policy embraces both its general foreign policy objectives (i.e., role-conception—whether it is state survival or diplomacy of development) and its specific behavior (i.e., role-performance or enactment—specific actions to promote an objective, whether it is the use of petrodollars or military means). Though foreign policy role-conception and role-performance are distinct components of this output, they are inseparable. By keeping them distinct, the observer can ascertain whether there is a gap between words and action in the country's foreign policy. If such a gap exists, the next step is to provide an explanation. This problematique helps the researcher to specify and classify the relevant foreign policy sources or determinants rather than to be content to merely list them.

2. Foreign policy *inputs*. In this respect we have reacted to the obsession of the literature with the impact of the "great man" at the top and an exclusive emphasis on idiosyncrasies. Indeed, in the literature on Third

World foreign policies, the leader is portrayed as the be-all and end-all. Even such pillars of foreign policy–theory-building as J. Rosenau and M. Brecher differed on many basics in their respective frameworks but agreed on the primacy of the man at the top.[1]

It is, of course, absurd to imagine the 1990–1991 Gulf crisis without giving due weight to the personality of Saddam Hussein. But the question is whether this crisis, together with the eight-year Iraq-Iran war preceding it, could be reduced to the personalities of Ayatollah Khomeini, Saddam Hussein, or Sheikh Jaber Al-Sabah. In our analytical framework we have tried to balance this onesidedness and obsession with idiosyncratic factors by attracting attention to global-systemic constraints, domestic structures, geopolitical context, and characteristics of state-formation—whether we are talking of Algeria, Sudan, or Syria. Our message is that the man at the top is to be analyzed not as a psychological atom but rather as a social phenomenon. His preeminence is part of the country's social dynamics and not a substitute for them. This preeminence itself varies. He could be an agenda-setter, arbitrator, or final decision-maker, which indicates that his greatest influence is not primarily in determining foreign policy in general but in taking—as distinct from making—decisions (mainly the ones important to him—usually "high politics" rather than technical or economic matters).

3. The decision-making process, or the *conversion of inputs into outputs*. This is where the "big man" exerts his maximum influence. But the leader's disproportionate influence is not due to his exceptional personal qualities as much as to the specific social context that allows him great latitude (like most developing countries, Arab countries are characterized by the lack of organized interest groups, a high level of illiteracy, a low level of bureaucratic development and communication facilities, modest resources at the disposal of civil society, and a personalized political culture). Though this decision-making aspect is the most revealing one of foreign policy, it is the most inaccessible because of the incompleteness and modest quality of data.

THE COMMON AND SPECIFIC ASPECTS
OF ARAB FOREIGN POLICIES:
DIALECTICS OF ORIENTATION AND BEHAVIOR

The application of the framework shows that Arab foreign policies reflect common characteristics among Arab countries as well as specificities of individual cases. All these countries share aspects of state-formation (e.g., the role of colonial powers), state functioning (e.g., predominant role of the military and/or other segments of the new middle class), problems of economic development and their social consequences, and Arab-Islamic political culture. But Arab countries also differ, whether in their specific geopolitical aspects (e.g., Morocco and Algeria are not front-line states with Israel as are Jordan or Syria), level and quality of resources (both human and primary products), specific social structure and organization (e.g., peasant versus bedouin), elite composition (e.g., ratio of ulama versus the secular managers), and of course specific problems faced (e.g., the South problem in the Sudan, state survival among the Gulf monarchies, or the debt problem for Egypt or Jordan). This mix of common and specific components in the situation of Arab foreign policy–making indicates why Arab countries historically share some aspects of foreign policy and differ on others. In this respect the common aspects have appeared most at the level of foreign policy orientation or role-conception and the differentiating elements in foreign policy behavior or role-performance.

For instance, at the international level, Arab countries have insisted on sharing a nonalignment *orientation*, whereas at the regional level, the insistence has been on Arab unity. This pattern was most apparent in the 1950s and 1960s. However, the 1990s are telling a different story. With the decline of bipolarity and the end of the cold war (but not the end of history!), the issue of nonalignment was bound to lose much of its value. Similarly, the issue of Arab unity has also ceased to be a war cry affecting the legitimacy of different political regimes. Since all declared their adherence to the principle, Arab unity lost salience as a controversial dividing issue. (The late 1980s showed, in contrast to the late 1970s, a consensus on accommodation with Israel. An example is the 1988 PNC declaration of a Palestinian state in coexistence with Israel.) With the passage of time, Arab foreign policy orientation toward Arab unity changed to emphasize not the one Arab state conception but a strategy of phases around subgroups (e.g., the 1981 Gulf Cooperation Council, the 1988 Union of Arab Maghreb, the 1989 Arab Cooperation Council). Moreover, the emphasis was then on ideological purity rather than on material and pragmatic interests as at present (e.g., relations between the "haves" and "have-nots" within the "Arab family"). Both the "historical" foreign policy orientation and its change bring to the fore two propositions for foreign policy analysis:

1. Elites' perceptions of the structure of the global system, of the norms governing its functioning, and of their position in it have greatly affected their foreign policy orientation of national self-assertion through nonalignment.
2. When the foreign policy elite of a developing country perceives the world as hostile, intense political competition leads the country toward a militant foreign policy that puts independence first. A less competitive situation will permit a policy that accords priority to the search for aid.

Briefly, global-systemic constraints and historical-regional patterns (e.g., belief in one Arab nation) clustered Arab foreign policy around a similar orientation, whether formal disengagement from cold war blocs or insistence on the oneness of "the Arab nation." It is revealing that even during the 1990–1991 Gulf crisis, supporters and opponents of Saddam Hussein's action have not questioned the principle of settling Arab affairs among Arabs. It is rather how this principle is interpreted, respected, or violated that divides the Arab countries. Hence the importance of dealing with how the consensual foreign policy orientation or role-conception is actually enacted in a specific foreign policy behavior.

It is indeed by dealing with foreign policy *behavior* of Arab countries that we realize the complexity of this subject matter. A first discrepancy is that on the whole Arab countries have insisted on *raison de la nation* (Arab nationalism) in justifying their foreign policy orientation but have practiced, more often than not, their foreign policy behavior in terms of *raison d'état*. For example, Egypt's intervention in the Yemeni civil war of 1962–1967 was officially in the name of *raison de la nation* and the promotion of Arab revolution and liberation, but it was equally, if not primarily, in defense of Egyptian regional leadership. Similarly, Saddam Hussein conducted both the war against Khomeini's Iran and the invasion of Kuwait in the name of the defense of basic Arab interests. But Iraq's specific moves are equally, if not primarily, the result of specific Iraqi needs and motivation, whether the perception of threat from Khomeini's Iran or the need—by invading Kuwait—to "correct" colonial history and Baghdad's economic conjuncture. A similar mix of explanation and motivation of foreign policy moves exists in Syria's intervention in Lebanon or Morocco's action toward the Western Sahara.

Contrary to the foreign policy orientation that is consensual in nature, foreign policy behavior can and does put Arab countries at cross-purposes. This is the case because foreign policy behavior—much more than orientation—gives reality to differences between Arab actors, e.g., their varieties of political regimes, geopolitical characteristics, and resource bases. In its behavior, Kuwait, for instance, is bound—because of its size and Iraqi claims—to emphasize the threats to its political independence and survival, whereas these issues are much less at stake in the case of Iraq itself, Morocco, or Egypt. In these last two cases, if survival is an issue at all, it is mainly at the economic level (e.g., worsening debt, IMF "advice" for structural adjustment, subsidy issues). The chapters on Jordan and the Sudan show that the threats to an actor's survival are in fact both political and economic.

As we can see, such differences are not a function of, or even primarily associated with, the man at the top. Thus Saudi Arabia practiced its nonalignment in a very peculiar way: Not having diplomatic relations with the erstwhile communist bloc on the ground that they were atheists, but then in the context of the Gulf crisis deciding to reestablish diplomatic relations with Moscow. Indeed, before the end of the cold war, Saudi Arabia purchased missiles from "communist" China and severed diplomatic relations with Taiwan.

Regional issues, too, bring into the open behavioral differences among Arab states. Thus the greatest contrast between orientation and behavior in the late 1970s was in relation to the Arab-Israeli conflict. Egypt practiced a go-it-alone policy, whereas the majority of Arab countries opposed this policy. Though the 1980s saw the continuation of the Egyptian/Israeli peace treaty, the issue did not prevent Egypt's reintegration into the Arab regional system and the appearance of an Arab behavioral consensus in accepting the State of Israel, especially after the 1988 Palestine National Council declaration of an independent Palestinian state. Similarly, the eight-year Iran-Iraq war manifested Arab differences. Whereas the majority of Arab countries—especially in the Gulf region—took Baghdad's side, Libya, Syria, South Yemen, and also Algeria sided with Teheran. Obviously, with Saddam Hussein's recent decision to settle pending issues with Teheran, the Iran-Iraq conflict is no longer a dividing behavioral issue among Arab actors. Instead, differences now appear in relation to Iraq's invasion of Kuwait, though with a different set of regional alliances, as we will see later.

Related to incongruence in role conception and performance are sudden changes, zigzagging, and improvisation in foreign policy behavior. In some cases, this is caused by despair at the gap between capabilities and objectives. In others, the cause is the complexity of international politics and the confusion between national dreams (which are by definition of a long-range nature) and objectives that must be related to operational capabilities.

The Arab world also provides an example of a state with no foreign policy. The Lebanese case is striking; a sovereign state, member of the United Nations and the League of Arab States, finds its territory the battleground of combating forces, none of which is present with Lebanese consent. Lebanon has become an arena for the foreign policies of other actors, rather than being able to choose a foreign policy of its own. To the extent that Lebanon has a foreign policy, it is a policy of survival.

This brings us to the actual making of foreign policy: the decision-making process.

THE DECISION-MAKING PROCESS

If foreign policy inputs emphasize the sorting out and classification of factors determining such a policy, decision-making is concerned with the chemistry of these factors, of their dynamic nature and their mingling process to produce the outcome: decision. Like almost all developing countries, Arab actors share the characteristics of the primacy of the executive and especially the personalized nature of the decision-making process (due mainly to lack of independent checks, legislative structures, or independently based political groups). The result is the prevalence of a neopatrimonial pattern of decision-making in which the distinction between public and private issues and their relationship is highly blurred. Consequently, it is not an individual's official position that could indicate relative status and influence in the making of decisions but rather his or her proximity to the top executive. This proximity could be physical (secretary or chef de cabinet) or social (friends, relatives, or wives). Thus acceptance of the leader as the final decision-taker[2] characterizes all Arab countries.

But differences still exist in the types of groups surrounding this leader. In Saudi Arabia, they are influential members of the royal family, tribal heads, ulama, or members of influential commercial families. In Libya and Algeria, they are ex-military revolutionaries. In Syria or Iraq, they are Ba'thist apparatchiks. Moreover, the type of leader may differ, as between the leader with the historical mission and hence a "mover," or the leader as purely the manager. Mubarak of Egypt symbolizes this last type, whereas Nasser, Sadat, Qaddafi, Saddam Hussein, or Tunisia's Bourguiba symbolize the former. The mover type does not necessarily and invariably take radical-nationalist foreign policy decisions, as the cases of Sadat and especially Bourguiba show. These two leaders befriended the dominant powers in their respective regions (whether the United States or France), and both proposed a political settlement with Israel (Sadat, contrary to Bourguiba's 1965 move, went beyond words to action by signing the 1979 peace treaty).

In addition, the presence of a historical mission for the leader is not a guarantee of his automatic monopoly of effective decision-making powers. There may even be checks on the leader to impose on him the necessity of consultation, bargaining, and search for consensus. On some occasions, this seems to be the case in Algeria, Syria, and especially the PLO. The main point is that contrary to the simplistic notion of a domineering leader or "commander of the faithful," with unchecked and unrestricted powers, the case studies of this book present a more sophisticated image of the decision-making process. In most cases, the leader is confronted by a complex situation of sociopolitical and economic constraints, military vulnerabilities, and a number of domestic political demands (on religious, national, or ethnic grounds).

Consequently the decision-making process in Arab countries can be approached from three perspectives: presidentialism, oligarchical-collective, and collegial collective. The first emphasizes the presidential center, which includes "the president as a person" and "the presidency as institution" (the presidential palace, advisers, offices, etc.). Nasser's and Sadat's Egypt comes closest to the presidential or leader-staff type of decision-making, which is characterized by an authoritarian decision-maker who can act alone without consultation with any political institutions other than a small group of subordinate advisers, typically appointed by the leader and lacking an autonomous power base of its own. Usually these advisers have no independent sources of information other than those available to the leader.

The leader-staff pattern is characterized by fragmentation of roles and responsibility on the part of the staff group, reliance on direct negotiation and personal diplomacy with foreign heads of state, and the ability to respond quickly to events and to make unconventional and bold decisions. Leaders often repeat their past behavior in similar situations, make important decisions without consulting the foreign minister or even the prime minister, and frequently use presidential emissaries (not necessarily career diplomats) in foreign policy assignments. This type of decision-making provides the opportunity for nonofficials to perform important roles due to their personal relations with the leader.[3]

At the other end of the spectrum is the collegial or delegate assembly type of decision-making, characterized by consultation, bargaining, and search for consensus. This pattern of decision-making—followed, for instance, by the PLO—may lead to immobility and an inability to innovate or adapt adequately to changing circumstances. When the challenge of change is no longer avoidable, the resulting decision could be improvised or hesitant. Yasser Arafat's decision to oppose condemnation of Iraq's occupation of Kuwait during the August 1990 Arab League Cairo Summit comes closest to this pattern. This brings us to the most difficult problem facing Arab foreign policies in the 1990s: the unavoidability of vertiginous change.

THE CHALLENGE OF CHANGE

It is this decision-making process—as a social, not only an idiosyncratic, process—that needs to be completed in the years ahead.[4] Indeed, the present context is one of increasingly dizzying change at the global, regional, and state levels. Consequently, the decision-making process is bound to be more complicated. Decision-makers are forced to mobilize the maximum capacity for creativeness and risk-avoidance.

The 1990s witnessed an unexpected bang at the global level (the end of the cold war), the origins of which were already in the making by the end of the 1980s. Thus 1989 started with the Soviet decision to pull out of Afghanistan,[5] the first such Soviet withdrawal decision since the beginning of the cold war, and ended with the fall of Romania's Ceausescu. In the intervening months upheavals ended the Soviet-led East European bloc and reached as far as the streets of China. The domino effect in favor of communism so feared earlier by President Dwight D. Eisenhower could also topple nations one after another away from communism. Thus constitutional clauses that guaranteed the upper hand for communist parties have been repealed, communist symbols have been removed, Soviet forces are leaving, and the drive toward restructuring of new trade relations and privatization is accelerating.

But much more foreboding than these concrete political changes was the questioning of long-held values and political convictions all over the world, especially in its "international periphery." Among these questions the most incessant and insistent one was whether there were still basic tenets of belief that applied everywhere.

There was the Chilean architect who recalled wistfully that he had "entered adolescence together with a woman who was beginning to mature and who was called the Cuban revolution." And . . . there was Mzala a 32-year-old South African living in London for whom Communism essentially meant an ideology that he thought bound him in communism with comrades around the world but which also most alarmed his enemies, the architects and technicians of apartheid. I think we are driven to our quest for Marxist theory by the South African Government itself because, from the time we became politically conscious in South Africa, the Government has been, and continues to be, at pains to show that, more than any other political entity, it opposes and it is afraid of the Communist Party.[6]

The sense of loss is, then, not only political but also ideological and could not but affect the Arab system, a region that is considered the most penetrated by external powers.

The degree of penetration is perhaps best measured by the extent to which differences between local, national, regional, and international politics become blurred. That is . . . politics . . . is not adequately explained—even at the local level—without reference to the influence of the intrusive outside system.[7]

The penetration is both historical (for geostrategic reasons) and contemporary (e.g., abundance of oil resources). In 1987, the region—in addition to Iran—exported a little more than half of world needs, possessed 67 percent of proven oil reserves, of which 40 percent were in the Arabian Peninsula and 24 percent in Saudi Arabia alone.[8] This importance of the Arab world to the global system explains the high level of attention directed to the region, as revealed for instance by the exports to the Arabs of increasingly sophisticated arms (50 percent of all arms exported to the Third World in 1986).[9]

This high global-regional interaction shows why the Arab system and the foreign policies of its components are going to suffer, in an acute way, the brunt of world changes. For instance, in the case of poor Arab countries dependent on international aid (e.g., Egypt, Syria, Yemen, Sudan, Morocco, Jordan), there could be a reduction or even absence of some sources of this aid. Aid sources from Moscow and East Europe are certainly diminishing and could even disappear altogether. Worse still, East European countries will not only disappear as sources of aid but will increasingly be rivals for credit at the international level. As for other international sources, they could be redirected to help East European economies and their integration in the world market. Thus, in the United States a preliminary program of aid for Poland and Hungary was adopted in 1989, with similar ones to follow for other East European countries. Robert Dole, head of the Republicans in the U.S. Senate, proposed formally at the beginning of 1990 the reduction of aid even to countries on the aid priority list (e.g., Egypt and Israel) by 5 percent to release aid resources for East Europe. West European countries were even faster in taking immediate action and early in 1990 established a European Bank for East European Reconstruction.

As Chapter 2 showed, many of the indebted Arab countries count on outside resources to balance their national budget and finance their basic food imports. Consequently, global changes that lead to aid reduction could be damaging even to their daily functioning. Even if sources of international credit increased substantially to cope with these rising global demands, conditions for eligibility would certainly be harder and might be difficult to meet for the have-nots among Arab countries.

At the political level, the effects of global change are equally inescapable. Perestroika is restructuring Soviet and East European foreign policy priorities and moves. For instance, though Soviet and East European basic support for Palestinian inalienable rights (principally the right for self-determination) is adhered to, alignment with Arab positions seems to be changing. Thus Moscow's present political discourse does not insist on "the consolidation of Soviet-Arab friendship" or the necessity "for all peoples to struggle against Israeli aggression." On the contrary, the insistence is increasingly on "political realism" and the necessity for a Palestinian political solution, even by stages and on the basis of mutual concessions. Already on October 13, 1988, Soviet Deputy Minister of Foreign Affairs Alexander Besmyostnykh incited the PLO to recognize Israel. This Palestinian accommodation was done as part of the November 1988 Palestinian Declaration of Independence. But then Moscow was not in a hurry to recognize the new Palestinian state. When this finally came out (November 24, 1988), the Soviet Foreign Ministry spokesman insisted that this recognition was of political rather than legal significance "for the USSR," he continued, "does not recognize occupied states which do not have a government."[10]

Moreover, at the behavioral level, there is a cooling in Arab–East European relations. The new leadership in East Europe is interested in new partners, especially since most Arab countries had close relations with the anciens régimes. Consequently, diplomatic relations are gradually being reestablished with Israel and visits are exchanged. During a UN vote in October 1989 that asked for the exclusion of Israel, the USSR, Poland, Bulgaria, and the ex–German Democratic Republic abstained, whereas Hungary and Romania voted against.

The most important direct effect of the policy change in East Europe for the Arab core issues is the opening of doors for Soviet Jews to immigrate to Israel. An average of 5,000 per month have left, and at least 750,000 are expected by 1995. The arrival of these new immigrants is bound to change the demographic balance between Palestinians and Israelis. The situation could become even more damaging to the Palestinians if these immigrants are settled in the occupied territories. This is why some Arab press reports are talking about a second Balfour Declaration, this time by Moscow. Moreover, in the attempt of the USSR and East European countries to become Westernized and accepted by the West as "reasonable" and "peaceful" states, the Palestinian cause is bound to pay part of the price. Given the weight of the Jewish lobby in the U.S. Congress and the keenness of Eastern countries to have U.S. aid, the support of those countries for the Palestinians is bound to diminish.

The change in East Europe may even have its effects on the internal politics of Arab states and thus influence both foreign policy and its making. For instance, the declining credibility of communism and socialism as alternative ideologies and development models will back up the drive toward economic privatization and influence relations between different interest groups, whether they are businesspersons or state managers. Egyptian *Infitah* has been a pacesetter in this respect, but the tempo at the regional level could increase now. Moreover, a liberalization process within "socialist" regimes of the area would not necessarily lead to Western-style democratization but could rather lead to Islamization. The Islamic groups could in fact present themselves as the only ideological alternative capable of defending "basic identity" in a context of flux and ideological lostness. If the experience of the Islamic Republic of Iran is any guide, foreign policy postures in the Arab world would then be more militant in their reaction to negative global changes. In this respect, global and regional changes could widen the gap between the global system and the regional one, adding to the dilemma of the policy-maker in the Arab countries. This brings us to regional changes.

REGIONAL CHANGES

The 1970s witnessed the rise of oil prices, the rise of militant Islam, Egyptian-Israeli peacemaking, and the exclusion of Egypt from Arab ranks. The 1980s, however, were dominated by the decline of oil prices, attempts to reintegrate Egypt into Arab ranks (and hence an implicit acceptance of a basic change in the fundamental Arab position toward Israel), the *intifada*, and especially the eight-year war between Iran and Iraq. This last element at least created for many Arab countries a dilemma about priorities in their foreign policies at the regional level.

As is well known, the Arab-Israeli conflict was not only the permanent item on the agendas of Arab meetings at the highest levels but was also usually presented as the most sacred cause in both the mass media and street parlance. But increasingly the Gulf was rising to preeminence to compete with the Palestinian issue as a regional policy priority. For after the ostracization of Egypt (hence the weakening of the Arab system by excluding its erstwhile leader and an influential member with one-third of the system's population), another influential member—Iraq— was distracted from a possible direct confrontation with the hereditary enemy, Israel. With the continuation and intensification of the Iran-Iraq war, the rich Gulf countries increasingly aligned themselves with Iraq and poured in massive financial and political influence. Though between

Scylla and Charybdis, the Gulf countries feared that victory of the Islamic Republic could send shock waves of instability throughout the region. But Iran's decision to accept a cease-fire, especially when set against the goals the Islamic Republic set itself during the conflict, was an implicit admission that Iraq had won on points: the admission that revolutionary, expansionist Islam could be contained and even moderated. Moreover, during the war Ba'thist Iraq seemed also to moderate its former radicalism and even signaled its intention to come to terms with Israel by accepting UN resolution 242.[11] But the second Gulf crisis—following the invasion of Kuwait—would change this impression.

In between these two Gulf conflicts came the *intifada*. Indeed, the *intifada* itself was both a consequence of the state of the Arab system and an input into its evolution. A consequence, because the Arab system of the mid-1980s seemed paralyzed in the face of what seemed the permanence of Israeli occupation and even annexation of the West Bank. Indeed, in addition "to the constant presence of the Israeli Defense Forces, some 67,500 settlers made their homes in more than one hundred and thirty settlements in what many Israelis regarded as 'Judea,' 'Somaria' and 'Gaza District.' "[12] Moreover, the situation became unbearable with the institutionalization of the Israeli Defense Forces' "iron fist" policy, the deteriorating economic situation, and the prevalence of incidents of "harrassment, arrest, physical abuse, confiscation, curfew or collective punishment."[13] The only remaining hope was that Arab foreign policy moves could improve this situation by mobilizing more pressure against Israel and its allies. The 1987 Arab summit in Amman put seriously in doubt the realization and even the realism of this hope.

The Arab foreign ministers who met in Tunis on September 20, 1987, and decided to hold the summit in early November in Amman indicated the change in priorities of many Arab foreign policies. Since the Gulf war constituted "the core of the Arab nation's concerns," the statement said, the summit would meet to "examine developments in the Iran-Iraq War from all angles, the persistent threats to Arab states of the Gulf region and the dangers aggravated by the continuation of these events."[14]

Due to Syria's threat (supported by Algeria and Libya) not to attend unless more emphasis was put on the Arab-Israeli conflict, the agenda was broadened. But some still did not turn up, e.g., Qaddafi and King Hassan.[15] Still, the Palestinian issue was certainly subordinated to the Gulf war. In fact, King Hussein, at the end of the conference, had to pay special attention to Arafat to attenuate the centrality of Gulf matters on the collective Arab agenda during summit discussion. On December 8, 1987, the *intifada* was sparked off. Disappointment with official Arab state foreign policies thus brought the Arab-Israeli conflict back to its historic communal origins and Palestinized it, endangering the legitimizing function of some of these policies.

The regional environment of Arab foreign policies was again thrown into drastic change by Iraq's invasion of Kuwait on August 2, 1990. It should be remembered that though the Iraq-Kuwait conflict dates back to the preindependence days of Kuwait in 1961, Iraq's military action jolted the Arab system because of both its rapidity and its potential consequences. Initially, Baghdad justified its action as a response to the demands of a new Kuwaiti government that overthrew the old order, but Baghdad finally finished by declaring Kuwait's simple "reintegration into the mother country." A new precedent was set in the pattern of Arab foreign policies: the weak or small Arab state could be swallowed up by its "big brother." Such a precedent—whatever the outcome of the ongoing Gulf crisis—is bound to change foreign policy priorities and their making in many Arab states. For instance, whether it is the Gulf countries or Jordan, the issue of state survival as an immediate foreign policy objective in Arab interaction could increasingly loom large. The survival dilemma is no longer limited to their interactions with Israel.

Consequently, the very normative basis of Arab togetherness could be seriously undermined, and the whole Arab system could become increasingly a satellite to non-Arab regional and international forces. After all, the Arab League is in limbo at the time this is written, with only part of it returning to its original headquarters in Cairo. That return could herald a return of Egypt's weight in regional politics. But the reemergence of the Egyptian pole could not be a pure and simple repetition of the regional environment of the 1950s and 1960s, for this potential reemergence is part of a new pattern of regional alliances and issues as well as international linkages. Egypt itself is not only crippled with more than a $50 billion debt but is too dependent on U.S. hegemony to have its regional leadership prestige untarnished.

Moreover, the invasion of Kuwait shows that the relationship between Arab governments and their grass roots is also changing. Many of these grass roots are attentive to Saddam Hussein's appeal of Arab political assertiveness and redistribution of (petrodollar) wealth within the Arab family, i.e., across state frontiers. The result is that in addition to the explicit return of high politics (issues of war/peace and state survival), there is a salience of so-called low politics (issues of economic inter-dependence, redistributive justice, and democratization). Consequently, regional change added to vertiginous global change could have a multiplier effect on the immediate environment of Arab foreign policies and their making in the 1990s.

The French thinker Raymond Aron said in the 1970s that policy-making is hellish for the practitioner but a study paradise for the analyst. Compared to the 1970s and even the 1980s, Arab and international environments of the 1990s may prove extremely arduous, indeed hellish, not only for the practitioner but also for the analyst.

NOTES

1. For details and critical evaluation of these theorists, see Bahgat Korany, *How Foreign Policy Decisions Are Made in the Third World* (Boulder, Colo.: Westview Press, 1986), pp. 39–61.

2. For the distinction between decision-making and decision-taking, see *ibid.*, pp. 166–183.

3. Charles Hermann, "Decision Structure and Process Influences on Foreign Policy," in Maurice East, Stephen A. Salmore, and Charles Hermann (eds.), *Why Nations Act: Theoretical Perspectives for Comparative Foreign Policy Studies* (Beverly Hills: Sage, 1978), pp. 69–102; Margaret Hermann, Charles Hermann, and Joe Hagan (eds.), *Leaders, Groups and Coalitions in Decision-Making* (forthcoming).

4. Bahgat Korany, *Dependent Development and Foreign Policy Change* (forthcoming).

5. Jacques Lévesque, *La retraite soviétique d'Afghanistan* (Bruxelles: Édition complexes, 1990).

6. Bernard Gwertzman and Michale T. Kaufman (eds.), *The Collapse of Communism* (New York: Random House [Times Book], 1990), p. 9.

7. L. Carl Brown, *International Politics and the Middle East* (Princeton, N.J.: Princeton University Press, 1984), pp. 4–5.

8. *Middle East and North Africa 1990* (London: Europa Publications, 1990), p. 13.

9. *Ramses 1990: Rapport Annuel Mondial sur le Système Économique et les Stratégies,* sous la direction de Thierry de Montbrial (Paris: Economica and Institut François de Relations Internationales, 1990), pp. 161–162.

10. See the documentary part in *Revue d'Études Palestiniennes* 31 (1989), p. 132.

11. David Bradshaw, "The Iran-Iraq Ceasefire and Its Regional Implications," *The Middle East Review 1989,* 15th ed. (Saffron Walden, Essex, England: World of Information, 1989), pp. 16–18.

12. Rex Brynen and Neil Caplan, "Introduction: The Palestinian Uprising," in R. Brynen (ed.), *Echoes of the Intifada: Regional Repercussions of the Palestinian-Israeli Conflict* (Boulder, Colo.: Westview Press, 1991), pp. 1–5.

13. *Ibid.*

14. Bruce Maddy-Weizeman, "Inter-Arab Relations," in Itamar Rabinovich and Haim Shaked (eds.), *Middle East Contemporary Survey* (Boulder, Colo.: Westview Press, 1989), pp. 117–152.

15. *Ibid.*

Abbreviations

AID	Agency for International Development (U.S.)
ALF	Arab Liberation Front
ALN	Armée de liberation nationale (Algeria)
AMIO	Arab military armaments organization
ANP	Armée nationale populaire (Algeria)
AWACS	Airborne Warning and Control System
bpd	barrels per day
CC	Central Council (PLO)
CIA	Central Intelligence Agency (U.S.)
CNRA	Conseil national de la révolution algérienne (National Council of the Algerian Revolution)
CNR	Conseil national de la révolution
COPDAB	Conflict and Peace Data Bank
DFLP	Democratic Front for the Liberation of Palestine
DUP	Democratic Unionist party (Sudan)
EEC	European Economic Community
EXCOM	Executive Committee (PLO)
FIS	Front islamique du salut (Algeria)
FLN	Front de liberation nationale (Algeria)
GC	Popular Front General Command
GCC	Gulf Cooperation Council
GCFR	General Command of the Forces of the Revolution (PLO)
GDP	gross domestic product
GNP	gross national product
GPRA	Gouvernement provisoire de la république algérienne (Provisional Government of the Republic of Algeria)
IMF	International Monetary Fund
INOC	Iraqi National Oil Company
IPC	Iraq Petroleum Company
LDI	Ligue de la Da'awa islamique (Algeria) (League of the Islamic Call)
LIBOR	London Interbank Offered Rate
LSP	Labor Socialist party (Egypt)
MNC	multinational company
NATO	North Atlantic Treaty Organization
NIEO	New International Economic Order
NPUP	National Progressive Unionist party (Egypt)

OAPEC	Organization of Arab Petroleum-Exporting Countries
OAU	Organization of African Unity
ODEP	open door economic policy
OECD	Organization for Economic Cooperation and Development
OPEC	Organization of Petroleum Exporting Countries
PAG	Parti de l'avant-garde socialiste (Algeria)
PDRY	People's Democratic Republic of Yemen
PFLOAG	Popular Front for the Liberation of Oman and the Arabian Gulf
PFLP	Popular Front for the Liberation of Palestine
PGC	People's General Congress (Libya)
PLA	Palestine Liberation Army
PLF	Palestine Liberation Front
PLO	Palestine Liberation Organization
PNC	Palestine National Council
PNF	Palestine National Fund
PNSF	Palestine National Salvation Front
PPSF	Palestine Popular Struggle Front
RCC	Revolutionary Command Council (Iraq; Libya)
SADR	Sahrawi Arab Democratic Republic
SIPRI	Stockholm International Peace Research Institute
SMC	Supreme Military Council (PLO)
SONATRACH	Société nationale de transport et de commercialisation des hydrocarbures (Algeria)
SPLM/SPLA	Sudanese People's Liberation Movement/Army
UAE	United Arab Emirates
UAR	United Arab Republic
UMA	Union du Maghreb Arabe (Arab Maghreb Union)
UNFA	National Union of Algerian Women

About the Book
and Authors

Middle East politics have been proverbial for their changeability. The 1970s ushered in petro-politics, for instance, but OPEC's international status declined markedly in the following decade. Similarly, the Arab world's ostracism of Egypt in the 1970s following its separate peace with Israel was turned around in the 1980s; the late 1980s also brought PLO acceptance of the State of Israel. Interstate relations were not the only arena to experience significant alterations; state-society relations also underwent dramatic changes, such as the acceleration of privatization in erstwhile socialist regimes. Then the 1990s opened with a political earthquake: the Gulf Crisis.

The second edition of this highly acclaimed text offers a penetrating analysis of trends in Arab foreign policies since the book was originally published in 1984, including an early analysis of the effects of Iraq's invasion of Kuwait and the subsequent coalition victory over Iraq. In addition, the authors have included new chapters on Jordan—at the heart of the Arab world—and on the Sudan—the region's link to sub-Saharan Africa. Their inclusion allows a fuller understanding of the foreign policies of states that occupy crucial geopolitical positions but wield little tangible power. Moreover, in many of its chapters the book raises the crucial question of how the foreign policies of these countries can cope with the prevalence of political change.

Bahgat Korany is director of the Arab studies program and professor in the Department of Political Science at the University of Montreal. **Ali E. Hillal Dessouki** is professor of political science at Cairo University and director of the Center for Political Research.

About the Contributors

Ahmad Yousef Ahmad is an associate professor in the Department of Political Science at Cairo University.

Gehad Auda is a senior researcher at the Centre for Political and Strategic Studies, Al-Ahram, Cairo.

Ali E. Hillal Dessouki is a professor of political science at Cairo University and director of the Center for Political Research.

Raymond A. Hinnebusch is an associate professor in the Department of Political Science at the College of Saint Catherine in Minnesota.

Karen Aboul Kheir is a Ph.D. candidate at the American University in Cairo.

A. G. Kluge, fellow in political science at Johns Hopkins University, is a Ph.D. candidate in international relations at the School of Advanced International Studies in Washington, D.C.

Bahgat Korany is director of the Arab studies program and professor in the Department of Political Science at the University of Montreal in Quebec, Canada.

Paul C. Noble is an associate professor of political science at McGill University in Montreal.

Mohamed E. Selim is an associate professor of political science at Cairo University.

I. William Zartman is director of African studies and professor of international politics at the School of Advanced International Studies of Johns Hopkins University in Washington, D.C.

Index

and Islam, 32, 150, 200
and Jordan, 5, 232–233
and Lebanon, 399
and new security arrangements,
90, 91
and oil resources, 4, 34–35
and PLO, 302–303, 415, 416
and regional alignment patterns,
83, 86, 90–93, 183–184, 421
and Saudi Arabia, 4, 91, 313, 348
Soviet role in, 322
Sudanese role in, 372
and Syria, 91, 383, 384, 399, 404
Gulf states, 90, 92
British withdrawal from, 312, 331
and Iran-Iraq war, 59, 86–87, 208,
230, 343, 344, 345, 402
and Iraq, 79, 80, 208
and PLO, 302–303
and regional alignment patterns,
84, 86–87, 184
and Saudi Arabia, 91, 351(n56)
Shi'i Moslems in, 54, 82, 230, 322,
344
See also Gulf Cooperation Council;
individual countries; Organization
of Petroleum Exporting
Countries

Habash, George, 382
Haddad, George M., 254
Haddad, Saad, 397
Al-Hafez, Amin, 298
Hagen, Joe I., 10
Haig, Alexander, 178, 385
Halliday, F., 17
Halpern, M., 332
Hamdan, Gamal, 158
Hamidi, Khuwaildi, 246
Hammouda, Yehia, 262, 276
Hamrouche, Mouloud, 129, 133
Harbi, Mohamed, 130
Al-Hasan, Hami, 301
Hashemites. *See* Iraq; Jordan
Al-Hassan, Bilal, 285
Hassan ibn Talal (crown prince of
Jordan), 225, 228
Hassan II (king of Morocco), 116,
141, 142, 149, 243, 420
Hawatema, Nayef, 293
Hegazi, Abdel-Aziz, 165

Heikal, Mohamed H., 172, 176, 237,
238
Al-Hendi, Al-Sharif Zien Al-Abdien,
365
Hermann, Charles, 170, 284, 285
Hizbullah, 313, 399, 401, 403
Hobeika, Elie, 399
Holocaust, 42
Holsti, Kal, 20
Hoss, Selim, 399
Hussein ibn Talal (king of Jordan),
225, 229, 230, 233, 402, 420
and PLO, 78, 232, 296, 297, 392,
393, 401
politics, 51–52, 222–224, 227, 228
and Syria, 231, 383, 401
See also Jordan
Hussein, Saddam, 32, 90, 91–92,
209, 233, 383, 411
and Arab-Israeli conflict, 6, 34
and decision-making process, 199,
200, 415
economy, 193, 205
and Europe, 203–204
and global system, 197, 198
and Iran, 208, 210
and Iraqi influence, 71, 79, 199
military, 194–195
politics, 53, 196–197
and United States, 201–202
See also Gulf crisis (1991); Iraq
Al-Hussein, Said Ahmed, 365

Ibn Abdallah, Fahd, 331
Ibn Al-Baz, Abdel-Aziz, 318
Ibn Saud, Abdel-Aziz (king of Saudi
Arabia), 311, 314, 316–317, 320,
324, 326, 330, 349(n16),
351(n56)
Ibrahim, Saad Eddin, 97(n54)
Ibrahimi, Ahmed Taleb, 125, 132,
149
IBRD. *See* World Bank
ICJ. *See* International Court of Justice
Ideology, 50, 51, 55, 74, 94(n12)
decrease in importance, 52, 75–76,
84, 88
and Palestinians, 266, 274, 278
See also Ba'thism; Iranian
revolutionary Islam; Islam; Pan-
Arabism; Transnational politics

and Western powers, 59, 71
Yemen War (1962–1967), 61, 331
See also Gulf Cooperation Council;
  Gulf states
Saud (king of Saudi Arabia), 311–
  312, 323, 324, 327, 333
Sayigh, Rosemary, 266
Second World War, 161, 197
Security/development dilemma, 11–
  12
Selim, M., 17
Selim, Mohamed, 14
Sendad, Ma'mon, 365
Senegal, 168, 244
Senussiya, 238–239
Seven Sisters, 27
Shaw, John A., 335
Al-Shazly, Saad, 173, 174
Shelli party (Israel), 279
Shell Oil Company, 313
Shevardnadze, Edvard, 338
Shihabi, Hikmet, 388, 390
Shi'i Moslems, 230, 275, 322, 344
  Iraq, 53, 54, 82, 93, 188, 195, 200,
    206
  See also Iranian revolutionary
    Islam; Islam
Shills, E., 8
Shoemaker, Christopher, 175
Al-Shukairy, Ahmed, 262, 263, 268,
  284, 290, 292
  and China, 293, 300
  on PLO goals and strategy, 276,
    280, 283
Shukry, Ibrahim, 165
Al-Siba'i, Yusuf, 300
Sidky, Aziz, 165
Silasy, Fikry, 363
SIPRI. *See* Stockholm International
  Peace Research Institute
Sirhan, Bassam, 265
Six-Day War. *See* June 1967 war
Smith, Adam, 41
Social structure, 9, 19, 50, 52, 106–
  107. *See also under individual
  countries*
Société nationale de transport et de
  commercialisation des
  hydrocarbures (SONATRACH)
  (Algeria), 114, 115, 128, 132, 134
Somalia, 15, 182, 340

SONATRACH. *See* Société nationale
  de transport et de
  commercialisation des
  hydrocarbures
South Korea, 340
South Yemen (People's Democratic
  Republic of Yemen) (PDRY), 76,
  77, 79, 84, 87, 241, 275
  and Arab-Israeli conflict, 85, 182,
    183
Soviet Union, 18, 34, 37, 322, 367
  Afghanistan invasion, 76, 202, 321,
    328, 338, 348, 416
  and Algeria, 118, 135–136
  and Arab-Israeli conflict, 90, 173,
    285, 418–419
  and Egypt, 76, 77, 156, 157, 161,
    166, 171–174
  and Iraq, 189, 201, 202–203, 204,
    205
  Jewish emigration to Israel, 90,
    202, 264, 418
  and Jordan, 222, 225, 229
  and Libya, 76, 173, 241, 242, 243,
    248, 249–251, 253
  and PLO, 276, 287, 292–293, 294
  and Saudi Arabia, 76, 320–322,
    338, 350(n34), 413
  and Syria, 293, 376, 386–387, 402,
    403
  See also Big powers; East-West
    conflict; Egyptian-Soviet relations
Spain, 205
Spanier, John, 175
SPLM/SPLA. *See* Sudanese People's
  Liberation Movement
Steadfastness Front, 244, 263, 299,
  401. *See also* Egyptian-Israeli
  relations
Stockholm Declaration, 282, 292
Stockholm International Peace
  Research Institute (SIPRI), 117–
  118
Sudan, 268, 354–372
  and Arab-Israeli conflict, 182
  decision-making process, 364–365
  domestic environment, 355–362
  economy, 360–361
  and Egypt, 171, 361–362, 363–364,
    368, 368–370
  foreign aid, 366, 370